GREEKS, ROMANS, JEWS

GREEKS, ROMANS, JEWS

Currents of Culture and Belief
in the New Testament World

James D. Newsome

Trinity Press International
Philadelphia

Cover designed by Brian Preuss.

This book is printed on acid-free paper.

Printed in the United States of America.

10 9 8 7 6 5 4 3 2 1

Trinity Press International, Philadelphia, Pennsylvania

For
Callie, David,
Laura, and Burns

CONTENTS

PREFACE

Several years ago, exhibiting more enthusiasm than prudence, I agreed to teach master of divinity students a course on New Testament backgrounds. In preparing for this venture, I soon discovered that while an abundance of fine scholarly literature existed on various topics related to the subject, there was no adequate (in my view, at least) textbook which addressed the entire field in terms suitable to my students. As so, eschewing Sirach's wisdom (32:8) to

> Be brief; say much in a few words;
> Be as one who knows and can still hold his tongue.

I began to prepare material that was designed to introduce my students to Jewish history, literature, and theology of the Greco-Roman period. It was my hope that this introduction would not only deepen their perspectives on both Old and New Testaments, but that they would be enticed into an enlarged appreciation of this fascinating world of thought and action for its own sake.

The present volume is a result of this endeavor. Since it began, other helpful contributions to fill the need for basic text in this area have been published, but is nonetheless my hope that these pages may be found useful both by students who are seeking academic degrees as well as by interested lay people who want to know more about the "world of the Bible."

A word is probably in order concerning terminology in this book. Many of the concepts referred to on these pages possess few theologically "neutral" terms in that both Jews and Christians have developed their own faith–vocabulary. A writer who, like myself, wishes to offend no one in his or her choice of words, must nevertheless rely upon an existing inventory of phraseology, some of which is theologically freighted. And so—for better or worse—in this volume the phrase Greek Bible refers to the Septuagint and/ or other Greek translations of the Hebrew scriptures into the Greek language made in antiquity. Hebrew Bible refers to the Palestinian tradition enshrined in the Masoretic text. While Old Testament refers to that part of the Christian canon of scripture (in whatever language) that, while it assumes somewhat different forms in various confessional traditions, is considered antecedent to and complementary of the New Testament.

Similarly, while the designations BCE (Before the Common Era) and CE (the Common Era) have contributed significantly to the language of scholarship and interfaith dialogue in recent years, there still appears to be a place for AD and BC. Because it seemed appropriate in the present context, this latter pair of terms has been utilized here.

No one works in a vacuum and, in typical fashion, I am indebted to a number of persons for their encouragement and assistance. Special mention should be made in this regard of Michael Goldberg, who read and criticized portions of the manuscript. His suggestions proved to be of great value, although he is by no means to blame for deficiencies that remain.

I am also grateful to my colleagues on the faculty and board of directors of Columbia Theological Seminary, who consented to a study leave during which much of the preparation for this volume was completed.

Finally, a special word of thanks is due my son, Burns, who helped in the preparation of the maps.

JAMES D. NEWSOME

Part One

THE HELLENISTIC PERIOD

Chapter 1

THE SPREAD OF HELLENISM

A. ALEXANDER THE GREAT AND THE HELLENISTIC KINGDOMS

1. *The Conquests of Alexander*[1] (336–323 BC)

The last half of the fourth century BC witnessed fundamental changes in the world of the ancient Near East, a series of events that profoundly altered the patterns by which ordinary men and women lived their lives. This reorientation began as a succession of military conquests by one of the most brilliant strategists of all time, but it continued in the form of new ways of writing, thinking, worshiping, playing, and creating art. The military leader was, of course, Alexander the Great, and the "new" culture was, in reality, the centuries-old culture of Greece, although shaped and adapted to a new environment. From the Mediterranean basin to the region of what today is northern India, entire populations embraced Hellenism, as the new culture came to be called (from the Greek word for Greece: *Hellas*). For the first time in human history something approaching a world culture was created, and not even Jerusalem's Jews were immune to its influences. Neither Second Temple Judaism nor New Testament Christianity can be understood without reference to the strong currents of Hellenism.

Alexander was born in the summer of 356 BC to Philip, ruler of the Greek kingdom of Macedon. At the time of Alexander's birth, the Greeks boasted traditions in the arts and sciences that had been developed over more than a thousand years. The great Greek writer, Homer, for example, who lived almost 500 years before Alexander, had told tales in his great epic poems, *Iliad* and *Odyssey*, about events surrounding the Trojan War, stories that were themselves a half millennium old when Homer heard them.[2] Various forms of Greek drama, sculpture, religion, philosophy, statecraft, and historiography were also venerable with age by the time of Alexander.

One thing, however, which the Greeks had never succeeded in achieving was lasting political unity. Greek communities in the Greek homeland, as well as those in western Asia Minor (which the Greeks called Ionia), governed themselves as independent city-states. They frequently quarreled and fought among themselves, forming ever-changing alliances against one another, conquering and being conquered by other Greeks in a seemingly endless chain of wars and insurrections. Only when threatened by some outside force, such as Persia, did they temporarily lay aside their rivalry and act for the common good, but such alliances were shaky and seldom lasted longer than the threat which called them into being. Sometimes not even external danger was enough to forge Greek unity, for the Persians often had little difficulty in recruiting Greek mercenaries to assist them in their efforts to conquer the world of the Greeks. Different city-states flourished at different times in Greek history, but those which are remembered as especially prominent include Sparta, famed for its military skill and endurance, and Athens, home of philosophy and the arts.

Macedon, as a glance at a map will show, lay near the fringes of the Greek world, north of the centers of power and culture, and for that reason was considered semibarbaric by many Greeks. And so it is somewhat ironic that it was out of Macedon that there arose the strong impetus which attempted and, in some important ways, succeeded in uniting not only Greece itself, but the entire "civilized" world. Alexander's father, Philip, inherited the Macedonian throne upon the death of an older brother in 359, and over the next two decades he engaged in a number of military campaigns which culminated, in 338, in the submission of virtually the entire Greek peninsula to his rule. The Persians still ruled east of the Aegean Sea and Philip was busy with preparations to invade Ionia when, in 336, he was dramatically assassinated before a large crowd in the Macedonian capital of Aegae, as he entered an outdoor theater to inaugurate an important festival.

Perhaps the Persians, alarmed at the growing Macedonian power, lay behind Philip's death. But many people have suspected that the instigator of the assassination was none other than Alexander. Philip had favored his son in a number of ways, providing him with the best education (the philosopher Aristotle was one of his tutors) and allowing him ample opportunity to develop the political and military skills necessary to succeed to the throne. Yet friction had developed between the two and, at the time of Philip's death, it was not a universally accepted fact that Alexander would, in due course, inherit the kingdom. And so Alexander's speedy execution of all political rivals (when added to the fact that the assassin himself, one Pausanias, was killed on the spot) has strengthened the suspicion of Alexander's guilt.

Not all of the Greek city-states which Philip had pacified were ready to accept Alexander's rule, and so some months were to elapse before the young Macedonian king was able to leave a relatively peaceful Greece behind him and resume his father's vision of an invasion of the Persian empire. In the spring of 334 Alexander and his army crossed the Hellespont into Asia and one of the most successful military campaigns in history was underway. Soon the first important engagement with the Persian army (which included many Greek mercenaries) had taken place at the river Granicus, where Alexander demonstrated his brilliant tactical skills by decisively winning a battle against a numerically superior enemy. The next twelve months were spent in subduing Asia Minor and it was during this period, at Gordium, that one of the legends about Alexander has its roots.

Gordium was the seat of the kingdom of Phrygia, whose most celebrated king, Midas, had been endowed by the god Dionysus (also called Bacchus) with the ability to transform ordinary substances into gold (the celebrated "Midas touch"). According to contemporary accounts, Alexander found Midas' carriage at Gordium, tied to its yoke by means of a very complex knot. Local lore had it that whoever could untie the knot would become ruler of the world, whereupon Alexander simply pulled out his sword and sliced the knot in two! Another account says that Alexander pulled out the yoke pin and revealed the concealed ends of the knot. Whatever truths or untruths may lie buried in the yarn of the Gordian knot, it was apparent to those who came in contact with Alexander—friend and foe alike—that this was a man of uncommon resourcefulness and skill.

In the autumn of 333 Alexander defeated the Persian king himself, Darius III, at Issus and, although the Persian ruler escaped to fight (and be defeated) another day, the way was now open for Alexander's army to march down the coast of the eastern Mediterranean. What is more, by subduing Asia Minor and its extensive coastline, important harbors had been denied to the powerful Persian fleet. Soon (the spring of 332) the Macedonian army was on the shore opposite the island city of Tyre, demanding its surrender. Tyre was a proud center of the Phoenicians, those kinfolk of the biblical Canaanites who, by means of their ships and skilled sailors, had maintained lucrative routes of commerce since before the days King Hiram, the friend of Israel's kings, David and Solomon (1 Kings 5:1ff., 1 Chron. 14:1ff.). When the Tyrians refused Alexander's ultimatum, the invaders laid a siege which lasted for seven months and which ended only after an impressive engineering feat on the part of Alexander's soldiers. This was the completion of an earthen rampart which stretched the half-mile distance between the shore and the island and which allowed the attackers to storm Tyre's walls. As punishment for the Tyrians' having slaughtered a group of Alexander's soldiers who had been taken prisoner, large numbers of men, women, and children were sold into slavery. One report, probably untrue, states that 2,000 Tyrian soldiers were crucified.

Next in Alexander's line of march lay Gaza, in earlier days an important Philistine city, but now the only significant Persian fortification protecting the satrapy of Egypt. With its fall in the autumn of 332 there was nothing to impede Alexander's triumphal entry into the land along the Nile, where he was warmly greeted by the people, many of whom had never reconciled themselves to Persian rule.

At some point in the year 332 a detachment of Alexander's troops almost certainly entered Jerusalem. Josephus, writing 400 years after the event, relates an extended tale in which he maintains that the Jewish high priest, accompanied by his fellow priests, all brilliantly arrayed in their robes of office, went out to meet Alexander. The conqueror was approaching Jerusalem at the head of his forces which were fresh from their victory at Gaza. So impressed was Alexander by this public acclaim that he praised the Jews and prohibited his soldiers—much to their disappointment—from violating any of the inhabitants of the city or their property. Alexander even joined the high priest in the worship of the God of the Jews! Shortly after this, Alexander received a delegation of Samaritans, whom he treated with respect, but from whom he withheld the warm praise he had lavished upon the Jews.[3]

However, this story is almost certainly a fabrication, either by Josephus or one of his sources. Contemporary Greek accounts record no such visit, and the truth would seem to be that, since Jerusalem was of no military or economic significance to the invaders, there was no reason for Alexander, his mind fixed on the riches of Egypt, to bother to go there in person. The one kernel of truth in the story is that at about the time of Alexander's occupation of Egypt, Jerusalem's Persian masters disappear and new ones arrive, speaking Greek.

Even before Alexander had made formal claim to Jerusalem, the Jews there must have watched the progress of his army down the Palestinian coast with great interest. And it may be that some anonymous Jewish poet recorded this fascination in Zechariah 9:1–10, a prophetic text which, if it does refer to Alexander's victories over Tyre (vv. 3–4), Gaza (v. 5) and other coastal citadels, describes the Macedonian warrior as a peacemaker sent from God.[4]

Alexander's stay in Egypt was brief, but highly significant. This conqueror who could, on occasion, be quite cruel, could also be deeply respectful of the traditions of art and religion. He reportedly went to Memphis and worshiped the important deity Apis (perhaps the inspiration for Josephus' story that he worshiped the God of the Jews in Jerusalem), thus winning the devotion of native Egyptians, who hailed him as the new pharaoh. In addition, Alexander made a celebrated journey into the Lybian desert to visit the then-famous shrine of the god Ammon, whom many in the Greek world believed to be a manifestation of the Greek high god Zeus and whose oracles were valued as being especially truthful. Alexander's ancient historians are vague about the details of this pilgrimage, but one story is that, while at the shrine, he received the title "Son of Ammon." This is one of many fantasies about Alexander that shed light on the nature of his authority. He had not only transformed the old model of the petty Greek ruler into that of autocratic world monarch, but he made no effort to suppress the frequent reports that he was divine. Both of these aspects of Alexander's political will would, in large measure, be taken up by certain of his successors, a reality with which Jerusalem's Jews would eventually have to reckon.

Alexander's most lasting achievement in Egypt, however, was his plan to build a new city in the Nile Delta which was to be named after himself. Its geographic location provided two excellent harbors and, by means of the Nile, easy access into the heart of Egypt. Alexandria in Egypt became the first and most important of the numerous cities of that name that the conqueror would sprinkle across his empire. Perhaps even Alexander could not foresee that, in time, it would become the richest city in the Greek-speaking world and would provide shelter and encouragement to the most dazzling collection of writers, artists, and scientists of antiquity. As we shall presently notice, it would also come to rival Jerusalem as the center of Jewish thought and life.

But the restless Macedonian could not remain in one place for long, especially when the King of Persia still presented a threat in the East. Alexander left Egypt in the late spring of 331 and marched toward Mesopotamia. By September he had crossed the Euphrates and the Tigris and, at Gaugamela, a short distance from the ruins of the old Assyrian capital of Nineveh, Alexander faced Darius' army once more. As at Issus, Alexander's victory over the Persian ruler was crushing, even more so here, as the flower of Persian nobility was now captured or killed. Although Darius himself once more escaped becoming Alexander's prisoner,[5] the empire founded by Cyrus the Great now lay at Alexander's feet. Babylon, Susa, Persepolis, Ecbatana—all of the most important Persian imperial strongholds were soon occupied by Alexander's invaders, an army which by this time included, along with its original Macedonians and their Greek allies, contingents from many of the conquered territories. This was a disciplined, but eclectic horde that was carried along by the greed of the men, accompanied by a growing number of women and children, who wished to indulge themselves in the riches of Persia. And indulge themselves they did. The destruction of Persepolis, the most radiant jewel in the Persian crown, was an extravagant example of the fierce looting which was accomplished many times and in many other places by Alexander's soldiers.

From the Persian heartland Alexander pushed eastward over the arid Iranian plateau and into the tortuous terrain of what is today Afghanistan. Those in Alexander's ranks who were perceptive may have sensed that bad times were ahead. Alexander's trusted friend Parmenion was accused of a plot against Alexander and was killed. The winter of 330–329 was spent under especially harsh conditions in Hindu Kush (the Afghan highlands). Two years of marching and fighting (329–327) produced more victories, but little in the way of the rich booty so adored by the soldiers. A disastrous defeat at the hands of Scythian tribesmen at Maracanda in Sogdiana was revenged, but the loss of life and prestige among Alexander's troops was deeply felt. In truth Alexander had pushed too far and too long, so it is perhaps not surprising that in 326, faced with the prospect of an invasion of India, Alexander's men refused to continue.[6]

The army returned to what was left of Persepolis by descending the river Indus and by enduring long marches over the arid region of what is today southern Pakistan and southern Iran. It was then on to Susa and, finally, to Babylon, with a great deal of merrymaking along the way. One of Alexander's closest subordinates, a general named Hephaestion, had died after over-indulging in wine (and perhaps other pleasures, as well), and once in Babylon, Alexander presided over an elaborate period of mourning. Plans were afoot for further military campaigns and for vast building programs. But on an evening in the late spring of 323 Alexander became ill of a fever and several days later he died. The cause of his death remains unknown to this day, although rumors that he was murdered have naturally persisted. The great Macedonian warrior had no ready heir, since his only son, by his wife Roxanna, a princess of Sogdiana, was an infant. His empire, held together by little more than his personal authority, soon began to fall to pieces, torn apart by his competing lieutenants. But the real significance of what Alexander had accomplished was only just beginning to be felt.

2. The Hellenistic Kingdoms

During the years following the death of Alexander the empire over which he had ruled experienced a series of military and political convulsions that largely grew out of the fact that none of his Greek or Macedonian followers could claim undisputed right to wear Alexander's mantle of authority. These Diadochi (meaning "Successors" of Alexander), as they were called, engaged in a prolonged struggle with one another, motivated by the desire of each to seize political power for himself. It was several years before new political structures and something approaching stability could be attained in the Hellenistic world. And even after the new contours of authority were clear there were many who wished to challenge them, so that peace was never a permanent state of affairs. Yet ultimately (by the year 301) there emerged three important power centers, each ruled by a family descended from one of the Diadochi: Macedonia, ruled by the Antigonids; Egypt, ruled by the Ptolemies; and Syria-Babylonia, ruled by the Seleucids. Of these, the Ptolemaic and Seleucid kingdoms were of particular importance for Jewish life.

a. *The Ptolemies and Egypt.*   One of the Diadochi who played a significant role in the years following Alexander's death was Ptolemy (ultimately Ptolemy I Soter [or "Savior"], who ruled 323–285 BC), who was Alexander's governor of Egypt. An ambitious man, he soon began to conduct his affairs of state in such a manner that it was apparent that he considered himself answerable to no one. The economy of Egypt that he organized in a tightly controlled, centralized manner, was managed by a small army of Greek and Macedonian bureaucrats who made sure that taxes were promptly paid. The state declared monopolies over some lucrative industries, among them the cultivation of certain oil-producing plants (sesame, castor, olive) and the excavation of some minerals. The result was a foundation of wealth that was to make of Ptolemaic Egypt the most powerful of the Hellenistic kingdoms during the third century BC.

To the economic and political base of Egypt proper Ptolemy added other lands. The confusion which reigned during the last quarter of the fourth century BC allowed him to extend his authority over Palestine as far north as Tyre and Sidon (including Jerusalem and Judaea), and into the southern Aegean Sea and eastern Mediterranean, as well, the islands of Rhodes and Cyprus becoming important Ptolemaic possessions. He also added territory to the west along the North African coast, including Cyrene. A glance at a map gives the impression that this kingdom was, geographically speaking, less than cohesive. But when one considers that almost all of the Ptolemaic territories were positioned either by the sea or along the Nile, it becomes apparent that communications and transportation were much less of a problem than in the vast Seleucid domains.

The heart of the Ptolemaic kingdom was the city of Alexandria, to which Ptolemy moved the capital from Memphis, and under his leadership and that of his son, Ptolemy II Philadelphus (285–246), the city attained a position of dominance in the Hellenistic world. The twin harbors were developed, thereby linking the economic wealth of the Nile valley with the entire Mediterranean basin. In commercial terms, Alexandria of the Ptolemies became the rival of great Carthage to the west. While in matters of science and letters, Alexandria became the "New Athens," as we shall presently discuss.

Alexandria is very important to the story of early Judaism (and in some ways, to that of early Christianity), because of the large numbers of Jews who lived there and because of their accomplishments in the fields of literature and religion. Jews had settled in Egypt as early as the Babylonian and Persian periods, yet it was the economic wealth of Ptolemaic Egypt which induced many Jews to migrate there from Palestine during the early years of the third century BC. These Alexandrian Jews would ultimately come to play a very important role in the development of Jewish thought and literature, both of which exercised important influences upon early Christianity.

After the reign of Ptolemy III Euergetes (246–221 BC), Egypt entered a period of weakness from which it never recovered. For reasons that are not clear Ptolemy IV Philopator (221–205 BC) armed native Egyptians in his struggle with the Seleucids at the battle of Raphia (in southern Palestine, near Gaza) in 217. Some historians see this as a sign of deterioration in the ability of the Ptolemies to control their own population and in their ability to wage effective war against their enemies. In 200 control of Palestine (including Jerusalem) was lost to the Seleucids and the balance of this century was marked by a succession of internal struggles for the Ptolemaic throne. Yet the dynasty managed to maintain itself in power (although a much more limited power than during the third century BC) until the coming of the Romans. The last Ptolemaic ruler was Cleopatra (actually Cleopatra VII—51–30 BC), mistress of Julius Caesar and, after that, wife of Marc Antony. Upon her death by suicide Roman control of Egypt was complete.[7]

b. *The Seleucid Kingdom of Syria-Babylonia.* At the time of Alexander's death one of his most respected officers was Seleucus, who commanded an elite unit of guardsmen. In the period following Alexander's death Seleucus (known as Seleucus I Nicator ["the Victor"], 312–281) consolidated a position for himself in the East, primarily Babylon, over which he ruled as satrap. At its greatest extent the Seleucid Kingdom bore a striking geographical resemblance to the old Persian Empire, stretching, as it did, from India to the Aegean Sea.

Initially the capital of the kingdom was a new city built for this purpose, Seleucia-on-the-Tigris, just to the north of Babylon. As Seleucid strength grew in the west, however, a new administrative center was constructed, Antioch-on-the-Orontes, in northern Syria. For a time, Seleucus I ruled from the new Antioch, while his crown prince, ultimately Antiochus I Soter (281–261), administered the affairs of the eastern realms from Seleucia-on-the-Tigris. But following his father's death, Antiochus vested almost all of the royal administrative presence in Antioch, a move which reflects the westward orientation of Seleucid interests during the third century BC and beyond.

The vastness of their kingdom's territory and the lack of homogeneity among its subject peoples proved to be a continuing cause of concern for all of the Seleucid rulers. Like the Persians before them (and unlike their Ptolemaic contemporaries), the Seleucids allowed a large degree of local autonomy among the diverse groups within their realm. Local governors and petty chieftains presided over the interests of their people, and peace was maintained with the central government by accommodating the ubiquitous tax collector. But restlessness was widespread, especially on the eastern and northern fringes of the kingdom. Some of the Seleucid rulers, especially Antiochus III the Great (223–187), devoted large amounts of energy and treasure to the subjugation of rebellious provinces, some of which were never permanently subdued.[8]

Northern Syria and, to a somewhat lesser extent, Babylon thus became the Seleucid heartland, over which were dispersed the colonies of Greek administrators and bureaucrats and, with them, the Greek merchants and traders who constituted the Seleucid presence. As in Ptolemaic Egypt, these people were a minority within the population, but they tended to be clustered in tight-knit communities which were strategically placed throughout the kingdom. Many of these were either older cities which had been refounded by the Seleucid authorities, or they were newly created towns altogether. This passion for the building of new cities was a distinctive feature of Seleucid policy, one in which they followed the example of Alexander. Also in keeping with Alexander's precedent, many of these new communities bore names of members of the Seleucid royal family, primarily Seleucus and Antiochus. In addition to Seleucia-on-the-Tigris, there was Seleucia-in-Pieria, -in-Susiana, -on-the-Erythraean Sea (the Persian Gulf), and others. The old Persian capital of Susa was refounded as Seleucia-on-the-Eulaeus. In addition to Antioch-on-the-Orontes, Seleucid authorities established Antioch-in-Persis, Anitoch-Nisibis, Antioch-Edessa and Antioch-in-Pisidia.[9]

In the third and early second centuries BC, Seleucid rulers mounted a number of campaigns against their stronger Ptolemaic rivals in a series of struggles which historians have termed Syrian Wars. In these conflicts, the Ptolemaic Kingdom at first prevailed, but in the Fourth Syrian War (219–217 BC), fought between Antiochus the Great and Ptolemy IV Philopator the pendulum began to swing. It was during this conflict that the Battle of Raphia, mentioned above, occurred which, although an Egyptian victory, revealed a growing weakness in Ptolemaic strength. A new campaign by Antiochus the Great (the Fifth Syrian War) took advantage of the fact that Ptolemy IV was dead and that his successor, Ptolemy V Epiphanes (205–180 BC), was a child aged five. Fighting was widespread throughout Palestine, and in 200 an especially important battle was fought at Paneas, northeast of the Sea of Galilee (near the site of the later community referred to in the New Testament as Caeseara Philippi; Matt. 16:13, Mark 8:27). When the campaign was concluded, Ptolemaic forces had been forced to withdraw to a point south of Gaza. All of Palestine, including the area east of the Jordan River, was in Seleucid hands.

In 175 a new Seleucid monarch, Antiochus IV Epiphanes (175–164 BC), came to the throne and was forced to deal with the weakness of the empire in the East, where rebellious tribes stirred up trouble, and in Asia Minor, where the Romans had gained a foothold. In 168 Antiochus Epiphanes invaded Egypt and effectively destroyed the army of Ptolemy VI Philometor (180–145 BC), but he was thwarted in his intention of adding Egypt to his kingdom by the presence of an ambassador from Rome. Rome's growing interests in the eastern Mediterranean dictated that no one power should dominate that area, lest its influence interfere with that of Rome. So, according to the account which has reached us from the historian Polybius,[10] the Roman ambassador, one Popilius, met Antiochus in the village of Eleusis, just inside Egypt. With none of the usual exchange of pleasantries, the Roman abruptly drew a circle in the sand around the Seleucid ruler and told him not to step out of it until he promised to withdraw his troops from Egypt. Antiochus, who had spent fourteen years in Rome as a hostage, feared Roman power and realized he had no choice but to comply. On his return home, he vented his frustration on the Jews of Jerusalem. The Seleucid army entered the city and slaughtered large numbers of the inhabitants and carried away as slaves many others. The Temple was looted of its treasures and profaned by the imposition of pagan sacrifices. Antiochus' violation of the city was one of the major causes of the Hasmonean revolt, an account of which we shall consider later.

The century or so following the reign of Antiochus Epiphanes was a period marked by internal struggles for the Seleucid throne, and by efforts of outsiders, notably the Ptolemaic rulers of Egypt, to limit Seleucid influence. It was also a period of continuing conflict between the leaders of the emerging Hasmonean state and the various Seleucid rulers, whose machinery of government grew progressively weak. In 64 the army of the Roman leader Pompey entered Antioch-on-the-Orontes, which was thereupon designated as the capital of the new Roman province of Syria. The Seleucid kingdom had ceased to exist.

B. Hellenistic Language, Literature, and Education

The process by which the literature, science, and arts of Greece came to be embraced—and in some ways recast—by the people of Alexander's dominions was complex. No two parts of what may by now be called the Hellenistic world reacted to this infusion of Greek ideas in precisely the same manner. Yet from India to Egypt to Greece itself men and women became, for the first time in human history on so grand a scale, citizens of the same world. And all of this occurred in spite of the deep political fragmentation that overcame Alexander's empire in the years following his death.

1. Language [11]

Alexander spoke in the tongue of Macedon, a language which, like the land itself, was not authentically Greek, but was a kindred speech within the larger family of Indo-European languages. But this warrior, who had sat at the feet of the great Aristotle, was by no means limited to the tongue of his native land and early in his political career it became apparent that the speech of Athens, not that of Macedon, would shape the language of his empire. It was a fortunate development and, although we cannot be sure of all the forces which motivated it, the ability of Attic Greek (Athens lay in the region of Attica) to convey a wide range of human thought and emotion must surely have played a prominent part. The fact that Attic Greek, more than any of the several other Greek dialects, was also the language of literature, philosophy, science, and the arts was to prove of profound significance. And as Alexander's soldiers spread across the face of western Asia the currency of communication thus became this dialect of the Greek language. As a consequence Aramaic was displaced in official correspondence, and thereby consigned to a long, slow decline, while Attic Greek filtered down from the military and diplomatic pouch into the places of business, the schools, the workshops, and the homes of ordinary people. This process had scarcely begun at Alexander's death, but it would continue over several centuries, even after Roman legions had laid claim to the lands of Alexander's former domains.

Before Alexander, Attic Greek had been the possession of a relatively small number of people, many of them well educated and steeped in the rich body of literature and art associated with the city of Athens. It is not surprising, then, that many who spoke and wrote in Attic Greek prided themselves not only in the power of their expression, but in its precision. An expansive vocabulary and a carefully guarded, sometimes complicated literary style were characteristic of Attic Greek. Yet, the world into which Alexander carried the language of Socrates and Plato was a rough-and-tumble arena, one where speech was often crude and direct, and where men and women were less concerned with expressing logical subtleties than in seeing that some task was performed quickly and efficiently. What is more, the people in Egypt and western Asia who now began to use Greek words and phrases were, in most instances, raised on a variety of other languages, each with its own vocabulary and rules of expression.

The result of this marriage between the language of Athens, on the one hand, and, on the other, the teeming world of the barracks, the vineyards, and the slave markets of the Near East was a new kind of Greek. It was, for the most part, terse and concise, only marginally concerned with order and precision, and always subject to influences from competing local languages. For all that, however, it inherited the vigor of Attic Greek and, even more important, it soon became the medium by which peoples of diverse backgrounds could stand on common ground and share mind and heart. In fact, the new dialect came to be called Common or Koine Greek.

It was not, however, simply the language of the deprived, although Koine Greek was widely used by people who were poor and dispossessed. It also became a medium of literary expression, as numerous writers of the Greek and Roman world used or were influenced by Koine Greek. Moreover, when the highly literate Jews of Alexandria in Egypt wished to translate their scriptures into a language their community could understand (since Hebrew was no longer in use among them) they used Koine Greek, the result being the Septuagint, a biblical translation of great importance.[12] And, of course, the New Testament demonstrates a variety of styles of Koine Greek, from the polished language of Luke and Acts to the less carefully drawn phrases of Mark. Koine Greek did not go unchallenged, for there were those in the Hellenistic world who continued to champion the cause of Greek dialects, primarily Attic. But Koine Greek was not to be dislodged. It not only survived the coming of the Latin-speaking Romans, but, like Aramiac, survived in some parts of the East after the Arab invasions of the seventh century AD.

2. Literature[13]

The Hellenistic period witnessed a remarkable outpouring of literary effort. The venerable traditions of classical Greek drama, philosophy, poetry, and historiography, now infused with literary forms and ideals from Egypt and Western Asia produced an eclectic and captivating body of literature. The names of more than a thousand writers who were active during the Hellenistic period have been preserved, although, sad to say, most of their literary output has been lost.

a. The Museum and Library of Alexandria.   Nothing reflects the importance of the written word in the Hellenistic world more than the museum and library of Alexandria, both of which were founded in the third century BC and made of Alexandria a "New Athens," the cultural and intellectual center of Hellenistic life. These institutions were the brainchildren of Ptolemy I Soter (323–285 BC), who seems to have been inspired to his project by a certain philosopher and literary critic, Demetrius of Phalerum, who arrived in Alexandria in 297 as a political refugee. But it was under the patronage of Ptolemy II Philadelphus (285–246) that the museum, and especially the library, achieved great distinction.

The museum,[14] literally, a seat of learning dedicated to the Muses, was a foundation which provided refuge and support to a variety of scholars. It was, in the words of a modern American writer, an ancient version of a "twentieth century think-tank,"[15] which fostered the study not only of what we would term the liberal arts, but of the sciences, as well.

The library,[16] housed nearby, was designed not only to facilitate the work of the scholars of the museum, but also to serve as a repository for at least one copy of every literary work which could be obtained. The political and financial strength of the Ptolemies was very important in this regard, and occasionally the gathering of new material could involve procedures which were ethically questionable. Ptolemy III Euergetes (246–221 BC), for example, is reported to have borrowed rare texts of the important Greek dramatists Sophocles, Euripides, and Aeschylus from the city of Athens, presumably, in order to have them copied. But instead, he had them placed in the library, and the Athenians had to content themselves with copies that the king provided (beautifully transcribed, it is said) and with the forfeiture of Ptolemy's funds that had been on deposit in Athens to insure the safekeeping of the original scrolls.

When the library's collection outgrew its original home, a second library building (perhaps the world's first "branch" library) was built in another part of Alexandria by Ptolemy II Philadelphus, and the total number of scrolls in both locations is reported eventually to have reached some 700,000. Since a modern bound volume might contain the equivalent of several ancient scrolls, this is not to be thought of as 700,000 books. Nevertheless, given the slow and expensive process by which scrolls were copied, this number represents a collection of enormous proportions, one that had never been achieved before and that would never be achieved again until the invention of the printing press.

Sometime during the reign of Ptolemy II Philadelphus the poet Callimachus drew up a catalog of the library's contents. Although this document no longer exists, several references to it by other writers have survived, and from these we know that it constituted not only an inventory of the library's possessions, but it was also an effort to organize all human knowledge into a series of categories which Callimachus had devised, an example of the kind of scholarship that the very existence of the library fostered.

Another such example may be found in the labors of the museum's literary scholars upon the texts of Homer's great epic poems, *Iliad* and *Odyssey*. Multiple copies of these extensive poems came, in time, to be lodged in the library, where it was evident that no two copies bore the exact text, for there were additions here, deletions there, and dialectal and spelling differences in abundance. In an attempt to standardize the texts of the Homeric epics, scholars of the museum mounted what is perhaps history's first large scale effort in the field of textual criticism, an enterprise with which all modern students of the Hebrew Old Testament and Greek New Testament are familiar.

The museum and library of Alexandria survived until 47 BC when they were destroyed by fire in the turmoil that accompanied the Roman conquest of Egypt. But for more than 200 years they had served as the focal point of vigorous literary and intellectual creativity on the part Hellenistic writers and thinkers. The claim in the Letter of Aristeas that the great translation of the Hebrew scriptures into Greek (the Septuagint) was begun as a result of Ptolemy II's wish to add the Jewish Torah to the library is certainly fictitious. Yet this assertion that the founder of the library and museum was also the patron of the Septuagint is a significant indication of the respect with which many Greek-speaking Jews viewed the Hellenistic literary establishment.

b. *Poetry*.   Among Hellenistic writers poetry was of primary interest, and Homer was often looked to as a model for style and subject matter. But there were many innovators whose fresh points of view helped to illustrate the spirit of the age. Among Alexandrian poets none was more influential than Callimachus, who was born in Cyrene on the North African coast just before 300 BC, but who moved to Alexandria as a young man. In addition to the catalog mentioned earlier, Callimachus composed more than 800 poems of various lengths and subject matter. Only a small part of this vast corpus has survived, but from these fragments, as well as from references to Callimachus' poetry by other writers, it is possible to appreciate the wide range of this poet's interests. Many of his poems have to do with themes from traditional Greek mythology, as this brief list of some of his titles will reveal: "Hymn to Zeus,"

"Hymn to Artemis" (Artemis is a daughter of Zeus), "Hymn to Demeter,"[17] "Hymn to Apollo," and the like. The collective title of these poems is *Homeric Hymns*, but Callimachus' approach to the old Greek pantheon is quite different from that of the more ancient Homeric tradition. The gods are not worshiped, or even held in awe.[18] Their stories simply become the vehicles by which Callimachus reflects on the nature of human life, on the origins of things, or on the function of poetry and art. Religion and mythology have been dismissed in favor of philosophy, science, and esthetics.

Other poets prominent during the Hellenistic period include Theocritus and Apollonius. Theocritus was born (c. 305 BC) in Syracuse, but spent his adult life in Alexandria and on the Aegean island of Cos. His interests include rural life, which he describes in a detailed, but romanticized fashion, an important early example of the bucolic style. He was also excessively complimentary of his sovereign, Ptolemy II Philadelphus, whom in his *Encomium to Ptolemy* he calls "savior god." Apollonius, who was born in Alexandria, but who later moved to the island of Rhodes, was first a pupil, then bitter rival of Callimachus. Apollonius' most important work was the *Argonautica*, a retelling of the story of Jason and the golden fleece. This work was executed in the grand epic style, in conscious imitation of Homer (possibly one of the reasons for Apollonius' conflict with Callimachus). Apollonius also elevated the theme of *eros*, or romantic love, and thereby influenced generations of poets to come, including many modern writers.

In summary, it may be said of poetry during the Hellenistic period that it was vigorous and reflective of a wide range of thought and feeling. Much of it probed the frontiers of human knowledge and belief, much of it attempted to teach manners and morals (or to undermine the traditional understanding of these qualities), while much of it simply tried to spin good tales for the enjoyment of a large reading public.

c. Drama and Romance.   The Hellenistic culture that flourished after the death of Alexander was heir to the first and, in some ways, the most brilliant blossoming of dramatic talent in history. In the earlier Golden Age of Greek drama Aeschylus (c. 525–456 BC), Sophocles (c. 495–406 BC), and Euripides (c. 480–406 BC) had given to the world their fine tragedies, while Aristophanes (c. 445–385 BC) pioneered the art of dramatic comedy. These writers, who laid foundations for all of Western drama, portrayed humankind on a vast canvas and, in their separate fashions, probed fundamental questions surrounding the nature and purpose of human life. During the Hellenistic and Roman periods their plays were copied and acted throughout the Greek- and Latin-speaking worlds. But although there were imitators in the Hellenistic period who attempted to carry on the lofty traditions of earlier Greek drama, their achievements were, on the whole, quite poor.

In the field of comedy, while several names have survived, one stands above the rest, that of Menander of Athens (c. 342–291 BC). The Athens of Menander's day was caught in the upheavals and dislocations that followed the death of Alexander. Perhaps as a response to a popular sentiment that the conditions of life were largely beyond the control of the individual, the focus of interest in Menander's plays is considerably more limited than was the case with the older comedy of Aristophanes. In keeping with the principles of what scholars now call the New Comedy, Menander's concern is with the private affairs of individuals (perhaps the one area which still *was* under personal control). Thus his plots contain elements which, although presented in exaggerated form, would touch the lives of most people within his audiences. Menander's themes include erotic love, domestic relationships, bravery in the face of great danger, and the like. Frequently there is a maiden-in-distress motif, which is resolved, of course, in favor of the maiden. And all of this is set within a framework of slapstick and comic hyperbole that must have caused the stone amphitheaters of the Hellenistic world to resound with laughter.

So popular was this Athenian playwright, that snatches of Menander's lines found their way into the ordinary conversation of people throughout the Greek-speaking world. One brief line from Menander's *Thais* even appears in the New Testament, as Paul reminds his Corinthian readers that "bad company ruins good morals" (1 Cor. 15:33).[19]

As for the other great dramatic form, tragedy, the writers of the Hellenistic period apparently included no one of the stature of Menander, unless one includes the Jewish tragedian Ezekiel, who is discussed in a later chapter. Ptolemy II Philadelphus created an actors' guild in Alexandria and sponsored dramatic contests. The tragedies of the great Golden Age were acted, and contemporary imitators were encouraged, some of whose names have survived. But of their dramatic output we know almost nothing.

Another literary genre which, according to some, may be an extension of drama, is the Hellenistic romance. Although some elements of the romance may be found in Greek literature of the Golden Age, there is nothing precisely like it before the third century BC. It is the result of a new consciousness among Greek-speaking peoples that they are citizens of a wider world, one filled with exotic dangers and mystery. Thus the romance is typically a travel tale, one in which an individual journeys to distant lands and overcomes a variety of obstacles to fulfill some goal, usually the reclaiming of a lost love. There are strong erotic elements in the Hellenistic romance (as with Menander, a possible protest against a view which sees life as beyond the control of ordinary individuals), as well as fanciful descriptions of ocean voyages to distant places, struggles against monsters, giants, and the like. Frequently, there is a detailed account of a wreck at sea from which the hero or heroine is saved (compare the account of Paul's shipwreck and subsequent adventures on Malta in Acts 27:13–28:10).[20]

d. *Historiography.*   There were many writers of the Hellenistic period whose interests turned to the story of past human affairs. Unfortunately—like that of the poets—most of their material has failed to survive into our own time. We know their names and, to some extent, their contributions largely through references by later writers.[21] Of the numerous Hellenistic historians, only two are represented by extensive existing material, Polybius and Diodorus Siculus (i.e., the Sicilian), yet even their extant works represent only a fraction of their total output.

The high esteem in which Polybius (c. 201–119 BC) was held in ancient times and which almost certainly helped to preserve at least some of his writings has been confirmed by modern scholars. Although strictly speaking a Hellenistic writer (he was a native of Greece and wrote in the Greek language), Polybius lived at a time when Rome was rapidly rising to its dominance of the Mediterranean basin. During the Roman wars to conquer his Greek homeland, Polybius, who had participated in the defense of his native city, was carried to Rome as a hostage. Later released, he decided to remain in Rome and to serve for a time in the Roman army, being present at the final destruction of Rome's great rival Carthage in 146 BC.

Polybius' subject is, in fact, the rise of Rome, which he chronicles in an extensive *General History,* the work for which he is best remembered, but of which less than half is extant. For Polybius human events reveal larger sociopolitical meanings, the most important of which is that the rule of Rome is of great benefit to the well-being of humankind. An important criterion by which truth may be understood, according to Polybius, is the faculty of reason, which he elevates to a universal virtue. Not a religious person himself, Polybius nevertheless employed reason (or the perceived lack of it in some people) in defense of the necessity of religion:

> My own opinion at least is that the Romans have adopted this course of propagating religious awe for the sake of the common people. It is a course which perhaps would not have been necessary had it been possible to form a state composed of wise men, but as every multitude is fickle, full of lawless desires, unreasoned passion, and violent anger, the multitude must be held in by invisible terrors and suchlike pageantry.[22]

Polybius' view on religion must have been shared by many educated people during the Hellenistic and Roman periods, for, while the old gods of the Greek and Roman pantheons could no longer command the devotion of literate people, their cults and those of the newer deities were generally tolerated.

Another historian of the Hellenistic period whose work has been partially preserved is Diodorus Siculus of Agyrion (in Sicily), who lived for some undetermined period during the first century BC.[23] Diodorus evidences little interest in the Jews, and such interest as there is is generally negative since he views them as rebels against, first, the Seleucids and, later, the Romans. The following passage reflects a remarkably different view of Antiochus IV Epiphanes' desecration of the Jerusalem Temple, the immediate cause of the Hasmonean revolt, than those found in 1 and 2 Maccabees (cf. 1 Macc. 1:20–28; 2 Macc. 5:15–21):

> Antiochus, called Epiphanes, on defeating the Jews had entered the innermost sanctuary of the god's temple, where it was lawful for the priest alone to enter. Finding there a marble statue of a heavily bearded man seated on an ass, with a book in his hands, he supposed it to be an image of Moses, the founder of Jerusalem and organizer of the nation, the man, moreover, who had ordained for the Jews their misanthropic and lawless customs. And since Epiphanes was shocked by such hatred directed against all mankind, he had set himself to break down their traditional practices. Accordingly, he sacrificed before the image of the founder and the open-air altar of the god a great sow, and poured its blood over them. Then, having prepared its flesh, he ordered that their holy books, containing the xenophobic laws, should be sprinkled with the broth of the meat; that the lamp, which they call undying and which burns continually in the temple, should be extinguished; and that the high priest and the rest of the Jews should be compelled to partake of the meat.[24]

Two other historians of the early Hellenistic period also deserve to be mentioned here, although their writings have entirely disappeared except for quotations in later works. One is Berossus, a Babylonian priest of the god Marduk, who lived during the third century BC and who wrote a history in Greek of his native land. The historians Josephus and Eusebius quote Berossus, whose work they probably do not know directly, but to whom they gained access through their reading of other Hellenistic historians, primarily Alexander Polyhistor.[25] Berossus is important because it was through him that many traditions about Babylon were disseminated in the Hellenistic world, including the legend of the famous Hanging Gardens of Babylon, which some Greeks and Romans considered to be one of the Seven Wonders of the Ancient World:

> Within this palace he [Nebuchadnezzar] erected lofty stone terraces, in which he closely reproduced mountain scenery, completing the resemblance by planting them with all manner of trees and constructing the

so-called hanging garden; because his wife, having been brought up in Media, had a passion for mountain surroundings.[26]

Another early Hellenistic historian whose work has been preserved only in quotations by later writers is Manetho, an Egyptian priest who was active in the adoption by Ptolemy I Soter of the cult of Serapis. His account of the history of Egypt is referred to by Josephus, who reports two interesting narratives from Manetho. One is that of the Hyksos rulers of Egypt, who may be connected in some ways with the Joseph stories in the Old Testament. The other is a narrative about Moses (called Osarsiph by Manetho), whom the Ptolemaic writer describes as a priest of the Egyptian city of Heliopolis and renegade leader of an unruly mob of social outcasts. The tone of both of these stories is strongly anti-Jewish, and Josephus cites them in order to contradict them.

e. *Biography and Aretalogy.* Biographical narrative came to classical Greece at a relatively late date, in spite of Homer's interest in great heros and their accomplishments. Xenophon (434–355 BC) wrote *Cyropaedia* (meaning "The Education of Cyrus") in which he charted some aspects of the life of the founder of the Persian Empire, and both he (primarily in a work entitled *Memorabilia*) and Plato (in *Apology*) sketched the significance of the life of the philosopher Socrates. In the early Hellenistic period a pupil of Aristotle, Aristoxenus of Tarentum (in central Italy, c. 370–322 BC), wrote biographies, now lost, of several notable individuals, among them Pythagoras, Socrates, and Plato.[27]

It was perhaps the deeds of Alexander the Great which provided the impetus to make of biographical literature the important genre that it became during the Hellenistic period. As we noticed earlier, several of Alexander's contemporaries wrote stories of his life, including his former subordinate Ptolemy I Soter, but all of these have now been lost and are known to us only through snatches quoted by writers of subsequent generations. But such biographies were popular and lives of Alexander inspired similar accounts of other rulers in both the Hellenistic and Roman periods. Plutarch's (c. 46–120 AD) *Lives* and Suetonius' (c. 69–140 AD) *Lives of the Emperors,* as well as other Roman-period biographies, stand firmly upon the foundations of biography as developed among Hellenistic writers.

Of more specific relevance to early Judaism and Christianity is a specialized type of biography, the aretalogy (meaning "story of virtue").[28] Here the emphasis is on praise of the subject (who is a god or some prominent human hero) for that one's divine qualities, a praise that is often mixed with admiration for the hero's frequently displayed miraculous powers. Plato's portrayal of Socrates seems to have served as a model for this type of literature, but other subjects included the mathematician-philosopher Pythagoras (sixth century BC) and the

Cynic philosopher Diogenes (412–323 BC), as well as the legendary Hercules and Dionysus. The Jewish-Hellenist writer Philo's (c. 20 BC–50 AD) *Life of Moses* includes elements of the aretalogy, and there is reason to believe that this genre is reflected in the four Gospels of the New Testament, as well, because of similarities between the portrait of Jesus and the so-called "Divine Man" of the Hellenistic aretalogy. Earlier in this century a scholar, with considerable exaggeration, wrote

> In form and content the tradition concerning Jesus stands considerably nearer to the legend of Pythagoras than it does to the history or the legend of a "Jewish Messiah." Jesus is, in terms of the history of religion, more a Pythagoras than a [second century AD Jewish zealot] Bar Kochba.[29]

That is hyperbole and should be understood as such, yet points of contact between the Hellenistic aretalogy and the New Testament Gospels, upon which this statement is based, should not be overlooked.

3. *Education: The Gymnasium*

As in many societies, the schools of the Hellenistic world were a primary transmitter of culture. As might be expected, some education was private, and tutors were often employed by parents of means to come into the home to teach the children of the family. But much education, while certainly not "public" in the American sense of that term, was socially visible. This was centered in the gymnasium, an institution that was part educational institution, part training center for young athletes. The meaning of the word *gymnasium* is connected with a Greek root which means *naked*, a reference to the state of undress in which athletic competition was carried on by Greeks in both classical and Hellenistic periods. This etymological association reflects that, originally, the emphasis in the gymnasia was upon *physical* education. But well before the end of the classical period the gymnasia in Greece proper and in the Greek city-states of Asia Minor had also become centers in which young boys were trained in the arts and sciences. When one remembers that in the Greek consciousness both athletic skills and the arts were related to the worship of the gods (i.e., the important games—Olympic, Pythian, Isthmian, etc.—were dedicated to various deities), this combination is not so unusual as might first appear. Also the ancient Greeks were as aware as many moderns that a sound body helps to make a sound mind.

In the Hellenistic kingdoms these gymnasia assumed a special role, in light of the numerical minority in which the Greek ruling classes often found themselves. The gymnasia became centers for the cultivation and perpetuation of all that was Greek: food, clothing (or the lack of it, in the case of athletic events), drama, literature, music, and so on. One of the ways in which affluent non-Greek families in the Hellenistic kingdoms who wished to assimilate into the (what must often have been to them) more elevated Greek social strata was to enroll their sons in a local gymnasium. There the youths became "Hellenized," a process by which, among other things, new social and financial opportunities became available to them which had not been available to their parents.

But the gymnasia never lost their original role as training centers for athletes. All of the traditional sports that the modern mind quite properly associates with ancient Greece—running, wrestling, discus and javelin throwing, and many more—were to be found on the playing fields of the gymnasia. For excellence in performance there were coveted awards, and the winners frequently had their names preserved in prominent locations for future generations to see, as for example the following inscription from the second century BC found at the site of the Hellenistic town of Cedreae in Asia Minor:

> The Confederation [or Guild] of the peoples of the Chersonese salutes Onasiteles the son of Onesistratus, victor in the furlong-race three times in the boys' category at the Isthmia, . . . [and here follows an extended list of Onasiteles' other triumphs].[30]

But the awards were not always for athletic acumen. We may imagine the pride with which these young men of the community of Magnesia on the Menander River in Asia Minor—and, of course, their parents—surveyed the stone which bore this inscription:

> For singing to the lyre: Dionysius son of Apollodurus,
>   Cleatus son of Morimus, Pythagoras son of Apollophanes.
> For painting: Apollonius son of Apollonius, Callistratus
>   son of Zophryus, Alcis son of Zopyrus.
> For arithmetic: Neoptolemus son of Admetus, Demetrius son of
>   Anaxicrates.[31]

The author of the confident statement in 2 Timothy, whatever else he may have been, was a good citizen of the Hellenistic world:

> I have fought the good fight, I have finished the race, I have kept the faith. From now on there is reserved for me the crown of righteousness, which the Lord, the righteous judge, will give me on that day, and not only to me but also to all who have longed for his appearing.
>
> (2 Tim. 4:7)

C. Hellenistic Philosophy and Religion

1. Philosophy[32]

The Greek-speaking men and women of the Hellenistic world inherited from the preAlexandrian Greeks a variety of rich traditions in philosophical and religious thought. They also inherited a fierce independence by which these philosophical and religious notions were forced to compete with one another in the marketplace of ideas. Although there was a pantheon of Greek gods that had been worshiped for centuries, by the time of Alexander few seriously believed in them. Their names might be invoked and temples built to their honor, but for the most part the Hellenistic world was a melting pot of diverse philosophical and religious teachings and, with some exceptions, men and women were generally free to choose whatever doctrines they pleased—or several doctrines at once! The narrative of Paul's encounter with the Hellenistic philosophers on the Areopagus in Athens well illustrates the kind of ideological give-and-take that was commonplace in the Hellenistic world (Acts 17:16–34).

This freedom of ideas stands, of course, in contrast to the conditions which prevailed in those empires which ruled the Ancient Near East before Alexander, particularly in the empires of the Egyptians, the Assyrians, and the Babylonians. There the worship of certain gods was closely tied to membership in the community of the nation-state, the king himself usually having certain responsibilities for the maintenance of the cult.[33] The authority of the state religion was an issue which would be raised again, by the Seleucid emperor Antiochus IV Epiphanes and by the later Roman cult of emperor worship, to name but two examples. But much of the Hellenistic world permitted the free flow of philosophical and religious teaching, a fact which bore profound consequences for both Judaism and Christianity, especially in the latter's early efforts at expansion.

A number of philosophical systems were important during the Hellenistic period and thereafter, but four are of special significance: Platonism, Epicureanism, Stoicism, and Cynicism. We shall deal briefly with these before turning to Hellenistic religions.

a. *Platonism.* The philosopher Plato (c. 427–347 BC), one of the most original thinkers who ever lived, spent most of his life in Athens where he was a pupil of the great Socrates and a teacher of Alexander's tutor, Aristotle. At his school in Athens, "The Academy," virtually every area of human knowledge was investigated: politics, art, ethics, and religion, among others. Central to Plato's teaching was his view that ultimate reality exists only in ideas, and that particular things we may experience with our senses are impermanent and unreal. The highest ideas are abstractions such as justice, beauty, truth, and goodness, and men and women achieve meaning in life by relying upon their powers of reason to incorporate these ideals into their day-to-day living.

One of Plato's more important teachings was that of the immortality of the soul. The soul of an individual corresponds to that person's body in somewhat the same way that the idea of a tree corresponds to the trunk, the branches and the leaves of the tree which we can see and touch. Since the soul has enjoyed a previous existence, upon a person's death, the soul returns to the realm of ideas from which it came. The following, from Plato's dialogue *Phaedo*, is part of a conversation which Socrates has with two pupils, Simmias and Cebes:

> Very true, said Cebes; about half of what was required has been proven; to wit, that our souls existed before we were born:—that the soul will exist after death as well as before birth is the other half of which the proof is still wanting, and has to be supplied; when that is given the demonstration will be complete.
> But that proof, Simmias and Cebes, has already been given, said Socrates, if you put the two arguments together—I mean this and the former one, in which we admitted that everything living is born of the dead. For if the soul exists before birth, and in coming to life and being born can be born only from death and dying, must she not after death continue to exist, since she has to be born again?[34]

The Platonic view of the immortality of the soul was to influence later Christian theology in profound ways, many Christians finding it a more satisfactory description of life after death than Paul's doctrine of the resurrection of the body (1 Cor. 15:1–58).

Plato did not deny the existence of the gods of Greek mythology. To the contrary he stressed the importance of their worship, and declared that atheism is a crime which the state must punish. Yet Plato's gods seem to be philosophical abstractions more than living beings, and one senses that Plato's pupils often gave their deities little more than lip service. Platonism continued as an important philosophical influence for many centuries, the Jewish writer Philo representing an interesting melding of Platonic and Jewish thought.

b. *Epicureanism.*   Epicurus (341–270 BC) was also a citizen of Athens who, like Plato before him, founded a school there, called "The Garden" because of its location. Yet Epicurus reached conclusions very different from those of Plato. For Epicurus the senses may be relied upon, therefore what we see, feel, hear, smell, and taste is true and real. In fact, ultimate reality is to be found in the world of matter, which is composed of minute particles called atoms (as had previously been taught by Leucippus of Miletus and Democritus of Abdera). Atoms are eternal and, because they differ in size, shape, and color, they form a material world of varying textures and patterns.

The highest good for men and women is to avoid pain and to achieve pleasure. But because human beings are rational beings, mental pleasure is superior to physical pleasure. And because most pleasures that are overindulged create pain, moderation in all things should be considered a goal of the rational person. The highest pleasure is friendship and, in light of this belief, many Epicureans lived in secluded communities to which were admitted only those who embraced their philosophy.

Epicurus affirmed the existence of the gods on the grounds that, since human reason is based on the senses, and the senses tell us what is true, human ideas of the gods must be based in reality. But the gods, like human beings, are composed of atoms and are therefore mortal. What is more, since the gods are not concerned about human life, men and women need have no concern about the gods.

Epicureanism spread throughout the Hellenistic world and was influential well into Roman times, although its adherants were often misunderstood and villified because of their tendency to seclusion. Almost none of Epicurus' writings have survived, but the Latin poet Lucretius (96–55 BC) eloquently espoused the Epicurean viewpoint in his long poem *On the Nature of Things* (*De Rerum Natura*). In the following excerpt from that work, one encounters not only the Epicurean teaching concerning pleasure and pain, but a certain attitude of self-congratulation which often characterized their outlook:

What a joy it is, when out at sea the stormwinds are lashing the waters, to gaze from the shore at the heavy stress some other man is enduring! Not that anyone's afflictions are in themselves a source of delight; but to realize from what troubles you yourself are free is joy indeed . . . But this is the greatest joy of all: to stand aloof in a quiet citadel, stoutly fortified by the teaching of the wise, and to gaze down from that elevation on others wandering aimlessly in a vain search for the way of life, pitting their wits against another, disputing for precedence, struggling night and day with unstinted effort to scale the pinnacles of wealth and power. O joyless hearts of men! . . . Do you not see that nature is clamoring for two things only, a body free from pain, a mind released from worry and fear for the enjoyment of pleasurable sensations.[35]

The presence of Epicurean and Stoic philosophers is noted by the Book of Acts (17:18) in connection with Paul's visit to Athens.

c. *Stoicism*.   The views of the Stoics may be traced to a certain teacher, Zeno of Citium on Cyprus (c. 335–265 BC), who came to Athens about the year 300. The name of this philosophical school derives from Zeno's favorite place for meeting with his pupils, the *Stoa Poikile*, or "Painted Porch" in the agora, or marketplace, in Athens. Like the Epicureans, the Stoics were materialists, but they went beyond the Epicureans to identify the material world with God. In other words, theirs was a type of pantheism which stressed the unity of all forms of being: mind, matter, God, man/woman—all constituted a unity. The duty of a person is to live rationally, that is, within the laws that govern the material world. These laws were understood by the Stoics to be the Divine Reason or *Logos* and the highest human good is attained by understanding the nature of *Logos* and by submitting to it. Human emotions are to the soul as diseases are to the body. One must attempt to be free of fear, desire, pleasure and the like if one is to attain the inner tranquility which permits one to live in harmony with *Logos*. [36]

The materialism and (as it would seem to many today) the fatalism of the Stoics did not prevent them from expressions of deep beauty and piety, as is demonstrated by the following lines from the *Hymn to Zeus* by the Stoic writer Cleanthes (d. c. 232 BC):

> Thou [Zeus] knowest (how) to make the crooked straight,
> Prune all excess, give order to the orderless;
> For unto thee the unloved still is lovely—
> And thus in one all things are harmonized,
> The evil with the good, so that one Word [*Logos*]
> Should be in all things everlastingly. [37]

d. *Cynicism*.   The Cynics preceeded the Stoics, to whom they were closely related, but are listed here because they represent less a philosophical system than a method of philosophical argumentation characterized by confrontation and polemic. A leading Cynic teacher was Diogenes of Sinope in Asia Minor (c. 412–323 BC) who taught in Athens in the fourth century BC. He is reported to have rejected all social conventions and values and to have lived in a tub. He bluntly reminded his fellow citizens that self control and the denial of physical comfort were goals to be attained, as were simplicity and honesty in personal dealings. One famous story about Diogenes is that he carried a lamp through the streets of Athens in an effort to locate an honest person. The straightforward nature of his social argumentation won a number of admirers—and probably more detractors. There is a tale (doubtless untrue) that Alexander the Great once came to see Diogenes, whom he discovered basking in the rays of the sun. "Ask any favor you wish," Alexander condescendingly invited the philosopher. "Get out of my sunlight," Diogenes is supposed to have replied. To which Alexander allegedly said, "If I could not be Alexander, I would like to be Diogenes." But other contemporaries, smarting from his bluntness, referred to Diogenes as a dog (*kyon*), presumably the origin of the word "Cynic."

2. Religion[38]

If the decay of confidence in the old gods of Mount Olympus had led, among the more rationally-inclined citizens of the Hellenistic world, to new forms of philosophy, those with a mystical bent were attracted to the new religions which flourished in the Hellenistic period and beyond. To a modern observer this teeming mixture of faiths and counterfaiths seems baffling and contradictory, but for the Hellenists themselves it was all a part of the robust, sometimes violent energy that characterized their lives. Although religious systems competed with each other and with the various philosophies for adherents, they could also be flexible and adaptive when the need arose. Consequently, it was often not considered unusual that a given individual might identify with more than one cult and/or philosophical system, or that the worship of a given deity in one place would have a quite different character from the worship of that same diety (who might, moreover, be known by a different name) in another place. Except for the state religions which, to one degree or another, regarded the ruler as god and which therefore had certain civil and political implications, there was usually no central hierarchy that defined "orthodoxy" or attempted to enforce it. Consequently, the lines between one Hellenistic system of faith and another are frequently blurred.

a. *The Mystery Religions.* Perhaps no other form of religious expression in the Hellenistic world was shaped to meet the needs of individual men and women more than the so-called Mystery religions, which enjoyed a wide following. The details of the manner in which each Mystery was observed was a closely held secret, the knowledge of which was limited to the initiates of that particular cult. The word *mystery*, in fact, seems to come from a Greek verb that means *to close*, in this case the lips. Because of this secrecy, what information we do possess about the Mysteries often comes from their detractors and, for this reason, must be carefully weighed. However, certain features are recognizable as common characteristics of the Mysteries as a whole. These include: (1) a rite of initiation or purification by which the individual is rendered worthy of participation in the activity of the Mystery; (2) a sense of personal relationship with a deity or group of deities whom the initiate now claims as his or her own; and (3) the hope of life beyond death. Some of the Mysteries were centered upon devotion to deities who had been venerated as part of the Greek pantheon for centuries before the Hellenistic period, while others focused upon gods and goddesses whose homes had originally been in the East or in Egypt. While there were many Mysteries, our discussion will be limited to two of the more prominent, the Eleusian and Dionysian Mysteries.

i. The Eleusian Mystery.   One of the more significant Mysteries was that practiced at a shrine in the community of Eleusis, near the city of Athens, and, to a lesser extent, at cultic centers in many places throughout the Hellenistic world. It is clear that, in the beginning at least, this was a fertility cult based upon devotion to the goddess of the grain harvest, Demeter, and her daughter Kore, who is also called Persephone. According to the myth surrounding these two figures, Kore was abducted from her mother at the time of the autumn harvest by Aidoneus (also called Pluto), king of the dead:

> Demeter of the beauteous hair, goddess divine, I sing,
> She and the slender-ankled maid, her daughter, whom the king
> Aidoneus seized, by Zeus' decree. He found her, as she played
> Far from her mother's side, who reaps the corn with golden blade.[39]

Demeter grieved for her daughter and searched far and wide in the hope of finding her. During this time (i.e., winter) the earth, symphathetic to Demeter's sorrow, was barren and refused to yield its fruit and produce. But ultimately Aidoneus released Persephone, whereupon Demeter, in her joy over having her daughter with her again, commanded the earth to bring forth its abundance once more:

> And immediately [Demeter] sent the corn sprouting in the fertile
>   fields,
> till the whole wide earth was heavy with leaves and flowers.[40]

What made the Demeter cult more than just another fertility religion, however, was the process of acceptance, by a rite of initiation, into membership in the cult. Several stages appear to have been involved in the new member's initiation, but a climax came in a grand procession in which the members of the cult walked from Athens to the shrine at Eleusis, a sacred parade which must have been an impressive sight to see and an even more impressive experience in which to participate. Membership in the Mystery implied more than a simple association of like-minded persons; it included the promise of release from earthbound concerns and of life beyond death. It may be that the Eleusian beliefs included some expectation of personal rebirth (as in the annual "rebirth" of the earth), but they certainly held out the promise that, for the believer, existence both in the present and beyond the grave was of a different order than for nonbelievers.

The Roman orator Cicero, who had been initiated into the Eleusian mysteries, described them in more than religious terms:

> They educated us out of a life of barbarous rusticity into civilization. The ceremonies are called initiations, and we recognize in them the first principles of living. We have gained from them the way of living in happiness and dying with a better hope.[41]

The fact that several Roman emperors, including Augustus, were initiated into the Eleusian Mystery offers evidence of its widespread acceptance.

ii. The Dionysian Mystery.   Dionysus, also called Bacchus, was the focus of another important Mystery Religion that was observed in many places in the Hellenistic world. So widespread and popular was the cult of Dionysus that many local varieties flourished, producing a great number of stories concerning this god and his adventures, not all of which may be reconciled with one another. The symbols of this diety of intoxication and fertility were the grape (or the wine goblet) and the ivy plant, while rebirth and intoxication—even madness—were experiences often associated with him.

There were several versions of the story of Dionysus' miraculous birth, the most often repeated of which went something like this: Semele, the daughter of King Cadmus of Thebes, fell in love with the great god Zeus, by whom she became pregnant. The majesty of Zeus, however, was too much for Semele and she died as a result of the brilliance of his presence. But Zeus claimed the fetus and sheltered it in the flesh of his own thigh until the child's birth. Because of this, Dionysus was widely referred to by the title, *Dithyrambos*, or "twice born one." And because of his special relationship with Zeus, Dionysus could also claim to be "god's son."[42]

As a youth Dionysus lived in Nysa, a vaguely identified rural region where he roamed the mountains and woodlands with friendly nymphs, cavorting and engaging in various kinds of pleasure. It was at this time, according to the myths, that Dionysus learned the art of making wine, and the young god was so charmed by the liquid's powers of intoxication that he traveled throughout the world to share this knowledge with human beings. During the course of these journeys he survived a number of incredible adventures, the stories of which grew more and more elaborate over the generations. He was even said to have traveled as far as India and to have taught the arts of civilization (including fermentation of the grape) in that distant land.

When he returned to Greece, he was often greeted with hostility, a feature of the stories about Dionysus that some scholars feel may reflect persecution of Dionysus' worshipers at the hands of their fellow citizens. A drama entitled *Bacchae* (meaning "Women Followers of Baccus/Dionysus") by the great

Athenian writer Euripedes (c. 485–406 BC) tells of one such incident. When Dionysus returns to Thebes, he is thrown into prison by the king, Pentheus. However, the god escapes and, in revenge, afflicts the women of Thebes, including Pentheus' mother, Agave, with madness. The women hurry to a nearby wooded mountain where they engage in the kind of orgies associated with Dionysus. When Penthus follows, Agave seizes and dismembers him, thinking that he is a lion. In the most compelling moment of the play, Agave proudly displays the head of this "lion," only then to be snapped out of her ecstatic trance and discover what she has done.[43]

One version of the stories about Dionysus spoke of his violent death at the hands of the god Perseus, who threw him into the sea. But in another version, he is raised to life by his father, Zeus, so that he becomes, in the words of the biographer Plutarch, "the god who is destroyed, who disappears, who relinquishes life and then is born again."[44]

Dionysus is mentioned in Greek literature as early as Homeric times, but not until Hellenistic and Roman times does his cult appear to gain wide popularity. There were several Dionysian festivals throughout the year, and there can be little doubt they were often debaucheries of the most extravagant kind. On one occasion (186 BC) the Roman senate enacted legislation to curb the excesses of the Bacchanalia, as these rites were called. But on a more positive note, the Dionysian rituals, which often involved role-playing by various participants, are credited with being one of the important foundation stones of Greek drama.[45]

It seems certain that some celebrations associated with Dionysus were little more than drunken brawls and orgies. Yet the veneration of this deity also functioned as a kind of Mystery through participation in which some hoped to gain immortality. The prominence of the Dionysian cult among Greek-speaking people is reflected in the report that, during the attempts to Hellenize Jerusalem which led to the Hasmonean revolt, the cult of Dionysus was among those forms of Hellenistic religious expression forced upon the Jewish peoples:

> On the monthly celebration of the king's birthday, the Jews were taken, under bitter constraint, to partake of the sacrifices; and when a festival of Dionysus was celebrated, they were compelled to wear wreaths of ivy and to walk in the procession in honor of Dionysus.
>
> (2 Macc. 6:7)

Recent archaeological excavations in the town of Sepphoris in Galilee have unearthed mosiacs which portray scenes associated with the myth of Dionysus and which date from the third century AD.[46]

b. *The Worship of the Ruler.*   There is one other form of religious expression in the Hellenistic world which should be included here, although its claims upon the allegiance of individuals was considerably different from those of other Hellenistic religions, and that is the worship of the ruler. It became an issue of special importance during the years following Alexander's death, and for some groups—especially Jews and, later, Christians—a focus of resistance to the will of the state.

There are at least two historical traditions at work in the rise to prominence of the cult of the ruler, the first of which is Greek. In the Greek mind a special place had always been reserved for the hero, that individual either human or divine who attained remarkable achievements. The Homeric poems and hymns are responsible for promoting this view, but even they rely upon a tradition which was centuries old before Homer lived and wrote. And they certainly inspired countless others—philosophers, poets, dramatists, and the like—who wrote in the shadow of Homer. Plato's vision of the philosopher-king, the individual of superior wisdom and skill who benevolently but firmly rules the state, is one form of the heroic ideal, and there were many, many others. The fact that in Greece of the classical period the strong ruler was generally not accorded the status of deity, and the absolute political power that usually accompanied such status, is probably a result of a deep commitment (among some Greeks, at least) to the principles of democracy. And it is interesting that, even when the idea of the divinity of the ruler had gained wide acceptance in the Hellenistic world, it took firmer root in those lands with large non-Greek populations than it did in the Greek homeland. There was already some evidence that the ruler cult was rising in influence before the end of the classical period, but the heroic dimensions in which Alexander was viewed, both in his own time and later, gave new strength to the idea that the ruler was also some kind of god. Sanctuaries and temples for the worship of the dead Alexander sprang up in many places within the Hellenistic world, most notably in Alexandria, the final resting place of his body.

The other influence at work in the rise of the ruler cult was the long history of the acceptance of such a view among some non-Greek peoples, most prominently the Egyptians. The pharaoh had been regarded as divine since deep antiquity, and although different generations of Egyptians nuanced their understanding of the pharaoh's divinity in various ways, he was usually identified either with the sun god Re or the ruler of the realm of the dead Osiris. Not even the monotheistic reforms of Akhenaton (Amenhotep IV [1369–1353 BC]) had succeeded in dislodging this view. In fact, Akhenaton seems to have made some concessions in this regard, for while he asserted that no god but Aton (the sun disk) was to be worshiped, he, Akhenaton, was to be the deity's devotee, while ordinary people were to channel their allegiance to Aton through the pharaoh himself. Such was the Egyptian commitment to the divinity of the king.

Alexander's conquest of Egypt, which resulted in his reception as the new pharaoh, quite logically meant that he was accorded divine status, as well. His visit to the shrine of Ammon/Zeus and his designation there as "Son of Ammon" was an early step not only toward his own deification, but toward divine status for the Greek-speaking monarchs of the Ptolemaic dynasty who were to come. Just as Ptolemy I Soter patronized the cult of the dead Alexander, so his son, Ptolemy II Philadelphus, would sponsor the worship of Ptolemy I and, upon her death, of his (Soter's) wife, the queen, whom Ptolemy II characterized as Savior Gods. Ptolemy II also elevated himself to divine status by proclaiming himself and his wife (who was also his sister) to be *theoi adelphoi*, the "Sibling Gods." As Ptolemaic political power waned, the emphasis upon the divinity of the king seems to have grown more urgent. Ptolemy IV Philopater claimed descent from the god Dionysus and is reported to have been tatooed with an ivy leaf (cf. 3 Macc. 2:29).

Among the rulers of the Seleucid kingdom, a comparable movement toward divinization may be found. Seleucus I Nicator was proclaimed divine by his son and successor Antiochus I Soter, while Antiochus III the Great conferred the rank of deity upon himself and upon his sister-queen Laodice. The great gods Zeus and Apollo, the chief deities of the Seleucid kingdom, were understood to be incarnate in Antiochus III, a political theology which was given a new impetus by Antiochus IV Epiphanes (meaning "manifest god") in his dealings with the Jews. Whereas the Seleucid realms generally enjoyed wide cultural and religious autonomy, Antiochus IV viewed the peculiar institutions of the Jews, including their monotheism, as seditious, and his attempts to enforce the worship of Zeus, which was also part of an attempt to impose his own political will, was a leading cause of the Hasmonean revolt.

Excursus

Non-Jewish Hellenistic Writers
Quoted in the New Testament

New Testament scholars have identified three non-Jewish writers who are quoted in the New Testament: Epimenides (quoted in Titus 1:12), Aratus (Acts 17:28) and Menander (1 Cor. 15:33), all of whom wrote in Greek.

Epimenides. The earliest of these is Epimenides of Crete, who was active during the late seventh and early sixth centuries BC and whose life story is only sketchily preserved. One legend is that while tending his father's sheep on Crete, he went into a cave to rest, but fell into a sleep that lasted for fifty-seven years. When he awoke and returned to his home, he was greeted as one who had returned from the gods. He seems to have lived for a time in Athens early in the sixth century, but according to one story he returned to Crete before his death. Another tradition alleges that he died and was buried in Sparta, while yet another legend says that he lived for more than 300 years.

What does seem certain is that Epimenides was a writer of considerable renown in the Greek-speaking world, perhaps his most important work being an account of the adventures of Jason in his search for the golden fleece. Unfortunately for modern readers who would wish to evaluate for themselves the work of this Cretan poet, none of his writings remain except for fragments quoted by later authors.

One of Epimenides' lines which seems to have attained something of the status of a proverb was this: "Cretans are always liars." This barb may have been popular because it was an ethnic slur that appealed to a prejudice held by nonCretan inhabitants of the eastern Mediterranean. But a large part of its attraction surely consisted in the fact that it presented to the rational Greek mind a self-negating statement. If "Cretans are always liars," Epimenides' statement to that effect could not possibly be true since he himself was a Cretan. Such were the games of logic that Greeks loved to play.

The popularity of Epimenides' axiom is reflected in a poem by Callimachus, the editor of the catalogue of the library in Alexandria and greatest of the Hellenistic poets. In his first *Hymn*, written about 280 BC, Callimachus

33

addresses the problem of the birth of Zeus, the circumstances of which were described in various ways by different myths of the great father of the gods. Callimachus ponders the matter in these words:

> Zeus, in Ida's mountains they say you were born,
> but also [others say], Zeus, in Arcadia. Which, Father, have lied?

Zeus then responds to this question by enigmatically quoting the axiom of Epimenides, which Callimachus then turns into a statement of his own concerning Zeus' immortality:

> "Cretans are always liars," [answers Zeus]. Yes, Lord, your tomb Cretans built [or so they say]; and you did not die—you are forever.[1]

The proverbial quality of Epimenides' statement is reflected in Titus 1:12–13, where the negative opinion of the Cretans' moral character is applied to certain unnamed opponents of the author of the letter.[2]

Menander.   We have already taken note of Paul's quotation from the play *Thais* by Menander of Athens (c. 342–291) in 1 Cor. 15:33: "Bad company ruins good morals." Very little is known of this comedy apart from a few references to it by other ancient writers and some seven lines which have been preserved. *Thais* seems to have been among Menander's early plays and to have focused upon the escapades of a beautiful, but unscrupulous woman (the title character) who sold her favors to the highest bidder. It is apparently one of Thais' suitors who speaks these four of the surviving lines:

> Sing to me, goddess, sing of such a one as she:
> audacious, beautiful and plausable withal; she does
> you wrongs; she locks her door; keeps asking you
> for gifts; she loveth none, but ever makes pretense.[3]

It is not known in what context the line cited by Paul appears in the comedy, but the words could well be a reflection of one of the play's characters concerning Thais' corrupting influence upon the innocent men in her life.[4]

Aratus.   One of perhaps two Hellenistic writers quoted in Acts 17:28, Aratus of Soli (in Cilicia, the native region of Paul) was active early in the third century BC. He worked as poet and physician at the court of the Macedonian king Antigonus II Gonatus (283–239), whose patronage attracted several artists and writers to the capital city, Pella. Aratus' literary output was wideranging in its subject matter, which included literary criticism and poetry, and frequently displayed influences from the Stoic philosophers. But it was as a scientific observer that his most popular work was done (and his only creation to be preserved to the present), a poem entitled *Phaenomena*, which dealt with astronomy and meteorology. *Phaenomena* was so popular in the Greco-Roman world that it was several times rendered into Latin translation, including one by Cicero (106–43 BC). In a manner not unusual for a Hellenistic scientific treatise, *Phaenomena* begins with a statement in homage to Zeus who, in the words of Aratus, "himself set the heavenly bodies in the sky" (*Phaen.* l. 10). In this introduction to his most widely read work, Aratus writes the line quoted by the author of Acts:

> From Zeus let us begin whom we mortals never
> leave unmentioned; full of Zeus are all the ways,
> and all concourse of men, and full is the sea
> and the harbors. Everywhere we all need Zeus.
> For we are also his offspring.[5]

In addition to the quotations from Epimenides, Menander, and Aratus, a fourth citation appears before the line from Aratus in Acts 17:28: "In him we live and move and have our being." One early tradition among Christian exegetes attributes this statement, like that in Titus 1:12, to Epimenides of Crete, an assertation that can neither be confirmed nor denied because of the loss of virtually all Epimenides' works. Another possibility, one based upon what seems to be the Stoic flavor of the statement, is that it is an additional line from a lost work of Aratus or that it is from some other Stoic poet, possibly Cleanthes of Assos (western Asia Minor—d. c. 232 BC), a poet of considerable reputation and successor to Zeno of Citium (in Cyprus—d. c. 265), founder of Stoicism.[6]

Chapter 2

JEWISH REACTIONS TO HELLENISM

A. THE HASMONEAN REVOLT

1. Background of the Hasmonean Revolt[1]

The end of Persian rule in Palestine and the beginning of that of the Greeks and Macedonians arrived violently for the citizens of the coastal cities of Tyre and Gaza, when those centers were besieged and captured by Alexander the Great. But for the majority of the region's inhabitants who lived inland and who thereby escaped the direct onslaught of Alexander's army, the transition was probably less traumatic. This included Jerusalem, of course, and those Jews who lived in and around their ancient capital city. Yet one very dramatic effect of Alexander's conquest must have been felt even by those of the interior: the increased presence of foreigners and of the influences which they brought to bear on daily life.

During the early years of the Persian period Jerusalem and Judaea had been somewhat removed from the main centers of political activity, since they lay near the imperial border with Egypt. Later, with the conquest of Egypt under the Persian king, Cambyses (529–522 BC), there was more traffic through the area, as Persian military detachments came and went, along with the inevitable cadres of bureaucrats, merchants, and opportunists. But with the establishment, following Alexander's death, of two strong Hellenistic kingdoms in the region, Ptolemaic Egypt to the south and Seleucid Syria to the north, Palestine was thrust to the center of the stage of conflict between the eastern Mediterranean's most powerful rivals. The area became the highway and frequently the battlefield between the two monarchies resident in Alexandria and in Antioch-on-the-Orontes.

For their part, the Ptolemies, who obtained that portion of Alexander's kingdom south of Tyre and Sidon, were apparently as tolerant of local customs and manners of life as the Persians had been before them. Although very little is known about the affairs of Ptolemaic Palestine in the third century BC, it is evident that the Ptolemaic tax collectors plied their trade there, as they did in Egypt proper. One collection of papyrus documents, the so-called Zenon Papyri,[2] records the visit to Palestine of a group of Ptolemaic officials about 259 BC. From these records it is clear that the native inhabitants of Palestine, including the Jews, were considered little more than serfs in that economic pyramid which placed the Greeks and Macedonians at the top. And yet there was apparently little of the kind of persecution which later came to be associated with Seleucid rule.

Some Jews, in fact, did quite well for themselves under Ptolemaic rule. One prominent Jewish family was that of the Oniads, who occupied the office of high priest and who claimed (whether correctly, we do not know) to be descended from Solomon's high priest, Zadok (1 Kings 2:35). As the position of high priest was heredity, it was one that gained great influence for the Oniad family, to say nothing of considerable wealth. That the Ptolemies seem not to have interfered with the Oniad succession over the several generations during which they ruled Jerusalem or with the religious ceremonies at the Temple is a commentary upon their attitude of religious tolerance.

Another important Jewish family of the period were the Tobiads, who also may have enjoyed ancient origins. One of the returned exiles (but one whose Jewishness was questioned) was named Tobiah (Ezra 2:60, Neh. 7:62), and another individual of that same name, called also "the Ammonite," appears later as a powerful adversary of Nehemiah (Neh. 2:10 and elsewhere). Ptolemy II Philadelphus (285–246 BC) appointed a certain Tobiah to an important military post in Transjordan (formerly Ammon), an individual whose name appears prominently in the Zenon Papyri. This Tobiah had a son, Joseph, who was prominent in political affairs and who also served as Ptolemaic tax collector in Palestine and was a bitter rival of the reigning Oniad high priest, Onias II.[3] That there were other Jews who gained wealth and some limited political influence during the Ptolemaic period is almost certain, although most Jews seem to have led lives that were unremarkable, apart from the economic oppression under which they lived.

With the explusion from Palestine of the Ptolemaic forces by Antiochus III the Great (223–187 BC) in 200 BC, a new era began in the lives of Palestine's Jews. This change may not have been immediately apparent. Although many Palestinian Jews suffered from the usual ravages of war, destruction was far from total, so that, for most, life under the Seleucids was little different from that under the Ptolemies. If anything, the Seleucid rulers had proven even more tolerant of local diversity than had the Ptolemies, in light of the wide range of cultural and religious expressions which prevailed throughout the Seleucid empire. The one group of Jews for whom the new state of affairs did bring significant changes, however, was that of people who had been politically active, either for or against their former Ptolemaic rulers. It was their reaction to the coming of Seleucid rule which helped to bring about that series of upheavals which we remember as the Hasmonean or Maccabean revolt.[4]

The convenient way in which the Hasmonean struggle for independence is often characterized is as a fight by those who wished to retain their freedom of worship against a tyrant who was attempting to deprive them of that right. That is true, but only partly so. The Hasmonean revolt, which itself was a series of complicated military and political movements, was the complex result of at least three additional factors: (1) struggles for power among prominent Jewish families (even among individuals within a given family), (2) political antagonism between pro-Ptolemaic and pro-Seleucid factions among the Jews, and (3) continuing conflict between the Ptolemaic and Seleucid kingdoms. Because the primary historical sources of this period are incomplete and partisan,[5] the detailed truth behind all of the events will never be known. But in broad outline the struggle seems to have progressed as follows:

During the reign of Seleucus IV Philopator (187–175 BC), successor to Antiochus III, one of the subordinates of the high priest, Onias III, a man named Simon who bore the title "captain of the Temple" (2 Macc. 3:4), denounced the high priest to the Seleucid authorities and described to them the large amount of wealth maintained by the high priest in the Temple treasury. A Seleucid official was sent to the Temple to confiscate the money, but returned empty handed.[6] It is not possible to determine all that motivated Simon to denounce Onias, but probably he was in league with one faction within the family of the Tobiads. Together they seem to have formed an alliance against Onias III and his friend Hyrcanus, the elder head of the Tobiad family and son of the now deceased Joseph. The apparent reason for this rift: Simon and the younger Tobiads were pro-Seleucid, Onias and the older Tobiad were pro-Ptolemaic. In the face of this challenge to his authority, Onias appealed to King Seleucus and traveled to Antioch to present his case before him in person.[7] About this time, however, Seleucus died and his brother Antiochus IV Epiphanes (175–164 BC) became the new king.

The portrait of this ruler which has endured across the centuries is far from flattering. Quixotic and moody, Antiochus was capable of displaying the kind of malicious cruelty that has been too often typical of absolute monarchs. Yet his dealings with Jerusalem's Jews, which were extreme in this regard, were not typical of his dealings with his other subject peoples, most of whom were treated in far less abusive ways. The likely explanation of his sadistic efforts to suppress the Jews and their traditions is to be understood in the context of those political circumstances in which Antiochus found himself. As we saw earlier, his outbursts toward the Jews came at a time when the eastern provinces of the Seleucid Empire were in disarray due to widespread revolt. Antiochus' efforts to compensate for the loss of the East by strengthening his position in the West had resulted in his humiliating rebuff by the Romans in Egypt.[8] Out of frustration and fear he then tried to consolidate his hold upon southern Palestine, with the tragic results for which subsequent generations remember him. Such an explanation will not exonerate Antiochus, but it may help to place his policies in some perspective.

As for those Jews who worked for accommodation with the forces of Hellenism, it must be remembered that our earliest primary sources (1 and 2 Maccabees) were written by their enemies and that no written record of their motives and hopes has survived. If we possessed such documents, they would no doubt speak of their authors' desires to live peaceably with their Greek masters and of the terrible persecutions inflicted upon them by their traditionalist fellow Jews who considered them traitors, such as the slaughter and forced circumcision triumphantly reported in 1 Maccabees 2:42–48. The story of the Hasmonean revolt, as it has come down to us, is a clear example of history written by the victors.

When Onias III arrived in Antioch-on-the-Orontes, he was detained, perhaps imprisoned, presumably because of his pro-Ptolemaic leanings. In his place as high priest, the Seleucid authorities installed his brother Jason, who, it should be noted, had paid a large sum of money for his new office (2 Macc. 4:7f.). In a manner unusual in the Hellenistic world, the bureaucracy of state had intervened in a local religious matter. However, Antiochus received not only Jason's silver, but he gained as well a political ally in this strategically sensitive area. Jason could be counted on to support Seleucid policy in southern Palestine, and he even went so far as to attempt to Hellenize Jerusalem.

> In addition to this [i.e., the money Jason paid for the high priesthood] he promised to pay one hundred fifty [talents] more if permission were given to establish by his authority a gymnasium and a body of youth for it, and to enroll the people of Jerusalem as citizens of Antioch. . . . He set aside the existing royal concessions to the Jews . . . [and] he took delight in establishing a gymnasium right under the citadel, and he induced the noblest of the young men to wear the Greek hat.
>
> (2 Macc. 4:9, 11a, 12)

Jerusalem was on its way to becoming a Greek city.

Opposition to Jason's scheme was not long in expressing itself, but it did so from an unexpected quarter—not primarily from anti-Hellenists, but from the competing party of Hellenists. The old enmity between Simon ("captain of the Temple") and the Oniad family flared again when Simon's brother Menelaus went to Antioch and outbid Jason for the high priesthood by offering to Antiochus IV Epiphanes 300 silver talents more than that offered by Jason (2 Macc. 4:24). For the first time in generations, a non-Oniad occupied the most sacred office among the Jews and, to make matters worse, Menelaus' descent was from what appears to have been a nonpriestly family. The population, already shocked by Jason's purchase of the office and by his Hellenizing policies, reacted strongly. The result was an intense, confusing conflict involving the two parties of Hellenistic Jews (the Oniads and some of the Tobiads on one side, and other Tobiads and the family of Simon and Menelaus on the other) and those Jews who wished to resist all Hellenistic influences in favor of the traditions of Israel. To add to the complexities of the moment, the anti-Hellenistic Jews were themselves represented by several groups, perhaps the most important of which were the Hasidim, or "pious ones," noted for their devotion to the Torah.[9]

The violence that erupted was to have a lasting effect upon Jerusalem and the affairs of the Jews. Antiochus Epiphanes was at this time campaigning in Egypt against the Ptolemaic rulers of that country, the adventure which would culminate in his embarrassing encounter with the Roman emissary, Popilius. Jason, encouraged by the rumor—false, as it turned out—that Antiochus had been killed, managed to confine Menelaus to the Seleucid military citadel in Jerusalem, the Akra, but Jason in his turn was driven out of the city to Egypt, apparently by the anti-Hellenistic faction (2 Macc. 5:5–10). The year was 168 BC and to Antiochus Epiphanes, fresh from his humiliation at the hands of the Romans in Egypt, the cause of Jason, and even that of the Hasidim and other anti-Hellenistic groups, must have seemed designed to return the area to the control of the Ptolemys, or to invite the intervention of Rome.[10] The king's fury was unbounded. He entered Jerusalem at the head of his army and proceeded to restore order in a most violent fashion. Jews were killed or enslaved in large numbers, and Antiochus violated the Temple by setting up an altar to Zeus and by sacrificing swine's flesh. He also carried off the Temple treasures (1 Macc. 1:20–23, 2 Macc. 5:11–6:2).[11] The author of 1 Maccabees sings a lament which captures the emotional impact of Antiochus' brutality.

He shed much blood,
  and spoke with great arrogance.
Israel mourned deeply in every community,
  rulers and elders groaned,
young women and young men became faint,
  the beauty of the women faded.
Every bridegroom took up the lament;
  she who sat in the bridal chamber was mourning.
Even the land trembled for its inhabitants,
  and all the house of Jacob was clothed with shame.
                    (1 Macc. 1:24b–28)

Some modern scholars have expressed doubts that the Jews and their religious institutions would have been subjected to a policy of systematic suppression, since this would have been contrary to the spirit of Hellenism and would have been out of character even for Antiochus Epiphanes. They suggest, instead, that much of the suppression of Jewish tradition was the natural result of the unruly behavior of the large number of Syrian troops stationed in the Akra, which was near the Jerusalem Temple.[12] Be that as it may, in the face of this terror, many Jews fled from Jerusalem and took refuge in the surrounding countryside, where the Seleucid military presence was less concentrated. And perhaps from such locations some few of them attempted to engage in a kind of guerrilla warfare against Seleucid troops (1 Macc. 1:62f.).

2. *Mattathias* (168 BC) *and Judas* (168–160 BC)[13]

The flashpoint of the Hasmonean revolt, and perhaps the most celebrated event from this period of Jewish history, occurred in the village of Modein, some fifteen miles northwest of Jerusalem. A priest, fleeing the turmoil in Jerusalem, had settled there, together with his five sons and, presumably, other members of their family. One day in 168 or 167 BC a group of Seleucid soldiers appeared for the purpose of enforcing Antiochus' new regulations concerning religious worship.[14] The priest, Mattathias, aided by his sons and other traditionalist Jews, attacked the soldiers and also fell upon other Jews present who were willing to comply with the Seleucid regulations. Mattathias' family then fled into the countryside where they were quickly joined by large numbers of traditionalist Jews, including many Hasidim. The area to which they fled was a mountainous, wooded region in the central hill country south of Shechem. Not long after this Mattathias died, apparently of natural causes, and the leadership of the revolt was vested in his son Judas, the most celebrated of the Hasmonean generals.

According to 1 Maccabees, Judas' military career (168–160 BC) may be divided into three phases: (1) his successful repulse of several Seleucid attempts to relieve Jerusalem of the threat posed by the presence of the Hasmonean army, a series of events that resulted in Judas' entry into Jerusalem and the reconsecration of the Temple, (2) campaigns of Judas and his brothers into areas outside Judaea proper, and (3) Judas' efforts to defend Jerusalem and his position in the central hill country, a series of battles which culminated in his death. But no simple schematic treatment of Judas' military campaigns can do justice to the genius of this leader, who utilized what few advantages he possessed—primarily, the total dedication of his followers—to thwart repeatedly an army that was numerically superior to and better equipped than his own. Upon Judas our sources confer the designation Maccabee or Maccabeus, probably meaning "the Hammer," a name by which this entire family—and the period—has sometimes been known. In view of his brilliant and courageous leadership, it is easy to understand, not only the devotion of his troops, but also the awe in which he has been held by generations of Jews, who have considered him to be, next to Moses and David, the greatest liberator of his people.

The first phase of Judas' military campaigns consisted of efforts by the Seleucids to reinforce Jerusalem and to drive a wedge between the city and

Judas' position in the central hill country. On the Seleucid side, these campaigns were characterized by an increasing investment of troops and equipment and—with each defeat administered by Judas—an increasing sense of
alarm with which the situation was viewed, as evidenced by the higher and
higher rank of the commanders who were sent to confront Judas. Battles at an
unnamed site (1 Macc. 3:10–12), at Beth-horon (1 Macc. 3:13–26), at Emmaus
(1 Macc. 3:38–4:25), and at Beth-zur all ended in Hasmonean victories, Beth-
zur being climaxed by the triumphant entry into Jerusalem of Judas and his
army (1 Macc. 4:26–5:59).[15] The Temple was reconsecrated, to a joy which the
author of 2 Maccabees makes no effort to conceal:

> They purified the sanctuary, and made another altar of sacrifice; then,
> striking fire out of flint, they offered sacrifices, after a lapse of two
> years, and they offered incense and lighted lamps and set out the bread
> of the Presence. When they had done this, they fell prostrate and im-
> plored the Lord that they might never again fall into such misfortunes,
> but that, if they should ever sin, they might be disciplined by him with
> forebearance and not be handed over to blasphemous and barbarous na-
> tions. It happened that on the same day on which the sanctuary had
> been profaned by the foreigners, the purification of the sanctuary took
> place, that is on the twenty-fifth day of the same month, which was
> Chislev. And they celebrated it for eight days with rejoicing, in the man-
> ner of the festival of booths, remembering how not long before, during
> the festival of booths, they had been wandering in the mountains and
> caves like wild animals.
>
> (2 Macc. 10:3–6)

The time was December 165 BC. More than two thousand years after the
event, this reconsecration of the Temple is celebrated by Jews at Hanukkah,
meaning *dedication*.

The second phase of Judas' career involved expeditions by Hasmonean
raiding parties into areas away from Jerusalem in which communities of Jews
were being persecuted by Seleucid authorities (2 Macc. 5:1–68). Notable in
this regard are Judas' campaign into Gilead (east of the Sea of Galilee) and his
brother Simon's campaign into western Galilee. As a result of these attacks,
which were mounted with great skill and courage, large numbers of Jews
were rescued and brought to Jerusalem for safety.

However, courage was not a monopoly of the Jews, and soon—the third
phase of Judas' career—Seleucid commanders resumed their efforts to crush
the Hasmonean rebellion. About this time (164 BC) Antiochus Epiphanes died
campaigning with his troops in the East, and his throne was mounted by his
son, Antiochus V Eupator (164–162 BC). The new king was still a boy, so affairs
of state were placed in the hands of trusted officials, the most important of

whom was the viceroy Lysias, who had been active in earlier campaigns against Judas (2 Macc. 3:32ff.). A garrison of besieged Seleucid troops still held the Akra in Jerusalem, having never been dislodged by Judas. With the intention of relieving them Lysias mounted a campaign which, among other things, included a number of elephants within the Seleucid contingent.[16] Lysias' army marched down the coastal plain and then turned and approached Jerusalem from the south. At Beth-zecharia Judas' army was defeated and the Seleucid forces besieged Jerusalem, finally breaking through the Hasmonean defenses to the relief of the long-suffering Seleucid garrison. The Hasmonean forces fled to the north, taking shelter in the same wooded hills in which they had found refuge following Mattathias' revolt at Modein. The Seleucid authorities were reluctant to reimpose the harsh mandates of Antiochus Epiphanes (by this time yet another Seleucid king, Demetrius I Soter [162–150 BC][17] was on the throne), so no effort was made to interfere with Jewish worship at the Temple or elsewhere. Some among Judas' followers, notably the Hasidim, felt that their goal of religious freedom had now been attained, and so they defected from Judas' army.

But Judas was still a force to be reckoned with. Two additional Seleucid campaigns against him were unsuccessful, both of which were led by the Seleucid general, Nicanor (1 Macc. 7:26–32 and 7:33–50). Nicanor had at his side a treacherous Jewish priest named Alcimus who was responsible for the murder of a group of Hasidim (1 Macc. 7:12–18) and who had persuaded King Demetrius to appoint him high priest. So hated were Alcimus and Nicanor that, following Nicanor's death in battle at Adasa, the Jews displayed his severed head and right hand outside the Jerusalem walls (1 Macc. 7:47).[18] It was about this time that, according to 1 Maccabees (8:1–32), the Roman Senate favorably received a delegation from Judas and struck a treaty of friendship with the traditionalist Jews.

But if the future now seemed bright for the fledgling independence movement, it was an illusion, for soon the Seleucid general Bacchides engaged Judas at Elasa (about ten miles north of Jerusalem) and defeated him there. Judas was killed in the fighting (160 BC) and his army routed. The story of how Judas was buried at Modein by his brothers Jonathan and Simon is retold in 1 Maccabees 9:19–22, and the brothers' sorrow that is described must have been accompanied by great secrecy in securing the burial. For the land was firmly in the hands of the Seleucid authorities, and it must have appeared that much for which Mattathias and Judas had fought had now been lost.

3. Jonathan (160–142 BC)

That the Hasmonean uprising did not die with Judas is primarily the result of two factors: the determination of the leaders of the revolt and of those closest to them to continue their cause, and political and personal animosities among the Hasmoneans' rivals that seriously impaired the unity of the Seleucid kingdom and prevented that state from prosecuting its enemies. Judas' place was taken by his brother Jonathan who, because of the superior Seleucid forces in Jerusalem and Judaea, was forced to lead his men to find refuge in the countryside. Small-scale guerrilla attacks were carried out by them from time to time, but Jonathan's weakened army was compelled to flee from any Seleucid attempts to engage them in a pitched battle. Once, the Seleucid commander Bacchides chased Jonathan and his men into the Judaean desert east of Bethlehem (1 Macc. 9:32–34). On another occasion, Jonathan's brother John was killed by local people while leading a group of Hasmonean followers in Transjordan (1 Macc. 9:35–42). Yet again, Jonathan's army was trapped by the Seleucid forces who caught them with their backs against the Jordan River, a situation from which the Jews escaped only by swimming across the stream (1 Macc. 9:43–49).

Jonathan's enemies, however, soon began to have troubles of their own. Bacchides, fearing Jonathan's military skills and his popularity among Jewish traditionalists, felt compelled to construct a string of fortifications around Jerusalem and, in addition, to strengthen the Seleucid garrison, the Akra, in the city itself (1 Macc. 9:50–53). Not long after this, the high priest Alcimus, who had alienated many of the Jews because of his Hellenizing policies, suffered a stroke and died (1 Macc. 9:55–56). The delicate balance of power between Hellenists and traditionalists may be seen in the fact that no successor to Alcimus was named, presumably because the Seleucid authorities and their allies among the Jews did not wish to alienate further the traditionalist Jews by naming a Hellenizing high priest, whereas for their part, the traditionalists did not yet possess the influence to force the appointment of one of their own party to the office. The result of this stalemate was a cessation of fighting that lasted for two years (160–158 BC).

The lull was broken when Bacchides suddenly returned to Judah with his troops and cornered Jonathan's forces in the Judaean wilderness at a place called Bethbasi.[19] The Maccabees were outnumbered, but countered the superiority of the Seleucid army by a clever stratagem. Jonathan slipped out of the camp with a few men and attacked Bacchides from the rear. When the Seleucid fighters turned to repulse Jonathan's men, Jonathan's brother Simon charged out from the camp and enabled the Maccabees to snare Bacchides in a pincers movement. The Seleucid army withdrew and soon peace descended upon Judaea once more, but not before a furious Bacchides had executed a number of Hellenized Jews who had led him to believe that his attack upon Jonathan would be successful (1 Macc. 9:62–69).

For the next five years (158–153 BC) there was no serious fighting in Judaea. The Seleucids were firmly in control of their fortified cities, including Jerusalem, but the Maccabees' influence continued to grow across the countryside. In language reminiscent of the Book of Judges, 1 Maccabees reports that "Jonathan settled in Michmash and began to judge the people; and he destroyed the godless out of Israel" (1 Macc. 9:73), this last phrase being a euphemistic way of saying that Jews who harbored Hellenistic sympathies were killed or exiled. Clearly, Jonathan was awaiting the time when he would be strong enough once more to engage the Seleucid authorities and their Jewish allies.

That opportunity came in 153 BC when the rule of the Seleucid king, Demetrius I Soter, was challenged by a pretender to the throne, a certain Alexander Balas who claimed to be the son of Antiochus IV Epiphanes and thus the rightful monarch. Alexander's cause was embraced by authorities in several nearby nations who wished to undermine Seleucid power, including Ptolemy VI Philometor (180–145 BC) and the senate of Rome. In the conflict that ensued, both sides attempted to find allies, and so the Hasmoneans were thrust into the unfamiliar role of being courted by their would-be enemies, in this case by both Alexander and Demetrius.

Demetrius, hoping to gain Jonathan's support, released certain traditionalist Jews who were being held prisoner in the Akra, and called home most of the Seleucid troops from Jerusalem and from the fortifications built by Bacchides, except for Beth-zur (1 Macc. 10:3–9). Soon Demetrius would also promise to abolish many forms of taxation which the Seleucid government imposed upon the Jews and to grant many other favors, as well (1 Macc. 10:25–45). Joyfully, Jonathan occupied Jerusalem (except for the Akra) and strengthened the city's fortifications. But Alexander Balas had an important gift of his own. He appointed Jonathan high priest, thus filling a vacancy left since the death of Alcimus seven years before (1 Macc. 10:15–20). And so, to add to their growing political power, the Maccabees now claimed this venerable office. Partly because Jonathan did not believe Demetrius' lavish promises and partly because he sensed the superior political and military strength of Alexander Balas, Jonathan declared for the latter. Thus when the forces allied to Alexander Balas defeated those of Demetrius, enabling Alexander to become Seleucid king in fact as well as in claim, Jonathan's position was greatly strengthened (1 Macc. 10:48–50). As for Alexander, he buttressed his pretentions to royal authority by marrying Ptolemy's daughter, Cleopatra.[20] Jonathan was one of the guests at the wedding, which took place at Ptolemais (modern Acre) on the Mediterranean coast north of Mt. Carmel, where he was accorded special honors by the groom (1 Macc. 10:51–66).

Jonathan's political power was now greater than had been that of his brother Judas, for, while Judaea was still nominally a part of the Seleucid kingdom, virtually all authority was vested in Jonathan. But Jonathan's position, which was based on his friendship with King Alexander Balas, was threatened anew when, in 147 BC Demetrius' son proclaimed himself Demetrius II and rightful king of the realm. During the four years of his reign (150–146 BC) Alexander had alienated many of his friends and subjects, thus a number of them went over to Demetrius to give him their support. Among these were Apollonius, the governor of Coele-Syria,[21] and Ptolemy VI Philometer (180–145 BC), who unceremoniously took his daughter away from Alexander and gave her in marriage to Demetrius. In fact, of the military and political leaders in the region, only Jonathan remained true to Alexander's cause, and in Alexander's name Jonathan waged successful warfare from Joppa to the former Philistine cities of the south (1 Macc. 10:70–89).

Ptolemy took advantage of this disarray within the Seleucid kingdom to send his own army northward along the Mediterranean coast and into Antioch-on-the-Orontes, where, with apparently no resistance, he crowned himself king of the Seleucid realm (1 Macc. 11:1–13). Alexander was away at that time, putting down a revolt in Cilicia, but, upon receiving the news concerning Ptolemy, he hurried home and engaged his former father-in-law in a battle that proved disastrous for them both. Ptolemy received wounds from which he died a few days later, while Alexander, with his army, was driven from the field and was killed by an otherwise unknown person named Zabdiel the Arab (1 Macc. 11:17).[22] The real winner of the battle thus became Demtrius, who was not even present. In 145 BC he became Demetrius II (145–139, 129–25 BC), nicknamed, with some irony, Nicator ("Victorious").

Jonathan now felt that the time was ripe for him to remove the last vestiges of Seleucid power in Judaea, and so he laid siege to the Seleucid citadel in Jerusalem, the Akra. The garrison held out against the Hasmonean fighters, but an angered (and doubtless anxious) Demetrius summoned Jonathan to Ptolemais, where a truce was arranged, according to the provisions of which Jonathan paid certain amounts into Demetrius' treasury, and Demetrius ceded to Jonathan (whom he recognized as high priest and as governor of Judaea) certain territories in Samaria (1 Macc. 11:20–30). As the record in 1 Maccabees makes no further mention of the siege of the Akra, it was presumably lifted as a part of the accord.

But the faction loyal to Alexander Balas still had one more card to play in the form of Alexander's young son, whom Alexander's former commander, Trypho, now (143 BC) put forward as the legal monarch Antiochus VI (143–142 BC). The population in Antioch, together with the military garrison there, had become alienated from Demetrius, and they thus saw this as an opportunity to rise against their king. Demetrius called for help from Jonathan who, before granting it, demanded the removal of the last Seleucid troops from Judaea, that is, those stationed at Beth-zur and in the Akra in Jerusalem. Demetrius consented, and Hasmonean forces under Jonathan marched into Antioch and restored order, thus (for the moment) sparing Demetrius his life and his throne. Thus according to the account in 1 Maccabees (and echoed in Josephus[23]), less than twenty years after the death of Judas, a Hasmonean army occupied the Seleucid capital city in defense of its king (1 Macc. 11:41–51).

But Demetrius had no intention of keeping his promises to Jonathan, and the Seleucid forces in the Akra and at Beth-zur were not withdrawn. Thus Jonathan, now back in Jerusalem, did not intervene when, some time after this, Trypho scattered Demetrius's army and captured Antioch, placing young Antiochus on the Seleucid throne.[24] Trypho made gestures of friendship toward Jonathan and, in the name of the new king, Jonathan expelled from the coastal cities of Ashkelon and Gaza forces loyal to Demetrius (1 Macc. 11:52–62). In Galilee, Jonathan, after suffering an initial defeat, expelled a large contingent of Demetrius' army, while to the south of Jerusalem, Jonathan's brother Simon captured the fortress of Beth-zur (1 Macc. 11:63–74).

Nominally, these were victories of young Antiochus VI, but in reality they were extensions of Jonathan's personal power and that of Judaea over important parts of Palestine. Jonathan now began even to act as a head of state, for he sent delegations to Rome and to Sparta to strike treaties of peace (1 Macc. 12:1–23). Further victories in the north by Jonathan carried Hasmonean arms as far as Damascus, while in the west Simon seized the Mediterranean port of Joppa (1 Macc. 12:24–34). Trypho, at the head of a large force, now met Jonathan's army near Beth-shan. As the two were supposedly allies, Jonathan allowed himself to be talked into accompanying Trypho to Ptolemais with only his (Jonathan's) personal guard.[25] Once inside the city, Jonathan's men were killed and Jonathan himself taken prisoner (1 Macc. 12:46–48). It was now (belatedly!) apparent that Trypho intended to brook no competition within the Seleucid kingdom, for his real intention was to seize power for himself (1 Macc. 12:39).

Trypho apparently felt that he could now march on Jerusalem, accompanied by his hostage Jonathan, and that the traditionalist Jews there would be too intimidated to resist. But Simon, who had assumed the role of leader following the capture of Jonathan, met Trypho with a large force before he could reach the city. Trypho sent word to Simon that he would release Jonathan in exchange for a hundred talents of silver and two of Jonathan's sons, who would take their father's place as hostages. Simon did not trust Trypho, but complied nonetheless, since failure to do so would have made it appear that he was an accomplice in Jonathan's continued captivity. Trypho accepted the treasure and the two new hostages, but did not release Jonathan. He then attempted to march against Jerusalem by a circuitous route from the south, but was thwarted in this effort by the weather.[26] Frustrated, Trypho murdered Jonathan and marched back to Antioch, whereupon Simon buried his brother's body among the family's graves in Modein. Not long after this, Trypho murdered young Antiochus VI and cast aside all pretense by proclaiming himself king (1 Macc 12:49—13:32).

4. *Simon* (142–135 BC)

It was natural that the last of old Mattathias' surviving sons should be looked upon as the successor of his brothers.[27] The position in which Simon found himself was considerably better than that of either Judas or Jonathan at the beginning of their periods of leadership, and Simon lost little time in exploiting his advantages. He strengthened the Hasmonean fortifications in Judaea and struck a treaty of friendship with Demetrius against their common enemy Trypho. In return for this support, Demetrius recognized the independence of Judaea, with Simon, whom Demetrius refers to as "high priest and friend of kings" (1 Macc. 13:36), as its chief of state. First Maccabees reports significantly that Jews now began to date their official documents in this manner: "In the first year of Simon the great high priest and commander and leader of the Jews" (13:42). The year was 142 BC and the dream long cherished by many Jews was now a reality, yet much more labor and suffering lay ahead for the citizens of the Jewish state and for their leaders.

Simon extended Jewish rule over a number of outlying areas,[28] and, in a very significant move, laid siege to the Akra in Jerusalem. Demetrius had either not fulfilled his promise to recognize the independence of Judaea by withdrawing Seleucid troops from the Akra or, more likely, he had no control over this fortress which was populated, in part at least, by local Hellenistic Jews. In any event, Simon starved the garrison into submission and then led his people into the citadel to the sounds of great rejoicing (1 Macc. 13:49–52). The last significant vestige of Seleucid rule in Jerusalem had been claimed by the traditionalists.

In words that resonate to the vision of the prophets of old (cf. Isa. 65:20–25, Zech. 8:4–8, 10:10), the author of 1 Maccabees celebrates these events and the period of tranquility that followed:

> Old men sat in the streets;
>   they all talked together of good things;
>   and the youths put on splendid military attire.
> He [Simon] supplied the towns with food,
>   and furnished them with the means of defense,
>   until his renown spread to the ends of the earth.
> He established peace in the land,
>   and Israel rejoiced with great joy.
> All the people sat under their own vines and fig trees,
>   and there was none to make them afraid.
> He gave help to all the humble among his people;
>   he sought out the law,
>   and did away with all the renegades and outlaws.
> He made the sanctuary glorious,
>   and added to the vessels of the sanctuary.
> (1 Macc. 14:9–12, 15)

It is doubtful that the Hasmonean state was ever as tranquil as these verses suggest, and the third from last line above makes it quite clear that the benefits of independence did not extend to Jews with Hellenistic sympathies. Yet it was a splendid time for traditionalist Jews and it must have seemed to many of them, as it did to the author of 1 Maccabees, that a kind of golden age had set in. At a great assembly of people (141 BC)[29] Simon was declared "leader and high priest forever, until a trustworthy prophet should arise, and that he should be governor over them . . . , and that he should be obeyed by all" (1 Macc. 14:41–43a).[30] Presumably, this meant that Simon's descendants would inherit his office until the return of the great prophet Elijah (Mal. 4:5). Bronze tablets inscribed with the assembly's decree were ordered placed in the courtyard of the Temple. It is interesting that there is no recorded attempt at any time during the Hasmonean period to restore the Davidic dynasty. Whether this is because there were no descendants of David known to be alive at the time, or that there was simply no longer significant interest in the Davidic model of kingship among traditionalist Jews is not clear.[31]

Sparta and, more importantly, Rome, who were happy to see any weakening of Seleucid strength, recognized the new state (1 Macc. 14:16–24, 15:15–21), but elements nearer at hand were not so pleased. Demetrius II had been captured while campaigning in the East, and his brother assumed the throne as Antiochus VII Sidetes (139–129 BC). Antiochus and Simon made a peaceful contract (again, their common enemy was Trypho) according to which the right of the Hasmonean state to mint its own coins was recognized (1 Macc. 15:1–9). But not long after this Trypho was defeated in battle against Antiochus' forces, and the Seleucid king was free to turn his attentions to the Hasmoneans who, in Antiochus' view, had usurped Seleucid sovereignty over important parts of his kingdom's domains. Antiochus demanded that Simon surrender control over Gazara, Joppa, and the Akra in Jerusalem or, in lieu of these places, surrender five hundred talents into Antiochus' treasury (1 Macc. 15:25–31). Simon refused to do either, so Antiochus sent an army into Judaea under the leadership of his general, Cendebeus. Simon, citing his old age, placed command of the Hasmonean army in the hands of two sons, Judas and John Hyrcanus. Although John Hyrcanus was wounded in the ensuing battle (which took place near Modein), the Hasmonean army was triumphant and the troops under Cendebeus were routed (1 Macc. 15:32—16:10).

The Hasmonean state now seemed secure, and Simon doubtless looked forward to a happy retirement in which he could savor the fruits of so many years' hardship. But he and two of his sons, Mattathias and Judas, were assassinated by Simon's son-in-law, Ptolemy,[32] a commander in the Hasmonean army who hoped, by removing Simon and his heirs, to become the leader of the Jewish state. Ptolemy had invited Simon and the two sons to his fortress of Dok, near Jericho, where he entertained them lavishly. But when they were drunk, Ptolemy's men attacked and killed them. John Hyrcanus, who was at

Gazara (perhaps recuperating from his battle wounds), learned of the murders and also discovered that assassins were on their way from Ptolemy to kill him. He had these men apprehended and executed before they could reach him, and then he marched quickly to Jerusalem where he was received as high chief priest and leader by the people, thus preventing Ptolemy's *coup d'etat* (1 Macc. 16:11–24).[33]

B. The Hasmonean State

1. *John Hyrcanus I* (135–104 BC)[34]

John Hyrcanus[35] was the first member of the Hasmonean family to inherit an independent state, and, although subsequent Jewish tradition has held him in high honor,[36] his rule was not an unqualified success. While he vigorously expanded the boundaries of the nation, he appears often to have been driven more by secular motives than by those arising out of devotion to the Torah and to the traditions of Israel. In this latter regard, he set an unfortunate precedent that many of his successors were all too eager to follow.

Simon's murderer Ptolemy, under military threat from Hyrcanus, fled from his fortress of Dok and found refuge in Rabbah, the old capital of the Ammonite kingdom, now (135 BC) called by its Hellenized name Philadelphia. But a greater threat to Hyrcanus' rule presented itself in the form of Antiochus VII Sidetes, who renewed his contest with the Hasmonean state, earlier thwarted by Judas' and Hyrcanus' defeat of the Seleucid general Cendebeus near Modein. Antiochus invaded Judah and was able to shut Hyrcanus and his army up within the walls of Jerusalem and to exact from them severe conditions for lifting the siege. Although the Jews were permitted to exercise their religion freely, Jerusalem's defenses were dismantled, heavy taxes were imposed, and the Jewish state was forced to contribute units of fighting men to Antiochus' army. The independence of the nation was thus seriously compromised, although Seleucid troops were not garrisoned in Jerusalem nor in the immediate countryside. Josephus mentions, with implied censure, that at this time Hyrcanus, in order to pay the necessary tribute to Antiochus and to pay his own mercenaries, looted the tomb of David of 3,000 talents of silver.[37]

Hyrcanus was then (129 BC) compelled to lead a contingent of Jewish troops within Antiochus' army when the Seleucid king challenged the control of the Parthians (who lived in what is today northern Iran) over upper Mesopotamia. This servitude of the Jewish state to Antiochus VII might have continued indefinitely, if a series of events had not intervened to weaken seriously the internal cohesion of the Seleucid state. Antiochus was killed in action against the Parthians, who about that time released from captivity Antiochus' brother, Demetrius II, who had been captured about 139 BC while fighting in the East. Demetrius (second administration: 129–125 BC), probably with Parthian sponsorship, reclaimed the Seleucid throne and mounted a military campaign against the forces of Ptolemy VII Neos Philopator or Physcon (meaning "Fat Paunch," 145–116 BC). Ptolemy countered by naming a rival claimant to the Seleucid throne, and for the balance of Hyrcanus' lifetime the Seleucid kingdom was so preoccupied with internal power struggles that the Hasmonean state was, for the most part, free from outside interference.[38]

Hyrcanus used this opportunity to expand the boundaries of the Jewish state. One campaign east of the Jordan River resulted in the capture of Medeba (in northern Moab), while another to the north brought about the subjugation of the Samaritans and the destruction of their temple.[39] A third campaign was mounted against the Idumaeans, a people who were descendants of the biblical Edomites and who had settled in the areas of Judaea south of Beth-zur. Hyrcanus overwhelmed their principal communities and forced them at sword point to become Jews.[40] About this time, the Hasmonean leader sent an embassy to Rome to renew the treaty of peace first struck during the time of Judas Maccabeus. As it had on previous occasions, the Roman senate, always anxious to subvert Seleucid authority in the area of the eastern Mediterranean, replied in friendly fashion. Toward the end of his reign, Hyrcanus sent his sons Antigonus and Aristobulus[41] to lay siege to the city of Samaria, which had been spared at the time of the destruction of the Samaritan temple. After the city was taken by the Jews, it was completely destroyed.[42]

One other significant development is reported by Josephus concerning Hyrcanus, this one of less hopeful portent for the future of the Jewish state: the high priest's rupture with the sect of the Pharisees. This is the earliest event in Jewish history which elicits from any ancient source a reference to the Pharisees or the Sadducees, groups which are familiar to readers of the New Testament. Although a more detailed treatment of these parties will follow,[43] a word or two about them is appropriate here, in order better to understand the significance of Hyrcanus' act.

Even before the time of Mattathias and the revolt at Modein, Jewish society was characterized by competing interest groups. Although there were many crosscurrents of emotion and belief, the primary lines of division were between traditionalist and Hellenistic Jews. The traditionalists were further split between those who sought religious freedom (the Hasidim) and those who intended to settle for nothing less than political independence (the Hasmoneans). To complicate matters more, some of those who struggled for independence within the Hasmonean ranks were motivated primarily by political concerns (and thus might be more willing to compromise on matters pertaining to Hellenistic culture), while the motivation of others was theological. For their part, the Hellenistic Jews were divided between pro-Seleucid and pro-Ptolemaic factions. During the wars for independence, most of the Hellenistic sentiments (political and otherwise) were suppressed, as we have seen, while tensions within the traditionalist camp were usually set aside in favor of the pursuit of common goals. But with the coming of peace, many of the areas of stress within Palestinian Jewish society reasserted themselves.

While very little is known of the early history of the Pharisees,[44] they appear to have emerged from those elements within Judaism, such as the Hasidim, which emphasized devotion to the Torah. For the most part the Pharisees were lay people, not priests, and commoners, not the traditional aristocracy, although there were many individual exceptions to this pattern. By the Roman period they had developed a body of tradition by which the Torah was to be understood and interpreted, a body of tradition which was regarded by them to be almost as authorative as the Torah itself. The extent to which the development of this tradition had advanced by the time of the Hasmonean state is a matter of uncertainty, but it was surely well underway.

The Sadducees,[45] on the other hand, appear during the Hasmonean times as the party of priests and of the aristocracy. As noted earlier, many of the wealthy priestly families prominent in the late third and early second centuries BC were strongly Hellenized, either with a pro-Seleucid or pro-Ptolemaic bias (e.g., the Oniads and the Tobiads).[46] And it is possible that the Sadducean party during Hasmonean times included many individuals who were as much at home among the traditions of the Greek world as among those of Israel. Certainly one suspects an inclination on the part of many Hasmonean Sadducees, if not toward Hellenism, at least toward secularism. That is, they sought to maintain by political means their privileged positions and the wealth to which those positions gave them access.[47] Yet it was not as secularists that they presented themselves, but rather as guardians of priestly ritual and of the Torah, but a Torah understood in its narrowest sense. If the Pharisees wished to develop a body of commentary on the Torah which attempted to apply the ancient teachings to everyday life, the Sadducees were willing to recognize as authorative only the letter of the Torah itself. If the Pharisees represented new ways of understanding Israel's ancient heritage, the Sadducees stood for the old way. Yet under the umbrella of this conservatism, they appeared willing—in a way the Pharisees were not—to accommodate themselves to the currents of the larger non-Jewish world in which they lived.

For some time (no one knows quite how long) important matters relating to the life of the Palestinian Jewish community had been decided by a priestly council. The Books of Ezra and Nehemiah, literature that describes the return from Babylonian exile, refer to the "elders of the Jews" (Ezra 5:5) and to "the priests, the nobles, the officials" (Neh. 2:16) of the nation. It is likely that, under a tolerant Persian rule and without a viable Davidic monarchy, responsibility for much of the day-to-day administration of the Jerusalem community was assumed by a council of priests and nobles, forerunner of the later Sanhedrin. If Josephus may be trusted on this point, a letter from Anitochus III the Great to his governor for Coele-Syria makes reference to a cordial reception of the Seleucid monarch by the Jewish council at the time of the Seleucid conquest of Palestine (c. 200 BC).[48] During the Hasmonean revolt, this council apparently continued to exist, functioning alongside the sons of Mattathias and supplementing their priestly and military roles by attending to the administrative and perhaps judicial tasks of government.

At the time of the Hasmonean revolt it is likely that a fundamental change took place in the nature of the council. Although the male members of the Hasmonean family were priests, they do not appear to have been wealthy or aristocratic. Mattathias and his sons were people of the land and, furthermore, were the sworn enemies of Hellenism. In all likelihood, therefore, their allies were more likely to be found among the ranks of the Pharisees than of the Sadducees. An important result of the Hasmonean revolt may have been the inclusion in the membership of the council of lay Pharisees, with their "progressive" views on the interpretation of the Torah. This is an indication not only of a new democratization among Palestinian Jews, but also of an intensified commitment to the written Torah, now expanded by a growing body of oral (and perhaps written) interpretation.

All of this is by way of introduction to what Josephus reports concerning Hyrcanus' break with the Pharisees.[49] According to that report, Hyrcanus, who "was a disciple of theirs and was greatly loved by them," invited a number of Pharisees to a banquet at which he requested their advice on any matter which concerned them. One Pharisee, a certain Eleazar, demanded that Hyrcanus give up the high priesthood and retain only the governorship because his ancestry was not purely Jewish.[50] A furious Hyrcanus suspected the entire Pharisaic party to be behind Eleazar's admonition, so he broke with them and joined the Sadducee party. It is even possible, although the fact is not reported, that at this time the Pharisees were forced from the council. Whatever else this falling out may signify, it is perhaps symptomatic of the worldliness of Hyrcanus' rule and of the continuing air of confrontation between Pharisees and Sadducees that lasted until the destruction of the Second Temple in 70 AD.

2. *Judas Aristobulus I* (104 BC)

John Hyrcanus' dispute with the Pharisees may have left its mark upon the Hasmonean leader, for in his will he stipulated that that the offices of high priest and governor should become separate. He further decreed that his eldest son, Judas Aristobulus, should become high priest, while the governorship should pass to his (John's) wife, the new high priest's mother. Hardly was John Hyrcanus in his tomb, however, than Aristobulus made it known that he had no intention of allowing his authority to be limited. He imprisoned his mother and three of his four brothers, subsequently allowing his mother to die of starvation, while he assumed the governorship for himself. To this office, and that of the high priesthood that he had inherited from his father, Aristobulus added the title king, perhaps the first Hasmonean leader to refer to himself by a designation that many considered to be reserved for a descendant of David.[51] The one brother whom Aristobulus loved and whom he did not imprison, Antigonus, was murdered by Aristobulus' bodyguards in circumstances which haunted Aristobulus to a premature death.

Antigonus had returned to Jerusalem at the head of a victorious Hasmonean army, which had been campaigning probably in Galilee or southern Lebanon. Many who were close to Aristobulus, who was ill at the time, were afraid of Antigonus and of what might happen to them should Antigonus replace his older brother on the throne. And so, in a fit of anxiety, they plotted Antigonus' death. They advised the king to invite Antigonus—who was celebrating the Feast of Tabernacles at the Temple—to visit his bedside in the nearby military compound the Baris, which, during Roman times, would be known as the Tower of Antonia.[52] At the behest of the plotters, which included the queen, Aristobulus ordered his brother to appear before him unarmed, as a sign of their friendship. But the plotters bribed the messenger to say that Antigonus should appear before Aristobulus fully armed, so that the king might admire his brother. Thus, when Antigonus approached the fortress with his weapons, Aristobulus' bodyguards, interpreting this as a threat, killed him.

Josephus adds that, some time after this, Aristobulus began to hemorrhage. A servant, carrying away a container of the king's blood, fell and spilled the blood on the very spot where the paving stones still showed the bloodstains of Antigonus. When Aristobulus learned what had happened, he interpreted it as a sign pointing to his guilt in the murder of his brother and mother and he fell into a deep depression from which he never recovered.[53]

In his brief reign of a year, Aristobulus added northern Galilee to the Hasmonean kingdom, either by leading an army there himself or by sending subordinates, such as Antigonus. The gentiles who lived there, like the Idumeans previously conquered by John Hyrcanus, were given the choice of deportation or conversion and, again like the Idumaeans, they opted to become Jews.[54] Thus under Aristobulus, two important developments that characterized the administration of John Hyrcanus were carried further: (1) the Hellenization of the Hasmonean state, in this instance through the establishment of the office of a king based not on the model of David, but on that of Alexander the Great and the Diadochi, and (2) the expansion of the territory of Judaea to include areas of the old Davidic kingdom. The manner in which both measures were taken indicate the increasing despotism of Hasmonean rule over both Jews and non-Jews within the realm. The Hasmonean state of Aristobulus would have been scarcely recognizable to Judas Maccabeus and his brothers, but worse was yet to come.

3. *Alexander Jannaeus* (104–78 BC)

Under Alexander Jannaeus (Jannaeus is a shortened, Hellenized form of the Hebrew name Jonathan) the Hasmonean state achieved its greatest territorial expansion and political power, but the same fierce energies that drove this leader into war against the nation's enemies also thrust him into unparalleled conflict with his own people. Upon the death of Aristobulus I, his widow Alexandra (or, to use her Hebrew name, Salome) freed from prison the king's three brothers, the eldest of whom became the new high priest and, in time, king. Although Josephus does not report the fact, it is probable that at this time Alexander also claimed Queen Alexandra as his wife.

The new Hasmonean leader set his attention to the task of expanding Judaea's borders, but his first adventures in this direction were less than successful. The Hasmonean army attacked the city of Ptolemais, but were in turn attacked by the forces of Ptolemy VIII Lathyrus (116–107, 88–80 BC), who had been expelled from Egypt by his mother Cleopatra III and was ruling Cyprus. Lathyrus soundly defeated the Hasmonean army, first in Galilee, then again in the Jordan valley, thus exposing all of Judaea to his advance. Only the intervention of Cleopatra, who now realized that her own borders were threatened by her son, saved Alexander. Cleopatra sent an army into Judaea frightening Lathyrus into retreat, whereupon the queen, content with the *status quo ante* and with a large payment from Alexander, recalled her forces and permitted peace to return to the land.[55]

But peace was far from Alexander's mind. He sent his reconstituted army into the rich commercial and agricultural areas east of the Sea of Galilee where, among other objectives, he claimed the important community of Gadara and another named Amathus, which Josephus describes as "the greatest stronghold of those occupied beyond the Jordan."[56] Alexander then marched to the southwest and carried out attacks against cities of the coastal plain, including Raphia and Gaza. The siege of Gaza seems to have been especially bitter and protracted, and Alexander is reported to have destroyed the town and many of its inhabitants in revenge for the defenders' stiff resistance. It may have been about this time (shortly after 100 BC) that Alexander assumed the title king. Coins from early in his reign bear the inscription (in Hebrew only): "Jonathan the High Priest and *Hever* [Council, later Sanhedrin] of the Jews." But later coins bear inscriptions in both Hebrew and in Greek, the first Hasmonean coins to be inscribed in Greek, so far as is known. The Greek reads: "King Alexander;" the Hebrew: "King Jonathan."[57]

The growing despotism of Alexander was resisted by the same group of Jews who had found his brother Aristobolus intolerable: the Pharisees. And out of the conflict between the two parties the long simmering tensions among Palestine's Jews boiled over into civil war, a bitter and protracted struggle that would leave deep and enduring scars within the nation. The immediate causes seem to have been at least three. (1) Many devout Jews, whose sons bore the brunt of Judaea's wars, must have seen a contradiction in the fact that the violent leader of the nation's campaigns of conquest also ministered before God as high priest. It was one thing for the early Hasmoneans to combine the offices of high priest and commander-in-chief, for then the nation was fighting for its life. But under Hyrcanus, Aristobulus and, now, Alexander, the wars of the nation had more and more become wars for empire.

(2) Virtually everything about the administration of Alexander smacked of Hellenism, most importantly his concept of what it meant to be a king. Pushed into the background was the theocratic ideal of old, that is, that the true king of the Jews was God. In its place was substituted the view that the Jewish state was the personal possession of the human king, a political concept that was the foundation of most of the Hellenistic kingdoms, including those of the Ptolemys and the Seleucids. As evidence of this, about the same time that Alexander begin to call himself king, he seems to have dissolved the council. Direct evidence of this is lacking, but the deletion of the phrase "Council of the Jews" from the Hasmonean coins strongly implies that such a step was taken.[58]

(3) Those Jews with whom King Alexander was most closely allied were the aristocrats, that is, the party of the Sadducees. It was they who stood most to gain from the nation's wars of conquest, and it was their understanding of the Torah—so narrow as to make the teachings of Moses nonapplicable to many areas of life—which appealed to a thoroughly secular ruler like Alexander. Although some Sadducees must have disagreed with Alexander's dissolution of the council, many pious Jews would have viewed the Sadducees' attitude toward the traditions of Israel and their openness to the influences of Hellenism as offensive. Thus the Pharisees' hostility to Alexander was part of their larger anger at the Sadducees.

Events took a tragic turn one autumn (in probably the year 94 BC) when King and High Priest Alexander attempted to preside over the celebration at the Temple of the Feast of Tabernacles. It was the custom for each worshiper to carry a palm branch and a lemon, and as Alexander stood before the altar to offer sacrifice, he was pelted with lemons and insulting cries from the crowd. Alexander was so enraged at this offense to his dignity that he ordered his troops to attack the crowd, with the result that, according to Josephus,[59] 6,000

Jews were massacred.[60] The rest presumably fled, many of these bearing a deeper hatred of Alexander than ever before and vowing to return to the struggle against the tyrant.

In the face of this dissent at home, Alexander pursued with new vigor his wars abroad, and he was soon expanding his territories in Moab and in Gilead, that is, in both southern and northern extremities of the area of the Transjordan. He was nearly killed in a battle east of the Sea of Galilee, and when he hurried home to Jerusalem for recovery, he was greeted by a hostile populace. Josephus, our most ancient source for these events, is vague on details, but states that in the civil unrest that followed and that lasted for six years (94–88? BC), 50,000 Jews lost their lives. When at length a weary Alexander asked what he could do to placate the rebels, they cried out, "Die!"[61]

The leaders of the revolt then did something that would have been unthinkable a generation before. They called for help from the Seleucid king Demetrius III Eukairos ("The Timely One," 96–88 BC) who had succeeded his father Antiochus VIII Grypus ("Hook-nosed," 126–96 BC). Demetrius came to meet the rebels, marching through Galilee and into Samaria, and adding the dissident Jews to his ranks. For his part, Alexander led his army, consisting of both non-Jewish mercenaries and native Jewish troops, out to meet Demetrius, and near Shechem the two forces (both of them a mixture of Jew and Hellene) fought a bloody battle. Demetrius' army prevailed, and a shattered Alexander retreated (Josephus says vaguely "fled to the mountains"), probably falling back in the direction of Jerusalem. Then a remarkable thing happened. Less radical Jews, who, in spite of their hatred of Alexander, feared a Seleucid invasion even more, rallied to Alexander's side. Faced with this toughened resistance, Demetrius returned home, where he had other problems,[62] and Alexander quickly overcame the Jewish rebels who remained behind.

Many of these rebels were killed in battle, but of those who survived a gruesome fate was in store. Alexander brought them back to Jerusalem where he crucified 800 of them. As they hung dying, the king arranged for their wives and children to be murdered before their eyes. As the terrible spectacle was played out, Alexander watched, probably from the Baris, near the Temple, while he feasted with his concubines.

It is possible that it was during the terrible oppression of Alexander that, among those fleeing from Jerusalem, some took refuge in a isolated settlement that had been established some years before in the forbidding countryside near the northwestern shore of the Dead Sea and that later would become known as the Qumran community. Literature from Qumran describes a painful struggle and an accompanying hatred which may reflect the war between pious Jews, including the Pharisees, and Alexander. The subject of Qumran is one to which we shall return.[63]

With the subjugation of the Jewish rebels, Alexander was able to devote the balance of his reign to fighting external enemies. As Seleucid influence had grown weak through constant dynastic struggles, new powers had arisen in the region. One of these was the Nabateans (an Arab tribe who lived south and east of the Dead Sea), who, during the time that the Jewish state was convulsed by its internal problems, had conquered Transjordan as far north as Damascus. They then invaded Judaea and inflicted a defeat on Alexander's army, but, for unexplained reasons, subsequently withdrew, leaving Judaea in peace. For the balance of his reign, Alexander appears to have directed his attentions to campaigning in the Transjordan, winning back the cities taken by the Nabataeans. The last three years of his life were marked by an illness induced, so says Josephus, by heavy drinking.[64] When he died in the Transjordan at age forty-nine, his body was returned to Jerusalem where he was buried amid lavish ceremonies.

The territory of the Hasmonean kingdom now extended (with some exceptions) from the border of Egypt in the southwest, to Mt. Carmel in the northwest, through northern Galilee and Golan to Trachonitis in the northeast (the area of the Decapolis, to use the New Testament term), to the lower Dead Sea region in the southeast. The lands of the kingdom of Alexander at the time of his death closely resembled those of the kingdom of David upon the accession of Solomon (1 Kings 4:21).

4. *Salome Alexandra* (76–69 BC)

With the death of Alexander Jannaeus, the Hasmonean throne passed to his widow, Salome Alexandra.[65] When this woman, who seems to have been wife to the Hasmonean state's first two kings, began to rule in her own right, it soon became clear that she intended to pursue a course different from those of either of her husbands, for she became a firm ally of the Pharisees. Josephus says that she was instructed by a dying Alexander Jannaeus to make peace with his enemies.[66] But rabbinic lore preserves what may be a more likely explanation for this shift in policy: the queen was a member of a Pharisaic family.[67] Whatever the reason, the return to prominence of the Pharisees and the corresponding exclusion from power of the Sadducees was the single most important event of the queen's reign. Former rebels were released from prison and permitted to return from exile, while leaders of the Sadducee party who had assisted in Alexander's persecution of the Pharisees were hunted down and killed. The council (Sanhedrin), which by now had been reconstituted, was firmly under the control of the Pharisaic party. In Josephus' words, "while she [the queen] had the title of sovereign, the Pharisees had the power."[68] As may be imagined, it was, in Pharisaic memory, a golden time:

It is told that in the days . . . of Queen Salome rain fell on Sabbath nights [when Jews did not venture out on the roads] until wheat grew to the size of kidneys, barley to that of olive berries, lentils to that of gold *denarii*.[69]

But the Sadducees, their influence on the wane and many of their number in fear of their lives, would doubtless have different memories.

The bitter sectarian struggles among the Jews were reflected in the tension between the two sons of Alexander Jannaeus and Salome Alexandra. The elder, Hyrcanus, was named high priest upon his father's death (thus becoming Hyrcanus II), and he apparently agreed with his mother's Pharisaic sympathies. The younger brother, Aristobulus, was allied to the Sadducees and, in addition, possessed a more aggressive temperament than his brother. He thus became a rallying point for the anger of the Sadducees who, because of their close ties with the military officer corps, still held important positions within the army. At one point (it is not known precisely when) Aristobulus complained bitterly to his mother over the alleged injustices to the Sadducees, in response to which she, perhaps fearing a Sadducean revolt, yielded command of important fortresses around the country to Sadducee commanders.[70] She also placed Aristobulus at the head of a fighting force sent to Damascus, an adventure, however, in which he gained no important successes.

Later, as the queen lay ill and apparently nearing death, Aristobulus left Jerusalem in order to rally his Sadducean allies into a *coup d' etat,* for it was important that the crown not pass to Hyrcanus. At first Queen Alexandra would not believe that her son was mounting a revolt, but as news arrived that first one, then another of the army's garrisons had gone over to him,[71] she imprisoned Aristobulus' wife and children in the Baris. As the rebel army neared Jerusalem, the frightened leaders of the city appealed to the queen for action, but she was too weak and tired and thus told them that, in effect, they would have to fend for themselves. Then, at age seventy-three, she died.

It was a terrible moment for the nation, but if anyone had had the foresight to do so, he or she would have looked beyond the immediate threat posed by Aristobulus' army and identified an even greater danger in the distance, that represented by the legions of Rome. Romans had long maintained a presence in the area of the eastern Mediterranean. Near the beginning of the second century BC they fought two wars (211–205 and 200–197 BC) against Philip V of Macedonia, ally of Rome's great enemy Carthage, and subsequently invaded Asia Minor, soundly defeating the Seleucid army of Antiochus III the Great at Magnesia in 188 (in which battle the future Antiochus IV Epiphanes was taken hostage). Macedonia became the first eastern Roman province in 148, while in 146 the city of Corinth was destroyed, marking the end of resistance to Roman rule on the Greek mainland. On the north African coast, the advance of Rome could also be traced. We have already noticed that as early as 168 Romans were influential enough in the Ptolemaic kingdom to humiliate an otherwise victorious Antiochus IV Epiphanes, while in the same year that Corinth was crushed, mighty Carthage was at last overwhelmed, after a struggle which had lasted intermittently for a hundred years. Josephus notes that, during the reign of Queen Alexandra, the Armenian king Tigranes overran Seleucid forces in Syria and was poised to invade Judaea. But at the last moment, Tigranes learned that the Roman general Lucullus had invaded Armenia, so he canceled his plans to invade Judaea and hurried away to defend his homeland.[72] Thus, at the death of Queen Alexandra the immanent danger to the Hasmonean state appeared to be the insurrection of Aristobulus and the anger of the aristocratic Sadducees that lay behind it. But the larger, although less visible threat, were the soldiers of Rome.[73]

5. *The Fall of the Hasmonean State: Aristobulus II* (69–63 BC)

It now became the responsibility of Hyrcanus to defend the Pharisaic interests against Aristobulus, but he was no match for his younger brother. A battle was joined near Jericho, where many of Hyrcanus' troops defected to Aristobulus apparently because they found him to be a more convincing leader. Hyrcanus retreated to Jerusalem, but surrendered himself and his high priestly office to Aristobulus, in return for the latter's assurances of favorable treatment. Aristobulus thus became king and high priest within weeks or even days of his mother's death.

This state of affairs might have continued until the arrival of the Roman army, had it not been for the influence upon Hyrcanus of a certain Idumaean named Antipater. This Antipater was the son of the governor of Idumea who had been appointed during the reign of Alexander Jannaeus and whose duties Antipater himself seems to have inherited.[74] But he was avaricious for greater power and, seeing in the weakness of Hyrcanus an opportunity for his own advancement, he soon began to manipulate the former high priest by advising him that his life was in danger as long as he submitted to the authority of Aristobulus. At first Hyrcanus dismissed the counsel of Antipater, but he was finally won over and, according to a scheme arranged by Antipater, Hyrcanus fled to Aretas III, the king of the Nabataeans, at his capital, Petra. (It is this same Antipater who becomes the father of the future Herod the Great.)

Hyrcanus and Aretas then struck an agreement, also arranged by Antipater, according to which Aretas would place Hyrcanus on the Hasmonean throne in return for the cities in Transjordan that had been in Jewish hands since the time of Alexander Jannaeus. The advantage to Antipater in all of this is that he apparently hoped by this means to become the real power in the Hasmonean state behind the pliable Hyrcanus. And so Aretas marched against Aristobulus, defeated his army in battle, and besieged him and his Sadducean allies on the Temple mount, the place to which they had fled for refuge. It was the time of Passover in the year 65 BC.

During the four years since the death of Queen Alexandra, the Roman advance into western Asia Minor and Syria had met considerable success. In 66 BC Mithradates, King of Pontus (just south of the Black Sea), a stubborn enemy of Rome, had been finally defeated, as had Tigranes, King of Armenia, whose earlier invasion of Judaea had been cancelled because of the approach of the Romans. The head of this Roman force was Pompey,[75] who dispatched his general, Scaurus, into Syria, where, in 65, he occupied Damascus. It was there that news reached Scaurus of the civil strife among the Jews, and so he marched into Judaea as quickly as possible, in order to exploit the Jews' weakness. Upon his approach, both Aristobulus and Hyrcanus offered Scaurus gifts and asked for his support. Scaurus declared in favor of Aristobulus[76] and warned Hyrcanus and his Nabataean allies to lift the siege of Jerusalem. As they were unable to defy the Romans, they obeyed, while Scaurus and his troops withdrew back into Syria. No sooner had the Romans departed, however, than Aristobulus pursued the withdrawing Hyrcanus and his Nabataean allies and overwhelmed them in battle. Among the 6,000 dead was Antipater's brother.[77]

For the next two years, Aristobulus ruled from Jerusalem relatively undisturbed, while Antipater and Hyrcanus plotted from exile. For his part, Pompey consolidated his hold upon Syria by subduing what remained of the Seleucid kingdom as well as petty local rulers who had assumed power in the final, faltering days of that monarchy. In 64, Antioch-on-the-Orontes was occupied and became the capital of the new Roman province of Syria,[78] and the next year Pompey arrived in Damascus. There he was visited by three delegations of Jews, all seeking his favor. The parties of both Aristobulus and Hyrcanus were present, each of whom argued that Pompey should acknowledge their patron as the rightful king of the Jews. A third delegation of Jews tried to convince the Roman leader that the Jews should have no king at all, but that the ancient theocracy, presided over by the priests, should be restored. The shrewd Pompey, not knowing where his and Rome's best interests lay, postponed a decision, but commanded all parties to keep the peace. He announced that, in the meantime, he intended to pacify the Nabataeans.

But Aristobulus would brook no delay in settling the matter between himself and Hyrcanus, and so he collected his army at the fortress of Alexandrium in the lower Jordan valley. Pompey interpreted this action as directed against himself, and he accordingly diverted his troops from their Nabataean campaign and into Judaea. It appeared at first that Aristobulus and Pompey would reach an accord, for, upon Pompey's demand, Aristobulus led his force peacefully out of Alexandrion and back into Jerusalem. Aristobulus was apparently unable to decide if his advantage lay in resistance to Pompey or in cooperation with him, but he eventually opted for the latter. He visited Pompey at his camp near Jericho where he promised subjection to the Romans, including the guarantee of unimpeded entrance by them into Jerusalem. But when Pompey's representative Gabinius arrived at the gates of the city, a frightened populace shut the gates and refused to admit him and his troops. Pompey, infuriated, then seized Aristobulus (who was still in his camp) and marched upon Jerusalem.

The citizens of the city were of two minds concerning Pompey's approach. The allies of Aristobulus wished to resist and possibly rescue their leader, whereas most of the people simply wanted to open the city to the powerful Roman army and thereby avoid destruction. The latter group thus threw wide the city gates, allowing the Romans to walk in, but the army of Aristobulus gathered on the Temple mount where they raised their fortifications and prepared for a siege. As the Temple mount consists of a ridge bordered on three sides by valleys and ravines, the open (northern) end was its most vulnerable point. Here, behind strong barricades, the partisans of Aristobulus held out for three months while the Romans erected earthen ramparts from which their siege engines could hurl missiles against the Jews.[79] On a sabbath day in the summer of 63 BC the defensive wall was breached and the legionnaires poured in, led by the son of the former dictator of Rome, Sulla,[80] an officer named Cornelius Faustus. Some Jews committed suicide, some were killed by fellow Jews hostile to Aristobulus while many others were slaughtered by the Romans, a total number of fatalities, according to Josephus, of about 12,000.[81] Among those to fall were a number of priests who were offering sacrifices and who refused to give up their sacred duties, so that they were murdered before the altar.

When the killing was over, Pompey inspected the scene, including the interior of the Holy of Holies, which he treated with respect, not allowing it to be looted. The next day he restored to Hyrcanus the office of high priest (but not that of the kingship) and instructed that the Temple sacrifices should be resumed. He executed surviving leaders of the resistance and awarded honors to Cornelius Faustus and others for their bravery. And in this manner the Hasmonean state came to an end, slightly more than one hundred years after Mattathias led the revolt at Modein, some eighty years after the proclamation of independence in the days of Simon. The territory of the former Hasmonean state was placed under the authority of Scaurus, the governor of the province of Syria, while Aristobulus II, in chains, was forced, with members of his family, to accompany Pompey back to Rome. There, two years later, he was among the royal prisoners of war paraded before the population in order to publicize Pompey's triumphs in the East.

Reflecting on these terrible events, the author of one of the Psalms of Solomon was to sing bitterly:

He entered in peace as a father enters his son's house;
  he set his feet securely.
He captured the fortified towers and the wall of Jerusalem,
  for God led him in securely while they wavered.
He killed their leaders and every [man] wise in counsel;
  he poured out the water of the inhabitants of Jerusalem like dirty
  water.
He led away their sons and daughters, those profanely spawned.

(Ps. of Sol. 8:18–21[82])

C. Jews of the Hellenistic Diaspora[83]

Perhaps it is inevitable that modern students of early Judaism think of Jewish life during the Hellenistic period primarily in terms of the Jews of Palestine. For one thing, as we shall later see, modern Judaism is largely a development of Pharisaism, thus the links between modern and ancient Judaism were, to a great extent, forged in Palestine. For another thing, meager as they are in many respects, the sources for our understanding of early Judaism are greater with respect to Palestinian Jewish life than for the life of the Hellenistic Diaspora. For all that, however, it is important to remember that during the Hellenistic period more Jews lived outside Palestine than in it, and that the rich traditions of Diaspora Judaism made important contributions not only to the life and thought of the larger Jewish community, but ultimately to that of the Christian community, as well.

The breaking down of time-honored political and cultural frontiers, which was one of the results of the conquests of Alexander the Great, plus the emergence of something approaching a world culture in the rise of Hellenism, opened new channels of communication and transportation throughout the Mediterranean basin and into the East (Mesopotamia and Persia) as never before. The relative ease by which peoples moved from place to place (either forced or of their own free will) undoubtedly contributed to the establishment of pockets of Jewish life throughout the Hellenistic world, a development which would gain even greater momentum with the subjugation of the Hellenistic kingdoms by the forces of Rome. During Hellenistic times, Jews began to live in significant numbers in Syria, Asia Minor, and Greece, and some Jews even found their way to the Greek colonies in Sicily and southern Italy (Magna Graecia). But by far the most important Diaspora communities were those of Babylon and Egypt.

The Babylonian Diaspora began with the deportations of Jews under Nebuchadnezzar in 597 and 587 BC. To be sure, these Jewish exiles had been preceded into the region by captives transported from the Northern Kingdom by the Assyrians after the fall of Samaria in 722 BC, fellow Israelites whose descendants, in time, would perhaps be assimilated into Jewish communities established in Mesopotamia by the Babylonians. But of these Northern Israelites there is scarcely a trace, so that the Babylonian exiles seem always to have thought of Jerusalem as home (Ps. 137). The capture of Babylon by Persian forces under Cyrus in 539 BC and the return of Jews to Jerusalem under Sheshbazzar (538 BC) and Zerubbabel (520 BC) by no means brought an end to Jewish life in Babylon, because most Jews, perhaps heeding the advice of Jeremiah (29:4–9), had by now made homes for themselves in this foreign land and entertained no intentions of leaving. Under the tolerant rule of the Persians that supplanted that of the Babylonians, Jews in Mesopotamia continued to flourish and Jewish settlers could be found over a wide area of the land drained by the Tigris and Euphrates rivers. When Seleucid rule arrived, it was, initially at least, no less tolerant, and the new capital city built by Seleucus I (312 BC), Seleucia-on-the-Tigris, soon outstripped Babylon as the chief metropolitan area in the region and, as such, could claim its own colony of Jews.

A special bond united the Jews of Babylonia with those of Palestine. The reasons seem to have to do with the fact that, since they lay nearer the fringes of the Hellenistic world, the Babylonian Jews were often freer to lay claim to their own traditions than were other Diaspora Jews. For example both Babylonian and Palestinian Jews spoke Aramaic (in somewhat different dialects), whereas for most Jews of Syria, Asia Minor, and Egypt, Greek had become a first language. But beneath the use of a common language there lay deeper bonds. Much of the Hebrew scriptures had been written or edited in Babylonia during the exile, and the form of the biblical canon in Palestine—at least as it was defined at Jamnia (Yavneh) in 90 AD[84]—was nearer the canon of Babylonian Jews than the canon of the Jews of the Greek-speaking Diaspora. Jewish families of a traditionalist bent in Palestine maintained ties with like-minded cousins in Babylonia, so that theological discourse between the two communities continued well into Roman times. One of the greatest of the Palestinian Jewish teachers during the first century AD was Hillel,[85] who had traveled to Palestine from his native Babylon. Important Babylonian Targumim were in use in Palestine, and by about the second century AD the Babylonian Talmud[86] had become a rich repository of Jewish teaching and lore embraced by Jews in Palestine and in the Diaspora alike.

Another important center of Diaspora life during the Hellenistic period was Alexandria, that glittering capital of the Greek-speaking world. Jews had been migrating to Egypt since at least the destruction of Jerusalem by

Nebuchadnezzar in 587 BC. That cadre of anti-Babylonian Jews who took the prophet Jeremiah hostage and forced him to accompany them to Egypt (Jer. 43:1–7) must have been only one of many groups of Jews who fled south rather than face the wrath of the Babylonians. By the early Persian period at least one military colony of Jews had been established in Egypt at Elephantine, while during the Ptolemaic rule over southern Palestine the relative ease of travel between Jerusalem and the more prosperous Nile valley must have made the relocation of Jews commonplace. The Seleucid invasion of Palestine at the beginning of the second century BC and the subsequent struggle over Hellenism gave pro-Egyptian Jews in and around Jerusalem the same reason to flee to Egypt that had compelled others to go there during the conquests of Nebuchadnezzar. It is in this context that Josephus reports the building of a Jewish temple by the high priest, Onias, in Heliopolis[87] to service the needs of the Jewish community there. That such Jews could rise to high rank is evidenced by the report of Josephus, mentioned earlier, that an Egyptian army sent into Palestine against Alexander Jannaeus was led by two Oniad brothers, Chelkias and Ananias, who, because of their loyalty to the reigning monarch, Queen Cleopatra III, were awarded special honors.[88]

The Jews of Egypt, therefore, often enjoyed economic and cultural advantages which were not always available to Jews elsewhere. To be sure, they were sometimes the objects of hostility and mistrust by their non-Jewish neighbors, as was the case in other parts of the Hellenistic world. The Egyptian historian Manetho, for example, writing in the third century BC, displays a decidedly anti-Jewish bias,[89] while during the reign of Ptolemy VI Philometor (180–145 BC) the Jews of Egypt suffered physical persecution. For all that, however, Egyptian Jews enjoyed a standing in society which was relatively favorable.

It is doubtless not accidental that the richest collection of literature from the Hellenistic Diaspora, the Septuagint, should have close ties to the literary and cultural center of Hellenistic life, Alexandria. No one will ever be sure of all the crosscurrents of influence and counterinfluence that flowed between writers of the Alexandrian Jewish community and their non-Jewish colleagues who worked in the museum and the library, but they were considerable. Whether written in the Diaspora or in Palestine, Jewish literature composed in the Greek language, including nonbiblical material, displays a fascinating variety, not only as to form, but also with respect to the manner in which it weaves together the colorful threads of Judaism and those of the Greek-speaking world.

Chapter 3

APOCALYPTIC

A. THE NATURE OF APOCALYPTIC[1]

Out of the turmoils of the Hasmonean era there emerged a theological perspective—and a literature which expresses that perspective—that was to have important consequences for Jews and, to an even greater extent, for Christians: apocalyptic. (The term comes from a Greek word, *apokalypsis*, meaning *revelation*.) The roots of apocalyptic are to be found in a number of strands of Old Testament thought,[2] perhaps the most important of which is prophecy. Those who fashioned apocalyptic writings in the second century BC and beyond took possession of major elements in the teaching of the Old Testament prophets, yet transformed these so that they became new and distinctive. In this task they were aided by the prophets themselves who, especially in the later stages of Old Testament prophecy, anticipated the directions in which apocalyptic was later to move. Primary theological principles in the prophetic view and their apocalyptic counterparts include the nature of evil, the certainty of judgment, and the course of future events. Alongside these primary characteristics of apocalyptic are a number of additional literary and theological features that are dependent upon them. These include: an extensive angelology and demonology (theological dualism), the figure of the messiah, belief in the resurrection of the dead, the periodization of history, an extensive use of symbols, the attribution of individual apocalyptic writings to earlier heroes of faith (pseudonymity) and a reliance upon dreams and visions as media of revelation.

1. *The Nature of Evil*

The prophets of Israel were deeply aware of the reality of evil. Nathan, who condemned David for the sordid affair involving Bathsheba and Uriah, her husband (2 Sam. 12); Hosea, who compared Israel to an unfaithful spouse (Hos. 2:2–13); and Jeremiah, who recited a litany of the nation's transgressions (Jer. 7:8–10) all stood squarely within the prophetic repudiation of evil. For these and other prophets, the evil which offends God consists of human perversion. It is the result of corrupted volition, that is, the purposeful disregard of the reality of God in human life and the frequent violation of the well-being of other persons. In

66

other words, people *choose* to do evil when they could choose good. In a powerful play upon the homophonic quality of his words Isaiah (or someone in the
Isaianic tradition) complained:

> He [Yahweh] expected *mishpat* (justice),
>   but saw *mishpach* (bloodshed);
> *sedaqah* (righteousness),
>   but heard *se'aqah* (a cry)!
> Isaiah 5:7

For the apocalyptists, on the other hand, evil assumed cosmic dimensions
that were, for the most part, unknown among the prophets. Because much apocalyptic literature was born in times of crisis, its authors attempted, among
other things, to reconcile two apparent contradictions: (1) human life is governed by a loving and benevolent God, and (2) the world is filled with apparently triumphant evil. For writers of apocalyptic materials, the reconciliation of
these opposites lay in identifying the origin of evil in the malicious activity of a
group of beings who are superior to human beings, but inferior to God: fallen
angels. The Book of Jubilees (second century BC) is typical in this regard in that
it identifies these angels with the "sons of God" of Genesis 6:2:

> And when the children of men began to multiply on the surface of the
> earth and daughters were born to them, that the angels of the Lord saw
> in a certain year of that jubilee that they were good to look at. And they
> took wives for themselves from all of those whom they chose. And they
> bore children for them; and they were the giants. And injustice in-
> creased upon the earth, and all flesh corrupted its way; man and cattle
> and beasts and birds and everything which walks on the earth. And
> they all corrupted their way and their ordinances, and they began to eat
> one another. And injustice grew upon the earth and every imagination
> of the thoughts of all mankind was thus continually evil.
> (Jub. 5:1–2)

The sinful initiatives of evil angels by no means excuse men and women of
the evils which they themselves perpetrate (Jubilees even retells the story
of the fall of Adam and Eve, Jub. 3:17–35), but ultimate culpability is clearly
with these other-worldly demonic powers. It is they who have befouled the
earth with sin and it is they who alienate human beings from God and from
one another. They presently hold the world in their evil grasp and no effort
short of the intervention of God will be able to break their power. This understanding of evil helped to explain why the best efforts of godly men and
women often fail, and why those who are faithful to God are often defeated
and humiliated.

2. *The Certainty of Judgment*

Just as the apocalyptists reshaped the prophetic understanding of the nature of evil, a similar change was effected by them on the prophetic view of the certainty of God's judgment. For the Old Testament prophets, particularly those who were active during the eighth through the sixth centuries, God's judgment upon human sin was seen to be the logical reaction of the Deity to the moral intransigence of men and women. Frequently (although not always) the prophetic proclamation of judgment was conditional, that is, it was promised *if* the people did not repent. On the other hand, if they did turn from their evil ways, there would be reconciliation.

> For if you truly amend your ways and your doings, if you truly act justly one with another, if you do not oppress the alien, the orphan, and the widow, or shed innocent blood in this place, and if you do not go after other gods to your own hurt, then I will dwell with you in this place, in the land that I gave of old to your ancestors forever and ever.
>
> (Jer. 7:5–6)

Second Isaiah even goes so far as to proclaim restoration for the people of God, who have already experienced the judgment of God, not because they have repented, but because it is the nature of God to redeem (Isa. 40:1–2, 43:22—44:8).

Out of this prophetic vision of the nature of God's judgment arose an apocalyptic understanding that was more radical both in terms of its inevitability and in terms of its finality. Already in the prophet Joel one may see this transformation taking place. What begins as a description of a locust plague (Joel 1:2–4) quickly becomes a promise of judgment (2:1–2). Yet it is not a judgment *within* history, but an eschatological judgment, that is, one that coincides with the end of history (Joel 2:30–32).

In much apocalyptic literature not only is the judgment of God portrayed as inevitable (judgment upon evil angels as well as upon human beings), but the entire course of human history is determined by God from the very beginning. The Testament of Moses (also called the Assumption of Moses) provides a succinct statement of this view:

> God has created all the nations which are in the world (just as he created) us. And he has foreseen both them and us from the beginning of the creation of the world even to the end of the age. Indeed, nothing, to the last thing has been overlooked by him. But, (rather), he has seen all things and he is the cause of all. [The Lord] has seen beforehand all things which may come to be in the world, and, behold, they have come to pass.
>
> (T. Moses 12:4–5)

In the context of this determinism judgment is promised. It is seen as the inevitable consequence not only of human sinfulness, but of the transcendent evil represented by the fallen angels. It is also portrayed as the only means by which the tyranny of the present evil age may be shattered. And because evil is a cosmic force, judgment is also cosmic in its scope. That is to say, it becomes more than a simple matter of chastising a wayward people. It becomes the destruction of cosmic evil root and branch. Not only are evil human beings to be destroyed, but the ranks of evil angels (the demons) are to be destroyed, as well. In some examples of apocalyptic, this judgment is the unmediated work of God, whereas in others judgment involves the work of an individual who comes with the authority of God. This individual is sometimes identified as an angel or other supernatural being, sometimes as the messiah.[3] Although the outcome is never in doubt (it has been pre-determined), the powers of cosmic evil fight fiercely before being subdued.

> At that time Michael, the great prince, the protector of your people, shall arise. There shall be a time of anguish, such as has never occurred since nations first came into existence. But at that time your people shall be delivered, everyone who is found written in the book.
>
> (Dan. 12:1)

3. The Course of Future Events

The prophets of the Old Testament frequently spoke of future events. Often, as we have noted, these statements had to do with God's judgment and were thus sometimes couched in conditional terms. At other times, however, the prophets spoke of a golden age to come, one in which human life would be lived according to the moral principles of the Torah (Jer. 31:27–34; Zech. 8:1–23, and elsewhere). This golden age and its benefits, however, would not be enjoyed by all people. It would be the heritage of the Jews and, according to some texts, those gentiles who had maintained peaceful relations with the Jews (Isa. 56:6–7), while other gentiles were to be destroyed. It is not always clear if these prophetic texts are speaking of a golden age within history, or of an eschatological paradise. In fact, as one reads certain of these prophetic texts, one may sense that he or she is standing in that area of transition in which the traditional prophetic vision of God's activity within human history is being altered into the apocalyptic vision of God's eschatological judgment and redemption.

Be that as it may, many apocalyptic writings clearly project the concepts of predetermined judgment and salvation to eschatological dimensions. Typically, human beings are to be raised from the dead at the time of judgment, the wicked to be damned eternally, the righteous to be conducted into never-ending paradise. This is a substantive leap from the prophetic view that human evil will be punished by, let us say, God's bringing a foreign invader into the land, or from the prophetic view that the faithful will be rewarded by God's allowing them to live a peaceful life in the Land of Promise (Isa. 1:18–20). For apocalyptic, judgment and redemption are decisive, final and universal.

> For first he will bring [the evil ones] alive before his judgment seat, and when he has reproved them, then he will destroy them. But in mercy he will set free the remnant of my people, those who have been saved throughout my borders, and he will make them joyful until the end comes, the day of judgment, of which I spoke to you at the beginning.
>
> (2 or 4 Esdras 12:33–34)

> In those days, angels shall descend into the secret places. They shall gather together into one place all those who gave aid to sin. And the Most High will arise on that day of judgment in order to execute a great judgment upon all sinners. He will set a guard of holy angels over all the righteous and holy ones, and they shall keep them as the apple of the eye until all evil and all sin are brought to an end.
>
> (1 Enoch 100:4–5)

4. Angels and Demons

As we have noticed, the apocalyptic worldview placed great importance upon an army of supernatural beings who, although creatures of God, were superior to human beings in power and influence. The Old Testament occasionally refers to angelic beings who serve before God (Isa. 6:1–8; Job 1:6, 2:1; cf. Gen. 6:1–4), and the importance of these beings seems to have increased in the Persian and Hellenistic periods as God, in the conception of many Jews, became increasingly majestic and thereby increasingly remote.[4] The tendency to fill the resulting vacuum with supernatural beings who were, in some ways, mediators between God and human beings may have been helped along by similar conceptions in Zoroastrianism and other eastern religions. Although God is in control of human and angelic/demonic affairs, the legions of supernatural beings, both good and evil, play important roles because of their ability to influence human life. Some examples of apocalyptic literature describe the organizational structure of angelic and demonic bodies in terms of ranks. An interesting passage in 1 Enoch 71 mentions, as angelic bodies, seraphim (literally: "burning ones"), cherubim ("intercessors") and ophanim ("wheels"). The same passage names as chief angelic individuals (archangels) Michael, Raphael, Gabriel, and Phanuel. Other apocalyptic texts provide different titles and proper names.[5] As for demons, they are sometimes referred to as "watchers," the corps of formerly good angels whose fall into sinfulness led to the corruption of human life

(Jub. 7:21). The primary demon is variously referred to as Satan,[6] Beliar (or Belial), Azazel, Mastema, and by other names.

The result of this intense interest in supernatural beings is a pronounced, although modified dualism. God's ultimate authority is never questioned and it is this authority that will be expressed in the final overthrow of evil in all its forms. But in the interim (the "present" of the various apocalyptic writers) the forces of evil are involved in a bitter struggle against the forces of good and have, for the moment, prevailed over them.

5. *The Messiah*

In some apocalyptic literature, but by no means all, the figure who embodies the righteous rule of God is not an angel, but a transcendent being of another kind who occupies a place very near God. Several titles are bestowed upon this being, including "son of man" and "messiah."

The phrase "son of man" appears a number of times in the Old Testament, as for example, in the Book of Ezekiel, where it is a frequently cited reference to the prophet (Ezek. 2:1, and elsewhere). In its usual Old Testament use, this title seems to be little more than a Semitism for "human being" or, collectively, "human beings" (cf. the phrase "sons of Israel," meaning "Israelites"). In certain apocalyptic writings, however, the words assume a greater significance and refer to a transcendent being who, in various ways, brings about the will of God. In that section of 1 Enoch referred to as the Similitudes of Enoch (chaps. 37–71), the son of man is described as a supernatural being who has been designated before the creation of the world as the one who will complete a work of God which, although it has not yet been revealed, is portrayed as being related in some manner to the final judgment (see esp. chaps. 46–49). The son of man is also called the Elect One, the Righteous One and the Anointed ("Messiah").[7]

The term "messiah," frequently used in the Old Testament, generally refers there to the Davidic king (2 Sam. 19:21), although in one interesting text the title is applied to Cyrus, the Persian emperor (Isa. 45:1). In some texts, although the word *messiah* itself does not appear, a portrait is painted of an ideal Davidic kingdom in which the kingly figure assumes more-than-human dimensions (Isa. 11:1–9, Ezek. 34:23–24). It is not surprising, therefore, that in some post-Old Testament apocalyptic literature, the *messiah* is described as a transcendent being who inaugurates the rule of God.

It should be noted here that in some apocalyptic writings the eschatological kingdom is described without reference to a messiah, an example being the Book of Daniel where, as noted above, "the great prince" Michael will lead the people of God into the consummation of their hope (Dan. 12:1).[8] But in other apocalyptic literature, the messiah, does assume a prominent role in the establishment of the divine kingdom. In literature that was written during the Hasmonean era, when Judah was ruled by a family of Levitical priests, the messianic figure was sometimes related, not to the family of David, but to that of Levi. The idealized description of the rule of Simon in 1 Maccabees 14:4–15, quoted in part above,[9] is quite similar to certain prophetic texts, just noted (Isa. 11:1–9, Ezek. 34:23–24) that portray the idealized Davidic kingdom, except that the Davidic figure has been replaced by a Levitical one. (As in the texts cited, the word *messiah* is lacking in the passage from 1 Maccabees). Of course, 1 Maccabees does not belong to the genre of apocalyptic, but a similar concept is sketched in the Book of Jubilees (31:13–15) and in the Testament of Levi (8:14) (which is one of the Testaments of the Twelve Patriarchs), literature which is decidedly apocalyptic in flavor.[10]

In other examples of apocalyptic, the messianic concept is based on a Davidic model. Noteworthy in this regard is the so-called Psalms of Solomon, apparently written in response to the fall of the Hasmonean dynasty at the hands of the Romans under Pompey. Psalm of Solomon 17 is especially specific:

See, Lord, and raise up for them their king,
    the son of David, to rule over your servant Israel
    in the time known to you, O God.
    *   *   *   *
He will gather a holy people,
    whom he will lead in righteousness;
and he will judge the tribes of the people
    that have been made holy by the Lord their God.
He will not tolerate unrighteousness (even) to pause among them,
    and any person who knows wickedness shall not live with them.
    *   *   *   *
And he will have gentile nations serving him under his yoke,
    and he will glorify the Lord in (a place) prominent (above) the
    whole earth.
And he will purge Jerusalem
    (and make it) holy as it was even from the beginning,
    *   *   *   *
And he will be a righteous king over them, taught by God,
There will be no unrighteousness among them in his days,
    for all shall be holy,
    and their king shall be the Lord Messiah.

                                                    (Ps. of Sol. 17:21–32)

Here the rule of the Davidic messiah is probably to be understood in historical, rather than in eschatological terms. But an eschatological version of the hope in a Davidic messiah seems to have been current among some writers of apocalyptic literature, as the close association between the titles son of man and messiah in 1 Enoch 48:10 would suggest. (Cf. Testament of Judah 24:1–6).

Yet it should be kept in mind that, in spite this association, son of man and messiah were separate concepts in the thought of many Jewish apocalyptic writers, the former term conveying an eschatological meaning that the latter frequently did not possess. In this context, it should be remarked that son of man was, according to the New Testament Gospels, Jesus' usual designation for himself, and one that was sometimes used in an eschatological manner (John 1:51). Yet, Jesus appears to have avoided the term Messiah (Mark 8:30).

To return briefly to the text quoted above from Psalm of Solomon 17, it should be noted that the conceptualization of the Davidic messiah in terms of a conquering military hero probably helped give rise to the work of various Zealot Messiahs (cf. Acts 5:36, 37; 21:38) as well as the tendency, noted in the Gospels, for Jesus' immediate disciples to see his work in those terms (Matt. 21:9, Luke 24:21).

6. *The Resurrection of the Dead*

For the writers of the Old Testament, there is little interest in or hope for life beyond death. The primary arena of God's activity is clearly *this* life, and most references to life beyond the grave are to Sheol, a dull and uninteresting place where all the dead, both good persons as well as evil, lead a vaguely defined and shadowy existence (Job 3:13–19). Only in late texts are there a few scattered allusions to a hope for life beyond the grave (Isa. 26:19, Dan. 12:1).

But the outlook is very different for the apocalyptic writers, and one of the most important of the differences is in the matter of the resurrection of the dead. Apocalyptic is virtually unanimous[11] in believing that the end of human history will be characterized by God's act of restoring to life those who have died. Yet this same literature provides a bewildering array of varying, sometimes contradictory views concerning the particulars of the resurrection. Sometimes the emphasis is upon the resurrection of the righteousness only, at other times the concern is with the resurrection of all persons. Frequently, resurrection is related to the final judgment, so that the righteous are raised into bliss, and the wicked into punishment. Yet even here there is a wide range of views concerning details. The extent to which foreign influences played a part in the development of a belief in resurrection among Jews (and, later, Christians) is a matter of debate. But it is quite possible that, whereas the hope for resurrection grew out of Israel's own theological traditions, that hope was stimulated and shaped by non-Hebrew, especially Persian and Greek, religious thought.

In spite of this diversity among the writers of apocalyptic in the manner in which resurrection is conceptualized, a hope in resurrection became an important element in second and first century BC Jewish thought and, it should be added, a point of controversy. The Sadducees were known for their denial of resurrection, on the grounds that it is not mentioned in the Torah. Whereas the Pharisees and other Jews[12] embraced the teaching and, to one degree or another, made it central to their doctrine (cf. Acts 23:8). As for the early Christians, Paul and others made the hope of resurrection a fundamental element in their eschatological views (1 Cor. 15:1–58).

7. *The Periodization of History*

There is an interest within some apocalyptic literature in viewing all or parts of human history in terms of a schematic division into various periods of time. Daniel, for example, identifies four sucessive world kingdoms (Dan. 7:17), whereas the Book of Jubilees (1:26) speaks in terms of weeks of years and jubilees. The Book of 1 Enoch includes the so-called "Apocalypse of Weeks" (chaps. 91–93) in which time is divided into periods of weeks, while 2 Enoch (33:1) surveys human history as occurring during eight millennia. The purpose of this periodization was not only to reaffirm the apocalyptists' conviction that God had ordained the events of human history from the beginning, but also to permit the reader to know where in this divinely appointed time-scheme he or she might happen to be. This method of viewing human history was to have considerable influence upon early Christian writers (cf. 1 Cor. 15:23–24, Rev. 20:4–6).

8. *Symbolism and Numerology*

Much apocalyptic literature is characterized by frequent use of symbols, animals of various kinds being a favorite symbolic medium. The origin of much of this symbolism is obscure, but the mythology of the ancient Near East seems to have played an important role in this regard. One of the most prominent symbolic motifs is that of the evil sea-dragon or serpent who, in the Babylonian creation epic, was killed as a first step in the creation of the heavens and the earth.[13] Because certain authors of apocalyptic material looked upon the final establishment of the rule of God as a climactic act of divine creation, the dragon reappears as the leader of the forces of evil, who must be overcome before the establishment of God's eschatological kingdom, that is, before God's act of re-creation. This motif is already present in the Old Testament itself, as for example in Isaiah 51:9,[14] and it reappears in certain apocalyptic writings, notably 1 Enoch (60:7–9) and 2 Esdras (6:47–52) where reference is made to not one, but two monsters, Behemoth and Leviathan. In 2 Baruch 29:3–4 Behemoth and Leviathan are both mentioned in connection with the coming of the messiah and the last judgment. In this passage, the two beasts provide meat for the redeemed at the eschatological banquet (cf. Ps. 74:14):

> And it will happen that when all that which should come to pass in these parts has been accomplished, the Anointed One [Messiah] will begin to be revealed. And Behemoth will reveal itself from its place, and Leviathan will come from the sea . . . And they will be nourishment for all who are left.
>
> (2 Baruch 29:3–4)

The text goes on to describe the resurrection of the dead and the final judgment (30:1–5). In the New Testament Apocalypse, the dragon is the symbolic representation of Satan who is overthrown and bound at the beginning of the millennium (Rev. 12:7–9, 20:1–3).[15]

Other prominent animal figures include sheep or lambs, who symbolize the righteous (Ezek. 34:11–16, 1 Enoch 89:16–18, and Rev. 14:1 and elsewhere [where the lamb represents Christ]), and various beasts and birds of prey, who symbolize gentiles and wicked people generally (notice especially Test. of Joseph 19:8, probably a Christian interpolation, where "all sorts of wild animals and reptiles" are conquered by a lamb who has come from a virgin). Among nonanimal symbols in apocalyptic literature the most important are celestial bodies. These frequently have a negative connotation, as in 1 Enoch 86:1–6 where they represent fallen angels, an idea perhaps based on Isaiah 14:12. But in the New Testament Apocalypse, the seven stars represent the angels of the seven churches (Rev. 1:20).

Numbers are also important symbols, especially seven and twelve, and multiples (and fractions) thereof. In Daniel 9:2 the seventy years (a Sabbath of decades) of Jeremiah 25:11–12 is recalled and, under the revelation of the angel Gabriel, Daniel understands this to mean seventy *weeks* of years (Dan. 9:20–24), or 490 years between the fall of Jerusalem and establishment of the rule of God. The number seventy is also prominent in 1 Enoch, and in the New Testament Apocalypse the number seven occurs fifty-four times.

9. Pseudonymity

It is a characteristic of apocalyptic to attribute various writings to remote figures of the past who were considered to be authoratative spokespersons for God. This feature is not unique to apocalyptic, for even in the Old Testament canon itself there are examples of this kind of attribution in the Song of Solomon and the Book of Ecclesiastes (also falsely attributed to Solomon), to name but two. But apocalyptic writers almost routinely practiced pseudonymity, favorite subjects being Enoch, who did not die (Gen. 5:24), as well as two personalities considered to be prominent scribes in recording the Word of God, Baruch (Jer. 36:4–8, 32) and Ezra (2 Esdras 14:37–48). This practice was probably not undertaken in an effort to deceive potential readers of this material, but was a curious (to modern women and men, at least) way of emphasizing the belief of the apocalyptic writers that they also conveyed a true message from God, as had those in whose name they wrote.

10. *Dreams and Visions*

The prophets of ancient Israel were frequently portrayed as speaking the Word of God out of divinely inspired dreams or trances.[16] The apocalyptic tradition, in turn, extended and amplified this view so that the (pseudonymous) spokesperson of God frequently is given certain truths only or primarily by means of a dream or a vision. For example, an entire section of 1 Enoch (chaps. 83–90) is devoted to a series of dreams and visions by which God shares certain truths with Enoch, while 2 Baruch 55:3 names the angel Ramael as the custodian of God's treasury of "true visions." Both major canonical apocalyptic works, Daniel in the Old Testament and Revelation in the New Testament, utilize the visionary experience as a primary medium by which divine truth is communicated (Dan. 2:36–45,[17] 7:1, and elsewhere; Rev. 1:9–16, 12:1, and elsewhere).

B. IMPORTANT INDIVIDUAL EXAMPLES OF APOCALYPTIC

Of the dozens of examples of early Jewish apocalyptic writings that have survived, several are of particular importance for the manner in which they illustrate various aspects of the apocalyptic worldview. In the discussion that follows five units of literature will be briefly examined not because they constitute an exhaustive survey, but because they illustrate the variety of methods by which apocalyptic ideals were expressed in the period of the second and first centuries BC. It should be remembered that many other examples of apocalyptic thought have survived in the literature of both the early Jewish and early Christian communities, some of which are discussed elsewhere in this volume.

1. *The Book of Daniel* [18]

Daniel is the most extensive, although by no means the only, example of apocalyptic literature found within the canon of the Old Testament.[19] The evidence within the book suggests that it achieved its present form during the early days of the Hasmonean struggle against the forces of Antiochus Epiphanes, the desecration of the Jerusalem Temple by that Seleucid monarch receiving particular attention (Dan. 11:31). It is written in both Hebrew and Aramaic languages and, although the reason for this peculiar feature has never been satisfactorily explained, it is not without significance for understanding the background of Daniel that both languages were in use among Palestine's Jews during the Hasmonean period.[20] There can be little doubt that the book was written for the purpose of giving encouragement to the traditionalist Jews in their fight against both Antiochus and those members of the Jewish community who were willing to set aside the traditions of Israel in favor of Hellenistic beliefs and customs. It attempts to accomplish this goal by citing examples of courageous behavior on the part of other faithful Jews, primarily the young man Daniel, during the time of the Babylonian and Persian periods and by promising the overthrow of Antiochus' kingdom in favor of the rule of God.

The book consists of two major sections. Chapters 1–6 contain six short stories concerning the faithfulness and courage of Daniel and of Daniel's close friends in the face of pressures placed upon them by foreign authorities, pressures which are intended to force the young men to abandon the traditions of the Jews in favor of those of their masters. Chapters 7–12, the truly apocalyptic section, record four visions of Daniel in which there is revealed to him the overthrow of the present tyranny and the establishment of the rule of God.

By way of example, the fourth and longest of these visions, chapters 10–12, describes how a bitter rivalry between the "king of the south" and the "king of the north" (the Ptolemys vs. the Seleucids) concludes with the victory of the "king of the north" (Dan. 11:14–16). In the place of the victorious "king of the north" (Antiochus III) "shall arise a contemptable person on whom royal majesty had not been conferred" (Dan 11:21, a reference to Antiochus IV Epiphanes who ruled in place of Antiochus III's son, Demetrius—later Demetrius I Soter—who was at this time held hostage by the Romans). This evil ruler will invade "the south" (11:29), but will be repulsed by the "ships of Kittim" (Antiochus was foiled by the Romans in his attempt to invade Egypt),[21] and

> he shall lose heart and withdraw. He shall be enraged and take action against the holy covenant. He shall turn back and pay heed to those who forsake the holy covenant. Forces sent by him shall occupy and profane the temple and fortress. They shall abolish the regular burnt offering and set up the abomination that makes desolate.
>
> (Dan. 11:30b–31)

There will follow a period of great suffering for the people of God when many will repudiate their faith (11:32–35), whereas the evil ruler will enjoy triumph upon triumph (11:40–45). Ultimately, however, Michael, "the great prince," will deliver the people of God, following which there will be a general resurrection when "some [shall awake] to everlasting life, and some to shame and everlasting contempt" (12:1–3).

Apocalyptic elements in the Book of Daniel include the following: (1) As may seen from the above discussion, the present time is considered to be in the grasp of evil forces that are so strong that they cannot be destroyed by anything other than the power of God. In the interim, even the most righteous of God's people will suffer, but they must be true to their faith even though they are killed, for they know that God will finally vindicate them and raise them to everlasting life. God's judgment, in other words, is sure.

(2) Although there is surprisingly little angel/demonology in Daniel, the archangel Michael is described as the instrument by which God's eternal rule is to be established (12:1).

(3) Dreams are a medium of revelation in two of the short stories (chaps. 2 and 4), while visions are prominent in the second half of the book (chaps. 7–12).

(4) There are a number of symbols. For example, the golden image of chapter 3 is emblematic of the statue of Zeus that Antiochus ordered erected in the Jerusalem Temple. Antiochus himself is symbolized by Nebuchadnezzar in chapter 4, where the story seems to have in mind a play upon words: instead of Antiochus Epiphanes ("manifestation [of Zeus]"), Antiochus Epimanes ("madman"). Other symbols include animal figures, such as the beasts in chapter 7 which represent the great world empires, and the ram and he-goat of chapter 8 which are emblematic of Persia and Greece. Numbers are prominent, as in "a time, two times, and half a time" (or one half of the "complete" number 7 [7:25; 12:7]), and as in the "two thousand three hundred evenings and mornings" (8:14, cf. 12:11, 12).

(5) The book is pseudonymous. There apparently was a figure known as Daniel in Hebrew and other Semitic lore, an individual remembered for the wisdom by which he judged his people (the name Daniel means "God judges"). Full accounts of this legendary person have not been preserved, as far as is known, but partial references are contained in the Ugaritic "Tale of Aqhat"[22] and in Ezekiel 14:14 and 28:3. The Book of Daniel portrays Daniel as an individual not only of exemplary righteousness (as in Ezek. 14:14), but also as a practitioner of Wisdom (as in Ezek. 28:3). In Daniel 2, Daniel proves himself to be wiser, in fact, that all the Wisdom scholars of Nebuchadnezzar's court. It is apparent, then, that the message of the author of the Book of Daniel was conveyed by relating it to a prominent figure of faith, as was done by many other apocalyptic writers.

Influence of Daniel upon the New Testament: The most prominent reference to the Book of Daniel in the New Testament is in Mark 13:14 and (its parallel passage Matt. 24:15). Here the "abomination that desolates" of Daniel 9:27, 11:31, 12:11 (the desecration of the Temple by Antiochus Epiphanes) is cited in reference to the destruction of Jerusalem in 70 AD.[23] It is interesting that the New Testament passage is also apocalyptic, the so-called "Little Apocalypse" of the Gospels.

Further along in the "Little Apocalypse" (Mark. 13:26–27, Matt. 24:30–31, Luke 21:27) the imagery and language of Daniel is utilized in order to describe the triumphant return of the transcendent Son of man:

I saw in the night visions,
and behold, with the clouds of
    heaven there came one like
    a son of man
and he came to the Ancient of
    Days and was presented
    before him.
And to him was given
    dominion and glory and
    kingdom, that all peoples,
    nations, and languages
    should serve him;
His dominion is an everlasting
    dominion which shall not
    pass away,
and his kingdom one that
    shall not be destroyed.

  *   *   *   *

But the saints of the Most High
shall receive the kingdom and
possess the kingdom for ever,
for ever and ever.
        (Dan. 7:13–14, 18; RSV)

Then they will see 'the Son
of Man coming in clouds' with
great power and glory. Then
he will send out the angels,
and gather his elect from the
four winds, from the ends of
earth to the ends of heaven.
        (Mark 13:26–27)

Other examples of Daniel's influence on the New Testament may be see in the following texts from the Book of Revelation (notice, as immediately above, the special importance of Daniel 7):

As I watched,
thrones were set in place,
    and an Ancient One took his
    throne,
his clothing was white as snow,
    and the hair of his head like
    pure wool;
his throne was fiery flames,
    and its wheels were burning
    fire.

(Dan. 7:9)

His head and his hair were
white as white wool, white as
snow; his eyes were like a flame
of fire, his feet were like
burnished bronze, refined as in
a furnace, and his voice was like
the sound of many waters.

(Rev. 1:14)

and [the saints] shall be given
    into [the evil king's] power
    for a time, two times and half
    a time.

(Dan. 7:25b)

But the woman was given the
two wings of the great eagle, so
that she could fly from the
serpent into the wilderness, to
her place where she is nour-
ished for a time, and times, and
half a time.

(Rev. 12:14)

As I looked, this horn made war
with the holy ones and was
prevailing over them.

(Dan. 7:21)

Also it was allowed to make war
on the saints and to conquer
them. It was given authority
over every tribe and people and
language and nation.

(Rev. 13:7)

until the Ancient One came;
then judgment was given for the
holy ones of the Most High, and
the time arrived when the holy
ones gained possession of the
kingdom.

(Dan. 7:22)

Then I saw thrones, and those
seated on them were given
authority to judge. I also saw
the souls of those who had been
beheaded for their testimony to
Jesus and for the word of God.
They had not worshiped the
beast or its image and had not
received its mark on their
foreheads or their hands. They
came to life and reigned with
Christ a thousand years.

(Rev. 20:4)

These final two texts from Revelation, with their interest in the
"tribulation" of the saints and resurrection of the righteous dead, also
reflect the influence of Daniel 12:1–2.

2. *One Enoch*[24]

This work, also known as the Ethiopic Book of Enoch (or sometimes simply as the Book of Enoch) is a composite whose earliest components date from the third century BC and whose latest are from the first century AD. Although originally written in Hebrew or Aramaic, 1 Enoch has survived from antiquity as a complete text only in the Ethiopic language, although fragments exist in Aramaic, Greek, and Latin. First Enoch apparently exercised a greater influence on the writing of the New Testament than any other noncanonical apocalyptic literature. From earliest times the book was considered to be canonical by the Ethiopic (Abyssinian) Church and its existence was known in the West, but it was not until 1773 that complete copies of 1 Enoch reached Europe, brought there by a Scottish traveler, James Bruce.

The book is composed of five major sections whose relationship to one another is frequently obscure, a reflection, no doubt, of the multiplicity of authors who contributed to it. The principal unifying factor, in addition to an apocalyptic outlook, is the figure of Enoch who, according to Genesis 5:24, "walked with God; then he was no more, because God took him." The righteousness of this man in an unrighteous time (before the flood) and his transcendence of the experience of death made of him an ideal subject for this and other pseudepigraphical works.[25]

The first section, the so-called "Book of the Watchers" (chaps. 1–36), is strongly eschatological in outlook. With Genesis 6:1–4 as a background, it describes the fall of angels (the "Watchers") and the subsequent corruption of humankind. Enoch attempts to intercede for the fallen angels and their leader, Azazel, and is conducted on a tour of the earth and of Sheol in the course of which there is revealed to him the nature of the final judgment.

> And he [the angel] said to me [Enoch], ". . . in the manner in which the souls of the righteous are separated (by) this spring of water with light upon it, in like manner, the sinners are set apart when they die and are buried in the earth . . . They will bind them there forever—even if from the beginning of the world . . . Such has been made for the souls of the people who are not righteous, but sinners and perfect criminals, . . . they shall be killed on the day of judgment, but will not rise from there.
>
> (1 Enoch 22:9–13)

The second section, the "Book of the Similitudes (or Parables) of Enoch" (chaps. 37–71), probably contains the youngest collection of texts, as it is the only section of 1 Enoch not discovered at Qumran.[26] It is also eschatological in emphasis in that it deals with the last judgment, the messiah and the resurrection of the righteous dead, among other topics. The association of the preexistent messiah, who is also termed the Son of Man and the Elect One, with the final judgment is of considerable importance:

> At that hour, that Son of Man was given a name, in the presence of the Lord of the Spirits [God], the Before-Time; even before the creation of the sun and the moon, before the creation of the stars, he was given a name in the presence of the Lord of the Spirits.
>
> (1 Enoch 48:2–3)

> The Elect One stands before the Lord of the Spirits; his glory is forever and ever and his power is unto all generations. In him dwells the spirit of wisdom, the spirit which gives thoughtfulness, the spirit of knowledge and strength, and the spirit of those who have fallen asleep in righteousness. He shall judge the secret things. And no one will be able to utter vain words in his presence. For he is the Elect One before the Lord of the Spirits according to his good pleasure.
>
> (1 Enoch 49:2–4)

> And he [the angel] said to me, "All these things which you have seen happen by the authority of his Messiah so that he may give orders and be praised upon the earth." Then this angel of peace answered, saying to me, "Wait a little and all secret things which encircle the Lord of the Spirits will be revealed unto you. As for the mountains which you have seen with your own eyes, . . . all of them, in the presence of the Elect One, will become like a honeycomb that melts before fire . . . It shall happen in those days that no one shall be saved either by gold or by silver, and no one shall be able to escape . . . when the Elect One shall appear before the face of the Lord of the Spirits.
>
> (1 Enoch 52:4–9)

The third section, the "Book of Astronomical Writings" (chaps. 72–82), contains an account of a series of revelations to Enoch by the angel Uriel, the subject of which is the nature and influence of celestial bodies.

The fourth section, the "Book of Dream Visions" (chaps. 83–90), is composed of two visions. In the first (chaps. 83–84) Enoch foresees the flood. The second vision (85–90) is a record of the history of Israel, which culminates in the establishment of the Hasmonean state and the ushering in of the messianic kingdom. In this series of visions, emphasis is placed on various kinds of animals as emblematic of various types of people (sheep = Israel, predators = gentile enemies of Israel, a black-horned bull = messiah, etc.).

> Then I saw that a snow-white cow was born, with huge horns; all the beasts of the field and all the birds of the sky feared him and made petition to him all the time. I went on seeing until all their kindred were transformed, and became snow-white cows; and the first among them

became . . . a great beast with huge black horns on its head. The Lord
of the sheep rejoiced over it and over all the cows. I myself became sati-
ated in their midst. Then I woke up and saw everything.

(1 Enoch 90:37–39)

The fifth section, the "Book of the Epistle of Enoch" (chaps. 91–104), is
Enoch's observations concerning the fate of the good and of the evil. Of particular interest are two short sections (91:12–17 and 93:1–10) referred to as the
"Apocalypse of Weeks" in which the final judgment and the events preceding
it are schematically represented within a time frame of ten and seven weeks,
respectively.

After that in the fifth week, at the completion of glory, a house and a
kingdom shall be built.
After that in the sixth week, those who happen to be in it shall all of
them be blindfolded, and the hearts of them shall all forget wisdom.
Therein, a (certain) man shall ascend. And, at its completion, the house
of the kingdom shall be burnt with fire; and therein the whole clan of
the chosen root shall be dispersed.
After that in the seventh week, an apostate generation shall arise; its
deeds shall be many, and all of them criminal. At its completion, there
shall be elected the elect ones of righteousness from the eternal plant of
righteousness, to whom shall be given sevenfold instruction concerning
his flock.

(1 Enoch 93:7–10)

The fifth section is followed by a brief appendix (chaps. 105–108), parts of
which may be from another apocalyptic work known as the Book of Noah.
A comparison of this outline of 1 Enoch with the list of characteristics of
apocalyptic, above, will make it quite clear that this work is apocalyptic in the
most basic and thoroughgoing sense. Beyond that, it is interesting to notice
that, in its concern to differentiate between the righteous and the wicked, the
latter are repeatedly portrayed as economic and political oppressors:

Woe to those who build oppression and injustice!
Who lay foundations for deceit.
They shall soon be demolished;
and they shall have no peace.
Woe to those who build their houses with sin!
For they shall all be demolished from their foundations;
And they shall fall by the sword.
Those who amass gold and silver,
They shall quickly be destroyed.

(1 Enoch 94:6–7)

Influence of 1 Enoch upon the New Testament: The eschatological "spectacles" through which the future is viewed, the identification of the Son of Man with the Messiah, that preexistent individual's participation in the final judgment and the equating of the rich and powerful in society with the wicked who will be judged by God are among the most obvious influences of 1 Enoch upon the New Testament. Another obvious influence is the citation of 1 Enoch 1:9 in Jude 14.[27]

Behold, he will arrive with ten million of the holy ones in order to execute judgment upon all. He will destroy the wicked ones and censure all flesh on account of everything that they have done, that which the sinners and the wicked ones committed against him. (1 Enoch 1:9)	It was also about these that Enoch, in the seventh generation from Adam, prophesied, saying, "See, the Lord is coming with ten thousands of his holy ones, to execute judgment on all, and to convict everyone of all the deeds of ungodliness that they have committed in such an ungodly way, and of all the harsh things that ungodly sinners have spoken against him." (Jude 14–15)

And there are other cases in which the very words and phrases of New Testament writers seem dependent upon I Enoch, as the following comparison will indicate:[28]

and pain shall seize them when they see that the Son of Man sitting on the throne of his glory. (1 Enoch 62:5)	"Truly I tell you, at the renewal of all things, when the Son of Man is seated on the throne of his glory. (Matt. 19:28)

This Son of Man whom you have seen is the one who would remove the kings and the mighty ones from their comfortable seats and the strong ones from their thrones. (1 Enoch 46:4)	He has brought down the powerful from their thrones and lifted up the lowly; . . . (Luke 1:52)

they shall not be able to behold
the faces of the holy ones,
for the light of the Lord of the
Spirits has shined
upon the face of the holy, the
righteous and the elect.

(1 Enoch 38:4)

For it is God who said, "Let
light shine out of darkness,"
who has shone in our hearts to
give the light of the knowledge
of the glory of God in the face
of Jesus Christ.

(2 Cor. 4:6)

Everything is naked and open
before your sight, and you see
everything; and there is nothing
which can hide itself from you.

(1 Enoch 9:5)

And before him no creature is
hidden, but all are naked and
laid bare to the eyes of the one
to whom we must render an
account.

(Heb. 4:13)

And to Michael God said,
". . . bind [the fallen angels] for
seventy generations underneath
the rocks of the ground until
the day of their judgment and of
their consummation, until the
eternal judgment is concluded.

(1 Enoch 10:11–12)

And angels who did not keep
their own position, but left their
proper dwelling, he has kept in
eternal chains in deepest darkness for the judgment of the
great Day.

(Jude 6)

Again I saw [a vision] with my
own eyes as I was sleeping, and
saw the lofty heaven; and as I
looked, behold, a star fell down
from heaven.

(1 Enoch 86:1)

And the fifth angel blew his
trumpet, and I saw a star that
had fallen from heaven to earth.

(Rev. 9:1)

A note of caution must be entered here. It has been suggested by some
scholars that the absence of the Similitudes of Enoch (1 Enoch 37–71) from the
Qumran library may indicate that that portion of 1 Enoch is later than the
New Testament and is thus influenced by the outlook of the early Christian
community. Although the weight of scholarly opinion is presently against
such a consideration, should it eventually be confirmed, our understanding of
the role of 1 Enoch in shaping the New Testament would be greatly altered,
especially with regard to the history of the phrase *Son of Man*.[29]

3. *The Testaments of the Twelve Patriarchs* [30]

This document purports to be the final testaments of the twelve sons of Jacob, modeled on that patriarch's last words as recorded in Genesis 49. It appears to have been written in Greek by a Jewish writer(s) during the second century BC who drew freely from an older "testamentary" tradition, Hebrew and Aramaic examples of which have been found at Qumran.[31] Like many other examples of early Jewish apocalyptic, the Testaments of the Twelve Patriarchs came to be valued among Christians, who are primarily responsible for its preservation and transmission (and for certain editorial interpolations).

Each of the twelve testaments describes how one of Jacob's sons, just prior to that son's death, makes his final testament to his heirs. Typically each testament contains a section devoted to the patriarch's life (drawn primarily from material in Genesis, but frequently embellished), a section (or more) of moral exhortation, and a section of predictions concerning the future of humankind, of Israel, and of the particular partiarch's tribe. The conclusion typically consists of an account of the patriarch's death and burial.

There are several apocalyptic features in the Testaments of the Twelve Patriarchs. (1) One is a theological dualism, as seen in the two kinds of spirits at work in human life: the spirits of truth (the spirits of the Lord) and the spirits of error (the spirits of Beliar). Human life is the arena of contest between these opposite and absolute realities:

> God has granted two ways to the sons of men, two mind-sets, two lines of action, two models and two goals. Accordingly, everything is in pairs, the one over against the other. The two ways are good and evil; concerning them are two dispositions within our breasts that choose between them. If the soul wants to follow the good way, all of its deeds are done in righteousness and every sin is immediately repented . . . But if the mind is disposed toward evil, all of its deeds are wicked; driving out the good, it accepts the evil and is overmastered by Beliar.
>
> (Test. of Asher 1:3–8)

(2) Another interesting feature of the Testaments of the Twelve Patriarchs is the document's cosmological views. Above the earth are tiered heavens. The first, in ascending order, is a heaven of water.

> The lowest [heaven] is dark for this reason: It sees all the injustices of humankind and contains fire, snow and ice, ready for the day determined by God's righteous judgment. In it are all the spirits of those dispatched to achieve the punishment of mankind.

The second heaven is one of light, described by the patriarch Levi (who, in a vision, had visited the three heavens) as "much brighter and more lustrous, for there was a measureless height in it."

> In the second [heaven] are the armies arrayed for the day of judgment to work vengeance on the spirits of error and of Beliar. Above them are the Holy Ones.

The third heaven is the most wonderful:

> In the uppermost heaven of all dwells the Great Glory in the Holy of Holies superior to all holiness. There with him are the archangels, who serve and offer propitiatory sacrifices to the Lord in behalf of all the sins of ignorance of the righteous ones . . . There with him are thrones and authorities; there praises to God are offered eternally.
> (all quotations are from Test. of Levi 2–3)

(3) As may be seen from these texts, a third apocalyptic feature of the Testaments of the Twelve Patriarchs is an interest in eschatology and the final judgment. Central to this work's eschatological hope is the figure of a Levitical priest who is described as the agent of God's judgment and of the establishment of the rule of God. It is he who will defeat Beliar and bring about the redemption of the people of God.

> The heavens shall greatly rejoice in his days
> and the earth shall be glad;
> the clouds shall be filled with joy,
> and the knowledge of the Lord will be poured out on the earth like
>   the water of the seas.
>
> *   *   *   *
>
> And the glory of the Most High shall burst forth upon him.
> And the spirit of understanding and sanctification shall rest upon
>   him.
>
> *   *   *   *
>
> In his priesthood sin shall cease
> and lawless men shall rest from their evil deeds,
> and righteous men shall find rest in him.
> And he shall open the gates of paradise;
> he shall remove the sword that has threatened since Adam,
> and he will grant to the saints to eat of the tree of life.
> (Test. of Levi 18:1–11)

Also active in the redemption of God's people is a kingly figure from the tribe of Judah, who, however, appears to have a less significant role than the eschatological priest from the tribe of Levi. Of this Judahite king God declares,

> Then he will illumine the scepter of my kingdom, and from your root will arise the Shoot, and through it will arise the rod of righteousness for the nations, to judge and to save all that call on the Lord.
>
> (Test. of Judah 24:5–6)

While some passages in the Testaments of the Twelve Patriarchs seem to have in mind two separate figures (e.g., Test. of Joseph 19:11), other texts blend the Levitical and Judahite saviors into one (e.g., Test. of Gad 8:1).

The tradition of portraying not a single messianic figure from the tribe of Judah, but a cooperating pair of divinely ordained agents may be grounded in Zechariah 6:9–14, where the priestly figure of Joshua and the kingly Zerubbabel appear to be described as jointly presiding over restored Jerusalem. It is also quite possible that the rise to prominence of the Hasmonean family during the second century BC kindled a hope in some Jewish quarters that this priestly family would be the agent by which God's final rule would be established. If so, the spectacular failures of the Hasmonean dynasty would have helped dash those hopes and refocus attention on the Davidic/Judahite line as that from which the messiah would finally appear.

A final note on the eschatological expectation of the Testaments of the Twelve Patriarchs: whereas there is no clear emphasis on the resurrection of the dead, occasional texts do give voice to this hope:

> Those who died in sorrow shall be raised in joy;
> and those who died in poverty for the Lord's sake shall be made rich;
> those who died on account of the Lord shall be wakened to life.
>
> (Test. of Judah 25:4)

(4) A fourth important feature of the Testament of the Twelve Patriarchs, although not one specifically relating to the document's apocalyptic outlook, is its ethical teaching, which has been compared to that of the Stoics. Among the virtues to be found are: integrity, piety, uprightness, honesty, generosity, compassion, hard work, self control, and love of neighbor.[32] Most ritual laws (circumcision, Sabbath observance and the like), while not repudiated, are neither emphasized. The point of greatest human weakness is sexual desire; women are linked with fallen angels (i.e., "Watchers") in their ability to seduce men into sin.

Influence of the Testaments of the Twelve Patriarchs on the New Testament:[33] The realization that this document was embraced and transmitted by early Christians forces one to be quite cautious in attempting to draw lines of influence from it to the New Testament, since one cannot always be sure in which direction the influence has flowed. Nevertheless, there are important parallels in which the Testaments of the Twelve Patriarchs appears to be antecedent to the New Testament. For example, the discussion, above, of the layered heaven, a feature found in other noncanonical apocalyptic literature,[34] calls to mind Paul's statement:

> I know a person in Christ who fourteen years ago was caught up to the third heaven—whether in the body or out of the body I do not know; God knows.
>
> (2 Cor. 12:2)

Another important possible influence by this book upon the New Testament is in its teaching concerning the importance of forgiveness, as in the following text, which R. H. Charles termed "the most important statement on the subject of forgiveness in all ancient literature," and which he compared to Luke 17:3 and Matthew 18:15, 35.[35]

> Now, my children, each of you love his brother. Drive hatred out of your hearts. Love one another in deed and word and inward thoughts . . . Love one another from the heart, therefore, and if anyone sins against you, speak to him in peace. Expel the venom of hatred, and do not harbor deceit in your heart. If anyone confesses and repents, forgive him. If anyone denies his guilt, do not be contentious with him, otherwise he may start cursing, and you would be sinning doubly.
>
> (Test. of Gad 6:1–4)

The linking of love for God with love for one's neighbor, an important element in the teaching of Jesus, is expressed several times in the Testaments of the Twelve Patriarchs.

Throughout all your life love the Lord,
and one another with a true heart.

(Test. of Dan. 5:3)

The Lord I loved with all my strength;
likewise, I loved every human being as I love my children

(Test. of Issachar 7:6)

He said to [the lawyer] "You shall love the Lord your God with all your heart, and with all your soul, and with all your mind." This is the greatest and first commandment. And a second is like it: "You shall love your neighbor as yourself."

(Matt. 22:37–39)

Other points of influence, both conceptual and verbal, include the following:

I was taken into captivity;
the strength of his hand came to my aid.
I was overtaken by hunger;
the Lord himself fed me generously.
I was alone, and God came to help me.
I was in weakness, and the Lord showed his concern for me.
I was in prison, and the Savior acted graciously in my behalf.
I was in bonds and he loosed me;
falsely accused, and he testified in my behalf.

(Test. of Joseph 1:6–7)

"For I was hungry and you gave me food, I was thirsty and you gave me something to drink, I was a stranger and you welcomed me, I was naked and you gave me clothing, I was sick and you took care of me, I was in prison and you visited me."

(Matt. 25:35–36)

And even if persons plot against [the good man] for evil ends, by doing good this man conquers evil, being watched over by God.

(Test. of Benj. 4:3)

Do not be overcome by evil, but overcome evil with good.

(Rom. 12:21)

There is a time for having intercourse with one's wife,
and a time to abstain for the purpose of prayer.

(Test. of Naphtali 8:8)

Do not deprive one another [in the matter of intercourse between husband and wife] except perhaps by agreement for a set time, to devote yourselves to prayer . . .

(1 Cor. 7:5)

4. Jubilees[36]

Like the Testaments of the Twelve Patriarchs, the Book of Jubilees is not, in form at least, an apocalyptic writing. It is an expansion of material found in the Books of Genesis and Exodus, a retelling, as it were, of the biblical story of God's activity in human life from creation to the time of Moses. But because of the prominence of certain apocalyptic features in Jubilees, it is appropriate to consider it here.

Jubilees, so-called because of its division of human history into "Weeks (of years) and their Jubilees," seems to have been written in the Hebrew language sometime near the end of the career of Judas Maccabeus, or about 160 BC. Its author was apparently someone close to the Hasidic movement, a fact which may help to account for the discovery of fragments of Jubilees at both Qumran and Masada.[37] He was almost certainly a priest, and his central concern is to demonstrate that faithfulness to the Torah characterizes the life of the true people of God.

The book's point of departure is God's revelation to Moses during the forty days and nights that he spent on Mt. Sinai (Exod. 24:18). According to Jubilees, God revealed to Moses at that time, through "the angel of the Presence" (Jub. 2:1), what had transpired since creation and why certain things occurred as they did. The biblical material is thus recast freely, the author reworking the texts in Genesis and Exodus in order to emphasize those concerns that are of particular importance to him. Some biblical material is omitted, but of greater interest are those expansions and additions to the biblical text. For example, the death of Abraham (Gen. 25:8) becomes an occasion for discussing the declining longevity of ancient human beings (Jub. 23:8–15), a fact which is laid to increasing human sinfulness, that is, disrespect for the Torah (Jub. 23:16–17). Then, in a celebrated digression, the future of humankind is described in which there is a return to the Torah, an event that results in the restoration of peace and joy to human life and which ushers in an age in which the human life span will again reach a millennium:

> And in those days, children will begin to search the law,
> and to search the commandments
> and to return to the way of righteousness.
> And the days will begin to increase and grow longer
> among these sons of men, generation by generation,
> and year by year, until
> their days approach a thousand years.
> (Jub. 23:26–27)

As may be seen from this example, while Jubilees is ostensibly about the past, it is really a statement about the author's present, namely, that those who are faithful to the Torah and to the priestly traditions of Israel stand in the line of the patriarchs and of Moses. It is they who, in the end, will be vindicated by God. This theological view is very similar, of course, to Daniel, a document written about the same time as Jubilees. But Jubilees is different from Daniel in that, unlike Daniel, Jubilees displays no sense of crisis. The author writes not as a member of a besieged minority, but as if he calmly took for granted that other Jews would consent to his view of the importance of the Torah and that these traditionalist Jews would prevail over their enemies.

The apocalyptic quality of Jubilees is to be found in its thoroughgoing theological dualism and in its portrayal of a vast world of angelic beings who attempt to influence human life for good or for evil. Evil entered God's good creation through the fall of one class of angels, the Watchers (Jub. 5:1–11).[38] These evil angels are led by their chief, Mastema or Satan, and it is they who, as demons, seduce human beings to do evil in order to destroy them (10:1). Ultimately, Mastema will be bound and imprisoned by God (48:15). Arrayed against the evil Watchers are two bands of good angels, the Angels of the Presence and the Angels of Sanctification. It is they who teach men and women the will of God (12:22) and come to the aid of those who are in moral or physical danger (48:4).

The Book of Jubilees is significant because it demonstrates how a Jewish writer of the second century BC, whose greatest interests lay in the Mosaic

---

Influence of Jubilees upon the New Testament: Echos of Jubilees are much fainter in the New Testament than those of Daniel, 1 Enoch, or the Testaments of the Twelve Patriarchs. But the following texts are of some interest:

But from the sons of Issaac one would become a holy seed . . . so that he might become a people [belonging] to the Lord, a special possession from all people, so that he might become a kingdom of priests and a holy people. (Jub. 16:17–18)	But you are a chosen race, a royal priesthood, a holy nation, God's own people. (1 Pet. 2:9) (Cf. Rev. 5:10)
for a thousand years are like one day in the testimony of heaven. (Jub. 4:30)	But do not ignore this one fact, beloved, that with the Lord one day is like a thousand years, and a thousand years are like one day. (2 Pet. 3:8)

Torah and in the priestly traditions of Israel, could, at the same time, be influenced by certain apocalyptic views. Yet this apocalyptic concept of the nature of good and evil is expressed without any apparent conviction concerning a traumatic and imminent end of human history.

5. *The Sibylline Oracles, Book 3*[39]

There are few writings that illustrate the influence of pagan literature and thought upon Jews and Christians more than the Sibylline Oracles. The original Sibyl, apparently mentioned first by the Greek writer Heraclitus about 500 BC, was a prophet of Cumae (near Naples), but over the generations the name was applied to prophetic figures (all women) in many parts of the Mediterranean world and the East (Mesopotamia and Persia). An extensive body of literature grew up that laid claim to being a record of the oracles of these Sibylls, and in Rome one such collection of Sibylline Oracles was declared to be official and was enshrined in the Temple of Jupiter, where it was consulted in moments of danger to the state. When the temple of Jupiter was destroyed by fire in 83 BC the oracles were lost, a fate shared by most of the literature associated with the Sibylls. Almost all of the pagan Sibylline material to survive from antiquity is fragmentary in nature.

There are at least two important characteristics of the pagan Sibylline Oracles. They frequently provide prophetic descriptions of events (often the foretelling of disasters and calamities) which, although they are portrayed as events yet to come, have actually already occurred. This *ex eventu* prophecy (which was also characteristic of Greek drama) was apparently of great appeal in the ancient world, for it could be read in such a manner as to cause it to appear to shed some light upon contemporary events. Another feature of the pagan Sibylline Oracles seems to be a tendency to divide history into a number of periods in a manner similar to Jewish and Christian apocalyptic. It is perhaps not surprising, therefore, that the Sibylline Oracles should attract the attention of Jews and, later, Christians. But what is somewhat unusual is that, in borrowing from this literary and mythological tradition, Jewish and Christian writers appropriated so much of its pagan language and imagery.

By at least as early as the second century BC Jewish writers had begun to employ the Sibylline Oracle, both in terms of its form as well as its content, and with the spread of Christianity into the Hellenistic-Roman world, Christian writers began to do likewise. In some cases, older pagan Sibyllines were rewritten by Jewish or Christian writers (who in turn frequently adapted each other's work), whereas in other cases, Jewish or Christian Sibyllines were new creations altogether. By the seventh century AD a body of this literature existed, which was collected and circulated as anthologies. Not all of the Jewish and Christian Sibylline Oracles have survived, but from two incomplete collections it has been possible to recover twelve books, plus additional fragments.[40] Among some Jews and Christians the Sibylline Oracles enjoyed great influence. In Jewish Sibylline lore, the Sibyl was said to be the daughter (sometimes the daughter-in-law) of Noah, and the early church fathers quoted the Sibylline Oracles extensively. Because of this early patristic favor and because of their thorough apocalpyticism, the Sibylline Oracles were especially popular in the medieval church where they helped to give rise to a strong interest in eschatology. Their role in this regard is perhaps best illustrated by lines from the most popular hymn of the Middle Ages, the *Dies Irae* traditionally attributed to Thomas of Celano (c. 1190–1260 AD).

> A day of wrath that day will be,
> It will dissolve the world into glowing ashes,
> As David and the Sibyl have testified.[41]

Book 3 of the Sibylline Oracles, while it is a composite piece of literature containing fragments from a number of different writers, is significant in that it contains perhaps the earliest examples of Jewish Sibylline literature. These originated in Egypt about the middle of the second century BC and were written in Greek. They were combined with other material in the Sibylline tradition (whether Jewish or pagan is not clear) about the beginning of the Christian Era, a collection to which was then prefixed a Jewish composition of the late first century AD to form the oldest complete book of Sibylline Oracles which has survived.

The part of Book 3 which dates from the second century BC has been referred to as the main corpus, and it is composed of five oracles, the first of which is a survey of human history from the Tower of Babel to the rise of Ptolemaic Egypt and then Rome. This oracle (lines 97–161) is not only significant in that it marks history into periods, each identified by the dominant kingdom (typically, as in this case, ten in number), but also because of use of figures from Greek mythology. After describing the confusion of tongues at Babel, the author turns to Greek lore to describe the divisions of humankind:

> Cronos and Titan and Iapetus reigned,
> The best children of Gaia and Ouranos, whom men called earth and
>   heaven, giving them a name
> because they were the first of articulate men.
> The portions of the earth were threefold, according to the lot of each
> and each one reigned, having his share, and they did not fight
> for there were oaths imposed by their father [Ouranos = Heaven] and
>   the divisions were just.
>
> (3:110–117)

But this peaceful relationship broke down upon the death of Ouranos, ushering in a history of conflict that involved humankind. Mythology gave way to history:

Then God inflicted evil upon the Titans and all the descendants of Titans and of Cronos died. But then as time pursued its cyclic course the kingdom of Egypt arose, then that of the Persians, Medes, and Ethiopians, and Assyrian Babylon, then that of the Macedonians, of Egypt again, then of Rome.

(3:156–161)

The other oracles of the main corpus (11. 162–195, 196–294, 545–656, 567–808) all contain similar outlines: human sin leads to great suffering and calamities, all of which are alleviated by the coming of a God-sent king. Some of the individual features within these oracles are of interest, such as the praise lavished upon the Jews, the following passage being significant for its interest in the Jerusalem Temple. Also, notice how the past is described as yet in the future.

There will again be a sacred race of pious men
who attend to the counsels and intention of the Most High,
who fully honor the temple of the great God
with drink offering, etc.
Sharing in the righteousness of the law of the Most High,
they will inhabit cities and rich fields in prosperity,
themselves exhalted as prophets by the Immortal
and bringing great joy to all mortals.
For to them alone did the great God give wise counsel
and faith and excellent understanding in their breasts.

(3:573–585)

Human sinfulness (frequently identified as idolatry and various kinds of immorality) will bring great suffering upon humankind:

Therefore the Immortal will inflict upon all mortals
disaster and famine and woes and groans
and war and pestilence and lamentable ills,
because they were not willing to honor the immortal Begetter
of all men, but honored idols
made by hand, revering them.

(3:601–606)

The description of normal pains of life, however, gives way to a portrait of the suffering of all creation at the end of time:

King will lay hold of king and take away territory.
Peoples will ravage peoples, and potentates, tribes.

(3:635–636)

Vultures and wild beasts of the earth
will ravage the flesh of some. Indeed when this is completed
the huge earth will consume the remains of the dead.
It itself will be completely unsown and unplowed,
wretched, proclaiming the curse of innumerable men.

(3:644–648)

There will also
be brimstone from heaven and stone and much
grevious hail. Death will come upon four footed creatures.
Then they will recognize the immortal God who judges these things.

(3:690–693)

God's response to human need is to send a savior king. In most of the oracles that form the main corpus, this is a Ptolemaic figure, probably Ptolemy
VI Philometer or his successor Ptolemy VII Psychon:

Every kind of deceit will be found among them
until the seventh reign, when
a king of Egypt, who will be of the Greeks by race, will rule.
And then the people of the great God will again be strong
who will be guides in life for all mortals.

(191–195)

But a transcendant, messianic king may be suggested by the following:[42]

And then God will send a king from the sun (or, from the east)
who will stop the entire earth from evil war,
killing some, imposing oaths of loyalty on others;
and he will not do all these things by his private plans
but in obedience to the noble teachings of the great God.

(3:652–656)

In the last of the five oracles within the main corpus of Book 3 the sending
of the savior ruler is followed by a time of great suffering (including an attack
upon the Temple), after which the Jews are to be saved:

And then all the islands and the cities will say,
"How much the Immortal loves those men!
for everything fights on their side and helps them."

(3:711–713)

Then comes the peaceful kingdom, characterized by harmonious human relations and by the worship by all humankind of the God of the Jews:

There will no longer be war or drought on earth,
no famine or hail, damaging to fruits,
but there will be great peace throughout the whole earth.
King will be friend to king to the end of the age.

*   *   *   *

And then, indeed, he [God] will raise up a kingdom for all
ages among men, he who once gave the holy Law.

*   *   *   *

From every land they will bring incense and great gifts
to the house of the great God. There will be no other
house among men, even for future generations to know,
except the one which God gave to faithful men to honor.

(3:767–775)

The fifth oracle ends with a description of the signs of the times:

I will tell you a very clear sign, so that you may know
when the end of all things comes to pass on earth:
when swords are seen at night in starry heaven
toward evening and toward dawn,
and again dust is brought forth from heaven
upon the earth and all the light of the sun
is eclipsed in the middle of the heaven.

(3:796–802)

The clear eschatological interest revealed in these lines is significant because of the locale from which it comes: Hellenistic Egypt. It is devoid of any
teachings concerning angels and demons, as well as of any hope in resurrection. However, although the opaque style of the writer causes one to be reserved in drawing conclusions of a sweeping nature, the eschatology of (at
least part of) Book 3 of the Sibylline Oracles has much in common with Jewish
apocalyptic, apparently including the figure of the messianic king. This material is also striking in that, although apocalyptic in outlook, it is remarkably
open to gentiles, a feature which has given rise to the suggestion that it may
have been written for gentile readers.

6. The Psalms of Solomon[43]

This collection of eighteen poems, many of them similar to certain Old Testament psalms, constitutes a response on the part of one or more pious Jews to the
capture of the Jerusalem Temple by Pompey in 63 BC. Like much other apocalyptic literature, the Psalms of Solomon are pseudepigraphical, although the reasons for their association with Solomon are unclear. In certain other respects,

however, this literature resists the apocalyptic label, in that much of its theological outlook is decidedly nonapocalyptic. Yet, its view of the nearness of the messianic kingdom is consistent with that of the apocalyptic tradition.

The author(s) of the Psalms of Solomon writes of the nation's suffering and distress. Faithful people of God are in anguish not only because of the fall of the sacred Temple, but because of the sinfulness of those Jews whose failure to be faithful to the traditions of Israel has resulted in this present calamity. The writer's understanding of the nature of evil is thus nearer that of the Old Testament prophets (and nearer deuteronomistic elements within the Old Testament) than it is to the dualistic, cosmic understanding of evil typical of apocalyptic. For this "psalmist," evil is human faithlessness and is to be punished by God in immediate and material ways (i.e., the sending of a conqueror):

> Arrogantly the sinner broke down the strong walls with a battering
>   ram and you [God] did not interfere.
> Gentile foreigners went up to your place of sacrifice;
>   they arrogantly trampled it with their sandals.
> Because the sons of Jerusalem defiled the sanctuary of the Lord,
>   they were profaning the offerings of God with lawless acts;
> Because of these things he said, "Remove them far from me;
>   they are not sweet smelling."
>
> (Ps. of Solomon 2:1–4)

The writer appears to consider the Hasmonean dynasty, with its tyrannous usurpations, as especially sinful. In place of the divinely ordained family of David, they have ruled with dishonor and have thus brought God's contempt upon themselves and upon the nation.

> With pomp they set up a monarchy because of their arrogance;
>   they despoiled the throne of David with arrogant shouting.
> But you, O God, overthrew them, and uprooted their descendents
>   from the earth,
> for there rose up against them a man alien to our race.
>
> (Ps. of Solomon 17:6–7)

But the writer of the Psalms of Solomon is convinced that God has not given up on the Jews. God is even yet in control of human affairs, and because righteousness, strength and mercy are essential elements in God's nature, the writer appeals to God to intervene on behalf of those Jews who continue to be faithful. In fact, the nearness of God to human life results in a virtual absence of interest in angels in the Psalms of Solomon, beings who, in other apocalyptic literature, are portrayed as the intermediaries between God and humankind. God is king, and to the Sovereign of the universe direct request is made for help in the nation's time of trouble.

> Do not neglect us, our God,
>   lest the gentiles devour us as if there were no redeemer.
> But you [have been] our God from the beginning,
>   and on you we have hoped, Lord.
> And we will not leave you,
>   for your judgments upon us are good.
>   (Ps. of Solomon 8:30–32)

Of greatest interest is the writer's belief that God is very soon to overthrow the power of the gentile rulers and establish the rule of the messiah. The messiah is called the "Son of David" and "Lord Messiah" and, although he is not a military leader in the sense that he establishes God's rule by means of his own powers, he is the human agent through whom God will work in establishing a kingdom of righteousness and peace. Jews of the Diaspora are to be returned to their homeland where they will live in concord and plenty with the Jews of Jerusalem, whereas the gentiles will be expelled.

> See, Lord, and raise up for them their king,
>   the Son of David, to rule over your servant Israel
>   in the time known to you, O God.
> Undergird him with the strength to destroy the unrighteous rulers,
>   to purge Jerusalem from gentiles
>   who trample her to destruction;
>   *   *   *   *
> He will gather a holy people
>   whom he will lead in righteousness;
> and he will judge the tribes of the people
>   that have been made holy by the Lord their God.
>   *   *   *   *
> And he will be a righteous king over them, taught by God.
> There will be no unrighteousness among them in his days,
>   for all shall be holy,
>   and their king shall be the Lord Messiah.[44]
>   (Ps. of Solomon 17:21–32)

Whereas the establishment of the messianic kingdom is to be an event within history, the writer of the Psalms of Solomon looked forward to the ultimate resurrection of the dead beyond the course of human history, although his interest in resurrection is secondary to his interest in the messianic kingdom. For the wicked there can be no destiny but destruction, whereas the righteous will be raised to live with God.

The destruction of the sinner is forever,
  and he will not be remembered when [God] looks after the righteous.
This is the share of sinners forever,
  but those who fear the Lord shall rise up to eternal life,
  and their life shall be in the Lord's light, and it shall never end.
                                                    (Ps. of Solomon 3:11–12)

Influence on the Psalms of Solomon the New Testament: The Psalms of
Solomon are instructive for what they tell us about the state of messianic
expectation on the part of at least some Jews approximately one-half
century before the birth of Jesus. Although not portrayed here as a transcendent being (as in 1 Enoch), the Messiah is nevertheless the unique
agent by which God establishes a kingdom of righteousness and peace.
As such, the Messiah's power and authority are irresistible. His Davidic
lineage is emphasized, as if the writer, who has found the Hasmonean
dynasty sinful and repugnant, wishes to dispell any thought of a Levitical Messiah (as in the Testaments of the Twelve Patriarchs and the Damascus Rule of Qumran). The messianic titles, "Son of David" and "Lord
Messiah," seem to have been used first in the Psalms of Solomon, and
both are to find later application in the New Testament in references to
Christ (Matt. 21:9, 15; Acts 28:31).

C. The Significance of Apocalyptic for
Early Judaism and Early Christianity

We have discussed in this chapter only six prominent examples of Jewish
apocalyptic literature that come, later additions aside, from the Hellenistic
and early Roman periods. We shall later investigate other examples of Jewish
literature which, in some form, exhibit apocalyptic features, including the
Testament of Moses,[45] the Apocalypse of Abraham, 2 (or 4) Esdras, 2 Baruch,
2 Enoch and the Treatise of Shem. Significant examples of apocalyptic material are also to be found among the discoveries at Qumran, discussed below.[46]

Several things emerge from this brief survey. For one thing, it is apparent
that the form of apocalyptic literature is not always the same. Daniel or, especially, 1 Enoch may approach what one may term a "pure" apocalypse, that is,
one that presents itself as a revelation from God to a divinely designated seer
of old (cf. the Book of Revelation in the New Testament). But Jubilees, on the
other hand, is a kind of free-flowing biblical midrash,[47] the Testaments of the
Twelve Patriarchs is related to that genre of testamentary literature that goes
back at least as far as Genesis 49, Book 3 of the Sibylline Oracles depends

upon non-Jewish literary models, while the Psalms of Solomon are clearly hymnic in nature. In other words, while there is such a thing as an apocalyptic form, apocalyptic views appeared in Jewish, and later, Christian literature of many different types.

A second feature worthy of note is the variety of theological views within the apocalyptic tradition. The complex of various understandings of the nature of God's messiah is but one of many examples of a basic concept that was comprehended in quite different ways by those who expressed an apocalyptic orientation. When one adds to this the fact that no two apocalyptic writers share identical concerns and beliefs (for Jubilees the end time is distant, for Daniel and Psalms of Solomon it is near; the Testaments of Twelve Patriarchs and 1 Enoch express a rich angel/demonology, a subject of little if any interest for Psalms of Solomon), it becomes apparent how rich and multifaceted is the early Jewish apocalyptic tradition.

As a further example of the variety within early Judaism, it will become clear as we proceed that that complex of theological ideas that we may term the "apocalyptic view" was not universally embraced within early Judaism, and alongside apocalyptic other viewpoints flourished that either ignored apocalyptic or repudiated it altogether. After about the second century AD Judaism would virtually abandon apocalyptic as a means of expressing views concerning the nature of good and evil, concerning the ultimate conclusion to human history and similar theological issues.

Apocalyptic is also significant because this complex of theological conceptions becomes normative for early Christianity. It is impossible to understand the New Testament or the early Christian hope without acknowledging that apocalyptic is the primary medium through which early Christianity understands the nature of God's work in Jesus Christ, the life of the church and the destiny of humankind. The transcendent nature of the son of man/messiah, the temporary state of this present world, God's ultimate victory over the transcendent forces of evil by means of a returning, victorious messiah, the resurrection of the dead, and the rewards/punishments of heaven/hell are only the most obvious of the many ways in which apocalyptic has shaped Christian belief.

Chapter 4

THE THEOLOGY OF PALESTINIAN JUDAISM: REFLECTION AND PRACTICE

A. TRADITIONS CONCERNING THE TORAH

1. The Centrality of the Torah[1]

Judaism of the Hellenistic period may be said to exhibit two characteristics that stand in some tension with one another: the centrality of the Torah and the existence of various sectarian groups. The increasing emphasis on Torah, that is, the biblical books of Genesis through Deuteronomy (also referred to as the Pentateuch), helped to provide Second Temple Judaism with an identity and a coherence, whereas the growth of the several sects, principally the Pharisees, Sadducees, Essenes, and Zealots, illustrates early Judaism's enormous variety.

The tendency to identify the Torah as the supreme written authority in matters of faith and life is evident even before the beginning of the exile. The "book of the law" that was uncovered during the reign of King Josiah, and that was almost certainly some form of the Book of Deuteronomy, was regarded by Josiah and his court as a special revelation of God, and on the basis of its teaching the life of the nation was reordered (2 Kings 22—23; 2 Chron. 34—35). The Josianic reformation, which lasted from 621 BC until that monarch's untimely death at the hands of the Egyptians in 609, is the earliest datable event in Israel's life that illustrates the priority of the Torah over other forms of revelation, although the even earlier prophetic elevation of the figure of Moses (cf. Hos. 12:13) helped pave the way for the events of 621–609 BC.

The supremacy of the Torah received additional impetus from the destruction in 587 of the Temple and of the priestly ritual that was practiced there. Although sacrifices may have constituted a form of worship among the Jews during the Babylonian captivity, the dislocation of the cult during those years caused Jews to turn with fresh vigor to the word, both written and spoken, as a primary medium of the revealed presence of God. The lengthy and complex priestly history, which was written during the exile, retold the story of God's activity in Israel's life from creation to the possession of the Land of Promise. Although it emphasized the importance of various cultic

acts (Sabbath observance, circumcision, various festivals, and the like), it itself—that is, the written word—began to become the vehicle by which Israel's
life was defined. And when, toward the end of the exile, the priestly history
was combined with other literary traditions to form what is now the Books of
Genesis through Deuteronomy, the Torah became fixed in form and content.
In other words, early Judaism was well on its way to becoming a religion of
the book. This book began to assume the qualities of sacred scripture in that
it, and it alone, was regarded as describing the divine ideal for human life as
to both belief and conduct. How did one express one's Jewishness, or respond
to the demands and expectations of God? By keeping the Torah, the Instruction of God. The canonization of the Torah, that is, the process by which the
biblical books of Genesis through Deuteronomy were considered to be a distinctive witness to the will of God, was complete by about the year 400 BC.[2]

When the priest Ezra determined to give new shape and direction to the
community of Jews in restored Jerusalem early in the fourth century BC, he
read in public assembly "the book of the Torah of Moses," to which the people emotionally responded by committing themselves to what they heard
(Neh. 8:1–18). Whether the "book" which Ezra read was the entire Torah or
only parts of it, the principal was reaffirmed that the written Torah stands
alone in its power to communicate the will of God. It was in the restored
Jerusalem community that the great "Torah Psalms" (Pss. 1, 19, and 119)
were written and used in Temple worship, psalms that lovingly describe the
place of the Torah in the heart of Israel:

> Give me understanding, that I may keep your law [Torah]
>   and observe it with my whole heart.
> *   *   *   *
> I will keep your law continually,
>   forever and ever.
> I shall walk at liberty,
>   for I have sought your precepts.
> *   *   *   *
> Oh, how I love your law!
>   It is my meditation all day long.
>   (Ps. 119:34, 44, 45, 97)

There must have been a special sense in which the teaching and interpretation of the Torah was, during the exile, a task of the priests. Not only was it at
this time that the Torah received its final form at the hands of the priests, but
the importance placed upon matters of a cultic and sacerdotal nature in many
Torah passages (e.g., Exod. 29, which describes the method of the priests' or-
dination) points to a close association between this literature and the priestly
class. But during the restoration of Jerusalem under the indulgent rule of the

Persians, a special class of Torah scholars began to emerge: the scribes. Although the scribes were initially drawn from the ranks of the priests, in time they came to include many laymen as well. Their task was not simply to copy the Torah, as their name might suggest, but to be its interpreters and teachers, as well. The priest Ezra is referred to as a "scribe skilled in the law of Moses that the LORD the God of Israel had given" (Ezra 7:6) and his role in the interpretation of the Torah was emulated by successive generations of scribes. During the Hasmonean Era, when many members of the priesthood were ready to accommodate the traditions of Israel to those of the Hellenistic world, the role of the scribes increased in importance among pious Jews because of their faithfulness to Torah as the only standard by which Israel was to live.

About the year 200 BC, even before the troubles of the Hasmonean Era, Jesus ben Sirach extolled the honored place of the scribe in Israel's life (Sir. 38:24—39:11). After discussing at length the importance of the scribe's vocation and how he must do no other work (in order not to be distracted from his main task), Ben Sirach writes:

> If the great Lord is willing,
>   [the scribe] will be filled with the spirit of understanding;
> he will pour forth words of wisdom of his own
>   and give thanks to the Lord in prayer.
> The Lord will direct his counsel and knowledge,
>   as he meditates on his mysteries.
> He will show the wisdom of what he has learned,
>   and will glory in the law of the Lord's covenant.
> Many will praise his understanding,
>   it will never be blotted out.
> His memory will not disappear,
>   and his name will live through all generations.
>   (Sir. 39:6–11)

By the first century AD it is the scribes, more than the priests, who are the teachers upon whom faithful Jews depend for proper instruction in the Torah, not only as to the content of religious belief, but especially as to matters of right conduct. It is in this sense that the New Testament calls them "lawyers" (Matt. 22:35, Luke 7:30, and elsewhere) and "teachers of the law" (Luke 5:17, Acts 5:34), for it is they who explain and enforce the legal provisions of the Torah. That they are sometimes not above practicing the kind of casuistry and hypocrisy for which some of the Pharisees were noted is indicated by Jesus statement:

> "Woe also to you lawyers! For you load people with burdens hard to bear, and you yourselves do not lift a finger to ease them."
>   (Luke 11:46)

But many, doubtless most of the scribes, even those whose primary task was the interpretation of the legal aspects of the Torah, were men of great integrity. One such example known to us is Gamaliel,[3] a Pharisee who was also a "teacher of the law" and a member of the Sanhedrin, whose wisdom and forebearance is portrayed in Acts 5:34–39. That there were many Gamaliels among the scribes of early Judaism is evident from the honored place these scholars of the Torah enjoyed among the people. The phrase "scribes of the Pharisees," which sometimes occurs in the New Testament (Mark 2:16, Luke 5:30, Acts 23:9), would seem to imply that, while some scribes were also Pharisees, there were other scribes who belonged to other sectarian groups or who were affiliated with no sect at all. In some passages, the scribes are associated with the chief priests and elders (Mark 8:31, Luke 22:66, Acts 4:5), groups with whom they may have formed a political alliance in the Sanhedrin.

The honor in which the teachers of the Torah were held is indicated by the special terms that were applied to them by the people. Perhaps the most important of these is the word rabbi, which literally means something like *My Great One*, or *My Master*. The word appears also to have had a pedagogical connotation comparable to the English *schoolmaster*. Just when the term came into general use is not known, but, if the New Testament may be taken as a guide, by the early first century AD it was employed as a form of address. Jesus is often addressed by others as "rabbi" (e.g., John 6:25) and it was apparently a term that at least some teachers greatly desired (cf. Matt. 23:7–8). Yet at this time the term is not used as a title, as was later the case. The phrase "Rabbi Jesus" is never used in the New Testament, nor are Hillel or Shammai, the great contemporaries of Jesus, referred to in this manner. But by the second century AD, the term rabbi is in use in a titular sense for teachers of the Torah, as in Rabbi Akiba (d. 135) or Rabbi Judah the Prince (d. 217).

During the Hellenistic and Roman periods Palestinian Jews lived under a civil and criminal law which was largely interpreted and administered by these teachers of the Torah. This was true to some extent even during those times when the political power of an occupying and alien force was most oppressive, and it was especially true when, as under the Hasmoneans, there was little or no interference in legal affairs from the outside. Thus the Torah scholars (be they termed scribes, rabbis, or whatever else) fulfilled the vital role in the life of the people of developing a legal system based upon the Torah and of helping to administer this system in the courts. Supreme in this regard was the work of the Sanhedrin which, because it deserves special consideration, is discussed later in this chapter.

But the teaching function of the Torah scholars was never entirely subordinated to their legal duties. Many scribes and rabbis attracted young people to their homes for study, and by the second century AD, or perhaps well before, certain schools existed called "Houses of Study," sometimes established in connection with a synagogue. Here pupils came together to be trained in the traditions of the Torah, which meant not only that they studied the biblical text itself, but that they committed to memory the growing traditions of Torah interpretation that as yet existed primarily in oral form. The methods of these schools were, of course, designed to achieve the particular purposes associated with Torah study. Unlike the earlier Greek schools (the academy of Plato, for example), there was little sense of a quest for undisclosed truth. Rather, the truth was affirmed to be at hand in the Torah, and the task was to elicitate that truth and to apply it to human life. A vast amount of time would thus have been spent in memorizing the great body of interpretation that generations of scribes and rabbis had placed around the Torah. The seriousness with which this aspect of Torah education was carried on may be seen in the following statement attributed to a certain Rabbi Dosthai, who spoke on the authority of Rabbi Meir and affirmed, "Whoever forgets one word of his instruction in the Torah, he is reckoned as though he had forfeited his life."[4]

This did not, however, mean that there was no debate in the schools of Torah instruction. Questions would typically be put to students on a variety of subjects, the answers to which were to come not out of the student's empirical observations nor his logical reflections, but from his knowledge of the Torah and of traditional Torah interpretation. It was just as important that a student not change scribal or rabbinic interpretation as it was that he learn it in the first place. It was this question-and-answer method of teaching that helped formulate the Mishnah (meaning "repetition"). Unlike the earlier midrash, which is Torah interpretation in the form of a commentary upon or expansion of the biblical text, the Mishnah, which achieved written form early in the third century AD, is a body of teaching which is organized according to various themes or subjects. An individual House of Study would reflect the views of its teacher or teachers, thus while many (or most) Houses were Pharisaic, Sadducee and Essene teachers were also active in the training of the young.

2. Midrash[5]

A principle vehicle for Torah interpretation that gained wide popularity during the Hellenistic period was termed midrash (meaning *study* or *investigation*). Midrash, which was tied to the biblical text, existed in two forms: *halakhah* and *haggadah*.

a. Halakhah (which means "walking") was concerned with legal texts of the Bible and their application to the lives of pious Jews. Frequently, however, halakhic midrash went beyond the simple exposition of the text and reported as law customs that had come to be considered as authorative simply because of their persistence or antiquity. In either case the purpose of halakhah was to guide the faithful in circumstances where the correct moral or legal action was not self-evident. Halakhah was both cumulative and open-ended, that is, it continued to transmit from one generation to the next the teachings of rabbis of the past, and it did so in the knowledge that its task was never completed. Thus it was constantly growing, rarely, if ever discarding bits of its collected wisdom, and continually adding new insights so that, by the time it was cast into written form in the second century AD, its various strata were so intertwined that it had become impossible to say with precision just which halakhic statements had emerged at what time. One modern writer has compared the effort to analyse the growth of halakhah to a person standing at the end of an assembly line in a factory trying to decide in what order the parts of the automobile or washing machine were put together.[6]

In constructing the halakhic midrash, the rabbis of the Hellenistic and Roman periods were fulfilling their function as the lawyers of the people of God. The weakness of halakhah is that, in their zeal for the Torah, the rabbis sometimes pushed too far their (or anyone's) ability to codify morality, that is, to define down to the least detail God's intention as to how women and men should act. And it was this excessive passion for legal minutiae that evoked Jesus' strong criticism of the Pharisees and other teachers of the Torah:

"Woe to you, scribes and Pharisees, hypocrites! For you tithe mint, dill, and cummin, and have neglected the weightier matters of the law: justice and mercy and faith. It is these you ought to have practiced without neglecting the others."

(Matt. 23:23)

Yet halakhah grew out of the conviction that no area of human life was exempt from the rule of God. Thus if the interpreters of the Torah sometimes erred in their excessive legalism, it was not because they wished to foster the tyranny of the law, but because they wished to repudiate the emptiness of a life lived apart from the will of God, a will which, in their view, was best expressed in the Torah.

"And I will glorify Him" [Exod. 15:2]. Rabbi Ishmael says: And is it possible for a man of flesh and blood to add glory to his Creator? It simply means: I shall be beautiful before Him in observing the commandments. I shall prepare before Him a beautiful *Lulab* [palm branch], a beautiful *Sukkah* [tent], beautiful fringes and beautiful phylacteries. Abba Saul says: O be like Him! Just as He is gracious and merciful, so be thou also gracious and merciful.

(Mekilta de-Rabbi Ishmael, Tractate Shirata[7])

b. *Haggadah* is the term applied to the other type of midrash (haggadah means *narration*), which was concerned with matters of doctrine and of historical tradition, and that often involved what amounted to a rewriting of the biblical text itself.

   i. Historical haggadah, like many other features of Judaism of the Hellenistic and Roman periods, has its roots in the time immediately following the exile. The Books of Chronicles, written in Jerusalem sometime during the Persian period, actually form a haggadic midrash upon the Books of Samuel and Kings, since whoever wrote Chronicles did so with a copy of Samuel-Kings as a reference, reproducing certain texts almost verbatim, yet rewriting others so as to provide an alternative point of view.

   With the passage of time, historical haggadah became ever more fanciful, displaying alternative versions of biblical texts that could not possibly have been based upon new "information," but could only represent the interests and views of their authors. Two examples from the second century BC, both of which are discussed more thoroughly later in this volume, will illustrate this tendency: Jubilees and the Genesis Apocryphon, the latter being one of the documents discovered at Qumran. It should be noted that both of these are expansions of the Book of Genesis, that is, a portion of the Torah.

   Jubilees elaborates the account of the first day of creation (Gen. 1:3–5) in the following manner:

> For on the first day [God] created the heavens, which are
> above, and the earth, and the waters and all of the spirits
> which minister before him:
>   the angels of the presence,
>   and the angels of sanctification,
>   and the angels of the spirit of fire,
>   and the angels of the spirit of the winds,
>   and the angels of the spirit of the clouds and darkness and snow
>   and hail and frost.
>
> (Jub. 2:2)

   The Genesis Apocryphon contains, among other things, a fanciful account in Abraham's own words of the near catastrophe that occurred when Abraham (Abram in the text below) attempted to pretend that his wife Sarah (Sarai) was his sister (Gen. 12:10–20). After Sarah has been taken into the harem of the unwitting pharaoh, (Gen. 12:15,17), Abraham recounts the following:

> And I, Abram, wept aloud that night, I and my nephew Lot, because
> Serai had been taken from me by force. I prayed that night and I begged
> and implored, and I said in my sorrow while my tears ran down:
> 'Blessed art Thou, O most High God, . . . Judge [Pharaoh] for me that I

THE THEOLOGY OF PALESTINIAN JUDAISM

may see thy mighty hand raised against him and against all his household, that he may not be able to defile my wife this night."

And during that night the Most High God sent a spirit to scourge [Pharaoh], an evil spirit to all his household; and it scourged him and all his household. And he was unable to approach [Sarai], and although he was with her for two years he knew her not.[8]

ii. Doctrinal haggadah is frequently found alongside historical haggadah, but is different in that its main concern is not historical "data," but the nature of belief and of pious devotion to God. In fact, there are many midrashic passages in which both types of haggadah, as well as halakhah, are placed side-by-side in such a manner that the distinctions among them are difficult to draw. The following passages from the Genesis Rabbah, an important midrash on the Book of Genesis, combines doctrine, history (the two forms of haggadah) and legal instruction (halakhah). These texts also demonstrate how biblical exegesis (including the use of one biblical text to elucidate another), legal and moral tradition, and legendary lore are all brought together in the composition of midrash. Like virtually all written forms of midrash, these passages date from a time later than that under discussion here, but they illustrate the methods of Torah interpretation developed by the rabbis of the Hellenistic and Roman periods. They all are part of a commentary on Genesis 2:3: "So God blessed the seventh day and hallowed it."

He blessed it with the distinction of robing (that is, a cloak should be worn on the Sabbath). Rabbi Huna said, "A man must change his garments on the Sabbath." Rabbi Hiyya said in Rabbi Johanan's name, "A man must mingle his garments. (That is, if he cannot afford a complete change, he must at least have something different to wear on the Sabbath with his week-day attire.)" Abin bar Hasde said, "He must let his cloak hang down (instead of tucking it up as on week-days, when he works in the fields)." Rabbi Jeremiah and Rabbi Zeira were walking together on the Sabbath, Rabbi Jeremiah's cloak being tucked up, whereupon Rabbi Zeira pulled it down. This shows that one must let his cloak hang down.

Rabbi Eliezer said, "He blessed it in the matter of a lamp (which was to be lighted before sundown at the beginning of the Sabbath), and this happened in my case: I once lit a lamp for the Sabbath and when I returned (twenty four hours later) at the end of the Sabbath, I found it still burning with none of its oil consumed."

Rabbi Hiyya bar Abba said, "I was once invited to dine by a man in Laodicea. They brought before us a table supported by sixteen poles, and on it was something of everything created in the first six days. A child sat in the middle of the table and recited, 'The earth is the Lord's and the fulness thereof' (Psalm 24:1). Why did he do this? So that the owner should not grow conceited. I said to him, 'My son, how did you obtain all this wealth?' 'I was a butcher,' he replied, 'and whenever I saw a choice animal, I set it aside for the Sabbath.'"

Rabbi Tanhuma said, "It once happened in Rome on the eve of the Day of Atonement that a certain tailor went to buy a fish. At the market he and the governor's servant began bidding for it until the bidding reached twelve dinars (an exhorbitant sum!), at which price the tailor bought it. At dinner the governor demanded of the servant, 'Why have you not served fish?' The servant replied, 'Sir, I will tell you the truth. A certain Jew out bid me for the fish at the market.' And then he asked, 'Did you really want me to bring you a fish for twelve dinars?' 'Who was this Jew,' the governor wanted to know, and the servant told him. The governor had the Jew summoned and asked him, 'How can a Jewish tailor eat fish at twelve dinar?' The Jew replied, 'Sir, we have one day when all our sins of the year are forgiven, and we honor it greatly.' When the Jew produced proof of his words, the governor let him go."

(Genesis Rabbah, Parashah 11[9])

Students of the New Testament who read passages such as the last two examples above, cannot help but be reminded of the narrative quality of some of the parables of Jesus, such as the parable of the unjust servant:

For this reason the kingdom of heaven may be compared to a king who wished to settle accounts with his slaves. . .

(Matt. 18:23–35)

Or the parable of the rich fool:

The land of a rich man produced abundantly. And he thought to himself. . .

(Luke 12:16–21)

3. *The Acceptance as Scripture of NonTorah Literature*

The Torah or Pentateuch is not, of course, the only collection of writings to have been considered sacred scripture by the early Jewish community. By the first century AD it is quite clear that, among Palestinian Jews, the Hebrew Bible had achieved the canonical shape with which we are familiar today, that is, Torah, Prophets, and Writings.[10] The conventional wisdom as to how this three-fold status was achieved goes something like this.

The prophetic literature had been accorded special honor for centuries because it recounted anecdotes from the prophets' lives and work, recorded the words of the prophets, and retold the history of the nation from a theological perspective that was distinctively prophetic. Books which contained anthologies of prophetic speech, such as Isaiah, Jeremiah, Ezekiel, and the Book of the Twelve (the so-called Minor Prophets) certainly fell into this category. But also the four divisions of the great Deuteronomistic History—Joshua, Judges, Samuel, and Kings—were also considered prophetic because they reflected a theological understanding of Israel's past that was deeply impregnated with prophetic views (as well as because they told the stories of Nathan, Elijah, Elisha, and other prophets). By about 200 BC this prophetic corpus had been accepted as equal (or nearly so) in authority with the Torah, the reason for the choice of this date being references in the Wisdom of Sirach (Ecclesiasticus) to prophetic individuals who stand among Israel's great figures of faith (chaps. 44–49).

Also venerated as possessing special authority were a variety of other literary works which were more or less independent of one another and that reflected a wide diversity of styles and theological viewpoints. This included the Psalms that had come to be the basic prayer and hymn book of the Second Temple, if the Books of Chronicles may be taken as a guide in the matter. Wisdom writings such as Proverbs, Job, and Ecclesiastes would also be a part of this group, as would the Book of Daniel. Chronicles, which, as we have noticed, is a kind of midrash on Samuel and Kings, was a part of this category, as were two short books that bear some literary relation (perhaps a common authorship) to Chronicles: Ezra and Nehemiah. Finally, five short pieces (*Megilloth* in Hebrew, meaning *scrolls*) that had come to be associated with festivals of the Jewish liturgical year: Song of Solomon (Passover), Ruth (Pentecost), Lamentations (the destruction of Jerusalem on the Ninth of Ab), Ecclesiastes or Qoheleth (Tabernacles), and Esther (Purim). These were considered so authoritative that, by about the year 140 BC, the grandson of Jesus ben Sirach, translating his grandfather's work into Greek and providing it with an introduction, would refer to the threefold division of the Hebrew Bible as "the law, the prophets, and the other books of our fathers." (RSV).

That, as stated above, is the conventional wisdom concerning the growth of the Hebrew canon, and it is doubtless one which, in general outline, is correct. It must be remembered, however, that this was not a uniform process to which all groups of Jews assented equally. The complexity of the patterns of growth of the Hebrew canon may be glimpsed when we remember that either a group of the enemies of Jeremiah (who died sometime after the fall of Jerusalem in 587 BC) or one of the editors of the book which bears that prophet's name could declare, "The law shall not perish from the priest, nor counsel from the wise, nor the word from the prophet" (Jer. 18:18 RSV). This is not identical to the threefold canonical division which is in evidence by the second century BC, but it is very close to it. On the other hand, as late as the time of the writing of the New Testament, some Christians (and presumably some Jews also) would refer to the Hebrew scriptures as simply "the law and the prophets" (Rom. 3:21, and elsewhere). There is no suggestion that Paul and others did not view the Writings as authoritative, but the persistence of the twofold designation for the Hebrew scriptures may indicate that an extended period of time had elapsed in which only the Torah and the Prophets were considered canonical, a period of sufficient duration for the phrase "the law and the prophets" to become a standard form of expression. (Cf. Luke 24:44 where the threefold division is referred to by the interesting phrase "the law of Moses, the prophets, and the psalms.") Josephus, writing toward the end of the first century AD, makes the point that the scriptures of the Jews are composed of twenty-two books.[11]

It is quite likely that the process of canonical growth corresponded, to some extent, to the lines of sectarian division.[12] The Pharisees, who accorded something like canonical status to the collected oral interpretation of the Torah, are the one group who perhaps would have been most open to the authority of the Prophets and the Writings. That they might have done this on the grounds that the Prophets and the Writings constituted a kind of commentary on the Torah is a possibility raised by later rabbinic literature in which the Prophets and Writings are often described as being ancillary and subordinate to the Torah. For example, according to one regulation, an individual might sell a scroll containing texts of the Prophets and the Writings and use the money to purchase a Torah scroll. But one could not sell a Torah scroll in order to purchase texts of the Prophets or the Writings.[13]

In their openness to the authority of the Prophets and the Writings the Pharisees would have been joined by the Essenes, assuming that the evidence from Qumran reflects general Essene practice, for the Qumran caves yeilded either fragments or entire copies of every book in the Hebrew canon except Esther. A third sect, the Zealots, also seem to have subscribed to the authority of non-Torah literature, for discoveries at Masada[14] yielded, in addition to fragments from Genesis and Leviticus, material from the Psalms and from the Wisdom of Sirach (Ecclesiasticus), Sirach, in fact, being represented by twenty-six large fragments. Thus we have the curious fact that the Masada zealots possessed a copy of a work that, while it failed to obtain canonical status among Palestinian Jews, was accorded that distinction by the Jews of Alexandria.

On the other hand, the Samaritans may have been less open to the binding authority of all non-Torah literature, insisting, instead, on the supremacy of Genesis through Deuteronomy. Although different from the Samaritans in many ways, the Sadducees would also have insisted upon the supremacy of the Torah, if not its absolute exclusivity.[15]

B. Jewish Sectarian Movements

Early Judaism was a lively admixture of beliefs and practices that were pursued with great passion, so much passion, in fact, that competing groups and sects often collided with one another with considerable energy. If the centrality of the Torah provided a focus, that focus did not obscure the wide variety of issues—theological and otherwise—which made the faith of these Jews a many-splendored thing. In fact, the very task of interpreting the Torah helped, along with other factors, to bring into existence two of the important sects of Second Temple Judaism, the Pharisees and the Sadducees. Although united in a common commitment to the Torah, they were often deeply divided as to how the Torah should be understood and applied to the lives of individual Jews.

1. The Pharisees

Mentioned by Josephus as the Jewish sect with the widest base of popular support, the Pharisees have left to subsequent generations more evidence concerning themselves than any other Second Temple Jewish sect, with the exception of the witness of the Qumran scrolls to the sectarian life lived in that community beside the Dead Sea. In addition to Josephus' interest in the Pharisees, a group of which he was once, according to his claim,[16] a youthful member (but which he does not always describe in flattering terms), there are two reasons for this relative wealth of information. First, the Pharisees are the only Jewish sect to survive in any significant numbers the destruction of Jerusalem in 70 AD and the Bar Kokhba revolt of 132–135 AD. Rabbinic Judaism, of which modern Judaism is a descendant, is in considerable measure the product of Pharisaism, which means that those who are responsible for our earliest information about the Pharisees were, to a large extent, sympathetic to the Pharisaic view. Second, the New Testament, while it describes tensions between Jesus and the Pharisees (a reflection, of course, of tensions between early Christians and Jews), nevertheless provides important information about some aspects of Pharisaic life (e.g., Acts 23:8). In addition, Jesus himself, a rabbi from Nazareth, expressed a view of the nature of God and of God's work in human life that in some respects is near that of the Pharisees (e.g., the reality of human sin, of God's final judgment, and of eternal rewards and punishments).[17] Moreover, Paul was a Pharisee (Phil. 3:5) and in certain important respects he continued to reflect Pharisaic teachings, even after his conversion to Christianity (e.g., 1 Cor. 15).

In spite of this important documentation, however, much less is actually known about the Pharisees than is sometimes claimed. Almost all written references to this sect (as well as to the Sadducees) were composed after the decisive events of 70 AD, thus scholars must admit the possibility that the descriptions of the role played by the Pharisees during the second and first centuries BC, and even the accounts of Pharisaic influence during the first seven decades of the first century AD, may be colored by the Pharisaic dominance of Jewish life in the decades after the destruction of the Temple by the Romans.

It is possible that the Hasidim, those allies of Judas Maccabeus who initially refused to fight on the Sabbath (1 Macc. 2:29–43), were the immediate predecesors of the Pharisees. The members of this group, unlike the Hasmonean party at whose side they fought, were interested in political and military affairs primarily to the extent that these impinged upon their central concern of faithfulness to the Torah, so that, when religious freedom was restored to the Jews during the time of Judas Maccabeus, the Hasidim were content to accept the political status quo and leave the fighting to the Hasmoneans, a decision that cost them their lives (1 Macc. 7:12–16). Their successors, the Pharisees (if successors they were), entertained a similar set of values. It is true that, when John Hyrcanus embraced a deeply Hellenized version of Judaism, the Pharisees revolted, and the hostility between them and, in turn, Hyrcanus, Aristobulus, and Alexander Jannaeus, illustrates their unwillingness to compromise with a version of Judaism that, in their view, was not faithful to the Torah.

It is often claimed that Pharisaism was a sect of the laity, and in general terms this is likely true. Although their teachings never repudiated the role of the priesthood, their ranks, while including priests, seem to have been composed primarily of lay persons. In at least the early days of the movement, these were individuals who were expected to support themselves in quite normal ways, while they carried on the study and teaching of the Torah. Yet as the corpus of Pharisaic intrepretation grew, only professional Torah scholars could be expected to master the increasing mass of material. The Pharisees never constituted a majority of the Jewish population, their number during the time of Herod the Great being estimated by Josephus at something more than six thousand.[18] Nevertheless, they spoke for more individual Jews than did any of the other sects, at least if Josephus may be trusted in the matter. For Josephus reports that

> so great is their influence with the masses that even when they speak against a king or High Priest, they immediately gain credence.[19]

For all that, however, they distinguished themselves from the mass of Jews, the "people of the land." "The garments of the 'people of the land' are unclean for the Pharisees," states the Mishnah. "A Pharisee does not enter the house of one of the 'people of the land' and does not accept him as a guest if the latter wears his own garments."[20] Whether, in their withdrawal from the 'people of the land,' their religious scruples were in many cases reinforced by a sense of personal superiority is difficult to know at this distance. But it was this attitude of separateness (the word Pharisee is presumably related to a word meaning *separation*), that formed the basis of their criticism of Jesus for "eating with sinners and tax collectors" (Mark 2:15–17, and elsewhere).[21]

But if they often separated themselves from other people, the Pharisees developed a strong sense of community among the members of the group. They bound themselves together by a common commitment to the strictest possible observance of the Torah, an observance that was, of course, understood in terms of their own body of Torah interpretation. Anyone who did not live up to the discipline of their teaching could not participate in their fellowship. It appears, in fact, that the term by which they originally referred to one another was not Pharisee, but *hever*, meaning *companion*.[22] In this respect Josephus compares them favorably to the Sadducees:

> The Pharisees are friendly to one another and cultivate harmonious relations with the community. The Sadducees, even towards each other, show a more disagreeable behavior and in their relations with their peers are as rude as to aliens.[23]

While we do not know as much as we would wish about the beliefs of this important sect, a few features deserve mention. (1) The first has to do with what, in later theological terms, would be termed the tension between the sovereignty of God and the free will of men and women. Josephus puts it like this:

> As for the Pharisees, they say that certain events are the work of Fate, but not all; as to other events, it depends upon ourselves whether they shall take place or not. The sect of the Essenes, however, declares that Fate is mistress of all things, and that nothing befalls men unless it be in accordance with her decree. But the Sadducees do away with Fate, holding that there is no such thing and that human actions are not achieved in accordance with her decree, but that all things lie within our own power, so that we ourselves are responsible for our well-being, while we suffer misfortune through our own thoughtlessness.[24]

It is doubtful that any of the sects referred to here ever discussed the role of "Fate." Rather, Josephus, whose intended readers were gentile, uses the language of Greek thought to express ideas of Jewish theology. When "translated," his remarks mean that, in the continuing debate over the role of God in human life, the Pharisees occupied an intermediate position between the deterministic Essenes and the nondeterministic Sadducees.

(2) Josephus' tendency to use the language of the Hellenistic world when discussing things peculiarly Jewish may be seen in another statement concerning the Pharisees.

> Every soul, they maintain, is immortal, but the soul of the good alone passes into another body, while the souls of the wicked suffer eternal punishment.[25]

When deprived of their Greek dress, Josephus' words are in fact attempting to say what the New Testament reports more directly: "The Sadducees say that there is no resurrection, or angel, or spirit; but the Pharisees acknowledge all three" (Acts 23:8). In other words, the Pharisees (and, as we shall see, the Essenes) disagreed with the Sadducees in that they accepted both the resurrection of the body and the world of angels and demons. Both resurrection and angel/demonology are, as we have noticed, essential elements in Jewish apocalyptic, elements that have roots in the Old Testament itself (cf. Dan. 12:1–2).

(3) The most important feature of Pharisaic life had to do with the study, interpretation, and teaching of the Torah. Again, Josephus:

> Of the two schools named first [i.e., the Pharisees and the Sadducees], the Pharisees are held to be the most accurate interpreters of the laws [i.e., the Torah] and are the leading sect.[26]

A principal quality which made the Pharisees distinctive in their activity as Torah scholars was their interest in setting forth as authorative not only the books of the Torah itself (i.e., Genesis through Deuteronomy), but a vast body of commentary upon the Torah. A great deal, if not most, of the activity relating to the interpretation of the Torah, discussed above, was carried on by Pharisaic scribes and rabbis. In addition, as we have noted, it is likely that the Pharisees, along with the Essenes, were more open to the authority of other literature, including the books of the Prophets and the Writings, than were the Sadducees, and certainly more open than the Samaritans.[27]

2. The Sadducees

The Sadducees were the sect with whom the Pharisees often found themselves involved in the greatest conflicts, tensions between these two groups having begun as early as the Hasmonean Era. In fact, Josephus' first mention of the Sadducees stresses the fractious nature of their relations with the Pharisees. Following his story of John Hyrcanus' dispute with the Pharisee

Eleazar, who demanded that Hyrcanus surrender the high priesthood, Josephus recounts that

> a certain Jonathan, one of Hyrcanus' close friends, belonging to the school of the Sadducees, who hold opinions opposed to those of the Pharisees, said that it had been with the general approval of all the Pharisees that Eleazar had made his slanderous statement.[28]

Whether this Jonathan's allegations were true or not, the incident became the flashpoint for the bloody struggle between the Hasmonean rulers and the Pharisees that would last until the time of Queen Alexandra.

Theological issues which set the Sadducees against the Pharisees included, as we have seen, the extent to which human beings are free from divine predestination, the existence of angels and demons and the reality of an final resurrection of the dead. But the theological focus of their debate and the one that received the most attention had to do with the manner in which the Torah was to be interpreted. As a matter of fact, most if not all of their theological differences, including those just enumerated, stemmed from this basic disagreement. The Sadducees apparently believed that the Torah alone, stripped of all encumberances of human interpretation, represented the revelation of God in Israel's life. The Torah itself, and not some human commentary upon the Torah, constituted the authoritative will of God for human life.

Given that distinction, however, many modern students of early Judaism would be hard pressed to identify either group as more or less legalistic, more or less casuistic than the other. In some matters the Pharisees, who were reknowned for their strictness in obeying the Torah, do indeed seem to be the more severe. But in other matters, the Sadducees can be equally or more demanding. The Mishnah, although written during the early third century AD and thus later than period under consideration here, contains what is doubtless an authentic tradition concerning the nature of the Sadducee-Pharisee debate even during the Hellenistic period.

On the question of whether a master can be held liable for damage caused by his servant:

> The Sadducees said: We must reprove you, Pharisees, for you say, if my ox or my ass cause damage, I owe compensation, and if my slave or my maid-servant cause damage, I am free. If I have to pay compensation for ox or ass, to which I have no legal obligations, how shall I not own compensation for my slave or maid-servant to whom I have legal obligations?
>
> [The Pharisees] answered: Not the same can apply to ox or ass which have no understanding as in regard to slave or maid-servant, who have understanding. For if I make [my slave] angry, he may go and set fire to another man's field, and oblige me to make restitution.

On the question of whether false witnesses in a capital case should be executed, even when their purjury was discovered in time (notice here the manner in which verses from the Torah are cited by both sides as proof of their
point of view):

> The Sadducees say: Only after [a person wrongly convicted in a capi-
> tal crime] has been executed [should the false witnesses be put to
> death]; as it is written, "Life for life" (Deut. 19:21).
> But the sages [of the Pharisees] said to them: Is it not also written,
> "Then you shall do unto him as he had planned to do to his brother"
> (Deut. 19:19)?[29]

In the first instance, the Sadducees seem to have taken a more demanding
position, insisting that an individual be responsible for the actions of his servants, but in the second example, the Pharisaic view is stricter, that is, that
false witnesses in a capital case be put to death solely on the grounds that
they *intended* that the accused be executed, whether the sentence has been carried out or not.[30]

But the tensions between Sadducees and Pharisees were caused not only by
differences in theology and in principles of Torah interpretation, but by a
whole complex of social and political matters. Simply put, whereas the Pharisees were predominantly a lay group, representing, to some extent at least,
Jews of modest economic means, the Sadducees were priestly and aristocratic,
and counted among their number families of rank and fortune. The Sadducees' very name seems to be derived from Zadok,[31] the name of the high
priest under David and Solomon (1 Kings 1:8) and the supposed ancestor of
the line of hereditary high priests who held power in Jerusalem before the
Hasmonean Era. They thus represented the interests of those who for generations had held both spiritual and, in a limited way, political power under Persian and Ptolemaic rule, since the high priest was also the head of the council
(later, the Sanhedrin). It was from the priests of the aristocratic families that
there came many (but not all) of those Jews who worked to accomodate the
laws and customs of Judaism to the models of Hellenism. Many of the Sadducees, as they would come to be called, were undoubtedly reserved or openly
hostile to the traditionalist movement led by Mattathias and his sons, especially since, at the time of Jonathan (153 BC), the high priesthood fell into Hasmonean hands. And it can hardly be accidental that the reemergence of this
group into a position of power as the allies of the Hasmoneans coincides with
the efforts of John Hyrcanus, Aristobulus, and Alexander Jannaeus to create a
kingdom constructed along Hellenistic models.

During the Roman period, the Sadducees endured limitations to their
power at the hands of Herod and the Romans. Nevertheless, they continued to
be influential in the Sanhedrin and to claim the allegiance of at least some

who held the office of high priest (Acts 5:17). The portrait of the Sadducees that tradition has preserved is of a worldly, religiously dispassionate group, more interested in privilege and wealth than in devotion to the true traditions of Israel. That is doubtless true, to some extent, and the marriage between a theological affirmation of Torah alone (thus, Torah removed from much of life) and the political affirmation of their own power (against the background of their affirmation of the freedom of the human will) was surely a convenient one. Yet the fact that much of what we know of the Sadducees was passed down by their opponents (the Pharisaic/rabbinic tradition and the early Christians) should cause one to be somewhat reserved in assenting completely to this traditional view. For among the Sadducees there must have been individuals who, political and social considerations aside, firmly believed that the priestly role in Israel was supreme and that, even in light of the importance of the Torah, the Temple and its cult formed the real meeting place between a Jew and her or his God.

In any event, with the destruction by the Romans of the Temple and its attending priesthood in 70 AD, the foundations of Sadducean life gave way and the sect disappeared from history.

3. The Essenes[32]

Although the Essenes constituted a sectarian group which, like the Pharisees and Sadducees, rose to prominence during Hasmonean times, they were distinctive in that they constituted a monastic community, or perhaps more accurately, a monastic movement represented by several communities. In other words, whereas both Pharisees and Sadducees were active in day-to-day life in Jerusalem and other parts of Palestine, the Essenes generally withdrew into their exclusive settlements, which perhaps helps to account for the fact that they are never mentioned in the New Testament. They are known to a number of ancient writers, however, and Philo and Josephus, as well as the Roman writer Pliny the Elder (23–79 AD), provide valuable information concerning the Essenes.[33] In addition, as we shall discuss below, there is good reason to believe that the members of the Qumran community were Essenes, thus their significant amount of literature that has survived, as well as archaeological information from the Qumran site, may help cast light on this group.

The details of Essene origins are obscure, even the derivation and meaning of their name constituting a mystery.[34] But it is a widely held view among scholars that they are ideological descendants of the Hasidim of the early Hasmonean Era, an ancestry they would thus share with the Pharisees and one that would help to explain the similarity of many of their views. If the evidence of the Qumran material is relevant, as seems most likely, the Essenes looked with deep hostility upon the Hasmonean assumption of the office of the high priest by Jonathan in the year 153 BC. The following passage from the Habakkuk *pesher* discovered at Qumran may characterize the Essene view of the so-called "Wicked Priest" whom a number of scholars identify with Jonathan:

> This [text, i.e., Hab. 2:5–6] concerns the Wicked Priest who was called by the name of truth when he first arose. But when he ruled over Israel his heart became proud, and he forsook God and betrayed the precepts for the sake of riches. He robbed and amassed the riches of the men of violence who rebelled against God, and he took the wealth of the peoples, heaping sinful iniquity upon himself. And he lived in the ways of abominations amidst every unclean defilement.
>
> Habakkuk *pesher*, 8[35]

The Essene response to the rule of the Hasmoneans apparently was to remove themselves from the Jerusalem community both physically (by leaving the city) and theologically (by repudiating the leadership of the Hasmonean-led Jerusalem priesthood). It is about this time that the Qumran site was constructed and settled[36] and probably about this time that other Essene communities were also established (none of which to this date has been discovered). Although they were in close contact with one another and, to some extent, with fellow Jews in Jerusalem and other towns and villages, they continued to dissent from mainstream Jewish life as long as a member of the Hasmonean dynasty ruled the life of the nation. Indeed, much of the evidence from Qumran strongly suggests that they considered themselves in a state of war with the reigning Hasmonean priesthood, a war which, in apocalyptic fashion, God would decide in their favor. They doubtless rejoiced over Pompey's capture of the Temple Mount in 63 BC and the unseating of the Hasmonean king (although Hyrcanus II continued in the office of high priest).

In Herod the Great they found a common ally against the Hasmoneans, for the Idumaean client king who ruled with the sufferance of the Romans feared the Hasmonean descendants as potential threats to his own authority. Thus Herod absolved the Essenes from taking an oath of loyalty (which, in any event, they would have refused to do) and, in the light of this, the Qumran community, and possibly other Essene settlements, may have been abandoned in order that the Essenes could return to Jerusalem and to other regular Jewish settlements. Herod's motive in permitting the Essenes this unusual freedom was undoubtedly his hope that they would be a political, perhaps even military, force against Hasmonean pretentions to power. Josephus' mention of a gate in the wall of Jerusalem at the time of its destruction in 70 AD named the "Gate of the Essenes,"[37] may suggest that the dwellings of Essene inhabitants of Jerusalem during the Herodian period were grouped together, thus perpetuating the sect's sense of community. The accommodation between the

Essenes and Herod is further suggested by a legend, recounted by Josephus, in which an Essene named Manahem prophesied to the young boy Herod that he would some day be king of the Jews. Many years later—so the story goes— Herod, now king, had the elderly Manahem brought before him and "from that time on he continued to honor all the Essenes."[38]

Herod's death, and the turmoil that followed, may have caused the Essenes once more to retreat into isolation, for at about this time evidence from the Qumran site again suggests signs of occupancy. Some Essenes, if not the group as a whole, appear to have been active in the revolt against Rome which resulted in the destruction of Jerusalem in 70 AD. One of the Jewish generals was an Essene named John,[39] and Josephus says of Essene captives taken by the Romans:

> Their spirit was tested to the utmost by the war with the Romans. They racked, twisted, burnt and broke them, subjecting them to every instrument of torture in order to make them blaspheme their Lawgiver [either Moses or the Righteous Teacher of the Qumran texts], or to eat something forbidden. Yet they did not yield to either demand, nor ever once did they fawn on their tormenters or shed a tear. Smiling in their agony and gently mocking their torturers, they cheerfully resigned their souls, confident that they would receive them back again.[40]

Qumran was destroyed at the time of the revolt against the Romans, and the sect was probably destroyed at this time, as well, although some Essenes may have been present to take part in the Bar Kokhba revolt of 132–135 AD.

Concerning their beliefs, Essenes have been referred to as "exaggerated Pharisees,"[41] for there is a certain commonality between the views of the two sects. Like the Pharisees, the Essenes believed in the supremacy of the Torah, and in the authority of the Prophets and the Writings, as well. Moses, in fact, was held in special awe by the Essene sectaries, and defamation of his name was punishable by death.[42] Philo describes the manner of their scripture study on the Sabbath, which was more intense than on other days, and says that "their . . . study takes the form of allegory, and in this they emulate the traditions of the past."[43] Philo seems to be referring to the belief of the Essenes that they were to be witnesses to many of the things foretold in scripture, and their ability to predict the future was a divine gift for which the members of the sect were apparently widely known. As to their use of allegory, this method of exegesis is confirmed by the Habakkuk *pesher* and other documents from Qumran.

The Essenes believed in demons and angels, in the resurrection of the dead,[44] and in a final judgment, while some Qumran literature portrays the role of a messiah (or perhaps two messiahs) in the establishment of the rule of God.[45] In terms of the debate between the proponents of divine predestination and of human free will, the Essenes, as we have seen, were convinced of the total rule of God over human life, another aspect of their theology that is consistent with that of much apocalyptic literature.

One of the most intriguing statements concerning the Essenes to come from the pen of an ancient writer is the following from the Roman geographer Pliny the Elder:

> On the west side of the Dead Sea, but out of range of the noxious exhalations of the coast, is the solitary tribe of the Essenes, which is remarkable beyond all the other tribes in the whole world, as it has no women and has renounced all sexual desire, has no money, and has only palm trees for company. Day by day the throng of refugees is recruited to an equal number by numerous accessions of persons tired of life and driven thither by the waves of fortune to adopt their manners. Thus through thousands of ages (incredible to relate) a race in which no one is born lives on forever: so prolific for their advantage is other men's weariness of life! Lying below the Essenes was formerly the town of Engedi, second only to Jerusalem in the fertility of its land and in its groves of palm-trees, but now, like Jerusalem, a heap of ashes. Next comes Masada, a fortress on a rock, itself not far from the Dead Sea.[46]

This description of the Essene community as lying on the northern end of a line that ran southward through Engedi to Masada sounds tantalizingly as if Pliny had the Qumran community in mind. Because of the significance of the discoveries at Qumran, over and above the light they may shed on the Essene movement, discussion of this community and its library are given special attention in the next chapter.

4. The Samaritans[47]

It may appear as less than logical to include the Samaritans in a discussion of Jewish sectarian groups. The ancient records are virtually unanimous is portraying the Samaritans as an independent ethnic-religious community that lived alongside of, but in deep hostility toward the Jews. The phrase "Samaritans and Jews" (or something similar) is consistently used in the New Testament and elsewhere to imply a polarity that would never occur in such unthinkable phrases as "Pharisees and Jews" or "Sadducees and Jews." The statement of the Samaritan woman to Jesus that "Jews have no dealings with Samaritans" (John 4:9) is a case in point. Yet when one considers that Samaritans and Jews share both a history and a rich literary-theological tradition, the fact of mutual animosity between the two groups in ancient times by no means rules out a consideration of them as closely related communities. The most powerful argument against the consideration of the Samaritans as a

Jewish sect is that such a conceptualization might imply that the Samaritans were a deviant branch from the main trunk of Israelite tradition whose normative representatives were the Jews (a view which has been traditionally held by both Jews and Christians). The Samaritans themselves, however—both ancient and modern—would stoutly resist such characterization and would maintain that their interpretation of the ancient Israelite tradition is the normative one, while it is the Jews (to say nothing of Christians and Muslims!) who are the false shoots. Perhaps it is not putting too fine a point on the matter, then, to say that the Samaritans represent a sect, if not of Judaism, at least of the larger Israelite tradition, in which case it seems appropriate to consider them here.[48]

The origins of the Samaritan community are irretrievably lost. To be sure, there is an account in the Hebrew scriptures, found in 2 Kings 17, that ties the beginnings of the Samaritans to the disruptions caused by the Assyrian conquest of the Northern Kingdom in 722 BC. Briefly, this version of Samaritan origins states that, following a seige of three years,

> the king of Assyria captured Samaria; he carried the Israelites away to Assyria. He placed them in Halah, on the Habor, the river of Gozan, and in the cities of the Medes.
>
> (2 Kings 17:6)

Then, faced with a population vacuum,

> The king of Assyria brought people from Babylon, Cuthah, Avva, Hamath, and Sepharvaim, and placed them in the cities of Samaria in place of the people of Israel; they took possession of Samaria, and settled in its cities.
>
> (2 Kings 17:24)

These new inhabitants from the East, who had brought their own deities with them, then intermarried with the few Israelites who had been allowed to remain on the land, with the result that a hybrid society emerged whose members worshiped Yahweh, the God of Israel, in a syncretistic mix that also included the gods of Babylon, Cuthah, and so on. The prejorative term "Cuthites" was even used by Jews of a later day to refer to these despised and, as they felt, semipagan Samaritans.

The Samaritan version of their origins is, as one might expect, quite different. Their literature calls attention to the references in the Torah to Mt. Gerazim (Deut. 11:29, 27:12) as a special place of worship for the people of God,[49] and maintains that, in violation of God's will, the priest Eli moved the ark of the covenant from the sacred mountain to Shiloh (cf. 1 Sam. 1:3), thus setting up an apostate cult. A Samaritan document, the Chronicle Adler,[50] puts it this way:

At that time Eli the son of Yafni went and made for himself an ark of gold, wherein he placed the books written in the handwriting of his ancestor, our lord Ithamar.[51] He also made for himself a tent and pitched it at Shiloh, because the children of Israel who were at that time in Shechem and in other cities of Palestine, had driven him from Mount Gerazim, together with those who joined him. There in Shiloh he built an altar and offered sacrifices upon it, and all the men of the tribe of Judah joined him, as well as many men from the other tribes.

In the Samaritan view, therefore, the Judaean cult, which later comes to be centered in Jerusalem, is a heterodox version of the true Israelite faith whose orthodox center is at Mt. Gerazim. As for the Assyrian deportations following the fall of Northern Kingdom in 722 BC, the Samaritan view of the Judahite tradition in 2 Kings 17 is that it exaggerates the numbers of captives who were removed from the cities of Samaria. Many citizens of the nation were allowed to remain in the land, and it is they—good Israelites and devout worshipers of Yahweh—who are the ancestors of the Samaritans. However—so goes the Samaritan argument—when the families of Judah returned from captivity in Babylon, the Judahite (Jewish) fiction of Samaritan apostasy was perpetuated by Ezra, Nehemiah, and others.

For modern Jews and Christians who are accustomed to the account in 2 Kings 17, the Samaritan version may seem farfetched, yet there are some facts which, if they do not demonstrate the validity of the Samaritan story, do demonstrate that the Jewish view was written for polemical purposes and is therefore partial and incomplete. For one thing, there are certain historical dislocations in the account in Kings (it was the Assyrian monarch Sargon, not Shalmaneser—as Kings would have it [2 Kings 17:3]—who captured Samaria). For another, Sargon boasts that he relocated 27,290 citizens of Samaria, a far smaller number than the total inhabitants of the land.[52] In view of the fact that ancient royal annals often exagerated but never denigrated the exploits of their kings, the figure furnished by the Assyrians must be taken seriously. Finally, there is the evidence of the Books of Chronicles, which takes a much more tolerant attitude toward the Samaritans than does Kings.[53] Chronicles, in describing the discovery of the "book of the law" during the reign of Judaean King Josiah (621 BC, a century after the fall of Samaria), refers to an offering sent to the Jerusalem Temple "collected from Manasseh and Ephraim [i.e., the Samaritan heartland] and from all the remnant of Israel" (2 Chron. 34:9).

The Books of Ezra and Nehemiah reflect growing animosity between the two communities during the Persian period. Ezra 4:1–3 tells of the effort of a group of "adversaries of Judah and Benjamin" (undoubtedly Samaritans) to participate in the Temple rebuilding project of the Jewish leader Zerubbabel,[54] an offer that was repudiated by the Jews, yet one that brought their reconstruction efforts temporarily to a halt. Nehemiah 2:19, 4:1–23, and 6:1–9 recount incidents growing out of the hostility between the Jewish governor Nehemiah and his Samaritan counterpart Sanballit. Later, when Sanballit's daughter marries one of the sons of the Jewish high priest, Nehemiah banishes the pair from Jerusalem (Neh. 13:28). It is to about this time that many scholars date the "final schism" between the Jews of Jerusalem and the Samaritans of Schechem-Mt. Gerazim, a time beyond which developments of a literary and theological nature take place in mutual independence. These tensions undoubtedly arose out of a sense of rivalry between the two communities as to which should occupy a commanding position in the affairs of Persian controlled Palestine.

At some time the Samaritans had built a temple on Mt. Gerazim. Josephus places the construction of this building to about 330 BC, but his report in this regard is sometimes regarded as unreliable.[55] What does seem certain is that this Samaritan temple was destroyed by the Hasmoneans under John Hyrcanus in 129 BC. We do not know how the Samaritans had responded to the influences of Hellenism or the precise nature of their relations with the Seleucid authorities during the reign of Antiochus Epiphanes, although 2 Maccabees 6:2 points out that one of Antiochus' agents transformed the Samaritan temple on Mount Gerazim into a shrine to Zeus. But it is clear that the Seleucid-Hasmonean conflict did not draw the Samaritan and Jerusalem communities closer to one another, and Hyrcanus' destruction of the Samaritan temple provides one more witness to the continuing hostility between them. During the Jewish War with Rome (66–74 AD), however, the Samaritans joined the struggle against the Romans, suffering a great massacre at the hands of Roman troops, who had trapped the main Samaritan body on the summit of Mt. Gerazim.[56] In this fight, the Samaritans acted not as allies of the Jews, but as a group drawn up into the general conflagration which flamed forth across Palestine.

Even with the Samaritan disaster at the hands of the Romans, the numbers of Samaritan population remained substantial during the first century AD and their presence (primarily between the two Jewish population centers of Judaea and Galilee) was a reality with which others in the area were daily forced to contend. But over the centuries of Roman, Byzantine, and Muslim rule which ensued, their numbers dwindled greatly because of persecution and conversion. Like the Jews, the Samaritans experienced their own Diaspora and, almost up to our own time, communities of Samaritans (showing some sectarian differences) could be found in Cairo, Gaza, Damascus, Athens, Corinth, Constantinople, and Rome. Early in our own century it was feared that the Samaritans would become extinct as an ethnic-religious entity, for in 1901 only 152 individuals could be identified, all living in Ottoman Palestine. But today there are several hundred Samaritans, about equally divided between two communities: Nablus, at the base of Mt. Gerazim, and the Tel-Aviv suburb of Holon.

Samaritan beliefs[57] are today defined by the corpus of existing Samaritan writings and by the liturgy observed in Samaritan places of worship.[58] But is very difficult to use this evidence to reconstruct the views of the Samaritans of the Hellenistic and Roman periods, because the literature, although it may contain very early traditions, dates from a much later time and suggests Islamic influences dating from the centuries of Arab and Ottoman rule. But some observations concerning the beliefs and practices of the ancient Samaritans may be made with certainty.

(1) Moses was regarded by them as the supreme prophet of Israel's God. This is consistent with the portrait in the Old Testament, which describes a theological outlook in the Northern Kingdom which focuses heavily on the work of the great lawgiver. This is apparent, among other places, in the books of both Deuteronomy and Hosea (see esp. Hos. 12:13), literature with a Northern or Israelite origin. It is also consistent with later Samaritan terminology, which speaks of Moses as the "exhalted prophet," the "seal of the prophets," and the like.

(2) The Torah, and only the Torah, was considered to be sacred scripture, all other literature, including the Prophets and the Writings of the Jewish canon, being of lesser authority or of no authority at all. A Samaritan version of the Pentateuch has been known by western scholars since 1616, and in the last 200 years has been subjected to critical analysis. Although existing copies are relatively late, the textual tradition of the Samaritan Pentateuch goes back to antiquity, in the view of many scholars. Differences between Jewish and Samaritan versions of the Pentateuch are minor, for the most part, but if the Samaritan text is anything like as old as the (Jewish) Masoretic Text, these variants must be seriously considered, even if they are ultimately judged to be later alterations. Of particular interest is the Samaritan Tenth Commandment (in the Samaritan Pentateuch the Ten Commandments of the Jewish tradition are compressed into nine). In the Masoretic Text the following words occur (in slightly different form) in Deuteronomy 27:2–7 (cf. Deut. 11:29), but in the Samaritan Pentateuch they constitute the Tenth Commandment.

> And when your God brings you into the land of the Canaanites which you are entering to take possession of it, you shall set up these stones and plaster them with plaster, and you shall write upon them all the words of the Law. And when you have passed over the Jordan, you shall set up these stones, concerning which I have commanded you this day, on Mount Gezirim [Mt. Ebal in Deut. 27:4]. And there you shall build an altar to the Lord your God.[59]

It has been suggested that some other variant readings in the Samaritan Pentateuch demonstrate affinities with certain texts from Qumran, an assertion that, if valid, would strengthen the argument for the antiquity of the Samaritan textual tradition.[60]

(3) The cult practiced at Mt. Gerazim was sacrificial in nature and was centered on the three main festivals of ancient Israel: Passover, Pentecost (Shavuoth), and Tabernacles (Sukkoth). Whereas the Jewish sacrificial system, including the priesthood, failed to survive the destruction of the Jerusalem Temple in 70 AD, the Samaritan priesthood continues to this day under the direction of a Samaritan high priest living in Nablus. The continuation of the Samaritan sacrificial system and the demise of the Jewish means, of course, that the observance of the great festivals by the Samaritans is closer to the biblical model than is their observance among the Jews. For example, the blood sacrifice of sheep still lies at the heart of the Samaritan Passover (Exod. 12:21–27), whereas the observance of the modern Jewish Passover is centered in the home.[61]

(4) A belief in angels (but not demons), in the resurrection of the dead, and in God's final judgment over humankind may have formed part of the corpus of belief of the ancient Samaritans. This is certainly so of modern Samaritans, who speak of God's Day of Vengeance and Recompense[62] and know of a universe filled with angelic creatures. Such a well-developed eschatology would seem to be inconsistent with the acceptance of only the Torah as the authoritative divine word (cf. the views of the Sadducees, above), and may represent borrowings from later Christian or Muslim teachings. But if the proposed affinities between the ancient Samaritans and the Qumran community are valid, this Samaritan eschatology could date from as early as Hellenistic times, for certain Qumran documents, as we shall see, display a strong eschatological hope.

C. INSTITUTIONS OF EARLY JUDAISM

1. The Synagogue [63]

The increasingly important role that the Torah assumed in Second Temple Judaism meant that, in addition to the rabbinic schools for training of young Torah scholars, some institution was necessary in which the larger community, especially its adult members, might study the Torah. Although it came in time to be regarded as a place of worship, the synagogue may initially have been this institution dedicated to the reading of and instruction in the Torah. The synagogue would be significant for the study of early Judaism, even if, like the Temple, it had failed to survive into modern times. In many communities, especially in the Diaspora, where Jews might find themselves a minority within the larger populaton, the synagogue became the center of Jewish social, as well as religious life, and it is in this context that it is often mentioned in the New Testament. But the synagogue takes on added significance from the fact that, with the destruction of the Temple in 70 AD, it became the place above all others where Jews met for worship, instruction, and fellowship. What is more, the synagogue provided the model for the earliest Christian congregations.

No one knows where or when the first synagogue was organized. It is tempting to believe that Jews in the Babylonian exile, deprived of their Temple as a place of social and religious gathering, established local houses of meeting and that from these the first synagogues were born. But there is no evidence for such a view other than the fact that it seems clear that the synagogue did not exist before the exile. All that can be affirmed with certainty is that the synagogue flourished during the Hellenistic and Roman periods first in the Diaspora, and only later in Palestine. By the first century AD synagogues existed in Galilee, Judaea, Egypt, Babylonia, and in virtually every other area where there were Jews, including Rome itself.[64] To this place on the Sabbath the faithful came together to hear the Torah, and frequently the Prophets, read and to be taught their meaning.

In communities in Palestine, where the population was almost entirely Jewish, the membership of the local synagogue would be nearly identical to membership in the Jewish community itself, so that the officers of the synagogue might also serve as the officials of the city. These included, first of all a council of elders, a body charged with general oversight of the affairs of the synagogue, including matters of discipline. Theirs was the power of excommunication (cf. John 9:22, 12:42, 16:2) as well as that of lesser penalties. In addition to the elders, each congregation was served by a "ruler" or "chief of the congregation" (Hebrew: *rosh hakeneset*; Greek: *archisynagogus*). This chief administrative officer, who in most cases probably came from the ranks of elders, appears to have had responsiblility for many of the details of synagogue life, as, for example, who would read the scripture and teach on the Sabbath. This "ruler" was not necessarily a scribe or rabbi, and there is no indication that he was expected to lead the synagogue service himself. Some synagogues seem to have more than one "ruler" (cf. Mark 5:22, Acts 13:15).

Beyond the elders and the "ruler" there was a "receiver of alms" (something like a treasurer) and a "servant of the congregation," who cared for the Torah scroll during the Sabbath service and who executed the administrative and disciplinary decisions of the elders. Undoubtedly there were other officers as the customs and needs of individual congregations required.

While there must have been local variations, a typical Sabbath service in a Hellenistic or Roman period synagogue proceeded in something like this order.[65] The people were seated in segregated fashion, the older and more important members of the community (presumably including scribes, rabbis, and—in Palestine—priests) to the front, the younger to the rear. Women probably (firm evidence is lacking) sat separately from men, and diseased or leperous persons were placed apart from the larger congregation. Elders sat facing the people, with their backs to the shrine or ark (chest) that housed the scroll of the Torah.

(1) The service likely began with a recitation of the *Shema* (meaning "Hear," the creed's first word), Israel's time honored confession of faith composed of Deuteronomy 6:4–9, 11:13–21 and Numbers 15:37–41. "Hear, O Israel, the LORD is our God, the LORD alone," begins this confession which, as an article of liturgy, was also in use in the Second Temple.

(2) The *Shema* might typically be followed by the Prayer, for which the people stood and faced the Holy of Holies of the Jerusalem Temple. The Prayer, probably fixed in form, was spoken by a designated leader who might be any person of the congregation, the congregation itself making appropriate responses. The precise wording of the Prayer for the period before about 100 AD is uncertain, but was undoubtedly similar to the *Shemoneh 'Esreh* (meaning *eighteen*, from the number of benedictions within the prayer), a widely used prayer from about the second century AD. In its Palestinian version, it begins in this manner:

Leader: Blessed art thou, Lord, God of our fathers, God of Abraham, God of Isaac and God of Jacob, great, mighty and fearful God, most high God who createst heaven and earth, our shield and the shield of our fathers, our trust in every generation.
People: Blessed art thou, Lord, shield of Abraham.[66]

(3) Readings from the Torah and, often, from the Prophets may have followed the Prayer. The Torah lections were arranged so that, over a three-year-period, the entire Torah would be read aloud. Readings from the Prophets, when they occurred, seem to have been less prescribed. Any person who was a rightful member of the congregation, or even a visiting Jew, could participate in these scripture readings, for which the reader stood at a podium facing the congregation. After the reading the text was frequently expounded or interpreted by the reader, who sat for this purpose. Luke 4:16–21, which recounts Jesus' reading and interpretation of a part of Isaiah 61, illustrates the procedure.[67]

In the Diaspora of the West, the language in which the scripture was read and interpreted was, for the most part, Greek, and in this regard the Septuagint translation must have received wide currency. In Palestine, as well, Hebrew was no longer the language of the Jewish people, thus the Torah and Prophets were translated into Aramaic for public reading, while the accompanying interpretation was likewise done in that language. Because Aramaic (in a somewhat different dialect) was also the language of the important Jewish community in Babylonia, Aramaic translations of the Torah and the Prophets were circulated there, as well. These Aramaic renditions of scripture, called Targumim[68] (sing: Targum, meaning *translation*), were extremely free, in some cases rather more of a paraphrase than a translation. The translator (called a meturgeman, from the same root as "Targum") was concerned to provide the biblical text and an appropriate interpretation that could be utilized in the Sabbath service of the synagogue. Over a period of time these Targumim settled into more or less fixed forms. These were handed down orally for many generations and did not achieve the written forms in which we know them until, in all likelihood, well after writing of the New Testament. Yet the written Targumim undoubtedly preserve the oral stage with considerable faithfulness, so it is instructive to read a selection from one of them, such as this Targum on Isaiah 11:1–6 (words that are unique to the Targum, i.e., not in the biblical text, are underlined):

> (11:1) And a *king* shall come forth from the *sons* of Jesse, and *the Messiah* shall *be exhalted* from *the sons of* his *sons.* (2) And *a* spirit *before* the Lord shall rest upon him, a spirit of wisdom and understanding, a spirit of counsel and might, a spirit of knowledge and the fear of the Lord. (3) And the Lord shall *bring him near to* his fear. And he shall not judge by the sight of his eyes, and he shall not reprove by the hearing of his ears; (4) but in *truth* he will judge the poor, and reprove with *faithfulness* for the needy of the *people;* and he shall strike *the sinners of* the land with the *command* of his mouth, and with *the speaking* of his lips the wicked shall *die.* (5) And *the* righteous shall be *all around* him, and *the* faithful shall be *brought near him.* (6) *In the days of the Messiah of Israel shall peace increase in the land,* and the wolf shall dwell with the lamb.[69]

At least two things become apparent in reading this Targum text. First, it is much less faithful to the Hebrew text of Isaiah than any good modern translation would dare to be. This is not to suggest that the Targum is in any sense incorrect. But it is to say that very different standards of translation were followed by the ancient meturgeman when compared to those in use today. Second, it is significant that an important theological idea, that of the messiah, is made explicit in the Targum, whereas in the biblical Isaiah text the messianic concept is only implied, if it is present at all.

For readers of the New Testament both of these elements are important. The ease with which the "translation" becomes a paraphrase perhaps helps to explain the difference between certain texts as they stand in the Old Testament itself and as they are quoted in the New Testament. Note, for example, the difference between Isaiah 6:9–10 and that same text as it is quoted by Jesus in Mark 4:12, then compare both with the Isaiah Targum of 6:9–10:

> (9) And he said, "Go, and speak to this people *that* hear *indeed,* but do not understand, and see *indeed,* but do not perceive. (10) Make the heart of this people dull, and their ears heavy and shut their eyes; lest *they* see

with *their* eyes and hear with *their* ears, and understand with *their* hearts, and repent and *it be forgiven them.*"[69]

Attention has been drawn to the fact that Mark 4:12 and the Isaiah Targum of 6:10, especially with respect to the final phrase, are nearer to one another than the Hebrew text of 6:10 ("and be healed"). Jesus and the New Testament writers were, of course, familiar with the Targumic tradition and they appear often to have been influenced by it in their quotation of Old Testament texts.

In addition, the tendency of the meturgeman to read certain texts with particular theological coloring (in the case of Isa. 11:1–6, messianically) is also a characteristic of the writers of the New Testament. Notice, for example, how Paul in Romans 15:7–13 understands Isaiah 11:10 (which he quotes—very freely—in Rom. 15:12).

(4) Finally, the Sabbath service in the synagogue was concluded, after the reading and interpretation of scripture, by a priestly blessing or, if no priest were present, by a benediction. The *Quaddish* (Aramaic for "holy") is a benediction that was perhaps often employed on such occasions, and which begins:

Exhalted and hallowed be His great name
in the world which He created
according to His will.
May He establish His kingdom
in your lifetime and in your days,
and in the lifetime of the whole house of Israel,
Speedily and at a near time.[70]

2. *The Sanhedrin*[71]

The most important administrative and legal assembly of Jews during the Hellenistic and Roman periods was clearly the Sanhedrin. Although rabbinic tradition states that such a body had existed in Israel from the time of Moses (citing Num. 11:10–25 as evidence), the truth would seem to be that the Sanhedrin can trace its origins to a time no earlier than the restoration of the Jerusalem community following the exile. The Books of Ezra and Nehemiah speak of various classes of Jewish officials who were active during the Persian period ("elders" in Ezra 5:5 and elsewhere; "the priests, the nobles, the officials" in Neh. 2:16), but, although the tolerant nature of Persian rule would make the existence of a Jewish administrative assembly quite possible, nothing is known of such a group. One argument in favor of a native Jewish assembly at this time is the fact that, when it is possible to identify a Jewish council during the Hellenistic period, it is aristocratic in nature, not democratic, as was the case in most native assemblies organized in cities under the rule of one of the Hellenistic powers.

Josephus' first mention of a Jewish administrative council occurs when he cites a letter reportedly written by Antiochus III the Great:

> Inasmuch as the Jews, from the very moment when we entered their country, showed their eagerness to serve us and, when we came to their city, gave us a splendid reception and met us with their senate . . . , we have seen fit on our part to repay them for these acts and to restore their city which had been destroyed by the hazards of war.[72]

The key word here, of course, is "senate," or *gerousia* in Greek, a term that may also be translated "council of elders." It is clear from this and other references in Josephus and elsewhere that this council of the early second century BC was composed primarily (if not exclusively) of aristocratic priests and that its presiding officer was the hereditary high priest.[73]

The Hasmonean revolt appears to have been a critical time in the life of the council in that the complex of tensions that racked the nation as a whole must have been reflected in this body. The disputes among the various priestly families, the rising influence of the laity, principally the Pharisees, and the increasing hostility between Pharisees and Sadducees—these and other factors must have introduced important changes into the life of the council of which we can have only the barest knowledge. The suppression of the Pharisees by John Hyrcanus, Aristobulus I, and Alexander Jannaeus, and their subsequent restoration by Queen Alexandra, must have been—on one level at least—a struggle for supremacy in the Sanhedrin. For it is clear that by Hasmonean times laymen as well as priests, Pharisees as well as Sadducees, played important roles in the council.

During the Roman period an important new element was introduced into the life and work of the council, that is, its authority was curtailed by a very powerful and alien oppressor. For reasons that are not clear, Josephus now begins to refer to this body as the *synedrion*, a Greek term which, in general use means something like *assembly*, but which in both Jewish and Christian literature refers particularly to the Jerusalem council. Because he saw it as a threat to his authority, Herod the Great, as one of his first acts, executed virtually all of the members of the Sanhedrin—if Josephus is to be believed in the matter.[74] Although a new Sanhedrin was constituted in place of the old one, its independence must have been severely limited. With the administrative changes instituted by the Romans following Herod's death, the authority of the Sanhedrin seems to have been limited to Judaea, although Jews living in Galilee and elsewhere would surely have looked to it and its decisions as an important influence upon their lives, an influence, however, which waxed or waned in a manner that reflected the political realities of a given moment.

The Mishnah states that the number of members of the Sanhedrin was seventy-one, a tradition which, like that concerning the origin of the Sanhedrin, has its eye upon Numbers 11:16, 24. Nearer the truth is that we do not know how many members the Sanhedrin contained (or indeed if there was any uniform number over the centuries of its existence), nor what methods were used in the members' selection. Somewhat more certain is the continuing role of the high priest as the presiding officer, and the fact that the rank-and-file were Jews of unquestioned genealogy. The Sanhedrin must always have contained members from the priestly and aristocratic groups, even during the times of greatest Pharisaic influence. Josephus and the New Testament both refer to the "chief priests" (e.g., Matt. 27:41, and elsewhere) as being active in affairs involving the Sanhedrin, and it is likely that this phrase refers to the established priestly and aristocratic families whose role in the Sanhedrin could be traced back for generations. These represented the Sadducean interests, of course, but its clear that, especially during New Testament times, other groups were represented on the Sanhedrin, as well: scribes, Pharisees, teachers of the law (these are not mutually exclusive groups) and others. There is some evidence, in fact, that in the period leading up to the destruction of Jerusalem in 70 AD, the Pharisees played a more dominant role in the Sanhedrin than did the Sadducees.

A building near the Temple Mount, the precise location of which is a matter of uncertainty, was the site of regular meetings of the Sanhedrin, at least during the Roman period. However, if Mark 14:53ff. may be used as evidence, extraordinary sessions could be held elsewhere, as, in this instance, at the palace of the high priest. The nature of the Sanhedrin's authority probably depended upon the nature of civil authority in general and upon the relationship between that authority (Hasmonean or Roman "king," Roman governor, or whomever else) and the Sanhedrin. As noted above, during the reign of Herod the Great the Sanhedrin's power appears to have been quite constricted, but after his death to have increased measurably. Certainly all matters of religious belief and conduct came under the jurisdiction of the Sanhedrin, as did a great many nonreligious matters, as well. In spite of the statement in John 18:31 in which the members of the Sanhedrin remind Pilate that "we are not permitted to put anyone to death," there is evidence that authority in some capital cases did reside in the Sanhedrin. The apostle Stephen, for example, is reported to have been excuted by the Sanhedrin with no involvement on the part of Roman authorities (Acts 6—7).

Chapter 5

QUMRAN

A. THE COMMUNITY AND ITS LIFE[1]

The discovery, shortly after the end of World War II, of the site of an ancient Jewish monastic community, together with much of its library, near the western shore of the Dead Sea caused a great deal of excitement on the part of both professional scholars and the general public. Although some of the more extravagant claims that were made at the time of the initial reports are now viewed more soberly, there is little doubt that the discovery of the Qumran[2] settlement and of the so-called Dead Sea Scrolls marked a major event in the study of Second Temple Judaism. The settlement and the nearby caves that contained the scrolls, located about a mile from the western shore of the Dead Sea and about ten miles south of Jericho, were discovered under circumstances that are now too familiar to bear repetition here. Suffice it to say that, once the remains of the ancient buildings had been thoroughly investigated and parts of the community's library had been carefully analyzed, it became apparent that Qumran had much to tell the world concerning at least two important subjects: the nature of Jewish life and belief during the period of the Second Temple, and the state of the text of the Hebrew scriptures and of related Jewish writings during the second and first centuries BC.

1. History of the Qumran Sect

Perhaps it is helpful to begin a discussion of Qumran not where the scholars were forced to begin their work—carefully analysing thousands of different bits of information and then attempting to form a coherent whole out of them—but by looking at the story of Qumran as the scholars have now been able to reconstruct it. Unfortunately, no one in the ancient world (to the best of our knowledge) ever wrote a history of the community. The author of 1 Maccabees, although relating events which may have led to the establishment of the settlement at Qumran, was either ignorant of the community's existence or, what is more likely, chose to ignore it. The most likely reference to Qumran from any ancient non-Jewish writer is the veiled comment of the Roman writer Pliny, quoted earlier, concerning the location of the "tribe of the Essenes."[3] Only Philo and Josephus, among ancient Jewish writers, made significant comments on the nature of the Essene sect, as noted in the previous chapter.[4] Therefore, in reconstructing a history of the community, one must piece together a number of references in the literature of Qumran and attempt to relate these to what is known of events in Palestine generally during the Hellenistic and Roman periods.[5]

There is no single, universally accepted account of the history of the Qumran sect. A key to uncovering that history, especially as it relates to the community's origins, lies in the identification of two figures repeatedly referred to in the community's writings, the Wicked Priest and the Teacher of Righteousness. The former has been variously identified as the Hasmonean leader Simon, his grandson Alexander Jannaeus, or Hyrcanus II, among other possibilities. In the sketch that follows, however, the Wicked Priest is understood to be the Hasmonean leader Jonathan, while (along with most other reconstructions) the Teacher of Righteousness is considered to be some otherwise unknown Jewish priest. Each theory of the sects's history has its strengths and weaknesses, but the following—occasionally referred to as the "Maccabean thesis"—is one which has much to commend it.[6]

It will be remembered that one of the groups that allied itself to Judas Maccabeus during the early days of the struggle against Seleucid tyranny was that of the Hasidim. These exceedingly devout Jews held certain principles in common with the Hasmoneans, primarily a fierce determination not to permit the Seleucid authorities to dictate to them in matters concerning the practice of their religion. But in other ways they were different and could, on occasion, demonstrate their independence. According to 1 Maccabees 2:29–38, initially they refused to fight on the Sabbath, even if attacked, but when that expression of their loyalty to the Torah produced fatal consequences, it was abandoned. Later, when the Seleucid general Bacchides pretended to permit the Jews to worship according to their own traditions, the Hasidim accepted this gesture by deserting the army of Judas (only to be murdered by Bacchides [1 Macc. 7:12–18]), while, for their part, the Hasmoneans vowed to fight on until political independence was achieved. Thus a certain tension was factored into Hasmonean-Hasidic relations from this time, one that later came to a head in the bitter hostilities between the Pharisees (who descended from the Hasidim) and successive Hasmonean rulers, primarily John Hyrcanus and Alexander Jannaeus.

But—according to the view favored here—another Hasidic group fell violently out with the Hasmoneans even before the rupture with the Pharisees. We cannot be certain of everything involved in this schism, but its flashpoint was likely the acceptance by Jonathan, the brother and successor of Judas Maccabeus, of the office of high priest (152 BC). It will be recalled that the office was offered to Jonathan by Alexander Balas, a pretender to the Seleucid throne, who, at that moment needed Jonathan's support in the fight against

Balas' rival, Demetrius II. Thus, it would have been offensive to many devout Jews that the office of high priest could be conferred by a pagan and that the individual who received the office was not even a member of the old Zadokite dynasty that had furnished the nation's high priests for generations. Beyond these circumstances, however, there were other causes for Hasidic disaffection, some of these having to do with aspects of worship, including the nature of the liturgical calendar, others having to do with apparent greed and corruption on the part of Hasmonean officials.

One of the Qumran documents, the Habakkuk *Pesher* or Commentary, in interpreting Habakkuk 2:5–6, lodges this protest against the Wicked Priest, presumably Jonathan:

> Interpreted, this concerns the Wicked Priest who was called by the name of truth when he first arose. But when he ruled over Israel his heart became proud, and he forsook God and betrayed the precepts for the sake of riches.[7]

Against what they viewed as combined greed and apostasy on the part of Jonathan, a group of Hasidim pursued an alternative vision of devotion to God under the leadership of an individual who is known in the Qumran literature as the Teacher of Righteousness (or, as the phrase may also be translated, the Righteous Teacher). Nothing is known of this Teacher beyond the very fragmentary information in the Qumran material, and efforts to identify him with some known contemporary of the high priest Jonathan have failed. In the view of the Qumran sectarians, however, the Teacher of Righteousness is the one chosen by God to lead the righteous remnant of Israel, a prophet on the model of Moses. In the words of the Qumran Damascus Rule:

> When they were unfaithful and forsook Him, God hid his face from Israel and His Sanctuary and delivered them up to the sword. But remembering the Covenant of the forefathers, He left a remnant to Israel and did not deliver it up to be destroyed. . . . And God observed their deeds, that they sought Him with a whole heart, and He raised for them a Teacher of Righteousness to guide them in the way of His heart.[8]

At some time after the installation of Jonathan as high priest, the sect disassociated itself from the Jerusalem establishment—so the theory goes—and moved to the barren shore of the Dead Sea where it took up permanent residence, a date of c. 150 BC being the approximate time. A settlement had existed on the spot some five centuries before, and the remains of the old buildings were restored and new ones added. In the years to come a complex of structures would be raised which, more than anything else, resembled a combined monastery and fortress. Ultimately there would be a large assembly and dining hall (measuring almost 75 × 15 feet) and a number of smaller rooms, including a laundry, a kitchen, a scriptorium (presumably where the scrolls were copied), and storerooms. Strong walls and a fortified tower were built to repel intruders, while an elaborate stone aqueduct drew water in the rainy season from a nearby waterfall into several cisterns for storage. A ritual bath was dug to be used for ceremonies of purification.

Although the sectarians were now physically removed from Jerusalem (some fifteen miles by crow flight), their controversy with Jonathan apparently continued, for there is an allusion in the Habakkuk Commentary to a visit by the high priest to Qumran. The text of the commentary is typical of much Qumran literature in that it refers to specific events in oblique and sometimes metaphorical language, the result being that it is impossible from this distance to know what happened. However, it would seem that Jonathan (or forces acting in his name) descended upon Qumran to taunt or perhaps to do physical harm to the Teacher of Righteousness:

> Interpreted, this concerns the Wicked Priest who pursued the Teacher of Righteousness to the house of his exile that he might confuse him with his venomous fury. And at the time appointed for rest, for the Day of Atonement, he appeared before them to confuse them, and to cause them to stumble on the Day of Fasting, their Sabbath of repose.[9]

The founder of the sect is portrayed in the Qumran literature as both priest and prophet. In the former capacity is he revered as the leader of the true Israel, and in the latter capacity as the ultimate interpreter of the Torah. His final fate is not disclosed by the scrolls. A number of the hymns or psalms in the Hymns Scroll (of which the Teacher or Righteousness may be the author) seem to speak of his suffering, yet the language is so much like the biblical Psalms of Lament that it is impossible to know if physical suffering is implied, much less whether it is suffering endured by the Teacher. The nearest the scrolls appear to come to a description of the death of the Teacher is contained in the final preserved words of the Commentary on Psalm 37, which interprets Psalm 37:22–23 in the following manner (brackets enclose material lost from the original document):

> Interpreted, this concerns the Wicked [Priest] who [rose up against the Teacher of Righteousness] that he might put him to death [because he served the truth] and the Law, [for which reason] he laid hands upon him. But God will not "abandon [him into his hand and will not let him be condemned when he is] tried." And [God] will pay him his reward by delivering him into the hand of the violent of the nations, that they may execute upon him [the judgments of wickedness].[10]

In connection with this last statement, it will be remembered that Jonathan was killed by the Seleucid general Trypho in 142 BC.

The members of the Qumran community in the generations after that of the Teacher of Righteousness continued to adhere to the founder's goal of the separation of the true remnant of Israel (themselves) from the apostate (the Hasmonean establishment in Jerusalem). There are few direct references to specific events or persons in the Qumran scrolls during these years, but one such allusion may be found in the Nahum Commentary. The Hasmonean king and high priest Alexander Jannaeus, it will be recalled, watched the crucifixion of 800 Pharisees in Jerusalem, while he banqueted. The Qumran sectarians apparently felt that such an outrage earned Alexander (the "furious young lion" in the text below) the wrath of God. (The phrase "those who seek smooth things" is an apparent reference to the Pharisees. The Qumran sectarians considered both Pharisees and Sadducees to be apostate, although they regarded the Hasmonean high priest as the greatest evil.)

> Interpreted, this concerns the furious young lion [who executes revenge] on those who seek smooth things and hangs men alive, [a thing never done] formerly in Israel. Because of a man hanged alive on [the] tree, He proclaims, "Behold, I am against [you, says the Lord of Hosts"].[11]

The Qumran sectarians apparently looked with some equanimity upon the capture of Jerusalem by Pompey in 63 BC. It was not, of course, that they loved the Romans, but they longed for the day when the Hasmonean high priesthood would be toppled, thus allowing them the opportunity to reestablish true worship in the Temple according to the teachings of the Teacher of Righteousness. The Habakkuk Commentary even cites Habakkuk 1:6 to prove that what is done by these foreigners is done in fulfillment of the will of God. (The "Chaldeans" [Babylonians] of the Hebrew text of Habakkuk have become the "Kittim" [Romans] in the Habakkuk Commentary, a word borrowed from Dan. 11:30.)

> *For behold, I rouse the Chaldeans, that [bitter and hasty] nation.*
>
> Interpreted, this concerns the Kittim [who are] quick and valiant in war, causing many to perish. [All the world shall fall] under the dominion of the Kittim, and the [wicked . . .] they shall not believe in the laws of [God].[12]

And yet if the members of the sect hoped for an early and triumphant return to Jerusalem they must have been disappointed, for the Hasmonean high priest, Hyrcanus II, was kept in office by the Romans, and the Temple rituals continued little changed. In their place in the desert, the members of the community were exhorted not to be discouraged and to await with patience the ultimate unfolding of the will of God. Again the Habakkuk Commentary on Habakkuk 2:1–3:

(On 2:1-2) And God told Habakkuk to write down that which would happen to the final generation, but He did not make known to him when time would come to an end.

(On 2:3a) Interpreted, this means that the final age shall be prolonged, and shall exceed all that the Prophets have said; for the mysteries of God are astounding.

(On 2:3b) Interpreted, this concerns the men of truth who keep the Law, whose hands shall not slacken in the service of truth when the final stage is prolonged. For all the ages of God reach their appointed end as He determines for them in the the mysteries of His wisdom.[13]

In 31 BC an earthquake did considerable damage to the buildings of the community, and it may be that about that time the site was abandoned. If so (and the matter is disputed), the members of the sect may have moved to Jerusalem where, as mentioned in the discussion on the Essenes, King Herod the Great would have been a friendly and anti-Hasmonean presence. But by early in the first century AD it is clear that the site had been reoccupied, assuming that it was abandoned in the first place, and it remained so until the great Jewish revolt which began in 66 AD. At that time it was destroyed by the Roman army and, presumably, its inhabitants along with it.[14] Just before that final destruction, the members of the community hid the contents of their library, presumably in the hope of recovering them upon their return, but in the caves of the surrounding limestone cliffs the scrolls would lie unattended for nearly 2,000 years.

2. Beliefs of the Community

Just as no contemporary attempted to write a history of the Qumran sect, no ancient writer has provided us with a systematic description of its beliefs. The effort to sketch the sect's theology, like that to provide its history, must be based on statements in the scrolls. Yet not only is the theology of the scrolls lacking a systematic structure ("systematic" theology is, for the most part, not a feature of ancient thought, including that of the Jews), it is frequently inconsistent or contradictory, reflecting the fact that the scrolls were produced by different writers over some two centuries. What follows is an effort to summarize the beliefs either stated or implied in the Qumran literature.

a. *Torah and Scripture.*   The Qumran sectarians held many beliefs in common with the larger world of early Judaism, including a commitment to the Torah as the supreme revelation of God's will. This is evident not only from the frequent references to the Law in the scrolls, but also from the physical remains of the library. Along with this emphasis upon the importance of the Torah, there is a view of Moses that considers him to be the chief of God's spokesmen upon earth. He is not only the Lawgiver, but is the Law's chief interpreter.

But Moses also stands at the head of a long tradition of prophets who have interpreted the Torah to the people. This tradition is contained in the prophetic books and reaches its climax in the Teacher of Righteousness, who is portrayed as a New Moses. We shall return to the Teacher of Righteousness in a moment, but it should be observed at this point that this acceptance of the prophets as interpreters of the Torah is a reminder that not only were the prophetic books of the Old Testament (Former and Latter Prophets) in use at Qumran, but that non-Torah literature that Jews (and Christians) were to include in the corpus of Writings in the Old Testament canon were known in the community, as well. In fact, every book in the Hebrew Bible (that is, in the Palestinian canon) is represented in the documentary discoveries at Qumran except the Book of Esther. The most numerous portions of text are from Psalms (27), followed by Deuteronomy (25).[15]

Moreover, it seems evident that literature that the mainstream Jewish community in Palestine would finally judge to be noncanonical was also in use at Qumran. The so-called apocryphal books of Sirach (Ecclesiasticus), Tobit, and the Letter of Jeremiah, all of which were included in the Greek Bible of the Alexandrian Jews, the Septuagint, but not in the final Palestinian canon, are represented among the Qumran scrolls. (One would not expect to find 1 or 2 Maccabees at Qumran, for they are quite pro-Hasmonean.) In addition, the presence of the Book of Jubilees and the Testament of Levi, which never gained canonical status among Jews generally, either in Palestine or the Diaspora, are not only represented among the Qumran manuscripts, but are referred to in the Damascus Rule as though they possessed the authority of scripture.[16]

What seems apparent from all of this is while the Qumran faithful would have been puzzled by the phrase "canon of scripture," a wide range of biblical, semibiblical, and nonbiblical writings were considered by them to be authoritative. Yet all literature was secondary to the Torah, the supreme written expression of God's will.

b. *Interpreting the Torah.*   As we have come to see, the manner in which the Torah was to be interpreted served as a catalytic element in the life of early Judaism, for upon this issue sectarian movements were born and flourished.

Thus it is no cause for surprise to learn that the Qumran sectarians were interested in this question, as well. As stated above, the supreme interpreter of the Torah was Moses, who was followed by a long line of prophets culminating in the Teacher of Righteousness. The Teacher of Righteousness was viewed not only as the finest interpreter of the Torah since Moses, but also (along with his followers) as the last in this noble prophetic line. In the highly apocalyptic thought of Qumran, God would soon bring an end to this present evil by establishing nothing less than the divine rule.

In the meantime, the Teacher of Righteousness gleaned from the Torah and from the previous prophetic interpretation of the Torah the message that God intended for the people. Frequently the prophet of old (Habakkuk, let us say, or Nahum) may not even have known the meaning of his own words; in any event, the interpretation of the Teacher of Righteousness was of even greater value than the prophetic words themselves. For it was the conviction of the Qumran sectarians that all prophecy was written with the present age in mind (*their* present age, of course), and that it was the special God-given ability of the Teacher of Righteousness to reveal that which had heretofore been secret. This ability to make clear the hidden secrets of God was handed on to the followers of the Teacher of Righetousness, those referred to in the scrolls as "the sons of Zadok, the priests who keep the Covenant."[17] And it was presumably they who, in the years following the Teacher's death, continued to contribute to the community's literature.

The form of instruction by the Teacher and his followers was often psalm-like, as in the Hymn Scroll, or of a narrative quality, as in the War Rule, or quasi-scriptural, as in the Genesis Apocryphon or (in a different manner) the Temple Scroll. But one of the most interesting (from a modern standpoint, at least) forms of scriptural interpretation was that of the so-called *pesher*, meaning *interpretation*. Although not unique to Qumran, the *pesher* is a type of running commentary on a biblical book that, in sequential fashion, quotes small portions of the biblical text (a phrase, or perhaps a sentence or two at a time) and then discloses the meaning of each quotation, a meaning that, as we have seen, may have been hidden until now. Then, having dealt with one bit of the text, the *pesher* then moves on to the next. In addition to the Habakkuk Commentary, there are (at least in fragmentary form) *pesherim* on Isaiah, Hosea, Micah, Nahum, and Psalm 37, examples from some of which have been quoted above. We shall presently look at other methods of commenting upon scripture practiced at Qumran.

c. *New Covenant and Holy War.*   Just as in the time of Moses, God had established a renewed covenant relationship with Israel, so now God had worked through the new Moses, the Teacher of Righteousness, to reestablish this covenant. But unlike the Mosaic covenant, which included all Israel, the New Covenant was extended only to those who responded to the Teacher's instruction and who rejected false teachers (the Jerusalem priestly "establishment," under the direction of the Hasmonean high priest). They, the "sons of light," were the true remnant of Israel, beloved by God. In the words of the Community Rule (also called the Manual of Discipline):

> He [the Master of the community] shall admit into the Covenant of Grace all those who have freely devoted themselves to the observance of God's precepts, that they may be joined to the counsel of God and may live prefectly before Him in accordance with all that has been revealed concerning their appointed times, and that they may love all the sons of light, each according to his lot in God's design, and hate all the sons of darkness, each according to his guilt in God's vengeance.[18]

The deep hostility that the Qumran covenant community exercised toward other Jews, referred to above, was a fundamental aspect of their self-understanding. Briefly put, they considered themselves the army of God in a Holy War against all forms of apostasy, a war in which God would actively intervene on the side of the "sons of light." The Holy War concept is, as noted earlier, found in certain parts of the Torah (e.g., Deut. 20), and is one that influences much of the community's thought. For one thing, good and evil are clearly defined and are mutually exclusive. Goodness consists in more than obedience to the Torah, as interpreted by the Teacher of Righteousness, although it is very much that. And for its part, evil is much more than disobedience. They are both cosmic forces ordained by God from the beginning. In fact, had it not been for the strong belief at Qumran in the majesty of God, one might sense in these words from the Community Rule a kind of moral and theological dualism:

> He [God] has created man to govern the world and has appointed for him two spirits in which to walk until the time of His visitation: the spirits of truth and falsehood . . . All the children of righteousness are ruled by the Prince of Light and walk in the ways of light; but all the children of falsehood are ruled by the Angel of Darkness and walk in the ways of darkness.[19]

Another aspect of the Holy War ideology is the sense of the role of the community which emerges from the Qumran writings. The sect itself is the gift of God, the means by which individuals avail themselves of God's truth and by which they live out their lives in obedient service. Unlike the older Mosaic covenant in which membership was a birthright, membership in the community of the New Covenant was the result of God's election of the individual, and in light of this, the initiate took an oath of obedience to the disipline of the community and to its teaching. In some of the sects of early Judaism there was often lively legal and theological debate, but the Qumran covenanters considered all matters to be settled, in that the tradition of interpretation associated with the Teacher of Righteousness (and supplemented by "the Sons of Zadok," about which more below) was unchangeable. Thus a strong sense of predestination pervaded the community's understanding of itself and its mission.

That mission was to bear witness to the truth revealed through the Teacher of Righteousness until the time when God would overthrow the apostate Jerusalem priesthood and all unrighteous gentiles (the "children of falsehood," "the children of darkness") and by means of the Qumran Elect ("the children of truth," "the children of light") reinstitute the divine rule. This aspect of the sect's Holy War ideology is seen best in the War Rule (also called The War of the Sons of Light Against the Sons of Darkness). This document describes in great detail the military aspects of the final eschatological battle, yet it should not be mistaken for a military document. It is, pure and simple, a theological statement that proclaims the victory of God over the forces of evil and that, until that day comes, calls upon the faithful to be courageous and obedient.

> Be strong and valiant; be warriors! Fear not! Do not be [confused and do not let your hearts be afraid!] Do not be fearful; fear them not! Do not fall back . . . for they are a congregation of wickedness and all their works are in Darkness; they tend toward Darkness. [They make for themselves] a refuge [in falsehood] and their power shall vanish like smoke. All the multitudes of their community . . . shall not be found. Damned as they are, all the substance of their wickedness shall quickly fade, like a flower in [the summertime].[20]

d. *Eschatology and Messianism.*   It is in the context of its strong eschatological hope that the sect's belief in a messiah, or more accurately messiahs, is to be found. The Damascus Rule[21] declares that after the death of the Teacher of Righteousness there will be a period of forty years, the "age of the wrath of God," in which the Elect community, led by "the Prince of Light" (also designated as Michael or Melchizedek), would be caught up in conflict with the forces of Satan. Whether the figure of forty years is meant literally or, as it frequently is in the Old Testament, symbolically, is uncertain. In any event, during these "last days," there are to be many who will join the ranks of the Elect, that is, the Qumran sect, if our understanding of the Messianic Rule (also called the Rule of the Congregation) is correct. Then the power of God will bring final victory to the Elect over all their (and God's) enemies.[22] Such seems to be the community's understanding of the "last days," although any reconstruction is difficult in view of the fragmentary nature of the discussion of this topic in the surviving Qumran literature.

(1) The community's messianic hope is outlined in no more systematic fashion than is its eschatological expectation. But there seems, first, to have been a priestly messiah, referred to variously as the "Messiah of Aaron," the "Priest," and the "Interpreter of the Law." For a community that placed strong emphasis upon the right interpretation of the Law and upon right worship (as we shall see below), it is not surprising that the most prominent messianic figure should be priestly (Aaronic) rather than royal (Davidic). The priestly messiah was to be the final Interpreter of the Law in the last days and would preside at the worship before the final battle. He would also serve as host at the eschatological banquet.

[This shall be the ass]embly of the men of renown [called] to the meeting of the Council of the Community when [the Priest-]Messiah shall summon them.

And [when] they shall gather for the common [tab]le, to eat and [to drink] new wine, when the common table shall be set for eating and the new wine, [poured] for drinking, let no man extend his hand over the first-fruits of bread and wine, before the Priest; for [it is he] who shall bless the first-fruits of bread and wine, and shall be the first to extend his hand over the bread.[23]

(2) A second messianic figure is royal and lay. He is called the "Branch of David," the "Messiah of Israel," the "Prince of the Congregation," and the "Scepter," and he is clearly subordinate to the priestly messiah and to the interpretation of the Law issued by the Qumran priests. One of the two fragmentary Isaiah Commentaries states, "as they [that is, the priests] teach him, so shall he judge."[24] The role of the royal messiah thus seems primarily judical and military, as is evident from one of the blessings recited by the master of the community:

The Master shall bless the Prince of the Congregation . . . and shall renew for Him the Covenant of the Community that he may establish the kingdom of His people for ever, [that he may judge the poor with righteousness and] dispense justice with [equity to the oppressed] of the land, and that he may walk perfectly before Him in all the ways [of truth], and that he may establish His holy Covenant at the the time of the affliction of those who seek God.

May you smite the peoples with the might of your hand and ravage the earth with your scepter; that you may bring death to the ungodly with the breath of your lips.[25]

(3) The possibility of a third messianic figure is raised in the Community Rule. He is the prophet who was to accompany the two messiahs in the last days, undoubtedly an allusion to God's promise to Israel, mediated through Moses, to "raise up for you a prophet like me from among your own people" (Deut. 18:15) and to the concluding words of the Book of Malachi concerning the return of the prophet Elijah (Mal. 4:5–6). His appearing is to be one of the signs of the end:

> [The Elect] shall be ruled by the primitive precepts in which the men of the Community were first instructed until there shall come the Prophet and the Messiahs of Aaron and Israel.[26]

It is quite possible that the prophet was identified with the Teacher of Righteousness, and that his leadership of the sect was interpreted as one of the signs of the "last days."

(4) A document composed of thirteen fragments and dealing with the figure of Melchizedek throws interesting light upon what may be an additional messiah-like individual who will act as God's judge at the end of time. Whether this is a fourth messiah or a different manner of describing the priestly messiah is unclear. In any event, it is he who will decree redemption for the faithful and who will consign Satan and his hosts to destruction:

> For this is the moment of the year of grace for Melchizedek. [And h]e will, by his strength, judge the holy ones of God, executing judgment as it is written concerning him in the Songs of David . . . And Melchizedek will avenge the vengeance of the judgments of God . . . and he will drag [them from the hand of] Satan and from the hand of all the sp[irits of] his [lot].[27]

As to the nature of the messianic kingdom, that is, the rule of God, the scrolls give little detail, except that it would certainly be characterized by faithfulness on the part of the Elect and by the reinstitution of true worship in the Temple. There is little mention of a future life in the scrolls, and it is not even clear whether Qumran beliefs in this regard could be characterized as a hope in the resurrection of the body or in the immortality of the soul. The reason for this lack of clarity seems to lie in the fact that the interest of the Qumran covenanters was not in their own well-being, but in the importance of faithfulness to the commands of a loving and almighty God. Thus the scrolls frequently describe the weakness and mortality of human flesh and the joy of the faithful over God's gracious act of electing them into the New Covenant. The final words of the Community Rule:

For without Thee no way is perfect,
  and without Thy will nothing is done.
It is Thou who has taught all knowledge
  and all things come to pass by Thy will.
There is none beside Thee to dispute Thy counsel
  or to understand all Thy holy design
or to contemplate the depth of Thy mysteries
  and the power of Thy might.

Who can endure Thy glory,
  and what is the son of man
  in the midst of Thy wonderful deeds?
What shall one born of woman
  be accounted before Thee?
Kneaded from the dust,
  his abode is the nourishment of worms.
He is but a shape, but molded clay,
  and inclines towards the dust.[28]

3. *Life at Qumran*[29]

The severity of the obligations that the Qumran covenanters took upon themselves is evident in almost every aspect of their common life. The scrolls portray the main features of that life, and on the basis of the information that they provide it is possible to sketch the nature of the sect's discipline and routine. As with any organizaton which exists for two centuries, the Qumran community probably witnessed modifications to its order over the years, but of the nature of these we are largely ignorant. Also, it appears that some aspects of the sect's life were more theoretical than actual, the imposition of the death penalty for certain offenses (at least among "town" sectarians) being one example. For all that, however, it is possible to establish some general portrait of the nature of life within the sect.

Membership in the Qumran community may have been been limited to males. That is certainly the impression frequently given by the scrolls, although the presence of a few female skeletons in the cemetary casts some doubt on that view. In any event, the postulant was forced to undergo an extended period of probation before being admitted to full membership in the sect. He first presented himself to the master or guardian (about whom more, below) who, if he was satisfied with the postulant's intentions, required from him an oath that he would

  return with all his heart and soul to every commandment of the Law of
  Moses in accordance with all that has been revealed of it to the sons of
  Zadok, the Keepers of the Covenant.[30]

A period of instruction followed that, if it was completed successfully, resulted in the postulant's acceptance into the community. That is to say, he was now a provisional member, although a continued novitiate was necessary before the postulant was admitted to "purity."

During this second stage of his novitiate, which lasted a year, the candidate underwent more instruction, followed by another examination. If he successfully stood this test, he surrendered his possessions (which, however, were not yet added to the property of the community) and he was admitted to partial purity in that he could now participate in the common meals of the sect, although he did not yet have access to the "drink of the Congregation."

In the final and third year there was more instruction and more examination. When this was mastered, the novice was admitted to full membership in the community. His possessions were absorbed into those of the sect, he participated fully in the common meals, and he was allowed the right to speak in the council of the community.

During his three-year apprenticeship, with its rigorous cycles of study and examination, the new member had discovered, among other things, the hierarchy according to which the community was organized. Of highest importance were the priests, referred to in the literature as the "Sons of Zadok." They were the direct spiritual heirs of the Teacher of Righteousness, and in them was vested the authority to make a number of decisions of the most wide-ranging nature, from the manner in which the Torah should be interpreted to the utilization of the community's property. As they were considered to be the true priests of Israel (the Jerusalem priesthood being apostate), they presided over the community's worship and study. No meeting of ten or more persons for purposes of Torah study or prayer was permissible without the presence of a priest.

The master or guardian was one of these Sons of Zadok. His task was primarily that of teacher and spiritual mentor to the entire community. It was he who taught the postulants, instructed the members, presided over meetings of the council and assessed the spiritual condition of the men of the order.

The council of the community was the deliberative assembly of the sect. It is unclear whether it was composed of all the members of the community or only certain representatives. When it met, its members were seated according to their rank: priests first, elders second, "and all the rest of the people according to their rank."[31] Perhaps the council's most time-consuming responsibility was judicial, for it was they who tried cases involving various offenses against the community. These might include, at one extreme, one who "murmers against the authority of the Community," or one who "deliberately or through negligence transgresses one Word of the Law of Moses," or one who speaks the name of God (Yahweh) "even while reading the Book [Torah] or praying." All of these offenses were punishable by permanent expulsion from the community. At the other extreme are offenses such as: deception of another (six-months penance), guffawing foolishly (thirty days), and interruption of another while speaking (ten days).

There is some evidence that, in addition to the hierarchy outlined above, there was another that, in a particular manner, reflected the sect's belief that it was the true Israel. According to this, the lay members of the group were divided into twelve tribes, after the Hebrew model, each of which was headed by one of the Sons of Zadok, collectively called the "twelve chief priests," who in turn were subordinate to a high priest, probably the same as the master or guardian. In addition to the tribal divisions, the laity were further divided into bodies of thousands, hundreds, fifties, and tens. As the total population at Qumran at any one time probably did not exceed 200, it is clear that this hierarchal arrangement was more theoretical than actual. Yet there may have been some effort to reproduce these ranks—symbolically, at least—during times of worship. The War Rule states

> They shall rank the chief Priests below the High Priest and his vicar. And the twelve chief priests shall minister at the daily sacrifice before God . . .[32]

Worship was a central aspect of the life of the sectarians, and in addition to daily sacrifices, there were daily prayers at sunrise and at sunset. As practiced at Qumran, worship was believed to be an earthly copy of the ritual of the angels in the heavenly temple and, as such, would replace the apostate liturgy of the Jerusalem Temple after the establishment of the rule of God. One of the essential differences between the Qumran liturgy and that of Jerusalem was the calendar. For the Jerusalem establishment the calendar was lunar, that is, it was based on phases of the moon, or to be more exact, the occurrences of the new moon. The result was a year of twelve months (each of 29 or 30 days), which totaled 354 days. (An extra month was inserted every three years to keep this calendar in sequence with the seasons.)

At Qumran, however, the calendar was solar, that is, it was based on the progression of the equinoxes. Yet rather than a true solar calendar of 365¼ days, the Qumran sectarians settled upon a year of 364 days, a period of time that could conveniently be divided up into exactly 52 seven-day weeks. The community must sooner or later have had to reckon with the discrepancy between their calendar and the true solar calendar, but there is no reference to this in the literature. The result of this difference in liturgical calendars was that the festivals of Judaism were observed at different times in Jerusalem (and other places where Jews lived) and at Qumran.[33] A feature of the Qumran calendar was that it allowed all annual festivals to fall on the same day of the week.

The most important festival for the sectarians seems to have been the Festival of the Renewal of the Covenant, celebrated on the fifteenth day of the third month (which was always a Sunday), the only Qumran ritual described in detail in the scrolls. It was one which placed emphasis on confession of the community's sins, and included a liturgy for the blessing of the community and one for the cursing of its enemies, especially anyone who would seek membership in the community out of unworthy motives. In addition, it is also apparent that the usual festivals of Judaism were also observed: Passover, Weeks, Booths, the Day of Atonement, and the like. Circumcision is generally taken for granted in the scrolls.

Communal meals were also of importance to the community, participation in them being, as we have seen, a sign of a person's membership. They were probably accompanied by ritual bathing and, in the mind of the sect, may have constituted a prefigurement of the coming eschatological banquet to be attended by the messiahs of Aaron and Israel.

From the Damascus Rule and the Messianic Rule it is clear that other members of the sect lived not at Qumran, but in ordinary towns and villages. To the extent possible in their nonmonastic environment, these members of the sect were bound to the same strict rules of Torah observance and obedience of the rules of the community. Yet they were married, rather than celebate, and they engaged in normal activities of agriculture, commerce, child-rearing, and the like. Some offenses which merited expulsion from Qumran carried the death penalty for the town sectarians, yet it is almost inconceivable that capital punishment could ever have been carried out since that was the prerogative of the civil authorities (and, under certain circumstances, of the Sanhedrin). It seems almost certain that the town sectarians looked upon Qumran as their spiritual center and it is probable that, from time to time, they traveled there for participation in the community's rites. The occasional presence of these pilgrims at Qumran may explain the few female skeletons in the cemetary of the Qumran monastery.

4. Qumran and the Essenes

In the discussion of the Essenes reference was made to the belief by many scholars that the Qumran sect was a community of Essenes. There is some speculation, in fact, that Qumran may have been the chief Essene community, the town sectarians forming satellite groups. The arguments for and against this identification may be summarized in the following manner:[34]

In support of the identification:

1. Pliny's statement placed the settlement of the "solitary tribe of the Essenes" on the "west side of the Dead Sea," and south of Jericho, but north of Engedi and Masada.

2. The archaeological evidence from Qumran coincides with Josephus' observations to the effect that the Essenes flourished between the time of the Hasmonean leader Jonathan and the Jewish revolt of 66–74 AD.

3. The beliefs and practices of the Qumran sectarians, as described in the scrolls, is remarkably similar to those of the Essenes, as gleaned from statements in Philo and Josephus.

The primary argument against the identification is that there are differences in detail between the scrolls' description of the Qumran covenanters and other ancient writers' descriptions of the Essenes. For example, Philo and Josephus make no mention of a major Essene community near the Dead Sea. Another example: Philo and Josephus write as if the common ownership of property was a normal feature of Essene life, whereas the town sectarians seem not to have followed the example of the Qumran community on this point. Still another example, Philo and Josephus seem to be ignorant of the role of the Teacher of Righteousness, a figure who looms large in the scrolls.

In summary, many scholars strongly argue that the differences in detail between the scrolls' portrait of the Qumran sectarians and that of the Essenes that emerges from Philo and Josephus may be attributed to several factors.

1. Philo and Josephus lived late in the period during which Qumran flourished and, as they were not members of the sect, may not have known of certain aspects of life and thought at Qumran, especially those that related to an earlier part of the Qumran period.

2. Because they were not sectarians themselves, Philo and Josephus may have been ignorant of some aspects of Essene/Qumran belief, since, to some extent, these beliefs were revealed only to those on the inside of these esoteric groups.

3. Philo and Josephus wrote for a largely gentile readership, whereas the scrolls were written for use by the sectarians themselves. Thus apparent differences in descriptions may be nothing more than different words and concepts being used to describe the same things.

On balance then, there are strong reasons for identifying the Qumran sectarians, both those of the Dead Sea community as well as those of the towns, with the Essenes.

5. *Qumran and the Old Testament*[35]

As stated previously, Hebrew texts loom large in the collection of scrolls in use at Qumran. These are basically of three types:

1. Copies of Hebrew texts. As noticed earlier, there is at least a fragment (in some cases much more) of every book in the Palestinian Jewish canon with the exception of Esther. These are usually in the form of straight-forward textual transcriptions in Hebrew, but there is one interesting Targum (Aramaic paraphrase) of the Book of Job.

2. Rewritings of biblical texts. It was not uncommon within early Judaism to embellish the biblical narrative with fanciful and legendary tales concerning important events and characters. Examples of this genre from Qumran include the Genesis Apocryphon, which contains elaborations upon the stories of the early patriarchs, Jubilees (also known in Ethiopic, Latin, and Greek translations before the Qumran discoveries) which retells events between creation and the giving of the Law, and the Words of Moses, which amplifies Moses' final words to the children of Israel as reported in Deuteronomy.

3. Commentaries on Old Testament books, as discussed earlier.

The significance of this material for the study of the Old Testament text is that it has provided us with copies of texts that, for the most part, are some 1,000 years older than anything previously known. In large measure, the Old Testament text in use at Qumran is remarkably similar to the Masoretic textual tradition in use by Jews in Europe and the West since at least the Middle Ages. But in places the Qumran scribes reveal their knowledge of other textual traditions also. For example, of three manuscripts of the Book of Jeremiah two follow the Masoretic tradition, but one seems dependent upon the shorter version of Jeremiah represented in the Septuagint. Fragments from Samuel, as another example, sometimes agree with the text of the Septuagint when that translation disagrees with the Masoretic Text. On occasion, an individual Qumran scribe will give evidence that he knows both Masoretic and Septuagint textual traditions, as when the Habakkuk Commentary interprets Habakkuk 2:16. In quoting the Hebrew text, the commentator agrees with the Septuagint: "Drink and stagger," but in interpreting that text, the commentator follows the Masoretic tradition, "Drink and show your foreskin," when he remarks that the Wicked Priest "did not circumcise the foreskin of his heart."[36] (Notice that the NRSV and some other modern translations follow the Septuagint tradition here, as it appears to make better sense.)

Textual traditions other than the Masoretic and Septuagintal are present in the scrolls. One fragment from the Book of Numbers provides readings that are nearer those of the Samaritan Pentateuch than to either the Masoretic or Septuagint traditions (e.g., Num. 27:13 is expanded by words borrowed from Deut. 3:21). Moreover, certain fragments of Samuel provide readings that are nearer Masoretic Chronicles than they are to Masoretic Samuel.

The picture of the Old Testament that emerges from Qumran is not only that of a canon that is unlike either the Palestinian (Masoretic) or Greek

(Septuagint) canons, but also of a variety of textual traditions in use side by side. In other words, the Qumran scrolls come from a time when neither the canonical form nor the content of the text (at least in all of its details) had been standardized.

6. Qumran and the Early Christian Movement

Almost from the time of the discovery of the Dead Sea Scrolls there has been speculation concerning a possible link between the Qumran covenanters and the early Christians. Some of the first pronouncements on the subject were more hastily than thoughtfully conceived, but with the passage of time a more mature assessment has become possible, one in which a number of fine scholars has participated. Yet nothing like unanimity of opinion prevails, and very many questions remain open. This brief discussion will do no more than outline some aspects of the debate, and the student who wishes to know more will consult the bibliography.

One striking association between the literature of Qumran and the New Testament is in the realm of vocabulary and imagery. Examples: (1) the "New Covenant" in which the sectarians considered themselves to be living is a phrase virtually identical to that which the early Christians used to refer to their own covenantal relationship with God and which becomes the name of the Christian scriptures, the "New Testament." (2) The words *light* and *darkness* are prominent in the Qumran literature as metaphors for good and evil, the same being true in the New Testament, especially in the Johannine literature. (The word *truth* is also prominent in both bodies of literature.) (3) In both the scrolls and the New Testament there is a great deal of apocalyptic imagery, some of which is remarkably similar, that is, the establishment of the Rule of God will feature an eschatological banquet presided over by the messiah or messiahs. Also, the messianic figure of Melchizedek may have influenced the New Testament Book of Hebrews (see esp. Heb. 6–7).

Another group of associations has to do with beliefs: (1) For both the Qumran sectarians and at least some (but not all) early Christians, the role of the Torah was of great importance. Both the sectarians and early Christians were at odds, separately, with Sadducees and Pharaisees over Torah interpretation, yet sectarians and Christians alike were convinced that in the teachings of their Master (the Teacher of Righteousness and Jesus) the Torah had been not abrogated, but fulfilled (Matt. 5:17). (2) Both the scrolls and the New Testament reflect a view of Hebrew prophecy that considers that prophetic statements were made with the events of the writers' days in mind. In this regard, there is a certain similarity between the exegetical method of, let us say, the Habakkuk Commentary, on the one hand, and the Gospel of Matthew and the Epistle to the Hebrews, on the other. (3) Both sectarians and Christians considered themselves to be the true Israel and, in quite diffferent ways, repudiated the sacrifical cult of the Jerusalem priesthood.

A final group of associations has to do with practices: (1) For both groups admission was not by birth, but was the result of a conscious commitment to a new way of life. (2) The use of water was important to the rites of both groups (at Qumran: ritual baths; for Christians, baptism). (3) The communal meal at Qumran and the eucharistic feast in the early church were both weighty in theological significance and were open only to members of the group. (4) The sharing of property was a feature of both groups (Acts 5:1–11).

This list of similarities between the Qumran sect and the early Christians could be extended, but it is probably sufficient to illustrate the point that, at least on a superficial level, the two groups held certain characteristics in common and that these were often features uncharacteristic of mainstream Judaism. Yet anyone who has followed this discussion concerning the nature of the Qumran sect and who is also familiar with the New Testament will quickly recognize that, for all their similarities, the differences between the groups were profound. To name but one example: Although both the Teacher of Righteousness and Jesus are looked upon by their followers as the ultimate interpreters of the Torah and as the persecuted founders of the New Israel, the scrolls—unlike the New Testament—make no claim that the Teacher of Righteousness is identical with the priestly or royal messiah, and there is no emphasis upon the messiah's death, to say nothing of resurrection or of a Second Coming.

In short, while there are fascinating parallels between the beliefs and practices of the Qumran sectarians and those of the early Christians, parallels which will engage the attentions of students for years to come, direct influences by Qumran upon the early church are yet to be proven. For the student of the New Testament, the main value of the Qumran material is that it provides another and richly documented example of the variety and diversity present in early Judaism.

B. THE LITERATURE OF QUMRAN

When investigators searched the caves in the vicinity of the Qumran settlement they discovered hundreds of documents, many of which were mere fragments, but some of which were complete scrolls. This material was, as has been noted, representative of a wide range of literary types including transcriptions of biblical books, biblical commentaries, apocryphal and pseudepigraphical writings, and compositions that dealt with the beliefs and discipline of the sect. This discussion of Qumran concludes with a brief survey of the more important documents.[37]

(For ease of identification scholars have assigned to each document a shorthand designation, which is indicated in parentheses. The number designates the cave in which the document was found. Q indicates that is from Qumran. Then there is usually an abbreviated form of the document's name. Thus 1QS identifies the Community Rule as coming from Cave 1, S being from the Hebrew title *Serekh ha-Yahad*.)

1. *The Community Rule (1QS), also known as the Manual of Discipline*

Several specimens of this document were recovered from the caves, including one nearly complete scroll. It appears to be one of the earliest of the sect's writings, having been composed sometime between 150 and 100 BC. It resembles nothing in the literary history of Judaism before this time and may therefore be considered to be perhaps the first representative of a type of sectarian or ecclesiastical order which, at a later time, is found in the Didache and other documents of the early church. It is quite possible that the Community Rule, or at least parts of it, is the work of the Teacher of Righteousness.

a. *Introduction*.   The Community Rule begins with a lengthy introduction that describes the standards for entrance into the community and enunciates the sect's views concerning the nature of good and evil:

[The Master shall teach the sai]nts to live [according to] the Book of the Community Rule, that they may seek God with a whole heart and soul, and do what is good and right before Him as He commanded by the hand of Moses and all His servants the Prophets.   (Col. I)

He shall admit into the Covenant of Grace all those who have freely devoted themselves to the observance of God's precepts . . . that they may love all the sons of light, each according to his lot in God's design, and hate all the sons of darkness, each according to his guilt in God's vengeance.   (Col. I)

He has created man to govern the world, and has appointed for him two spirits in which to walk until the time of His visitation: the spirits of truth and falsehood . . . All the children of righteousness are ruled by the Prince of Light and walk in the ways of light, but all the children of falsehood are ruled by the Angel of Darkness and walk in the ways of darkness.   (Col. III)

But in the mysteries of His understanding, and in His glorious wisdom, God has ordained an end for falsehood, and at the time of the visitation He will destroy it forever.   (Col. IV)[38]

b. *Rules of the Order.*   The heart of the Community Rule spells out the regulations concerning the life of the sect. First, the hierarchical nature of the community is emphasized, with special attention drawn to the the priestly office of the community's leaders, but with prominence also given to the virtues by which the members are to live.

> They shall separate from the congregation of the men of falsehood and shall unite, with respect to the Law and possessions, under the authority of the sons of Zadok, the Priests who keep the Covenant, and of the multitude of the men of the Community who hold fast to the Covenant. Every decision concerning doctrine, property, and justice shall be determined by them.

> They shall practise truth and humility in common, and justice and uprightness and charity and modesty in all their ways. No man shall walk in the stubbornness of his heart so that he strays after his heart and eyes and evil inclination, but he shall circumcise in the Community the foreskin of evil inclination and of stiffness of neck that they may lay a foundation of truth for Israel, for a community of the everlasting Covenant.   (Col. V)[39]

Next, the Community Rule enumerates the regulations that the members of the community are to observe, together with penalties for their violation, items discussed earlier.

c. *Regulations for the Master.*   A brief section contains special regulations concerning the manner in which the Master's responsibilities are to be carried out.

> He shall do the will of God according to all that has been revealed from age to age.
> He shall measure out all knowledge discovered throughout the ages, together with the precept of the age.
> He shall separate and weigh the sons of righteousness according to their spirit.
>   *   *   *   *
> He shall judge every man according to his spirit. He shall admit him in accordance with the cleanness of his hands and advance him in accordrance with his understanding. And he shall love and hate likewise.
>   *   *   *   *
> He shall conceal the teaching of the Law from men of falsehood, but shall impart true knowledge and righteous judgment to those who have chosen the Way . . .
> Everlasting hatred in a spirit of secrecy for the men of perdition.
> (Col. IX)[40]

d. *A Hymn.* The final section contains a lengthy hymn similar to some of the material in the Hymn Scroll. Here someone, presumably the master, speaks in the first person, praising God and describing his commitment to the godly life. There are very beautiful passages in the hymn, such as the following, which alludes to the periods of morning and evening prayer at Qumran:

> I will sing with knowledge and all my music shall be for the glory of
>   God.
> [My] lyre [and] my harp shall sound
>   for his holy order
> and I will tune the pipe of my lips
>   to His right measure.
> With the coming of day and night
>   I will enter the covenant of God,
> and when evening and morning depart
>   I will recite his decrees.
> I will place in them my bounds without return.   (Col. X)[41]

2. *The Temple Scroll*[42] *(11Q Temple)*

The most recent of the major scrolls from Qumran to be published, the Temple Scroll, exists in a single, considerably damaged copy (plus detached fragments) that came to light in the 1960s. It is also the longest of the scrolls, in that it measures twenty-seven feet in its existing condition, in other words some five feet longer than the great Isaiah Scroll (1QIs^a). Although the manuscript that has survived to the present was probably copied during Herodian times, the document itself apparently dates from the middle decades of the second century BC, and may be the work of the Teacher of Righteousness, in view of the importance of its contents and the place it is likely to have held in the esteem of the community.

The Temple Scroll dwells upon a number of subjects, of which the most important is the temple itself (hence the name of the document). Elaborate details are provided for the plans of the temple to be built by the children of Israel. Drawing upon biblical descriptions of the tabernacle in the wilderness and of Solomon's Temple, upon Ezekiel's vision of the eschatological Temple (Ezek. 40–48), and perhaps upon traditional reminiscences of the nature of Solomon's Temple,[43] the author of the Temple Scroll nevertheless portrays a sanctuary and its complexes not altogether like any of his models. For example, the temple is to be surrounded by a ditch 150 feet in width (100 cubits) in order that it not be approached in haste or by accident.

Also prominent in the Temple Scroll are the prescriptions for sacrificial worship in the temple, the festivals to be celebrated there, and the statutes relating to the duties of the king. In presenting these matters, the Temple

Scroll relies heavily upon the Priestly stratum of the Pentateuch, as well as upon the Book of Deuteronomy. Yet the material is often conflated or reshaped to reflect the special concerns of the Qumran community. For example, pentateuchal passages in which God is referred to in the third person are often rewritten in the first person (e.g., "and I said . . ."), thus having the effect of increasing the document's inspired authority.

The scholar primarily responsible for the publication of the Temple Scroll, the late Yigael Yadin, concluded that the scroll played so prominent a place in the life of the Qumran community that it was considered part of the Torah itself.

(1) The first section of the Temple Scroll (Cols. II–XII), after relating God's words to Moses concerning the divine covenant with Israel (reproduced from Exod. 34:10–16) and the command to build the temple, provides details of the temple edifice. The author of the scroll apparently considered his document to contain that information concerning Solomon's Temple referred to in 1 Chronicles 28:19 (a passage without parallel in the Old Testament), which states that "all this, in writing at the LORD's direction, he made clear to me [David]—the plan of all the works."

The temple in view here is not the eschatological temple that, according to Jubilees 1:15–29, is to be built by God at the time of the new creation. Rather, this is the earthly temple that will foreshadow the eschatological temple, as is made clear near the end of the scroll:

> And I will consecrate my [t]emple by my glory, (the
>   temple) on which I settle
> my glory, until the day of blessing on which I will
>   create my temple
> and establish it for myself at all times, according
>   to the covenant which I have made with Jacob at
> Bethel.   (XXIX, 8–10)[44]

(2) The second section (Cols. XIII–XXIX) details commandments relating to the nature of sacrifices to be offered on the Sabbath and on other special occasions, such as Unleavened Bread, Weeks (Pentecost), and the like. Of interest here is the introduction of festivals unknown to the Old Testament: the New Barley Festival, the New Wine Festival, the New Oil Festival, and the Wood Offering Festival.

(3) The third section (Cols. XXX–XLVI) returns the attention of the reader to the temple complex in that it describes the courts and their construction. The section concludes with a discussion of steps to be taken to insure that persons who are ritually unclean do not violate the temple or its courts.

(4) The fourth section (Cols. XLVII–LV) continues the theme of ritual cleanliness by identifying those things that render a person unclean, such as a

nocturnal emission, leprosy, contact with the dead, and so forth. Instructions are given for making sure that such persons do not defile the temple or its courts. Of great interest in this section is the feature that, unlike the Jerusalem priesthood, the Temple Scroll considers the entire city of Jerusalem and not just the temple complex to be subject to the laws of ritual cleanliness. In addition, no distinction is made in respect to matters of ritual cleanliness between the priests and the population as a whole.

(5) The fifth section (Cols. LVI–LIX) relates the duties of the king. In a manner similar to that employed in the reference to the plans for the temple referred to in 1 Chronicles 28:19, the author of the scroll apparently felt that he was providing here a document mentioned in 1 Samuel 10:25: "Samuel told the people the rights and duties of the kingship; and he wrote them in a book and laid it up before the LORD." The statutes of the king in the Temple Scroll are also written with an eye upon Deuteronomy 17:14–20, which is reproduced with subtle but significant changes. For example, Deuteronomy 17:18, which explains how the king

shall have a copy of this law written for him in the presence of the levitical priests.

is altered to read:

they shall write for him this law in a book from that which is in charge of the priests.   (LVI, 20–21)[45]

The significance of this emendation appears to be that it reveals a view among the Qumran sectarians that the king was to be guided not by a copy of the original Torah, but that an additional law (including, presumably, the words of the Temple Scroll itself) exists alongside the "canonical" Torah.

(6) A final section (Cols. LX–LXVII) of miscellaneous texts concludes the Temple Scroll.

3. *The Damascus Rule (CD), also known as the Zadokite Document*

In 1896–97 two medieval copies of the same document were discovered in the geniza (storeroom) of an old synagogue in Cairo. They were published in 1910 by S. Schechter under the title *Fragments of a Zadokite Work*,[46] and their contents aroused speculation that they were somehow connected with the Essenes of early Judaism. When a number of fragments of this same work came to light at Qumran, the relationship between the document and the Qumran sect was made evident. The title Damascus Rule stems from references in the work to a time of exile in Damascus, but whether that is meant literally or figuratively is unclear. The alternative title, Zadokite Document, reflects the importance placed upon the work of the priests. The document may have been composed about 100 BC.

There are two main sections, a series of exhortations and a list of the legal statutes by which the life in the community is to be conducted.

a. The Exhortation. This section is essentially a retelling of the history of Israel, with emphasis placed upon the manner in which God has always rewarded the faithful and punished the unfaithful. It is in the context of this historical survey that important statements are made concerning the origins of the Qumran sect, as we have earlier discussed. Parts of this section form a running commentary upon selected biblical texts, of which the following is an interesting example (the biblical texts are in italics, chapter and verse references have of course been added by the modern editor):

> And all those who despise the commandments and the statutes shall be rewarded with the retribution of the wicked when God shall visit the Land, when the saying shall come to pass which is written among the words of the prophet Isaiah son of Amoz: *He will bring upon you, and upon your people, and upon your father's house, days such have not come since the day that Ephraim departed from Judah* (Is. 7:17). When the two houses of Israel were divided, Ephraim departed from Judah. And all the apostates were given up to the sword, but those who held fast escaped to the land of the north; as God said, *I will exile the tabernacle of your king and the bases of your statutes from my tent to Damascus* (Amos 5:26).   (Page VII)[47]

With respect to the interpretation of the text from Amos 5, it is interesting that the Damascus Rule transforms a statement, which in its Old Testament context is a promise of judgment, into one of salvation. Students of the New Testament may wish to compare the similar manner in which Matthew 1:23 transforms Isaiah 7:14.

b. The Statutes. The concluding section contains regulations for community life. These are somewhat different from those in the Community Rule in that they are apodictic in nature and specify no penalties. Also, many of them are a classical type of halakhah in that they attempt to relate specific biblical texts to the life of the sect, such as the regulations below concerning the Sabbath. But perhaps the biggest difference is that the statutes of the Damascus Rule, unlike those of the Community Rule, are concerned with the town sectarians.

> No man shall work on the sixth day from the moment when the sun's orb is distant by its own fulness from the gate (wherein it sinks); for this

is what He said, *Observe the Sabbath day to keep it holy* (Deut. 5:12). No man shall speak any vain or idle word on the Sabbath day. He shall make no loan to his companion. He shall make no decision in matters of money or gain. He shall say nothing about work or labor to be done on the morrow.

No man shall walk abroad to do business on the Sabbath. He shall not walk more than one thousand cubits beyond his town.

   *   *   *   *

No man shall chide his manservant or maidservant or laborer on the Sabbath.

   *   *   *   *

No man shall assist a beast to give birth on the Sabbath day. And if it should fall into a cistern or a pit, he shall not lift it out on the Sabbath.

   *   *   *   *

No man shall profane the Sabbath for the sake of riches or gain on the Sabbath Day. But should any man fall into water or fire, let him be pulled out with the aid of a ladder or rope or (some such) tool.   (Pp. X, XI)[48]

4. The War Rule (1QM), also referred to as the War of the Sons of Light Against the Sons of Darkness

This is an extended account of the final battle between the forces of God and those of Satan, which results in the victory of the former. Because of a lack of continuity between certain sections of this document, as well as because of a number of repetitous passages, the literary unity of the War Rule has been questioned.

No other Qumran scroll is more apocalyptic in character. Belief in predestination, in the cosmic nature of evil, in the importance of angels and demons, in the leadership of the messiah, and in the intervention of God in bringing evil to a final end are all present. Present also is a detailed attention to the logistics and weaponry of war that, although reflecting the Old Testament's Holy War traditions, also betrays a knowledge on the part of the writer(s) of the conditions of contemporary warfare. Because it is likely that the military references in the War Rule have been influenced by Roman military practices, the composition of the document is often placed in the last decades of the first century BC or the first decades of the first century AD. The influence of the Book of Daniel has been detected also, as in the reference to the forces of evil as the Kittim (cf. Dan. 11:30).

Because of the frequently disconnected and repetitous nature of the War Rule an outline of the document is difficult. Generally speaking, however, the narrative moves from a declaration of war against the Kittim, through an account of that war (including a schematic description of its forty-year duration), to a celebration of the war's triumphant conclusion.

a. *Declaration of War.* Here is heralded a proclamation of hostilities against the Kittim. Prominent themes include the conviction that the war and its outcome have been ordained by God from the beginning, the cosmic nature of the contest, and the suffering of the faithful before their final vindication by God:

> On the day when the Kittim fall, there shall be battle and terrible carnage before the God of Israel, for that shall be the day appointed from ancient times for the battle of destruction of the sons of darkness. At that time the assembly of (pagan) gods and the hosts of men shall battle, causing great carnage; on the day of calamity the sons of light shall battle with the company of darkness amid the shouts of a mighty multitude and the clamor of gods and men to (make manifest) the might of God. And it shall be a time of [great] tribulation for the people which God shall redeem; of all its afflictions none shall be as this, from its sudden beginning until its end in eternal redemption.   (Col. I)[49]

b. *The Conduct of the War.* The manner in which the war is carried on is narrated in considerable detail, in that various kinds of trumpets and standards are described, together with the inscriptions they bear (all of which emphasize Holy War themes). In addition, there is information on the deployment of the several kinds of military units and on the priests who serve as commanders. Attention is also devoted to the implements of this eschatological warfare:

> The Rule for the ordering of the battle divisions to complete a front formation when their host has reached its full number.
>
> The formation shall consist of one thousand men ranked seven lines deep, each man standing behind the other.
>
> They shall all hold shields of bronze burnished like mirrors. The shield shall be edged with an interlaced border and with inlaid ornament, a work of art in pure gold and silver and bronze and precious stones, a many-colored design worked by a craftsman. The length of the shield shall be two and a half cubits and its width one and half cubits.   (Col. V)[50]

If the references to shields made of precious stones and metals did not inform the reader that this battle is not to be a normal military engagement, but an eschatological climax, the following account of the ages of the combatants surely would do so. The soldiers can be old men because the real victor in the struggle is God.

> The men of the army shall be from forty to fifty years old. The inspectors of the camps shall be from fifty to sixty years old. The officers shall be from forty to fifty years old. The despoilers of the slain, the

plunderers of booty, the cleansers of the land, the keepers of the baggage, and those who furnish provisions shall be from twenty-five to thirty years old.   (Col. VII)[51]

The messiah is mentioned, but here (Col. XI) his role seems to be that of one who reveals the outcome of the final battle, rather than that of an eschatological military leader. That task is attributed to the angel Michael (cf. Dan. 12:1):

This is the day appointed by Him for the defeat and overthrow of the Prince of the kingdom of wickedness, and He will send eternal succor to the company of His redeemed by the might of the princely Angel of the kingdom of Michael.   (Col. XVII)[52]

Then there is the description of the battle itself:

The Priests shall sound to marshall them into the divisions of the formation; and at the sound of the trumpets the columns shall deploy until [every man is] in his place. Then the Priests shall sound a second signal on the trumpets for them to advance, and when the [foot-]soldiers approach throwing distance of the formation of the Kittim, every man shall seize his weapon of war. . . . they shall begin to bring down the slain. And all the people shall cease their clamor, but the Priests shall continue to blow [the trumpets of Massacre and battle shall be fought against the Kittim.]   (Col. XVII)[53]

c. *Celebration of the War's Conclusion.*   The conclusion of the battle is cause for great celebration on the part of the triumphant people of God. There are several hymns of praise in the War Rule (one of which appears twice), each calling attention to the power of God and to God's goodness to the faithful remnant of Israel.

And when they have risen from the slain to return to the camp, they shall all sing the Psalm of Return. And in the morning, they shall wash their garments, and shall cleanse themselves of the blood of the bodies of the ungodly. And they shall return to the positions in which they stood in battle formation before the fall of the enemy slain, and there they shall all bless the God of Israel. Rejoicing together, they shall praise His Name, and speaking they shall say:

Blessed be the God of Israel
    who keeps mercy towards his Covenant,
and the appointed times of salvation
    with the people he has delivered!

(Col. XIV)[54]

5. *The Messianic Rule (1QSa), also termed the Rule of the Congregation*

A brief document of two columns attached to the Community Rule, the Messianic Rule is significant for its description of a banquet presided over by dual messiahs, one priestly, the other lay (perhaps Davidic). Because of similarities to the War Rule, it is dated, like the latter document, to the late first century BC or early first century AD.

> [This shall be the ass]embly of the men of renown [called] to the meeting of the Council of the Community when [the Priest-]Messiah shall summon them.
>
> He shall come [at] the head of the whole congregation of Israel with all [his brethren, the sons] of Aaron the Priests, [those called] to the assembly, the men of renown; then they shall sit [before him, each man] in the order of his dignity, And then [the Mess]iah of Israel shall [come], and the chiefs of the [clans of Israel] shall sit before him, [each] in the order of his dignity, according to [his place] in their camps and marches. And before them shall sit all the heads of [family of the congreg]ation, and the wise men of [the holy congregation,] each in the order of his dignity.
>
> And [when] they shall gather for the common [tab]le, to eat and [to drink] new wine, when the common table shall be set for eating and the new wine [poured] for drinking, let no man extend his hand over the first-fruits of the bread and wine before the priest; for [it is he] who shall bless the first-fruits of bread and wine, and shall be the first [to extend] his hand over the bread. Thereafter, the Messiah of Israel shall extend his hand over the bread, [and] all the Congregation of the Community [shall utter a] blessing, [each man in the order] of his dignity.

The final words of the Messianic Rule make it clear that the daily meals of the community are to be observed in a manner which anticipates this messianic feast:

> It is according to this statute that they shall proceed at every me[al at which] at least ten men are gathered together.[55]

6. *The Hymns (1QH), also called the* **Hodayoth** *or the Thanksgiving Hymns*

A badly preserved scroll from Cave One contains a number of hymns which, in certain respects, are similar to Psalms of Lament and Psalms of Thanksgiving in the Old Testament. Because of the state of the text it has not been possible to establish just how many hymns the scroll contains, but at least twenty-five have been identified. Principle themes are thanksgiving to God for having saved the hymnist from some distress (often imposed by his enemies) and for having imparted to the hymnist knowledge of the divine mysteries. Because of a virtual absence of historical allusions, dating the hymns is very difficult, although the scroll itself seems to come from the first century AD.

Many of the hymns begin with the phrase, "I thank thee, O Lord," as does the following example. This fragment is one of many in which the hymnist expresses gratitude to God for having saved him from his enemies:

> I thank thee, O Lord,
>   for thou hast [fastened] Thine eye upon me.
> Thou hast saved me from the zeal
>   of lying interpreters,
> and from the congregation of those
>   who seek smooth things.
> Thou has redeemed the soul of the poor one
>   whom they planned to destroy
>   by spilling his blood because he served Thee.   (Col. II)[56]

Apocalyptic images, very similar to those which appear in the War Rule, are present in the following passage, which also reflects the language of Job 26:6 and 28:22.

> The torrents of Satan shall break into Abaddon
>   and the deeps of the Abyss shall groan
>   amid the roar of heaving mud.
> The land shall cry out because of the calamity
>   fallen upon the world,
>   and all its deeps shall howl.
> And all those upon it shall rave
>   and shall perish amid the great misfortune.
> For God shall sound his mighty voice,
>   and His holy abode shall thunder
>   with the truth of his glory.
> The heavenly hosts shall cry out
>   and the world's foundations
>   shall stagger and sway.
> The war of the heavenly warriors shall scourge the earth;
>   and it shall not end before the appointed destruction
>   which shall be for ever and without compare.   (Col. III)[57]

The hymnist's thanksgiving to God over his having received from God the secrets of the divine mysteries takes many forms. In this passage, this gift is compared to God's gift of water in a desert land. Notice here also that the hymnist looks upon this knowledge as a divine gift that is to be shared with others. This element in some of the hymns, along with other characteristics, has led some scholars to suggest that the Teacher of Righteousness may have written some or all of the hymns, a theory, however, that cannot be established with certainty. The literary inspiration for this hymn may have been Psalm 1, one of the Torah Psalms.

> I [Thank thee, O Lord,
>   for] Thou hast placed me beside a fountain of streams
>   in an arid land,
> and close to a spring of waters
>   in a dry land,
> and beside a watered garden
>   [in a wilderness.]
>   *   *   *   *
> But Thou, O God, hast put into my mouth
>   as it were rain for all [those who thirst]
>   and a fount of living waters which shall not fail.
> When they are opened they shall not run dry;
>   they shall be like a torrent [overflowing its banks]
>   and like the [bottom]less seas.
> They shall suddenly gush forth
>   which were hidden in secret.   (Col. VIII)[58]

The weakness and mortality of the hymnist is a frequent theme, one that is contrasted to the power and goodness of God.

> Clay and dust that I am,
>   what can I devise unless Thou wish it,
>   and what contrive unless Thou desire it?
> What strength shall I have
>   unless Thou keep me upright,
> And how shall I understand
>   unless by (the spirit) which Thou hast shaped for me?
> What can I say unless Thou open my mouth
>   and how can I answer unless Thou enlighten me?   (Col. X)[59]

If, as mentioned above, some of the hymns do reflect the personality of the Teacher of Righteousness, the passage that follows may refer to an otherwise unknown revolt by members of the sect.

> [All who have ea]ten my bread
>   have lifted their heel against me,
> and all those joined to my Council
>   have mocked me with wicked lips.

The members of my [Covenant] have rebelled
   and have murmured round about me;
they have gone as talebearers
   before the children of mischief
   concerning the mystery which Thou hast hidden in me.   (Col. V)[60]

7. The Genesis Apocryphon (1QapGen)

A badly damaged scroll which contains legendary anecdotes relating to the lives of the partiarchs, the Genesis Apocryphon has been dated by scholars to late in the second century or early in the first century BC (although the scroll itself seems to have been copied late in the first century BC). It is written in Aramaic, and is akin to the haggadah that developed as a result of rabbinic interpretation of the Torah in synagogue services. The stories are colorful and provide details missing from the biblical narrative itself, the kind of material that would have appealed to curious listeners (and readers) who wished to know more about the founders of their traditions. Frequently the anecdotes in the Genesis Apocryphon project moral and spiritual ideals for the faithful to follow, although this document is different from many of the Qumran scrolls in that contains no views that are essentially sectarian. For this reason, it may have had its origin outside the Qumran community.

The beginning and end of the Genesis Apocryphon are missing, as are several of its interior columns. The remaining material may be outlined as follows:

1. Lamech's story of the unusual birth of his son Noah (Gen. 5).
2. Abraham's journey to Egypt (Gen. 12).
3. Abraham's settlement in Canaan and his wars against the four kings (Gen. 13–14).

The anecdotes are narrated in the first person by the patriarch.

(1) Lamech is disturbed when he learns that his wife, Bathenosh, is pregnant, for he fears that the child (Noah) had been conceived with the aid of one of the "Watchers" or "Holy Ones," that is, a fallen angel (see Gen. 6:1). When he questioned his wife, she replied,

I swear to you by the Holy Great One, the King of [the heavens] . . . that this seed is yours and that [this] conception is from you. This fruit was planted by you . . . and by no stranger or Watcher or Son of Heaven.   (Col. II)[61]

Lamech then reports that he told this news to his father Methuselah, who advised him to go to his grandfather Enoch. Lamech finds Enoch, but at this point the preserved text breaks off.

(2) We have referred earlier to the account of Abraham's journey to Egypt in the Genesis Apocryphon. The narrative thread follows that of the Genesis account, except that it is much embellished. The preserved portion begins with a report by the Egyptian courtier Harkenosh to the pharaoh (whose name is Zoan) concerning Sarah's beauty:

> How fair are her breasts and how beautiful all her whiteness! How pleasing are her arms and how perfect her hands, and how [desirable] all the appearance of her hands! How fair are her palms and how long and slender are her fingers! How comely are her feet, how perfect her thighs. No virgin or bride led into the marriage chamber is more beautiful than she; she is fairer than all other women.   (Col. XX)[62]

Pharaoh is deceived into thinking that Sarah is Abraham's sister, and she is thus added to the royal harem. But an agitated Abraham prays to God, who sends an evil spirit to keep the pharaoh from Sarah, the account of which was quoted previously.[63] For two years the plagues continue until Lot tells Harkenosh that they are caused by the pharaoh's keeping of Sarah, who is really Abraham's wife. When the suffering pharaoh learns of this, he restores Sarah to Abraham and implores him to intervene with God so that the evil spirit will be withdrawn.

> So I prayed [for pharaoh] . . . and I laid my hands on his [head]; and the scourge departed from him and the evil [spirit] was expelled [from him], and he lived. And the king rose to tell me . . . and the king swore an oath to me that . . . and the king gave her much [silver and gold] and much raiment of fine linen and purple . . . And Hagar also . . . and he appointed men to lead [me] out [of all the land of Egypt]. And I, Abraham, departed with very great flocks and with silver and gold, and I went up from [Egypt] together with my nephew [Lot].   (Col. XX)[64]

(3) The final existing section of the Genesis Apocryphon parallels Genesis 13:14—15:6. One important expansion of the text, however, is the geographic detail given to Abraham's survey of the land, referred to in Genesis 14:17. As described in the Genesis Apocryphon, the Land of Promise includes all of Syria-Palestine as far west as Mesopotamia and the Persian Gulf as far south as the Red Sea. But perhaps of most interest is the account of Abraham's battle with the four kings (in the course of the narrative of this section there is an

unexplained shift from the first person to the third), an account which parallels Genesis 14:14–16:

> Abraham wept because of Lot his nephew. Then he braced himself; he rose up and chose from among his servants three hundred and eighteen fighting men trained for war, and Ornam and Eshkol and Mamre went with him also. He pursued them until he came to Dan, and came on them while they were camped in the valley of Dan. He fell on them at night from four sides and during the night he slew them; he crushed them and put them to flight, and all of them fled before him until they came to Helbon which is north of Damascus. He rescued from them all their captives, and all their booty and possessions. He also delivered Lot his nephew, together with all his possessions, and he brought back all the captives which they had taken.   (Col. XXII)[65]

8. *The Habakkuk Commentary (1QpHab)*

Reference has been made several times to this *pesher* on the first two chapters of the Book of Habakkuk. The scroll on which it is written is in a relatively good state of preservation, and it seems evident that the author either did not know of the third chapter of the canonical Habakkuk or chose not to utilize it, as there is a vacant space on the scroll that could have accommodated at least the beginning of that chapter. The purpose of reproducing part of the pesher here is to give an indication of its running style. The following example relates to Habakkuk 1:6–9a:

> *For behold, I rouse the Chaldeans, that [bitter and hasty] nation* (1:6a).

> Interpreted, this concerns the Kittim [who are] quick and valiant in war, causing many to perish. [All the world shall fall] under the dominion of the Kittim, and the [wicked . . .] they shall not believe in the laws of [God . . .]

> *[Who march through the breadth of the earth to take possession of dwellings which are not their own]* (1:6b).

> [Interpreted, this concerns . . .] they shall march across the plain, smiting and plundering the cities of the earth. For it is as He said, *To take possessions of dwellings which are not their own.*

> *They are fearsome and terrible; their justice and grandeur proceed from themselves* (1:7).

> Interpreted, this concerns the Kittim who inspire all the nations with fear [and dread]. All their evil plotting is done with intention and they deal with all the nations in cunning and guile.

Their horses are swifter than leopards and fleeter than evening wolves. Their horses step forward proudly and spread their wings; they fly from afar like an eagle avid to devour. All of them come for violence; the look on their faces is like the east wind (1:8–9a).

[Interpreted, this] concerns the Kittim who trample the earth with their horses and beasts. They come *from afar*, from the islands of the sea, to devour all the peoples *like an eagle* which cannot be satisfied, and they address [all the peoples] with anger and [wrath and fury] and indignation. For it is as He said, *The look on their faces is like the east wind.* (Cols. II, III).[66]

Chapter 6

ADDITIONAL JEWISH LITERATURE
OF THE HELLENISTIC PERIOD (1)

In this chapter and that which follows we shall conclude our discussion of Judaism during the Hellenistic period by focusing attention upon some of the community's literature that we have not yet examined. It is difficult to reconstruct with precision the history of this body of literature for the reason that much of it is difficult to date or to place in a specific geographical or cultural context. Furthermore, in many cases, an initial nucleus of composition has been expanded over the years by various copiers and redactors so that, as a whole, the writing can be assigned no specific date. To further complicate matters, the writings of some Jews of the Hellenistic period are known only because fragments have been quoted by others, thus rendering even more difficult the attempt to place them in their proper historical setting. Acknowledging these problems, however, it is possible to project approximate contours of the several literary traditions which emerged within Hellenistic Judaism. We have attempted to do this with by no means all known documents of the period, but with several of the more significant. If they do nothing else, these literary creations will remind one of the fascinating diversity within early Judaism, both that of Palestine and that of the Diaspora.

A number of writings has already been investigated in the discussions of Apocalyptic and of Qumran. The problems encountered in categorizing that literature into clearly defined literary and theological types will be apparent here, as well. For sake of convenience, however, and with an eye on the danger of oversimplification, the literary works discussed here are brought together under the following categories: biblical translation, expansions of biblical material, testamentary literature, wisdom, historiography, epic poetry, stories and legends, drama, and Hellenistic philosophy. A final excursus (at the conclusion of the next chapter) focuses upon expressions of messianism in Jewish literature of the period.

A. BIBLICAL TRANSLATION: THE SEPTUAGINT
(3D TO 2D C. BC)[1]

The most significant literary achievement of the Jews of the Greek-speaking Diaspora was the translation of the Hebrew scriptures into the Greek language, a Bible known as the Septuagint (from the Greek term for "seventy") because of the legend surrounding its origin. The Septuagint (often abbreviated LXX) is important not solely for what it tells us about the text of the Old Testament and its process of canonization, but also because this translation into Greek, and not the Hebrew scriptures themselves, became the Bible of the early Christian church.

A document known as the Letter of Aristeas[2] (often referred to as Pseudo-Aristeas) purports to tell how the Septuagint came to be. According to this "letter," the celebrated librarian of Alexandria, Demetrius of Phalerum,[3] informed his king, Ptolemy II Philadelphus (285–246), that the library contained no copy of the Jewish Torah. The king, in order to redress this deficiency, drafted a letter to the high priest in Jerusalem in which he asked for seventy-two Jewish scholars (six from each tribe) to come to Alexandria to produce a copy of the Torah. (Aristeas, the purported author of the "letter," is one of those who carried the king's request to Jerusalem.) The king accompanied his letter with valuable gifts to the Jerusalem Jews and, at home, demonstrated his good will by freeing more than a 100,000 Jewish slaves. The high priest complied with the king's request and the scholars, once they were in Egypt, were set to their task. In seventy-two days the work of translation was completed and a copy of the Torah, so faithfully translated that it was never to be altered, was presented to the library.

Thus goes the tale of the Septuagint's origin. In years to come, this story was to be expanded by others, including Philo,[4] who described the whole Bible, not just the Torah, as the subject of the translation. Some later accounts even go so far as to say that the seventy-two scholars worked independently of one another, but when their work was compared, it was found to be identical in every respect!

As interesting as it is, the Letter of Aristeas (to say nothing of the later embellishments to its story) is a fiction that tells us more of the need felt by some anonymous Alexandrian Jew of the second century BC to write a document that portrayed a favorable attitude toward the Jews by the ruling Ptolemys than it tells us of the origin of the Septuagint. It is possible to demonstrate that the Greek Bible was written over a number of years, and that it was produced by a variety of translators who possessed widely differing levels of skill as well as different concepts of the purposes a translation was to serve. The Pentateuch (Torah) was translated first about 250 BC, while the Prophets followed shortly after and were certainly in use during the early years of the second century. The Writings and the Apocrypha (those books and additions to books not found in the Hebrew scriptures) seem to have been added over a longer period of time, some texts perhaps not appearing before the late second or early first century BC.

The first thing which strikes the reader of the Septuagint is a difference in content when compared with the Palestinian (Hebrew) canon, the Septuagint being considerably more inclusive. Works that appear in the Septuagint canon, but not in that of the Palestinian Jews include 1 Esdras, Tobit, Judith, The Wisdom of Solomon, Sirach, Baruch, The Letter of Jeremiah, 1 and 2 Maccabees, and additions to Daniel and Esther. Some of these writings originated in Palestine (1 Maccabees and Judith, for example) and the anomaly that literature of a Palestinian origin should be excluded from the Palestinian canon, but accepted into that of the Greek-speaking Diaspora is not yet fully understood.

On the other hand, while there are no books in the Palestinian canon which are missing from the Septuagint, some books are present in the Septuagint in abbreviated form. For example, the Greek version of Job is approximately one sixth shorter than the Hebrew version. The Septuagint of Jeremiah is also briefer than its Hebrew counterpart by about 2,700 words[5] and displays a different order, in that the oracles against foreign nations, which in the Hebrew text occur after chapter 45, are inserted into chapter 25 in the Septuagint. One other example of an interesting omission in the Septuagint relates to 1 Samuel 17, the story of David and Goliath, as a large number of Septuagint manuscripts omit 17:12–31 and 17:55—18:5. The Septuagint 1 Samuel therefore knows nothing of David's journey to the Hebrew encampment to take food to his brothers, of Saul's offer to give his daughter to the man who will slay the Philistine giant, or of Eliab's scornful words to David. It is likewise ignorant of the conversation between Saul and Abner concerning David's identity and of the new friendship between David and Jonathan.

It should not be concluded from this, however, that the text of the Septuagint or of the Hebrew manuscripts from which it was translated are necessarily inferior to the Hebrew of the Palestinian tradition (the so-called Masoretic text). There are points where it seems apparent that the Septuagint has transmitted a text in better condition than the Hebrew, the Books of Samuel, in fact, being a case in point. For example, the context of 1 Samuel 12:15 strongly suggests that the Hebrew text,

then the hand of the LORD will be against you and your ancestors.

is inferior to the text of the Septuagint:

then the hand of the Lord will be against you and your king.

It is interesting to thumb through a modern translation of Samuel that is equipped with marginal notes, such as an annotated NRSV, and notice how many times the translators have turned to the Greek text to help them make sense of the Hebrew.

To make matters even more interesting, discoveries of fragments of Samuel at Qumran have provided evidence of a Hebrew text that is nearer the Septuagint than it is to the traditional Masoretic text. A fragment of Samuel from Cave 4 (4QSam[b]) has been published,[6] which contains ten points at which the Septuagint and the Masoretic Text disagree. In eight of these cases, 4QSam[b] agrees with the Septuagint, and in only two with the Masoretic text. The conclusion drawn from this and similar evidence by many scholars is that there were at least three Hebrew language textual traditions in currency during the second century BC. One of these is preserved in the Masoretic Text, another in the Septuagint and a third (confined to the Torah) in the Samaritan Pentateuch.

As stated above, the Septuagint is important to modern students for several reasons. In addition to giving us information concerning a different textual tradition from that contained in the Masoretic text, the Septuagint also reminds us that the process toward the canonization of the scriptures did not follow the same paths among all Jews. As has been pointed out by many scholars, before there existed the unity of the canon to which both modern Jews and Christians are accustomed, there was wide diversity, a fact to which the use of the scriptures at Qumran is also evidence. The implications of this axiom are yet to be fully explored by biblical theologians in our time.[7]

As for students of the New Testament, the Septuagint has always provided a rich field of inquiry because it became the Bible of the early church. The very first Christians were Jews, of course, and the Bible with which they were familiar was the Hebrew text and, to an even greater degree (since Hebrew had declined as an everyday language in Palestine) the Aramaic Targumim.[8] As we noticed earlier, it is not surprising to find in the New Testament references to the manner in which the Targumim were used in synagogue services, as well as quotations of Old Testament texts in the style of the Targumim. But as the church spread beyond the Aramaic-speaking population of Palestine and into the larger world (which in spite of Roman military domination continued to speak Greek as a primary language), the scriptures to which the growing Christian community increasingly turned was the Greek Bible of the Diaspora Jews. Time and again, therefore, when New Testament writers quote the Old Testament, their text is either taken from the Septuagint directly or is strongly influenced by it.

Statistics in this matter are difficult to arrive at because it is not always easy to distinguish a quotation of an Old Testament text from a mere allusion to it. But it has been calculated that, while 212 Old Testament texts cited in the New Testament diverge from the Hebrew (Masoretic) text, only 185 diverge from the Septuagint.[9] It may surprise some that either of these figures is so high, but it must be remembered that the Targumic tradition of free renditions of scriptural texts was very strong among writers of the New Testament. The real lesson to be learned from the numbers is that, of the various textual traditions of the Old Testament known in the first two centuries AD, the Septuagint was a principal source of Old Testament quotations by the New Testament writers. Among many examples of exact or near exact quotations of the Septuagint in the Synoptic Gospels alone are Mark 7:10, 7:6, 10:6–9, 11:17, 12:10, 12:29–30, 12:31, 12:36, 13:14 (including parallels).

This reliance upon the Septuagint by the early church continued into the patristic era. It was not until Jerome (c. 340–420) successfully argued for the superiority of the Hebrew Old Testament and based his new translation (the Vulgate) upon it that the Septuagint began to lose its influence among Christian writers and preachers.

Before concluding our discussion of the influence of the Greek Bible, brief comments are in order about Greek-language successors to the Septuagint. By early in the second century AD the Septuagint had begun to lose favor among Jews. One reason for this was that rabbinic teaching, based largely upon Palestinian textual traditions (Hebrew Bible, Aramaic Targumim, and various forms of halakhah and haggadah) were in some tension with certain Septuagint texts. But another cause for Jewish dislike of the Septuagint was its use by Christians for purposes of anti-Jewish apologetic. Therefore, the second century AD saw the appearance of three additional translations of the Hebrew scriptures into Greek, all the work of Jews (with the possible exception of Theodotion).

The first of these is associated with an individual who, according to the tradition which has been preserved about him, was a Jewish proselyte from Christianity, a native of Pontus in Asia Minor named Aquila. About 130 AD he produced a version of the Hebrew scriptures in Greek that was not only an attempt to create a more literal (and therefore, faithful) translation than the Septuagint, but one that would deny to the Christians some of their cherished Old Testament texts. For example, in Isaiah 7:14 Aquila followed the Hebrew text and used a word meaning "young woman" instead of the Septuagint's "virgin" apparently because of the insistence of some Christians that Jesus' virgin birth had been foretold in the Old Testament (see Matt. 1:23).

Aquila's translation was followed later in the second century (about 180 or 190) by another Greek version, that of Theodotion. Little is known of this individual, although some have suggested that he may have been a Christian because of the popularity of his translation among certain Christian writers. That, however, is disputed by, among others, Irenaeus (c. 130–200 AD) who describes him as a Jewish proselyte. Theodotion's translation may actually have been a revision of an even earlier and now unknown Greek Bible (referred to by modern scholars as pre-Theodotion), a conclusion based upon the fact that Old Testament quotations in the New Testament Book of Revelation agree with Theodotion in a large number of cases. One interesting feature of Theodition was his tendency to transliterate certain Hebrew words into Greek characters, thus providing helpful clues to the manner in which Hebrew was pronounced in the second century AD. The popularity of Theodotion in some Christian circles is seen in the large number of references to this translation in the Greek "fathers" and in the fact that in many copies of the Septuagint, the Book of Daniel is replaced by its counterpart from Theodotion. What is more, some of the deficiencies in the Septuagint text, texts missing from Job, for example, are often supplied by texts from Theodotion.

About the time of the appearance of the translation of Theodotion, another Greek Old Testament came into use, that associated with the name of Symmachus. Little is known of this individual, although the style of his translation would suggest that he was a Jew, in that it seems to give evidence of the influence of rabbinic exegesis. Symmachus seems to have known and used the translation of Aquila against whose literalness he attempts to set out a freer translation that sometimes lapses into paraphrase.

Aquila, Theodotion, and Symmachus were all included in the great Hexapla of the Christian scholar Origin (c. 185–254). However, only fragments of them have survived into the present.

B. Expansions of Biblical Material

We have already observed in discussing Jubilees and the Genesis Apocryphon from Qumran a tendency on the part of certain Jewish writers to expand or, in some cases, to rewrite the biblical text. Similar efforts are to be found in the Letter of Jeremiah, the writings of Artapanus, The Martyrdom of Isaiah, The Prayer of Manasseh and Additions to the Books of Esther and Daniel.

1. *The Letter of Jeremiah* (late 4th, 3d or 2d c. BC)[10]

At some time during the Hellenistic period, a Jewish writer who had been inspired by Jeremiah 10:2–15 (a polemic against idolatry) and 29:1–28 (Jeremiah's letter to the exiles), wrote a purported letter in Hebrew from Jeremiah to the Babylonian captives. More a repetitious sermon than a letter, its single focus is on the futility of the worship of idols. Lack of any historical references in the work and the frequency with which idolatry was practiced by neighbors of the Jews render it virtually impossible to date the composition of the letter with any precision or to be sure that its author lived in Palestine, although that seems likely.

Since a fragment of the letter was found at Qumran, and as it is referred to in 2 Maccabees 2:1–2, one may assume that the work was in use among Jews during the second century BC not only in Palestine, but in the Diaspora. In the community of Alexandrian Jews it was regarded as canonical, and in Christian Era copies of the Septuagint it is placed either after Lamentations (also regarded at the time as a work of Jeremiah) or as a final part (a sixth chapter) of Baruch.

A brief introduction (vv. 2–7—the letter is but a single chapter) alerts the reader to the danger posed by the ubiquitous presence of idols. Otherwise, there is little structure to the letter apart from a refrain which repeats the same thought in a variety of words, as in v. 16: "Therefore they evidently are not gods, so do not fear them."

Between the refrains, the author uses irony and simile to drive home his point, but his primary technique is a simple negative indicative. The following is representative of the style and content of the letter:

> For they [i.e., the idols] cannot set up a king over a country or give rain to people. They cannot judge their own cause or deliver one who is wronged, for they have no power; they are like crows between heaven and earth. When fire breaks out in a temple of wooden gods overlaid with gold or silver, their priests will flee and escape, but the gods will be burned up like timbers. Besides, they can offer no resistance to king or enemy. [The refrain: Why then must anyone admit or think that they are gods?
>
> (vv. 53–56)

2. *Artapanus* (3d to 2d c. BC)[11]

During the first century BC a Greek historian named Alexander Polyhistor[12] compiled a number of documents relating to the Jews. Polyhistor, who was a native of Miletus (in Asia Minor), had spent some time as a slave in Rome before being given his freedom and was thus in touch with Roman cultural tastes. He seems to have worked less as a genuine historian in the style of, say Herodotus or Thucydides, and more as a collector of the words of others, which he often seems to quote verbatim. One whose work Polyhistor reproduced is that of a third or second century BC Jewish writer named Artapanus.

To further complicate matters, not only has Artapanus' work not survived in an independent form, but even the writings of Alexander Polyhistor have also perished. All that remains are quotations of Polyhistor (including his quotations of Artapanus) in the writings of the Christian, Eusebius of Caesarea

(c. 260–340 AD). Even so, there is good reason to believe that the few words of Artapanus and other Jewish writers that have been preserved in this manner have survived in a condition very similar to their original state, as both Polyhistor and Eusebius seem to have taken pains to transmit precisely that which they received from others.

Although the Jews of Egypt seem generally to have been held in high regard by their neighbors, there were occasional outbursts of anti-Jewish feeling in the Ptolemaic kingdom. As we have mentioned before, the Egyptian historian Manetho[13] (third century BC) doubtless expressed the view of many of his compatriots when he portrayed Moses and his people as barbarians, and there were serious efforts to Hellenize the Jews of Egypt by force during the reign of Ptolemy IV Philopater (221–205 BC). Josephus felt the attacks of Manetho to be sufficiently serious to try to refute them four centuries later,[14] and in doing so, he may have been inspired by the work of Artapanus, an earlier apologist for the Jews.

Artapanus lived in Egypt probably toward the end of the third century BC. Although he wrote in Greek and was surely influenced by literary circles in Alexandria, there are hints in his work that he may have lived in a rural area. His choice of words reflects a knowledge of classical Greek literature, yet he writes in the Koine dialect of the Hellenistic world and at several points demonstrates a knowledge of the Septuagint, which he occasionally quotes directly. His purpose in writing seems to have been to present a favorable view of Jewish life in Egypt, as his subjects (to the extent that his work has been preserved) are those Jews of the past who had important contacts with Egypt: Abraham, Joseph, and Moses. He appears to have written with many of Manetho's defamations in mind for, although he does not refute the Egyptian directly, he presents alternative versions of many of the incidents raised by Manetho.

Artapanus' accounts are, in some ways, scarcely recognizable to those familiar with the books of Genesis and Exodus. For example, Joseph, knowing that he was about to be harmed by his brothers, requests a group of Arabs to carry him to Egypt, not, as in Genesis 37:25–28, being forced to go there against his will. Moses is described as the teacher of Orpheus, the Greek god of music, and was himself believed by the Egyptians of his day to be Hermes, the messenger of the gods (later called Mercury by the Romans). Moses' slaying of the Egyptian (whose name is Chenephres in Artapanus' account) is in self-defense, rather than as a response to the man's striking of a Hebrew, as in Exodus 2:11–12. When Moses tells the king that he must release the Jews, the king has him thrown into prison. But that night Moses is miraculously released when the doors to the prison are thrown open, while some of the guards are struck dead and others are rendered unconscious. After the Israelites cross the Red Sea (in one of two versions of the Exodus in Artapanus), the pursuing Egyptians are destroyed not only by the returning waters, as in Exodus 14, but also by a miraculous fire.

As mentioned above, there is good reason to believe that Artapanus' work influenced that of Josephus, but beyond that the importance of this Egyptian Jew seems to lie in the fact that he represents an interesting synthesis of the traditions of Judaism with those of the Hellenistic world. In this regard, he anticipated the work of Philo (first century AD), whom we shall discuss in a subsequent chapter.[15] Artapanus is also noteworthy because he reflects Jewish sensitivity to anti-Jewish polemic, a sensitivity that in this case attempts to disarm that polemic by recasting the historical record to make it more palatable to non-Jews. It is not known if Artapanus' work was in circulation in Palestine during the first half of the second century, but if so, it would represent the kind of accommodation to Hellenism so despised by the Hasidim and others.

There are three fragments of Artapanus' writings preserved by Polyhistor/Eusebius. The first deals with Abraham and is so brief that it may be quoted in full.

Artapanus says in his *Judaica* that the Jews are named "Hermiouth," which, translated into Greek, is "Jews." They were called Hebrews after Abraham. He says that the latter came to Egypt with all his household to the Egyptian king Pharethothes, and taught him astrology, that he remained there twenty years and then departed again for the regions of Syria, but that many of those who came with him remained in Egypt on account of the prosperity of the land.

(Fragment 1)

The second fragment concerns Joseph and reads, in part:

He came to Egypt, was recommended to the king, and became administrator of the entire land . . . This man (Joseph) was the first to divide the land and distinguish it with boundaries. He made much barren land arable and allotted some of the arable lands to the priests.

This man also discovered measurements and on account of these things he was greatly loved by the Egyptians. He married Aseneth, the daughter of a Heliopolitan priest, and begot children by her.

The third and most extensive fragment tells of Moses. Unlike the other two fragments, this one is cited by Clement of Alexandria (c. 150–220 AD).[16]

As a grown man he [Moses] bestowed many useful benefits upon mankind, for he invented boats and devices for stone construction and the Egyptian arms and the implements for drawing water and for warfare, and philosophy. Further, he divided the state into 36 nomes [i.e. districts] and appointed for each of the nomes the god to be worshiped, and for the priests the sacred letters, [i.e. the heiroglyphs] and that they should be cats and dogs and ibises.

But when Chenepheres [the king] saw the excellence of Moses he was envious of him and sought to destroy him on some specious pretext. Once indeed when the Ethopians campaigned against Egypt, Chenepheres supposed he had found a convenient opportunity and sent Moses against them as a general with an army. But he put together a host of farmers for him, supposing that he would be easliy destroyed by the enemy on account of the weakness of the soldiers.

When Moses came to the district called Hermopolis, with about a hundred thousand farmers, he pitched camp there. He sent generals to blockade the region, and these gained notable advantage in battles.

Those around Moses founded a city in that place on account of the size of the army, and made the ibis sacred there because it destroys the creatures which harm men. They called it Hermopolis (the city of Hermes).

The Ethopians, even though they were his enemies, loved Moses so much that they learned the circumcision of the genital organs from him, and not only they, but also all the priests.

3. *The Martyrdom of Isaiah* (2d c. BC)[17]

A document has survived from ancient times that tells of the execution of the prophet Isaiah by the wicked Judaean king Manasseh and that also narrates a series of visions which the prophet earlier experienced during the reign of good Hezekiah. It is clear that the portion of the document that deals with the visions is a Christian addition to an earlier Jewish work that was concerned with Isaiah's martyrdom, and that this addition at one time circulated independently. What is more, the section dealing with the prophet's martyrdom is interrupted by another expansion, also demonstrating Christian beliefs. The entire document has been named the Ascension of Isaiah, while the various parts are

The Martyrdom of Isaiah (1:1—3:12; 5:1–16)

The Testament of Hezekiah (3:13–4:22)

The Vision of Isaiah (6:1—11:43)

We shall be concerned here only with early Jewish section, the Martyrdom. It was probably written in Hebrew about 165 BC, although existing copies are in Ethiopic, Latin, and Slavonic. (A fragment in Greek, containing 2:4—4:4, has survived from the fifth or sixth century.)

The Old Testament makes no mention of Isaiah's death. The last dated activities of the prophet are associated with the reign of King Hezekiah (Isa. 36—39, paralleled in 2 Kings 18—20). Of Hezekiah's evil son, however, it is reported that "Manasseh shed very much innocent blood, until he had filled Jerusalem from one end to another" (2 Kings 21:16). The Martyrdom of Isaiah connects these two traditions and not only reports that Isaiah was one of Manasseh's victims, but provides details of his execution.

The narrative begins with Hezekiah's admonitions to Manasseh to be a righteous and faithful king. It then continues:

> And it came about that after Hezekiah had died, and Manasseh had become king, [Manasseh] did not remember the commands of Hezekiah his father, but forgot them; and (the demon) Sammael dwelt in Manasseh and clung closely in him. And Manasseh abandoned the service of the Lord of his father, and he served Satan, and his angels, and his powers.
>
> (2:1–2)

Because of Manasseh's evil and his "persecution of the righteous," Isaiah and other faithful people flee from Jerusalem and seek refuge "on a mountain in a desert place." In addition to Isaiah, the refugees include the prophets Micah and Habakkuk. However, their whereabouts are disclosed to Manasseh by an evil Samaritan, Belkira, and Isaiah is seized and brought back to Jerusalem.

> Beliar [i.e, Satan] was angry with Isaiah, and he dwelt in the heart of Manasseh, and he sawed Isaiah in half with a wood saw. And while Isaiah was being sawed in half, his accuser, Belkira, stood by, and all the false prophets stood by, laughing and [maliciously] joyful because of Isaiah . . . And Belkira said to Isaiah, "Say, 'I have lied in everything I have spoken; the ways of Manasseh are good and right, and also the ways of Belkira and those who are with him are good.'" . . . And Isaiah answered and said, "If it is within my power to say, 'Condemned and cursed be you, and all your hosts, and all your house?' For there is nothing further that you can take except the skin of my body."
>
> (5:1–10)

Several elements in this narrative are of interest, of which one is the demonology. Beliar is a frequent designation in apocalyptic literature for the chief demon, who is also called Satan and Sammael in the Martyrdom. It is he who captures the heart of Manasseh and who instigates the king's evil deeds.

Another point of interest is the anti-Samaritan polemic. It has been suggested that the name of the Samaritan informer, Belkira, is a play upon a Hebrew phrase that means "the elect of evil."

Of primary importance is the nature of Isaiah's death. Some scholars have linked the prophet's martyrdom to the sufferings of the Qumran community, but a better suggestion seems to see the story as a response to the persecutions of Antiochus Epiphanes. The Books of Daniel (chaps. 3, 6) and 2 Maccabees (6:18—7:42) offer similar stories, except that here the emphasis is upon the prophet's acceptance of his fate as the price he must pay for faithfulness to God.

Those scholars are probably correct who see a reference to the Martyrdom (or perhaps to another version of the same story) in Hebrews 11:36–37:

> Others suffered mocking and flogging, and even chains and imprisonment. They were stoned to death, *they were sawn in two.*

4. *The Prayer of Manasseh* (2d c. BC to 1st c. AD)[18]

Two contrasting accounts of the character of Judaean king Manasseh are contained in the Old Testament. The Deuteronomistic History roundly condemns this monarch, who, in the seventh century BC, enjoyed the longest reign of any Davidic king. He was so thoroughly evil that the guilt for the fall of Jerusalem in the early sixth century BC is laid at his feet (2 Kings 23:26–27; cf. 2 Kings 21:11–15). Chronicles, however, has a different view. Second Chron. 33:1–10 reports the wickedness of this king in almost the same words as 2 Kings 21:1–10, but then goes on to add that, after he had been taken prisoner by the Assyrians, Manasseh repented of his former evil.

> While he was in distress he [i.e., Manasseh] entreated the favor of the LORD his God and humbled himself greatly before the God of his ancestors. He prayed to him, and God received his entreaty, heard his plea, and restored him again to Jerusalem and to his kingdom. Then Manasseh knew that the LORD indeed was God.
>
> (2 Chron. 33:12–13)

Some time after the writing of Chronicles (fifth-fourth century BC) it seems that some pious Jew set a hand to expand the story of Manasseh's repentance, just as some other Jew had attempted to add to the story of Isaiah by recounting the circumstances of that prophet's death. Where or when that Jew lived is impossible to know, although Palestine of the second century BC is quite possible. On the other hand, the author of the Prayer of Manasseh may have lived in the Diaspora and could have worked as late as the first century AD. It is also unknown whether the prayer was written in a Semitic language (Hebrew or Aramaic) or Greek. The oldest existing copies are in Syriac and Greek.

Whoever this person was, the result of his or her work is strikingly beautiful. In its brief course of fifteen verses, the Prayer of Manasseh, using language

similar to that of the Psalms (esp. Ps. 51), describes the mercies of a loving God
and the renewing experience of God's forgiveness. One may wish to compare it
with the Prayer of Azariah, another expansion of the biblical text, described
later.

The Prayer of Manasseh begins with a statement of praise:

O Lord Almighty,
God of our ancestors,
of Abraham and Issac and Jacob
and of their righteous offspring;
you who made heaven and earth
with all their order;
who shackled the sea by your word of command.

(vv. 1–3a)

Against anyone who would protest that the one praying these words is too
wicked to receive the forgiveness of a just and mighty God, the author offers
this thought:

Therefore, you, O Lord, God of the righteous,
have not appointed repentence for the righteous,
for Abraham and Issac and Jacob, who did not sin against you;
but you appointed repentence for me, who am a sinner.

(v. 8)

Then the sinner asks for God's forgiveness:

I am not worthy to look up and see the height of heaven
because of the multitude of my iniquities.
*   *   *   *
And now I bend the knee of my heart,
imploring you for your kindness I have sinned,
O Lord, I have sinned,
and I acknowledge my transgressions.

(vv. 9b–12)

As the author anticipates living a changed life because of the redemptive
power of God, the prayer concludes:

I will praise you continually all the days of my life;
For all the host of heaven sings your praise,
And yours is the glory forever. Amen

(v. 15)

Although the Prayer of Manasseh was not a part of the Septuagint (nor, of course, of the Palestinian Jewish canon), it attained a near canonical status in some Christian circles. It was included in the Codex Alexandrinus (a Christian Bible of the fifth century) and was praised by both Thomas Aquinas and Martin Luther. On the other hand, there is no record of its extensive use by Jews.

5. *Additions to Esther* (2d or 1st c. BC)[19]

The Hebrew Book of Esther, which was accorded canonical status by the Jews of Palestine, has the distinction of being one of only two books of the Bible which never refer directly to God (the other being the Song of Solomon). This omission is more than a matter of semantics or literary style, for Esther is also interestingly deficient in any sense of faithfulness to the Torah or to the traditions of Israel in general. It is, simply put, a thoroughly secular tract which advocates the survival of the Jews, a character which has caused questions to be raised concerning the appropriateness of its canonical status.[20]

Near the turn of the second/first century BC, one or more pious Jews of Egypt, who were attracted to the nationalistic qualities of Esther, but displeased by its secularism, set themselves to the task of rewriting the book to bring it into line with traditionalist Jewish theology, a task which they accomplished by introducing several new passages into the existing text. Their work may have coincided with the translation of the Hebrew original into Greek, although it is probable that an unexpanded Greek Esther circulated in Egypt for a period before the additions were affixed. The additions were probably written in Greek (although some may have had Hebrew originals), and they were inserted at appropriate places into the translated Greek text of canonical Esther, the receiving text being rewritten at points to make it more compatible with the additions. It was in this form that the Book of Esther was included in the Septuagint. The additions constitute six passages, containing a total of 107 verses, not found in the Hebrew text. Beyond injecting a strong note of piety into the story of Esther (in the additions there are more than fifty occurrences of "God" or "Lord"), the additions also contain a stronger element of anti-gentile feeling than the canonical Esther, a feature that doubtless reflects the periods of Jewish-gentile tension which were sometimes present in Egypt.

The six additions are as follows:

A. The first addition tells, in apocalyptic language, of a dream of Mordecai in which two dragons fight (11:2–12). It also relates how Mordecai revealed a plot against the king, an act for which he is rewarded by the king, but hated by Haman (12:1–6).

At this point the canonical Esther begins, where one reads of the manner in which Esther becomes queen and of Haman's plot, born of his hatred of Mordecai, to destroy the Jews. (1:1—3:13)

B. The second addition contains the text of the king's proclamation that the Jews be destroyed (13:1–7).

The second addition is followed in canonical Esther by a description of Mordecai's distress and of his appeal to Esther to intervene with the king (3:14—4:17).

C. The third addition contains prayers by Mordecai and by Esther for God's help in the present crisis (13:8—14:19).

D. The fourth addition (which immediately follows the third) paints in colorful detail Esther's approach to the king (15:1–15). It takes the place of 5:1–3 in canonical Esther, verses that are omitted.

The fourth addition is followed in canonical Esther by the unraveling of Haman's plot and his death. The king issues a further decree permitting the Jews to defend themselves (5:3—8:12).

E. The fifth addition contains a copy of the king's decree (16:1–24).

The fifth addition is followed in canonical Esther by the story of the Jews' massacre of their enemies and of the institution of the feast of Purim (8:13—10:3).

F. The sixth addition contains the interpretation of Mordecai's dream told in the first addition (the two dragons are said to be Mordecai and Haman). A postscript purports to give the name of the translator of the "Letter of Purim," that is, the Book of Esther (10:4—11:1).

(A note about chapter and verse numbers within the additions: Jerome, the translator of the Vulgate, removed the first five additions from the text of Esther and collected them at the end, thus causing them to be placed immediately after the sixth addition, which Jerome left undisturbed. Subsequently, the five displaced additions received chapter numbers that were in sequence with the canonical text + the sixth addition. Thus:

End of canonical Esther: 10:3
Sixth addition: 10:4—11:1
First addition: 11:2—12:6
and so on.

These rather illogical chapter and verse divisions have been maintained to the present time.)

In spite of the fact that the additions are almost certainly the product of the community of Egyptian Jews, there is little trace of accommodation to

Hellenistic thought, the piety of the additions having a very traditionalist Jewish character. God is One who hears the prayers of faithful Jews and responds to their needs. The God of Israel is also One who favors the Jews above the rest of humankind. Although they seem to come from the same general environment, the additions to Esther and the Letter of Aristeas exhibit two very different answers to the problems posed by the presence of a Jewish minority within a gentile society.

In the additions, the following texts may be read, first, from the second addition that purports to give a copy of the king's proclamation that the Jews are to be destroyed. This text presents the kind of slander with which Jews of the Diaspora were sometimes familiar:

> Haman . . . pointed out to us that among all the nations in the world there is scattered a certain hostile people, who have laws contrary to those of every nation and continually disregard the ordinances of kings, so that the unifying of the kingdom that we honorably intend cannot be brought about. We understand that this people, and it alone, stands constantly in opposition to every nation, perversely following a strange manner of life and laws, and is ill-disposed to our government, doing all the harm they can so that our kingdom cannot attain stability.
>
> (13:3–5)

The following passage, from the third addition, portrays Esther's deep piety, a trait of character completely missing from the canonical Esther:

> Then Queen Esther, seized with deadly anxiety, fled to the Lord. She took off her splendid apparel and put on the garments of distress and mourning, and instead of costly perfumes she covered her head with ashes and dung, and she utterly humbled her body . . . She prayed to the Lord God of Israel and said: . . . "And now we have sinned before you, and you have handed us over to our enemies, because we glorified their gods. You are righteous, O Lord! . . . O God, whose might is over all, hear the voice of the despairing, and save us from the hands of evildoers. And save me from my fear!"
>
> (14:1–3a, 6–7, 19)

Esther's piety is contrasted, in the fourth addition, with her beauty and cleverness. The splendor of the king is also heightened:

> On the third day, when she ended her prayer, she took off the garments in which she had worshiped, and arrayed herself in splendid attire. Then, majestically adorned, after invoking the aid of the all-seeing God and Savior, she took two maids with her; on one she leaned gently for support, while the other followed, carrying her train.

She was radiant with perfect beauty, and she looked happy, as if beloved, but her heart was frozen with fear. When she had gone through all the doors, she stood before the king. He was seated on his royal throne, clothed in the full array of his majesty, all covered with gold and precious stones. And he was most terrifying.

(15:1–6)

The fifth addition, containing the text of a second proclamation of the king, sets the matter straight concerning the character of the Jews.

"But we find that the Jews, who were consigned to annihilation by this thrice-accursed man, are not evildoers, but are governed by most righteous laws and are the children of the living God, most high, most mighty, who has directed the kingdom both for us and for our ancestors in the most excellent order."

(16:15–16)

Finally, words of anti-gentile feeling from the sixth addition:

"The Lord has saved his people; the Lord has rescued us from all these evils; God has done great signs and wonders, wonders that have never happened among the nations. For this purpose he made two lots, one for the people of God, the other for all the nations."

(10:9–10)

6. The Prayer of Azariah and the Song of the Three Jews (2d or 1st c. BC)[21]

The popularity of the Book of Daniel during the Hasmonean Era is made clear by a number of additions which pious Jews made to the Hebrew and Aramaic apocalypse of the Old Testament. One of these is (in the text of the Septuagint) inserted after Daniel 3:23, which records the consignment of Shadrach, Meshach, and Abednego to the fiery furnace. It consists of a prayer by Azariah (Abednego's Hebrew name) in which he petitions God for help and, after a brief narrative link, of a hymn of praise by the three young men. The literary history of the Prayer of Azariah and the Song of the Three Jews is uncertain, but it is likely that they existed as separate documents before being brought together in this addition to Daniel.

The prayer (vv. 3–22) is a statement of confidence in God's goodness and a confession of the nation's sin, similar in certain respects to Daniel 9:4–19 and Baruch 1:15—3:8 (see discussion in the next chapter). It is significant, however, that it is not Azariah's present distress that is the focus of concern, but the weakness of the people. Because of God's judgment, they are in dire straits:

For we, O Lord, have become fewer than any other nation,
  and are brought low this day in all the world because of our sins.
In our day we have no ruler, or prophet, or leader,
  no burnt offering, or sacrifice, or oblation, or incense,
  no place to make an offering before you and to find mercy.
(vv. 14–15)

But the prayer affirms the penitent spirit of the people and calls on God to save them, and to do so in such a manner that the gentiles will know of the power of the God of Israel:

Deliver us in accordance with your marvelous works,
  and bring glory to your name, O Lord.
Let all who do harm to your servants be put to shame;
  let them be disgraced and deprived of all power.
  and let their strength be broken.
Let them know that you alone are the Lord God,
  glorious over the whole world.
(vv. 20–22)

The date and circumstances for the composition of the prayer are not totally clear, but the references to "no ruler, or prophet, or leader, no burnt offering, . . ." in v. 15 suggest a time just subsequent to Antiochus' desecration of the Temple, but before the revolt of Mattathias and the leadership of Judas.

The Song of the Three Jews (vv. 29–68) appears to depend upon Psalm 148, for it is a carefully structured hymn in which all creation is called upon to praise the Lord. The hymn begins with a doxology (vv. 29–34) to the sovereign God who dwells in the heavenly Temple:

"Blessed are you, O Lord, God of our ancestors,
  and to be praised and highly exalted forever;
Blessed are you in the temple of your holy glory,
  and to be extolled and highly glorified forever."
(vv. 29, 31)

The balance of the hymn calls upon, in order, the heavens and celestial objects, the earth and terrestrial objects, and finally humankind, (especially Israel) to praise the Lord. This order is strikingly similar to that in Psalm 148, although the phraseology here is more repetitious (cf. Ps. 136):

"Bless the Lord, you heavens;
  sing praise to him and highly exalt him forever.

Bless the Lord, you angels of the Lord,
  sing praise . . .
Bless the Lord, all you waters above the heavens;
  sing praise . . . ."

"Let the earth bless the Lord,
  let it sing praise . . .
Bless the Lord, mountain and hills;
  sing praise . . .
Bless the Lord, all that grows in the ground;
  sing praise . . . ."

"Bless the Lord, all people on earth;
  sing praise . . .
Bless the Lord, O Israel,
  sing praise . . .
Bless the Lord, you priests of the Lord;
  sing praise . . . ."

(vv. 36–38, 52–54, 60–62)

The subject matter of the song is too general to permit any identification of the date and place of its composition.

The prose narrative (vv. 23–28) that connects the prayer to the song describes the ferocity of the flames into which the three men have been cast and contains this interesting sentence:

But the angel of the Lord came down into the furnace to be with Azariah and his companions, and drove the fiery flame out of the furnace, and made the inside of the furnace as though a moist wind were whistling through it. The fire did not touch them at all and caused them no pain or distress.

(vv. 26–27)

This sentence, or perhaps the entire prose link, may have been adapted from a missing portion of the text of Daniel, since the arrival of the angel is implied in Daniel 3:24, but is stated nowhere in the existing text of the book.

The Prayer of Azariah and the Song of the Three Jews may have been written in Hebrew or Aramaic, but the oldest existing copies are in Greek. The Septuagint version of Daniel was discarded by the second century AD in favor of the Greek translation of Theodotion,[22] and it is in copies of Theodotion's Daniel (bound with the Septuagint) that the earliest extant copies are to be found. A ninth century copy of the Septuagint version of Daniel, however, also contains this addition, thus raising the likelihood that the prayer and the song were added to Daniel at the time of its translation into Greek or shortly thereafter.

All of the additions to Daniel have been widely read and used in Christian circles, the song having gained a special place in the liturgy of some Christian communions.

C. Testamentary Literature: The Testament of Moses (2d c. bc to 1st c. ad)[23]

The Testaments of the Twelve Patriarchs, discussed earlier because of its apocalyptic content, is the most extensive example of Jewish testamentary literature to come out of the Hellenistic period. Another document that belongs to this genre is the Testament of Moses.

The final chapters of the Book of Deuteronomy, 31–34, are a narrative of Moses' farewell to his people just prior to their entry into the Promised Land. An interesting document has survived from antiquity that records the efforts of a Palestinian Jew to expand this account by providing details of Moses' testamentary speech to Joshua (Deut. 31:7–8, 23). This Testament of Moses was probably written in either Hebrew or Aramaic and was later translated into Greek. The single ancient copy that has been preserved, however, is in Latin and is seriously defective in that its conclusion is absent, with perhaps one third to one half of the document having been lost prior to its discovery by modern scholars.

There is wide disagreement concerning the literary history of this document. One body of opinion holds that the Testament of Moses was written during the period of the Hasmonean revolt and that important additions were made during the first century AD. A second view is that the work comes from early in the first century AD. A third conclusion is that it is the product of the Bar Kokhba revolt of 132–135 AD. The view adopted here is the first of these, but the student should bear in mind that the issue is far from settled.

The theological themes of the Book of Deuteronomy and of the Deuteronomistic History are prominent in the Testament of Moses, especially the cycle of sin-punishment-repentance-salvation. But to these themes is added an outlook that is clearly apocalyptic in nature: God will deliver the faithful people by overthrowing the devil and establishing the divine rule. In anticipation of this day, the people of God must be courageous in the face of suffering, even to the point of martyrdom.

The Testament of Moses begins as Moses tells Joshua of the experiences that the people will have in the Land of Promise. This is basically a brief recapitulation of the history of Israel until the time of the return from exile, an event that is portrayed (as it is in the Old Testament) as an act of God's grace. Once they are back in the land, however, the people, or at least their leaders, return to sinful ways. In language that sounds as if it has been written with Hellenizing Jews in mind, the testament predicts:

> they will pollute the house of their worship with the customs of the nations; and they will play the harlot after foreign gods. For they will not follow the truth of God, but certain of them will pollute the high altar by [several letters lost] the offerings which they place before the Lord. They are not (truly) priests (at all), but slaves, yea sons of slaves.
>
> (5:3–4)

God's reponse to this sin is one of severe punishment that comes in the form of sufferings inflicted by a "king of the kings of the earth," language that is reminiscent of Daniel 7:17. Presumably this is a reference to Antiochus Epiphanes and the forces at his command.

> And there will come upon them [. . .] punishment and wrath such as has never happened to them from the creation till that time when he stirs up against them a king of the kings of the earth who, having supreme authority, will crucify those who confess their circumcision. Even those who deny it, he will torture and hand them over to be led to prison in chains. And their wives will be given to the gods of the nations and their young sons will be cut by physicians to bring forward their foreskins. [This last reference is unclear, but it seems to have to do with some kind of prohibition against circumcision.]
>
> (8:1–3)

At this point there is introduced into the narrative the story of one, Taxo, who, with his seven sons, chooses self-imposed exile and death, rather than deny the traditions of Israel. The story of Taxo (9:1–7), which may not be an original part of the Testament of Moses, is remotely similar to that of the Jewish mother and her seven sons in 2 Maccabees 7:1–42 who bravely endured torture rather than renounce their beliefs.

This is followed by an eschatological hymn that, in the language of apocalyptic, describes God's overthrow of the forces of evil:

> Then his kingdom will appear throughout his whole creation
> Then the devil will have an end.
> Yea, sorrow will be led away with him
>
> Then will be filled the hands of the messenger, [probably Michael]
>   who is in the highest place appointed.
> Yea, he will at once avenge them of their enemies.
>
> For the Heavenly One will arise from his kingly throne.
> Yea, he will go forth from his holy habitation
>   with indignation and wrath on behalf of his sons.

For God Most High will surge forth,
  the Eternal One alone.
In full view he will come to work vengeance on the nations.
Yea, all their idols he will destroy.

Then you will be happy, O Israel!
And you will mount up above the necks and the wings of an eagle.
Yea, all things will be fulfilled.

(10:1–3, 7–8)

The existing manuscript comes to an end with Moses reassuring Joshua that God is sovereign and that sin will be punished, while faithfulness will be rewarded. Among other things, this final section (12:1–13) contains a statement of predestinarian belief that will be familiar to readers of apocalyptic literature:

God has created all the nations which are in the world (just as he created) us. And he has forseen both them and us from the beginning of the creation of the world even to the end of the age. Indeed, nothing, to the last thing, has been overlooked by him. But (rather) he has seen all things and he is the cause of all.

(12:4)

According to the theory followed here, a second writer about 30 AD updated the testament by inserting material having to do with the Herod and the Romans (chaps. 6 and 7).

Some scholars have pointed to possible influences by the Testament of Moses upon the New Testament Book of Jude. Jude 9, for example, refers to a dispute between Michael and the devil over the body of Moses. It has been suggested that such a dispute may have been described in the lost ending of the testament, although that is a matter of conjecture.

Another possible point of contact may be reflected in Jude 12–13 that uses the images of natural catastrophe to describe evil in a manner similar to the way in which T. Moses 10:5–6 describes the eschaton:

The sun will not give light.
And in darkness the horns of the moon will flee.
Yea, the will be broken in pieces.

It will be turned wholly into blood.
Yea, even the circle of the stars will be thrown into disarray.

And the sea all the way to the abyss will retire,
  to the sources of waters which fail.
Yea, the rivers will vanish away.

(T. Moses 10:5–6)

> These are . . . waterless clouds, carried along by the winds; autumn trees without fruit, twice dead, uprooted; wild waves of the sea, casting up the foam of their own shame; wandering stars, for whom the deepest darkness has been reserved forever.
>
> (Jude 12–13)

D. Wisdom Literature: The Wisdom of Jesus the Son of Sirach, also called Ecclesiasticus (early 2d c. bc)[24]

Early in the second century BC a Palestinian Jew composed in Hebrew an extended collection of his thoughts on the nature of God and the nature of human life, an anthology that is cast in the literary forms and conceptual mold of Wisdom literature. Near the end of his work the author affixes his name,[25] and although subsequent copyists spoiled the text of the line so that modern readers cannot be sure precisely what the name was, it appears to have been "Jesus son of Eleazar son of Sirach of Jerusalem" (50:27). For reasons of brevity, he is often called Ben (son of) Sirach, or sometimes simply Sirach. His anthology of Wisdom reflections was probably composed shortly after the death of the high priest Simon II, who died about 195 BC and whom he eulogizes (50:1–24).

Although Ben Sirach was aware that certain contradictions in life will always frustrate the human mind in its quest for truth, one should not be distracted by these paradoxes.

> Neither seek what is too difficult for you,
>   nor investigate what is beyond your power.
> Reflect upon what you have been commanded,
>   for what is hidden is not your concern.
> Do not meddle in matters that are beyond you,
>   for more than you can understand has been shown you.
>
> (3:21–23)

In short, it is possible to know what one needs to know, thus little accommodation is made to the "skeptical" school of Wisdom (represented by the Wisdom Books of Job and Ecclesiastes) and to its probing of Wisdom's fundamental assumptions. Ben Sirach accepts those assumptions and, in a wide-ranging discourse that often reminds one of the Book of Proverbs (upon which Ben Sirach modeled his work), he shapes them to meet his own particular concerns. Yet, for all his "orthodoxy," Ben Sirach is far from provincial or cloistered. In one place (34:9–12) he refers to his travels and to adventures that have brought him close to death, and he remarks that such experiences are necessary for an educated man. There are even references which suggest his absorption into Hellenistic literature (cf. 13:2 and Aesop's fable of the pot and the kettle). When all is said and done, however, the only way in which God's truth may be known is through Israel's Wisdom. In fact, this emphasis on the supremacy of Israel's Wisdom teaching may have been intended as a quiet reminder to Jews faced with the lures of Hellenism that *their* allegiances should be to the traditions of Israel.

A wide range of topics is addressed in the Wisdom of Ben Sirach. There are practical admonitions concerning unbridled anger (1:22), filial loyalty (3:8), slander (5:14), marital relations (9:1), friendship (12:8), strong drink (19:1) and the like. There are also reflections upon human freedom (15:11–20), the irresistible power of God (43:1–33), the mercy of God (18:1–14), and similar themes. But clearly Ben Sirach's greatest interest is in the power of Wisdom itself to shape human life for good and to provide answers to the heart's deepest questions. Taking his cue from Wisdom writers of the Persian period (Prov. 1:7, Job 28:28), Ben Sirach affirms

> All wisdom is from the Lord
>   and with him it remains forever.
>
> To fear the Lord is the beginning of wisdom;
>   she is created with the faithful in the womb.
>
> To fear the Lord is the root of wisdom,
>   and her branches are long life.
>   (1:1, 14, 20)

But not only is love of God the foundation of Wisdom for Ben Sirach, he goes farther than any Wisdom writer before him in identifying Wisdom with the Torah. Other writers had spoken of Wisdom as one of the original creations of God (Job 28:23–28) or had personified Wisdom as a companion of God at creation (Prov. 8:22–31). Ben Sirach, however, goes beyond them and, by allowing Wisdom to speak for herself, describes her (Wisdom is always feminine in Hebrew thought) as roaming the world since creation in search for her own people:

> Alone I compassed the vault of heaven
>   and traversed the depths of the abyss.
> Over the waves of the sea, over all the earth,
>   and over every people and nation I have held sway.
> Among all these I sought a resting place;
>   in whose territory should I abide?
>   (24:5–7)

Then, at the direction of God, Wisdom was sent to Israel as an eternal gift:

Then the Creator of all things gave me a command,
    and my Creator chose the place for my tent.
He said, "Make your dwelling in Jacob,
    and in Israel receive your inheritance."
Before the ages, in the beginning, he created me,
    and for all the ages I shall not cease to be.
                                        (24:8–9)

Ben Sirach then permits Wisdom to describe how she became resident in the Jerusalem Temple and, in a shift of metaphors, how she became a tree, bearing delicious fruit. Wisdom then invites Israel to sustain itself with this fruit.

Come to me, you who desire me,
    and eat your fill of my fruits.
For the memory of me is sweeter than honey,
    and the possession of me sweeter than the honeycomb.
Those who eat of me will hunger for more,
    and those who drink of me will thirst for more.
Whoever obeys me will not be put to shame,
    and those who work with me will not sin.
                                        (24:19–22)

The part of the poem in which Wisdom speaks in the first person comes to an end, but Ben Sirach makes obvious what has been implicit all along: Wisdom is the Torah of Israel.

All this is the book of the covenant of the Most High God,
    the law that Moses commanded us
    as an inheritance for the congregations of Jacob.
                                        (24:23)

Referring to the rivers which surrounded the Garden of Eden (Gen. 2:10–14) as well as to other streams, Ben Sirach emphasizes the life-sustaining qualities of the Torah:

It overflows, like the Pishon, with wisdom,
    and like the Tigris at the time of the first fruits.
It runs over, like the Euphrates, with understanding,
    and like the Jordan at harvest time.

It pours forth instruction like the Nile,
  like the Gihon at the time of vintage.
The first man did not know wisdom fully,
  nor will the last one fathom her;
For her thoughts are more abundant than the sea,
  and her counsel deeper than the great abyss.
                                        (24:25–29)

Ben Sirach's view of the Torah, while deeply felt, betrays none of the sectarian views on Torah interpretation that were later to cause such deep divisions within early Judaism. It is a devotion to the Torah for its own sake that motivates this cultured Jew of the early second century BC.[26]

Toward the end of that century the grandson of Ben Sirach, who had settled in Egypt, made a translation of his grandfather's work into Greek and added to it a brief prologue. In this prologue he expresses the hope that Ben Sirach's work will inspire Diaspora Jews to lead lives based on the Torah.

It seemed highly necessary that I should myself devote some diligence and labor to the translation of this book. During that time I have applied my skill day and night to complete and publish the book for those living abroad who wished to gain learning and are disposed to live according to the law.

Two fragments of Ben Sirach's anthology were found at Qumran and one at Masada, thus indicating its acceptance by at least some Palestinian Jews during the Hellenistic period. In Egypt, the Wisdom of Ben Sirach became a part of the canon of the Septuagint, and has thus enjoyed canonical and deutero-canonical status among Christians.

Influence upon the New Testament:[27] Scholars have long drawn attention to striking parallels between Ben Sirach and the New Testament, especially the Letter of James. Below are a few of the texts that strongly suggest that the author of that letter was influenced by Ben Sirach:

My child, when you come to
  serve the Lord,
  prepare yourself for testing.
Set your heart right and be
  steadfast,
and do not be impetuous in
time of calamity.
        (Ben Sirach 2:1–2)

My brothers and sisters,
whenever you face trials of any
kind, consider it nothing but joy,
because you know that the testing of your faith produces
endurance.
                    (James 1:2–3)

Do not say, "It was the Lord's
doing that I fell away";
for he does not do what he
hates.
Do not say, "It was he who led
me astray";
for he has no need of the
sinful.

If you choose, you can keep the
commandments,
and to act faithfully is a
matter of your own choice.
(Ben Sirach 15:11–12, 15)

My child, when you are ill, do
not delay,
but pray to the Lord, and he
will heal you.
(Ben Sirach 38:9)

No one, when tempted, should
say, "I am tempted by God"; for
God cannot be tempted by evil
and he himself tempts no one.
But one is tempted by one's own
desire, being lured and enticed
by it.
(James 1:13–14)

Are any among you sick? They
should call for the elders of the
church and have them pray over
them, anointing them with oil
in the name of the Lord. The
prayer of faith will save the
sick.   (James 5:14–15)

In addition to these and other parallels between Ben Sirach and
James, there is reason to believe that Ben Sirach 11:18–19 may have provided the model for Jesus' parable of the Rich Fool in Luke 12:16–21:

One becomes rich through diligence and self-denial,
and the reward allotted to him is this:
when he says, "I have found my rest,
and now I shall feast on my goods!"
he does not know how long it will be
until he leaves them to others and dies.
(Ben Sirach 11:18–19)

Finally, it should be noted that the section 44:1—50:24, which begins
with the summons: "Let us now sing the praises of famous men," is a
roll of Israel's heroes of faith that may have inspired Hebrews 11:1–40.

E. Historiography

Both Jews and Greeks possessed honored traditions in the writing of history. Among the Jews the Yahwist, the Elohist, the Deuteronomistic Historians, and the authors of the Priestly History are only some of those whose work became part of the canon of scripture. Among the Greeks, as we have seen, Herodotus, Thucydides, Polybius, and others helped to shape the collective memory of the Hellenistic world. Given these facts, it is curious that there is so little writing of history by Jews of the Hellenistic period. Palestinian Jews of this era are represented primarily by 1 Maccabees and by an earlier historian whose work has survived in only fragmentary form, Eupolemus, while the Diaspora produced the five-volume account of the Maccabean wars by Jason of Cyrene, known to us in its abbreviated form 2 Maccabees.

1. *Eupolemus* (2d c. BC)[28]

Like Artapanus, the work of the Jewish historian Eupolemus is known to us primarily through Alexander Polyhistor/Eusebius. Polyhistor (according to Eusebius) recorded four fragments from a work by Eupolemus on the history of the Jews, probably entitled On the Kings in Judaea. A fifth fragment is contained in a brief summary of a part of Eupolemus' work found in Stromata of the Christian writer Clement of Alexandria (c. 150–216). In this fragment (which is not recorded in Polyhistor/Eusebius) Eupolemus calculates the number of years from Adam to the fifth regnal year of the Seleucid ruler Demetrius I Soter (162–150 BC), thereby providing reason to believe that Eupolemus worked about 157 BC. This date is three years after the death of Judas Maccabeus, thus giving rise to the possibility that the author of On the Kings in Judaea may be the same Eupolemus sent by Judas as ambassador to Rome (1 Macc. 8:17f and 2 Macc. 4:11).

As Josephus was later to do, Eupolemus retold Jewish history by combining the biblical narrative with certain flights of fancy. He seems to have relied both on the Hebrew text and on the Septuagint, and to have preferred the text of Chronicles to that of Samuel-Kings. For example, he calls the King of Tyre Souron, from Chronicles' Hebrew version Churam (Kings: Hiram), but other proper names reflect the style of the Greek Septuagint.

Alexander Polyhistor, as quoted by Eusebius, appears to have transmitted the words of Eupolemus with some exactitude, altering them only to couch them as indirect discourse. The early history of Israel seems to have been treated by Eupolemus in summary form, as his primary interest was apparently in the Davidic monarchy. In the first fragment it is interesting that Eupolemus knows of the role of the Phoenicians in teaching the alphabet to the Greeks, but he attributes prior knowledge of the alphabet to Moses.

And Eupolemus says that Moses was the first wise man, that he first taught the alphabet to the Jews, and that the Phoenicians received it from the Jews, and the Greeks received it from the Phoenicians, and that Moses first wrote laws for the Jews.

(Fragment 1)

Fragment 2 is the longest and carries the history of the people from the time of Moses to the building of the Temple by Solomon. Again, much of this is in summary form, except for some of the details surrounding the building of the Temple. One interesting feature of this fragment is copies of correspondence purported to have passed between Solomon and Vaphres, King of Egypt, and between Solomon and Souron, King of Tyre, in which Solomon requests the help of his fellow monarchs in the Temple project (cf. 1 Kings 5:2–9). Both kings agree to help after they have lavished praise upon Solomon:

King Vaphres to Solomon the Great King, greetings! When I read the letter from you, I rejoiced greatly, and I and all my administration celebrated a feast day in honor of your reception of the kingdom from a man who was so noble and approved by so great a God.

*   *   *   *

Souron to Solomon the Great King, greetings! Praised be the God, who created heaven and earth and who chose a noble person, the son of a noble man. As soon as I read the letter from you, I rejoiced and praised God for your reception of the kingdom.

(Fragment 2)

Fragment 4 contains lore about the prophet Jeremiah not found in the Old Testament. The name of the Judaean king, Jonachim, is apparently a corrupted form of Jehoiakim (2 Kings 23:34—24:7).

Then Jonachim (became king). During his reign Jeremiah the prophet prophesied. Sent by God, he caught the Jews sacrificing to a golden idol, whose name was Baal. He disclosed to them the coming misfortune. Jonachim attempted to burn him alive, but he [i.e. Jeremiah] said that, with this wood, as captives they would prepare food for the Babylonians, and dig the canals of the Tigris and Euphrates.

(Fragment 4)

2. One Maccabees (late 2d c. or early 1st c. BC)[29]

Our discussion of the Hasmonean revolt referred on a number of occasions to 1 Maccabees as a primary source of knowledge of these events. Because of those references the reader will already be aware, in general terms, of the contents and style of this important work. However, a few words are in order here concerning its literary history and significance.

One Maccabees follows in orderly fashion the progress of the revolt, beginning with an introductory account of its background and causes (1:1–64), which includes a description of Antiochus' desecration of the Temple (1:21–28). Then follows, in succession, narratives of the campaigns of resistance waged by Mattathias (2:1–70), Judas (3:1—9:22), Jonathan (9:23—12:53), and Simon (13:1—16:24). The book concludes with the death of Simon and the assumption of leadership by his son John Hyrcanus.

The author of 1 Maccabees, assuming that he was not a participant in the revolt himself, seems to have drawn on information provided by eyewitnesses to the struggle, a judgment based upon apparently authentic detail incorporated in the narrative (e.g., the descriptions of battle in chap. 4). But it is also apparent that certain written sources were available to the writer, in particular, documents that contained the contents of various letters (5:10–13, 12:6–18, and elsewhere) and one inscription (14:27–45).

The First Book of Maccabees was almost certainly written in Hebrew, and its style is generally simple and unadorned. The author not only records noteworthy events, but in the manner of a true historian, he frequently attempts to interpret them. He considers the Hasmonean fighters to be "seeking righteousness and justice" (2:29) and their enemies, including Jewish opponents, are "renegades" and "wrongdoers" (9:23), while he characterizes the energy with which the revolt is carried on as the result of "zeal for the law" (2:26). It is also clear that he considers the Hasmonean succession to be legally and morally right (13:7–8). Surprisingly, however, there is not a single direct mention of God, although several occurrences of the euphemism Heaven (3:18, 4:10 and elsewhere).

In contrast to 2 Maccabees, which frequently invokes the element of the miraculous, 1 Maccabees is very reserved in this regard. Events happen as a result of normal cause-and-effect sequences, although there is no doubt that the author considers the Hasmoneans to be doing the will of God. As a corollary to this sober style, there is very little effort to play upon the emotions of the reader (again, unlike 2 Maccabees). Because references to the Romans are not unfavorable, 1 Maccabees was almost certainly written before 63 BC, and the lack of detailed references to John Hyrcanus or his successors may imply an even earlier date. The author was perhaps a Sadducean supporter of John Hyrcanus or Alexander Jannaeus.

In spite of the presence of 1 Maccabees in the Septuagint, and thus in the earliest Christian canon, the book has not received a great deal of attention from Christians. Among Jews, interest has been stimulated in our time by the emergence of Zionism, which has drawn a parallel between the Hasmonean warriors of old and those who have fought for the modern State of Israel.

In addition to the quotations from 1 Maccabees given earlier, the following are submitted as examples of the style of this important history of the Hasmonean revolt. First, on the slaughter of the Hasidim during the time of Mattathias:

> At that time many who were seeking righteousness and justice went down to the wilderness to live there, they, their sons, their wives, and their livestock, because troubles pressed heavily upon them. And it was reported to the king's officers, and to the troops in Jerusalem the city of David, that those who had rejected the king's command had gone down to the hiding places in the wilderness. Many pursued them, and overtook them; they encamped opposite them and prepared for battle against them on the sabbath day. And they said to them, "Enough of this! Come out and do what the king commands, and you will live." But they said, "We will not come out, nor will we do what the king commands and so profane the sabbath day." Then the enemy quickly attacked them. But they did not answer them or hurl a stone at them or block up their hiding places, for they said, "Let us all die in our innocence; heaven and earth testify for us that you are killing us unjustly." So they attacked them on the sabbath, and they died, with their wives and children and livestock, to the number of a thousand persons.
>
> (2:29–38)

On the rededication of the Temple:

> Early in the morning on the twenty-fifth day of the ninth month, which is the month Chislev, in the one hundred forty-eighth year, they rose and offered sacrifice, as the law directs, on the new altar of burnt offering that they had built. At the very season and on the very day that the Gentiles had profaned it, it was dedicated with songs and harps and lutes and cymbals. All the people fell on their faces and worshiped and blessed Heaven, who had prospered them. So they celebrated the dedication of the altar for eight days, and joyfully offered burnt offerings; they offered a sacrifice of well-being and a thanksgiving offering. They decorated the front of the temple with golden crowns and small shields; they restored the gates and the chambers for the priests, and fitted them with doors. There was very great joy among the people, and the disgrace brought by the Gentiles was removed.
>
> (4:52–58)

On the death of Judas:

> Judas saw that Bacchides and the strength of his army were on the right; then all the stouthearted men went with him, and they crushed the right wing, and he pursued them as far as Mount Azotus. When

those on the left wing saw that the right wing was crushed, they turned
and followed close behind Judas and his men. The battle became desperate, and many on both sides were wounded and fell. Judas also fell and
the rest fled.

Then Jonathan and Simon took their brother Judas and buried him in
the tomb of their ancestors at Modein, and wept for him. And all Israel
made great lamentation for him; they mourned many days and said,
> "How is the mighty fallen,
> the savior of Israel!"

Now the rest of the acts of Judas, and his wars and the brave deeds that
he did, and his greatness, have not been recorded, but they were very
many.

(9:14–22)

3. Two Maccabees (2d c. BC)[30]

Together with 1 Maccabees and Josephus, the 2 Maccabees constitutes our earliest source of information concerning the Hasmonean revolt. Unlike 1 Maccabees, however, which narrates events concerning the activities of Mattathias
and his three sons, Judas, Jonathan and Simon, 2 Maccabees focuses upon
events leading up to the armed insurrection and upon the career of Judas until
the time of his victory over the Seleucid general Nicanor (cf. 1 Macc. 7). It is
silent concerning Judas' death and all subsequent events. Again unlike 1 Maccabees, which seems to have been preserved in more or less its original literary
unity, 2 Maccabees is a summary of a longer work (now lost) in five volumes
(scrolls) by an otherwise unknown Jason of Cyrene. Jason's writing was apparently done in the last quarter of the second century BC and in the Greek language, while the person responsible for the summary of Jason's work, our
2 Maccabees, may have been active early in the first century BC. Because the
name of this latter individual is not known, he is called simply "the epitomist."

The Second Book of Maccabees in the form in which it has reached us begins with two letters (1:1–9, 1:10—2:18) from Jews of Jerusalem to their counterparts in Egypt, passages that appear to have been added after the epitomist
completed his work. Both of these letters urge the keeping of the feast of
Tabernacles, and the second, which may be a composite literary creation, is
noteworthy because it relates a miracle by which Nehemiah obtained fire for
the altar of the Temple.

The document proper begins with a prologue by the epitomist (2:19–32) in
which he tells of his desire to set forth a faithful, but condensed version of the
work of Jason of Cyrene.

we have aimed to please those who wish to read, to make it easy for
those who are inclined to memorize, and to profit all readers. For us

who have undertaken the toil of abbreviating, it is no light matter but calls for sweat and loss of sleep.

(2 Macc. 2:25–26)

It has been observed that the historical account that ensues has been erected upon a theological framework of sin, followed by punishment, followed by both judgment (for the faithless) and salvation (for the faithful):

1. Blessing: Jerusalem during the priesthood of Onias III (3:1–40)
2. Sin: Hellenization of Jerusalem under Jason and Menelaus (4:1—5:10)
3. Punishment: Antiochus' reprisals (5:11—6:17)
4. Turning point: Deaths of the martyrs and prayers of the people (6:18—8:4)
5. Judgment and salvation: The victories of Judas (8:5—15:36)[31]

Finally, there is a brief epilogue from the epitomist (15:37–39) in which he expresses the hope that readers will enjoy his work:

If it is well told and to the point, that is what I myself desired; if it is poorly done and mediocre, that was the best I could do. For just as it is harmful to drink wine alone, or, again, to drink water alone, while wine mixed with water is sweet and delicious and enhances one's enjoyment, so also the style of the story delights the ears of those who read the work.

(2 Macc. 15:38-39b)

The epitomist's style, perhaps reflecting that of Jason of Cyrene, is indeed calculated to gain the attention and sympathy of the reader. The evils of the Hellenists—their persecution of faithful Jews, for example—are etched in bold strokes, as are the virtues of the brave fighters for freedom—that is, their fortitude under torture. Nor does the epitomist confine his remarks to the narration of events, but goes to great pains to reveal the inner emotions of the parties to the conflict. Even God is described as a participant in the struggle, not only as the Sustainer of the faithful, but also as One who intercedes on their behalf by means of miraculous events. Those who fall on behalf of the traditions of Israel are assured of resurrection (7:22–23, and elsewhere). All of these characteristics are, of course, quite different from the sober, reserved style of 1 Maccabees.

The question of a literary relationship between 1 and 2 Maccabees has been discussed by scholars, but no clear answers have been forthcoming. The general agreement between the two documents in matters which they treat in common may be the result of their mutual dependence upon the same historical sources, rather than the dependence of 2 Maccabees upon 1 Maccabees. It has been said that, if 1 Maccabees is a Sadducean account of the Hasmonean revolt, 2 Maccabees may be that of a Pharisee, in light of the interest in miracles and resurrection. But 2 Maccabees could just as easily represent an Essene point of view, since the document's failure to treat Jonathan would coincide with the rejection of his high priesthood by the Essenes, assuming, that is, that he is the "Wicked Priest" of the Qumran scrolls.[32]

The Second Book of Maccabees has been used by some Christians to support belief in prayers for the dead (12:43–45) and intercessory prayers by the departed saints (15:12–16).

A few examples of the style of 2 Maccabees, first the account of the miracle that prevented the Seleucid agent, Heliodorus, from looting the Temple treasury:[33]

> Heliodorus went on with what had been decided. But when he arrived at the treasury with his bodyguard, then and there the Sovereign of spirits and of all authority caused so great a manifestation that all who had been so bold as to accompany him were astounded by the power of God, and became faint with terror. For there appeared to them a magnificently caparisoned horse, with a rider of frightening mien; it rushed furiously at Heliodorus and struck him with its front hoofs. Its rider was seen to have armor and weapons of gold. Two young men also appeared to him, remarkably strong, gloriously beautiful and splendidly dressed, who stood on each side of him and flogged him continuously, inflicting many blows on him. When he suddenly fell to the ground and deep darkness came over him, his men took him up, and put him on a stretcher, and carried him away.
>
> (3:23–28a)

Concerning Antiochus' desecration of the Temple:

> Not content with this, Antiochus dared to enter the most holy temple in all the world, guided by Menelaus, who had become a traitor both to the laws and to his country. He took the holy vessels with his polluted hands, and swept away with profane hands the votive offerings that other kings had made to enhance the glory and honor of the place. Antiochus was elated in spirit, and did not perceive that the Lord was angered for a little while because of the sins of those who lived in the city, and that this was the reason he was disregarding the holy place. But if it had not happened that they were involved in many sins, this man would have been flogged and turned back from his rash act as soon as he came forward, just as Heliodorus had been, whom King Seleucus sent to inspect the treasury.
>
> (5:15–18)

Concerning martyrs:

> It happened also that seven brothers and their mother were arrested and were being compelled by the king, under torture with whips and thongs, to partake of unlawful swine's flesh. One of them, acting as their spokesman, said, "What do you intend to ask and learn from us? For we are ready to die rather than transgress the laws of our ancestors."
> The king fell into a rage and gave orders to have pans and caldrons heated. . . .
> And when he [the second brother] was at his last breath, he said, "You accursed wretch, you dismiss us from this present life, but the King of the universe will raise us up to an everlasting renewal of life, because we have died for his laws." . . . The king fell into a rage, and handled him [the last brother] worse than the others, being exasperated at his scorn. So he died in his integrity, putting his whole trust in the Lord.
> Last of all, the mother died, after her sons.
>
> (7:1–41)

F. Epic Poetry

Poets of the Greek tradition often wrote with the model of Homer before them, either to emulate the epic style, as Apollonius of Rhodes, or to react against it, as Callimachus of Cyrene, both of whom we discussed earlier. But it is somewhat surprising to find the epic style practiced, not only by poets of the museum in Alexandria, but by Jews whose subject matter, at that, was the traditions of Israel. But that seems to be what we have in the work of Philo and Theodotus.

1. *Philo the Epic Poet* (3d to 2d c. BC)[34]

An Egyptian Jew, who lived sometime before the end of the second century BC in (probably) Alexandria, wrote a poem of unknown length dealing with the traditions of the Jews. The poet's name was Philo and, to distinguish him from the Jewish writer of that name who was active in the first century AD, he is usually referred to as Philo the Epic Poet or Philo the Elder. The Christian writer Eusebius, depending upon the historian Alexander Polyhistor, is our only source of what survives of the text of Philo the Epic Poet.

Polyhistor/Eusebius report that Philo's work was entitled On Jerusalem and, as the surviving fragments all seem to relate in some manner to the traditions surrounding that city, it probably constituted the subject of Philo's poem. It is not surprising that Jerusalem should occupy the thoughts of an

Egyptian Jew since, even in the Diaspora, Jerusalem was looked upon as the symbolic home of all Jews. Of the extent of this poem nothing is known.

The significance of Philo the Epic Poet is not in any fresh light he throws upon the traditions of the Jews, but upon the fact that his work is cast in a thoroughly Hellenistic form of poetry, making is an excellent example of cultural syncretism. Although it is more self-conscious and pedantic than much Greek poetry written in Alexandria, On Jerusalem obviously attempts to emulate that style. Like many other Hellenized Jews, Philo's sympathies were nevertheless with his people, "the offspring of that awesome born one (i.e., Issac) [who] have won far-hymned praise."

Four fragments of Philo are preserved by Polyhistor/Eusebius, the first two of which are here quoted in full. They are part of Philo's account of the near sacrifice of Isaac, a story that is associated with Jerusalem through the identification of Mt. Moriah (the site of the incident, Gen. 22:2) with the location of Solomon's Temple (2 Chron. 3:1). For those who have read *Iliad* and *Odyssey* Philo's style, while less lucid than Homer's, will nevertheless be familiar.

A thousand times I have heard in the ancient laws how once (when you achieved something) marvelous with the bonds' knot, O far-famed Abraham, resplendently did your God-beloved prayers abound in wondrous counsels. For when you left the beauteous garden of dread plants, the praiseworthy thunderer quenched the pyre and made his promise immortal. From that time forth the offspring of that awesome born one have won far-hymned praise.

And so forth, to which he adds after a short while: as mortal hand readied the sword with resolve, and crackling (wood) was gathered at the side, he brought into his hands a horned ram.

(Fragments 1 and 2)

2. *Theodotus* (2d c. BC)[35]

Another Jewish poet who composed in the Greek epic style is Theodotus, who was active in the second century BC and whose work, like that of Artapanus, Eupolemus, and Philo the Poet, is also preserved in Polyhistor/Eusebius. Polyhistor says that Theodotus penned a work entitled On the Jews, but whether the poet produced other writings is unknown. Also uncertain is the precise extent of On the Jews, since the surviving fragments deal only with the story of the rape of Dinah (Gen. 34). However, it is quite likely that it was a much longer work and may indeed have constituted something of a true epic, not only with respect to its poetic style, but also to its scope.

Polyhistor/Eusebius preserved eight fragments of Theodotus' On the Jews. These do not constitute a continuous narrative, but are connected by means of prose summaries (apparently composed by Polyhistor) of intervening events. As for the poetic fragments, the manner in which the city of Shechem is described has caused some modern scholars to suggest that Theodotus may have been a Samaritan, since Shechem was a Samaritan center in the second century BC. While that may or may not be true, the poet does seem to have known the community at firsthand. Furthermore, Theodotus makes reference to the Shechem city wall that was destroyed in 190 BC, thus giving some clue to the time when he lived.

The eight fragments strongly suggest that Theodotus was influenced by the deep respect for Homer and for the epic tradition that was common in Hellenistic literary circles, especially among some of those who worked in the museum and library in Alexandria. Theodotus may thus have lived part of his life in Egypt and may even have composed On the Jews there. Yet there is no evidence that he drew upon the language of the Septuagint, the Greek Bible used by Alexandrian Jews, in his recasting of the story of Dinah.

Theodotus' fragments betray a knowledge of traditions concerning the story of Dinah and Shechem that do not occur in the biblical account, but that are found in other Jewish literature of the Second Temple period. For example, the view that the destruction of the Shechemites was more than a matter of simple revenge (as in Gen. 34), but that it was also the judgment of God is found in Framents 6 and 7 of Theodotus, as well as in Judith (9:2), Jubilees (30:6–7) and the Testament of Levi (5:1–5; 6:8, 11).

The significance of Theodotus is that, like Philo the Poet, he represents a blending of Jewish historical and theological traditions with those of Hellenistic poetry, for in Theodotus (at least to the extent that his writings have survived), there is no hint of the tensions between traditionalist and Hellenistic Jews that so inflamed his century. He apparently considered it not unusual at all that the story of the Jews should be cast in the language and poetic forms akin to those of Homer. His regard for the Law and for the rite of circumcision, as well as his belief in God's justice leave no mistake concerning his allegiance to the traditions of Israel. Yet his use of the Greek epic style suggests that he may have written for those who were just as much at home in the gymnasium as in the synagogue.

In the selections below, the italicized text represents the connecting narrative of Alexander Polyhistor.

Theodotus in On the Jews *says that Shechem took its name from Shechem, the son of Hermes, for he also founded the city. He says that the city is situated in the land of the Jews in the following manner:*

Thus the land was good and grazed upon by goats and well watered. There was neither a long path for those entering the city from the field nor even leafy woods for the weary. Instead, very close by the city appear two steep mountains, filled with grass and woods. Between the two of them a narrow path is cut. On one side the bustling Shechem appears, a sacred town, built under (i.e. the mountain) as a base; there was a smooth wall around the town; and the wall for defense up above ran in under the foot of the mountain.

(Fragment 1)

Then a little below he [i.e. Jacob] says concerning circumcision,

Once (God) himself, when he led the noble Abraham out of his native land, from heaven called upon the man and all his family to strip off the flesh (i.e. the foreskin), and therefore he accomplished it. The command remains unshaken, since God himself spoke it.

(Fragment 5)

God sent this thought [to kill the Shechemites] into them [i.e. the sons of Jacob] because those in Shechem were impious. He (i.e.Theodotus) says,

God smote the inhabitants of Shechem, for they did not honor whoever came to them, whether evil or noble. Nor did they determine rights or laws throughout the city. Rather deadly works were their care.

(Fragment 7)

Chapter 7

ADDITIONAL JEWISH LITERATURE
OF THE HELLENISTIC PERIOD (2)

G. STORIES AND LEGENDS

Jewish writers of the Hellenistic period sometimes turned their hand to the creation of brief tales of adventure or of faith. Although Hellenistic literary influences may often be detected in these stories and legends, they are for the most part thoroughly Jewish in outlook.

1. *The Letter of Aristeas* (3d c. BC to 1st c. AD)[1]

Our earlier discussion of the Septuagint referred to the Letter of Aristeas as the source of a legendary account of the origin of the Greek Bible. Although scholars are agreed that the narrative contained in the letter is largely fiction, it has not been possible to identify the letter's author nor to know exactly when he worked. The best indications to his identity point to his being an Alexandrian Jew. As for the time of his activity, he could have flourished no earlier than about 250 BC (because of his references to Ptolemy II Philadelphus) and no later than about 100 AD (because of references to the letter in Josephus). A majority of scholars favors a time in the second century BC.

The purpose of the letter, which was written in Greek, seems to be to portray relationships between the Alexandrian Jewish community and the Ptolemaic intellectual and political establishment in a cordial light. Demetrius of Phalerum, the librarian of Alexandria, and the king himself demonstrate a sincere willingness to protect the traditions of Israel under the umbrella of the royal patronage by including a copy of the Torah in the library. For their part, the Jews recognize the authority of the king and attempt to cooperate with him in every way. It has therefore been reasoned that the letter may have been written during a period of strained relations between Jews and their Ptolemaic masters for the purpose of urging tolerance upon both sides. One interesting proposal is that the letter was written during the time of the Hasmonean revolt which, although confined to Palestine, may have produced anxiety in Egypt concerning relations between Jews and non-Jews.

208

The document purports to be a letter and begins with the kind of salutation (vv. 1–8) common to personal communications in the Hellenistic age (cf. Luke 1:1–4, Acts 1:1). Both Aristeas, the writer of the letter, and Philocrates, its recipient, are presumed to be fictions.

> A trustworthy narrative has been complied, Philocrates, of the meeting which we had with Eleazar, high priest of the Jews, arising out of your attaching great importance to hearing a personal account of our mission, its content and purpose.
>
> (v. 1)

The letter recounts how the king, at the request of Demetrius of Phalerum, decreed that the books of the Jewish Law should be translated and added to the library (vv. 9–12). After a lengthy digression (vv. 13–27) dealing with the release of Jewish slaves in Egypt, the text of the king's letter is given (vv. 28–40).

> King Ptolemy to Eleazar the high priest, hearty greetings. It is a fact that a large number of the Jews settled in our country after being uprooted from Jerusalem by the Persians during the time of their ascendancy, and also came with our father into Egypt as prisoners . . . We have freed more than a hundred thousand prisoners, paying their captors the price in silver proportionate to their rank . . . It is our wish to grant favors to them and to all Jews throughout the world, including future generations. We have accordingly decided that your Law shall be translated into Greek letters from what you call the Hebrew letters, in order that they should take their place with us in our library with the other royal books.
>
> (vv. 35–38)

The king's letter concludes with the request for six scholars from each of the twelve Hebrew tribes to do the work of translation. The offer is accepted and implemented (vv. 41–82).

The letter continues with a description of the Temple and of the services held there (vv. 83–120).

The high qualifications of the translators are affirmed (vv. 121–127), following which there is an explanation of certain aspects of the Jewish legal system in a tone which suggests that it is intended for gentiles (vv. 128–172).

The translators, accompanied by the king's agents, Aristeas and Andreas, arrive in Alexandria and are immediately welcomed by the king (vv. 173–181).

> The king was anxious to meet the members of the deputation, so he gave orders to dismiss all the other court officials . . . The unprecedented nature of this step was very clear to all, because it was an established

procedure that important bona fide visitors should be granted an audience with the king only four days after arrival . . . However, he deemed the present arrivals to be deserving of greater honor . . . When the king saw the delegates, he proceded to ask questions about the books, and when they had . . . unrolled the parchments, he paused for a long time, did obeisance about seven times, and said, "I offer you my thanks, gentlemen, and to him who sent you even more, and most of all to the God whose oracles these are." They all, visitors and court present alike, said together and with one voice, "It is well, O King." At this the king was moved to tears, so deeply was he filled with joy.

(vv. 174–178)

The king then provides a wonderful banquet to celebrate the arrival of the Jewish scholars (vv. 182–186).

In a lengthy section, the letter describes the questions put by the king to each of the translators over a period of seven days (vv. 187–300). This section is more an explication of Hellenistic practical philosophy than of Jewish theology.

The work of translation is addressed and completed (vv. 301–311):

Three days afterward, Demetrius [of Phalerum] took the men with him, traversed the mile-long jetty into the sea toward the island, crossed the bridge, and went in the direction of the north. There he assembled them in a house . . . , a magnificent building in a very quiet situation . . . , all that they would require being handsomely provided . . . The result [of their work] . . . was made into a fair copy by Demetrius . . . The outcome was such that in seventy-two days the business of translation was completed, just as if such a result was achieved by some deliberate design. When it was completed, Demetrius assembled the company of the Jews in the place where the task of the translation had been finished, read it to all, in the presence of the translators, who received a great ovation from the crowded audience for being responsible for great blessings. Likewise they gave an ovation to Demetrius.

(vv. 301–309)

The king participates in the joy over the completion of the project and

said to Demetrius, "How is it that after such great works were (originally) completed, none of the [gentile] historians or poets took it upon himself to refer to them?"

(v. 312)

Demetrius' answer is that the Jewish Law is so holy, that unclean gentiles who have attempted to use it for unworthy purposes have been punished by God, sometimes to the point of death (vv. 309–312). The king then orders that the books of the Law be treated with great reverence and sends the scholars home with valuable gifts (vv. 313–321).

2. *Tobit* (late 3d or early 2d c. BC)[2]

After the return from Babylonian captivity, some literature of the Jews reflected growing tensions with the Samaritans, noteworthy examples being the canonical books of Ezra and Nehemiah. Not only are the Samaritans themselves rarely mentioned in a favorable light, but their Israelite ancestors of the Northern Kingdom are also generally portrayed in negative terms as schismatics and idolaters. The Book of Tobit, therefore, is something of a rarity in that it constitutes a sympathetic story of Israelites exiled to Assyria after the fall of Samaria in 722 BC, although, to be sure, their virtue consists in their continued faithfulness to the traditions of Jerusalem (i.e., the Jews).

Tobit is almost certainly a composition from the Diaspora, a conclusion based on the several expressions of concern within the book about relations with a gentile majority in society, and repeated stress on the importance of good relations, including marriage, within the faith. Furthermore, its author appeared to live in a cosmopolitan literary environment because of reflections within the document of various non-Jewish influences. That he was familiar with Hellenistic romances may be detected in his interest in creating a sense of wonder within his readers, while the presence of magic and of a personal angel and demon suggest Persian influences. The references to Ahikar in the postscript (chap. 14) are reminiscent of tales of such a personality contained both in Aesop's *Fables* and in the *Arabian Nights*.[3]

Nevertheless, Tobit is a thoroughly Jewish document. Its purpose is to remind the reader of the importance of the traditions of Judaism, especially the giving of alms and the proper burial of the dead. There is also a theological outlook which goes back at least to the Book of Deuteronomy, that is, that God will sustain those who are faithful and obedient, in spite of all misfortune. Perhaps the nucleus of the book's message is contained in the long prayer of chapter 13:

> If you turn to him with all your heart and with all your soul,
>   to do what is true before him,
> then he will turn to you
>   and will no longer hide his face from you.
>
> (13:6)

This axiom of faith is borne out by the experiences of the cousins Tobit and Raguel and their families, dramatic episodes that are narrated with considerable subtlety and skill. Yet Tobit is a story not of individuals, but of the nation, a theme that becomes more clearly defined toward the end of the narrative. A brief history of Judah's captivity and restoration is recited, to which is attached a statement concerning the conversion of the gentiles at the end of history.

> Then the nations in the whole world will all be converted and worship God in truth. They will all abandon their idols, which deceitfully have led them into their error; and in righteousness they will praise the eternal God.
>
> (Tob. 14:6–7a)

Tobit's interest in eschatology, as well as its angel/demonology, betray the influence of Jewish apocalyptic, although Tobit cannot be termed apocalyptic per se. There is no sense of crisis in the document, as the sufferings of its characters are those of Jews anywhere in the gentile world, not just those under persecution.

The book appears ignorant of the events of the Hasmonean revolt, and therefore may be dated before 168 BC, most scholars preferring a time around 200. The original language of Tobit was Aramaic, but it was translated at an early time into Hebrew and into Greek, and found its way into inclusion in the Septuagint. Aramaic and Hebrew fragments were recovered from the library at Qumran, a fact which demonstrates, of course, that, in spite of its origin in the Diaspora, Tobit was in use in Palestine in the Hellenistic and/or Roman periods. Because of various shifts in style and emphasis within the book, some scholars have suggested composite authorship.

The book opens with two parallel stories of undeserved suffering. Tobit, a pious Israelite of the Assyrian captivity (1:1–22), earns the scorn of his neighbors by burying the body of a murdered Israelite and, as an indirect cause of his charity, is blinded by sparrow droppings (2:1–11). In his incapacity he is reproached by his wife and he prays to God for deliverance (2:11—3:6).

At the same time, but unknown to Tobit, the daughter of his cousin Raguel in far away Ecbatana is also praying for deliverance. An evil demon named Asmodeus has killed each of her seven husbands on their wedding bed and the woman, Sarah, is driven by the taunts of her maids to petition God for help (2:7–15). One scholar has pointed out the manner in which the author has erected parallel literary structures to emphasize the similarity of Tobit's and Sarah's misfortunes:

Tobit's piety = Sarah's innocence

Tobit's blindness = Sarah's demon

Reproach of Tobit's wife = Reproach of Sarah's maids

Tobit's prayer = Sarah's prayer.[4]

The narrator now tells us that God's mercy will rectify the injustices suffered by Tobit and Sarah, even to the providing of details:

> At that very moment, the prayers of both of them were heard in the glorious presence of God. So Raphael [meaning "God heals"] was sent to heal both of them: Tobit, by removing the white films from his eyes, so that he might see God's light with his eyes; and Sarah, daughter of Raguel, by giving her in marriage to Tobias son of Tobit, and by setting her free from the wicked demon Asmodeus. For Tobias was entitled to have her before all others who had desired to marry her. At the same time that Tobit returned from the courtyard into his house, Sarah daughter of Raguel came down from her upper room.
>
> (3:16–17)

Tobit summons his son Tobias to tell him about a sum of money he had entrusted to a certain Gabael, an Israelite (from his name) of Media. Blind Tobit assumes his death is near, and he admonishes his son (4:1–21):

> "Revere the Lord all your days, my son, and refuse to sin or to transgress his commandments. . . . for those who act in accordance with truth will prosper in all their activities. To all those who practice righteousness give alms from your possessions, and do not let your eye begrudge the gift when you make it. Do not turn your face away from anyone who is poor, and the face of God will not be turned away from you."
>
> (4:5–7)

These words strengthen the reader's impression of Tobit's faith, for he does not yet know, as does the reader, that God's act of redemption has already been set in motion. He is waiting, in fact, for death.

Tobias complains that he needs help in recovering the money, so Tobit sends him out to hire an assistant. When he returns, he is accompanied by the angel Raphael, who appears to be an ordinary mortal. When Tobit questions him about his ancestry, Raphael assures Tobit that he is a good Israelite (5:1–15). Tobit then charges Tobias in words whose gentle irony permits the reader to be assured of that which Tobit himself does not yet know:

> Then he called his son and said to him, "Son, prepare supplies for the journey and set out with your brother. May God in heaven bring you safely there and return you in good health to me; and may his angel, my son, accompany you both for your safety."
>
> (5:17)

A moment later, Tobit comforts his sobbing wife. The previous irony about the angel is repeated and is, indeed, compounded in that Tobit's reference to his wife's eyes constitute an (unknown to him) promise concerning the restoration of his own sight.

> Tobit said to her, "Do not worry; our child will leave in good health and return to us in good health. Your eyes will see him on the day when he returns to you in good health. Say no more! Do not fear for them, my sister. For a good angel will accompany him; his journey will be successful, and he will come back in good health."
>
> (5:21–22)

As Tobias and Raphael journey to distant Media to recover Tobit's funds, they catch a marvelous fish. Raphael (whom Tobias still believes to be a human being) tells his companion that the heart and liver of the fish have power to ward off demons and evil spirits, while its gall can cure blindness. He further tells Tobias that he is to marry his kinswoman Sarah and, in spite of Tobias' protests about the evil demon who is in love with the girl, assures the young man that by means of the miraculous fish Tobias can exorcise the demon (6:1–17).

When they arrive at the home of Raguel, Tobias, using Raphael as his spokesman, proposes marriage to Sarah. Raguel, after explaining his daughter's tragic history, agrees and preparations are made, including a wedding feast (7:1–18).

> When they had finished eating and drinking they wanted to retire; so they took the young man and brought him into the bedroom. Then Tobias remembered the words of Raphael, and he took the fish's liver and heart out of the bag where he had put them and put them on the embers of the incense. The odor of the fish so repelled the demon that he fled to the remotest parts of Egypt. But Raphael followed him, and at once bound him there hand and foot.
>
> (8:1–3)

Meanwhile, Raguel and his wife assume that Tobias will meet the same fate as Sarah's previous husbands, and so they prepare his grave. But when a servant slips into the wedding chamber and finds the bride and groom safe and asleep, the family is ecstatic (8:9–14). Raguel praises God:

> "Blessed are you O God, with every pure blessing;
>   let all your chosen ones bless you.
>   Let them bless you forever.
> Blessed are you because you have made me glad.

It has not turned out as I expected,
but you have dealt with us according to your great mercy."

(8:15–16)

After Raphael secures the money from Gabael (9:1–6), he, in the company of the bride and groom, returns to Nineveh. There Tobias uses the gall of the magic fish to restore the sight of his father (10:1—11:19). Then Raphael urges Tobit and Tobias to be faithful and just:

"Bless God and acknowledge him in the presence of all the living for the good things he has done for you . . . Do good and evil will not overtake you. Prayer with fasting is good, but better than both is almsgiving with righteousness . . . Those who give alms will enjoy a full life, but those who commit sin and do wrong are their own worst enemies."

(12:6–9)

The angel thereupon reveals his true identity (12:15).

Tobit utters an extended prayer of thanksgiving to God (14:1–18) and, in his old age, advises Tobias to

serve God faithfully and do what is pleasing in his sight . . . So now, my son, leave Nineveh; do not remain here. On whatever day you bury your mother beside me, do not stay overnight within the confines of the city.

(14:8, 9–10)

Tobias heeds his father's instructions and, after the old man's death at age 158, the family goes to Ecbatana to live with Raguel. There Tobias' mother dies as do, years later, Sarah and Tobias himself.

He died highly respected at the age of a hundred seventeen years. Before he died he heard of the destruction of Nineveh . . . Before he died he rejoiced over Nineveh, and he blessed the Lord God forever and ever. Amen.

(14:14–15)

That the story of Tobit was known and enjoyed in Hellenistic-Roman Palestine is evidenced not only by the discoveries at Qumran, but by possible influences exerted by Tobit upon other Jewish literature. Scholars have suggested that Tobit was known to the authors of Daniel, and of some of the later Psalms, and Jubilees, while its echoes may also be heard in the New Testament.[5] In this last regard, attention has been drawn to structural parallels between Raphael's commission and ascension

(12:16–22) and those of Jesus as described in the Gospels (Matt. 28:18–20). Similarities between Tobit and the pastoral epistles have also been noted (especially the use of the unusual phrase "King of the ages" in Tob. 13:6 and 1 Tim. 1:17), as have possible parallels between Tobit's description of the eschatological Jerusalem and that in the Book of Revelation.

The gates of Jerusalem will
  be built with sapphire
  and emerald,
  and all your walls with
  precious stones.
The towers of Jerusalem will
  be built with gold,
  and their battlements with
  pure gold.
The streets of Jerusalem will
  be paved
  with ruby and with stones
  of Ophir;
The gates of Jerusalem will
  sing hymns of joy,
  and all her houses will cry,
  "Hallelujah!
Blessed be the God of Israel!"
  and the blessed will bless the
  holy name forever and ever.
              (Tob. 13:16c–17)

and showed me the holy city Jerusalem coming down out of heaven from God. It has . . . a radiance like a very rare jewel, like jasper, clear as crystal. It has a great, high wall with twelve gates.
              (Rev. 21:10–12)

  *   *   *   *

After this I heard what seemed to be the loud voice of a great multitude in heaven, saying, "Hallelujah! Salvation and glory and power to our God."(Rev. 19:1)

3. 1 Esdras, including the Story of the Three Guardsmen (2d c. BC)[6]

During the Persian period various stories of the return from exile were compiled in Palestine into (what came to be) the Old Testament Books of Ezra and Nehemiah. Stories of the return were also current among Hellenistic Jews in Egypt, as is clear from the inclusion of Ezra and Nehemiah in the Septuagint, but they also seem to have circulated independently of the biblical version. At some time during the second century BC an Egyptian Jew recast stories of the exile into a Greek narrative which parallels 2 Chronicles 35—36 (Josiah's reinstitution of Passover), all of Ezra and Nehemiah 7:73—8:13 (where the text breaks off in mid-sentence). The many points of correspondence between this document and its biblical counterparts suggest that its author worked with the biblical material before him. On the other hand, the rather extensive manner in which the sequence of the biblical narrative is reorganized suggests either that the Egyptian Jew intentionally rearranged his version of events, or that he also worked from sources independent of the biblical texts. Because the style of his Greek is similar to that of the Septuagint books of Esther and Daniel, it has been proposed that the author or translator of this variant collection of tales of the return and the translator of Daniel and Esther may have been the same person. In time, this alternative collection of tales of the return was incorporated into the Septuagint under the title Esdras A ("Esdras" being the Greek form of "Ezra"), while the Greek translation of the canonical Ezra and Nehemiah was entered as Esdras B.[7] In most modern collections of the Apocrypha the alternative version is known as 1 Esdras.

In addition to the different manner in which material common to Ezra and Nehemiah is presented, the most striking feature of 1 Esdras is its inclusion of a tale unknown to the Old Testament. This story, which constitutes 1 Esdras 3—4, concerns Zerubbabel and purports to describe the manner in which he was chosen to lead a delegation of Jews from Babylon to Jerusalem. In this sense it may be regarded as an expansion of a biblical narrative. But because this story contradicts the literary context in which it is laid in several important ways, it is sometimes argued that it must have existed independently before it was attached in 1 Esdras to other tales of the return, thus its inclusion here in the category of stories and legends. In fact, because it is similar in certain respects to Daniel and its additions (e.g., the superior wisdom of the hero), the proposal has been made by some that its original subject was Daniel and not Zerubbabel at all.

This Story of the Three Guardsmen, as it is called, is significant not because of any theological insights it affords, but because it provides one more example of the fertile creativity of Hellenistic Judaism, this time working in the categories of Wisdom thought.

Three young bodyguards of Persian king Darius devise a contest among themselves, according to which each will write on a piece of paper that which is the strongest thing in the world. These bits of paper are to be put under the pillow of the sleeping king who, upon awakening will, in consultation with his nobles, decide who has written correctly. The winner is to awarded gifts and honors.

> The first [guardsman] wrote "Wine is strongest." The second wrote, "The king is strongest." The third wrote, "Women are strongest, but above all things truth is victor."
>
> (3:10–12)

The reader is not told how the king is advised of the contest or why it is in his interest to participate. Nevertheless, upon awakening and being given the pieces of paper, the king calls a convocation of his nobles to decide the matter. Each of the three young men is called in to explain his statement.

Then the first, who had spoken of the strength of wine, began and said: "Gentlemen, how is wine the strongest? It leads astray the minds of all who drink it. It makes equal the mind of the king and the orphan, of the slave and the free, of the poor and the rich."

(3:17–19)

Then the second guardsman, who had written that the king is strongest, was summoned.

"Gentlemen, are not men strongest, who rule over land and sea and all that is in them? But the king is stronger; he is their lord and master, and whatever he says to them they obey. If he tells them to make war on one another, they do it; and if he sends them out against the enemy, they go, and conquer mountains, walls, and towers."

(4:2–4)

Finally, the third guardsman is summoned, he who had written that women and truth are strongest. We are now told that this young man is Zerubbabel. He says,

"Gentlemen, is not the king great, and are not men many, and is not wine strong? Who is it, then, that rules them, or who has the mastery over them? Is it not women? Women gave birth to the king and to every people that rules over sea and land. From women they came; and women brought up the very men who plant the vineyards from which comes wine. . . . Therefore you must realize that women rule over you!"

(4:14–16, 22)

Then the king and the nobles looked at one another; and he began to speak about truth: "Gentlemen . . . , truth is great and stronger than all things. The whole earth calls upon truth, and heaven blesses her. . . . Wine is unrighteous, the king is unrighteous, women are unrighteous, all the sons of men are unrighteous . . . But truth endures and is strong forever, and lives and prevails forever and ever. . . . To it belongs the strength and the kingship and the power and the majesty of all the ages. Blessed be the God of truth!"

(4:33–40)

Darius and his court agree that truth is strongest, so the king says to Zerubbabel,

"Ask what you wish, even beyond what is written, and we will give it to you, for you have been found to be the wisest. And you shall sit next to me, and be called my Kinsman."

(4:42)

When Zerubbabel reminds Darius of his vow to restore Jerusalem, the king commissions Zerubbabel to go to Jerusalem at the head of a group of Jews and provides him ample resources for the task of rebuilding.

> When the young man went out, he lifted up his face to heaven toward Jerusalem, and praised the King of heaven, saying, "From you comes the victory; from you comes wisdom, and yours is the glory. I am your servant. Blessed are you, who have given me wisdom; I give you thanks, O Lord of our ancestors."
>
> So he took the letters, and went [from the Persian court] to Babylon and told this to all his kindred. And they praised the God of their ancestors, because he had given them release and permission to go up and build Jerusalem and the temple that is called by his name; and they feasted, with music and rejoicing, for seven days.
>
> (4:58–63)

4. *Judith* (2d c. BC)[8]

Sometime around the year 150 BC a Jewish writer who was committed to the authority of the Torah—perhaps a Pharisee—wrote a short story which, although it contains echos of the Old Testament (especially the Book of Judges) is framed in the style of a Hellenistic novella. The frequent use of speeches and prayers (2:5–13, 5:5–21, and elsewhere)[9] as well as attention to narrative detail (e.g., the descriptions of Judith's beauty) suggest the author's familiarity with Hellenistic literature. This writer also was alert to the facts of history, for he borrowed the names of two of his characters (Holofernes and Bagoas) from officials who served the Persian king Artaxerxes III Ochus (359–338). Yet the story is fiction, and the reader is signaled that this is so by inconsistencies so glaring (e.g, Nebuchadnezzar is "king of the Assyrians" [2:1]) that it seems that the author took some pains to insure that the tale not be misunderstood as reportage. Its point is basic: God will save those pious Jews who, convinced of the authority of the Torah, will go to any lengths to defend their traditions.

Yet this simple lesson is contained in a very sophisticated work of literature. Structurally, the story is designed to hold the attention of the reader as the action moves toward a clear climax and denouement. The characters are strongly delineated and the description of certain details—especially the effect of Judith's beauty—are skillfully crafted. The moral of the tale is contained not only in the action, but also in the speeches of Achior (5:5–21) and Judith (8:11–34, and elsewhere). Yet speeches of the heroine, in spite of their high moral and spiritual purpose, are characterized by clever double meanings, as in 12:4 where Judith's reference to "what he [God] has determined" means one thing upon Judith's lips, but quite another as heard by Holofernes.

The purpose of the story of Judith is almost certainly to encourage Jews to resist the forces of the Seleucid kingdom. The importance of fidelity to the Torah is illustrated by Judith's own observance of various ritual regulations (prayer, sabbaths, New Moon, consumption of only ritually clean foods), while her assassination of Holofernes reminds one of Jael's assassination of Sisera (Judg. 4, 5) and was doubtless projected as a example to be followed by all devout Hasmonean fighters. The almost certain identification (on the basis of its description) of the fictitious town of Bethulia with the Samaritan center of Shechem was probably intended to send some type of message concerning the Samaritan-Jewish problem, but the nature of that message remains a riddle.

Judith (which means "Jewess") is one of three important stories to come out of the Second Temple period in which the heroine is a courageous woman, the others being Esther and Susannah. In two of these (Judith and Esther) the bravery of the woman results in the salvation of the people. But unlike Esther (which could claim a connection with the Festival of Purim), Judith was never accepted into the Palestinian Jewish canon, although it does appear in the Septuagint and was frequently utilized in rabbinic circles. Jerome records that Judith was declared canonical by the Council of Nicea, and it is still regarded thusly by Roman Catholic and Greek Orthodox churches. In most Protestant Bibles, Judith is included in the Apocrypha.

The first part of the story describes the military situation. Chapters 1–3 tell the story of Nebuchadnezzar's campaign in the West, while chapters 4–7 describe the siege that Nebuchadnezzar's general, Holofernes, lays to the Jewish town of Bethulia. Here we read the speech of Achior, the Ammonite leader who has been interrogated by Holofernes concerning the nature of his adversaries (5:1–21). Its point is this:

"So now, my master and lord, if there is any oversight in this people and they sin against their God and we find out their offense, then we can go up and defeat them. But if they are not a guilty nation, then let my lord pass them by; for their Lord and God will defend them, and we shall become the laughingstock of the whole world."

(5:20–21)

To which Holofernes snaps, "What god is there except Nebuchadnezzar?" (6:2).

It is at this point (chap. 8) that we meet Judith, a pious widow. The narrator remarks that "no one spoke ill of her, for she feared God with great devotion" (8:8). When Judith discovers that the people of Bethulia are about to surrender their city, she addresses them and sternly summons them not to despair, but to put their trust in God. When reminded by one of the magistrates, Uzziah, that noble words are no substitute for a miracle from God, Judith replies,

"I am about to do something that will go down through all generations of our descendants. Stand at the town gate tonight so that I may go out with my maid; and within the days after which you have promised to surrender the town to our enemies, the Lord will deliver Israel by my hand. Only, do not try to find out what I am doing; for I will not tell you until I have finished what I am about to do."

(8:32–34)

In preparation for her ordeal, Judith prays an extended prayer, which contains these words:

"For your strength does not depend upon numbers, nor your might on the powerful. But you are the God of the lowly, helper of the oppressed, upholder of the weak, protector of the forsaken, savior of those without hope. Please, please, God of my father . . . Let your whole nation and every tribe know and understand that you are God, the God of all power and might, and that there is no other who protects the people of Israel but you alone!"

(9:11–14)

Judith, accompanied by her maid and dressed in her most seductive finery, leaves Bethulia and makes her way to the camp of the Assyrians where the guards, stunned by her beauty, usher her into the presence of Holophernes. The general is also smitten by Judith and, although he treats her kindly, he secretly hopes to possess her. Judith pretends to be a defector from her people and tells Holophernes that Achior had earlier spoken the truth, that the Jews are impregnable as long as they are faithful to their law. However, she goes on to say, the siege has reduced them to such a level that they are about to eat food that has been set aside to the Lord, an act that will surely bring judgment upon them. Judith promises, in return for Holophernes' grant of free passage in and out of the Assyrian camp, to inform the general when the Jews make themselves vulnerable.

Four days later Holophernes arranges to be alone with Judith. The author describes the climax of the adventure in these words:

Then Judith came in and lay down. Holofernes' heart was ravished with her and his passion was aroused, for he had been waiting for an opportunity to seduce her from the day he first saw her. So Holofernes said to her, "Have a drink, and be merry with us!" Judith said, "I will gladly drink, my lord, because today is the greatest day in my whole life." Then she took what her maid had prepared and ate and drank before him. Holofernes was greatly pleased with her, and drank a great quantity of wine, much more than he had ever drunk in any one day since he was born . . . Judith was left alone in the tent, with Holofernes stretched out on his bed, for he was dead drunk. . . . [Then Judith] went up to the bedpost near Holofernes head, and took down his sword that hung there. She came close to his bed, and took hold of the hair of his head, and said, "Give me strength today, O Lord God of Israel!" Then she struck his neck twice with all her might, and cut off his head. Next she rolled his body off the bed and pulled down the canopy from the posts. Soon afterward she went out, and gave Holofernes head to her maid, who placed it in her food bag.

(12:16—13:10)

When Holofernes' head is displayed from the walls of Bethulia, the citizens of the city fall upon the dismayed and bewildered Assyrians and deliver their town. Judith is showered with honor for having saved not only Bethulia, but also the Temple, as Jerusalem lay next in the path of Holofernes' army. The story ends on a note of joy.

No one ever again spread terror among the Israelites during the lifetime of Judith, or for a long time after her death.

(16:25)

5. *Susannah* (2d c. BC)[10]

The story of Susannah is, as it stands, a brief tale about the vindication of a righteous woman by the young man Daniel. At first reading it appears well integrated in literary terms, the product of a skillful storyteller who also wished to drive home an important moral. But a close analysis of the text suggests a complex literary history involving more than one writer and more than one moral or theological purpose. For one thing, although the most ancient existing manuscripts are in Greek, a Semitic original (Hebrew or Aramaic) seems to underly the Greek text. Yet at an important point in the story, there are key wordplays upon Greek terms, suggesting that a second writer(s) rewrote an earlier tale. For another thing, the figure of Daniel, who is not introduced until the story is more than half told (v. 45), seems like an intrusion, and may indicate that an earlier version of the story existed that knew nothing of Daniel's role. In brief, it is difficult to know precisely when, where, or by whom the original Susannah was composed, although by the first century BC it was well enough known to be included in the Septuagint.

The moral of the story is, like the tale itself, more complex than first appears. Its lesson seems to be that God will protect and vindicate those who obey the Torah. Susannah is described in the very beginning of the narrative as an observant Jew: "Her parents were righteous, and had trained their daughter according to the law of Moses" (v. 3). At the moment when she is forced to make her crucial moral decision, she opts for the Torah, unlike the two wicked judges, who flout it. Yet she is saved, while they are condemned; thus obedience to the Torah is vindicated.

But is that all? Some readers have sensed an allegorical meaning, Susannah representing persecuted Jews generally (or the persecuted church, in some later Christian exegesis) whose devious enemies are judged by God. Others, in one of the more interesting interpretations of the book, see the tale as a reflection of the struggle between Sadducees and Pharisees. Earlier, we made reference to a difference between these sects in regard to the Torah's teaching concerning false witnesses.[11] The Sadducees claimed that false witnesses in capital cases should not themselves be executed unless their intended victim had received the death penalty as a result of their false testimony, whereas the Pharisees argued that false witnesses in capital cases should be executed because of their perjury, regardless of the fate of their intended victim. One view of Susannah, therefore, is that it is a Pharisaic document intended to poke ridicule at the Sadducean position.

And how does Daniel fit in to the story? Those scholars are probably correct who see his presence as the result of a secondary writer who introduced this hero into the story in order to provide another example of Daniel's God-given skills. If that is so, this author chose an excellent vehicle for this purpose, as it coincides with Daniel's reputation as a wise judge (Ezek. 28:3, Dan. 2:13), to say nothing of the fact that Daniel means "God judges."

In the oldest Christian-Era copies of the Greek Bible, where the translation of Theodotion's Daniel was preferred to the Daniel of the Septuagint, Susannah is often placed before Daniel 1, thus forming a kind of preface to Daniel that explains his rise to prominence in Babylon (something unexplained in the Hebrew-Aramaic Daniel [i.e., the Daniel of the Palestinian Jewish canon]). However, in the Septuagint Daniel, Susannah appears to have been attached to the conclusion of Daniel 12.

Although its inclusion in the Greek Bible led to its acceptance as canonical among early Christians, Susannah never gained wide use in either the synagogue or the church.

The story is this: Susannah, the wife of a Jew of the Babylonian exile, a man named Joakim, is not only a paragon of virtue in that she scrupulously observes the Torah, but of beauty as well. However, two wicked elders of the Jewish community are enamored of her to the point that they plot to rape her. When Susannah is alone, bathing in her garden on a hot day, the elders, who had previously hidden themselves among the plants, emerge.

When the maids had gone out, the two elders got up and ran to her. They said: "Look, the garden doors are shut, and no one can see us. We are burning with desire for you; so give your consent and lie with us. If you refuse, we will testify against you that a young man was with you, and this was why you sent your maids away."

Susannah groaned and said "I am completely trapped. For if I do this, it will mean death for me; if I do not, I cannot escape your hands. I choose not to do it; I will fall into your hands, rather than sin in the sight of the Lord."

(vv. 19–23)

Susannah cries out, but when the two elders are discovered, they make good on their threat and claim to have seen Susannah making love to an unknown young man. A trial follows at which Susannah is convicted on their testimony and, as adultery is a capital offense, she is sentenced to death. But Susannah prays to the Lord for help and

The Lord heard her cry. Just as she was being led off to execution, God stirred up the holy spirit of a young lad named Daniel.

(vv. 44–45)

Daniel demands a new trial at which he examines each of the two wicked judges separately. The Greek text of their contradictory testimony, followed in each case by Daniel's judgment upon them, contains the play upon words referred to earlier.

When [the two elders] were separated from each other, [Daniel] summoned one of them and said to him, "You old relic of wicked days, your sins have now come home, . . . Now then, if you really saw this woman, tell me this: Under what tree did you see them being intimate with each other?" He answered, "Under a mastic tree [schinon]. And Daniel said, "Very well! This lie has cost you your head, for the angel of God has received the sentence from God and will immediately cut [schisei] you in two.

Then, putting him to one side, he ordered them to bring the other. And he said to him, "You offspring of Canaan and not of Judah, beauty has beguiled you and lust has perverted your heart. . . . Now then, tell me: Under what tree did you catch them being intimate with each other?" He answered, "Under an evergreen oak [prinon]." Daniel said to him, "Very well! This lie has cost you also your head, for the angel of God is waiting with his sword to split [prisai] you in two, so as to destroy you both."

(vv. 52–59)

The two wicked elders are led out to their execution "in accordance with the law of Moses" (v. 62), while the people rejoice and praise God. Susannah's reputation is restored, and as for Daniel: "And from that day onward Daniel had a great reputation among the people" (v. 64).

6. *Bel and the Dragon* (2d or 1st c. BC)[12]

An interesting pair of stories centering on the figure of Daniel was composed sometime after the writing of the Book of Daniel for the purpose of attacking the worship of idols. Although each story is self-contained, the probability that they were composed by the same author is raised not only by their common style and subject matter, but by the fact that the two incidents involved (the discovery of the hoax concerning Bel and the slaying of the dragon) are brought together in the text itself (v. 28). However, a secondary element does seem to be the role of the prophet Habakkuk, and it is quite possible that the narrative of his involvement in feeding Daniel in the lions' den was substituted in favor of an original statement (now discarded) between v. 32 and v. 40 to the effect that God closed the mouths of the lions. Because they may stand alone as narratives, Bel and the Dragon are included in this section of our discussion, although there is an important sense in which they may be considered extensions of the story of the biblical Daniel.

The narratives constitute a polemic against the worship of idols and, although the setting of the stories is the Babylon of Cyrus the Persian (v. 1), their theology would be equally appropriate in any context in which idolatry posed a threat to the worship of the God of Israel. The contest between Hellenism and traditional Judaism is the likely environment in which Bel and the Dragon were composed, and a date sometime in the Hasmonean Era is the most likely time, since the tales are quite obviously dependent upon the Book of Daniel, especially the episode concerning the lions' den (vv. 31–42, cf. Dan. 6). The original language may have been Hebrew or Aramaic, although the oldest existing copies are in Greek. Suggestions have been made that the dragon may be a reflection of the chaos dragon, Tiamat, from the Babylonian creation myth,[13] but direct evidence for such a connection is lacking.

In the Septuagint, Bel and the Dragon were placed at the conclusion of Daniel 12, but in Theodotion these stories occur after Daniel 6 and, in this fashion, they came into the early Christian canon of scripture. However the tales have received little attention in either Jewish or Christian communities.

In the story concerning Bel, Daniel challenges the king by declaring that the god Bel, worshiped by the Babylonians, is no god at all, but merely inanimate clay and brass. The aroused king, pointing out that Bel consumes a great quantity of food each evening, arranges for a test of the god's validity, not knowing that seventy priests and their families enter the shrine each evening by a secret door and eat the food. The king and Daniel agree that the king shall set out the food that evening and that the doors to the shrine shall then be sealed. If the food is gone the next morning, it will prove that Bel is real. The priests are dismissed and

> After they had gone out, the king set out the food for Bel. Then Daniel ordered his servants to bring ashes, and they scattered them throughout the whole temple in the presence of the king alone. Then they went out, shut the door and sealed it with the king's signet, and departed.
>
> (v. 14)

The priests and their families slip into the shrine that night, as was their custom, and eat all the food. When the king unseals the doors the next morning, he is overjoyed to find the food gone and proclaims the praise of Bel.

> But Daniel laughed and restrained the king from going in. "Look at the floor," he said, "and notice whose footprints these are." The king said, "I see the footprints of men and women and children."
>
> (vv. 19–20)

The enraged king has the priests and their families slain and permits Daniel to destroy the idol and its temple.

The story of the dragon is so brief as to be more an anecdote than a developed narrative. A great dragon that is worshiped by the Babylonians is shown to Daniel by the king, who invites the Jew to worship it. Daniel naturally refuses and then

> Then Daniel took pitch, fat, and hair, and boiled them together and made cakes, which he fed to the dragon. The dragon ate them, and burst open. Then Daniel said, "See what you have been worshiping!
>
> (v. 27)

The entire narrative concludes with Daniel's being cast by the king—who has been urged on by an angry mob—into a den of hungry lions, where he stays for six days. He is then miraculously saved when an angel of the Lord seizes the prophet Habakkuk by the hair of his head and carries him from Judaea to Babylon. Habakkuk has in his hand food which he had been taking to workers in the field, and he gives this to Daniel. Daniel eats the food, while the angel carries Habbakuk back to Judaea. (It is curious that Daniel is saved by having his own hunger assuaged, not that of the lions.) When, on the seventh day, the king discovers that Daniel is still alive, he brings him out of the den, praises Daniel's God, and executes Daniel's enemies.

7. 3 Maccabees (1st c. BC)[14]

Although the Jews who lived in Ptolemaic Egypt fared relatively well in their relations with the gentile majority, there were nonetheless times of oppression. Although these persecutions were not systematically documented by the Egyptian Jewish community, evidence of them may be seen in various places, one of which is 3 Maccabees.

The title of this story is a misnomer, in that it has nothing to do with the Hasmonean family. It is rather a mostly legendary account of an unsuccessful attempt to eradicate the Jews of Egypt by Ptolemy IV Philopator (221–205 BC). Scholars have theorized that it may have received its title (which was bestowed upon it in antiquity) because it describes events just prior to the Hasmonean revolt, or because it was placed next to 1 and 2 Maccabees in some copies of the Septuagint. But, in truth, no one really knows the reason.

Another mystery concerns its date of composition. Although it is clear that 3 Maccabees originated in Egypt, it may have been written there as early as a time not long after the Battle of Raphia,[15] to which it refers (217 BC), or as late as the time just prior to the destruction of the Temple (70 AD), an event of which 3 Maccabees appears ignorant. Most scholars, however, prefer a date sometime during the first century BC.

Its author (or authors) had access to certain valid historical records. The description of the Battle of Raphia, for example, is faithful enough to suggest dependence on some accurate source, while the story of the use of elephants to kill the Jews is very similar to one told by Josephus[16] (which, however, is placed during the reign of Ptolemy VII Physcon or more than a half century later than the setting of the story in 3 Maccabees).

Nevertheless, 3 Maccabees appears to be mostly legendary. Like 2 Maccabees, by which its author was influenced, 3 Maccabees attempts to involve the sympathies of the reader on the side of the Jews by means of an emotive and self-conscious literary style (which often appears to be an artificial effort to copy the style of classical Attic Greek), and by means of descriptions of miraculous events, which may stretch the credulity of the reader, but which are intended to convey to him or her that God is clearly the champion of the Jews. Furthermore, as might be expected of a document dealing with the persecution of the Jews, the gentiles are held up as an object of scorn.

The theological outlook of 3 Maccabees is one of absolute faithfulness to the traditions of Judaism, including obedience to the Torah, dependence upon prayer as a means of reaching God, and a reverent regard for the Jerusalem Temple as the most important venue of Jewish worship. Its author is convinced that faithfulness to God results in blessing, while unfaithfulness brings God's punishment. The book is opposed to all forms of syncretism and appears to be interested in no type of accommodation to the forces of Hellenism, which must have dominated the thought-world in which its author lived. In fact, Hellenized Jews are held in even greater contempt than gentiles.

There is no certainty that 3 Maccabees was widely circulated in antiquity, as it does not always appear in copies of the Septuagint. It was omitted from Jerome's Vulgate, and seems to have been generally ignored in rabbinic and patristic circles. However, because it is present in a few Septuagint manuscripts (e.g., the important fifth century AD uncial manuscript Alexandrinus), 3 Maccabees is sometimes included in collections of the Apocrypha.

The story begins abruptly, a feature that has caused some to speculate that its original beginning may have been lost. When Ptolemy IV Philopator, at the Battle of Raphia (in southern Palestine), is saved from a plot against his life by a Jew, he visits the Jerusalem Temple where, in spite of protests by the priests, he announces his plans to enter the sanctuary (1:1–29). The high priest Simon offers a prayer to God (2:1–20), the elaborate and pious language of which is typical of much of 3 Maccabees:

> "Lord, Lord, king of the heavens, and sovereign of all creation, holy among the holy ones, the only ruler, almighty, give attention to us who are suffering grievously from an impious and profane man, puffed up in his audacity and power."
>
> (2:2)

God then answered Simon's prayer by miraculously thwarting Ptolemy's intentions:

> Thereupon God, who oversees all things, the first Father of all, holy among the holy ones, having heard the lawful supplication, scourged him who had exalted himself in insolence and audacity. He shook him on this side and that as a reed is shaken by the wind, so that he lay helpless on the ground and, besides being paralyzed in his limbs, was unable even to speak, since he was smitten by a righteous judgment.
>
> (2:21–22)

When the king recovers, he is so angry that he returns home, vowing revenge against the Jews. One of the indignities with which he threatens them is that they "be branded on their bodies by fire with the ivy-leaf symbol of Dionysus" (2:29). In the face of this and other intimidations, many of the Jews "have been initiated into the mysteries," (2:30), but most remain faithful to the traditions of their people (2:21–33).

This infuriates Ptolemy all the more and he decrees the death of all the Jews in the country. Since the peculiar habits of diet and worship observed by the Jews are repugnant to the general population, the king's order to arrest the Jews, the text of which is provided, is expected to encounter no popular resistance (3:1–30). However, penalties are provided for any effort to protect a Jew against the royal wrath:

> "But those who shelter any of the Jews, whether old people or children or even infants, will be tortured to death with the most hateful torments, together with their families. Any who are willing to give information will receive the property of those who incur the punishment, and also two thousand drachmas from the royal treasury, and will be awarded their freedom. Every place detected sheltering a Jew is to be made unapproachable and burned with fire, and shall become useless for all time to any mortal creature."
>
> (3:27–29)

In highly emotive language the plight of the Jews is described as they are brought from all over Egypt to the hippodrome in Alexandria for their public execution (precisely how all the Jews of Egypt could be collected into this arena 3 Maccabees 4:1–21 does not say). The king orders that the herd of royal elephants is to be made drunk with wine and frankincense and, the next morning, turned loose upon the Jews. But when the keeper of the elephants arrives in the morning to receive the final order from the king, he cannot awaken him:

> But the Lord sent upon the king a portion of sleep, that beneficence that from the beginning, night and day, is bestowed by him who grants it to whomever he wishes. And by the action of the Lord he was overcome by so pleasant and deep a sleep that he quite failed in his lawless purpose and was completely frustrated in his inflexible plan.
>
> (5:11–12)

For the moment at least, the Jews are saved (5:1–20).

The next morning, all is in readiness once more as the drunken elephants are in position to be let loose upon the bound and helpless Jews. Again, however, when the keeper of the elephants appears before the king for his final command, God performs a miracle, this time by striking the king with amnesia:

> But [the king], on receiving the [elephant keeper's] report and being struck by the unusual invitation to come out—since he had been completely overcome by incomprehension—inquired what the matter was for which this had been so zealously completed for him. This was the act of God who rules over all things, for he had implanted in the king's mind a forgetfulness of the things he had previously devised. Then Hermon [the elephant keeper] and all the king's Friends pointed out that

the animals and the armed forces were ready, "O king, according to your eager purpose." But at these words [the king] was filled with an over-powering wrath, because by the providence of God his whole mind had been deranged concerning these matters.

(5:27–30)

Once more, the Jews are temporarily saved (5:21-35).

A third time plans are made to kill the Jews. By now, however, the king's friends have grown irritated and, when they remonstrate with the king over the continued delay, the angry monarch vows not only to kill the Jews of Egypt, but also to invade Judaea and destroy the Temple (5:36–47). The next morning, as the elephants are about to be set loose upon the Jews, the captives pray to God for help, one of their number, a priest named Eleazar, offering a particularly emotional plea (5:48—6:15). The result is another miracle:

Just as Eleazar was ending his prayer, the king arrived at the hippo-drome with the animals and all the arrogance of his forces. And when the Jews observed this they raised great cries to heaven so that even the nearby valleys resounded with them and brought an uncontrollable ter-ror upon the army. Then the most glorious, almighty, and true God re-vealed his holy face and opened the heavenly gates, from which two glorious angels of fearful aspect descended, visible to all but the Jews. They opposed the forces of the enemy and filled them with confusion and terror, binding them with immovable shackles. Even the king began to shudder bodily, and he forgot his sullen insolence. The animals turned back upon the armed forces following them and began trampling and destroying them.

(6:16–21)

The remorseful king now declares freedom for all the Jews (6:22–29), who celebrate with great joy and make preparations to return to their homes (6:30–41). The text of the king's decree is recorded in which he proclaims tol-eration for the Jews (7:1–9):

"For you should know that if we devise any evil against them or cause them any grief at all, we always shall have not a mortal but the Ruler over every power, the Most High God, in everything and inescapably as an antagonist to avenge such acts. Farewell."

(7:9)

After insisting that the king punish those Jews who had abandoned obedi-ence to the Law in order to escape the royal decrees, the Jews witness the execution of more than 300 of their apostate brothers (7:10–15). Then they return to their homes after having celebrated a festival to commemorate their divine deliverance (7:16–23).

H. DRAMA: EZEKIEL THE TRAGEDIAN (2D C. BC)[17]

It will be recalled from our discusson of Hellenistic literature that, in spite of the rich traditions of dramatic comedy and tragedy that had been forged by such classical Greek writers as Aeschylus (d. 456 BC), Sophocles (d. 406), Euripides (d. 406) and Aristophanes (d. 385), Greek writers of the Hellenistic period produced relatively little in the way of drama.[18] The comedian Menander of Athens (d. 291) is one exception, and his writings proved so popular in the Hellenistic-Roman world that, as noted earlier, one fragment of his *Thais* found its way into Paul's First Letter to the Corinthians (15:33).[19] Another exception, this one representing the genre of tragedy, may be found in the Jewish writer Ezekiel.

Just where and when Ezekiel lived is uncertain. Since he was familiar with both the Septuagint and the great Greek dramatists, he was probably a citizen of Alexandria, although other centers of Hellenistic culture have been suggested. He worked after the completion of the Septuagint translation of Exodus (c. 250, upon which he depends), but before the historian Alexander Polyhistor (c. 50 BC), a date in the second century BC being favored by several scholars. Like other Jewish writers whom we have discussed, it is because of Alexander Polyhistor and Eusebius that fragments of Ezekiel's work have been preserved, although he is also cited less extensively by Clement of Alexandria (d. 150–220 AD).

The significance of Ezekiel lies in the manner in which he combined the forms of classical Greek tragedy with the biblical story of the Exodus. His one (partially) surviving drama is, in fact, titled *Exagoge,* or "Leading Out" and, with the exception of a few interesting interpolations into the plot, it appears to follow the main thread of the biblical narrative. Yet Ezekiel's *Exagoge* is written in the iambic trimeter of classical Greek tragedy and appears to have been composed with the intention of emulating the tragedians of classical Athens. It also seems to have been designed to be acted before an audience, an inference drawn from the fact that certain events that would have been difficult to stage (e.g., the plagues, the drowning of Pharaoh's army) are narrated by the principals in the drama. Whether it was actually presented in this form is unknown, but if so, the celebration of the Passover would have been a possible time.[20]

Exagoge appears to have been composed in a prologue and five acts, a standard form among Greek tragedians:

Prologue: A monologue by Moses in which he narrates the circumstances leading up to the action of the drama, beginning with the story of Jacob's journey into Egypt:

And when from Canaan Jacob did depart,
with threescore souls and ten he did go down
to Egypt's land; and there he did beget
a host of people: suffering, oppressed,
ill-treated even to this very day
by ruling powers and by wicked men.

(lines 1–6)

Act One: Moses flees to the land of Midian where he meets the seven daughters of the priest, one of whom is named Sepphorah (Zipporah in the Hebrew, Exod. 2:16–17). Almost all that remains of this act is a fragment of Sepphorah's speech about her father:

This land, O stranger, all bears Libya's name,
but tribes of sundry races dwell throughout;
the dark-skinned Aethiops. Yet there is one
who rules, prince and sole commander, he
rules all this state and judges mortal men;
a priest, the father of myself and these.

(ll. 60–65)

Act Two: Moses marries Sepporah (Exod. 2:21) and has a dream in which he is transported to the summit of Mt. Sinai where he has a vision of God who seats Moses on a throne and places a crown upon his head. Moses's father-in-law subsequently interprets the dream in these words:

My friend, God gave you this as sign for good.
Would I might live to see these things transpire.
For you shall cause a mighty throne to rise,
and you yourself shall rule and govern men.
As for beholding all the peopled earth,
and things below and things above God's realm:
things present, past and future you shall see.

(ll. 83–89)

By introducing the element of a dream which reveals the future, Ezekiel departs from the biblical story and draws upon a favorite device of classical Greek dramatists. But he is probably also utilizing certain nonbiblical traditions about Moses and about the enthronement of important figures current in the Diaspora.

Act Three: Moses encounters God at the burning bush and is commissioned to confront Pharaoh (Exod. 3). There follows a description of the plagues and of the institution of the Passover (Exod. 7—12). God's statement at the burning bush that he is invisible may be a theatrical device calculated to avoid an awkward anthropomorphism and, if so, is another clue that *Exagoge* was written to be staged:

> Stay, Moses, best of men, do not come near
> till you have loosed the bindings from your feet;
> the place on which you stand is holy ground,
> and from this bush God's word shines forth to you.
> Take courage, son, and listen to my words;
> as mortal man you cannot see my face,
> albeit you have power to hear my words,
> and for this very reason I have come.
> God am I of those, your fathers three,
> of Abram, Issac, Jacob, I am He.
>
> (ll. 96–105)

Act Four: The Hebrews flee through the Red Sea, whose waters drown the pursuing army of Pharaoh. In the play the scene is described by a surviving Egyptian soldier:

> From heaven, then, a shining light like fire
> appeared to us, so we were led to think
> that God was their defense. For when they reached
> the farther shore a mighty wave gushed forth
> hard by us, so that one in terror cried,
> "Flee back before the hands of the Most High;
> to them he offers succor, but to us,
> most wretched men, destruction he does work."
> The sea-path flooded, all our host was lost.
>
> (ll. 234–242)

Act Five: All that remains of the rest of the drama is a description of the Hebrews' encampment at the oasis of Elim (Exod. 15:27) which, although barely mentioned in the Bible, becomes for Ezekiel a type of Paradise. Part of the surviving fragment is devoted to the wonderous Egyptian bird of legend, the Phoenix:

> Another living creature there we saw,
> full wonderous, such as man has never seen;
> 'twas near in scope to twice the eagle's size,
> with plumage iridescent, rainbow-hued.
> Its breast appeared deep-dyed with purple's shade,
> its legs were red like ochre, and its neck
> was furnished round with tresses saffron hued;
>
> *   *   *   *

Exceeding all, its voice pre-eminent;
of every other winged thing, the king,
it did appear. For all the birds, as one,
in fear did haste to follow after him,
and he before, like some triumphant bull
went striding forth with rapid step apace.

(ll. 254–269)

I. HELLENISTIC PHILOSOPHY: ARISTOBULUS (2D C. BC)[21]

One of the truly distinctive contributions of classical Greek civilization was in the area of philosophical thought. For all its infinite variety, Greek philosophy was based on the assumption that reality is rational and that, by applying the faculty of logic, truth may be discovered by human thinkers. Although that assumption bears a certain similarity to Hebrew Wisdom teaching, the religious traditions of Israel and the philosophical traditions of Greece generally had little in common, the nature of God (or the gods) and the question of revelation being two areas in which Jerusalem and Athens were particularly far apart. The pressures of Hellenization that resulted from the advance of Greek culture into the East brought these differences in philosophical/theological outlook into sharp focus, differences that contributed to the continuing conflict between traditionalist Jews, on the one hand, and, on the other, gentiles and nontraditionalist Jews alike. We have noticed, in the Letter of Aristeas, one attempt by a Jewish writer to reconcile differences between Jew and gentile by promoting the pious fiction that Ptolemy II Philadelphus coveted a copy of the Torah for the library in Alexandria. In the work of Aristobulus of Alexandria we find another such effort on the part of a Jew, this time directed toward fashioning a synthesis between the teaching of the Greek philosophers and the Law of Moses.

Aristobulus, who, according to Eusebius, dedicated his work to "King Ptolemy," was probably active during the reign of Ptolemy VI Philometor (180–145) and is presumably the same person of that name mentioned in 2 Maccabees 1:10. On the basis of his belief that truth is a unitary whole, Aristobulus taught that there is no basic contradiction between the teachings of the Greek philosophers and those of Israel's great law-giver Moses. Pythagoras,[22] Socrates, and Plato, in fact, all knew the Mosaic law and learned from it, as did the poet Aratus and the songwriter-god Orpheus. Greek and Hebrew thought are different only in respect to language and form; in content they both express the same fundamental reality.

Aristobulus is also significant, not only because of his efforts to erect a synthesis between Greek and Hebrew thought, but because of his pioneer work in what today would be termed biblical hermeneutics. Aristobulus requests that his readers understand scripture not in mythological or even in literal fashion, but "according to the laws of nature," by which he means that human understanding must be allowed to interpret the text. When he sets his hand to the actual task of interpretation, it is clear that Aristobulus considers the allegorical method to be the key to the text's "elevated meaning," a characteristic in which he follows the Stoics.[23]

In the fragments of Aristobulus' work which have been preserved, the Alexandrian philosopher demonstrates interest in several subjects. He takes pains to explain to gentile readers the anthropomorphisms in the Bible, a feature that would have been repugnant to cultured Hellenists. He does this in allegorical fashion by claiming that references to the parts of God's body (hands, voice) are metaphors for divine characteristics or attributes. Aristobulus is also interested in the date of the Passover and of the Sabbath, and is perhaps the first Jewish-Hellenistic thinker to reflect on the theological significance of the logos.[24]

Perhaps Aristobulus' primary influence is to be seen as one who laid the foundations for the later work of Philo of Alexandria (first century AD), who is discussed in a subsequent chapter. But he should also be credited with helping to establish allegory as a method of biblical interpretation that not only found favor among some of the rabbis, but became the primary method of Christian biblical exegesis until the time of the Protestant Reformation.

Five fragments of Aristobulus' work have been preserved by Eusebius, and he is also cited, but less faithfully, by Clement of Alexandria. Aristobulus' work takes the form of a series of answers to the king's questions, although it may be doubted that he was really the king's tutor, in spite of the fact that that is the characterization in 2 Maccabees 1:10.

According to Aristobulus, the key to understanding Moses is to realize that he spoke in terms of metaphor and allegory. Those who have read Moses in this manner have laid claim to great truths.

> For our lawgiver Moses proclaims arrangements of nature and preparations for great events by expressing that which he wishes to say in many ways, by using words that refer to other matters (I mean matters relating to ourward appearances). Therefore, those who are able to think well marvel at his wisdom and at the divine spirit in acordance with which he has been proclaimed as a prophet also. Among these are the philosophers already mentioned and many others, including poets who took significant material from him and are admired accordingly.
>
> (Fragment 2:3–4)

Aristobulus illustrates his method of interpreting scripture by allegory and metaphor when he attempts to explain the references to the "hands" of God in the law of Moses.

> Now "hands" are clearly thought of even in our own time in a more general way. For when you, being king, send out forces, wishing to accomplish something, we say, "The king has a mighty hand," and the hearers are referred to the power which you have.
>
> Now Moses indicates this also in our Law when he speaks thus: "God brought you out of Egypt with a mighty hand," and again when he says that God said to him, "I will send forth my hand and I will strike the Egyptians" . . . so that it is necessary that the hands be explained as the power of God. For it is possible for people speaking metaphorically to consider that the entire strength of human beings and their active powers are in their hands.
>
> Therefore the lawgiver [Moses] has employed a metaphor well for the purpose of saying something elevated, when he says that the accomplishments of God are his hands.
>
> (Fragment 2:7–9)

For the teachings of the Greek philosophers Aristobulus demonstrates the greatest respect. Yet he maintains that their teaching was not entirely original, for they had access to the Torah and from its truths they enhanced their own views. Aristobulus, in the passage below, not only demonstrates that he knows the legend about the translation of the Pentateuch reported in the Letter of Aristeas, but he states that there was a previous Greek translation of the Mosaic law, a view not confirmed by any known evidence. Nor is it likely that Plato or Pythagoras had ever read the Pentateuch.

> It is evident that Plato imitated our legislation and that he had investigated thoroughly each of the elements in it. For it has been translated by others before Demetrius Phalereus, before the conquests of Alexander and the Persians. . . . So it is very clear that the philosopher mentioned above took many things (from it). For he was very learned, as was Pythagoras, who transferred many of our doctrines and integrated them into his own system of beliefs.
>
> But the entire translation of all the (books) of the Law (was made) in the time of the king called Philadelphus, your ancestor. He brought greater zeal (to the task than his predecessors), while Demetrius Phalereus managed the undertaking.
>
> (Fragment 3:1–2)

In passages that appear to have been invented by him, Aristobulus attributes quotations to famous Greek writers, the purpose of which is to corroborate his argument that the Greeks knew and were dependent upon Moses. In Fragments 4 and 5 he attributes such pseudoverses to Homer (ninth century BC?), Hesiod (eighth century BC?) and, in the following example, to the mythic Orpheus. This pseudo-Orphic hymn is noteworthy because here Aristobulus links the philosophical principle of logos, with the creative "Word" of God in Genesis 1.

> And it seems to me that Pythagoras, Socrates, and Plato with great care follow him [i.e., Moses] in all respects. They copy him when they say they hear the voice of God, when they contemplate the arrangement of the universe, so carefully made and so unceasingly held together by God. And further, Orpheus also imitates Moses in verses from his books on Holy Logos. He expresses himself thus concerning the maintaining of all things by divine power, their being generated and God's being over all things.
>
> (Fragment 4:4)

The theological outlook which sees an identification of the logos with the divine Word spoken at creation is one which, as we shall see, is present also in Philo of Alexandria. For readers of the New Testament its most familiar expression is that in John 1.

J. Mixed type: Baruch (2d c. bc)[25]

While it is true that many examples of Jewish literature from the Hellenistic period exhibit characteristics of more than one type of literature, some works are so diverse as to defy easy categorization. One such is the Book of Baruch, which contains, among other features, elements of prayer, Wisdom and hymnody.

The Book of Baruch, also referred to as 1 Baruch, is a collection of (probably) liturgical material of somewhat diverse character that, if it is not the work of a single person, has been carefully arranged so as to present the form of a unified whole. The evidence points to its composition in Hebrew during the Hasmonean Era, but subsequent to the writing of Daniel upon which Baruch is dependent. It was attributed to Baruch, the scribe of Jeremiah, and in this manner came to be attached to the Book of Jeremiah in some copies of the Septuagint, appearing between Jeremiah and Lamentations. There is, in fact, evidence to suggest that the Septuagint translation of Jeremiah and that of Baruch were executed by the same person. This association with the Book of Jeremiah led some

Christians to consider Baruch canonical, even when other apocryphal literature had been relegated to a deuterocanonical status.

There is a brief introduction (1:1–14) which states that Baruch read the
contents of this book to an assembly of exiles in Babylon, following which
he returned to Jerusalem with the vessels taken by the Babylonians from
the Temple and with an offering from the exiles to the inhabitants of
Jerusalem. The Jerusalemites are asked to "pray for the life of King Nebuchadnezzar of Babylon, and for the life of his son Belshazzar" (1:11) and to
pray for the exiles, an exhortation that reflects the influence of Jeremiah
(Jer. 29:7)

Then follows a lengthy prayer (1:15—3:8) that contains both a confession of
sin (1:15—2:10) and a petition for forgiveness (2:11—3:8), and that is heavily
dependent upon certain Hebrew texts, especially Daniel's prayer in Daniel
9:4–19.

> The Lord our God is in the right, but there is open shame on us today,
> on the people of Judah, on the inhabitants of Jerusalem, and on our
> kings, our rulers, our priests, our prophets, and our ancestors, because
> we have sinned before the Lord.
>
> (1:15–17)

The third section (3:9—4:4) is a Wisdom poem, similar in certain respects
to the Wisdom of Ben Sirach 24 and to Job 28. As in the Sirach text, Wisdom is
personified and is identified with the Torah:

> She is the book of the commandments of God,
>   the law that endures forever.
> All who hold her fast will live,
>   and those who forsake her will die.
>
> (4:1)

In the fourth and final section (4:5—5:9) Zion is personified as a mother
exhorting her children to be courageous in the face of the (unidentified) enemy. In courage and faith in God there is comfort:

> Take off the garment of your sorrow and affliction, O Jerusalem,
>   and put on forever the beauty of the glory from God.
>
> (5:1)

The section (and the book) end in a declaration of hope (5:5–9) that is strikingly similar to Psalm of Solomon 11:2–7 and that may have been composed at
a time subsequent to other parts of Baruch (compare also Isa. 40:4–5):

Arise, O Jerusalem, stand upon the height
  look toward the east,
and see your children gathered from west and east,
    at the word of the Holy One,
    rejoicing that God has remembered them.
For God has ordered that every high mountain and the
    everlasting hills be made low
    and the valleys filled up, to make level ground,
    so that Israel may walk safely in the glory of God.
                                  (5:5, 7)

Excursus

MESSIANISM IN THE LATE
HELLENISTIC PERIOD[1]

B efore bringing the discussion of Jewish literature of the Hellenistic period to a close, we would do well to gather together in brief fashion expressions of messianic hope contained in writings we have examined. The purpose is not to provide a systematic summary of messianic thought, but to illustrate the abundant diversity that characterized Judaism on the eve of the rise of Christianity. It was, of course, out of this rich mixture that the early Christians drew the vocabulary and thought forms which they used to express their understanding of the nature of Jesus of Nazareth and the significance of his life and work.

It should be observed at the outset that hope in a messiah was by no means characteristic of all of Hellenistic period Judaism, for one may see that a number of documents express no interest in the matter at all. Second Maccabees, for example, although it describes a crisis event in Jewish life, the Hasmonean revolt, and does so by means of a theology which relies heavily upon a belief in the direct intervention of God in human affairs, expresses no form of messianic hope. Likewise, the Additions to Daniel, although appended to a book that contains a bold vision of the coming kingdom of God, betray no interest in messianism. Nor is this lack of interest in the messiah simply a feature of Diaspora literature, for the same could be said of 1 Maccabees, Sirach, and Judith, to name but three examples of Palestinian provenance.

Having said that, however, one must admit that it is not always possible to know with precision when a text is expressing a messianic hope (in the sense of anticipating the sending of God's special agent to rule over the end time) and when it is not. To take a pair of examples from the Book of Isaiah: it is often asserted that the two hymns, Isaiah 9:2–7 and 11:1–9, are messianic in nature, in spite of the fact that the word messiah (Hebrew for *anointed one*) occurs nowhere. On the other hand, there are few who would maintain that Isaiah 45:1, which refers to Cyrus the Persian as Yahweh's messiah, is messianic in the sense described above. Or, to refer to two other texts from the Persian period, should one infer that Haggai (Hag. 2:20–23) and Zechariah (Zech. 6:9–14) are expressing a messianic hope, or simply a royalist (i.e., political) expectation centering on the person of Zerubbabel?

240

This is not the place to discuss the questions raised by these and similar texts, but they are cited here for the purpose of reminding one that a messianic text is not always easily identified, nor is it always a simple matter to comprehend the nature of the messianic hope that a given literary work expresses. This discussion focuses upon texts whose messianic content it seems possible to identify. Each of these writings has been discussed previously, and the reader is encouraged to consult the page numbers indicated.

1. *The Book of Daniel* (see pages 76–80)

It may be debated that Daniel contains a messianic hope, but there is little question that Daniel's teaching concerning the coming of the rule of God gave new impetus to messianism during the Hellenistic period. In the case of Daniel, we run straight way into a problem concerning words. In spite of the reference to an "anointed prince" in Daniel 9:25, where the phrase seems to refer either to Zerubbabel or to his colleague Joshua (Ezra 3:2), there seems to be no reference in Daniel to a messiah in the sense of a transcendent individual agent of God (notice that the "anointed one" of Dan. 9:26 is probably the high priest Onias III). On the other hand, there is ample hope expressed in a coming kingdom of God.

A "time of anguish" (Dan. 12:1) has set in upon Israel with the persecutions and sacrilege of Antiochus Epiphanes. In response to this evil, God has promised to judge the nations of the world and to uproot iniquity for ever. The establishment of the divine kingdom will be the result of the sending of "one like a son of man" (NRSV: human being)

[who will be given] dominion
  and glory and kingship,
that all peoples, nations, and languages
  should serve him.
(Dan. 7:13–14)

But this figure almost certainly is to be understood not as a reference to an individual, but to the "holy ones of the Most High" (Dan. 7:18, 22, 27). It is they who, in a corporate sense, will preside over "a kingdom that shall never be destroyed" (Dan. 2:44). Just as the beasts in Daniel's dream (7:1–8) represent the political (i.e., human) kingdoms of the earth, so the "one like a son of man" represents the saints:

"As for these four great beasts, four kings shall arise out of the earth. But the holy ones of the Most High shall receive the kingdom and possess the kingdom forever—forever and ever."
(Dan. 7:17–18)

These saints are not just those faithful to God who are presently alive, but the faithful dead as well, whose resurrection will be presided over by the angel Michael (Dan. 12:1).

In summary, Daniel expresses a hope in a righteous kingdom established by God, over which the faithful people of God will preside for ever. To the extent that messianism is present in Daniel, it would seem to be of a corporate nature.

2. *The Qumran Scrolls* (see pages 153–169)

In our discussion of the eschatology and messianism at Qumran we noticed a distinctive characteristic of the messianic expectation of that community: a plurality of messiahs. The Messianic Rule (1QSa), for example, appears to describe an eschatological banquet presided over by a messiah of the house of Aaron and a "Messiah of Israel." The latter is perhaps a military figure for he sits at the head of the assembled hosts, whereas the Aaronic messiah, who appears superior to the "Messiah of Israel," is to bless and serve the bread and wine. A fragment entitled (by modern scholars) Midrash on the Last Days seems to describe two messiahs (the "Branch of David" and the "Interpreter of the Law") in this manner:

> He is the Branch of David who shall arise with the Interpreter of the Law [to rule] in Zion [at the end] of time. As it is written, "I will raise up the tent of David that is fallen" (Amos 9:11). That is to say, the fallen "tent of David" is he who shall arise to save Israel.
>
> (Mid. on the Last Days I)[2]

The plurality of messiahs is made even more complex by a statement in the Community Rule which appears to refer to three messianic figures:

> They [the members of the sect] shall depart from none of the counsels of the Law to walk in the stubbornness of their hearts, but shall be ruled by the primitive precepts in which the men of the Community were first instructed until there shall come the Prophet and the Messiahs of Aaron and Israel.
>
> (1QS 9:11)[3]

It is not clear how these three figures are related to one another, but their coming is apparently connected with the end time. The figure of the eschatological prophet is almost certainly drawn from Deuteronomy 18:15–19. There is also a fragmentary midrash on the heavenly Prince Melchizedek who may constitute a fourth messianic figure.[4]

In summary: Not all Qumran documents reveal messianic expectations, but among those that do, the dual messiahship of the Aaronic and Davidic figures appears normative. The images of dual leadership on the part of Aaron and Moses and on the part of Joshua and Zerubbabel, plus the priestly self-consciousness of the Qumran community, seem to lie behind this unusual messianic conceptualization. Isolated texts suggest the possibility of a third or even a fourth messianic personality.

3. The Similitudes of Enoch (see pages 81–85)

As discussed earlier the substance of 1 Enoch's messianic expectation, which is quite elaborate, is contained in the so-called Book of the Similitudes (chaps. 37–71), apparently the last part of 1 Enoch to be composed. The final judgment, at which the wicked (included demons) will be destroyed and the faithful people of God raised from the dead (51:1–5), will be presided over by a special agent from God, whose names are Elect One (45:3), Son of Man (46:3), and Messiah (52:4). His preexistence and his transcendence stress the fact that he is a more-than-human figure, while his power over both good and evil reveal that he functions as none other than the representative of the living God.

The many parallels between 1 Enoch and the New Testament suggest that this pseudepigraphon was widely known and used in the early church and that, therefore, much of the New Testament's language concerning the Jesus the Messiah was drawn from the Similitudes. While that is likely true, the fact that the Similitudes alone, of the various parts of 1 Enoch, was not found at Qumran, raises the possibility, however unlikely, that the Similitudes post-dates the New Testament. In this case, of course, it would be the New Testament that has influenced the Similitudes.

In summary: In its description of the nature of the messiah and in the titles conferred upon him, the Similitudes of Enoch are nearer the New Testament than any other literature, canonical or noncanonical.

4. The Testaments of the Twelve Patriarchs (see pages 86–90)

In a manner similar to documents from Qumran, the Testaments of the Twelve Patriarchs also describes the supremacy of a priestly messiah who is instrumental in bringing in the rule of God. He will inaugurate an age of peace and will overcome the forces of evil:

> And Beliar shall be bound by him.
> And he shall grant to his children the authority to trample on wicked
>   spirits.
>   (Test. of Levi 18:12)[5]

In a less important role is a messiah from Judah who will rule in the name of the Lord.

> And you, my children, honor Levi and Judah, because from them shall arise the salvation of Israel.
>
> (Test. of Joseph 19:11)[6]

Although these two messiahs are distinct figures in these texts, other texts within the Testaments of the Twelve Patriarchs appear to merge their identities into one:

> Tell these things to your children as well, so that they will honor Judah and Levi, because from them the Lord will raise up a Savior for Israel.
>
> (Test. of Gad 8:1)[7]

A further similarity to Qumran is found in a passage in the Testament of Benjamin that, like the Community Rule, speaks of an eschatological prophet to come:

> The twelve tribes shall be gathered there (at the Temple) and all nations, until such time as the Most High shall send forth his salvation through the ministration of the unique prophet.
>
> (Test. of Benj. 9:2)[8]

In summary: The description of the messiah in the Testaments of the Twelve Patriarchs is far from uniform. What is striking is its affinity with messianic views of the Qumran documents.

5. *Jubilees* (see pages 91–93)

The Book of Jubilees might be characterized as "restrained apocalyptic," in that there is no sense of urgency or crisis that permeates its portrayal of the end time. While the role of the messiah is not large, there are one or two texts which reflect an expectation concerning a messianic figure from the House of Judah (i.e., David). At the end of time there will be a state of well-being and peace as life is lived under the Torah:

> And all of their days they will be complete
> and live in peace and rejoicing
> and there will be no Satan and no evil (one) who will destroy
> because all of their days will be days of blessing and healing.
>
> (Jub. 23:29)[9]

And the tribe of Judah will be the instrument through which God's salvation will come:

> And to Judah he (Jacob) said:
> *   *   *   *
> Be a prince, you and one of your sons for the sons of Jacob;
> may your name and the name of your son be one which travels and
>   goes about in all the lands and cities.
> Then may the nations fear before your face,
> and all of the nations tremble,
> And with you will be the help of Jacob
> and with you will be found the salvation of Israel.
>
> (Jub. 31:18–19)[10]

In summary: Jubilees appears to expect the coming of a messiah from the tribe of Judah, but such an expectation is not central to its understanding of the future of the people of God.

6. Book 3 of the Sibylline Oracles (see pages 93–97)

As we discussed earlier, the final oracle of the so-called main corpus of Sibylline Oracle 3 describes the overthrow of the evil nations of the earth by the power of God and the establishment of a divine kingdom. There are five lines which either precede this hymn or constitute its beginning which may be a reference to a messianic figure:

> And then God will send a king from the sun (or "from the east")
> who will stop the entire earth from evil war,
> killing some, imposing oaths of loyalty on others;
> and he will not do all these things by his private plans
> but in obedience to the noble teachings of the great God.
>
> (Sib. Orac. 3:652–656)[11]

On the basis of the fact that this king is never again referred to in the oracle that follows, this is probably, like other statements in the main corpus of Book 3, a reference to a Ptolemaic king.

In succeeding lines (3:657–808), the oracle describes an assault upon the Temple by evil "kings of the peoples" (3:663), a sacrilege to which God responds by sending a universal judgment (3:669–701).

> But the sons of the Great God will all live
> peacefully around the Temple, rejoicing in these things
> which the Creator, just judge and sole ruler, will give.

For he alone will shield them, standing by them magnificently
as if he had a wall of blazing fire round about.

(3: 702–706)[12]

These faithful people will worship and praise God, gathering the fallen
weapons of their foes, while gentiles will be moved to join this worship
(3:702–731).

A time of peace will ensue in which the earth will bring forth its produce
in abundance and in which "king will be friend to king to the end of the age"
(3:741–761). God will provide the light for the citizens of this kingdom that is
described, in dependence upon Isaiah 11:6–8, as a place where "wolves and
lambs will eat grass together in the mountains" (3:767–795). The sign that the
end is near is described:

I will tell you a very clear sign, so that you may know
when the end of all things comes to pass on earth:
when swords are seen at night in starry heaven
toward evening and toward dawn,
and again dust is brought forth from heaven
upon the earth and all the light of the sun
is eclipsed from the middle of the heaven, and the rays
of the moon appear and return to the earth.

*   *   *   *

This is the end of war which God, who inhabits heaven, is
accomplishing.
But all must sacrifice to the great king.

(3:796–808)[13]

In summary: Book 3 of the Sibylline Oracles presents the establishment of
the kingdom of God as the direct activity of God, apparently without reliance
upon the aid of a messiah, unless—as appears unlikely—the "king from the
sun" is a messianic figure.

7. The Psalms of Solomon (see pages 97–100)

We noticed an interest in a messiah in the Psalms of Solomon, especially in
Psalm of Solomon 17. Because of Israel's sin, God overthrew the original
Davidic dynasty:

Lord, you chose David to be king over Israel,
and swore to him about his descendants forever,
that his kingdom should not fail before you.

> But (because of) our sins, sinners rose up against us,
> > they set upon us and drove us out.
> > > (Ps. Sol. 17:4–5)[14]

The present distress (presumably the conquest of Jerusalem by Pompey) is part of this judgment of God, and in order to obtain the salvation of the nation the author prays for a new Davidic king to destroy the oppressive gentile forces. This Davidic ruler will "gather a holy people" and will establish Jerusalem as the center of a new kingdom of righteousness and peace. This sinless messiah will be an individual of compassion and strength, of hope and faithfulness:

> He shall be compassionate to all the nations
> > (who) reverently stand before him.
> He will strike the earth with the rod of his mouth forever;
> > he will bless the Lord's people with wisdom and happiness.
> And he himself (will be) free from sin, (in order) to rule
> > a great people.
> > > *   *   *   *
> Faithfully and rightously shepherding the Lord's flock,
> > he will not let any of them stumble in their pasture.
> He will lead them in all holiness
> > and there will be no arrogance among them,
> > that any should be oppressed.
> This is the beauty of the king of Israel which God knew,
> > to raise him over the house of Israel
> > to discipline it.
> > > (Ps. of Sol. 17:34–42)[15]

In summary: A single messiah of the House of David will establish an earthly kingdom of justice and peace.

In conclusion it may be observed that among Jewish writers of the late Hellenistic period who express a messianic hope, there is little consensus concerning the nature of the messiah. He is to be either one, two, or three persons, or, in the case of Daniel, the entire family of the saints. He is to be either Aaronic or Davidic. He is to be either the force by which God brings in the kingdom, or the agent of God who presides over that kingdom. What seems to be commonly held is that the messiah's coming will coincide with the end of time and the overthrow of the powers of evil. At his coming the faithful people of God will experience salvation.

Part Two

THE ROMAN PERIOD

Chapter 8

Roman Rule Comes to Palestine

The penetration of the East by the legions of Rome, an event both feared and resisted by the rulers of the Hellenistic kingdoms, appears all but inevitable to an observer in our own time. Antiochus IV Epiphanes hurried to Egypt in 169 BC in the express hope of thwarting a Roman presence on his southern border only, as we have seen, to be surprised and rebuffed there by the Roman ambassador Popillius. In 146 BC Corinth was destroyed and Greece was designated the Roman province of Achaia (note Acts 18:12), while Antioch-on-the-Orontes became the capital of Roman Syria in 64 BC. That Jerusalem should fall to Roman control in 63 was, in a certain respect, merely a closing of the pincers.

The coming of the legions was as decisive for the peoples of the region, including the Jews, as had been the march of Alexander's Macedonians in the fourth century BC. But though equally profound, the nature of Roman influence was remarkably different, as will be noted. The currents of Hellenistic culture, instead of being dispelled, were largely redirected, often with fresh energies to urge them forward. This new Greco-Roman world was, of course, an environment in which early Judaism flourished, in spite of intense, often violent conflict. And it was also the cradle of early Christianity.

The period of early Roman domination of Palestine was also a time of momentous change in Rome itself, the death of the republic and the birth of the empire (27 BC) being the most conspicuous of these changes. The reverberations of Roman politics were felt no less in Palestine than in other lands conquered by Rome, thus introducing additional elements of uncertainty into the lives of those who lived there.

In this chapter we shall survey events in Roman political and cultural history from the time of Julius Caesar and the First Triumvirate through the first quarter of the second century AD, the setting for the revolt of the Palestinian Jewish leader Simon bar Kokhba. We shall then turn our attention to the early years of Roman occupation of Palestine before, in the next chapter, discussing the rule of Herod the Great and subsequent events of importance to both Christians and Jews.

A. ROME: THE REPUBLIC BECOMES AN EMPIRE

1. *To the Death of the Republic* (27 BC)[1]

a. *The First Triumvirate (60 BC).* The advance of Roman military power throughout the Mediterranean world in the second and early first centuries BC had not resulted in political tranquility in Rome itself. Although theoretically enjoying a republican form of government in which power was balanced between two elected executives called consuls, who were advised in matters of state by a senate, Rome was often torn by deep political conflicts that arose out of the personal greed and vanity of the city's politicians. The army, whose courage and professional skills had created a highly efficient fighting force, was nevertheless composed of individual soldiers whose first loyalty was not to the Roman government, but to their own commander. Thus, even while it continued to expand Rome's influence abroad, the army was often a destabilizing factor in Roman domestic affairs.

A politician of unusual skill who wished to bring greater political and social order into Roman life and, not incidentally, to further his own ambitions, was Gaius Julius Caesar (c. 100–44 BC). Caesar, who had served Rome in a number of civic capacities, established, in collaboration with two political allies, Marcus Licinius Crassus and Gnaeus Pompeius (Pompey), a committee designed to exercise supreme authority over the Roman government, a group commonly referred to by historians as the First Triumvirate (60 BC). Crassus (c. 112–53 BC), a wealthy political and military leader, is remembered for having crushed a revolt led by the famous gladiator Spartacus in 71 BC. Later, he would win the contempt of the Jews for looting the Jerusalem Temple in order to help finance his war against the Parthians (53 BC). Pompey (c. 106–48 BC), in addition to his military victories in the East, including Jerusalem, was well known to the Roman population for having cleared the Mediterranean of pirates in 67 BC. The members of the First Triumvirate hoped to establish a strong government that would end the divisiveness in Roman politics.

If anything, however, their attempt succeeded in establishing deeper hostilities than before. By the time Crassus was killed in his Parthian campaign, Pompey had become alarmed over Caesar's growing power. The latter had conquered Gaul (the basis of his great *Commentaries on the Gallic War*) and had pushed Roman frontiers to the Rhine Valley and across the English Channel into Britain. In 49 BC Caesar was summoned home by the Roman government, a move that had been abetted by new political alliances erected by Pompey and threatened Caesar's downfall. But in a bold move, Caesar instead marched against Rome, his crossing of the Rubicon River (which separated the provinces from Italy), being perhaps the most decisive moment in his political career. Caesar's army defeated that of Pompey, which fled with its commander to the Balkans. But Caesar, in pursuit, finally routed Pompey's forces at the important Battle of Pharsalus (48 BC) in Greece. Pompey once more tried to escape, this time to Egypt, only to be murdered there by Caesar's friends. Before learning of his adversary's death, Caesar arrived in Egypt, remaining long enough to meet and be seduced by the last Ptolemaic ruler, Cleopatra VII.

Back in Rome, Caesar briefly enjoyed political supremacy before being murdered by a group who had grown to fear his power and skill. This celebrated event, which took place on March 15 (the Ides of March), 44BC, was primarily the work of two former followers of Pompey, Marcus Junius Brutus and Gaius Cassius, both of whom Caesar had pardoned after the Battle of Pharsalus.

b. The Second Triumvirate (43 BC).   Caesar's closest lieutenant at the time of his death was Marc Antony (c. 82–30 BC), who entertained thoughts of inheriting his leader's mantle. But Caesar's great-nephew and adopted son, Octavian (63 BC–14 AD), challenged Antony and defeated him in battle in 43 BC. Octavian was thereupon elected consul and, with Antony and a general named Aemilius Lepidus (d. 13 BC), formed the Second Triumvirate. The murderers of Caesar were punished and administration over the provinces was divided among the members of the new Triumvirate, with Antony ruling in the East, Octavius in the West, and Lepidus in Africa.

Antony married Octavian's sister, Octavia, in 40 BC, but abandoned her when, in Egypt, he, too, fell under the spell of Cleopatra VII. When Antony later gave large territories in the East to Cleopatra and their children, Octavian set out to overthrow Antony and claim the East for himself. The naval Battle of Actium (off the western coast of Greece) in 31 BC, in which the ships of Octavian defeated a combined fleet of Antony and Cleopatra, attained that goal. Antony committed suicide and, as the weak Lepidus was no longer a factor, Octavian was soon named "first citizen" (*princeps*) of Rome.

In 27 BC the senate conferred upon Octavian a title never before borne by a Roman leader, Augustus (meaning *Exalted One*). Although the forms of republican government were retained, Rome had now become an empire, its ruler a virtually absolute monarch.

2. The Empire (27 BC and after)

Although this is not the place to trace the history of imperial Rome, it is perhaps in order to mention a number of important early Roman emperors who presided over events which touched the lives of the Jewish and Christian communities.

a. *Caesar Augustus (27 BC–14 AD).* Julius Caesar's adopted son is considered by many to be the greatest of the rulers of the Roman Empire. His reign coincided with the beginning of a 200-year-period of peace, the *Pax Romana* (Peace of Rome), during which, in spite of local disturbances, both Rome and its provinces were secure as never before. Augustus was a ruler of great skill, and the efficiency of his government, which created an unparalleled system of roads, harbors, and trade, brought considerable prosperity to the merchantile classes in all parts of the empire. Yet this expanding economy, which was dependent upon a large pool of cheap labor, caused slavery and other forms of social and economic exploitation to be widespread.

The Augustan Age also produced great flowerings in the arts and literature, for during this period Virgil wrote the *Aeneid,* Horace his *Odes,* Ovid the *Metamorphoses* and Livy his outstanding history, *The Annals of the Roman People.* The city of Rome was beautified by splendid monuments and buildings, while new aqueducts, bridges, amphitheaters, and temples appeared throughout the empire.

In Roman Palestine, the first two and a half decades of Augustus' reign coincided with the rule of the client king, Herod the Great. Herod emulated the architectural triumphs in metropolitan Rome by a number of splendid building enterprises of his own, the most celebrated being Caesarea Maritima (named for Augustus and possessing one of the finest harbors in the Roman world) and the Temple complex in Jerusalem. Readers of the Gospel of Luke are familiar with the fact that it cites Caesar Augustus as the regnant monarch at the time of the birth of Jesus (2:1).

b. *Tiberius (14–37 AD).* Tiberius Claudius Nero was stepson and successor to Augustus. A military leader who had led important campaigns in the East and against German tribes, Tiberius was forced by Augustus to divorce his wife and marry Augustus' daughter Julia, an unhappy union which led Tiberius to leave Rome and settle for seven years on the island of Rhodes in the Aegean Sea. From there he was recalled by Augustus and, having been designated heir to the throne, Tiberius resumed his successful military career, becoming emperor upon Augustus' death.

During the early years of his reign, Tiberius was popular and successful. The government, especially in the provinces, was efficiently organized, and skillful diplomacy was employed in the maintenance of peace with peoples beyond the frontiers of the empire. But in his later years, Tiberius relinquished much of his authority to a lieutenant, Sejanus, who imposed harsh measures upon the people. Tiberius himself was accused of murder in the death of his nephew and heir-apparent Germanicus. Yet at Tiberius' death, the empire remained politically and militarily strong.

Tiberius was emperor during the adulthood of Jesus and at the time of the birth of the Christian church. About 20 AD, Herod Antipas, tetrarch of Galilee and Peraea, constructed a city on the western shore of the Sea of Galilee that he named in honor of the emperor. Tiberias, with a mixed Jewish and gentile population, soon became the most important commercial and social center in the region and the capital of Galilee. Curiously, it is never mentioned in the New Testament, in spite of the fact that it lay in the heart of the area of Jesus' Galilean ministry.[2]

c. *Caligula (37–41 AD).*   Gaius Caesar Augustus Germanicus was the great-grandson of Augustus and son of the successful general Germanicus (the possible murder victim of Tiberius). As a child he received the affectionate name of Caligula ("Little Boots") from his father's soldiers because of his habit of wearing miniature military boots. Caligula was adopted by Tiberius and, upon the latter's death, became emperor.

Initially, Caligula ruled well, but it soon became apparent that he was mentally ill, one of the more notorious symptoms of his condition being the severe cruelty which he inflicted upon many of his subjects. He wasted the public resources in senseless ways and acted in such an irrational manner (he proclaimed his horse consul and threatened to kill the members of the senate) that he was eventually assassinated by members of the Praetorian Guard.

Caligula took seriously the proclamation of his own divinity (see below), and was particularly angry at the Jews for their refusal to worship him. In 38 AD he instigated severe anti-Jewish persecutions in Alexandria, and ordered a statue of himself to be set up in the Jerusalem Temple. When these plans became known, Jews in Palestine threatened revolt, but the governor of Syria, Publius Petronius, skillfully delayed implementation of the emperor's command. Caligula, angered at the delay, was determined to see the matter through and dispatched a message to Petronius that he should commit suicide. But before the order reached the governor, Caligula was killed and, as Petronius learned of the emperor's death before he received his own death warrant, he wisely disregarded the latter when it arrived.

d. *Claudius (41–54 AD).*   Tiberius Claudius Drusus Nero Germanicus, the son of Augustus' niece Antonia (daughter of Mark Antony and Augustus' sister Octavia), was considered in his youth something of an embarrassment to the imperial family. He had a speech impediment and a retiring personality, and because of this he was kept away from the public during his formative years. He read avidly, however, and was to write several important historical works, among them a history of Carthage (now lost). He is said to have become emperor by accident when the members of the Praetorian Guard, following the assassination of Caligula, came across Claudius in the imperial palace. As a new candidate was needed for the imperial throne, the forty-nine-year-old uncle of the dead emperor was chosen on the spot. One of those who became his close political ally at this time was the Herodian king, Agrippa I, whom Claudius would reward by the addition of Judaea and Samaria to his kingdom.

In spite of any personal weaknesses he may have had, Claudius ruled well, one of his most important accomplishments being the establishment of a professional civil service, which was to provide much needed stability to the Roman government in the years ahead. Highways and aqueducts were constructed and new cities were built, including Colonia Agrippina (named for Claudius' last wife) in Germany, known today as Cologne. And during his reign the town of Ostia, near the mouth of the Tiber River, was developed into an important port for the city of Rome.

Several parts of the empire that had been ruled by the client kings were placed by Claudius under direct Roman administration. Upon the death of Claudius' friend, Agrippa I, Judaea received a Roman governor, an unfortunate event (as it turned out) for Palestine's Jews, and one that might have been averted, had not Agrippa's heir, the future Agrippa II, been so young (about sixteen years of age).[3]

Claudius' domestic life was less successful than his career as emperor. Messalina, his third wife (out of a total of four), was killed upon the orders of the emperor after she engaged in a public love affair with an imperial official, Silius. His last wife Agrippina, was a sister of Caligula and therefore Claudius' own niece. A brutal woman, she managed to have Claudius promise that her son, Nero, would inherit the throne, in spite of the fact that Claudius' own son, Britannicus, was in line to become emperor. In order to insure that the succession would occur as she intended, Agrippina poisoned Claudius.

e. *Nero* (54–68 AD).   Nero Claudius Caesar Drusus Germanicus was the son of Agrippina, sister of Caligula, and the last member of the family of Julius Caesar to rule Rome. As a child, he was placed under the supervision of several teachers, one of whom was the great Roman philosopher Seneca. These tutors encouraged Nero's artistic inclinations, so that music, the theater, and sports were among his interests as an adult. Nero's father died when the child was young and in 49 AD Agrippina married the emperor Claudius who, as we have noted, adopted Nero and designated him his heir. Upon Claudius' death by poisoning at the hand of Agrippina, Nero became emperor.

Although Nero was in certain respects a good administrator, he is best remembered for his extravagance and cruelty. Nero murdered his mother and, a few years later, his wife Octavia, the daughter of Emperor Claudius, this latter crime being committed in order that he might take a new wife, Poppaea Sabina. In 62 Nero put to death a number of nobles whom he considered his enemies, and later (65 AD), he ordered the suicide of his mentor, Seneca. His financial irresponsibility led to serious economic problems, including high rates of inflation. In 67–68 Nero traveled to Greece in order to participate in public musical competitions and, while he was away, a tide of opinion rose against him in both Rome and the provinces because of his excesses. He was declared a public enemy by the senate and, faced with the desertion of the Praetorian Guard, he committed suicide.

It was to Nero that Paul appealed, when brought before the Roman Procurator of Judaea, Porcius Festus (Acts 25:10). And it is likely that in the Neronian persecutions both Paul and Peter met their deaths, although there is no evidence that the emperor was personally involved. A great fire which burned part of Rome in July of 64 AD was popularly believed to have been started by Nero and, while that charge is probably false, Nero used the conflagration as an occasion for widespread persecution of Christians (perhaps the context of the martyrdom of Paul and Peter). There is reason to believe, so feared was Nero by the Christian community, that it is he who is represented by the beast of Revelation 13:11–18.

During the reign of Nero the Jewish revolt broke out in Palestine (66 AD) as a result of continuing indignities inflicted upon the people, an event traced in the next chapter in some detail.[4]

f. *Vespasian* (69–79 AD).   The brutal and wasteful reign of Nero resulted in the near breakup of central Roman authority, and his death was followed by a chaotic period in which three Roman generals succeeded one another upon the imperial throne during the space of only two years. Each of these emperors was forcefully deposed and was either killed or forced to commit suicide. It was the general sent by Nero to quell the Jews, Titus Flavius Sabinus Vespasianus, known simply as Vespasian, who restored the office of emperor and the authority of the central government.

Vespasian was not of noble birth, but his skills as an administrator and military strategist won for him important responsibilities in the government and the army. Among other public activities, he had commanded troops in Germany and Britain, had served as consul under the emperor Claudius, and as proconsul of Africa under Nero. He had accompanied Nero to Greece in 67 and from there he was dispatched by the emperor to suppress the Jewish rebels in Palestine with three legions at his command. As the political situation deteriorated at home following the death of Nero, those around Vespasian (and apparently the general himself) began to think of him as in imperial candidate. Josephus describes how he predicted to Vespasian's face that he would become the next to wear the imperial purple[5] (a prescience that resulted in Josephus' gracious treatment at the hands of the Flavian family of emperors), and not long afterward Vespasian's devoted soldiers in Alexandria proclaimed him emperor. Vespasian left his son Titus in command of the legions in Palestine and proceeded to Rome where he was greeted with great popular enthusiasm.

Vespasian's reign of a decade was an efficient and honest administration. The finances of the imperial government were reorganized, and many public services that had ceased during the last years of Nero and the two turbulent years following his death were restored. A number of important building enterprises, including the Forum and the Colosseum in Rome, were begun during this time. Vespasian, for all his triumphs, was a modest man and refused to take seriously the popular view that the emperor was a god. During Vespasian's rule Titus destroyed Jerusalem, including the Temple (70 AD), crushed the final Jewish rebels, and (according to some sources) persecuted the surviving Palestinian Jews.[6] Upon Vespasian's death, his deity was proclaimed by the senate.

g. *Titus (79–81 AD).* Vespasian's eldest son, who bore the same full name as his father but who was known popularly as Titus, had been designated by Vespasian as his heir and, thus, became emperor upon Vespasian's death. Like his father, Titus enjoyed an illustrious military career in which the capture of Jerusalem (70 AD) was the most renowned accomplishment. His brief reign was characterized by a certain paradox in that, while he was self-indulgent with respect to his own appetites, he demonstrated a great affection for the common people and their needs. In the summer of 79 Mt. Vesuvius erupted, burying the thriving city of Pompeii as well as neighboring Herculaneum, the most noteworthy event of Titus' brief reign.

h. *Domitian (81–96 AD).* Titus Flavius Domitianus Augustus, the second son of Vespasian, became emperor upon his brother's death. The first year of his rule saw the completion of the Titus Arch, a public monument begun by Vespasian to celebrate Titus' capture of Jerusalem. Tough and resolute, Domitian attempted to expand the borders of the empire, especially in the Rhine and Danube valleys, where he constructed a string of fortifications. He equated loyalty to Rome with devotion to himself as a god, and after the year 89, when he put down a revolt against his rule, he cruelly suppressed those whom he considered seditious, including many Jews and Christians. Since the time of the destruction of the Jerusalem Temple, Jews had been forced to send the former Temple tax to Rome, and Domitian's agents collected this tax with harsh determination. Many Jews and Christians refused Domitian's demand that he be addressed as *Dominus et Deus* (Lord and God) and for this defiance they were often subjected to imprisonment and death.

Some have suggested that Domitian's niece, Flavia Domitilla (a granddaughter of Vespasian), may have been a Christian, for she was exiled from

Rome and her husband killed. Many others whom Domitian or his agents suspected of disloyalty, because of their religious or political views, were also severely persecuted. This reign of terror may be reflected in the sufferings described in the Book of Revelation, which was completed near the end of Domitian's reign, and it certainly contributed to the emperor's downfall. He was assassinated as a result of a conspiracy against him, among whose participants was his wife.

i. *Trajan (98–117 AD)*.   Marcus Ulpius Trajanus, a popular and successful Roman military leader, was adopted by the emperor Nerva (96–98 AD) and designated as his heir. As emperor, Trajan is best remembered for his successful military campaigns, his construction of public buildings, and his efforts at financial reform within the empire. The most famous visible reminder of his reign is Trajan's Column in Rome (dedicated in 113 AD) that commemorates the emperor's victories in Dacia (modern Rumania). Although once crowned with a statue of Trajan, this 100-foot-high column has, since 1588, supported a statue of St. Paul.

During the latter years of Trajan's reign, Jewish uprisings broke out in the North African provinces of Egypt and Cyrenaica. It took the efforts of one of Rome's most skilled generals, Marcus Turbo, to suppress these violent revolts, which did not end (c. 117) until the death of thousands of those who were loyal to the Jewish "king," Lucuas. Jewish revolts also took place about the same time on Cyprus and in Mesopotamia.[7]

j. *Hadrian (117–138 AD)*.   Publius Aelius Hadrianus was a nephew of Trajan who, upon the death of his father, was adopted by the emperor and designated his successor. Intelligent and able, Hadrian codified Roman law into a more manageable form and reorganized the empire's systems of transportation and communication. A patron of the arts, Hadrian was also a skilled diplomat who negotiated treaties of peace with many of the peoples against whom Trajan had campaigned. He constructed a fortified wall between Roman Britain and the unconquered tribes of the north, a barrier that ran the width of Britain and whose considerable remains may still be seen in the north of England.

A violent exception to the generally peaceful reign of Hadrian was the Palestinian Jewish revolt of 132–135 AD, led by the legendary Simon Bar Kokhba. Jerusalem was still in ruins from the destruction by Titus' army in 70, and Hadrian's plan to rebuild the site as a Roman city, plus a ban on circumcision, seem to have led the Jews to take up arms against the Romans. Three and a half years of fighting ensued, during which thousands of lives were lost and the land was left in desolation, before Bar Kokhba was killed and the revolt crushed. Jerusalem then arose as the Roman city Aelia Capitolina, a community from which all Jews were expelled and whose most prominent religious sanctuary was a temple to Jupiter erected on the site of the former Temple of the Jews. Hadrian himself may have been present for the Roman campaign of pacification, events we shall trace in the next chapter.

B. Literature, Philosophy, and Religion of the Early Roman Empire

Although the cultural traditions of Rome were quite old at the time of Rome's rise to political dominance of the Mediterranean basin, many of these were either set aside in favor of the traditions of Greece, or were given new expressions highly colored by Greek influences. For example, although Latin was the tongue of Rome, during the time of the late republic and early empire most educated Romans were also fluent in Greek, while in the provinces Greek, more often than Latin, was the language of choice. In addition, Roman literature, art, and architecture came to depend upon Greek models, which had become familiar to many Romans, long before the conquest of Greece, through the influences of Hellenized communities in southern Italy and Sicily (Magna Graecia). Because many Roman citizens considered Greek cultural traditions superior to their own, Roman political domination of the Mediterranean world, instead of acting as a restraint upon the spread of Hellenism, was a means of its further spread, although in somewhat altered form.

1. Literature[8]

As noted above, the late republic and early empire were times of energetic artistic expression during which some of Rome's finest writers flourished. Cicero set new standards in political oratory; Virgil, Horace, and Ovid excelled in poetry; while Livy, Tacitus, Plutarch, and Suetonius wrote enduring history and biography.

a. Political Oratory. Marcus Tullius Cicero (106–43 BC) was the son of a prosperous family from Arpinum, near Rome, who, after a formal education in Roman law and Greek philosophy and literature, turned to a career as a statesman. He won wide popular acclaim for his role in two celebrated events. In 70 BC he succeeded in prosecuting the corrupt governor of Sicily, who was forced into exile as a result of Cicero's exposure. In 63 BC, Cicero, now consul, thwarted a conspiracy led by an ambitious politician, Catiline, who plotted to kill Rome's leading officials and seize control of the government. In crushing the Catiline conspiracy, Cicero relied upon his enormous powers of oratory in denouncing the rebellion before the senate.

Review with me now, Catiline, the events of the night before last . . . I say that the night before last you came into the Street of the Scythemakers (I will not deal in general terms), you came to the house of Marcus Laeca; to the same place came many of your allies animated by the same madness and wickedness. You do not dare to deny it, do you? Why are you silent? I will convict you if you do deny. For I see here in the senate some who were there with you. O ye immortal gods! Where in the world are we? What sort of commonwealth do we possess? In what city are we living? Here, here in our very midst, [fellow senators,] in this most sacred and dignified council of the whole world, are men who plan for the destruction of all of us, who plan for the destruction of this city and even the destruction of the whole world.[9]

In both of these episodes Cicero revealed his deep affection for republican political principles, and his dedicated opposition to despotism and public corruption. Because he refused to cooperate with the members of the First Triumvirate he was briefly banished from Rome. He condoned the murder of Julius Caesar in 44 BC, although he did not participate in it, because he considered Caesar a tyrant. After Caesar's death, Cicero bitterly attacked Marc Antony (then, Caesar's heir apparent) in a series of speeches before the senate known as the Philippic Orations, so named because of their similarity to attacks upon Philip of Macedon by the Athenian orator Demosthenes (c. 383–322 BC). Not surprisingly, he was condemned to death by the Second Triumvirate and assassinated.

Cicero's contribution to the craft of political oratory lay in his emphasis upon the need for factual accuracy and logical clarity in arguing one's position, a method which, in his view, required the widest possible knowledge of philosophy and literature on the part of the orator. Cicero's skillful blending of the traditions of Greek learning with the legal principles of the Roman republic not only resulted in an oratorical style of considerable power, but, in addition, helped shape Latin prose into a medium of great expressiveness. His philosophical essays reveal eclectic interests on Cicero's part, with perhaps an important inclination toward Stoicism, while his letters provide valuable insights into the nature of Roman daily life in the twilight years of the republic.

b. *Poetry*.   Quintus Horatius Flaccus (65–8 BC), known as Horace, was a native of Venosa in northern Italy who had commanded a legion in the army of Brutus at the Battle of Philippi. He was later befriended by the emperor Augustus (to whom he dedicated several of his verses) and by a wealthy Roman, Maecenas, to whom he was introduced by his friend Virgil and whose gifts enabled Horace to achieve considerable financial independence. Much of Horace's poetry (all of which is in Latin) exhibits the self-confidence of the new age which, at the same time, is respectful of the traditions of the past, but is anxious to move forward to new accomplishments. For example, in one

poem, which has been titled "To Augustus, Explaining the Modern Literary
Attitude Toward the Ancient Greeks," Horace pokes fun at the idea that the
older a poem is, the better:

> A writer that has lived a hundred year
> is old and is a classic, 'twould appear.
> Well, in which category shall we place
> A man that has a month, a year, lived less?
> Among the ancient poets, or with them
> That this and future ages may condemn?[10]

Horace's subjects included romantic love (his famous "Lydia" poems) and
the joys and trials of daily life, themes which he explored through various
poetic forms: satire, ode, poetic letter, and the like. In one of his satires, he
describes with considerable humor his efforts to be rid of a boring
acquaintance, while in others he ridicules the avarice of his contemporaries
and praises the contentment that comes from the pursuit of simple pleasures.
His work frequently possesses a proverbial quality, such as the following:

> If you study the history and records of the world you must admit that
> the source of justice was the fear of unjustice.[11]

> You must make frequent use of the eraser if you want to write some-
> thing that deserves a second reading.[12]

His often quoted sentiment, "It is sweet and fitting to die for one's country,"
reflects the deeply felt pride in itself of the Augustan Age.[13]

Virgil (Publius Vergilius Maro, 70–19 BC) represents the height of poetic
achievement during the early empire, and is regarded by many as the greatest
poet of the Latin language. Like his friend Horace a north Italian, Virgil modeled his work closely along the lines of earlier Greek poetry. Yet his origi-
nality of thought prevented his poetry from becoming mere imitation and
allowed it to rise to new levels of creative expression. His *Eclogues*, early poems (about 40 BC) glorifying the shepherd's life, are based upon the pastoral
poems of the third century BC Greek writer Theocritus of Syracuse (in southern Italy). Of these the most celebrated is the Fourth Eclogue, where Virgil
acknowledges his indebtedness to the Sibylline[14] tradition for the poem's central idea—the dawning of a golden age:

> We have reached the last era in Sibylline song. Time has conceived and
> the great sequence of the ages starts afresh.

The new age is described in language reminiscent of the Book of Isaiah
(Isa. 11:6–9):

The goats, unshepherded, will make for home with udders full of milk, and the ox will not be frightened of the lion for all his might . . . The snake will come to grief, and poison lurk no more in the weed.

But perhaps most striking is the poem's declaration that the golden age will dawn with the birth of a holy child:

The firstborn of the New Age is already on his way from high heaven down to earth . . .

*   *   *   *

Enter—for the hour is close at hand—on your illustrious career, dear child of the gods, great increment of Jove. Look at the world, rocked by the weight of its overhanging dome . . . See how the whole creation rejoices in the age that is to be.[15]

Although Virgil is almost certainly extolling the growing power and influence of Rome, and the unidentified child is a personification of the Roman political leader, some Christians were later to see in Virgil a pagan confirmation of the messianic role of Christ.[16]

Virgil's most important work, however, is the *Aeneid*, an epic poem in twelve books, the first six of which are based on Homer's *Iliad* and the rest on the *Odyssey*. The *Aeneid*, written between 30 and 19 BC, describes the adventures of Aeneas, a Trojan hero who, after the fall of Troy, sets out to establish a new home for his people and their gods. By means of divine guidance and protection, Aeneas ultimately makes his way to Italy, where he establishes a community which later produces Rome. The *Aeneid* is thus an important political statement in which Rome is described as the divinely ordained heir and successor of heroic Troy, while Augustus is portrayed as the direct descendant of Aeneas.

In Book VI of the *Aeneid*, Aeneas' father, Anchises, permits his son a vision into the future of the nation he is helping to create:

Let now thy visionary glance look long
On this thy race, these Romans that be thine.
Here Caesar [Augustus], of Julius' glorious seed,
Behold ascending to the world of light!
Behold, at last, that man, for this is he,
So oft unto thy listening ears foretold,
Augustus Caesar, kindred unto Jove [i.e., Jupiter].
He brings a golden age; he shall restore
Old Saturn's septre to our Latin land.
                    (VI, 1021–1029)[17]

Ovid (Publius Ovidius Naso, 43 BC–c. 17 AD), was a third important poet of the early Roman empire. Less concerned with Rome's new place in the world than were Horace and Virgil, Ovid expressed a deep interest in the themes of human love and in Greco-Roman mythology. His love poems, including a work in three books entitled *The Art of Love*, were so realistic as to cause offense in some quarters, and may have helped Augustus decide to send Ovid into exile. Whatever the reasons for his banishment from Rome in 8 AD (the historical record is not clear), the last decade or so of the poet's life was spent in what is now Rumania, on the shore of the Black Sea.

Ovid's most important work, *Metamorphoses,* combines his interest in love and mythology in a collection of 250 tales, arranged in chronological order from the beginning of the world to the time of Julius Caesar. The title is drawn from a common feature found in the stories, which recount how the subject is transformed from one thing into something else (e.g., Julius Caesar is changed into a star). The *Metamorphoses* are important to students of classical literature because they provide one of our best sources of information concerning the content of Greek and Roman myths, and are also significant because of their influence upon many later writers.

An example of Ovid's style may be seen in this excerpt from his tale of how the nymph Daphne was transformed into the laurel tree in order to escape the amorous designs of the sun god Apollo. Under Ovid's pen, Cupid possessed two arrows, one of which generates love in the person it strikes, the other disgust.

> cleaving the air with his beating wings, he [Cupid] stood upon the shady heights of Parnasus, and drew two weapons out of his arrow-bearing quiver, of different workmanship; the one repels, the other excites desire. That which causes love is gold, and is brilliant, with a sharp point; that which repels it is blunt, and contains lead beneath the reed. This one the god fixed in the Nymph [Daphne], the daughter of Peneus, but with the other he wounded the very marrow of Apollo, through his bones pierced by the arrow. Immediately the one is in love; the other flies from the very name of a lover.[18]

c. *Historiography and Biography.*   From the period of the early empire the work of two important historians who wrote in Latin has survived, Livy and Tacitus. Livy's (Titus Livius, 59 BC–17 AD) extensive *History from the Founding of the City* traced the growth of Rome from its beginnings to the death in 9 BC of the Roman general Drusus, brother of the (later) emperor Tiberius. Like the poets Horace and Virgil, and the Greek-language historian Polybius,[19] Livy felt that Rome's mastery of the world was of great benefit to humankind, and the historian was especially flattering of his patron, Augustus. But in literary terms, Livy demonstrated an indebtedness to Cicero, and it was Livy's willingness to explore further the new possibilities of Latin prose which, in part at least, contributed to his greatness as a writer. Less than half Livy's history has survived, but the contents of much of the lost sections have been partially preserved through summaries prepared in antiquity for readers who did not possess the time or the funds to have access to the original work.

In Book II of his work, Livy tells the celebrated story of Horatius Cocles ("Horatius at the Bridge"), the brave Roman who single-handedly withstood an invading army. The story is set in Rome's legendary past and, if it is true, may perhaps be dated to about the sixth century BC. Livy's narrative tells how all the Romans fled into the city at the advance of the Etruscan army, except Horatius:

> Then, striding to the head of the bridge, conspicuous among fugitives who were clearly seen to be shirking the fight, he covered himself with his sword and buckler and made ready to do battle at close quarters, confounding the Etruscans with amazement at his audacity . . . Then, darting glances of defiance around at the Etruscan nobles, he now challenged them in turn to fight, now railed at them collectively as slaves of haughty kings, who, heedless of their own liberty, were come to overthrow the liberty of others . . . [Horatius held off the enemy until the bridge collapsed, whereupon] he leaped down into the river, and under a shower of missiles swam across unhurt to his fellows, having given a proof of valor which was destined to obtain more fame than credence with posterity.[20]

Cornelius Tacitus (c. 55–117 AD), a politican whose historical writings are concerned with the administrations of various Roman emperors, was critical of the abuses of power which often characterized Roman imperial government. Tacitus' *Histories*, which chronicle the reigns of emperors from Galba through Domitian, and his *Annals*, which take as its subjects the emperors of the Julian line, are preserved only in part. But the surviving fragments reveal an attitude toward the imperial rule that condemned extravagance and tyranny and that looked back with approval to the moral values of the lost Roman republic. For example, in the midst of his description of the career of the emperor Otho (69 AD), Tacitus digresses to discuss the causes of the earlier Roman civil wars:

> The old greed for power, long engrained in mankind, came to full growth and broke bounds as the empire became great. When resources were moderate, equality was easily maintained; but when the world had been subjugated and rival states or kings destroyed, . . . then the first attempts at civil war were made. The same wrath [which now drives the army of Otho], the same human madness, the same motives to crime drove them on to strife. The fact that these wars were ended by a single blow, so to speak, was due to the worthlessness of the emperors.[21]

Tacitus is also the source of much of our information relating to the early persecution of Christians, whom he refers to in one place as followers of "a foreign and deadly superstition."[22] In one celebrated passage he relates how, during Nero's reign, some Christians were covered in the skins of wild animals before being set upon by vicious dogs and how others were burned alive, the light of the flames serving to illuminate Nero's gardens.[23]

(In addition to Livy and Tacitus, mention should also be made here of the Jewish historian Josephus [c. 37–100 AD], who had won the patronage of the emperors of the Flavian family and who was active in Rome after 70. Because of his importance in contributing to our knowledge of Jewish life during the Hellenistic and Roman periods, he is discussed in the final chapter.)[24]

An important biographer of the early Roman Empire was Plutarch (c. 46–120 AD), a native of Boeotia in southern Greece. As a young man, Plutarch studied philosophy in Athens, where he gained a deep reverence for the teachings of Plato[25] and where, as well, he was impressed with the ability of the individual to shape human events, either for good or evil. His knowledge of history and culture was deepened by means of extensive travels in Asia Minor, Egypt, and Italy, including Rome, where he lived for some time and where he gained fame as a philosopher. Plutarch returned to Greece, where he spent the latter years of his life as a priest of Apollo at Delphi, and it was probably there that he did much of his writing, all of it in the Greek language.

A large part of the work of Plutarch consists of essays on a wide range of topics, which are collectively referred to as the *Morals*. Here Plutarch gave voice to his Platonism and to his views on human life and behavior. One of the most charming of these essays is that entitled "Concerning Talkativeness." It begins like this:

> It is a troublesome and difficult task that philosophy has in hand when it undertakes to cure garrulousness. For the remedy, words of reason, requires listeners; but the garrulous listen to nobody, for they are always talking. And this is the first symptom of their ailment: looseness of the tongue becomes impotence of the ears. For it is a deliberate deafness, that of men who, I take it, blame Nature because they have only one tongue, but two ears.[26]

But Plutarch is best known for his *Parallel Lives of Illustrious Greeks and Romans*, biographical sketches that often take the form of a comparison between a famous Greek and a famous Roman (e.g., Theseus, the legendary founder of Athens, is paired with Romulus, the legendary founder of Rome; Alexander the Great with Julius Caesar). While much of what information—either factual or legendary—we possess concerning certain ancient personalities has come to us through Plutarch (who often quotes previous writers), Plutarch's interest is not simply in historical events. Rather, the *Lives* are frequently a forum for the expression of his philosophical, religious, and social opinions, as in the following consideration from his *Life of Solon*.

It is irrational and ignoble to renounce the acquisition of what we want for fear of losing it; for on this principle a man cannot be gratified by the possession of wealth, or honor or wisdom, for fear he may be deprived of them.[27]

Another biographer/historian of the period is Suetonius (Gaius Suetonius Tranquillus, c. 69–140 AD), who served as private secretary to the emperor Hadrian. Much of Suetonius' work has been lost, but of that which has survived the most important is his *Lives of the Caesars,* biographical sketches of twelve emperors from Julius Caesar to Domitian. Suetonius is one of the first historians who was neither Jew nor Christian to refer to the growing conflict between synagogue and church. In his sketch of the emperor Claudius, Suetonius tells us that "since the Jews constantly made disturbances at the instigation of Chrestus, he (Claudius) expelled them from Rome."[28] Some scholars feel that the "disturbances" were really between Jews and Christians (followers of "Chrestus") whom Suetonius has lumped together here as "Jews." In another place, however, Suetonius is quite clear about the distinctive nature of the early church, as he calls the Christians whom Nero persecuted "people who held a new and impious superstition."[29]

d. *Letters.* Personal correspondence was a significant part of the literature of the Greco-Roman world, the collection of Paul's letters in the New Testament constituting the example of this genre most widely read today. Letter writing was, indeed, a common enterprise of the day, and reference has earlier been made to the letters of Cicero, which provide for modern readers valuable insight into daily life in the closing years of the Roman republic. An important letter writer of the early empire was Gaius Plinius Caecilius Secundus (c. 61–113 AD), usually referred to as Pliny the Younger in order to distinguish him from his important uncle who bore the same name.

This uncle, Pliny the Elder (c. 23–79 AD) had been a distinguished writer in the fields of natural science and military strategy, and was a close friend of the emperor Vespasian, whom he often engaged in lengthy conversations. He was killed during the eruption of Mt. Vesuvius when the younger Pliny was eighteen, but as the older man had named his nephew as his heir, the younger man assumed his uncle's name, his own father having died when the future letter writer was a child. From his uncle the younger Pliny also received a love of literature, but he chose Cicero as model on which to pattern his own life and work. Like Cicero, he, too, became a skillful orator and politician and, in time, a famed letter writer. But Pliny was prepared to follow Cicero only to a degree, for he showed none of the republican's fiery independence nor depth of intellectual power. Whereas Cicero wrote out of a moral and political passion and was willing to die for his beliefs, Pliny the younger was an adroit politician who survived the terrors of Domitian's reign unscathed and who often wrote with an eye to pleasing his readers.

Yet Pliny's letters are significant because of their descriptions of contemporary persons and events, some ordinary, some extraordinary. In a letter to the historian Tacitus, for example, Pliny describes his uncle's death and, in the process, provides us with what amounts to an eyewitness account of the famous eruption of Vesuvius in 79 AD. Pliny and his mother were at nearby Misenum at the time (where his uncle was in command of part of the Roman fleet), and what he did not himself observe of the cataclysm, he would easily have heard from others. Parts of his description read like this:

> In the meantime Mount Vesusius was blazing in several places with spreading and towering flames, whose refulgent brightness the darkness of the night set in high relief . . . The house now tottered under repeated and violent concussions, and seemed to rock to and fro, as if torn from its foundations. In the open air, on the other hand, they [the uncle and his companions], dreaded the falling pumice-stones, light and porous though they were; yet this, by comparison, seemed the lesser danger of the two; a conclusion which my uncle arrived at by balancing reasons, and the others by balancing fears. They tied pillows upon their heads with napkins; and this was their whole defence against the showers that fell round them.[30]

Of perhaps more interest are portions of a letter written by Pliny to the emperor Trajan about 111 AD. Trajan had appointed Pliny governor of the Roman province of Bithynia (in northwestern Asia Minor) where, among other things, Pliny found himself in the position of having to pass judgment upon Christians brought to him for trial. His letter to the emperor requests guidance in the matter and states the method, in dealing with Christians, Pliny had followed to date.

> In the meantime, the method I have observed towards those who have been denounced to me as Christians is this: I interrogated them whether they were Christians; if they confessed it I repeated the question twice again, adding the threat of capital punishment; if they still persevered, I ordered them to be executed. For whatever the nature of their creed might be, I could at least feel no doubt that contumacy and inflexible obstinacy deserved chastisement.

In the course of his letter to Trajan, Pliny reports what some of the accused have said to him concerning the nature of their faith:

> They affirmed, however, the whole of their guilt, or their error was, that they were in the habit of meeting on a certain fixed day before it was

light, when they sang in alternate verses a hymn to Christ, as to a god, and bound themselves by a solemn oath, not to any wicked deeds, but never to commit any fraud, theft or adultery, never to falsify their word, nor deny a trust when they should be called to deliver it up; after which it was their custom to separate, and then to reassemble to partake of food—but food of an ordinary kind.[31]

Pliny's letter to Trajan constitutes one of the earliest known references to the Christian movement by a non-Christian writer.

2. *Philosophy*

In certain respects, Roman philosophy appears less vigorous than the Greek philosophy upon which much of it is based. Roman awe of Greek culture, combined with a less theoretical cast of mind on the part of the Romans, created a philosophical literature that often attempted to reformulate the ideas of the classical schools of Greece. We noticed earlier how the poet Lucretius (c. 96–55 BC) had embodied Epicurean principles in his *On the Nature of Things*,[32] while Plutarch popularized the widely shared ideals of Platoism. That the most convincing Latin spokesmen for the older Greek philosophers were also among Rome's finest men of letters is no better illustrated than in the work of the Stoic dramatist Seneca, to whom we shall turn in a moment.

Yet if the distinctions between philosophy and the literary arts seemed softened to one side, to the other the boundary between philosophy and religion also seemed less than clear. To be sure, even among the Greeks, much philosophical discourse had possessed a large religious component, as the dialogues of Plato—among many other examples—makes clear. But in the period of Roman rule, that which passed for philosophy was often framed not in the elevated discourse of the Athenian schools, but in popular terms designed to appeal to the masses. In addition, practitioners of the many and varied religions often competed in the same arena of popular opinion as did the advocates of the several philosophies, and at a level of intensity only slightly less than that which charged the contests among the gladiators (Acts 17:16–34; 2 Cor. 10:3–6).

Of the various philosophical traditions inherited from Greece, that of the Stoics,[33] with their concern for logic and law, seemed particularly suited to the Roman mind, and the outstanding proponent of the Stoic position in the early imperial period was the dramatist Seneca. Lucius Annaeus Seneca (c. 4 BC–65 AD), the son of a eminent Roman legal scholar and historian, was born in Spain, but moved to Rome as a young man, where he, too, entered the legal profession. His work as a scholar and dramatist won a wide circle of friends and readers in Rome, and in 49 AD, when the emperor Claudius adopted the young

Nero as his son and heir, Seneca was called to be the lad's tutor. When the seventeen-year-old Nero became emperor in 54, Seneca remained at court as one of his chief advisors. As Nero's rule degenerated, however, Seneca fell out of favor and was accused by the emperor of plotting to murder him. As a consequence, Nero ordered Seneca to commit suicide.

In part, Seneca's fame rests upon his work as a playwright. He was the author of nine tragedies, crafted in the classical Greek dramatic traditions, with subject matter drawn largely from Greek lore (e.g., Hercules, Oedipus, Medea, Agamemnon). But even here Seneca's Stoic principles are evident, as in his often stated view that tragedy results in human life when reason is overcome by emotion. Seneca's letters (124 of which have survived) and essays (12) also reflect his Stoic teachings, as this example from one of his letters illustrates:

> Hold fast, then, to this sound and wholesome rule of life; that you in-
> dulge the body only as far as is needful for good health. The body
> should be treated more rigorously, that it may not be disobedient to
> your mind. Eat merely to relieve your hunger; drink merely to quinch
> your thirst; dress merely to keep out the cold; . . . Despise everything
> that useless toil creates as an ornament and an object of beauty. And
> reflect that nothing except the soul is worthy of wonder; for to the soul,
> if it be great, naught is great.[34]

3. *Religion*[35]

Like many other aspects of Roman life, Roman religion was deeply influenced by Greek models. To the original Roman gods, who themselves were conceived more and more in terms of their Greek counterparts (Jupiter is a Romanized Zeus), Greek deities were added, specifically Hermes (who became Mercury), Poseidon (Neptune), Hades (Pluto) and Aphrodite (Venus), to name but a few. As in Greece itself, these traditional deities continued to be publicly wor-shiped in Rome and their intentions probed by augury and divination long after they had lost the allegiance of the population as a whole. In the place of the old faiths, many people in the time of the late republic and early empire turned to the religions and popular philosophies of the East for help and in-spiration. In part, this was a result of Rome's openness to the ways of Hel-lenism, which had already been deeply influenced by Eastern religious views. But at a deeper level it bespoke the inability of traditional religion and philos-ophy, either Greek or Roman, to meet the needs of men and women whose views on the nature of the human experience transcended the old answers.

With the dominance of the legions over the empire of Alexander and its successor kingdoms, the Mystery religions found fertile new fields for

missionary activity and, by the time of the early empire, the Mysteries surrounding Dionysus, Isis, Asclepius, and many other figures were flourishing
as never before.[36] To be sure, their progress did not always march unchallenged. The Roman senate had attempted to outlaw the excesses of the Bac-
canalia as early as 186 BC, while temples to Isis were repeatedly destroyed by
senatorial and, later, imperial, decree. But the missionaries of the newer
"philosophies" and religions, themselves sometimes confused with the deities
they claimed to represent (Acts 14:11–13), went from town to town, each
preaching the power of his or her Mystery and claiming converts. They competed not only with the old faiths, but with each other in a teeming marketplace of religious ideology where supreme value was often placed upon the
ability of the Mystery to benefit in immediate ways the life of the individual.
In such an atmosphere it is not surprising that appeal was frequently made by
means of magic and miracle, since that preacher or philosopher who could not
heal a sick body or fill an empty purse was often considered the representative of a puny deity, indeed (Acts 3:1–10). Yet many of the newer faiths also
spoke to the human longing to find some kind of meaning in life and to
achieve victory over the grave.

Not all of the popular faiths of Rome had been strong before the march of
the legions. Four philosophical or religious systems, in particular, deserve
special mention here because, although their roots ran deeply into the religious soil of Greece and the East, they flowered in especially significant ways
during the time of the early empire: Neopythagoreanism, Mithraism, Gnosticism, and the worship of the emperor.

(In historical terms, Christianity is, of course, one of the important new
faiths of the early empire and, as such, has a claim to be considered here. But
that vast subject is considered to be outside the scope of the present volume.)

a. Neopythagoreanism.   Pythagoras, perhaps from the island of Samos in the
Aegean Sea, was a famed mathematician and philosopher who had lived during the sixth century BC. Very little is known of this scholar's life, in that he
left no known body of writings and is remembered only through the recollec-
tions of others, chiefly Aristotle. Yet Pythagoras' accomplishments apparently
included the formulation of that theorem that bears his name: the square of
the hypotenuse of a right triangle equals the sum of the squares of the other
two sides. As a philosopher, Pythagoras proposed a mathematically-based understanding of reality in which the numbers one through four were of special
significance. These may have been related to the four prime elements (earth,
air, fire, and water), or they may have been regarded as levels of deity. In any
event, Pythagoras taught that there were multiple deities and that the human
soul was immortal, passing from one body to another in a continuing series of
transmigrations.

After traveling in Babylon and Egypt, Pythagoras settled in Crotona in southern Italy (Magna Graecia), where he formed a society of like-minded individuals whose common life was characterized by asceticism and by a concern for ethical values. But the Pythagoreans became embroiled in local political disputes and, in the ensuing violence, many of them were killed, while their organization itself was destroyed. It is not known whether Pythagoras himself was a victim of this turmoil.

Pythagoras' teachings, however, survived both their author and the society which he founded, and by the first century AD they had been reclaimed by a group to which modern scholars refer as Neopythagoreans. The extent to which these Neopythagoreans of the early empire reflect the teachings of the sixth-century mathematician is a matter of some debate, for they actually seem to have embraced an eclectic philosophy shaped by a number of influences. An ascetic style of life (including a vegetarian diet); a concern for the well-being of others; a reverence for the gods that was expressed not through animal sacrifice, but by means of self-denial; a fear of demons; the use of magic to cure demon possession and disease; and a willingness to undertake long and difficult journeys to preach their beliefs to others—these were among the characteristics of Neopythagorean belief and practice. Although they appear not to have promoted the existence of organized communities, their presence was widespread during the early imperial period, and Neopythagorean "evangelists" could be found in many communities of the Mediterranean world.

b. *Mithraism.* Mithras was the name of a being worshiped in Persia, before and during the time of the Persian Empire, who was known as an angel of light in the Zoroastrian hierarchy and whose veneration moved westward with Persian armies under Cyrus and his successors. His importance during the second and first centuries BC is clear from the use of his name in that of the ruling house of Parthia at the time (i.e., Mithradates). Precisely how the worship of this Indo-Iranian deity reached Rome is not clear, but it is likely that, perhaps during the first century BC, it was brought into the empire by soldiers stationed along the eastern frontier or by slaves and traders from the East who were Mithras devotees.

In Roman hands Mithraism became a Mystery religion, that is, a means by which the individual was spiritually reborn. As Roman Mithraism was open to males only, it became a favorite among soldiers and sailors, and, although sanctuaries to Mithras were plentiful in Rome itself by the late first century AD, it remained especially attractive to individuals stationed on the outposts of the empire. Sites of worship have been discovered from Mesopotamia to Germany.

As with most Mystery religions, the details of the Mithraic creed and cult are only imperfectly known, but it is clear that the sun and other celestial bodies played a part. Mithras is reputed to have been born on December 25 (near the winter solstice) and, after having killed a bull (perhaps to gain the animal's strength and procreative powers), Mithras and the sun enter into a covenant over a meal of the animal's meat and blood. This suggests that in some manner Mithras, as well as those who worshiped him, achieved the sun's power to move beyond death into a new life. In the Mithras cult, the rebirth of the individual occurs when he takes a vow to become a soldier of Mithras, and from the level of an initiate he moves upward through seven stages (corresponding to the seven visible celestial bodies) to a final union with the sun and, perhaps, to a kind of immortality.

During the second and third centuries AD, Mithraism was very popular throughout the empire and served as one of the strongest rivals of Christianity.

c. Gnosticism.[37]   During the time of the early Roman Empire, perhaps even before, a cluster of philosophical and religious beliefs achieved great popularity, beliefs that are collectively referred to by modern scholars as Gnosticism (from the Greek word *gnosis:* knowledge). Our two primary sources of information concerning Gnosticism are both later than the period with which we are concerned, yet they undoubtedly reflect views which, in some fashion, were current in the first century AD. The first of these is the writings of certain church fathers from Irenaeus (late second century) and after, who identified Gnosticism as a dangerous heresy that must be suppressed. As might be expected, the description of Gnosticism from this source is almost entirely negative. The second important source for our understanding of Gnosticism, one which has only recently come to light, is a body of writings by Gnostic authors, a corpus of literature that, again understandably, views Gnostic teaching quite positively. By far the most important collection of Gnostic material is that discovered since World War II near the Egyptian town of Nag Hammadi, texts that in their present form appear to date from the fourth century AD, but contain much older material.

Although there are a great many unanswered questions concerning Gnosticism, some things seem evident. One is that Gnostic teaching was expressed in a wide variety of sectarian versions. For example, a certain Basilides, who was active in Alexandria in the second century AD, taught a system of Gnostic belief that was, in some respects, very different from that of his contemporary Valentinus, perhaps the greatest of the Gnostic teachers, an Egyptian who taught in Rome. In addition, while many of the Gnostic advocates, like Basilides and Valentinus, considered themselves Christian (and thus earned the wrath of Irenaeus and other church fathers), there were also Jewish and pagan Gnostics, a fact made quite clear by the Nag Hammadi texts. To further add to this complexity, it may also be noted that some important writers, while not completely committed to the Gnostic philosophy (or perhaps, more appropriately, mythology), nevertheless exhibited significant Gnostic influences. One such teacher is perhaps Marcion (second century AD), whose sharp distinction between the Creator God and the Father of Jesus Christ is similar to the typical Gnostic dualism (see below).

In spite of this wide diversity, however, there does appear to have been a central core of Gnostic belief that included the following elements:

1. The transcendent God, who is good, is a Spirit whose nature is incomprehensible to ordinary men and women. This God is often referred to in terms of negation: unknowable, indescribable, and the like.

2. The world in which men and women live is evil and is the creation of an inferior supernatural being (the Demiurge).

3. The spirit of the individual person is related to the transcendent God, but has become trapped in the created world and in all of its evil.

4. A savior sent from God is the only power capable of breaking through the evil world and of kindling in the individual an awareness of his or her true condition.

5. Only through the knowledge (*gnosis*) that this savior brings can the individual be restored to a condition of harmony with God.

Before the discovery of Gnostic texts, when our only important source of information concerning Gnostic teaching was the fathers of the church, it was widely assumed that the origins of Gnosticism were in Christian teachings that had been influenced by Greek philosophy and, perhaps, by other factors. But the Nag Hammadi texts have cast that conclusion into considerable doubt, so that today there is no general concensus concerning the origins of this body of belief. The possibility has been raised that Gnosticism, at least in some form, may be older than Christianity, and may have roots not only in Greek philosophy (Plato's world of ideas?), but in one or more of the religions of the East (perhaps Zoroastrian dualism). Scholars will be addressing these problems for some years to come, and it is hoped that out of this work will emerge a better understanding of the nature of early Gnostic belief and its place in the religious world of the late Roman republic and early empire.

d. *Worship of the Emperor.* We have noticed earlier that, under the influence of Greek conceptions concerning the hero and non-Greek beliefs regarding the divinity of the monarch, certain rulers in the Hellenistic kingdoms were accorded divine honors.[38] Because Rome's transition from republican to imperial forms of government coincided, in general terms, with its conquest of the Hellenistic East, it is perhaps to be expected that the early emperors would be attracted to the godly roles of those Hellenistic rulers whom they had conquered, in spite of the fact that there was little in the Roman tradition itself that would have led to the deification of the ruler. Subjects of the former Hellenistic kingdoms would, quite naturally, refer to their new masters from Rome by means of all of the old titles of divinity that they had once lavished upon their now deposed monarchs, even if these expressions were only formalities. And so it was apparently only a matter of time until the Romans themselves began to take these accolades seriously. In taking the step to confer deity upon the emperor, the way was eased for some Romans by the view, expressed by Virgil and others, that the mission of the empire (and thus of the emperor) was divinely sanctioned. Yet the notion of a divine ruler was not one that settled easily into the Roman mind, and some, even among the emperors themselves, resisted this deification.

As had been the case in certain of the Hellenistic kingdoms, the first official proclamations that the ruler was also a god were bestowed posthumously. The senate added Julius Caesar to the state pantheon after his murder and provided an altar in the city of Rome where he might be worshiped. For his part, Augustus, although he flirted with divine status by referring to himself as "Son of the Divinized One," did not proclaim himself to be a god, a distinction that, however, was awarded by the senate after his death. Augustus' successor, Tiberius, refused all divine honors.

The first serious efforts by a living emperor to be regarded as a god were made by Caligula, who accompanied his demands with the cruel and irrational behavior which characterized many of his other policies. His self-divinization resulted in serious conflicts with others, including the Jews, in that he demanded a degree of veneration of himself that forced the denial of local religious loyalties, something that had not been a feature of the emperor cult before his time. Although other factors may also have been involved, the extensive outbreak of violence against the Jews of Alexandria in 38 AD was due in large measure to Caligula's determination in the matter. While his insistence that a statue of himself be set up in the Jerusalem Temple, referred to earlier, would undoubtedly have resulted in great bloodshed, had it been implemented.

Neither Claudius nor Nero was officially deified during his lifetime, although the veneration of deceased emperors continued to be a feature of the state religion. However, Nero's cruel and quixotic temperament evoked excessive flattery among his subjects, some of whose expressions of loyalty lapsed into statements of religious devotion. Nero's persecution of Christians in Rome, while severe, was conducted on other grounds than their unwillingness to recognize him as divine, and was at least partly the result of his precarious mental state.

Vespasian, a tough and pragmatic military hero, turned a deaf ear to all efforts to transform him into a god and, instead, promoted a conservative view of the state religion in which only deceased rulers, officially divinized by the senate, were venerated. This remained the policy of all emperors in the period under consideration here, except for Domitian. His insistence that he be recognized as *Dominus et Deus* (Lord and God) led, as under Caligula, to strife with a number of groups, including Jews and Christians, these latter now being of sufficient number in the empire to constitute at least a perceived threat to the state by their refusal to participate in the worship of the emperor. Romans were generally tolerant of other religions and were at a loss to understand why some of their citizens and subjects would not worship the emperor alongside their own God.

C. Events in Palestine From the Capture of Jerusalem by Pompey to the Rise of Herod the Great (63–37 bc)

Until Pompey's triumphant assault upon Jerusalem in 63 BC, the Jews, no matter how divided they might be over matters of theology and tradition, stood the chance of holding alien powers at bay, often by playing them one against the other. But Rome was to prove itself an irresistible political and military force not only for the Jews, but for almost all of the peoples in the region, a presence which neither courage in battle nor cleverness in the games of statecraft would repel. From this point forward the Jews of Palestine would be ruled, either directly or through client princes, by Rome, and, in the end, their unwillingness to accept this form of domination would lead to the virtual annihilation of the Palestinian Jewish community.

Of course, not every aspect of life was equally effected by the coming of the legionaires. That great cultural complex, Hellenism, continued to thrive for generations, being embraced even by the Romans themselves. The Greek language continued to be the currency of international communications. Greek literature continued to provide inspiration for writers of the early Empire in matters of content, form and style. Roman gods were largely the gods of Mt. Olympus with Latinized names and, like the Olympian deities, were generally remote from the drama of everyday life. The primary difference imposed by Rome was in the kindred areas of law and military rule, but what a difference that was! This was a leaden hand which fell heavily upon both Jews and, in time, the early Christians. Yet it was a hand which could occasionally be grasped and used to great advantage.

1. *The High Priesthood of Hyrcanus II* (63–40 bc)

The immediate result of Pompey's capture of Jerusalem (63 BC) was a brief period of peace. Aristobulus, whose struggles with his brother Hyrcanus provided the military weakness in the Hasmonean state that Pompey had exploited, was carried to Rome as a captive, there to be paraded before the people in Pompey's victory procession. Hyrcanus was allowed to continue in the capacity of high priest, but not as king. However, in 57 BC Aristobulus' son Alexander, like his father a Roman captive, escaped to Palestine where he attempted to rouse his father's partisans to revolt. Only after hard fighting, led on the Roman side by Gabinius, the Roman proconsul of Syria (in whose jurisdiction Palestine lay), and by the rising Marc Antony, was Alexander's revolt put down. Another revolt, this one by Aristobulus and his son Antigonus, both of whom had eluded their Roman captors and made their way back to Palestine, followed in the next year, but it, too, was crushed. And still a third attempt to restore Aristobulus' family to power was made (again!) by Alexander in 55 BC. During this time Hyrcanus ruled as high priest under the growing influence of the Idumaean Antipater, who was regarded by the proconsul Gabinius as a friend of Rome and as a personal ally because of Antipater's support of Gabinius during the latter's military campaign in Egypt in 55 BC.

The degree to which Antipater's friendship toward the Roman authorities was shared by the common people cannot be precisely measured, but the popular feeling could not have been very warm because of, for no other reason, the heavy taxes which Gabinius imposed. But in 54 BC Gabinius was replaced as proconsul of Syria by M. Licinius Crassus (the same Crassus who was a member of the First Triumvirate) who, in order to help finance his campaign against the Parthians, looted the Temple of its treasures, an outrage that not even Gabinius had dared. Jewish hatred of the Romans seethed, and when Crassus was killed in battle (53 BC), not a few Jews must have rejoiced.

In 49 BC Julius Caesar crossed the Rubicon and the Roman civil wars began. All of the provinces were to feel the consequences of these turbulent events, but none more than the provinces of the East, including Syria, for it was primarily in the East that the armies of the principal rivals confronted one another. With each change in the political winds provincial leaders were forced to scramble in forging new alliances, lest they run the risk of deposition or death. The political survival of the Idumaean Antipater and his son Herod is due in no small measure to their ability adroitly to align themselves with the successive winners in the contests for power in Rome.

Soon after Julius Caesar marched on Rome, forcing Pompey to flee to Greece, he released Aristobulus from prison with the intention of sending him to Syria in order to rouse his (Aristobulus') followers there against the forces of Pompey, which were strong in the area. But before the former Hasmonean king and high priest could leave Rome, he was assassinated by a group of Pompey's followers. Josephus reports that Aristobulus

> was buried by those who favored Caesar's cause, his corpse lying preserved in honey for a long while, until Antony [Caesar's lieutenant] finally sent it back to Judea and had it placed in the royal sepulchres.[39]

At about the same time, Pompey ordered the execution by beheading of Aristobulus' son Alexander, who, after two unsuccessful revolts against Roman authority, had been imprisoned in the provincial capital, Antioch-on-the-Orontes.

Pompey's defeat by Caesar at Pharsalus, and his subsequent murder in Egypt, forced Antipater and Hyrcanus to seek the favor of Caesar, now the undisputed ruler of Rome. When Caesar went to war with Ptolemy XII Theos Philopator I (51–47 BC), Antipater sent 3,000 Jewish troops from Palestine to aid Caesar's cause and was himself prominent in the fighting. He was also instrumental in swaying the sympathies of local Egyptian Jews to support Caesar. For his pains, Antipater received Roman citizenship from Caesar and exemption from all taxation. In addition, he was designated procurator of Judaea. Hyrcanus, who was also present in Caesar's army, was confirmed as high priest and ethnarch of the Jews. Antipater and Hyrcanus were also permitted to rebuild the walls of Jerusalem, destroyed by Pompey. The Jews of Egypt and Asia Minor were recognized by Caesar and assured of their right to follow their own traditions.

Antipater, who had once worked solely through Hyrcanus, now began to exercise his newly conferred authority in a manner increasingly independent of Hyrcanus, whom he found, in the words of Josephus, "dull and sluggish."[40] He appointed two of his sons to high office: Phasael, the eldest, became governor of Jerusalem, and Herod, governor of Galilee.[41] The energetic Herod, who now becomes for the first time a principal figure in Palestinian Jewish affairs, lost little time in assuming his responsibilities. A band of robbers under the leadership of a certain Ezekias was terrorizing the country, and these criminals were hunted down by Herod and brought to justice, many of them, including Ezekias, being executed. The people in the region of Galilee were delighted with Herod's treatment of the brigands. But members of the Sanhedrin in Jerusalem, many of whom were already suspicious of the motives of Antipater (no less so because of his Idumaean blood), were alarmed at the skill and decisiveness of Herod. On the complaint that he should not have put the criminals to death without a trial, the Sanhedrin forced Hyrcanus to summon Herod to appear to answer charges of murder.

Instead of presenting himself before the Sanhedrin as a defendant, however, Herod, upon the advice of his father, appeared clothed in royal purple and surrounded by his bodyguard. The council was awed into submission and, as Hyrcanus had been warned by Sextus, the governor of Syria, to see that no harm befell Herod, the matter might have ended with Herod's acquittal. But a council member named Samaias arose and spoke, indicting the council and Hyrcanus for their timidity of the face of Herod's effrontery. This speech roused the passions of the Sanhedrin against Herod, but Hyrcanus, who as high priest was the presiding officer, postponed the trial, thus allowing Herod time to leave Jerusalem in safety. Herod went to his friend Sextus who, in return for a bribe, appointed Herod governor of Coele-Syria (in modern Lebanon). Thereupon the young Idumaean, still smarting from his treatment by the Sanhedrin, gathered his army and marched against Jerusalem, but was disuaded from attacking the city by his father and his brother Phasael. But Herod had only postponed his revenge, for in describing Herod's appearance before the Sanhedrin, Josephus reports that the hostility generated by this encounter was one of the reasons for Herod's later murder of the members of this body (including Hyrcanus), only Samaias being spared because of his bravery.[42]

In 44 BC Julius Caesar was assassinated in Rome by the band of conspirators led by Brutus and Cassius. When Caesar's lieutenant Marc Antony took steps against the murderers, Cassius fled to Syria, where the army swore its allegiance to him. Crippling taxes were leveled against the people of the province, including Palestine's Jews, but Antipater and his sons, adjusting to this shift in the political winds, made their services available to Cassius and helped in the collection of the taxes. However, one of Antipater's many enemies, an otherwise unknown individual named Malichus, arranged to have Antipater murdered.

When Brutus and Cassius were defeated in Philippi in 42 BC, the East fell to Marc Antony. Herod and Phasael were forced to defend their conduct in the face of charges by their enemies, who attempted to utilize the new political realities as a fresh opportunity to unseat the sons of Antipater. But, somewhat surprisingly, Hyrcanus testified before Antony to the worthiness of Herod and Phasael. And the Roman leader (now a member of the Second Triumvirate), recalling an earlier time when he and Antipater had been comrades-in-arms under Gabinius, proclaimed Herod and Phasael tetrarchs of Judaea, although Hyrcanus as ethnarch and high priest was apparently still regarded as chief of state.

Antony did not remain in Syria, however, and in 40 BC, while he was occupied in his famous liaison with Cleopatra in Egypt, the Parthians invaded Syria in the company of their ally, Antigonus, the son of Aristobulus, who still coveted the Hasmonean crown. As the Parthian army advanced upon Jerusalem, Hyrcanus and Phasael, who had been invited to negotiate with the Parthians, were captured and handed over to Antigonus. Antigonus cut off Hyrcanus' ears, thus rendering him ritually unfit for the high priesthood, and Phasael committed suicide. The Parthians proclaimed Antigonus king and high priest.

Herod, suspecting a trap, had tried to dissuade his brother from meeting with the Parthians. So at the news of the treachery, Herod fled to the south, leaving his family under the protection of his brother Joseph at the fortress of Masada, and making his own way to Egypt.

2. *Antigonus II, King and High Priest* (40–37 BC)

The fortunes of Herod were now at low ebb. However, he was not without friends, nor had he lost his knack for bending the currents of politics in his favor. With considerable difficulty, Herod made his way to Rome where he presented himself to Mark Antony. Angered over Antigonus' alliance with the troublesome Parthians, Antony was happy to support Herod's claims, and went so far as to influence Octavian (with whom he was still on good terms) in Herod's behalf. Octavian recalled Antipater's help to Julius Caesar in Egypt and together the two Roman leaders arranged for the senate to declare Herod king of Judaea.

Armed with the full weight of Roman authority, Herod returned to Palestine in 39 BC, at about the time a Roman army under Antony's lieutenant Ventidius was engaging the Parthians in Syria. After a great deal of campaigning, during which Herod's family was freed from their isolation at Masada, Herod's army, with Roman support, surrounded Jerusalem.

Josephus reports[43] that at this time Herod was married for the second time. His first wife, Doris, was "a plebian woman of his own nation"[44] (whether that meant that she was Jewish or Idumaean is not clear) who bore him a son, Antipater. Now, however, Herod marries into the Hasmonean family, for his new bride, Mariamme (referred to as Mariamme I to distinguish her from another of Herod's wives of the same name) is the granddaughter of both Hyrcanus II and Aristobulus II,[45] and thus the niece of the very Antigonus whom Herod has now besieged within the walls of Jerusalem.

After offering tenacious resistance for two months, Antigonus' army was overwhelmed and Jerusalem became the prize of Herod and the Roman general Sosius. Herod was now king in deed as well as in word. The Romans carried away the captive Antigonus to Antioch-on-the-Orontes, where Marc Antony was temporarily headquartered. Herod bribed Antony to have Antigonus executed, this being the first instance in which the Romans had executed a vanquished monarch.

Chapter 9

FROM HEROD THE GREAT TO THE REVOLT OF BAR KOKHBA (37 BC–135 AD)

A. HEROD THE GREAT, KING OF JUDAEA (37–4 BC)

1. Herod Consolidates His Rule (37–25 BC)

Although Herod enjoyed the support of Marc Antony, ruler of the Roman East without whose patronage Herod's position would not have been tenable, the Idumean possessed many enemies among the Jews. His most formidable opponents, either real or potential, included remaining members of the Hasmonean family and the members of the Sanhedrin, and these he took steps to crush. Herod, a hard and driven man, thirsted for absolute power and bent his considerable physical energy and cunning to achieve that goal. A strategy that had been used effectively by his father, Antipater, was to be mastered by the son: those under his authority were bent totally to his will, while his superiors were plied with flattery and bribes. In an age that was soon to see the outrages of Caligula and Nero, Herod's cruelty and cynicism were by no means unique. Yet he must certainly rank among the more brutish and self-serving of those who, in the long history of the Jews, have presided over their affairs. There is no evidence that Jewish traditions had the slightest meaning for him. Rather, he regarded Judaea and its inhabitants as no more than a personal fiefdom within the larger Roman world.

Hyrcanus II, still a captive of the Parthians, was carried to Babylon (at this time a part of the Parthian kingdom) where he was released into the custody of the large Jewish community there. His physical mutilation was apparently not regarded by the Babylonian Jews as an impediment to his high office, for they received him warmly and acknowledged his authority over them as high priest and king. Herod, who had been treated kindly by his father's old ally, apparently feared that Hyrcanus's popularity among the Babylonian Jews might incite unrest against his own rule at home, and he therefore invited the aging Hasmonean to return to Jerusalem. After Hyrcanus arrived there, Herod at first treated him graciously, but that cordiality only masked Herod's true feelings, which would soon surface.

Herod also brought from Babylon an otherwise unknown Jewish priest named Hananel, whom he installed as high priest. But this so enraged the members of the Hasmonean family, who considered the office to be theirs by hereditary right, that Herod was forced to back down. His primary opposition in the matter came from Mariamme's mother, Alexandra, the daughter of Hyrcanus II, who coveted the office for her son Aristobulus (known to history as Aristobulus III), then a lad of sixteen. Alexandra wrote to Cleopatra, Antony's lover, and requested her help in influencing the Roman to order Aristobulus' consecration as high priest. At first Antony paid no attention to the matter, which must have seemed to him quite trivial, but when one of Antony's friends described to him the beauty of both Aristobulus and his sister Mariamme, Antony's legendary lust was aroused and he requested Herod to send Aristobulus to him in Egypt "for erotic purposes," as Josephus delicately puts it.[1] Because Herod feared letting Aristobulus leave the country (and thus his control) and because Mariamme was also pressing Herod on behalf of her brother, Herod summarily removed Hananel and installed Aristobulus as high priest. In so doing, Herod may have mollified the Hasmonean family for the moment, but many traditionalist Jews must have been horrified over this political interference in the high priestly succession.

But Herod had more schemes afoot. A few months after the accession of Aristobulus III as high priest, Herod arranged the young man's murder. Aristobulus' handsome features, in addition to his Hasmonean lineage, led to his great popularity among traditionalist Jews, and this, in turn, to Herod's growing jealousy. A banquet was hosted in Jericho by Alexandra and, the day being hot, a number of the revelers went swimming in the large baths of the palace, one of whom was Aristobulus. In response to a bribe, several of the swimmers, who appeared simply to be playing in jest, held Aristobulus' head under water until the youthful high priest was dead. In spite of Herod's public show of mourning, many suspected the truth. Grief and anger consumed Alexandra and other members of the Hasmonean family, while public disgust over Herod intensified.

Alexandra appealed, through Cleopatra, to Antony and, when the Roman leader traveled through Syria in 34 BC on his way to a military campaign against the Armenians, Herod was summoned to appear before him. As he had now become skilled at doing, Herod vindicated himself before Antony by his smooth tongue and expensive gifts. But before leaving home, Herod had entrusted the beautiful Mariamme to his uncle Joseph (Antipater's brother) with secret instructions that, in the event he did not return from his audience with Antony, she should be killed, for Herod was aware that the lascivious Antony might imprison him simply in order to obtain the favors of Mariamme. Upon his return, Herod was informed by Joseph's wife, Salome (who was also Herod's sister), that Joseph and Mariamme had become lovers in

Herod's absence. When confronted with these accusations by the violently jealous Herod, Mariamme denied them to the apparent satisfaction of Herod. But when Mariamme later reproached Herod for having secretly provided for her execution, Herod knew that information could have come only from an infatuated Joseph. And so Herod's uncle was killed without a trial.

A new danger to Herod's authority arose when, about 36 BC, Antony awarded to Cleopatra possession of vast territories in the province of Syria, including Herod's fertile lands in and around Jericho. Herod concealed his anger against the Ptolemaic queen when she passed through Judaea on her return from a visit to Antony, who was engaged in fighting the Armenians. But he had the good sense to resist her sexual advances, because he feared she might later use any weakness on his part to incriminate him before Antony.

When hostilities broke out between Antony and Octavian in 32 BC, Herod, instead of being allowed to ingratiate himself to Antony by joining the fighting, was sent, at Cleopatra's instigation, to campaign against the rebellious Nabataeans. Herod was eventually successful, but not before a great deal of blood was shed. While the campaign against the Nabataeans was in progress, Judaea was devastated by an earthquake (31 BC), evidences of which have been discovered at Qumran.[2]

In the fall of 31 BC, the battle of Actium paved the way for the overthrow of Antony and of Cleopatra, the last Ptolemaic ruler of Egypt, and for the control of Egypt by the army of Octavian. Herod now realized that he must transfer his allegiance to a new Roman master. Perhaps because he felt that his own position in dealing with Octavian would be stronger if the Hasmonean house could produce no viable candidate for the throne of Judaea, Herod arranged for the murder of Hyrcanus II. The indictment brought against Hyrcanus was that he had secretly sided with the Nabataeans during Herod's campaigns against them, but the charge was undoubtedly trumped-up. Nevertheless, the old man was strangled. Josephus, after describing with considerable sympathy Hyrcanus' long career,[3] sums up his account in these words.

> But what was most painful of all, as we have said before, was that in his old age he [Hyrcanus] came to an unworthy end. For he seems to have been mild and moderate in all things and to have ruled by leaving most things for his administrators to do, since he was not interested in general affairs nor cleaver enough to govern a kingdom. That Antipater and Herod advanced so far was due to his mildness, and what he experienced at their hands in the end was neither just nor an act of piety.[4]

When Herod met Octavian on the island of Rhodes in 30 BC, the king of Judaea, while admitting his former friendship with Antony, stressed his ability to serve Octavian, now in undisputed control of the provinces of the East and soon (27 BC) to be proclaimed Augustus by the Roman senate. Octavian apparently saw the usefulness of Herod, for he confirmed his title and restored and enlarged the lands under Herod's control.

Not long after Herod's return to Jerusalem, his mother, Cyprus, accused Mariamme of infidelity during his absence. When the charge appeared true, Herod, in a fit of jealous rage, had Mariamme executed (29 BC), only to grieve deeply over her faithlessness and death.[5] The execution of the vexatious Alexandra followed (28 BC), as did that of a prominent Idumaean, Costobar, who was Herod's governor of Idumaea and husband (since the execution of Joseph) of Herod's sister Salome (c. 27 BC).

Herod's hold upon the throne of Judaea was now secure.

2. *Herod's Supremacy in Judaea* (25–13 BC)

At its greatest extent, Herod's kingdom included not only Judaea and Idumaea, but also Samaria and Galilee, as well as regions such as Gaulanitis, Batanaea, Auranitis, and Trachonitis to the north and east of the Sea of Galilee, and Peraea, just east of the Jordan. It was a kingdom of mixed Jewish and gentile composition, with the Jews being in the majority only in Judaea and parts of Galilee and Peraea.

Herod belonged to that class of local client kings upon whom the Romans conferred the title "friend and ally of Rome."[6] Although their authority was limited and always dependent upon the emperor's goodwill, there was much that lay within the grasp of these local rulers, especially in the area of domestic affairs. Perhaps their most important functions lay their ability to levy taxes within their kingdoms, to raise armies, and to maintain order among their people. In effect, therefore, while subservient to the imperial will, they enjoyed virtually unrestrained power over the lives of their own people, including the right to impose the death penalty.

In the case of Herod, it is not entirely coincidental that his period of greatest strength also marked the beginning of the *Pax Romana*. The end of the Roman civil wars meant that the Idumaean, as long as he maintained the favor of Octavian—now Caesar Augustus—was free to conduct the affairs of his kingdom with minimal interference from Rome and without the preoccupation of having to flatter successive Roman generals and politicans. Since his domestic enemies were, for the most part, either dead or silenced, he was able to shape the life of Judaea in his own image.

That image was largely Hellenistic, with a decided infusion of the culture of imperial Rome. Herod built a theater, an amphitheater, and a hippodrome in Jerusalem and inaugurated the custom of holding athletic contests every four years in honor of Augustus. He also established competitions in music and other arts, in chariot racing, and even went so far as to stage contests between wild animals and condemned criminals. The splendid new structures in which these events took place were lavishly decorated with inscriptions honoring Augustus and with golden and silver trophies emblematic of the emperor's military victories. In doing these things, Herod was by no means alone, for cities and petty kingdoms throughout the empire competed with one another in similar extravagant measures intended to flatter Augustus and to parade their own wealth. But in Judaea such things kindled among traditionalist Jews intense anger, as they remembered the terrible desecrations of the past associated with Antiochus Epiphanes and other Hellenists. There were protests against Herod's pagan displays and, although the king rescinded some of the more offensive practices, an abortive attempt was made to assassinate him.

Jewish hatred for Herod was not confined to any one sect or party. The Sadducees despised the king because of his suppression of their allies, the Hasmonean family. And as for the Pharisees, who perhaps more than any other group molded the opinions of the population as a whole, their enmity was insured by Herod's disregard for the Torah and for other sacred traditions of Judaism. A ruler as clever as Herod knew that he presided over a heated cauldron whose lid must be kept firmly in place, and the Idumaean took every step possible to see that that was done. Members of the Sanhedrin were killed, and the council itself seems to have been dissolved,[7] at least for a time. What is more, the countryside was dotted with fortresses, some of which were reconstructions of older fortifications, but all of which were primarly intended not to repel invasion from abroad, but to suppress dissent within Judaea itself. Earlier, when Marc Antony ruled the East, Herod rebuilt the old fortress just north of the Temple and named it Antonia in honor of his then patron.[8] To this were now added—to name only the most important—the former Hasmonean strongholds of Alexandrium and Hyrcania (both destroyed by Gabenius), as well as Macherus,[9] Masada, and Herodium, these last three containing royal palaces.

The army, composed largely of mercenaries from abroad, but also containing Jewish and gentile conscripts from Herod's own kingdom, was kept at a high level of readiness. Herod's military strength was employed in enforcing the king's many stringent laws, including those against most forms of public assembly, while a network of spies informed against seditious plots, both real and imagined. Occasionally, the king demonstrated some act of kindness toward his subjects, as on the occasion in 25 BC when, in the face of a severe famine, he contributed royal gold and silver to help buy grain from Egypt. But such gestures were rare, so that the bitter relationship between ruler and subjects continued, and order was maintained only by Herod's ubiquitous soldiers and spies. And if Herod sought not to offend the religious sensitivies of traditionalist Jews, a step which he took on several occasions, it was simply a concession by the ruler to avoid open conflict.

Herod engaged in a number of ambitious building projects during this time, in addition to his new and reconstructed fortresses, and it is for these that he won perhaps his greatest acclaim throughout the Roman world and for which he earned the distinction "Great."[10] A new royal palace in Jerusalem and one in Jericho were erected. Cities that had fallen into decay were rebuilt to grand proportions, including Samaria (destroyed by John Hyrcanus), which Herod renamed Sebaste in honor of the emperor (sebastos is the Greek form of the Latin augustus: exhalted one), whereas others were constructed on sites no previous community had occupied. Temples were raised in predominately gentile areas of his kingdom and even in neighboring Syria, all of which were pagan and most of which were dedicated to the emperor. But of all Herod's architectural and engineering feats, none were more imposing than the new city of Caesarea on the Mediterranean coast and the new Jerusalem Temple.

For centuries the western Mediterranean coast had looked out upon the busy sea lanes which connected Egypt in the south with Phoenicia, Asia Minor, and Greece to the north. In an age in which maritime navigation was accomplished primarily by simply following the coastline to one's destination, and in which flimsy vessels were often no match for storms of the sea, safe anchorages were of great importance. Between Dora and Joppa (roughly, the coast of Samaria) lay a stretch of forty miles of forbidding coastline with no natural harbors, a maritime gauntlet where ships were often driven onto the rocks by the frequent gales from the west. Here,[11] about 23 BC, Herod began construction of a harbor that, when completed, would be one of the finest in the Mediterranean basin, attracting ships from all parts of the Roman world and beyond. In addition to serving as a safe haven from the tempests of the sea, this splendid port opened up Herod's kingdom to commerce and trade in a manner not otherwise possible.

Since the topography of the land offered no natural anchorage, Herod constructed one. An enormous stone breakwater, 200 feet in width, was sent out into the Mediterranean for a distance of more than 1,500 feet, at which point it curved, elbow-like, to the north. To a spot near the tip of this arm a second breakwater extended from the shore, forming an enormous U-shaped barrier, which was complete except for a gap between the two stone arms. Into this shelter, ships could sail in defiance of the Mediterranean's frequent wrath either to ply their trade or simply to ride out a storm. On the sturdy breakwater handsome buildings were erected that contained shops and dwellings for transient seamen. Josephus declares that Herod's harbor was grander than Piraeus, the famed port of the city of Athens,[12] and when one considers the feats of engineering involved (for example, the stones for the breakwater had to be transported many miles), the accomplishment was all the more impressive. The harbor itself was dedicated, like so many other of Herod's enterprises, to the emperor and named in his honor: Sebastos.

But the spectacular port facility was only part of Herod's enterprise, for next to it he built a glittering city made of the most expensive materials by the finest artisans Herod could employ. Again, with Augustus in mind, Herod named the city Caesarea, now almost uniformly referred to as Caesarea Maritima, to distinguish it from other dedicated municipalities, such as Caesarea Philippi. Covering an area of more than 160 acres (in antiquity a large city would occupy approximately fifty acres), the new metropolis would, in time, boast an amphitheater, a hippodrome (for chariot races), a royal palace, temples, and public buildings in abundance, an aqueduct to bring fresh water from Mt. Carmel, a system of sewers that were regularly flushed by the changing tides, vaulted warehouses for the storage of goods in shipment, and an imposing defensive wall. But perhaps the most eye-catching edifice in Caesarea was a temple that Herod built on a hill overlooking the harbor and in which he placed a huge statue of Augustus. The temple, like much of the city, was built of white marble, so that it glistened from far out at sea, a welcome beacon to many a weary sailor.

Caesarea was twelve years in building and, with great ceremony, the city was dedicated to its patron in 10 BC.[13] It would later become the residence of the Roman procurator of Judaea and thus the seat of Roman government (Acts 12:19–23). In the New Testament Caesarea is mentioned several times. It was the site of a sermon by Philip (Acts 8:40), and the military base to which was attached a centurion whom Peter converted (Acts 10:1–48, 11:11). Paul, like many tens of thousands of other travelers, passed through the city on several occasions (Acts 9:30, 18:22, 21:8). It was here that he was imprisoned and brought before Felix and Festus (Acts 23:31—25:12), and from Caesarea Paul set out for Rome (Acts 25:13—27:2).

The other building enterprise of Herod which is of special significance is the Jerusalem Temple. The Second Temple, dedicated by Zerubbabel in 515 BC (Ezra 6:16–18), would have seemed cramped and shabby to many who had admired the pagan temples with which Herod was endowing his realm—most of all to Herod himself. And so in 20 BC, work on a new Temple was begun.

The Jews were not entirely pleased with this ambitious program. For one thing, it would have been clear to them that Herod's motives were far from pure and, for another, many feared that, once undertaken, the construction would have to be abandoned because of its great expense, the result being that the Jews would have no Temple at all. But, as he usually did, Herod prevailed and, partly because of the king's smooth persuasions and partly because they had little choice, the Jews joined in. The statistics that Josephus (who knew Herod's Temple firsthand) cites relative to the construction are impressive:

> [Herod] prepared a thousand wagons to carry the stones, selected ten thousand of the most skilled workmen, purchased priestly robes for a thousand priests, and trained some as masons, others as carpenters,

and began the construction only after all these preparations had been diligently made by him.[14]

Priests were involved in the work, of course, because the most sacred parts of the Temple could be entered by no one else.

The result of this project was a Temple building of unusual grandeur. White stones were used in the construction of the walls, which were 100 cubits long (about 150 feet) and 100 cubits high—much larger, it may be assumed, than the Zerubbabel Temple. The doors into the Temple, which were as high as the building itself, were embellished with rich fabrics of many colors, while under the cornice was sculpted a large grape vine of gold, bearing huge golden grapes, "a marvel of size and artistry," wrote Josephus, "to all who saw with what costliness of material it had been constructed."[15]

The area around the Temple was greatly expanded and was largely given over to the Court of the Gentiles, a spacious esplanade of more than twenty acres which was paved with beautiful stones. On three of the four sides of the Court of the Gentiles was a lengthy colonnade or portico, each with a double row of marble columns twenty-five cubits (37 feet) high. On the fourth (southern) side of the Temple enclosure was the Royal Portico, which merits description in Josephus' own words:

> The fourth front of this [court], facing south, also had gates in the middle, and had over it the Royal Portico, which had three aisles, extending in length from the eastern to the western ravine. It was not possible for it to extend any further. And it was a structure more noteworthy than any under the sun. For while the depth of the revine was great, and no one who bent over to look into it from above could bear to look down to the bottom, the height of the portico standing over it was so very great that if anyone looked down from its rooftop, combining the two elevations, he would become dizzy and his vision would be unable to reach to the end of so measureless a depth.[16]

Josephus adds that each of the columns of the Royal Portico were so large "that it would take three men with outstretched arms touching one another to envelope it."[17]

Such was the complex that Herod presented to his Jewish subjects. Although the Temple building was dedicated within a year and half of the start of construction (Herod himself sacrificing 300 oxen on the occasion), work on the edifice continued over many years and may even have been in progress at the time of the destruction of Jerusalem by Titus in 70 AD. This was, of course, the Temple known to Jesus and the earliest Christian community.[18]

For all the beauty of the Temple, however, Herod was not one to let his subjects forget who their master was. So in the perhaps the most conspicious place possible, atop the main gate of the Temple, the king erected a golden eagle. This symbol of Roman and Herodian authority was doubly offensive to pious Jews because, in direct contravention of the Law, it stood within the Temple enclosure as the likeness of a living creature.

3. Herod's Final Years (13–4 BC)

The last decade of Herod's life is marked by intense strife within the king's family. Herod is known to have had at least ten wives, of whom the names of eight have survived, and, as has often been the case, intrigue within the king's harem resulted in anguish for the monarch and in turmoil within the kingdom (cf. 2 Samuel 13—1 Kings 2). We have already referred to Herod's first two wives, Doris and Mariamme, and jealousy between their sons now came to preoccupy the king. Doris' son was also Herod's eldest and, like his grandfather, bore the name Antipater. Mariamme, it will be recalled, was of Hasmonean blood, and her two sons by Herod were also endowed with family names, Alexander and Aristobulus. The struggle to succeed Herod that was waged between Antipater (often called Antipater III), on the one hand, and Alexander and Aristobulus, on the other, was thus a feud between the Idumaean and Hasmonean bloodlines within the royal family. The plots and counterplots may be read in Josephus in all of their depressing detail,[19] but the first result was that, in 7 BC, Alexander and Aristobulus were executed, after having been found guilty of treason. Even with his major rivals out of the way, however, Antipater continued to scheme, and in 5 BC was tried and condemned to death for plotting against his father.

It was now clear that Herod, who was almost seventy, was ill and near death. A rebellion broke out under the leadership of two rabbis named Judas and Matthias, the mob tearing down the golden eagle that stood mockingly over the main gate of the Temple. But the uprising was suppressed and its leaders burned alive. Those who believed in omens must have been disturbed by the occurrence, on the night of the executions, of an eclipse of the moon.[20]

Herod soon ordered that the death sentence against Antipater be carried out. And he further directed that, upon his own death, leading Jews should be executed in order that the nation's impending period of mourning should be genuine, a command that, fortunately, was ignored. Thus in the spring of 4 BC, five days after the execution of his eldest son, Herod died in the royal palace at Jericho, to the regret of almost no one.

B. FROM THE DEATH OF HEROD TO THE JEWISH WAR WITH ROME (4 BC–66 AD)

The family turmoil that marked Herod's final years complicated the question of political succession in Judaea. The final version of Herod's will had left power distributed among his favorite surviving children, but they were, for the most part, not willing to share their father's legacy. In addition, many Jews felt that the abuses they had endured under Herod could be avoided in the future only if the family were deposed and the nation placed under direct Roman rule. Because the question lay entirely in the hands of Augustus to decide as he pleased, delegations of Jews arrived in Rome, each to plead it's particular case, among whom were Herod's sons Archelaus and Antipas, who argued their own merits before the emperor.

While Augustus pondered Judaea's future, violence flared in the nation itself. Several mobs took up arms, some in an effort to place their own "king" on the throne of the nation, others simply to express their hatred of the Romans, still others to rob and plunder their fellow subjects. But these were vigorously suppressed by legions sent from Syria and led by the governor of that province, Varus. During fighting in Jerusalem at the Pentecost season in 4 BC, when thousands of visiting Jews had crowded into the city for the festival, part of the Temple complex, including the splendid porticoes, were destroyed by fire.

When Augustus announced his decision concerning the political future of Herod's former kingdom, Herod's final will was, in general terms, upheld. Herod's son Philip (his mother: Cleopatra of Jerusalem) became tetrarch of important regions north and east of the Sea of Galilee, including Batanaea, Trachonitis, Aurantis, Gaulanitis, and Panias.[21] Another of Herod's sons, Antipas (mother: Malthace, a Samaritan) was named tetrarch of Galilee and Peraea. A third son, Archaleaus (his mother: Malthace) was designated ethnarch (a slightly superior title to tetrarch) of Judaea, Samaria, and Idumaea. Herod's sister, Salome, was given jurisdiction over the cities of Jamnia, Azotus, and Phasaelis. For the moment, Herod's former kingdom had ceased to exist and, with it, the office of a Jewish king.

1. *Philip* (4 BC–33 AD)

Philip, who in addition to his tetrarchy, had received 100 talents from Augustus, enjoyed the most peaceful reign of any of Herod's successors. Josephus, in fact, remarks on Philip's benign disposition and on his accessibility to the people, characteristics that apparently made him a favorite among his subjects, of whom there were more gentiles than Jews.[22] He was also a favorite among the Romans, who considered him a loyal client king. To demonstrate his admiration of Roman rule, he named a new city he had built in the Greco-Roman style Caesarea Philippi (cf. Mark 8:27 and parallels), "Philippi" being added to distinguish it from the great port constructed by his father, Caesarea Maritima. Philip also appears to have possessed an interest in scientific matters, for Josephus describes how he proved that a certain spring near his new city was one of the sources of the Jordan River. He did this by throwing straw into the spring, which then emerged several miles downstream at Caesarea Philippi.[23]

When Philip died, his tetrarchy was added to the province of Syria. But in 37 AD, the new emperor Caligula bestowed Philip's former territory upon Herod's grandson Agrippa (Agrippa I), who, in addition, received the title king (see below).

2. *Antipas* (4 BC–39 AD)

The tetrarch of Galilee and Peraea, who ruled during the lifetime of Jesus, presided over a territory whose two parts were separated by the Decapolis, a region of autonomous cities that had been built east of the Jordan during the Hellenistic period. The richer of the two parts of the tetrarchy was Galilee, whose extensive agricultural base supported a mixed Jewish and gentile population. Antipas considered the building of new cities and their dedication to the emperor an important form of flattery, a view he shared with his father and with his brother Philip. However, his new capital, Tiberias, was more readily accepted by Antipas' gentile subjects than by the Jews, as parts of it were constructed on the site of an old cemetery, a sacrilege in Jewish eyes. At first, it was necessary to conscript people to settle in the town, but in time, Tiberias became the thriving center of Galilean commerce and the site of Antipas' court.

Perhaps in an effort to compensate for the unfortunate division of his territories and to guard against invasion from the south, Antipas married the daughter (unnamed in Josephus) of the king of the Nabataeans, Aretas IV. Toward the end of his reign, however, Antipas felt the full wrath of Aretas, whose daughter he had now scorned in favor of his own half-sister Herodias. Aretas humiliated Antipas in battle so decisively that Antipas could only call for help from Tiberius. But before Aretas could be punished for his treatment of Antipas, the emperor was dead.

The scandal of Antipas' marriage to Herodias is, in fact, one of the more noted events of his rule, receiving attention from both Josephus and the New Testament. In the course of a trip to Rome sometime after about 30 AD, Antipas fell in love with the wife of his half-brother Herod, son of Mariamme II (called "Philip" in Mark 6:17, Matt. 14:3), a woman who was his own half-sister, Herodias.[24] (Herodias was a daughter of Herod's son Aristobulus whom the father executed about 7 BC.) Antipas' plans to marry Herodias, which caused the daughter of Aretas to flee to her father, were consummated upon his return to Tiberias. According to Mark 6:14–29 (paralleled by Matt. 14:1–12), the immorality of this action was denounced by John the Baptist, who was thereupon imprisoned by Antipas (called "Herod" in the New Testament passages) primarily as a result of Herodias' anger over John's charges. The passage in Mark goes on to describe how, some time later, Antipas, who feared a public upheaval should John be executed, was tricked into taking the Baptist's life. Herodias' daughter so captivated Antipas by her dancing that, at the instigation of her mother, the girl replied to Antipas' invitation that she should request some favor of him by asking for the Baptist's head.[25] Antipas reluctantly complied.

Josephus' account of the incident is so interesting that it deserves to be quoted in full. Referring to Antipas' defeat by the Nabataean king, Aretas, Josephus reports:

> But to some of the Jews the destruction of Herod's [i.e., Antipas'] army seemed to be divine vengeance, and certainly a just vengeance, for his treatment of John, surnamed the Baptist. For Herod had put him to death, although he was a good man and had exhorted the Jews to lead righteous lives, to practise justice towards their fellows and piety towards God, and so doing to join in baptism. In his view this was a necessary preliminary if baptism was to be acceptable to God. They must not employ it to gain pardon for whatever sins they committed, but as a consecration of the body implying that the soul was already thoroughly cleansed by right behavior. When others too joined the crowds about him, because they were aroused to the highest degree by his sermons, Herod became alarmed. Eloquence that had so great effect on mankind might lead to some form of sedition, for it looked as if they would be guided by John in everything that they did. Herod decided therefore that it would be much better to strike first and be rid of him before his work led to an uprising, than to wait for an upheaval, get involved in a difficult situation and see his mistake. Though John, because of Herod's suspicions, was brought in chains to Machaeruus, the stronghold that we have previously mentioned, and there put to death, yet the verdict of the Jews was that the destruction visited upon Herod's army was a vindication of John, since God saw fit to inflict such a blow on Herod.[26]

Josephus has emphasized Antipas' fear of John's power over the masses as the reason for the Baptist's imprisonment, whereas the New Testament emphasizes Herodias' anger (Mark 6:19). The two accounts, however are not contradictory, as even Mark acknowledges Antipas' fear of John's authority (Mark 6:2). One additional difference is that Josephus tells nothing of Herodias' daughter's involvement in John's death.

Antipas is referred to in two other New Testament passages. In Luke 13:31–32 Jesus, during the period of his Galilean ministry, is warned by some Pharisees that Antipas wants to kill him. To this Jesus replies by calling Antipas a "fox" who should be informed of Jesus' powers over evil and disease and of the fact that his (Jesus') death will take place only in Jerusalem.

In Luke 23:6–12, Jesus, who is being tried by the Roman governor Pilate (Judaea is now under direct Roman control, see below), is sent to Antipas for interrogation, since the tetrarch of Galilee happens to be in Jerusalem. Luke describes the meeting between Jesus and Antipas in this terse passage (vv. 8–9):

> When Herod [i.e., Antipas] saw Jesus, he was very glad, for he had been wanting to see him for a long time, because he had heard about him and was hoping to see him perform some sign. He questioned him at some length; but Jesus gave him no answer.

The passage goes on to state that Pilate's gesture resulted in a reconcilaton between himself and Antipas, ending a period of estrangement.

Antipas' career ended unhappily. When Caligula became emperor upon the death of Tiberius in 37 AD, he appointed Agrippa, a (full) brother of Herodias to be ruler over the former territories of the tetrarch Philip and, what is more, conferred upon him the title "king." At Herodias' urging, Antipas went to Rome to petition Caligula that he, too, might receive a royal title. But Antipas and Herodias were confronted there by charges of treachery brought by Agrippa, whose representative alleged (whether truly or not we do not know) that Antipater had collaborated with Tiberius' now-disgraced lieutenant Sejanus[27] and, in addition, had had secret dealings with the Parthian enemies of Rome. Caligula was convinced in the matter and Antipas was exiled to Gaul, to be accompanied there (of her own choice) by Herodias. To compound Antipas' disgrace, his former tetrarchy was added to the new kingdom of Agrippa.

3. *Archelaus* (4 BC–6 AD)

The son whom Herod's final will had designated to be King of Judaea received Samaria, Judaea, and Idumaea from Augustus, but not the title "king." As ethnarch, he ruled his lands with much the same love of luxury that characterized his father's administration, and with much the same disregard for the rights of the people. Of his father's royal palaces, he seems to have favored that at Jericho, for he expanded and beautified the site and built a new aqueduct to bring fresh water to nearby palm orchards he had planted. Just north of Jericho he constructed a new town which he named for himself, Archelais.

Archelaus aroused the resentment of devout Jews by his unlawful marriage to a Cappadocian princess named Glaphyra (she had been married twice before, he once). In addition, the ethnarch twice deposed the high priest for reasons having more to do with politics than with religion, and apparently committed other outrages, as well. After almost a decade of his misrule, a delegation of Jews traveled to Rome to charge Archelaus with "cruelty and tyranny" (Josephus' words[28]) before Augustus. The emperor listened sympathetically and, as Caligula was later to do in the case of Antipas, banished his client king to Gaul. Archelaus' territories were placed under the direct rule of Rome, where they would remain for the next thirty-five years (6–41 AD).

4. *Judaea under Roman Governors* (6–41 AD)

If Herod the Great had shown systematic disregard for the rights of the people, he at least knew that there were limits beyond which they would not be pushed without protest. Moreover, his frequent violation of the rights of his Jewish subjects was often counterbalanced by a clumsy, but effective, public display of support for their religious feelings, as, for instance, his deference to priestly law during the construction of the Temple. The example of Archalaus' inability to rule the most Jewish of his father's lands should have served as a signal to the governors whom Rome now placed over Judaea that Jewish toleration of oppressive government was not infinite. But that, as well as many other examples of Jewish willingness to resist despotism, seems to have escaped the Roman governors of Judaea, whose policies drove the Jews of Palestine toward certain revolt.

Judaea (including Samaria and Idumaea) was placed under the general oversight of the governor of the province of Syria, but was given a governor of its own.[29] This official normally resided at Caesarea Maritima, which thus served as the captial of the province, but he could also be found pursuing his military or judicial responsibilites in any one of the several fortified sites or former royal palaces in the region. In this regard, the Fortress Antonia, just north of the Jerusalem Temple, was especially important, and the governor, in the company of a large military escort, could often be found there at the times of the important Jewish festivals, when crowd control was essential to the task of maintaining public order. (It seems to have been this arrangement that resulted in the presence in Jerusalem of Pontius Pilate for the Passover celebration at the time when Jesus was arrested and tried. However, whether the *praetorium* mentioned in the Gospels [Mark 15:16, and elsewhere] was a part of the Fortress Antonia or part of Herod's former palace, west of the Temple, is not clear.[30])

The governor's responsibilities as commander of the military forces involved not only protecting the province from threats from outside (a number of semiautonomous client kingdoms still existed in the region), but also the suppression of revolt from within. The Roman army in Judaea was, for the most part, composed of gentile natives (Jews were exempt from service because of their unwillingness to fight on the Sabbath), since the professional legions made up of Roman citizens were stationed in the province of Syria and were brought into Judaea only as needed. As the province's chief judicial officer, the governor decided important cases of law which, in most instances, involved Roman citizens only. The Sanhedrin (presided over by the high priest) served as the most important tribunal for cases involving Jews, and only if a Jew were involved in a matter relating to the Roman government would he likely be found before a Roman tribunal. Only Roman citizens enjoyed the right to appeal any decision of the governor directly to the emperor (Acts 25:11). A third important responsibility of the Roman governor was that of chief financial officer, whose primary task in this regard was to see to the collection of taxes. The actual receipt of taxes was contracted to local subjects over whom little supervision was employed, except to see that the government received what it demanded. The resulting system was open to much graft and corruption, and permitted petty officials to extort large sums from the population, much of which was quite poor. Readers of the New Testament are familiar with the opprobrium attached to the title "publican" or "tax collector" (Matt. 9:10, and elsewhere).

In some ways the Romans attempted to make allowances for the peculiar customs of the Jews, especially those involving religious matters. The observance of the Sabbath by Jews was sanctioned not only in Judaea, but throughout the empire. In addition to exempting Jews from service in the Roman army, this tolerance also permitted Jews to escape forced participation on the Sabbath in many civic and legal matters, as, for example, appearing in a court of law. And as long as Jews were willing to pray and sacrifice to God for the emperor's welfare, as they did twice each day in the Jerusalem Temple, Roman authorities were content, for the most part, not to push too hard on the matter of emperor worship. Only under Caligula was a serious effort made to suppress the traditional Temple ritual in favor of undivided devotion to the emperor, as we earlier noticed.

Yet in everyday affairs Roman rule could be harsh and demanding. Following the deposition of Archelaus, the newly appointed governor of the province of Syria, Quirinius, decreed a census for Judaea.[31] Because the purpose of such a census could only be to create a more effective method of collecting taxes in this province now coming under direct Roman rule, the people were frightened and angry. Yet they grumblingly submitted to Quirinius' edict, largely as a result of the mediating efforts of the high priest, Joazar. But a small group of resisters led by two individuals, Judas of Gamala and Zaddok, a Pharisee, took up arms against the Romans. Their efforts met with little success, but these rebels are significant in that, according to Josephus, they laid the seeds of the Zealot movement, that group of Jewish patriots whose determination to end Roman rule eventually led to the devastating Jewish War of 66–74 AD. Josephus refers to the Zealots as "an intrusive fourth school of philosophy"[32] (in addition to Pharisees, Sadducees, and Essenes), and comments

This school agrees in all other respects with the opinions of the Pharisees, except that they have a passion for liberty that is almost uncon-
querable, since they are convinced that God alone is their leader and
master. They think little of submitting to death in unusual forms and
permitting vengeance to fall on kinsmen and friends if only they may
avoid calling any man master.[33]

That the hand of the Zealots was strengthened in the decades that followed
the census of Quirinius was due in large part to the foolish policies of the
Roman governors of Judaea, many of whom extended their disregard of Jewish
feeling to matters other than taxation. Of particular interest in this respect
were the actions of Pontius Pilate, who served from 26 to 36 AD. We are given
some insight into the character of this man, known to us from his part in the
trial of Jesus (Matt. 27:2, and elsewhere), through a letter purportedly written
by Pilate's contemporary, Agrippa (later, King Agrippa I), to the emperor
Caligula in which he describes the Roman as "a man of inflexible disposition,
harsh and obstinate."[34] This assessment is supported by Josephus, who reports several outrages by the Roman governor. In one instance, Pilate ordered
his troops to march into Jerusalem carrying standards that bore images of the
emperor, knowing full well that previous governors had commanded their
troops to keep such standards out of sight in light of the intense Jewish feeling against the display of images, especially in the Holy City.[35] Seeing what
had happened, a throng of Jews went to Caesarea Maritima to protest to Pilate
himself, who, after turning a deaf ear to the Jews for five days, ordered his
soldiers to surround the delegation with drawn swords. But the Jews lay
down before the soldiers, whom they dared to kill them, whereupon Pilate,
his bluff having been called, ordered the offending images be brought back to
Caesarea.

On another occasion, Pilate ordered the confiscation of funds from the
Temple treasury to build an aqueduct for Jerusalem. When he visited the city,
the governor was surrounded by a large crowd of Jews who shouted their com-
plaints in full voice. But Pilate, who had known what was coming, had planted
some of his own soldiers in the crowd, dressed in street clothing, and, when
Pilate gave the signal, these men began to beat every Jew within reach, so
protesters and bystanders alike were injured and killed. On this occasion,
Pilate prevailed.[36]

In the end, not even the Romans themselves could tolerate Pilate's repres-
sive methods, and an incident involving the Samaritans resulted in his removal from office. There was a legend among the Samaritans to the effect that
Moses had buried a number of sacred vessels on Mt. Gerizim. A false prophet
(unnamed by Josephus, who relates the tale[37]) aroused the Samaritan people
to a high pitch of excitement by promising them that, if they would meet him

there, he would lead them to the holy objects that would then be uncovered. At the appointed time a large crowd gathered and began to walk up the mountain, only to be met by a detachment of Pilate's heavily armed soldiers, who, presumably expecting an insurrection of some kind, began to attack the crowd. Many of the Samaritans were killed and injured, while a number of those who were captured were executed. When the Samaritans complained to the Roman governor of Syria, Vitellius, Pilate was ordered to go to Rome to explain his conduct to the emperor Tiberius. Vitellius sent a new governor for Judaea, but before Pilate reached Rome Tiberius died, so he presumably never stood trial for his crimes. Beyond this time we know nothing of Pilate's life.

The New Testament alludes to another outrage committed by Pilate, although modern readers are tantalized by the lack of detail in this reference. Luke 13:1 relates that "at that very time there were some present who told him [Jesus] about the Galileans whose blood Pilate had mingled with their sacrifices." Although it sounds as if Galilean pilgrims to the Jerusalem Temple were murdered for some reason, nothing is known of the incident beyond these words.

In connection with his discussion of events during the governorship of Pilate, Josephus briefly refers to Jesus and to the early Christian movement. Whether the text is actually from the pen of Josephus or is, as some have argued, a Christian interpolation, is a matter that has generated a great deal of scholarly debate.[38] It goes like this:

> About this time there lived Jesus, a wise man, if indeed one ought to call him a man. For he was one who wrought surprising feats and was a teacher of such people as accept the truth gladly. He won over many Jews and many of the Greeks. He was the Messiah. When Pilate, upon hearing him accused by men of the highest standing amongst us, had condemned him to be crucified, those who had in the first place come to love him did not give up their affection for him. On the third day he appeared to them restored to life, for the prophets of God had prophesied these and countless other marvelous things about him. And the tribe of the Christians, so called after him, has still to this day not disappeared.[39]

5. *Agrippa I (37–44 AD) and Agrippa II (c. 50–95 AD)*

Agrippa, grandson of Herod the Great by Aristobulus, one of the sons executed by Herod, was something of a ne'er-do-well. Educated in Rome, he grew so accustomed to luxury that he exhausted his finances and was forced to return to Palestine to seek the aid of family members. He was given the post of overseer of markets in the city of Tiberias, but a quarrel with his uncle, the tetrarch Antipas, ended that arrangement. He later made his way back to Rome, where he became friends with Caligula who, as noted earlier, granted him the former tetrarchy of Philip, over which he ruled as king. His continuing quarrel with Antipas resulted in Antipas' banishment to Gaul and in the addition of Galilee and Peraea to Agrippa's kingdom. In 41 AD, Agrippa happened to be in Rome at the time of the murder of Caligula, and he quickly allied himself to Claudius, the new emperor, for whom he performed valuable services during the precarious early days of Claudius' rule. Claudius rewarded this loyalty by adding Judaea, Samaria, Idumaea, and other territories to Agrippa's kingdom, so that for the first time since the death of Herod the Great, all his former territories were united under the rule of a member of his family.

Agrippa began his reign over Judaea with acts of piety that must have come as a welcome change to devout Jews. He presented a golden chain that he had received from Caligula to the Temple priests and, at the same time, offered sacrifices of thanksgiving for God's goodness to him, acts that omitted "none of the ritual enjoined by our law," in the words of Josephus.[40] The new king of Judaea made Jerusalem his home and the Temple his regular place of worship. When a group of gentiles set up an image of the emperor in a synagogue in the coastal city of Dora, near Caesarea, Agrippa interceded with the governor of Syria to have the offense removed and the perpetrators punished. And his efforts to strengthen the walls of Jerusalem won him the admiration of many Jews, although the project was overruled by the governor of Syria, who feared Agrippa's independent ways.

According to Acts 12:3, it was Agrippa's desire to please his Jewish subjects that led him to persecute Christians, so he ordered the execution of James, the brother of John, and the imprisonment of Peter. According to the account in Acts 12:1–19 (where Agrippa is referred to as "Herod"), after Peter was miraculously delivered from his cell, Agrippa had the prison guards killed.

The rule of this king, so popular with his Jewish subjects, was not to last, for in 44 AD he died while in residence at Caesarea. According to Acts 12:20–23, he was struck down by an angel while seated on his throne making a speech, because he received the acclaim of the people, who stated that he was a god. According to Josephus, Agrippa became mortally ill during his attendance at a festival, after having seen an owl (an omen of death).[41] Josephus' narrative is interesting in that it, too, relates that Agrippa willingly received the flattery from the crowd that he was a god.

After Agrippa's death, all of his kingdom came under direct Roman rule, as had earlier been the case with Judaea, Samaria, and Idumaea. The emperor Claudius, in keeping with a policy—applied to various parts of the empire—by which client kingdoms were dissolved in favor of immediate

Roman administration, appointed a governor (*procurator*) for Judaea who was to be answerable to the governor of the province of Syria.

Agrippa had a son of the same name who might have been appointed his father's successor by Claudius, had it not been for the emperor's preference for direct Roman rule, as well as for the intervention of some of the emperor's counselors, who were fearful of placing a youth on the throne of Judaea (he was about sixteen years of age at the time of his father's death). Instead, Agrippa II received the Kingdom of Chalcis (in Lebanon) about 50 AD following the death of his uncle, the ruler. Later, (53 AD) he was given the former tetrarchy of Philip, in exchange for Chalcis, and to those territories were added parts of Galilee and Peraea, including the city of Tiberias. Upon him was also conferred the right to supervise the affairs of the Jerusalem Temple and to appoint the high priest.

Like many of the Herodians, Agrippa II considered himself more Roman than Jew. He renamed his capital city (Caesarea Philippi) in honor of the reigning emperor, Nero (Neronias). And he was completely supportive of the Roman cause during the Jewish War, which began in 66 AD. Yet he was often responsive to Jewish concerns as well, coming to the aid of the Temple, when its substructures began to sink, by providing massive timbers from Lebanon for a new foundation (the outbreak of the war prevented the completion of this project). After the war both Agrippa II and his queen, Bernice, spent a great deal of time in Rome, where it was an open secret that Bernice was a mistress of the emperor Titus. She had had a previous affair with the Roman in Palestine when he was there on military service.

The historical record is unfortunately silent on the later life of Agrippa II. He probably died sometime in the last decade of the first century AD, the last descendant of Herod the Great to rule. His kingdom apparently came under the direct rule of the Roman governor of Syria.

According to Acts 25:13—26:32, Agrippa II and Bernice heard the defense of the apostle Paul in Caesarea, where they had come to welcome the new governor, Porcius Festus, who was appointed about 60 AD.

6. *Palestine under Roman Governors* (44–66 AD)

The tensions that had existed between the Jews of Judaea and their earlier Roman governors, including Pilate, were to be intensified in the two decades following the death of Agrippa I. Among the more notorius of the Roman governors after 44 AD are Cumanus, Felix, and Festus.

a. *Ventidius Cumanus* (c. 48–52 AD).   Josephus has related three incidents during the governorship of Ventidius Cumanus that illustrate the growing hostility between Roman and Jew. During a celebration of the Passover, when thousands of Jewish pilgrims thronged the Temple area, a Roman soldier, one of the large contingent of troops stationed to keep the peace, was for some reason motivated to show his scorn of the worshipers. Accordingly, he bent over in public view and bared his naked buttocks, making, at the same time, "a noise as obscene as his attitude."[42] In the ensuing riot, thousands of Jews were killed.

In another incident, a slave traveling in the service of the emperor was robbed by bandits on a highway near Jerusalem. In revenge, Cumanus ordered the looting of some villages in the vicinity, presumably hoping to discover the stolen items. In the process, a Roman soldier came upon a scroll of the Torah that, in a public display of contempt, he tore to pieces. The Jews of the village were so angered that they traveled to Caesarea Maritima to protest to the governor, who, fearing that the intensity of the Jews' feelings would spark a revolt, ordered that the soldier be put to death.[43]

Some time later there occurred yet another episode. A number of Jewish pilgrims from Galilee, who were traveling through Samaria to attend the Passover celebrations in Jerusalem, were murdered by Samaritans. A delegation of Galilean Jews thereupon traveled to Caesarea Maritima and angrily demanded that Cumanus punish the criminals. They did not know that the governor had been bribed by the Samaritans and they were thus enraged even further when he took no action. A group of Zealots from Jerusalem quickly took matters into their own hands and went to Samaria to avenge the murders, which they did by burning several Samaritan villages and murdering their inhabitants. To quell the disturbance, Cumanus sent troops to the area who killed many of the Jews, while others were forced into hiding from which they carried on a kind of guerrilla warfare against the Romans. After delegations of both Jews and Samaritans had appealed to the governor of Syria, that official, Ummidius Quadratus, came to Samaria in person to investigate. He ordered the executions of many of the Jewish leaders of the disturbance, and dispatched important Roman, Samaritan, and Jewish officials to the emperor for further inquiry, among whom were the Jewish high priest and Cumanus. The emperor Claudius found the Samaritans guilty and ordered three of their leaders to be killed, while Cumanus was banished.[44] In the course of telling this story, Josephus notes ominously that "from that time the whole of Judaea was infested with bands of brigands."[45] Many of these were simple lawbreakers, but others appear to have been political rebels.

b. *Antonius Felix (c. 52–60).*   Cumanus was succeeded as governor of Judaea by Antonius Felix, whose brother Pallas was a freed slave of Antonia, sister-in-law to the emperor Tiberius, and, as such, was a trusted member of the imperial household. For reasons that are not clear, Felix's appointment had been urged by the high priest, Jonathan, while the latter was in Rome for the inquiry into the matter involving the Samaritans. The selection of the new governor was not a fortunate one, for Felix was brutal and arrogant in his policies and his misrule contributed greatly to the growing Jewish hatred of the Romans. The historian Tacitus, always quick to identify despotism in a ruler, said of Felix (in apparent reference to his family's history), "Practicing every kind of cruelty and lust, he wielded royal power with the instincts of a slave."[46] Of Felix's three wives, one was the daughter of Agrippa I, Drusilla, whose marriage to the Roman governor must have outraged many pious Jews.

One of Felix's first tasks was to clear the countryside of the "bandits," whose growing boldness threatened not only Romans, as they went about their daily affairs, but law-abiding Jews, as well. "Not a day passed," asserts Josephus, "but that Felix captured and put to death many of these impostors and brigands."[47] Apparently the governor felt that any means justified his ends, because after he promised safe conduct to the most celebrated of these outlaws, a certain Eleazar, he arrested him and packed him off to Rome. Not even the high priest, Jonathan, was immune to Felix's treachery. Jonathan often counseled moderation in Felix's handling of public affairs because, since it was widely known that the high priest had recommended Felix to the emperor in the first place, he feared that the increasing hatred of the governor would be turned against him as well. Felix arranged for a group of Jewish Zealots, who despised Jonathan precisely because of his ties to the Roman government, to be allowed to enter Jerusalem. The Zealots, masquerading as religious pilgrims, concealed daggers in their clothing and, mingling in the crowd, were able to get near enough to the high priest to stab him to death.

In abetting this murder, Felix had unwittingly made Judaea vulnerable to a new terror. Since the countryside was becoming a more dangerous place for rebels and bandits to operate, many of them now adopted the tactics of Jonathan's assassins. As Josephus put it,

As the murder [of Jonathan] remained unpunished, from that time forth the brigands with perfect impunity used to go to the city and, with their weapons similarly concealed, mingle with the crowds. In this way they slew some because they were private enemies, and others because they were paid to do so by someone else. They committed these murders not only in other parts of the city but even in some cases in the temple; for there too they made bold to slaughter their victims, for they did not regard even this as a desecration.[48]

These terrorists, known as *sicarii* from the short daggers (*sicae*) that they carried, sowed such panic among the people in Jerusalem that even old friends began to avoid each other, since no one could be sure who the next target would be.

There were continuing efforts to channel the seething hatred of Rome into more organized forms of resistance, all of which Felix suppressed. Perhaps the most infamous such example was that of an Egyptian (whose name has not been recorded), who gathered a large crowd on the Mount of Olives with the promise that the walls of Jerusalem would fall down before their advance and that the city would be theirs. Felix intercepted the throng with a large detachment of calvary and infantry, killing 400 and taking 200 prisoners.[49] The Egyptian escaped, never, so far as is known, to be heard from again. But many of his followers who escaped with him were almost certainly among those who continued to plot against the Roman authority. Shortly after this, Paul, who had been arrested on what turned out to be his last trip to Jerusalem, was mistaken for this Egyptian by one of his Roman guards (Acts 21:38).

Josephus sums up the situation in Judaea at this time in the following words:

> No sooner had these troubles died down than the inflammation, as in a sick man's body, broke out again in another quarter. The impostors and brigands, banding together, incited many to revolt, exhorting them to assert their independence. They threatened to kill any who submitted willingly to Roman domination and to suppress all those who would accept servitude voluntarily. Then, deployed in gangs throughout the country, they looted the houses of the nobles and killed their owners. They set villages on fire, so that all Judaea felt the effect of their frenzy and day by day the fighting blazed more fiercely.[50]

Tensions mounted on every side, and Josephus takes note not only of a serious conflict between Jewish and gentile citizens of Caesarea Maritima,[51] but also of violence between the aristocratic supporters of the high priest, whose name was Ishmael, and the rest of the Jerusalem priesthood, this latter turmoil caused by economic exploitation of the poor by officials of the high priest.[52]

The events recorded in Acts 21—24 may be seen against the background of this near anarchy. It is interesting that Paul is said to have spoken to Felix and Drusilla about "justice, self-control, and the coming judgment" (24:25), concerns that were notably absent from the governor's mind, in response to which Felix was "frightened and said, 'Go away for the present.'" About 60 AD, Felix was recalled by Nero, but was followed to Rome by a delegation of Jews who wished to bring charges against him before the emperor. But Felix's brother Pallas, still in a position of some authority in the imperial court, intervened, so that the Jews were not able to press the matter. Back in Caesarea Maritima Paul was still in prison, having been left there by Felix in one of his last efforts to "grant the Jews a favor" (Acts 24:27).

c. *Porcius Festus (c. 60–62).* By now the situation had deteriorated too far to be brought under control, but Festus, the new governor appointed by Nero, attempted to do so, nonetheless, sending out the army against rebels and outlaws with some success. The quarrel between Jewish and gentile elements in Caesarea Maritima was decided by Nero in favor of the gentiles, apparently as a result of a large bribe paid by the gentiles to one of the close advisors of the emperor. Jewish sentiments were enraged by this, nor did an incident in Jerusalem serve to mollify them, although it turned out in the Jews' favor. There a dispute arose involving Agrippa II, who was frequently in the city in his capacity as overseer of the traditions of the Jews. Agrippa made a habit of taking his meals on a balcony of Herod's former palace, from which vantage point he enjoyed an unrestricted view of the Temple and its adjoining structures. This was regarded as an unwelcomed intrusion by many devout Jews, so a wall was built on the west side of the Temple compound to block the royal gaze, a step that angered not only Agrippa, but Festus as well, since the new wall impeded the work of the Roman sentries posted at times when large crowds gathered. The wall was ordered down, but the Jews gained Festus' permission to appeal to Nero, who then decided in their favor.

The Book of Acts (chaps. 25—26) tells how Festus, after having gone to Jerusalem to invite witnesses to come to Caesarea Maritima to testify against Paul, hears the apostle's defense and acknowledges his right to appeal to the emperor. "You have appealed to the emperor; to the emperor you will go" (25:12). Festus then consults with Agrippa II, who, with his wife Bernice, has just come to the city. When Agrippa expresses an interest in hearing Paul, the apostle is allowed to present his defense a second time before the king. Festus decides that Paul is mad, but Agrippa responds enigmatically, "In a short time you think to make me a Christian" (26:28 RSV). According to the narrative, both rulers agree that Paul has done nothing worthy of death, but, as he has appealed to Rome, he must be sent there.

Festus' two successors, Albinus (62–64 AD) and Gessius Florus (64–66 AD), were little more than common criminals. Albinus accepted bribes from various quarreling factions and, as he had no intention of imposing discipline on those who paid him, he allowed civil order to deteriorate to dangerous levels. When he learned that he was being replaced as governor, he emptied the prisons of their inmates, including the most dangerous. For his part, Florus engaged openly in those practices which Albinus did in secret, since he pillaged cities and sent their inhabitants into exile. Josephus, without offering many details of Florus' malfeasance, says that, "So wicked and lawless was Florus in the exercise of his authority that the Jews, owing to the extremity of their misery, praised Albinus as a benefactor."[53]

7. *The Jewish War with Rome* (66–74 AD)

To many it must have seemed that open rebellion against Roman authority was inevitable, given the lawlessness of many of the Jews and the corruption of the Roman officials. Josephus, in fact, alleges that Florus calculated a plan to cause an insurrection in order that his own misdeeds would never be called up for scrutiny before the emperor, as had been the case with some of his predecessors.[54] If that is so, the governor succeeded in achieving his purpose, perhaps more thoroughly than he expected. The proverbial straw that broke the camel's back was a deed of no little significance in itself, yet when compared with other crimes that both preceeded and followed it, it was a minor affair. However, it could later be looked back upon as the beginning of the rebellion that was to last for eight years and would cost an incalculable sum in lives and treasure. Florus confiscated seventeen talents from the Temple funds on the pretext that they were needed by the government.[55]

a. *The Rebel's Seizure of Jerusalem and Much of the Countryside* (66 AD).   In response to the expected protest against this outrage, Florus, happy to have an excuse to terrorize the emperor's Jewish subjects, brought his army against Jerusalem and allowed it to indulge in an unpercedented rampage of destruction and death. In a single day 3,600 Jews were murdered, many of them Jewish nobles who also enjoyed Roman citizenship, and who were, like many ordinary citizens, publicly whipped and crucified. The next day prominent Jews, including the chief priests, tried to calm the crowd in order to prevent the incitement of further barbarities. Fresh troops sent from Caesarea Maritima by Florus were even treated courteously by the Jews, but when the Romans replied with insults, fierce fighting broke out in the city. To what must have been Florus' great surprise, the Jewish throng managed to gain control of the complex of Temple buildings, and to separate Florus from part of his army. The governor then withdrew his forces, except for one cohort of troops, which was left in the city with the consent of the chief priests and the Sanhedrin. Not long afterward, a group of Jews surprised the Roman garrison at Masada, the mountaintop fortress overlooking the eastern shore of the Dead Sea, and seized the bastion. About the same time, the daily Temple sacrifices for the welfare of the emperor were discontinued, a conspicuous act of defiance.

Many of the aristocratic members of the priesthood, the "chief priests" in the language of Josephus, became alarmed over the course of the rebellion, fearing that hotheads among the insurgents would push the nation into a hopeless and ruinous war. Shortly after the withdrawal of Florus, King Agrippa II had appeared in the city to appeal for calm, but had been vigorously rejected. So now the peace party requested military help, from Florus, who proved indifferent to even well-meaning Jews and so did nothing, and from Agrippa II, who sent a large body of cavalry from his own kingdom. With the aid of these troops, the peace party gained control of the upper city while confining the Zealots and their allies to the lower city and the area surrounding the Temple. But in the week of fierce fighting that followed, the hardcore insurgents proved stronger than Agrippa's horsemen, so that the latter were expelled from Jerusalem. The victorious rebels burned the palace of Ananias the high priest and that of Agrippa, as well as parts of the former palace of Herod. Ananias himself was killed along with other members of the peace party and, as evidence of the character of the rebellion, the insurgents even began fighting among themselves so that one of their most important leaders, a Zealot named Menahem (who had led the assault on Masada), was also murdered. As for the remaining Roman soldiers that Florus had left in the city, they were also butchered, after having been assured that they could lay down their arms and peacefully leave the city.

The revolt had now reached such proportions as to command the attention of the Roman governor of Syria, Cestius Gallus, who marched on Jerusalem with a sizeable force of cavalry and infantry. After entering the city from the north, where he set fire to a district named Bezetha, Cestius attempted an assault on the Temple mount, which was crowded with worshipers who were present for the celebration of the Feast of Tabernacles. In spite of his superior military force, Cestius was repulsed and, in the course of their retreat, which became a rout, the Romans abandoned a large amount of their supplies and equipment, to the delight of the rebels.

In the meantime, violence between Jews and gentiles had broken out in a number of communities, including some beyond the borders of Palestine such as Tyre and Alexandria, where numbers of Jews were killed. In some local conflicts nearer Jerusalem, where the Jewish population was predominant, the result of the fighting was that the community, with its resources, went over to the rebels, two such examples being the bastion of Cyprus, near Jericho, and the old Herodian fortress of Machaerus, on the northeastern shore of the Dead Sea. In this way, much of the Jewish heartland, including Galilee, was now in revolt.

b. The War in Galilee (67 AD).   In spite of their serious internal divisions, the rebel leadership in Jerusalem addressed itself to the task of planning for the defense of the country, since it was obvious that Nero would soon attempt to avenge the defeat of Cestius. Even after the bitter fighting between the largely aristocratic peace party and the Zealots it is noteworthy that aristocratic elements were still present in the rebel camp, some of these persons in positions of responsibility. One of these individuals was the former Pharisee, Josephus, later the historian of this war, to whom was now entrusted command of the rebellion in Galilee. Of all of the military commissions granted at this time, this was perhaps the most important because Galilee would likely be the battlefield upon which the Jews would meet an advancing Roman army from Syria. What Josephus lacked in military experience (he had none!) could be compensated for by his sharp wits—at least that appears to have been the hope of the rebel authorities in Jerusalem.[56]

Josephus went into Galilee at once to begin preparations for the fight. He organized local citizens into administrative and judicial councils, and oversaw efforts to fortify a number of strategic locations, and initiated the training of an army of 100,000, which he organized on the model of the Roman army. But his first serious challenge came not from the Romans, but from a Zealot warrior named John of Gischala (a village in northern Galilee). In a manner that echoed the earlier struggle in Jerusalem between the fanatic supporters of the rebellion and the aristocratic moderates, John now attempted to undermine Josephus by urging the Jews of Galilee to repudiate his authority, and he was successful enough in this effort to place Josephus' life in danger on more than one occasion. He then managed to have Josephus' commission withdrawn by the Jerusalem authorities, but Josephus intercepted the messengers who were bringing him this word and had them returned to Jerusalem. Added troubles arose in the form of local defiance of Josephus' authority when the cities of Tiberias and Sepphoris revolted and had to be forcefully returned to rebel control.

While these things were going on, Nero placed prosecution of the Jewish War in the hands of Vespasian, a veteran soldier who had distinguished himself in combat in Germany and Britain. This crusty commander was soon in Syria, where he readied a large force, consisting of more than three legions (to which a fourth was later added). As Vespasian began to move south, Sepphoris revolted again and asked for Roman protection, a request that the Roman commander was all too glad to grant with a garrison of 7,000 men. In light of this strong Roman presence in the heart of Galilee, many in Josephus' army deserted, so that he was forced to call for more and better fighters from Jerusalem. But before any reinforcements could arrive, Vespasian decided to attack Josephus' main force, which had stationed itself behind the stout walls of Jotapata, a town a few miles north of Sepphoris.

The siege that now began was to last for some six weeks, during the course of which barbarities typical of this brutal war were commonplace. The Romans brought to bear their most dreaded engines of war, including the catapult and the battering ram, while the Jews responded with ingenious stratagems to deflect the Roman might. Acts of great bravery were common to both sides, Vespasian himself being wounded by an arrow in the thick of the fight. In the end, however, it was sheer exhaustion that caused the Jews' defeat, for in the dead of night, Vespasian's son Titus scaled the walls with a small contingent of men, killed the sleeping sentries, and opened the city to the rest of the Roman army. The town was destroyed, and its defenders killed or imprisoned.

Josephus and a number of other superior officers escaped and hid in a cave, where Josephus advised that they surrender. The others would have nothing of such talk, however, and insisted they all commit suicide. When Josephus reminded them that suicide is a sin in the eyes of God, a compromise was reached in which, according to an order established by lot, each person would kill a designated colleague before himself being slain by another. Whether by luck or trickery—Josephus doesn't say[57]—Josephus' turn to die was last (or possibly next to last). So he and a remaining Jew walked out of the cave and into the hands of the Romans.

Josephus was carried to Vespasian, who was doubtless anxious to have a look at this adversary who had withstood his legions for such a long time. There, according to his own testimony, Josephus piqued the interest of the Roman general even further by predicting that he and his son Titus would be elevated to the imperial throne. Vespasian was apparently flattered by the prophecy, for, although he did not release Josephus from his chains, he presented him with gifts and treated him with consideration.

c. *From the Fall of Jotapata to the Destruction of Jerusalem (67–70 AD).* Jotapata collapsed in July of 67, and by the end of the year all of northern Palestine was in Roman hands. However, the Jews of Jerusalem, instead of planning together to meet the coming Roman assault, began a series of recriminations based on the old socioeconomic divisions, in that the Zealots accused the aristocrats (once the party of peace) of responsibility for the fall of Galilee, in light of the fact that Josephus was one of their number. These embers were fanned by the arrival in Jerusalem of Josephus' enemy, John of Gischala, who had escaped the Roman seige of his native town and had made his way south, in the company of many of his followers, to the Holy City. A reign of terror was soon inaugurated in Jerusalem in which many of the leading citizens of the city were murdered, including a member of the Herodian family named Antipas, and two high priests (who had served successively), Ananus and Jesus ben Gamaliel.

Vespasian felt it best to allow the Jews to exhaust their resources and, as a consequence, he spent the first half of 68 in campaigns of pacification in Peraea, the Jordan valley and along the coastal plain. When at length he was ready to lay siege to Jerusalem, word arrived of Nero's death, and Vespasian felt compelled to postpone the assault in order to await developments in Rome. Because of the confused situation there (the new emperor, Galba, was almost immediately assassinated) and because Vespasian saw no urgency in advancing against a deeply divided enemy, an entire year was to elapse before the Roman army would assume operations again. But it was not to be under

Vespasian's command, for in July of 69 the veteran commander was acclaimed emperor by his troops, first in Egypt and, following that, in Palestine and Syria. And so he left the military situation in Judaea in charge of Titus and set out for Rome.

In the meantime, the relationships among Jerusalem's Jews had grown even more fractious. A certain Simon bar Giora, who, like John of Gischala, had been a Zealot warrior in the field, had also been forced into the city by the Romans, and hostilities soon broke out between his followers and those of John. In time, a third Zealot splinter group formed under Simon's son, Eleazar, and the three warring parties each took possession of a different part of the city. In their senseless fighting, the Zealots destroyed by fire large quantities of grain that had been stored in the city. Their motive, which was to starve each other into submission, in the end served only the purposes of the Romans.

Titus and the four legions that had been placed at his disposal arrived before Jerusalem's walls just prior to the Passover celebration of 70 AD and they immediately set to work preparing a siege. In order to avoid having to advance against the city's defenses by scaling the steep slopes that surround much of Jerusalem, Titus attacked from the North and West, where the terrain is the most level. This line of assault meant that the Temple lay roughly in the path of Titus' main force, yet protected by three stout walls. By using their powerful battering rams, the Romans penetrated the first, northernmost wall, in two weeks time. Ten days later the second wall was successfully breached, allowing Titus' troops to advance to the edge of the Temple mount and to the walls of the Fortress Antonia.

Now began the most difficult part of the siege for, with less area to defend, the Jews fought more effectively, a truce having been worked out between the Zealot factions. Roman attempts to force their way past the third wall were repulsed, by the Zealots of John of Gischala who stood in defense of the Fortress Antonia, and by those of Simon bar Giora who were stationed in the upper city. (The splinter group led by Eleazar bar Simon had by this time been crushed by John of Gischala.) Their advance frustrated, the Romans resorted to both reason and terror. Josephus appeared and, standing just beyond the range of the Jews' missiles, urged the defenders to surrender in order that no harm should come to the Temple. But the rebels, who looked upon Josephus with the same hatred that they viewed Titus and his legions, turned a deaf ear. The terror took the form of a stone or earthen dike with which the Romans encircled the entire city and that served to let no one in or out without the Romans' permission. The object, which was immediately apparent to the defenders, was to bring about their submission by starvation.

The weeks that followed were a terrible time for the Jews trapped inside the city. Josephus describes some of the horrors in this manner:

The roofs were full of women and infants in the last stages of exhaustion, the alleys with the corpses of the aged; children and young men,
swollen with hunger, haunted the market places and collapsed wherever
faintness overtook them . . . And throughout these calamities, no
weeping or lamentation was heard: hunger stifled the emotion; and
with dry eyes and grinning mouths those who were slow to die watched
those whose end came sooner. Deep silence blanketed the city, and
night laden with death was in the grip of a yet fiercer foe—the brigands.
They broke as tomb plunderers into the houses, rifled the deceased and
stripped the coverings from their bodies, then departed laughing; they
tried the points of their swords on the corpses, even transfixed some of
the wretches who lay prostrate but still living, to test the steel, and any
who implored them to . . . end their misery, they disdainfully left to
perish with hunger.[58]

Around the perimeters of the rebels' defenses, the fighting continued without remission, especially around the Fortress Antonia, where the Romans had
now concentrated their attack. On the seventeenth of the Jewish month Tam-
muz (June-July), the daily sacrifices in the Temple had to be discontinued, as
all able-bodied men were at their stations of battle. This was a tragedy of great
proportions in the eyes of devout Jews, and the morale of many of the city's
defenders, already sapped by lack of food and rest, sank even lower. On the
eighth day of Ab (July-August), Titus' soldiers succeeded in burning down
the great gates leading into the outer court of the Temple, and the next day
were able to force an entry through this opening. In the fighting that followed
the Temple was destroyed by fire (ninth of Ab), in spite of Titus' express command that it should be spared.[59] Josephus takes note of the tragic irony that
the Romans destroyed the Second Temple on the same day that the Babylonians destroyed the First.[60]

In spite of the great massacre that accompanied the destruction of the
Temple, Jewish resistance did not end. The Zealots under John of Gischala
and Simon bar Giora fought on for another month until the upper and lower
cities were in Roman hands. On the eighth of Elul (August-September) the last
defenders were overwhelmed, five months after Titus' siege began. Almost all
of the city had now been destroyed by fire; most of the Jews killed, either by
the Romans or by other Jews. The only structures on any consequence left
standing were three towers of Herod's former palace. As for John of Gischala
and Simon bar Giora, they were both taken prisoner.

Leaving one legion in Jerusalem, Titus returned with the rest of his army,
prisoners and booty in hand, to Caesarea Maritima where 30,000 Jewish captives were sold into slavery. Then it was on to Caesarea Philippi and festival
games where, with King Agripa II looking on, 2,500 Jewish fighters were killed
in gladitorian combat. The next year Titus returned to Rome for a triumphant

celebration that included a grand procession through the city in which prominent Jewish prisoners, including Simon bar Giora, were displayed, as well as
artifacts from the Temple, including the Table of the Shewbread and the Seven-
branched Candlestick. At the conclusion of the procession, Simon bar Giora, as
the ranking enemy commander, was executed, according to Roman custom. Vespasian immediately laid plans for a commemorative structure, the so-called
Titus Arch, which still stands on the site of the Roman Forum.

d. *From the Destruction of Jerusalem to the Fall of Masada (70–74 AD).* The
collapse of Jerusalem left only three strongholds in the hands of the Zealots:
Herodium, Machaerus, and Masada. The first two of these bastions fell to
the Romans with only minimal effort, the command of the army now being
entrusted to the governor of Judaea, Lucilius Bassus. The fall of Machaerus
was effected by a cruel, but effective method. One of the leading rebels had
been captured by the Romans, a young man named Eleazar, who was led
before the walls of the Machaerus where, in full view of the defenders, he
was whipped. The distressed Jews then watched as a cross was set up for the
evident purpose of crucifying the young man. But rather than let this happen, the rebel soldiers surrendered, an act, however, that did not prevent the
massacre of 1,700 male citizens of Machaerus and the enslavement of their
wives and children.

Masada, the last Jewish stronghold to fall, was a virtually impregnable fortification that overlooked the Dead Sea and that rose more than 600 feet above the
desert floor, being accessible only by a nearly vertical ascent. With painstaking
difficulty, the Romans, under the new governor of Judaea, Flavius Silva (Bassus
had died), began to build an earthwork up the steep side of Masada, at a point
where the angle of ascent was the least precipitous. Slowly they worked their
way upward, the Roman engineers laboring under the protection of a wooden
tower covered with iron plates from which Roman missiles could be directed at
the defenders on the walls above. At length, the earthwork was capable of sup-
porting a battering ram that was then brought against the wall with the desired
effect, so that Roman troops poured into the fort. A second wall, constructed of
wood, was subsequently torched by Silva's men.

Realizing that the situation was hopeless, the Zealot commander urged the
defenders to commit suicide rather than to fall into the hands of their enemies. They complied, 960 Jews in all, with the exception of two women and
five children who had gone into hiding and who emerged only when it was
possible to give themselves up to the Romans. The date was the fifteenth of
the month Nisan (March-April), in the year 74.[61]

Josephus reports that some Jewish fanatics managed to escape to Egypt,
where there were further disturbances. But in reality, the long Jewish War
with Rome was finally at an end.

C. From the Jewish War With Rome to the
Revolt of Bar Kokhba (74–135 AD)

As Josephus' narrative of events in Palestine comes to an end with his account of the war with Rome, and, as no other writer, either Jewish or gentile, attempted to write a similar history for the post-war years, we are very much in the dark concerning developments in Judaea after 70. Thanks, however, to a few references by Roman writers, to several inscriptions and documents unearthed by archaeologists, and to the written traditions of the rabbis some things are evident.

Jerusalem was allowed to remain in its devastated state. For the first time since the days of King David, the Holy City could claim no Jewish inhabitants, with the possible exception of a few hardy souls who may have tried to squeeze out an existence amid the scorched rubble. Instead, the remains of the palace of Herod and a part of the western wall became a camp for the legion Titus had left behind to keep the peace. In one of Josephus' final comments on the fall of Jerusalem, he observes that

> all the rest of the wall encircling the city was so completely leveled to the ground that no future visitors would believe that it had once been inhabited.[62]

No less traumatic than the physical devastation was that inflicted upon the soul of the Jews. Unlike the destruction of Jerusalem by the Babylonians in 587 BC, the calamity of 70 AD resulted in the death of major Jewish institutions, for with the razing of the Temple the office of the priesthood was destroyed, as well. Because the venue of priestly worship was now gone, the great festivals of Judaism, once celebrated by pilgrims bands who converged upon the Temple, now found other settings in the synagogue and the home. The synagogue, in fact, now takes on added importance as the primary place where the community comes together for the worship of God.

The collapse of the priesthood also signaled the end of the Sadducees, most of whom were probably dead by now because of the vicious persecution of the aristocracy by Jewish Zealots during the war. The Essenes also are lost at this time, unless a few lived on in to the time of Bar Kokhba. As for the Zealots, the embers of their hatred of the Romans continued to smolder and were to be fanned by Bar Kokhba and others into a raging new inferno in the next century. Primarily in the Pharisees are there the signs of the new life that will reinvigorate Judaism and begin to shape it into the vital reality it has remained during the almost two millennia since the fires of 70. With the approval of the Romans, the coastal town of Jamnia (also called Yavneh or Jabneh) becomes a seat of Pharisaic learning, and here, under the leadership of the scholars Johanan ben Zakkai and Gamaliel II, the Torah is read and expounded with a new earnestness. In Jamnia is located a new Pharisaic council, the *Bet Din* (House of Judgment) to which Jews begin to look for leadership in place of the defunct Sanhedrin, which has perished along with its Sadducean and priestly membership. Thus from Jamnia fresh light is infused into Jewish communities not only in Palestine, but throughout the Roman world, developments we shall pursue in the next chapter.

Of social and political events in Judaea over the next decades we know very little. Judaea continued to be a Roman province ruled, as before, from Caesarea Maritima. Also, as before, local matters having to do with public affairs and with the administration of justice were largely left to local Jewish communities, except that now the academy at Jamnia functioned as a kind of final authority, in place of the lost Sanhedrin. In one particular community, however, there was introduced a significant change that must have rankled devout Jews. The former Temple tax was now directed to Rome where, by order of the Flavian emperors (Vespasian, Titus, Domitian), it was used to support the activities of the cult of Jupiter. There must have been other indignities directed at the Jews, whom the Romans viewed as especially troublesome, but of these we are largely ignorant. Beginning in 115 AD, during the reign of Trajan, serious rioting by Jews erupted in several parts of the empire, including Egypt, Cyrene, Cyprus, and Mesopotamia. While this may have stimulated disturbances in Palestine, there are no details in the historical record to help us know how these may have transpired.

But there can be no doubt that there was a very serious insurrection during the second quarter of the second century, a conflict generally refered to as the revolt of Bar Kokhba, which probably took place 132–135 AD. Our primary witness to this revolt is an account of only a few hundred words from the Roman historian Cassius Dio (c. 155–230 AD), a politician from Bithynia (in Asi Minor) who wrote a history of Rome. The church historian Eusebius of Caesarea Maritima (c. 260–340) also refers briefly to the revolt, and there are fragmentary references in other Greek and Latin authors, as well as brief rabbinical memories contained in the Talmud. In recent years, the existence of the so-called Bar Kokhba has been confirmed by the discovery of coins and manuscripts that bear his name.

The revolt was probably rooted in multiple oppressions, some of which we may never know. A prohibition against circumcision, issued during Hadrian's reign, would have offended all devout Jews. Although a number of people in the empire practiced circumcision, the Romans considered it a barbaric custom similar to castration, which was also proscribed. But the fact that the ban also applied to many of their neighbors would not have mollified the feelings of the Jews in the matter.

More serious, however, seems to have been a plan by Hadrian to rebuild Jerusalem as a pagan city and to install on the former Temple mount a shrine dedicated to the worship of Jupiter.[63] Hadrian may not have considered this measure as especially anti-Jewish, since the refounding of cities and their rededication to Greco-Roman gods had been going on since the time of Alexander the Great. But we may be sure that it was an outrage to the Jews, who still considered Jerusalem a site holy to the God of Israel and who still hoped that it would be restored some day as a center of Jewish life.

Dio states[64] that the leaders of the rebellion suppressed their anger as long as Hadrian was in the vicinity (he was in Egypt in 130 and in Syria in 131 AD), but that, as soon as he left the East, they began their attacks upon the Romans. Virtually nothing has come down to us concerning the nature of this war. Dio etches a kind of guerrilla war in which the Jews use weapons discarded as inferior by the Romans, and in which the rebels, rather than risk a frontal attack upon the enemy, employed hit-and-run tactics, hiding in caves and subterranean tunnels between engagements.

> At first the Romans took no account of them. Soon, however, all Judaea had been stirred up, and the Jews everywhere were showing signs of disturbance, were gathering together, and giving evidence of great hostility to the Romans, partly by secret and partly by overt acts.[65]

The leader of the rebellion emerges only slightly from the shadows of time. Eusebius refers to him by the name Bar Chochebas, but then adds that this means *star*. As other Christian writers refer to him as Bar Kokhba (literally, son of a star), Eusebius' version is seen to be a corruption of this latter designation. In rabbinic sources (all written well after the time of the rebellion) he is designated as Bar Koziba ("son of a lie"). However, coins and documents from this period discovered by modern archaeologists give us his true name, Simon bar Kosiba, and make clear that both Christian and Jewish writers are employing derogatory puns in the names they bestow. The Christians probably called him "Son of a Star" in ridicule over his messianic claims (or perhaps claims made in his behalf by others), apparently in reference to Numbers 24:17, "a star shall come out of Jacob." This seems confirmed by Eusebius, who writes:

> The Jews were at that time led by a certain Bar Chochebas, which means "star," a man who was murderous and a bandit, but relied on his name, as if dealing with slaves, and claimed to be a luminary who had come down to them from heaven and was magically enlightening those who were in misery.[66]

Yet in employing the designation "Son of a Star" the Christian writers were following the lead of Bar Kosiba's own followers, among them the important rabbinic sage Akiba, who used the term quite seriously (see the next chapter). For the Jews, the "Son of a Lie" may also have been a derogatory epithet for a failed messiah.

We do not know the extent of Bar Kosiba's victories, but they must have been impressive, for it appears that a very large Roman military presence was required to suppress the rebellion. Eusebius names as commander of the Roman forces a certain Rufus, undoubtedly the same as the Q. Tineius Rufus who was governor of Judaea at the time. Although Eusebius describes Rufus' victories over the rebels, it is likely that he was defeated, for Dio affirms that the governor of distant Britain, a certain Julius Severus, was called to lead the Roman troops. Dio implies that other Roman commanders followed Severus, although he does not provide their names, and it is quite likely that even the presence of the emperor was required.

It seems evident that the Jews intended to set up an independent state with Bar Kosiba as its head. Coins were minted bearing the inscription "Simon, Prince of Israel," some of which also exhibit a star. Documents reflect an organizational structure in which commanders have been placed over local districts, and which proclaim the beginning of the revolt as a new era in the lives of the Jews. One papyrus fragment begins:

> The twentieth Sabbath in the second year of the liberation of Israel, by the authority of Simon bar Kosiba, prince of Israel.[67]

Where the theaters of combat may have been located is uncertain, although all indications point to the Judaean desert as the stronghold of the rebels. There is no direct evidence that Jerusalem was captured by them, although that is by no means out of the question, as it would surely have been one of the rebel's goals. What does seem clearer is that a very great deal of destruction accompanied the fighting, and the devastation of some areas may have approximated that of Jerusalem in 70. At least that is the opinion of Dio, who writes that "nearly the whole of Judaea was made desolate."[68]

The rebels were finally besieged in a mountain fortress named by Eusebius as Beththera or Bethar, which has been identified as modern Bettir, six miles southwest of Jerusalem.[69] The fighting was intense and protracted, but in the end the determination of the Jews could not match the superior power of Rome. Eusebius says that

> the siege lasted a long time before the rebels were driven to final destruction by famine and thirst and the instigator of their madness paid the penalty he deserved.

But the Romans paid dearly as well, since Dio remarks that, in his commu-
nique to the Senate, the emperor omitted the customary formula, "I and the
legions are in health."[70] But the rebellion, begun in 132 AD, was at long last
now, in 135, at an end.

Hadrian was now free to pursue his plan to raise Jerusalem as a Roman
city. It was rebuilt in the Greco-Roman style of architecture and named Aelia
Capitolina (Aelius was Hadrian's family name, Capitolina a reference to the
patron deity of the new city, Jupiter). No Jew was allowed even to go near the
city, whose gentile population, according to Eusebius, included some Christians. We know very little of the nature of Aelia (as it was commonly called),
except that it boasted very beautiful buildings. A temple to Jupiter was
erected on the site of the former Jewish Temple and contained, among other
objects, a statue of Hadrian. According to Jerome, who visited the city in the
late fourth century, the southern gate of Aelia was surmounted by an image of
a pig. A small sixth-century church in the village of Madeba, east of the Dead
Sea, possesses a moasic representation of Aelia Capitolina and its buildings.
Although details are difficult to distinguish, what appeares to be a grand
colonnaded avenue, similar to those known from other Greco-Roman cities,
runs through the heart of the city.[71]

Not only was the name Jerusalem expunged by the Romans, but that of
Judaea, as well, in that the former province was renamed Syria-Palestina. Circumcision was forbidden, while the study and teaching of the Torah became a
crime punishible by death.

Chapter 10

PALESTINIAN JEWISH THEOLOGY AND LITERATURE TO THE REVOLT OF BAR KOKHBA

A. THE RABBIS AND THEIR TEACHINGS

Earlier (chapter 4), we attempted to trace the movement within Jewish theology that gave central place to the authority of Torah, and we considered, as well, the various sectarian schools that emerged in large part as a result of differences over how the Torah should be interpreted and applied to daily life. It is clear that, while these developments were impacted in special ways by the pressures exerted from the forces (cultural and otherwise) of Hellenism, the developments themselves had their origins in the Persian period and continued well into the time of Roman rule. Therefore, those contributions to theological thought made by the rabbis of the Roman period should be understood to be a continuation of that stream of Jewish reflection and practice that arises after (or perhaps even during) the exile and flows vigorously through the era of the Hellenistic kingdoms.

The Jewish memory of the manner in which the life of the spirit was conducted in Roman period Palestine focuses largely upon individual sages and teachers, rabbis they would come to be called, who were instrumental in giving the theology of early Judaism much of its character and content. But in considering these individuals we run into two serious problems. The first is that the reminiscences of these rabbis, including the things they said and did, received the written forms that we know at a time later than that in which they lived. The task, therefore, of separating the actual words and deeds of these teachers from the creative additions of their faithful disciples is not unlike the task faced by students of the Gospels in separating the words and deeds of the historical Jesus from contributions of the early Christians. A second problem is that these sources tend, on the whole, to be the work of sages of the Pharisaic tradition, in light of the reality that Sadducean and Essene interpretations of Judaism died out under the tragic force of two failed rebellions against the Romans. Therefore, those individual teachers who were active in Palestine during the two centuries after

316

Pompey's conquest of Jerusalem in 63 BC and who have been enshrined in the Jewish memory are, by and large, Pharisaic teachers. Had there been an enduring Sadducean or Essene tradition into the third century AD (the date of the earliest written rabbinic sources), our picture of Jewish theology during the time of Herod and the Roman governors would doubtless exhibit more diversity than is the case.

The names of the most prominent of the sages known to us include: Hillel (c. 70 BC–10 AD); Shammai (c. 50 BC–30 AD); Gamaliel the Elder, or Gamaliel I (c. 25 BC–50 AD); Johanan ben Zakkai (c. 1–80 AD); Gamaliel the Younger, or Gamaliel II (c. 30–100 AD); and Akiba (c. 50–135 AD). Some indication of the importance which the rabbinic tradition placed upon these teachers is the following statement from a later midrash, the *Sifre* on Deuteronomy (on this, see below):

> "And Moses was a hundred and twenty years old." [Deut 34:7] He was one of four who died at one hundred twenty, and these are they: Moses, and Hillel the Elder, and Rabban Johannan ben Zakkai, and Rabbi Akiba.[1]

They and their followers would be called *tannaim* (meaning *repeaters* or *teachers*), thus this era in Jewish thought (to about 200 AD) came to be known as the Tannaitic period.

1. *Hillel* (c. 70 BC–10 AD)[2]

Hillel, sometimes referred to as Hillel the Elder to distinguish him from a later teacher of the same name, was a native of Babylonia. Although the rabbinic tradition gives few clues to his early life, it is assumed by many that Hillel had studied under important teachers in the Jewish community in Babylon before making his way to Judaea, and that this early training helped to shape his own teaching in significant ways. In this connection, it will be remembered that Babylonian Jews had long since developed a life of faith and practice in which Temple worship, and the priesthood that presided over that worship, were absent. It is possible that Hillel's own thought, influenced by such circumstances, began to prepare Judaism for a day when the sacrificial system would be only a memory. For example, a dispute over the proper manner to observe the Passover when that festival fell upon a Sabbath (see below) elicited the following from Hillel:

> They [Hillel's opponents] said to him: What will be for the people who have not brought knives and [sacrificial animals] to the sanctuary [on the mistaken belief that the usual Passover rules did not apply].

He said to them: Let them alone. The holy spirit is upon them. If they
are not prophets, they are sons of prophets.[3]

If Hillel's teaching did prepare Jews for worship in a world without Temple or
priesthood, such a goal was accomplished as a result of the tragic events that
were to transpire after Hillel was dead, and certainly not as a result of pre-
meditation on his part. Yet it may help to explain why Hillel's teaching, which
in the years soon after his death seems to have been considered by many to be
inferior to that of his contemporary Shammai (see below), ultimately came to
exercise much greater influence among Jews.

Whatever experiences he may have had in Babylonia, Hillel came to
Jerusalem as a young man where he studied under the influential sages
Shemaiah and Abtalion. The tradition seems unanimous in remembering his
kind and gentle spirit, and his interest in finding ways in which people might
live together in peace and justice. One story about him tells how he obtained
a horse and a servant that he placed at the disposal of a poor man who had no
other means of getting around to attend to his daily affairs. One day the servant failed to appear, and so Hillel himself took the place of the servant and
walked before the poor man's horse.

It is in the accounts of his teaching, however, more than in personal anecdotes, that one finds Hillel's concern for kindness and equity. Yet even the
stories concerning his teaching often contrast Hillel's gentle disposition with
that of his more irritable contemporary Shammai (see below). On one occasion
a gentile approached Shammai and promised that he would become a Jew if
Shammai could teach him the entire Torah while the man stood on one foot.
Shammai responded to the gentile's insolence by throwing a carpenter's tool
at him. But when the same man posed the same challenge to Hillel, Hillel
(who was more open to gentiles than were many other Jews) is reported to
have replied, "What is hateful to you, do not unto your neighbor. That is the
whole Torah; while the rest is commentary thereof; go and learn it."[4] (Cf. Matt.
22:34–40).

A similar anecdote purports to reveal the nature of Hillel's teaching and
his patience, and it also tells us a great deal about the Pharisaic attitude toward the traditions of halakhah and haggadah, which are here termed the *oral
Torah*.

A certain man once stood before Shammai and said to him: "Master,
how many Torahs have you?"

"Two," Shammai replied, "one written and one oral."

Said the man, "The written one I am prepared to accept, the oral one
I am not prepared to accept."

Shammai rebuked him and dismissed him in a huff.

He came before Hillel and said to him, "Master, how many Torahs were given?"

"Two," Hillel replied, "one written and one oral."

Said the man, "The written one I am prepared to accept, the oral one I am not prepared to accept."

"My son," Hillel said to him, "sit down."

He wrote out the alphabet for him (and pointing to one of the letters) asked him, "What is this?"

"It is *alef*," the man replied.

Said Hillel, "This is not *alef*, but *bet*. What is that?" he continued.

The man answered, "It is *bet*."

"This is not *bet*," said Hillel, "but *gimmel*."

(In the end) Hillel said to him, "how dost thou know that this is *alef* and this *bet* and this *gimmel*? Only because so our ancestors of old handed it down to us that this is *alef* and this *bet* and this *gimmel*. Even as thou has taken this in good faith, so take the other in good faith."[5]

Hillel also effected legal reforms which indicate the temper of his spirit. According to the Torah (Deut. 15:2), each sabbatic year brought about the cancellation of personal debts, a practice that had originally been intended to prohibit the virtual enslavement of poor Jews. But in the capital intensive economy that came with Roman rule, this tradition had a negative effect, since lenders, in the late stages of the seven-year cycle, were unwilling to let their money out for fear that it would never be repaid. Hillel devised a system that, while it left the tradition itself unchanged, ensured the eventual repayment to the lenders of their funds.

Another reform had to do with the sale of houses. Leviticus 25:29 permits the seller of a house to repurchase the building within a year of the sale, the intent being to protect the poor person, who may have been forced into the sale by a momentary need for funds, from losing his or her patrimony. But in Hillel's day, the spirit of the law was being circumvented by buyers who would disappear before the first anniversary of the sale, thus preventing the original owner from reclaiming his or her home. Hillel decreed that in such circumstances, the seller could redeem the home by depositing the necessary funds in the Temple treasury.

It is clear that only a teacher of exceptional authority could institute such reforms, and the esteem in which Hillel was held resulted in his being bestowed with the title *nasi*, meaning *prince* or *patriarch*. A story about how he received such an honorific also says something about Hillel's method of teaching and about how that method contrasted with that of many of his fellow Pharisees. It seems that one year Passover was to fall on the Sabbath day, and so a dispute arose whether the effort involved in sacrificing the Passover lamb violated the prohibition against labor on the Sabbath. Hillel was called for and, by detailed arguments from scripture and the tradition (written and oral Torah), he declared that the sacrifice was permissible and necessary. But the Pharisees who were present took exception to this opinion and further argumentation ensued, during which Hillel continued to press his interpretation by logical means. When it became apparent that this method would produce no results, Hillel declared simply that he knew his interpretation to be true because he had learned it from his teachers, the esteemed Jerusalem Pharisees, Shemaiah and Abtalion. Hillel's opponents, who would not yield to his logic, gave way in the face of this appeal to authority, whereupon he was declared *nasi*. But—according to the tradition—Hillel then rebuked them for their ignorance of the Torah and their unwillingness to permit the Torah to be followed to its logical conclusions.[6]

It is in Hillel's method of theologizing, which he may have learned in Babylonia, that his most important contribution to Jewish thought lies. He became the exponent of a system of logical thought, based largely on inductive principles that, in time, was profoundly to shape the manner in which the Pharisees conceptualized their beliefs. Whereas others were content to appeal to authority (sometimes scripture, but more often previous Pharisaic pronouncements), Hillel worked from both scripture and tradition to hammer out new insights into the manner in which the life of faith must be lived. Analogy (where an ethical or theological problem described by scripture or the tradition—and the solution applied to that problem—was compared to a contemporary problem) and argumentation from a particular principle to a general application were among the cornerstones of Hillel's method.

A modern scholar has summarized Hillel's contribution to Pharisaic Jewish thought by comparing those who came before Hillel to

> primitive chemists deprived of catalytic agents. Phenomena surrounded them, but they suggested nothing new. Facts existed, but were were incapable of reproducing anything surpassing themselves. Hillel recognized that tradition by itself was insufficient . . . Its components had to be united . . . so that men would not be helpless when history was silent and they were left to their own resources.[7]

After Hillel's death it was said of him "that it was fitting that the *Shekinah* (the presence of God) should rest upon him." A group of Pharisees called the House of Hillel perpetuated his memory and his teaching.

2. *Shammai* (c. 50 BC–30 AD)[8]

Shammai is remembered as an important contemporary of Hillel, and one who founded a school (the House of Shammai) that opposed the House of Hillel for many generations. The rabbinic tradition records almost nothing of

Shammai's origins beyond the fact that he was a builder by trade and a native Judaean. As noted above, he was said to be of a more acid temperament than Hillel, although one statement for which he is remembered would seem to contradict that, for he is reported to have observed:

> Make your study of the Torah a matter of established regularity, say little and do much, and receive all men with a friendly countenance.

Few of Shammai's teachings have been preserved and, among those that are, almost all have to do with ritual matters, such as the legality of setting out on a sea voyage when one knows that one will still be at sea on the Sabbath, or the question of fighting an offensive war on the Sabbath. The rabbinic tradition gives greater attention to the decisions of the House of Shammai in its disputes with the House of Hillel, than it does to the teachings of Shammai himself. But if these later disputes may be used as a measure of Shammai's own thought (and it is not certain to what extent they may), Shammai appears to be more strict than Hillel in most cases, but by no means in all. It may be that in whatever disputes the two sages engaged, Shammai represented the more traditional Pharisaic outlook, in light of the manner in which Hillel revolutionized Pharisaic methodology. The House of Shammai was apparently the more influential school up to the time of the destruction of the Temple, but the House of Hillel was dominant in the period thereafter.

3. *Gamaliel the Elder* (c. 25 BC–50 AD)[9]

This Gamaliel, who may have been a grandson of Hillel and who was, according to rabbinic tradition, president of the Sanhedrin (although this office was usually held by the high priest), was the first in a long line of rabbinic teachers who bore this name. He was apparently the first on whom was conferred the title Rabban, a word that enjoys the same etymological foundation as rabbi (*rab: great*), but that seems to have been somewhat more honorific. There are several traditions that portray Gamaliel as a confidant and teacher of his contemporary, King Agrippa I. In his judgments, Gamaliel seems to have been compassionate and tolerant, as indicated by his teaching that a widow might remarry on the basis of only a single witness to the fact that her husband had died, a judgment that Rabbi Akiba was later to dispute.[10] He also liberalized divorce proceedings in favor of women.

Gamaliel's tolerant attitude is further evidenced by his unwillingness to deal harshly with the Christians brought before the Sanhedrin (Acts 5:33–39). The New Testament reports that this Gamaliel was the teacher of Saul of Tarsus (Acts 22:3), although it is difficult to reconcile Gamaliel's irenic spirit with the persecuting zeal of the pre-Damascus-Road Saul.

The great honor in which Gamaliel was held by the Pharisaic tradition is evidenced by the statement: "When Rabban Gamaliel the Elder died the glory of the Torah ceased, and purity and saintliness perished."

4. *Johanan ben Zakkai* (c. 1–80 AD)[11]

The most important Pharisaic sage at the time of the destruction of the Temple, Rabban Johanan ben Zakkai, had been a teacher in Lower Galilee before going to (perhaps, returning to) Jerusalem to live and work about 40 AD. According to tradition, he had been a pupil of Hillel, although for that to have been the case, Hillel's death would have had to occur later, or Johanan's birth earlier, than is commonly supposed. More likely, Johanan was trained by scholars of the House of Hillel.

In Jerusalem before the beginning of the war with Rome he distinguished himself in his disputations with the Sadducees and with the Temple authorities by his interpretations of halakhic and haggadic traditions.[12] Although the record is sketchy concerning his teachings at this time, his usual place was "in the shadow of the Temple," where he appears to have made the special privileges of the priests one of the objects of his concern. Of their practice of exempting themselves from the obligatory offerings to the Temple he is reported to have said, "Any priest who does not pay the shekel is guilty of a sin." He also reprimanded upper-class Jews for their lax attitude toward the Torah:

Keep children away from the proud, and separate them from the householders, because the householders draw a man far from words of Torah.[13]

The Torah was considered by Johanan as the God-given center of life which one could neither neglect nor utilize as a source of false pride:

If you have learned much Torah, do not ascribe any merit to yourself, since it was for this that you were created.

Johanan gathered a large body of pupils to his side, and these he taught firmly but compassionately by means of a method similar to that of Hillel. The bonds that held this group together would survive the destruction of Jerusalem and would go far in helping to insure continuity of Pharisaic teaching in the world of Palestinian (and ultimately, Diaspora) Judaism after the disaster of 70 AD.

Whatever suspicion Johanan may have harbored toward the aristocrats of Jerusalem, the sage did not identify himself with the Zealot cause and seems to have viewed with alarm the growing tensions with Rome. The tradition attests that when Vespasian came to Jerusalem to beseige the city, Johanan escaped and went out to the Roman leader. The time was probably 68 AD, after the Roman intentions had become clear and before siege itself had begun, but when the Jews inside Jerusalem's walls were locked in some of their most violent struggles with each other. Several versions of the meeting between Johanan and Vespasian have been preserved[14] and, while differing in detail, they agree that Johanan asked and won Vespasian's permission to travel to Jamnia (also known as Yavneh or Jabneh), a city almost due west of Jerusalem on the coastal plain untouched by the war. The tradition also indicates that Johanan, like Josephus the year before, promised Vespasian that he would become emperor of Rome.

Johanan may have escaped the destruction of Jerusalem, but the emotional impact of the tragedy weighed as heavily upon him as upon any Jew. One story has it that, as the fighting in Jerusalem grew ever more intense,

> Rabban Johanan [who was now in Jamnia] sat and watched in the direction of the wall of Jerusalem to learn what was happening there, even as Eli sat upon his seat by the wayside watching [2 Sam. 4:13]. When Rabbi Johanan ben Zakkai saw that the Temple was destroyed and the *heikhal* (gates) burnt, he stood and rent his garments, took off his *tefillin* (phylactery), and sat weeping, as did his pupils with him.

But another anecdote reveals that, in spite of his attachment to the Temple, Johanan knew that the life of faith did not depend even upon this holy building and its sacrificial system.

> Once when Rabbi Johanan ben Zakkai was leaving Jerusalem, Rabbi Joshua was walking behind him and saw the Temple in ruins. Rabbi Joshua said, "Woe are we that this has been destroyed, the place where atonement was made for the sins of Israel." "No, my son, [responded Johanan] do you not know that we have a means of making atonement that is like it? And what is it? It is deeds of love, as it is said [Hos. 6:6], 'For I desire kindness and not sacrifice.'"

It would seem evident that it was teachings like this that helped the Jews of the day to maintain the integrity of their faith in a world in which the Temple no longer stood.

Other Pharisaic teachers gathered around Johanan at Jamnia and soon gave new life to the already existing council of religious leaders there, the *Bet Din* (House of Judgment), over which Johanan began to preside. In the years to come, since the Sanhedrin was to perish with the disaster of 70, Jews from all over Palestine and, ultimately the Diaspora, would consider as binding the interpretation of the Torah that issued from the House of Judgment at Jamnia. The dominance of the sages of Jamnia was not accepted immediately, and

Johanan was to pass from the scene before the House of Judgment that he directed was to reach the height of its influence. But under the leadership of other scholars, primarily Rabban Gamaliel II, most Jews eventually looked to Jamnia for definitive answers concerning their beliefs and practices. In Johanan's day the most pressing issues were, as might be expected, those that arose as a result of the loss of the Temple and its priesthood. As an example, priestly law had mandated that, when the New Year's day fell on a sabbath, the shofar (ram's horn) should be sounded only in the Temple. Now, however, Rabban Johanan decreed that the shofar should be sounded in any community where there was a local council, or House of Judgment.

Johanan, like other scholars of his day, attributed the destruction of the Temple to the Jews' disobedience of God, and he apparently viewed the Romans as the divine agents sent for this purpose. Such a view, of course, was grounded in the prophetic response to the destruction of the first Temple by the Babylonians in 587 (cf. Jer. 32:26–44). But like the prophets of old, Johanan was convinced that God still had a future in store for Israel.

Just as the supremacy of the teachers of Jamnia was not gained immediately, however, so Johanan himself seems to have met opposition from within his own circle. We cannot know the reasons for this, but he may have been perceived by some as too friendly to the Romans, given his appearance before Vespasian. In any event, in the decade of life left to him after the destruction of Jerusalem, he moved away from Jamnia, and made his home in the village of Beror Hayil in the Judaean foothills to which scholars came from all Judaea to hear him teach. By about 80 AD he was dead, but his momnument, the *Bet Din* of Jamnia was only then beginning to exercise its lasting influence over Jewish life.

5. *Gamaliel the Younger, or II* (c. 30–100 AD)[15]

The successor of Johanan ben Zakkai at Jamnia was the grandson of Gamaliel the Elder, who seems to have succeeded to the leadership of the House of Judgment at Jamnia upon Johanan's retirement or death. As one might expect, he embodied the teaching of Hillel (his great-grandfather, according to some traditions) and is reported to have conducted his affairs with a gentle, but firm spirit. He is called Rabban Gamaliel by the tradition, while the scholars at Jamnia recognized him as their *nasi*.

His rise to a position of authority, however, was bitterly contested by other rabbis, some of whom resisted the growing influence of Jamnia because of their loyalty to their own local Houses of Judgment. But others contested Gamaliel's teaching itself, with the result that bitter divisions developed among the scholars of Jamnia. Most celebrated in this connection was Gamaliel's dispute with a certain Rabbi Joshua ben Hananiah over the matter of the liturgical calendar. While we do not know all that was said or done during this affair, the tradition states that Gamaliel ordered Joshua to conform to Gamaliel's interpretation of the date of the Day of Atonement by demonstrating his acceptance in public.

> I charge you to appear before me with your staff and your money [items which one could not lawfully carry on the Day of Atonement] on the day which according to your reckoning should be the Day of Atonement.

When, upon the counsel of other rabbis, Joshua complied, we are told that Gamaliel received his opponent with a kiss and said,

> Come in peace, my teacher and pupil—my teacher in wisdom and my pupil because you have accepted my decision.

But in spite of this show of concord, hard feelings remained. Joshua's allies succeeded in having Gamaliel removed from the office of *nasi* and, thus, from his responsibilities as head of the Jamnia House of Judgment. But this title, as well as Gamaliel's duties, were later restored.

Gamaliel's intellectual powers were widely recognized and admired, even by his enemies. Still unsettled were many issues relating to matters of worship that had been raised by the destruction of the Temple, and Gamaliel's decisions regarding these were to influence Jewish life from his time forward. His instructions concerning the Passover celebration are especially important, and he is credited with formulating the definitive version of the *Shemoneh 'Eshreh* (Eighteen Benedictions), which constituted early Judaism's most important prayer and, along with the *Shema*, amounted to early Judaism's creed.[16] The significance of Gamaliel's teaching may be seen in the fact that it formed the basis of the Mishnah, that collection of rabbinic teaching drawn up about 200 AD under the leadership of Rabbi Judah the Prince (*Nasi*) and one of the chief documents of rabbinic Judaism.

Two actions of the Jamnia rabbis at this time have been frequently cited as being of special significance for Christians. The first of these is the institution of a prayer, the *Birkat ha Minim* (Benediction Against the Heretics), in which God is petitioned to foil the plans of heretics and sectarians. Scholars have traditionally understood this intercession as directed against the growing number of Jewish Christians, many of whom still worshiped in local synagogues. Since they could not join in the offering of this prayer, it has been argued, the effect was to force these Christians out of the synagogues and, thus, out of fellowship with the Jewish community. Evidence for this movement to evict Jewish Christians from the synagogue has been cited from New Testament passages such as John 9:22, 12:42, and 16:2. But this interpretation of the purpose of the Benediction Against the Heretics has been cast into doubt by the work of some recent scholars.[17]

Another action of the Jamnia rabbis under the leadership of Gamaliel had to do with the shape of the biblical canon. As we have discussed earlier,[18] during most of the period of the Second Temple a number of different writings other than the Torah were considered, to one degree or another, to be authoritative in matters of faith and life. But this literature was not viewed in the same manner in all parts of the Jewish community, in that—to name but one example—Palestinian Jews tended to give little or no weight to literature written in Greek, while Egyptian Jews were much more open to such material. In their role as Judaism's definitive teachers, the rabbis of Jamnia turned their attention to this matter. Their decisions, it must be stressed, had for the most part been reached beforehand, by means of a widely held consensus among Palestine's Jews as to what literature could be regarded as having similar authority as the Torah. But the results of their deliberations were nonetheless significant in that, among other things, they decided (as Hillel had earlier taught) that Ecclesiastes and the Song of Solomon should be considered authoritative, while the Wisdom of Ben Sirach (Ecclesiasticus) as well as all Christian literature should be considered as nonauthoratiative. Since the time of Jerome (c. 340–420 AD) some Christians, primarily Protestants after the sixteenth century, have considered this rabbinic definition of the Hebrew scriptures to be the superior form of the Old Testament, in contrast to the Septuagint Old Testament of the early church.

Gamaliel's attitude toward gentiles was remarkable, in light of the tensions that characterized Jewish-Roman relations in his day. He permitted, perhaps encouraged, the study of the Greek language at Jamnia, and, was once known to bathe in the public bathhouse in Acre dedicated to the goddess Aphrodite. The rabbinic tradition asserts that he sealed documents with seals that bore small figures (Jews normally shunned images), and he appears to have read widely in Greek literature, especially that of a scientific nature. He accepted recognition by the Roman governor of Syria as the leader of his people, and on one occasion even traveled to Rome on an affair of state.

The time of Gamaliel's death is not known, but he was apparently spared news of the Jewish revolts throughout the Diaspora that occurred during the time of Trajan, knowledge of which would have saddened him greatly.

6. *Akiba* (c. 50–135 AD)[19]

A younger contemporary of Gamaliel II, Rabbi Akiba ben Joseph is distinctive among the sages discussed here in that he suffered martyrdom at the hands of the Romans. Because of that, his cherished memory has possibly received more legendary embellishment in the rabbinic tradition than has that of other sages. In any event, his was a colorful life, even if some exaggeration has occurred in its telling.

Akiba was born of poor Judaean peasant stock and, as a young man, was hired by one of Jerusalem's most wealthy men to work as a shepherd. When he married the man's daughter, both he and his bride, Rachel, were cut off from her family and reduced to a level of bare subsistance. According to the tradition, Rachel once was forced to cut off her hair and sell it for food. But she was a devout woman and, through her influence, Akiba was brought to the study of the Torah. In time he became what he had once despised, a rabbinic sage. (He is quoted as having said in later life, "When I was poor, I said, 'Had I a scholar in my power, I would maul him like an ass.'")

Akiba's studies demanded many years, during most of which time he was separated from his beloved Rachel. Initially, he worked at Lydda (near Jamnia), and later at the school at Jamnia, where he learned from Gamalial. Ultimately, however, he presided over his own circle of scholars at Bene Berak, between Lydda and the coast, but continued his association with Jamnia, where he seems to have been a member of the House of Judgment.

The great contribution of Akiba to the development of rabbinic Judaism consists in the organization that he brought to the corpus of halakhic teaching, as it existed in his time. Efforts in this direction had been mounted by others, but it was Akiba's great accomplishment to arrange the body of Halakhah, which exhibited great diversity of subject matter, into six major divisions, each of which contained a number of subdivisions. That which had been a diffuse body of teaching by the sages now came to have the character of a code, and Akiba's system would be followed by those who formalized rabbinic teaching into the Mishnah (c. 200 AD).

In the debates within the House of Judgment at Jamnia, Akiba appears to have often sided with the opponents of Gamaliel. When Gamaliel excommunicated his own brother-in-law, Eliezer ben Hyrcanus, it was Akiba who was chosen to go to Eliezer with the news. And when the allies of Joshua ben Hananiah temporarily ousted Gamaliel from leadership in the House of Judgment, Akiba was considered as Gamaliel's possible successor. On another occasion he is known to have rebuked Gamaliel when the latter attempted to thwart the will of the majority of Jamnia's rabbis in a matter before consideration by the House of Judgment.

Akiba appears as a leader of that group that won the acceptance of the Song of Solomon into the canon of scripture, and in so doing he revealed a mystical quality to his faith. He argued for an allegorical interpretation of the song in which the text is understood to speak of God's love for Israel (an allegory that has come into Christian exegesis as one between Christ and the church). "All the Writings are holy," he is recorded as saying, "but the Song of Songs is the Holy of Holies."

Akiba's mysticism may also be responsible for the manner in which he treated the text of the Torah. He viewed every word as inspired by God and even argued that any pecularities in spelling or syntax were also God-given.

Akiba went so far as to claim theological significance for that particle (*et*) that, in Hebrew, signifies that a word or phrase functions as the definite article within a sentence. This was in opposition to some of his contemporaries who argued that the language of the Torah functions no differently from any other human language. Akiba is thus one of the founders of that tradition within both Judaism and Christianity that places great theological importance upon the literal form of the text of scripture.

It is said that one of Akiba's disciples was the Aquila, a convert from Christianity, whom we discussed earlier.[20] Aquila's translation of the Hebrew scriptures into Greek was made not only to furnish the Jewish community with a distinctive Greek Bible (since the Christians had adopted the Septuagint), but also to provide a biblical text more compatible with Akiba's interpretation, which it reflects in many ways. Some scholars have proposed, for example, that the literal method of translation employed by Aquila reflects Akiba's attention to the very words and letters of the biblical text.

Whereas the leaders of the rabbinic school at Jamnia had attempted to cooperate with the Roman authorities, Akiba was hostile to their presence and viewed them as an oppressive force to be overcome. Thus, unlike many of his contemporaries, he greeted Bar Kosiba as the Messiah and saw in him the fulfillment of the promise of Numbers 24:17.[21] He probably took no part in the actual fighting because of his advanced age, but he was arrested by the Romans because of his sympathies and because he violated a ban in effect at the time against teaching the Torah. Although treated with some leniency at first, he was ultimately tortured to death by his captors.

7. *Traditions of the Rabbis After 135 AD*

In the aftermath of the Bar Kokhba revolt, which appears to have been fought primarily in Judaea, the focal point of rabbinic activity shifted to the north. Many rabbis, like Akiba, had doubtless died in the fighting or in the Roman efforts to suppress Jewish religious observance, but even in the face of Roman persecution (which lasted until the time of Emperor Antoninus Pius [138–161 AD]), the rabbis who survived continued to study and to teach. Ultimately, Tiberias became the most important center of rabbinic activity, and there and in other Jewish communities the scholars preserved the traditions associated with Jamnia and elsewhere. About 200 AD one of the most important formulations of rabbinic material was compiled, as we have noted earlier, under the leadership of the noted sage, Rabbi Judah the Prince. This was the Mishnah, an anthology of rabbinic reflection and law that became the primary authority for rabbis and their students in both Palestine and Babylonia. Its six divisions, which apparently may be traced back to Akiba, give some indication of the Mishnah's contents:

1. Seeds: concerning agricultural matters
2. Festivals: on matters relating to the liturgical calendar
3. Women: on family life and vows
4. Damages: on civil and criminal law
5. Hallowed Things: concerning sacrifice and rituals of worship
6. Cleanness: involving discussions of that which is clean and unclean

Notice should be taken of the fact that there is very little abstract theological reflection contained in the Mishnah and only one subdivision, the tractate *Avoth* (meaning *fathers*), contains serious efforts at moral philosophy. Rather, the primary concern is how to apply the rabbinic rules to everyday life. So wide-ranging are the Mishnah's interests and so great did its authority become that it, along with the Bible, became one of the two pillars of Jewish belief and practice.

During the lifetime of Rabbi Judah, relations between Jews and Romans had grown particularly cordial, and the rabbinic tradition even describes close relations between Rabbi Judah and the imperial family in Rome. Some have pointed out that, just as the Jewish theological and legal tradition was codified at this time in the Mishnah, Roman law was reorganized and codified about the same time under the Emperor Septimus Severus (193–211 AD). However, evidence for direct connections between these two events is lacking.

In addition to the Mishnah several midrashim appear to have been compiled about this time, predominantly legal commentaries on portions of the Torah. Among these are *Mechilta* (meaning *measure*), a commentary on portions of Exodus; *Sifra* (*book*) on Leviticus; and *Sifre* (*books*), a composite commentary on Numbers and Deuteronomy.

A further collection of material similar to the Mishnah that was compiled about this time is called the *Tosefta* (meaning *additions*). The origin of this anthology is uncertain, as is its relation to the Mishnah.

The Mishnah, with the later Talmudim (Palestinian or Jerusalem Talmud, third-fourth centuries AD; Babylonian Talmud, third-sixth centuries AD) constitute the basic corpus of rabbinic teaching, and it is primarily from this literature that we learn of the sayings and deeds of the rabbis whose contributions to Jewish life and thought have been traced here.

B. SOME JEWISH LITERATURE OF PRESUMED PALESTINIAN ORIGIN WRITTEN BEFORE 135 AD

1. *Apocalyptic*

In addition to the developing rabbinic theology, other strands of thought may be identified in Palestinian Judaism of the Roman period. In light of the growing conflict with the Roman authorities, it is little wonder that at least some of this took the form of apocalyptic speculation, as evidenced by the following examples. It is only by the most remarkable of circumstances that this litera- ture has survived, so one may only wonder at the nature of those writings that may have been lost and at the character of the larger spectrum of reflec- tion that they may have represented. This literature is discussed here not only because of the interest it generates in and of itself, but also because it serves as reminder that sages of the Pharisaic-rabbinic tradition were not alone among Palestinian Jews of the Roman period in creating models of theological reflection.

a. *The Apocalypse of Abraham (late first or second century AD).*[22]   A Jewish document with Christian interpolations has been preserved in the Eastern church, its oldest existing copies dating from the fourteenth and fifteenth centuries and written in Old Slavonic. Because the document has received relatively little scholarly attention, systematic attempts to reconstruct its lit- erary history remain yet to be done. However, studies to date suggest that its original language was Semitic, probably Hebrew, and that its author was a Palestinian Jew. Because the Apocalypse of Abraham refers to the destruc- tion of the Temple by the Romans in 70 AD, it must date from a time subse- quent to that event.

The significance of the Apocalypse of Abraham lies in its eschatological speculations. Like many other examples of apocalyptic literature, this docu- ment sees the world in terms of sharply drawn distinctions between good and evil, with angels and demons abounding. Yet the dualism is limited, for God is clearly in control over even the chief of demons, Azazel. History is divided into distinct periods of time, twelve in all (29:2), which will be cli- maxed by the last judgment. Then God's chosen one (31:1) will be sent who will gather the scattered people of God, while at the same time, evil will be destroyed in that the enemies of God will be condemned to a subterranean torment. Although there is no mention of the resurrection of the body, it is evident that the author assumed the continuing existence of the righteous (21:6).

Two themes receive special attention in the Apocalypse of Abraham. The first of these is idolatry, which is identified as a chief sin of the godless and a concern for which occupies the first section of the document. The second is the importance of Israel as God's chosen people and the problem of the na- tion's continuing oppression by gentile powers. This problem is resolved by portraying Israel's suffering as the result of her sin and by the promise of the eventual overthrow of wicked gentile powers.

The first section (chaps. 1–8), reminiscent of passages in Daniel 1–6 and the Additions to Daniel, [23] tells how Abraham, still living with his father Terah, ponders the significance of the idols that his father manufactures. In a series of anecdotes, the foolishness of venerating these idols is illustrated. In one incident, perhaps inspired by Isaiah 44, Abraham places a small idol named Barisat beside a fire over which he intends to cook a meal, and then instructs the idol to blow on the fire if it appears to be in danger of dying. Abraham returns, only to find that the wooden god has fallen into the fire, thereby kindling the flames. When the meal is ready,

> I carried the food to my father to eat. I gave him wine and milk, and he drank and enjoyed himself and he blessed Muramath his god. And I said to him, "Father Terah, do not bless Muramath your god, do not praise him. Praise rather Barisat, you god, because, as though loving you, he threw himself into the fire in order to cook your food." And he said to me, "Where is he now?" And I said, "He has burned in the fierceness of the fire and become dust." And he said, "Great is the power of Barisat! I will make another today, and tomorrow he will prepare my food."
>
> (5:12–17)

Abraham, however, recognizes the foolishness of depending upon such false gods.

The second section is the apocalypse proper (chaps. 9–32), containing several subsections. Initially (9–14), God appears to Abraham, in a scene dependent upon Genesis 15, and commands the angel Iaoel to consecrate Abraham as "friend of God" (9:5). Abraham is then (15–18) carried to heaven in the company of Iaoel who commands Abraham to sing a song of praise to God:

> Eternal One, Might One, Holy El [God], God autocrat
> self-originate, incorruptible, immaculate,
> unbegotten, spotless, immortal,
> self-perfected, self-devised,
> without mother, without father, ungenerated,
> exalted, fiery, . . .
>
> (17:8–11)

A series of visions follows (19–26) in which, among other things, Abraham is shown the various degrees of heaven and their angelic inhabitants (19). A vision of the Garden of Eden, which includes the presence of Azazel, is transposed into a vision of the judgment and of a scene of the division of humankind into the good and the evil (21–23). Abraham's question about the introduction of evil into human life brings God's response, which is couched not in terms of an explanation of the origin of evil, but in terms of further visions of evil deeds (24–25). Abraham is told that, ultimately, the ways of

God are an unfathomable mystery (26). A vision of the destruction of the Temple and its attendant suffering (27) prompts Abraham to ask how long the people's distress will last, but God's reply to the question is difficult to understand, perhaps because of the poor state of the received text (28).

After a Christian interpolation into the text, the final days are described (29). Abraham is told that the evil gentiles will be punished, but

> from your seed will be left the righteous men in their number, protected by me, who strive in the glory of my name toward the place prepared beforehand for them . . . And they will rejoice forever in me, and they will destroy those who have destroyed them, they will rebuke those who will rebuke them through their mockery, and they will spit in their faces.
>
> (29:17–21)

This scene concludes Abraham's visions, but when the patriarch is returned to earth, his dialogue with God continues (30–32). God promises to send his "chosen one"[24] to gather the scattered redeemed (31:1). In the judgment scene that follows, the wicked are dealt with in this manner:

> I [God] will burn with fire those who mocked them [God's people] and ruled over them in this age, and I will deliver those who have covered me with mockery over to the scorn of the coming age. Because I have prepared them to be food for the fire of Hades, and [to be] ceaselessly soaring in the air of the underworld [regions] of the uttermost depths, to be the contents of a wormy belly . . . For they shall putrefy in the belly of the crafty worm Azazel, and be burned by the fire of Azazel's tongue . . .
>
> (31:2–8)

With an apparent reference to the author's own situation, the document concludes.

> "Therefore, hear, Abraham, and see, behold your seventh generation shall go with you. And they will go out into an alien land. And they will enslave them and oppress them as for one hour of the impious age. But of the nation of whom they shall serve I am the judge." And the Lord said this, too, "Have you heard, Abraham, what I told you, what your tribe will encounter in the last days?" Abraham, having heard, accepted the words of God in his heart.
>
> (32:1–6)

b. 2 or 4 Esdras[25] (late first or early second century AD).[26]   About the year 100 AD a Palestinian Jew wrote in Hebrew an apocalyptic treatise that attempts to deal with the theological problem of the continued oppression of the Jewish people by the Romans. In so doing, this individual drew upon the character of Ezra, the scribe and priest who had been instrumental in shaping the life of restoration Jerusalem during the Persian period, and around this figure wove a tale of visionary experiences that were intended to communicate certain truths to Palestinian Jews. Although ostensibly set during the time when the Jews were suffering under Babylonian rule, the book clearly uses the figure of the Babylonian destruction of Jerusalem (3:1) as symbolic of the Roman destruction of the city in 70 (compare the manner in which Daniel and Revelation, the primary canonical apocalypses, also use Babylon as a thinly veiled figure for a present oppressor).

At a time subsequent to the circulation of this apocalypse within the Palestinian Jewish community, it was adapted by a Christian writer who, probably late in the second century, added an introduction (chaps. 1–2). In perhaps the third century another Christian added a conclusion (15–16), and in this expanded form, the book achieved deuterocanonical status within the church. It was included in the Vulgate (the oldest extant texts of 2/4 Esdras are in Latin) and thus passed into the Apocrypha of Protestant Bibles. In this regard 2 or 4 Esdras enjoys the distinction of being the only deuterocanonical book that did not appear in the Septuagint. Our discussion will be concerned only with the Jewish apocalypse.

The significance of 2/4 Esdras lies in the fact that it is an important response to the destruction of the Temple by the Romans in 70. In this regard it is to be compared with such documents as the Apocalypse of Abraham and 2 Baruch, writings with which 2/4 Esdras shares certain features in common. It is also one of the latest examples of a Jewish apocalypse. (The crushing of the revolt of Bar Kokhba would effectively put an end to apocalyptic speculations concerning the future of Israel, but even now, perhaps thirty-five years before Bar Kokhba, much rabbinic thought coursed in nonapocalyptic channels, a tendency that doubtless received at least some of its impetus from the strong apocalyptic flavor of early Christian theology.) The themes of the present evil age and of the coming of the kingdom of God, which are evident in 2/4 Esdras, are typical apocalyptic concerns, as are the final judgment and the role of the Davidic messiah in the establishment of the kingdom.

The book falls rather neatly into a series of seven visions. In the first (3:1—5:20), Ezra, who is in Babylon, laments the sufferings of his people. He acknowledges their innate sinfulness, but protests that they are no more evil than the triumphant Babylonians, thus suggesting that the fault for the Jews' distress may lie with God who has punished the people because he did not lift the burden of sin from them.

Yet you did not take away their evil heart from them,
so that your law might produce fruit in them.
(3:20)

To the angel Uriel, who now appears, Ezra repeats the question with added force (4:22–25). The answer he receives contrasts the present age of suffering with the future age:

> this age is full of sadness and infirmities. For the evil about which you ask me has been sown, but the harvest of it has not yet come.
>
> (4:27–28)

When Ezra wants to know how long before the coming of the new age, Uriel replies that the time is in God's hands (4:33–43), but that the new age will be preceded by terrifying signs (4:44—5:13).

The second vision (5:21—6:34) repeats Ezra's questions and, as before, an angel appears to provide answers. In response to Ezra's attempts to understand the ways of God, the angel provides a Job-like response.

> [God] said to me [Uriel], "At the beginning of the circle of the earth, before the portals of the world were in place, and before the assembled winds blew . . . then I planned these things, and they were made through me alone and not through another; just as the end shall come through me alone and not through another."
>
> (6:1–6; cf. Job 38—41)

In the third vision (6:35—9:25) the question of the final judgment is raised. To this Uriel responds in terms of God's messiah:

> For my son the Messiah shall be revealed with those who are with him, and those who remain shall rejoice four hundred years. After those years my son the Messiah shall die, and all who draw human breath. Then the world shall be turned back to primeval silence for seven days, as it was at the first beginnings, so that no one shall be left.
>
> (7:28–30)[27]

When the punishment of all evil persons is promised, Ezra, in a remarkable plea for the universal salvation for all humankind, expresses the hope that, on the judgment day, the righteous may be able to intercede for the unrighteousness (7:102–103, 132–140). But Uriel's answer is firm:

> The Most High made this world for the sake of many, but the world to come for the sake of only a few . . . Many have been created, but only a few shall be saved.
>
> (8:1–3)

The fourth vision (9:26—10:59) marks a transition from Ezra's grief, out of which his questions have emerged, to a new sense of hope. Ezra sees a woman in lamentation over her son. But as he speaks with her, she is transformed into a city. The passage that describes this change is pivotal for the entire book:

> While I was talking to her, her face suddenly began to shine exceedingly; her countenance flashed like lightening, so that I was too frightened to approach her, and my heart was terrified. While I was wondering what this meant, she suddenly uttered a loud and fearful cry, so that the earth shook at the sound. When I looked up, the woman was no longer visible to me, but a city was being built, and a place of huge foundations showed itself.
>
> (10:25–27)

Suffering Israel has become the New Jerusalem.

The fifth vision (11:1—12:39) is, like Daniel 7, an allegory of human history. Here an eagle represents the Roman Empire and a lion the messiah of God:

> And as for the lion whom you saw rousing up out of the forest and roaring and speaking to the eagle and reproving him for his unrighteousness, and as for all his words that you have heard, this is the Messiah whom the Most High has kept until the end of days, who will arise from the offspring of David, and will come and speak with them. He will denounce them for their ungodliness and for their wickedness, and will display before them their contemptuous dealings. For first he will bring them alive before his judgment seat, and when he has reproved them, then he will destroy them.
>
> (12:31–33)

The sixth vision (13:1–58) also concerns a messianic figure, in this case a man rising from the turbulent sea. From the top of Mt. Zion he will destroy the enemies of God.

The final vision (14:1–48) portrays Ezra as a new Moses who is commissioned by an angel to record the scriptures. He gathers five scribes and goes with them into a field.

> The Most High gave understanding to the five men, and by turns they wrote what was dictated, using characters that they did not know. They sat forty days; they wrote during the daytime, and ate their bread at night. But as for me, I spoke in the daytime and was not silent at night. So during the forty days, ninety-four books were written. And when the forty days were ended, the Most High spoke to me, saying, "Make public the twenty-four books that you wrote first, and let the worthy and the unworthy read them; but keep the seventy that were written last, in order to give them to the wise among your people. For in them is the

spring of understanding, the fountain of wisdom, and the river of
knowledge. And I did so.

(14:42–48)[28]

There are several interesting points of contact between 2/4 Esdras
and the New Testament, although direct influence of one upon the other
is impossible to establish.[29] The statement that "many have been created,
but only a few shall be saved" (8:3) is similar to Matthew 22:14 and Luke
13:23–24, while Ezra's wish to know the time remaining until the coming of the new age (4:33) is reminiscent of the question of the disciples in
Luke 21:7. Comparison may also be made between 12:42, where Ezra is
described as "a lamp in a dark place," and the "lamp shining in a dark
place" of 2 Peter 1:19. The figure of the redeemed community as a new
city (10:25–27) is parallel to the New Jerusalem of Revelation 21:2.

---

c. *Two Baruch (late 1st or early 2d c. AD).*[30]   Yet another apocalyptic Palestinian Jewish response to the destruction of Jerusalem in 70 AD is 2 Baruch.
Although the oldest copy is a Syriac manuscript of the sixth or seventh century AD, the work was probably composed in Hebrew near the beginning of
the second century. It is likely the creation of more than one author.

As in 2/4 Esdras, a figure from the Babylonian period is chosen as the prin-
cipal for this apocalypse, in this case Jeremiah's friend and scribe (Jer. 36:4).
And although the action purportedly takes place after the destruction of 587
BC, it is clear that the disaster of 70 AD is the focus of concern.

To the pressing problem of the destruction of the city and Temple, 2 Baruch
replies that the tragedy was the work of God, not only as punishment for the
sin of the people, but—more importantly—as a step toward the establishment
of the New Jerusalem, a heavenly city planned by God from the beginning
and revealed to Adam, Abraham, and Moses (4:2–7). During the interim between the present evil age and the wonderful age to come, God's people must
be faithful to the Torah, for out of that faithfulness comes eternal life (32:1,
38:1, and elsewhere). Also prominent in the outlook of 2 Baruch is the role of
the messiah, whom God will send at the end of the present suffering (29:3) to
establish God's kingdom of righteousness and peace. The messiah will destroy the evil nations (39:7–8, and elsewhere) and will establish a time of great
abundance for the righteous (29:4–7, 73:2—74:4).

The structure of 2 Baruch is somewhat complex, but eight major sections
may be identified. The first section (chaps. 1–9) describes the destruction of
the Temple. In response to Baruch's questions when he learns that the city is
to be destroyed, the Lord responds that the destruction is not to be permanent, but should be understood as preparation for the establishment of the
heavenly Temple.

It [the true Temple] is not this building that is in your midst now; it is that which will be revealed, with me, that was already prepared from the moment I decided to create Paradise. And I showed it to Adam before he sinned. But when he transgressed the commandment, it was taken away from him—as also Paradise. After these things, I showed it to my servant Abraham in the night between the portions of his victims [cf. Gen. 17]. And again I showed it to Moses on Mount Sinai when I showed him the likeness of the tabernacle and all its vessels. Behold, now it is preserved with me—as also Paradise.

(4:3–6)

The second section (10–12) contains a lament by Baruch, while the third (13–20) records a dialogue between God and Baruch that contains affirmations concerning the importance of the Torah and assurances that the present suffering will not continue forever:

Therefore, the days will come and the times will hasten, more than the former, and the periods will hasten more than the ones which are gone, and the years will pass more quickly than the present ones. Therefore, I now took away Zion to visit the world in its own time more speedily.
(20:1–2)

The fourth section (21–34) contains a lengthy prayer by Baruch (21), continued discussion between him and God (22–30), and an address by Baruch to the people (31–34) in which he tells them that he must go away for a time, but that he will return (34). This is one of several points in the text (cf. 43:1–3) where 2 Baruch alludes to the leadership vacuum among Palestinian Jews caused by the destruction of the Sanhedrin and the high priesthood, a vacuum that apparently not everyone considered to be filled by the rabbis of Jamnia. Of more importance in the section, however, is the portrait of the messiah and of the age of peace and prosperity that he will inaugurate.

And it will happen that when all that which should come to pass in these parts has been accomplished, the Anointed One [i.e., Messiah] will begin to be revealed . . . The earth will also yield fruits ten thousandfold. And on one vine will be a thousand branches, and one branch will produce a thousand clusters, and one cluster will produce a thousand grapes . . .

And it will happen after these things when the time of the appearance of the Anointed One has been fulfilled and he returns with glory, that then all who sleep in hope of him will rise . . . But the souls of the wicked will the more waste away when they see all these things. For they know that their torment has come and that their perditions have arrived.
(29:3—30:5)

The fifth section (35–47) bears interesting similarities to 2/4 Esdras 11–12 in that it concerns an allegory upon Rome. As in Esdras, 2 Baruch declares that the power of this oppressive nation will be broken by the messiah, whose "dominion will last forever until the world of corruption has ended" (40:3).

The sixth section (48–52) contains a prayer by Baruch and more dialogue between him and God in which God provides further details concerning the final judgment (50–51). The prayer contains one of the book's several descriptions of the role of the Torah in the life of the people of God.

> In you we have put our trust, because, behold, your Law is with us,
> and we know that we do not fall as long as we keep your statues.
> We shall always be blessed; at least, we did not mingle with the
>   nations.
> For we are a people of the Name;
> We, who received one Law from the One.
> And that Law that is among us will help us,
> and that excellent wisdom which is in us will support us.
>
> (48:22–24)

The lengthy seventh section (53–75) provides Baruch's final vision and its interpretation, and it reiterates many of the themes already addressed. Of special interest is the condemnation of those who have oppressed Israel.

> After the signs have come of which I have spoken to you before, when the nations are moved and the time of my Anointed One comes, he will call all nations, and some of them he will spare, and others he will kill. These things will befall the nations which will be spared by him. Every nation which has not known Israel and which has not trodden down the seed of Jacob will live. And this is because some from the nations have been subjected to your people. All those, now, who have ruled over you or have known you, will be delivered up to the sword.
>
> (72:2–6)

The final section (78–87) contains a letter sent by Baruch to the tribes in exile which urges them (in reality, the Jews living throughout the Roman world) not to forget the traditions of Israel.

> And remember Zion and the Law and the holy land and your brothers and the covenant and your fathers, and do not forget the festivals and the sabbaths. And give this letter and the traditions of the Law to your children after you as also your fathers handed down to you.
>
> (84:8–9)

There are a number of parallels between 2 Baruch and the New Testament, the role of the messiah in the establishment of the kingdom of God being among the more prominent (Mark 13:26, and elsewhere). And mention may also be made of more subtle similarities, such as that between Jesus' high priestly prayer (John 17) and Baruch's intecessory prayer in chapter 48.

2. *Expansions of Biblical Material: The Life of Adam and Eve* (first c. BC to second c. AD)[31]

Because of the interest displayed by Jewish writers of the Hellenistic and Roman periods in employing biblical personalities as the vehicles for their own theological speculations (and often simply as the subjects of their entertaining tales), it is not surprising that the original human beings, Adam and Eve, should play a role in the literature of this era. How many stories of the parents of humankind may have circulated in unknown, but one cycle of such tales appears to have been preserved in a pair of documents, one of which has been transmitted in Greek, the other in Latin. Both seem dependent upon a Hebrew original that was probably composed in Palestine, perhaps during the first century AD. These documents purport to narrate events in the lives of Adam and Eve subsequent to their expulsion from the Garden of Eden, including the murder of Abel and the deaths of Adam and Eve. By means of flashbacks, events relating to the fall of Adam and Eve and their expulsion from the garden are also described.

The Latin document, commonly referred to as The Life of Adam and Eve, is the more inclusive of the two, and will form the basis for the discussion here. The Greek document, traditionally but erroneously entitled The Apocalypse of Moses,[32] contains an important section not included in the Latin recension, one that will receive our attention after our consideration of the Latin version. The relationship of the two documents to one another is not altogether clear, nor their relationship to the common Hebrew original. It is significant, however, that recent scholarship has demonstrated that certain elements within the Life are expansions of material also found within the Apocalypse.[33]

In theological terms, The Life of Adam and Eve projects views common within nonsectarian Judaism of the Roman period. While God is a figure of majesty and splendor, anthropomorphisms similar to those of Genesis 2–3 convey God's nearness to and involvement in the life of the first human family. Angel/demonology is striking, the archangel Michael serving as God's chief emissary, while Satan—a fallen angel—attempts to corrupt the life of humankind. Sin entered human life through the weakness of Eve (Life, 18:1), but repentance leads to salvation for both Adam and Eve, described as, in the case of Adam, the transportation of the soul to the third heaven (Apoc. 37:5). (Adam's body is subsequently buried, as is that of Eve, after "she gave up her spirit to God," Apoc. 38–43.) The resurrection of the righteous dead is a frequent theme in both the Life and the Apocalypse. Paradise is a matter of special emphasis in that it exists in two manifestations, the earthly paradise from which Adam and Eve have been expelled, but where their bodies are buried, and the Paradise of the third heaven, the home of the souls of the righteous dead. There is no trace of messianism in either recension.

In the Latin version, the narrative begins with an account of the repentance of Adam and Eve after their expulsion from the garden (1–8). They are driven to turn to God because of a lack of food and they make their repentance by standing neck-deep in water, Eve in the Tigris River, Adam in the Jordan (9). (This unusual form of penitence may reflect the practice of some Jewish or Christian group that used and copied the Life and, if so, is one of the few sectarian touches in the document). But Satan appears to Eve disguised as an angel and tricks her into obeying him.

> The Lord . . . sent me to bring you up from the water and give you food which you had in Paradise, and for which you have been lamenting. Now therefore come out of the water and I will lead you to the place where your food has been prepared.
>
> (9:4–5)

Satan leads Eve to Adam, who recognizes Satan and who berates Eve for being deceived by him (10–11).

In the ensuing conversation between Adam and Satan, Satan describes how he rebelled against God and was expelled from heaven (12–17), a fall from grace that preceeded and led to the fall of Adam and Eve. The point of Satan's disobedience, as it turns out, is that he refused Michael's order to worship Adam, a creature formed in the image of God.

> And when Michael kept forcing me to worship, I said to him, "Why do you compel me? I will not worship one inferior and subsequent to me. I am prior to him in creation; before he was made, I was already made. He ought to worship me."
>
> When they heard this, other angels who were under me refused to worship him. And Michael asserted, "Worship the image of God. But if now you will not worship, the Lord God will be wrathful to you." And I said, "If he be wrathful with me, I will set my throne above the stars of heaven and will be like the Most High."
>
> (14:3—15:3)

When Adam learns the reasons for Satan's fall, he cries to God for help, whereupon Satan disappears. But Adam continues to stand penitently in the Jordan for forty days (17).

In a brief section (18–24), the birth of Cain is described, after which Michael brings seeds to Adam and instructs him how to grow food. Abel is subsequently born and, at age 122, is murdered by Cain (23:5).[34] Additional sons and daughters are born to Adam and Eve, including Seth.

Next, Adam describes to Seth how, following his and Eve's expulsion from the earthly paradise, he was carried up into the heavenly paradise (25–29). There he saw the Lord, whose appearance "was unbearable flaming fire" (25:3), as well as thousands of angels. Adam receives the sentence of judgment from God, but, in response to Adam's pleading, God promises not to "abolish from your seed forever [those who would] serve me" (27:3).

> After I had worshiped the Lord, Michael the archangel of God immediately took hold of my hand and ejected me from the Paradise of visitation and of God's command. And Michael held in his hand a rod and touched the waters which were around Paradise and they froze. I crossed over and Michael with me, and he took me to the place from where he had seized me.
>
> (29:1–3)

During Adam's final illness (30–44) he gathers his sons about him and tells them the story of his and Eve's fall. God divided paradise into two parts, one of which as Adam's responsibility, the other Eve's.

> The Lord God appointed two angels to guard us. The hour came when the angels ascended to worship in the presence of God. Immediately the adversary, the devil, found opportunity while the angels were away and deceived your mother so that she ate of the illicit and forbidden tree. And she ate and gave to me.
>
> (33:1–3)

The pain of Adam's illness (part of God's judgment upon him) is so intense that he sends Eve and Seth back to paradise.

> Put dust on your heads and prostrate yourselves to the ground and mourn in the sight of God. Perhaps he will have mercy and send his angel to the tree of his mercy, from which flows the oil of life, and will give you a little of it with which to anoint me, that I might have rest from these pains by which I am wasting away.
>
> (36:1–2)

But as they go along, Seth is bitten by a serpent that, when reproached by Eve, answers her that the bite was intended for her, since she first ate the forbidden fruit. But Seth rebukes the serpent, and it leaves (37–39). When they arrive at paradise, they pray for "the oil from the tree of mercy," but instead receive Michael's word that Adam is about to die. Eve and Seth return home with aromatic spices, with which they apparently intend to anoint the body. When Adam is told about the incident with the serpent, he promises that pain, labor, and evil will be the constant companions of humankind (40–44). Adam then dies at age 930 and is buried in the presence of Michael, Uriel, and "all the ranks of angels" (45–48).

> Then Seth saw the extended hand of the Lord holding Adam, and he handed him over the Michael, saying, "Let him be in your custody until the day of dispensing punishment at the last years, when I will turn his sorrow into joy. Then he shall sit on the throne of him who overthrew him.
>
> (47:2–3)

Six days after Adam's death, Eve summons her children and directs them to write the story of their father's and mother's life upon clay tablets for all future generations. She then dies and is buried by her children (49–51).

> After this all her children buried her with great weeping. Then, when they had mourned for four days, the archangel Michael appeared to them and said to Seth, "Man of God, do not prolong mourning your dead more than six days, because the seventh day is a sign of the resurrection, the rest of the coming age, and on the seventh day the Lord rested from all his works." Then Seth made the tablets.
>
> (51:1–3)

In the Greek recension, The Apocalypse of Moses, the same general story line is followed, with details sometimes more, sometimes less elaborately related. Three sections that appear in the Life, however, are omitted from the Apocalypse: (a) the narrative of Adam's repentance up to and including the birth of Cain (Life 1—21); (b) Adam's reminiscences to Seth concerning his expulsion from paradise (Life 25—29) and (c) Eve's directions to her children just before her death (Life 49:1—50:2).

On the other hand, an extended section appears in the Apocalypse that is absent from the Life and in which Eve relates to her children the story of the fall (Apoc. 15–30). She begins by telling how the devil enticed the serpent to rebel against God.

> And the devil spoke to the serpent, saying, "Rise and come to me, and I will tell you something to your advantage." Then the serpent came to him, and the devil said to him, "I hear that you are wiser than all the beasts; . . . Rise and come and let us make him to be cast out of Paradise through his wife, just as we were cast out through him.
>
> (Apoc. 16:1–3)

Then the devil, speaking through the serpent, encounters Eve and entices her to eat of the forbidden fruit (17–19). Before giving it to Eve, however, Satan makes her promise that she will also give it to her husband.

> When he had received the oath from me, he went, climbed the tree, and sprinkled his evil poison on the fruit which he gave me to eat which is his covetousness. For covetousness is the origin of every sin. And I bent the branch toward the earth, took of the fruit, and ate.
>
> (Apoc. 19:3)

Immediately, Eve is overcome with the terrible reality of what she has done, but, true to her word, she calls Adam and invites him to eat, as well. At first, he refuses, but then gives in to her insistence. He, too, realizes the awful truth, and rebukes Eve.

> Then I quickly persuaded him. He ate, and his eyes were opened, and he also realized his nakedness. And he said to me, "O evil woman! Why have you wrought destruction among us? You have estranged me from the glory of God."
>
> (Apoc. 21:5–6)

God appears in paradise, causing all the flowers to bloom. But when God cannot find Adam, he calls to him and, when Adam confesses his nakedness, God realizes what the man and woman have done (22–23). Then, in a passage that closely follows the thought of Genesis 3:14–19, God curses (in this order) Adam, Eve, and the serpent (24–26). God then orders the angels to cast the man and woman from paradise, but when Adam begs for mercy and asks for fruit from the tree of life, God denies his request, yet promises:

> But when you come out of Paradise, if you guard yourself from all evil, preferring death to it, at the time of the resurrection I will raise you again, and then there shall be given to you from the tree of life, and you shall be immortal forever.
>
> (Apoc. 28:4)

After recounting how God allowed Adam to take sweet fragrances out of paradise, Eve ends her story with an admonition to her listeners.

> Now then, my children, I have shown you the way in which we were deceived. But you watch yourselves so that you do not forsake the good.
>
> (Apoc. 30:1)

A number of interesting parallels may be found between The Life of Adam and Eve and The Apocalypse of Moses, on the one hand, and the New Testament on the other. Because of the difficulty in knowing precisely when the Adam and Eve stories were written, however, it is not possible to establish the influence of one upon the other. It is likely that both the New Testament and the Life share elements which were to some degree current in the first and second centuries AD.[35]

The thought that God's angels should worship the firstborn is present both in the Life (13–14, where Adam is intended) and Hebrews (1:6, where Christ is meant). Eve is presented as the cause of the fall (Apoc. 21:6; 2 Cor. 11:3), while Satan appears as a bright angel (Life 9:1; Apoc. 17:1; 2 Cor. 11:14). The location of paradise in the third heaven is another element in common (Apoc. 37:5; 2 Cor. 12:2), as is the identification of covetousness as the root of human sinfulness (Apoc. 19:3; Rom. 7:7–8).

Chapter 11

SOME JEWISH LITERATURE OF PRESUMED DIASPORA ORIGIN WRITTEN BEFORE 135 AD

Non-Palestinian Jews of the Roman period also suffered conflicts with their rulers, as the widespread disturbances under Trajan attest, the difficulties suffered by Egyptian Jews being especially notable. Yet many Jews of the Roman period Diaspora lived relatively tranquil lives and managed to remain faithful to their traditions at the same time. This variety of experiences is reflected in the wide range of types of literature to come out of the Diaspora, to say nothing of the diversity of points of view this literature exhibits. Noteworthy in this regard is the work of Philo and Josephus, the two most influential Jewish writers of the time who lived outside Palestine.

A. APOCALYPTIC: 2 ENOCH (1ST C. AD)[1]

Earlier in our discussion,[2] we noted the importance of that apocalypse that is termed by modern scholars 1 Enoch. In that work, the core of which dates from about the second century BC, the figure of the patriarch Enoch is elevated to a position of great importance, and by means of a miraculous journey, he becomes a revealer of important truths, especially of an eschatological nature. The author(s) of the present document, also called the Slavonic Apocalypse of Enoch (because of the language of its oldest extant copies), knew either 1 Enoch directly or many of the traditions concerning the patriarch which that writing contains, for a number of features of the older document are incorporated in 2 Enoch, although there are a great many significant differences.

The literary history of 2 Enoch appears to be extremely complex. It is uncertain when or where the document was composed, or in what language. However, a number of scholars believe that it is the work of an Egyptian Jew or Jews writing in the first century AD. Evidences of both Greek and Semitic elements may be discovered in the Slavonic manuscripts, resulting in scholarly arguments in favor of both Greek and Hebrew (or Aramaic) as the original language. But the presence of these elements may also be accounted for if

the Slavonic textual tradition we possess is based on an earlier Greek translation of a Semitic original.

To complicate matters further, 2 Enoch has come down to us in two versions, one much longer than the other. There is wide scholarly judgment that
the shorter form of the text is nearer the original, although the relationship
between the two versions continues to be a matter of uncertainty. The discussion here is based on the shorter version.

There are three major sections in 2 Enoch. In the first section (chaps. 1–37)
Enoch is approached by three "huge men" who are described in language
reminiscent of Daniel 10:6 and Revelation 1:12–16:

> Their faces [were like the shining sun;
> their eyes were] like burning lamps;
> from his mouth (something) like fire was coming forth;
> their clothing was various singing;
> and their arms were like wings of gold.
>
> (2 Enoch 1:5)

These creatures carry Enoch to the first of seven heavens where he is introduced to the "elders" (i.e., angels) who rule over the celestial bodies. Enoch is
next conducted to the second heaven where

> they showed me prisoners under guard, in measureless judgment. And
> there I saw the condemned angels, weeping. And I said to the men who
> were with me, "Why are they tormented?" The men answered me,
> "They are evil rebels against the Lord, who did not listen to the voice of
> the Lord, but they consulted their own will."
>
> (7:1–3)

In the third heaven, Enoch is shown paradise, a lovely garden that is described in terms of the garden in Genesis 2:

> Every tree was in full flower. Every fruit was ripe, every food was in
> yield profusely; every fragrance was pleasant. And the four rivers were
> flowing past with gentle movement.
>
> (8:2)

Enoch is told that this paradise is preserved for the righteous, but he is also
shown, on the northern side of the third heaven, a place of punishment for the
unrighteous where "a black fire blazes up perpetually, and a river of fire coming out of the whole place, with cold ice" (10:2).

In the fourth heaven Enoch is introduced to the mysteries of the movements of the sun and moon, and in the fifth he meets the Grigori, a race of

giants who mourn for their brothers, the fallen angels whom Enoch has met in the second heaven.

In the sixth heaven Enoch sees the seven angels who are responsible for the orderly patterns of celestial bodies and earthly seasons. In the seventh heaven, Enoch witnesses the dazzling court of God.

> They showed me from a distance the Lord, sitting on his throne. And all the heavenly armies assembled, according to rank, advancing and doing obeisance to the Lord. And they withdrew and went to their places in joy and merriment, but gloriously serving him.
>
> (20:3–4)

Then the archangel Vereveil tells Enoch "all the deeds of the Lord" (23:1), which Enoch records in 360 books. And next the Lord expounds to Enoch the mysteries of creation, an account that has little to do with Genesis 1 or other Old Testament creation texts, but that emphasizes the roles of the mythological figures Adail and Arukhas. (The longer version contains a much more elaborate—and presumably later—mythic account of creation.)

The second section (chaps. 38–67) relates how Enoch, upon God's command, returned to his children and instructed them in the things he had learned. Much of this instruction is highly eschatological in nature and has to do with heaven, hell and the future judgment.

> From there I was brought down and I came to the place of condemnation, and I saw hell open, and I saw there a certain [plain], like a prison, a unbounded judgment. And I descended and I wrote down all the judgments of the judged, and I knew all their accusations. And I sighed and wept over the condition of the impious. And I said in my heart, "How blessed is he who has not been born, or who, having been born, has not sinned before the face of the Lord, so that he will not come into this place nor carry the yoke of this place.
>
> (40:13—41:2)

*   *   *   *

> And from there I went up into the paradise, even of the righteous, and there I saw a blessed place, and every creature is blessed, [and] all live there in joy and in gladness and in immeasurable light and in eternal life. Then I said, my children, [and now] I say it to you: Happy is he who reverences the name of the Lord, [and] who serves ceaselessly in front of his face, and who organizes the gifts, offerings of life, and who will live his life and dies. Happy is he who carries out righteous judgment.
>
> (42:3–7)

The moral tone of this section of 2 Enoch is lofty:

> [Happy is he who] clothes the naked with a garment, and to the hungry gives his bread! Happy is he who judges righteous judgment for orphan and widow, and who helps anyone who has been treated unjustly.

> *   *   *   *

> Happy is he in whom is the truth, so that he may speak
>   the truth to his neighbor!
> Happy is he who has compassion, truth and gentleness
>   in his lips!
>
> (42:8–14)

Enoch also addresses Mefusalem (Methuselah) and his brothers, as well as the elders of the people (chaps. 57—63), and finally an assembly of 2,000 men (64—66), before being taken back to heaven (67).

A third section (68—73), which may once have had an existence independent of the rest of 2 Enoch, tells of the death of Methuselah and the miraculous birth of Melkisedek (Melchizedek). This latter individual is born to Sothonim, the wife of Methuselah's friend Nir. After a miraculous conception ("Nir the priest had not slept with her" [71:2]), the heretofore barren woman gives birth to the future priest on her deathbed. When the child is forty days old, God instructs the archangel Gabril:

> Go down onto the earth to Nir the priest, and take the child Melkisedek, who is with him, and place him in the paradise of Eden for preservation. For the time is already approaching, and I, I will pour out the water onto the earth, and everything that is on the earth will perish. And I will raise it up again in another generation, and Melkisedek will be the head of priests in that generation.
>
> (72:1–2)

The significance of 2 Enoch lies in its sharply drawn eschatological portrait of good and evil, of heaven and hell. Those angels and human beings who live in obedience to God are commissioned by a sovereign God to live in eternal bliss, while the disobedient are consigned to unending torment. Yet obedience and disobedience are couched in highly ethical terms. Because man and woman have been created in the image of God, the manner in which one treats one's fellow human beings is in reality the manner in which one treats God.

> The Lord with his own two hands created mankind; and in a facsimile of his own face. Small and great the Lord created. Whoever insults a person's face insults the face of the Lord; whoever treats a persons face

with repugnance treats the face of the Lord with repugnance. Whoever treats with contempt the face of any person treats the face of the Lord with contempt.

(44:1–2)

There are many parallels between the thought of 2 Enoch and that of the New Testament, the strongly eschatological hope, the ethical view of obedience to God (cf. Matt. 25:31–46) and the special place accorded Melchizedek (Heb. 5) being among the more obvious. But all of these elements were present elsewhere in Jewish and Christian thought, so it is impossible to draw direct lines of contact between 2 Enoch and the New Testament.[3]

B. Expansions of Biblical Material:
Joseph and Aseneth (first century bc to second century ad)[4]

One of the most enjoyable tales to come out of the Diaspora of the Roman period is the story of Joseph and Aseneth, written in Greek by an Egyptian Jew sometime between the circulation of the Septuagint (with which the author was familiar) and the early second century AD. The narrative's point of departure is the statement in Genesis 41:45 that Pharaoh gave to Joseph a bride, "Asenath (Aseneth in Greek), the daughter of Potiphera, priest of On." The marriage of a devout Hebrew to the daughter of a pagan priest posed something of a problem for later Jews, and there is evidence that more than one attempt was made to invent stories designed to resolve this dilemma. Joseph and Aseneth was the most successful of these efforts, to judge from the number of copies that have survived from antiquity.

Although the author was a devout Jew, there is little sectarian theologizing in the story or, for that matter, little interest in specific Jewish rituals or traditions. Rather, the author was a member of that group of Hellenized Jews who, while valuing their Jewishness, embraced much of the culture in which they lived, including its literary values. Like Ezekiel the tragedian, Philo the epic poet, and Philo of Alexandria, the author of Joseph and Aseneth used models of Greek literature and thought to spin his tale about the superiority of the God of Israel and the importance of the worship of this God. In this case, the literary vehicle was the Hellenistic romance, with its elements of eroticism and adventure.[5]

One of the purposes of Joseph and Aseneth, if not its main purpose, was social in nature. The author seems concerned to demonstrate that, while Jews might live in peace wit the gentile majority in society, they must not become merged into that majority, but must preserve the distinctiveness of their traditions, including the worship of the God of Israel. Thus, the marriage of

Aseneth to Joseph is impossible until the beautiful young woman converts to Judaism. The Judaism to which she converts, while open to proselytes, does not seek them. It is not militant in its attitude toward gentile society, nor is it excessively defensive. There is no sense of urgency in Joseph and Aseneth that might suggest a period of persecution, such as that reflected in 3 Maccabees. (The violence surrounding the abduction of Aseneth is not that of gentile against Jew, but primarily Jew against Jew.) Rather, the document quietly congratulates itself upon the rightness of Judaism's ways and upon the superiority of the Jews (Joseph becomes king, in the end), gently rebuking the religious practices of its non-Jewish neighbors, and thus displaying the kind of attitude one might expect from a Jew living in a nonthreatening gentile environment.

The theology of Joseph and Aseneth might be described as moderate in its tone. God is the creator and sustainer of all, but there is little interest in the Torah or the cult. Human life is permeated by sin, which is usually equated with idolatry, a senseless form of worship that is perhaps more the result of ignorance than of a corrupted will. Only those who, like Aseneth, do not worship the true God are in need of salvation.

Just as the story was popular in antiquity, it also became a favorite among many Christian readers, particularly in the Armenian church of the Middle Ages, as well as in Europe.[6]

The plot of Joseph and Aseneth falls into two main sections, the first (chaps. 1—22) describing the conversion of Aseneth and her marriage to Joseph, the second (23—29) a plot against Joseph and Aseneth by the son of Pharaoh.

The story begins by introducing Aseneth, the seductively beautiful daughter of the priest Pentepheres (Potiphera of Gen. 41:45). Although she is wooed by suitors from all parts of the realm, she scorns them all and lives a secluded life in the luxuriously appointed tower provided by her father, where she worships the idols of her people (1—2). When Pentepheres learns that he is to be visited by the mighty Joseph, who is traveling throughout Egypt gathering grain, the priest declares his intention to give Aseneth to Joseph to be his bride (3—4). But the young woman angrily protests.

> Why does my lord and my father speak words such as these, to hand me over like a captive, to a man [who is] an alien, and a fugitive . . . No, I will be married to the king's firstborn son, because he is king of the whole land of Egypt.
>
> (4:9–12)

But when Joseph arrives, Aseneth is overcome by the sight of him.

And Aseneth saw Joseph on his chariot and was strongly cut [to the heart], and her soul was crushed, and her knees were paralyzed, and her entire body trembled, and she was filled with great fear.

(6:1)

Joseph enters Pentepheres' home and refreshes himself by eating at a special table ("because Joseph never ate with the Egyptians," [7:1]). He sees Aseneth staring at him from the window of her tower, but he is afraid to meet her because he is so often subjected to unwelcome advances by Egyptian virgins. When Aseneth is presented to Joseph (8), she tries to kiss him, but Joseph resists her.

And as Aseneth went up to Joseph, Joseph stretched out his right hand and put it on her chest between her two breasts, and her breasts were already standing upright like handsome apples. And Joseph said, "It is not fitting for a man who worships God, who will bless with his mouth the living God . . . to kiss a strange woman who will bless with her mouth dead and dumb idols.

(8:5)

Joseph, who is nevertheless moved by the sight of the girl, then prays for her conversion.

Aseneth returns to her tower where she repents of her idolatry, covering herself with sackcloth and ashes, and fasting (10). In response to her repeated prayers (11—13), "a man came to her from heaven" (14:3), in reality, an angel.

His face was like lightening, and his eyes like sunshine, and the hairs of his head like a flame of fire of a burning torch, and his hands and feet like iron shining forth from a fire, and sparks shot forth from his hands and feet.

(14:9)

The angel declares that Aseneth's repentance has been accepted by God and that she is to marry Joseph. Not only that, but her name is to become "City of Refuge," signifying the fact that she has become the model for all proselytes to Judaism (15:7). Then the man miraculously provides Aseneth with a honeycomb, which they both eat together (16), symbolic of the fact that Aseneth, who may now eat the food of the angels, has also, like them, gained eternal life (cf. the "bread from heaven" in John 6:25–59).

Joseph and Aseneth are soon married.

And after this Pharaoh gave a marriage feast and a great dinner and a big banquet for seven days. And he called together all the chiefs of the land of Egypt and all the kings of the nations and proclaimed to the whole land of Egypt saying, "Every man who does any work during the seven days of Joseph's and Aseneth's wedding shall surely die."

And it happened after this, Joseph went into Aseneth, and Aseneth conceived from Joseph, and gave birth to Manasseh and Ephraim, his brother, in Joseph's house.

(21:8–9)

The second section describes how the son of Pharaoh, lusting after the lovely Aseneth, schemes to do harm to Joseph, apparently because he suffers the injured pride of a jilted lover. After unsuccessfully attempting to involve Simeon and Levi in his plot, the prince turns to Dan, Gad, Naphtali, and Asher (22—24). He lyingly tells them that Joseph plans to kill them and invites them to ambush Joseph and Aseneth, killing Joseph, but saving Aseneth to be his wife. In the meantime, he himself is to kill Pharaoh, who is part of Joseph's alleged plot against his brothers, thus allowing him, the prince, to assume the throne of Egypt.

The scheme, however, goes awry when the prince fails to kill his father and when Joseph leaves Aseneth to attend to his duties (25—27). But Aseneth is captured and, in the melee, Dan, Gad, Naphtali, and Asher decide to kill Aseneth and escape.

And Aseneth saw them and was exceedingly afraid and said:

Lord my God, who made me alive again and rescued me from idols and the corruption of death, who said to me, "Your soul will live forever," rescue me from the hands of these wicked men.

And the Lord God heard Aseneth's voice, and at once their swords fell from their hands on the ground and were reduced to ashes.

(27:10–11)

Dan and his evil brothers beg for mercy from Aseneth, who then protects them against the wrath of Simeon and Levi (28). Pharaoh's son, who had been seriously wounded in the fighting by young Benjamin, is about to be slain by the youth. But Levi intervenes to save the prince's life, and when Pharaoh's heir is presented to his father, "Pharaoh rose from his throne and prostrated himself before Levi on the ground" (29:6). But Pharaoh's son dies of his wounds, and shortly thereafter, the monarch himself succumbs to complications brought on by his grief.

And Pharaoh died at a hundred and nine years, and left his diadem to Joseph. And Joseph reigned as king in Egypt for forty-eight years, and after this he gave the diadem to Pharaoh's younger offspring, who was at the brest when Pharaoh died. And Joseph was like a father to Pharaoh's younger son in the land of Egypt all the days of his life.

(29:9)

Curiously, Aseneth's original wish, that she marry into the royal house (4:12), has now been fulfilled, but in a manner vastly different from that in which she earlier hoped.

C. TESTAMENTARY LITERATURE

1. *The Testament of Job* (first century BC to the first century AD)[7]

In discussing the Testaments of the Twelve Patriarchs and the Testament of Moses[8] we noted an important genre of Jewish literature that, in a fashion similar to Genesis 49, purports to give the last words of significant figures from the Old Testament. The Testament of Job is another example of this literature, one which appears to have been composed in Greek by an Egyptian Jew, perhaps a member of the Essene-like sect called the Therapeutae who are known from the writings of Philo. Although this document betrays a knowledge by its author of the Septuagint translation of Job (which in some significant ways is different from the Hebrew Job), and thus could not have been written before about 100 BC, the specific date of its composition is impossible to identify. The Testament of Job was known by some early Christian writers, including Tertullian (c. 160–220) and Eusebius (c. 260–340), yet it never received wide approval among either Christians or Jews.

The Testament of Job, like other examples of testamentary literature, greatly expands the biblical text. In a manner quite foreign to the biblical Book of Job, the Testament is filled with apocalyptic elements. There is a highly developed angelology, while Satan assumes a much more menacing role than in the canonical story. Satan frequently attempts to attack Job and to take his life, often appearing in various disguises. He is referred to not only as Satan (3:6), but as the devil (3:3), the enemy (47:10). The implied dualism, however, is not complete, for God's authority is superior to that of Satan (8:13), over whom God will ultimately triumph. While there is mention in the document of the resurrection of the dead (4:9), members of Job's family (39:12) and ultimately Job himself (52:10) are carried directly to heaven at the time of their deaths.

The Testament of Job is also noteworthy because of the prominence of women within the narrative, Job's wife, Sitis (who is, of course, unnamed in the Bible), playing as especially important role in the narrative. Job 2:9 becomes in the Testament of Job 24—25 an extended speech by Sitis (one of the points where the Testament reflects a knowledge of the Septuagint Job), while elsewhere in the Testament Sitis is portrayed as one who suffers with her husband (21—26), in that she is forced into slavery and must sell her hair for food. In addition to the interest in Sitis, the document displays an interest in the mourning of widows (53:3) and, more importantly, in the transformation of Job's daughters. These three women are given cords from the phylactery previously given to Job by God, the effect of which is miraculous, for the daughters, Hemera, Kasia, and Amalthiea's Horn, experience an ecstatic vision of God and sing hymns in the language of the angels (46—50).

After a brief introduction in which Job (Jobab in the text) calls his children around him (chap. 1), the patriarch tells how an angel appeared to him and told him that the idolatrous house of worship next to which he lived was in reality the place of Satan. In spite of the angel's warning that Job's destruction of the building will incur the terrible wrath of Satan, Job gathered a crowd of fifty youths and destroyed the evil temple (2—5).

The next major section (6—27) describes Satan's assault upon Job. First Satan appears to Job in the disguise of a beggar and plays upon Job's generosity, which is described at length, as is his former wealth.

> I used to have 130,000 sheep; of them I designated 7,000 to be sheared for the clothing of orphans and widows, the poor, and the helpless. And I had a pack of 80 dogs guarding my flocks. I also had 200 other dogs guarding the house. And I used to have 9,000 camels; from them I chose 3,000 to work in every city. After I loaded them with good things, I sent them away into the cities and villages, charging them to go and distribute to the helpless, to the destitute, and to all the widows.
>
> (9:2–5)

But Satan, who in the meantime has received authority from God to attack Job directly, causes his wealth to be destroyed, his children to be killed and his health to be broken (16—20). Job and Sitis are now reduced to the lowest levels of poverty, and even those who knew of his former generosity will not help him (21). When Satan appears to Sitis disguised as a bread merchant, she allows him to cut off her hair in return for three loaves, but as he gives her the bread, he also incites her to complain to Job over their miserable condition (23—25). But Job gently rebukes Sitis and emphasizes the need for patience (the italicized words are taken by the author of the Testament of Job from the biblical text).

> So I answered her, "Look, I have lived seventeen years in these plagues submitting to the worms in my body, and my soul has never been depressed by my pains so much as by your statement, 'Speak some word against the Lord and die.' . . . Why have you not remembered the many

good things that we used to have? *If we have received good things from the hand of the Lord, should we not in turn* endure *evil things?* Rather, let us be patient til the Lord, in pity, shows us mercy. Do you not see the devil standing behind you and unsettling your reason so that he might deceive me too? For he seeks to make an exhibit of you *as one of the senseless women* who misguide their husband's sincerity."

(Test. of Job 26:1–6)

At that, Satan comes out from behind Sitis and, comparing himself to an exhausted wrestler (a Hellenistic metaphor), he admits temporary defeat (27).

The four friends of the biblical Job (including Elihu) now appear as four kings (28—45) who are so astonished by the condition of Job (whom they refer to as "King of all Egypt" [28:7]) that they cannot believe that it is he. Eliphas laments the condition to which Job has fallen (32), but Job responds with a hymn in which he affirms that his throne is not upon earth, but in heaven.

My throne is in the upper world, and its splendor and
majesty come from the right hand of the Father.
    The whole world shall pass away
    and its splendor shall fade. And those who heed it
    shall share in its overthrow.
But my throne is in the holy land, and its splendor is in the
world of the changeless one.

(33:3–5)

However, statements like this cause Baldad to question Job's sanity (35—38), yet Job continues to insist that his afflictions are bearable because they come from the hand of God.

"I do have my wits about me, and my mind is sound. Why then should I not speak out the magnificent things of the Lord? . . .

"Now then, so that you may know that my heart is sound, here is my question for you: Food enters the mouth, then water is drunk through the same mouth and sent into the same throat. But whenever the two reach the latrine, they are separated from each other. Who divides them?"

An Baldad said, "I do not know."

Again I replied and said to him, "If you do not understand the functions of the body, how can you understand heavenly matters?"

(38:1–5)

At this point Sitis reappears, in what appears to be an interpolation into the original text of the document (39—40). When the kings recognize her, she begs them to dig through the rubble of the family home, which had fallen upon her children, so that their bodies might be recovered. Job forbids this, saying, "You will not find my children, since they were taken up into heaven by the Creator their King" (39:12). When Sitis and the kings ask for proof, Job directs their gaze upward where the children may be seen, "crowned with the splendor of the heavenly one" (41:3). Sitis then dies in peace and is mourned by the entire city.

The argument between Job and the kings resumes (41) when Elihu, who has been "inspired by Satan," berates Job for the "boastful grandeur" (41:4) with which he has spoken. As in the biblical Job (38:1), Elihu's speech is followed by the appearance of the Lord, who rebukes the kings. Job intercedes for Eliphas, Baldad, and Sophar, and offers sacrifices on their behalf (42). But as for Elihu, his kingdom is destroyed because he worked as the agent of Satan. Eliphas sings a hymn that concludes with these words:

> Let the holy ones rejoice, let them leap for joy in their hearts,
>   for they have received the splendor they awaited.
> Gone is our sin, cleansed is our lawlessness.
> And the evil one Elihu has no memorial among the living.
>   (43:15–17)

Job is now restored (44), and as he lies dying he speaks his testament to his family.

> And now, my children, behold I am dying. Above all, do not forget the Lord. Do good to the poor. Do not overlook the helpless. Do not take to yourselves wives from strangers. Look, my children, I am dividing among you everything that is mine, so each one may have unrestricted control over his own share.
>   (45:1–4)

In the final major section in the Testament (46–50), Job gives to his daughters the cords from the phylactery he had received from God, with the result described above.

In a brief conclusion, (51—53) Job dies and his soul is received by God.

2. *Testament of Abraham* (1st or 2d c. AD)[9]

Although not strictly belonging to the testamentary genre because of an absence of anything resembling the testament of the patriarch, the Testament of Abraham is so-called because of the prominence of the theme of the patriarch's death. The document, which was almost certainly composed in Greek, has come down from antiquity in two versions, the longer of which seems to be more original (and that will constitute the basis of these comments). Scholarly opinion concerning the place and time of its composition has varied widely, some commentators dating the document as early as 200 BC, others as late as the second century AD. However, the suggestion that it originated in Egypt during the first or second centuries AD has much to commend it.

The Testament of Abraham is almost certainly the work of a Jewish writer, a conclusion based on the centrality of the figure of Abraham and on the lack of any specifically Christian content (aside from one or two glosses inserted by Christian scribes who copied the manuscript). Yet the document is curious in that very few distinctively Jewish traditions may be identified. There is no effort to differentiate between Jew and gentile in describing the human condition, while the theological/ethical ideals of the Testament are more humanitarian than biblical (no mention of circumcision, of Jewish festivals and the like, but condemnation of robbery, murder, and warfare). Salvation seems available to anyone, upon the condition that they repent or, in some cases, that they die a premature death. The final judgment, in fact, seems to be of particular interest to the author, and it is described in the simplest of terms: those whose sins are more numerous than their good deeds are to be condemned, while those with predominately good deeds will be saved. A special category is those in whom good and evil are equally balanced and who can be saved by the intercessory prayers of the righteous living (14:6). In all of this, the emphasis is upon the mercy of God who condemns individuals only if they are beyond redemption, a quality that stands in some contrast to the rigorous views of Abraham, who desires the death of anyone caught in a state of sin (10:12–13).

The portrait of the patriarch is itself curious in that, although he plays a central role in the narrative and is referred to in elevated terms ("honored father, righteous soul elect of God, true friend of the heavenly One [2:3]), Abraham is less virtuous and obedient than one might expect. He stoutly refuses God's command that he die and be transported to heaven, while his zeal for moral behavior has to be curbed by God lest he destroy all of humankind.

Recent scholarship has pointed out that the Testament of Abraham consists of two cycles of narrative that are quite similar in their movement.[10] In the first cycle (chaps. 1—15) God sends the archangel Michael, who is referred to as God's "commander-in-chief," to tell Abraham that he is to prepare for death. Abraham resists and, after a series of events that includes a tour of heaven from which Abraham can see all of humankind engaged in various activities, Michael returns to heaven, his mission unfulfilled. In the second cycle (16—20) God sends Death to Abraham to repeat the demand, but this messenger is likewise rebuffed. After a series of experiences involving Death, which in certain respects parallel those that Abraham had with Michael, Abraham dies and is taken to heaven.

The first cycle opens as God commissions Michael to go to Abraham, who has "lived the measure of his life, 995 years" (1:1), to tell him that he is to prepare for death (1). In a narrative that seems to have Genesis 18:1ff. in mind, we are told how Michael visits Abraham and his family at Mamre, but is unrecognized by them (2—5). After Isaac experiences a revelatory dream, Michael identifies himself and tells Abraham that he must prepare to die.

> And now know, most honored Abraham, that at this time you are about to leave the earthly life and journey to God. And Abraham said to the Commander-in-chief, "O most surprising wonder of wonders! And is it you, then, who are about to take my soul from me?" The Commander-in-chief said to him, "I am Michael, the Commander-in-chief who stands before God, and I was sent to you that I might announce to you the mention of death. And then I shall return to him just as we were commanded." And Abraham said, "Now I do know that you are an angel of the Lord, and you were sent to take my soul. Nevertheless I will not by any means follow you, but you do whatever he commands."
>
> (7:9–12)

Abraham then asks for a tour in order to see "all the inhabited world and the created things" (9:6), a request that is granted. The archangel places Abraham in a heavenly chariot that he then leads over the world in such a manner that the patriarch is permitted to see men and women engaged in a variety of activities: working in the fields, dancing, playing games, burying their dead, celebrating marriages: "In a word he saw everything that was happening in the world, both good and evil" (10:3). But then come scenes of warfare, robbery, murder, and sexual immorality. Abraham asks that these evildoers be killed and such is his standing before the Lord that his wishes are granted:

> And Abraham said, "Lord, Lord, heed my voice and command that wild beasts come out of the thicket and devour them." And as he was speaking, wild beasts came out of the thicket and devoured them.
>
> (10:6–7)

But God becomes alarmed at Abraham's righteous indignation and he commands Michael to bring the tour to a halt "lest he [Abraham] should see the entire inhabited world" (10:12). God then points to his own merciful attitude toward humankind.

> For behold, Abraham has not sinned and he has no mercy on sinners. But I made the world, and I do not want to destroy any one of them; but

I delay the death of the sinner until he should convert and live. Now conduct Abraham to the first gate of heaven, so that there he may see the judgments and the recompense and repent over the souls of sinners which he has destroyed.

(10:14–15)

Abraham is then permitted to view the scenes of God's judgment, which are cast in typical apocalyptic imagery (11–13). There are three levels of judgment, each person being forced to confront, first, Abel (apparently representing all the human victims of sin), second, "the twelve tribes of Israel" and, third, "the Master God of all" (13:5–7). Abraham and Michael pray for the dead and, as a result, the soul of one person who was hanging in the balance is saved (14). Abraham once more refuses to follow Michael to heaven, whereupon the archangel returns to God (15).

In the second cycle God sends death to Abraham to repeat the demand that he prepare for death, but the patriarch still will not comply (16). However, Death is persistent and, whereas he had first appeared to Abraham in a bright and beautiful form, he is now transfigured.

Then Death put off all the bloom of youth and beauty and all the glory and the sunlike form which he had worn and he put on (his) robe of tyranny, and he made his appearance gloomy and more ferocious than any kind of wild beast and more unclean than any uncleanness.

(17:12–13)

When this happens, Abraham's servants die, but Abraham and Death pray for them and they are restored to life (cf. Abraham's and Michael's prayer for the dead, above, one of several parallel features between the first and second cycles). But in the end, Death is too powerful for Abraham, and the patriarch begins to die.

And Abraham entered the depression of death. And Death said to Abraham, "Come, kiss my right hand, and may cheerfulness and life and strength come to you." For Death deceived Abraham. And he kissed his hand and immediately his soul cleaved to the hand of Death. And immediately Michael the archangel stood beside him with multitudes of angels, and they bore his precious soul in their hands in divinely woven linen . . . [and] the undefiled voice of the God and Father came speaking thus, "Take, then, my friend Abraham into Paradise, where there are tents of my righteous ones and . . . where there is no toil, no grief, no moaning, but peace and exhultation and endless life."

(20:7–14)

D. Historiography:
Josephus (c. 36–100 AD)[11]

During the course of our discussions, especially in those sections relating to the history of the Jews in Palestine, we have frequently invoked the name of Josephus. The reason for the prominence of this Roman-Jewish historian in any attempt to understand the period under survey here is quite simple: Josephus has provided the only existing sequential account of the life of Palestinian Jews during the era of Second Temple. While there are a number of surviving examples of contemporary literature that provide indirect knowledge of the history of Second Temple Judaism (the Qumran scrolls, for example), and a few pieces of historical writing that survey limited horizons (1 and 2 Mac.), only Josephus steps out of the period itself to describe it to us. He may not have been alone in his efforts, for the work of Eupolemus was certainly more extensive than the few fragments that have survived,[12] and the number of other Jewish historians who labored during this period, only to have their works completely lost or destroyed, is something we shall never know. Josephus' rival, Justus of Tiberius (see below), of whose work we are aware only because it is mentioned by Josephus, is representative of this unfortunate group. Be that as it may, however, only in Josephus is there anything like a systematic overview of the events within Palestinian Judaism from Zerubbabel's dedication of the Second Temple in 515 BC to Titus' destruction of it in 70 AD.

Precious jewel that it is, Josephus' work is not without its serious flaws. For one thing, Josephus had a number of axes to grind. Because he was in the employment of the Flavian family of emperors (Vespasian, Titus, and Domitian), he it at pains to portray Rome, in general, and the Flavians, in particular, in the best possible light. Because he lived, during his creative years, at least, as a member of the Jewish minority in Rome, he was concerned to portray the traditions of his people in the most positive manner. And because much of his attention is devoted to controversial events in which he himself was a participant, namely, the Jewish War of 66–74 AD, his own actions are described in often flattering terms. In addition, the numerous contradictions and inconsistencies between parallel accounts in, for example, his Life and the Jewish War have caused many readers so question his truthfulness, his memory, or both.

Having acknowledged these things, however, one is forced to admit that, although it is impossible to verify many of Josephus' claims, there is little reason to doubt the main threads of his narratives. The result is that, although the modern reader consumes Josephus with a certain grain of salt, we find him to be dependable, on the whole, and our most complete source of information concerning an era of great importance to both early Judaism and early Christianity.

What we know about Josephus comes from his own hand, primarily from his *Life* and from references to himself in the *Jewish War*. He was born about 36 AD, the son, so he claims, of a Jerusalem priest named Matthias, one of whose ancestors had been a daughter of the high priest Jonathan, brother of Judas Maccabeus.[13] Thus his veins carried Hasmonean blood, an object of pride to many devout Jews. As a young man he became interested in various sects and studied the beliefs and practices of the Sadducees, Essenes, and Pharisees. He even lived the life of a hermit, attaching himself for three years to a recluse named Banus, perhaps a solitary Essene, before returning to Jerusalem and submitting himself to the order of the Pharisees. The frequently critical attitude toward the Pharisees in his writings, however, suggests that his commitment to this sect was either superficial or temporary.

In his twenty-sixth year he traveled to Rome to assist in the release of certain Jewish priests who had been sent there by the governor, Felix, to answer charges (the nature of which Josephus doesn't tell us) before Nero. The brief story of this trip in *Life* contains, in the fashion of a typical Hellenistic romance, an account of Josephus' ship being wrecked at sea and of his successful rescue. Also successful was his mission, for he tells us that, through the friendship of the emperor's wife, Poppea (to whom he was introduced by a Jewish actor), he obtained the liberty of the priests.

When Josephus returned to Jerusalem, he found the country preparing for war. He describes how he tried to discourage his compatriots from taking up arms against the Romans, for, fresh from his visit to their great city, he knew that their superior might would crush any Jewish revolt. "But I could not persuade them," he writes, "for the madness of desperate men was quite too hard for me."[14] When the attempted intervention by Cestius, the Roman governor of Syria, failed, Josephus had little choice but to cast his lot with the rebels. It was soon after this that he was made commander of the Jewish resistance in Galilee, the consequences of which, including his declaration to Vespasian that he was to be the new emperor, we have already noted.[15]

Because of his prophecy about Vespasian and because he cooperated with the Romans during the siege of Jerusalem, Josephus was carried by Titus to Rome at the conclusion of the war. There he was granted Roman citizenship and endowed with a state pension, and there he assumed the name of his patron and came to be called Flavius Josephus. That he had earned the hatred of many Jews is understandable, and there were numerous attempts to undermine his reputation, such as the accusation before a Roman tribunal by a Jewish rebel from Cyrene in North Africa that Josephus had secretly supplied him with arms. But the emperor Vespasian was not distracted from his support of Josephus, who was provided residence in an imperial palace and who was given land in Judaea, from which he drew revenues. After the death of Vespasian, the new ruler, Titus, continued these favors. But with the

accession of Domitian, to whom Josephus expresses his gratitude for perpetuating his special relationship with the Flavian house, it is possible that Josephus' support began to be eroded. How he fared under the new dynasty that
arose with Nerva (96 AD) is unknown. It is likely that he died shortly after
the year 100 AD.

The *Jewish War* was Josephus' first literary work, begun shortly after his
arrival with Titus in Rome. The first draft was composed in Aramaic, but, in
order to insure a larger circulation, the work was revised in Greek. For this
purpose, Josephus had at his disposal Greek scribes, since his own facility in
that language was limited. The work is divided into seven books and covers
the period between the capture of Jerusalem by Antiochus Epiphanes and its
destruction by Titus. The primary purpose of the *Jewish War* seems to have
been, not only to glorify Vespasian and Titus, but to demonstrate the folly of
resisting the power of Rome.

Josephus' next work was his *Antiquities of the Jews*, written in Greek
(again, with assistance) during the reign of Domitian and modeled on the
Roman Antiquities of the first century BC historian Dionysus of Halicarnas-
sus (on the Aegean coast of Asia Minor). Like Dionysus' work, Josephus' *Antiquities* is composed of twenty books, the first ten of which retell the
history of Israel to the Babylonian captivity, while the last ten relate events
to the beginning of the war with Rome. This latter section is of great interest because it is the only material we possess that comes near to being a
systematic account of events in Palestine up to the time of Antiochus
Epiphanes. In addition, although events relating to the Hasmonean and
Herodian kingdoms had been previously described in *Jewish War*, they are
often treated in *Antiquities* by means of additional detail. The sources of information that Josephus employed in writing the *Antiquities* were both Jewish and non-Jewish, among which were two he credits directly, Nicholas of
Damascus, a Greek historian who was a friend of the emperor Augustus
and of Herod the Great, and the Greek writer Strabo (c. 63 BC–24 AD). The
mood of the *Antiquities* is less pro-Roman than *Jewish War*, since Josephus'
primary purpose is to demonstrate to the Roman world the lofty and venerable nature of the traditions of the Jews.

To the *Antiquities* Josephus added an appendix, a brief document entitled
Life of Flavius Josephus, in which the historian deals primarily with events
during the war with Rome. The *Life*, however, is of further interest in that it
provides a summary biography of Josephus as a young man. It was written in
response to charges from a certain Justus of Tiberias, whose own history of
the war with Rome had portrayed Josephus in an unflattering manner.

Josephus' final completed work is a defense of Judaism entitled *Against
Apion*. Here Josephus skillfully attempts to demonstrate the superiority of the
Torah to the moral and religious standards of the gentile world.

In the concluding sentences of the *Antiquities* Josephus declares his intention to write a history of the Jews from the time of the destruction of Jerusalem to the reign of Domitian, as well as

> a work in four books on the opinions that we Jews hold concerning God and His essence, as well as concerning the laws, that is, why according to them we are permitted to do some things while we are forbidden to do others.[16]

But these ambitious plans were apparently never fulfilled.

E. HELLENISTIC PHILOSOPHY

1. *The Wisdom of Solomon* (1st c. BC–1st c. AD)[17]

During some period of persecution of the Jewish community in Egypt one (or possible more) of the members of that community penned an exhortation to his fellow Jews in which he appealed for faithfulness to the God of Israel. Although influenced by the thought-world of Hellenism, the writer's emphasis upon Widsom as God's creative and redemptive force in life reveals that he stands in a tradition that extends back through such writings as Sirach and Job to the Old Testament Proverbs. And, in keeping with his loyalty to traditions of the Jews, he exhorts his readers to avoid the seductions of idolatry and the power of those who practice it. The specific crisis that called forth this appeal is unknown, but the time of the tribulations of Egypt's Jews during the persecutions under Caligula (37–41 AD) has been suggested.

The theology of the Wisdom of Solomon repudiates the notion that evil people can exercise ultimate power over God's faithful people. Neither torment nor death can separate the righteous from God and, in the end, it is they who will preside over the destruction of their oppressors.

> Then the righteous will stand with great confidence
> in the presence of those who have oppressed them
> and those who make light of their labors.
> When the unrighteous see them, they will be shaken with dreadful
> fear,
> and they will be amazed at the unexpected salvation of the
> righteous.
>
> (5:1–2)

As for Wisdom, it is praised in language that makes it clear that this quality is nothing other than God at work in the arena of human life, something closely akin to the Christian understanding of the work of the Holy Spirit. Building upon an obvious knowledge of Proverbs 8 and Sirach 24, the author describes Wisdom in terms of an elaborate personification (7:22—9:18).

The philosophical views of the Wisdom of Solomon are as significant as its theology, the interplay between philosophy and theology being of particular fascination to scholars.[18] Elements of Stoic thought as well as the Isis mystery have been detected, but it is perhaps the influence of Platonism that is most significant. Dame Wisdom (*Sophia* in Greek) is, in philosophical terms, the emanation of the glory of God (7:25), the mind of God at work (8:4). She is also to be identified with the *logos* principle, the "Word" by which God created the world.

"who have made all things by your word,
and by your wisdom have formed humankind.
(9:1–2)

In these and in other respects, the Wisdom of Solomon bears remarkable similarities to the thought of Philo of Alexandria, the greatest synthesist of Jewish theology and Hellenistic philosophy, whom we shall consider just below. Whether Philo and the author of the Wisdom of Solomon exercised influence upon one another, or whether they both drew from a common body of Hellenistic-Jewish thought is difficult to know, primarily because of the scholarly uncertainty over the precise date of the Wisdom of Solomon.

There are three rather distinct divisions within this document. The first section (1:1—6:11), which has been referred to as the book of eschatology, is concerned with divine rewards and punishments. The section is bracketed by appeals to the ruling (Roman?) authorities that they learn God's Wisdom and that they practice the justice and righteousness that Wisdom teaches (1:1, 6:1–11).

Love righteousness, you rulers of the earth,
think of the Lord in goodness
and seek him with sincerity of heart; . . .
(1:1)

Between these brackets, the author parodies the thought of the wicked, who tell themselves that

our life will pass away like the traces of a cloud,
and be scattered like mist
that is chased by the rays of the sun
and overcome by its heat.
(2:4)

Because they have concluded that life is evanescent and that they are account-
able to no one, they feel free to persecute the righteous.

What they do not know, however, is that

> But the souls of the righteous are in the hand of God,
> and no torment will ever touch them.
> In the eyes of the foolish they seemed to have died,
>
> *   *   *   *
>
> but they are at peace.
> For though in the sight of others they were punished,
> their hope is full of immortality.
>
> (3:1–4)

The second section (6:12—9:18) describes Wisdom in terms of an elaborately crafted personification. Again, there is an appeal to the governing authorities to heed Wisdom's ways:

> Therefore if you delight in thrones and scepters, O monarchs over the
> peoples,
> honor wisdom, so that you may reign forever.
>
> (6:21)

King Solomon begins to describe his personal quest for Wisdom (thus the
text assumes the authority of Israel's king to speak to the rulers of Rome) to
whom he was led by God. Although the connection with Israel's Wisdom tradition is clear, it is here that the thought-world of Hellenistic philosophy is
most evident.

> For she is a breath of the power of God,
> and a pure emanation of the glory of the Almighty;
> therefore nothing defiled gains entrance into her.
>
> Although she is but one, she can do all things,
> and while remaining in herself, she renews all things;
> in every generation she passes into holy souls
> and makes them friends of God, and prophets;
> for God loves nothing so much as the person who lives with wisdom.
>
> (7:25, 26–28)

Wisdom is then compared to a bride whom Solomon loved from his youth
(8:1). To love her is to acquire four cardinal virtues so important to Stoic
philosophers: self-control, prudence, justice, and courage (8:7). Only by means
of the presence of Wisdom is it possible for the ruler to govern in a manner
acceptable to God (9:10–12).

The final section (10–19) deals with the place of the Jews in a hostile gentile world and recalls the themes of justice and retribution prominent in 1:1—6:11. The section begins by recalling that it was Wisdom who guided the lives of important figures from Israel's past (10), and then calls attention to the manner in which God defended the Israelites from the Egyptians at the time of the exodus (11). A principal sin of the Egyptians is that of idolatry, which is thoroughly denounced in an extended passage (11:15—15:19) that often seems to depend upon the Second Isaiah (cf. Isa. 44:9–20).

A skilled woodcutter may saw down a tree easy to handle
* * * *
[and] make a useful vessel that serves life's needs,
and burn the cast-off pieces of his work
to prepare his food, and eat his fill.
But a cast-off piece from among them, useful for nothing,
a stick crooked and full of knots,
he takes and carves with care in his leisure,
* * * *
he forms it like the image of a human being,
* * * *
and sets it in the wall, and fastens it there with iron,
* * * *
When he prays about possessions and his marriage and children,
he is not ashamed to address a lifeless thing.
(13:11–17)

In the remaining chapters (16–19) the text returns to contrasting God's treatment of Israel with that of the Egyptians at the time of the exodus, demonstrating that God repeatedly saved the former, while inflicting punishment upon the latter.

When they had resolved to kill the infants of your holy ones,
and one child [i.e., Moses] had been abandoned and rescued,
you in punishment took away a multitude of their children,
and you destroyed them all together by a mighty flood.
(18:5)

The section and the entire document conclude with a statement designed to encourage the people of God in the troubled times through which they were living.

For in everything, O Lord, you have exhalted and glorified your
people;
and you have not neglected to help them at all times and in all places.
(19:22)

Several scholars have commented upon similarities between the thought of the Wisdom of Solomon and aspects of the New Testament.[19] Since the New Testament nowhere quotes the Wisdom of Solomon directly, immediate influence is beyond proof, so the possibility remains open that both this document and the writers of the New Testament were drawing upon common sources. However, the following parallels are striking.

(1) Observations concerning God's protection of the righteous in the Wisdom of Solomon and the statement of the bystanders at the crucifixion in Matthew 27:

> For if the righteous man is God's son he will help him, and will deliver him from the hand of his adversaries.
>
> (Wis. Sol. 2:18; RSV)

> He trusts in God; let God deliver him now, if he wants to; for he said, "I am God's Son."
>
> (Matt. 27:43)

(2) The possibility of knowing God through the perception of the natural world, a subject also discussed by the Stoics, receives attention in the following texts:

> For all people who were ignorant of God were foolish by nature;
> and they were unable from the good things that are seen to know the one who exists,
> nor did they recognize the artisan while paying heed to his works.
>
> (Wis. Sol. 13:1)

> Ever since the creation of the world his eternal power and divine nature, invisible though they are, have been understood and seen through the things he has made. So they are without excuse; . . .
>
> (Rom. 1:20)

(3) The image of the potter and the clay (cf. Jer. 18:1–11):

> A potter kneads the soft earth
> and laboriously molds each vessel for our service,
> fashioning out of the same clay
> both the vessels that serve clean uses
> and those for contrary uses, making all alike;
> but which shall be the use of each of them
> the worker in clay decides.
>
> (Wis. Sol. 15:7)

> Has the potter no right over the clay, to make out of the same lump one object for special use and another for ordinary use?
>
> (Rom. 9:21)

2. *Philo of Alexandria* (c. 20 BC–50 AD)[20]

The history of Judaism during the Hellenistic and Roman Periods is peppered with examples of attempts by faithful Jews to accommodate their traditions to the powerful intellectual and cultural appeal of Hellenism. Of the various means by which this effort was mounted none is more fascinating than that represented by the philosopher Aristobulus[21] and by the writer of the Wisdom of Solomon, both of whom attempted to reconcile the traditions of Jewish theology and Greek philosophy. The supreme example of this type of Jewish-Hellenistic fusion, however, is to be found in the Alexandrian philosopher-exegete Philo, sometimes called Philo Judaeus, whose influence upon successive generations of religious thinkers, especially Christian, is of the highest order.

Next to nothing is known of the life of this extraordinary individual. In his own words, Philo tells of having been a part of a delegation of Alexandrian Jews who went to Rome in 40 AD to seek the help of the emperor Caligula in putting a stop to the persecution of the Jewish community in Egypt.[22] He also mentions a visit to the Jerusalem Temple, which took place on another occasion. We may guess that his family, thus he himself, occupied a place of leadership within the community of Alexandrian Jews and that he was an individual of some financial independence, in light of the fact that his brother Alexander was one of the richest men in the empire.

It is apparent from reading his works that Philo was thoroughly educated in the literature of the Hellenistic world. He is familiar at firsthand with the philosophers, poets and dramatists who wrote in the Greek language, a language of which he himself was a master. The extent of his exposure to the traditions of the Jews is less clear, however, for in many ways he seems distant from the developing Palestinian rabbinic theology. He apparently saw no need to learn Hebrew, since he considered the Septuagint to be inspired in its every word, and his indebtedness to this translation he demonstrates time and again. That he was aware of the work of other Hellenized Jews, such as Aristobulus and the author of the Letter of Aristeas, there can be little doubt. It is less certain that he knew the Wisdom of Solomon, as we have noted, or 4 Maccabees.

For all the greatness of his contribution, however, Philo is difficult to categorize, especially in philosophical terms. The basic core of his outlook is Platonic, yet so many and varied are the components of his teachings that he has often been accused of simply picking and choosing those elements out of the Hellenistic philosophical tradition that appealed to him at the moment. An alternative view, however, is that Philo's apparent eclecticism is, in reality, the eclecticism of the Platonism of his day, the so-called Middle Platonism[23] that, since the days of the Academy in Athens, had grown to include elements from the teachings of the Stoics, the Neopythagoreans and many others. In any event, Philo strongly argues, in a manner reminiscent of Aristobulus, that of all the philosophers the greatest is Moses, and the Torah is the highest expression of those truths that the world of Greek philosophy had attempted to elucidate. The intellectual skill and the variety of arguments with which he drives this point home constitute one of the truly remarkable aspects of the work of this creative thinker.

Another significant feature of the thought of Philo is his mysticism. God is not simply an abstraction to be intellectually apprehended, but is the object of the devotion of the soul. For Philo, God relates to the creation in an ongoing manner by means of a hierarchy of beings in which the intermediary between God and creation is the *logos*. The *logos*, which is fashioned in the image of God, is that force that gives to the world its form and order, but at the same time mediates God's attributes of grace, mercy, and justice. Thus, by means of the *logos* men and women may know that One who is basically unknowable, whose being is beyond the power of thought to contain and who may be embraced only by the love of the soul. For the individual, the result of this mystic engagement with God is peace, yet it is a peace characterized by ecstatic flights of joy.

> When soaring upward the mind has spied the atmosphere and its changes, it is borne yet higher to the ether and celestial revolution, and is carried around with the dances of the planets and fixed stars, in accordance with the laws of perfect music, following the love of wisdom that guides it. When it has transcended all sensible substance . . . it is possessed by a sober intoxication . . . and inspired, filled by another sort of longing and a more fitting desire. Escorted by this to the uppermost vault of things intelligible, it seems to be on its way to the Great King himself . . .[24]

A third way in which Philo profoundly influenced later thinkers and exegetes was his manner of interpreting scripture. On one level Philo was ready to admit the literal or common sense meaning of a scriptural passage, that is, that there really was an Abraham and a Moses and a David who did the things attributed to them in the Bible. But on another, higher level, the text was to be read allegorically; that is, its essential meaning lay hidden and must be coaxed from the text by the skills of the interpreter. In identifying allegory as the key to scripture, Philo enjoyed ample precedent in both Hellenistic (e.g., the Stoics) and Jewish (e.g., Ezekiel) traditions. Yet the creativity that Philo brought to the allegorical task surpassed that of most interpreters and laid a foundation upon which Christian exegetes were to build for centuries. The nature of Philo's allegorical method, and the extent to which he depended

upon the very words of the Septuagint, are illustrated in the following passage. (Note that only the Septuagint uses the phrase "you shall die the death."
The Hebrew text says simply, "you shall die.")

> He [Moses] says further, "In the day that you eat of it, you shall die the
> death" (Gen. 2:17). And yet after they have eaten, not only do they not
> die, but they beget children and become for others the cause of life.
> What then is to be said? That death is twofold, one of men in general,
> the other of men in particular. The death of man is the separation of the
> soul from the body, while the death of the soul is the destruction of
> virtue and the acquisition of vice. Therefore he says not only "die" but
> "die the death," indicating not the common death, but that special death
> truly so called, that of the soul becoming entombed in every sort of pas-
> sion and vice.[25]

The corpus of Philo's writings has been fairly well preserved, although
some individual units of his work have been lost, while others have survived
only in fragmentary form. Three types of writings are commonly recognized,
the first being *Questions and Answers to Genesis and Exodus*, a midrash on scripture that typically proceeds in verse-by-verse fashion, providing, first, a literal interpretation of the text, then a more extended allegorical exegesis.
Questions and Answers has survived in fragments only, smaller sections in
Greek, larger sections in the Armenian language.

A second body of exegesis is that of the *Allegory of the Law*, a group of treatises that were originally at least ten in number: *On the Creation of the World,
Concerning Abraham, On Joseph, Life of Moses, On the Decalogue, On the Special
Laws, On the Virtues, On Rewards and Punishments, On Isaac* (now lost), and *On
Jacob* (also lost). Less midrashic than *Questions and Answers, Allegory of the Law*
appears to have been written for those who, like himself, were open to the
claims of both the Bible and the Hellenistic philosophers. It is principally here
that Philo argues for the superiority of the Torah and that he lifts the great
ancestors of Israel—primarily Moses—as persons endowed with special
power to lead men and women into a mystic relation to God.

A third group of Philo's writings contains treatises that, in one form or
another, are intended to justify Judaism to gentile intellectuals. This category
includes *Apology for the Jews*, as well as *Against Flaccus* and *Embassy to Gaius*,
both of which deal with the persecution of the Jews under Caligula and with
Philo's journey to Rome. *The Contemplative Life* describes a group known as the
Therapeutae, a sect similar to the Essenes of which Philo may have been a
member. Other writings of a philosophical nature include *That Every Good
Man is Free, On the Eternity of the World,* and *On Providence*.

Although Philo's work was considered of little value by those in the mainstream of rabbinic Judaism, early Christian thinkers praised him highly, an

esteem that resulted in the preservation of most of his works. The church historian Eusebius of Caesarea (c. 260–340 AD) records a tradition that Philo was influenced by Paul and that not only was Philo's teaching about the *logos* identical to the Christian doctrine of the Trinity, but that the Therapeutae were a Christian sect. Whatever the value of this doubtful memory, it is obvious that the early Christian exegetes were deeply impressed by Philo's allegorical method since it allowed them to shape texts, particularly from the Septuagint, to meet their own theological agenda. The result was that, not only did Jerome list Philo among the church fathers, but allegory became the principal method of Christian biblical interpretation until the Reformation of the sixteenth century. Philo is also credited with exercising an important influence upon medieval Jewish mysticism.

These few examples of Philo's work should provide additional evidence of his style and his teaching. Concerning the significance of Moses and the Torah, he writes:

> I intend to record the life of Moses, whom some consider the lawgiver of the Jews, others as the interpreter of the Holy Laws, a man who is in every respect the greatest and most perfect, and whom it is my wish to make known to those who deserve not to be uninformed of him. For while the fame of the laws he left behind has traveled throughout the inhabited world and reached the ends of the earth, the man himself as he was in reality is known to few. This was due to the unwillingness of Greek men of letters to consider him worthy of mention, probably through envy . . .

> But Moses' laws alone, firm, unshaken, unswerving, stamped as it were by the seals of nature herself, remain solid from the day they were first enacted to now, and there is hope they will remain for all future ages as though immortal, as long as the sun and moon and the entire heaven and universe exist.[26]

Philo's allegorical method and his commingling of the Hellenistic philosophical tradition (in this case, the four Stoic virtues) with the biblical message (the story of the Garden of Eden) is in evidence in the following passage, a commentary on Genesis 2:10–14. Note also the reference to Wisdom (*Sophia*).

> "A river issues from Eden to water the garden, and there it is separated into four heads; the name of the one is Pheison; that is that which circles about the whole land of Evilat, there is where the gold is; and the gold of that land is good; and there is the ruby and the emerald. And the name of the second river is Geon; this skirts all the land of Ethiopia. And the third river is Tigris" [Gen. 2:10–14]. By these rivers he [Moses] wishes to indicate the particular virtues. These are four in number, wisdom, self-control,

courage, justice. The largest river, of which the four are effluences, is generic virtue, which we have called goodness. Generic virtue takes its beginning from Eden, the wisdom of God, which is full of joy, brightness and delight, exulting in and priding itself only on God its Father; but the four specific virtues derive from the generic virtue, which like a river irrigates the right conduct of each of them with the abundant flow of noble actions.[27]

This final passage describes the role of the *logos*.

To his chief messenger and most venerable Logos, the Father who engendered the universe has granted the singular gift, to stand between and separate the creation from the Creator. This same Logos is both suppliant of every anxiety-ridden mortal before the immortal and ambassador of the ruler to the subject. He glorifies in this gift and proudly describes it in these words, "And I stood between the Lord and you" [Deut. 5:5], neither unbegotten as God, nor begotten as you, but midway between the two extremes, serving as pledge for both . . . .[28]

3. *Fourth Maccabees* (first century AD)[29]

The stories of the martyrs Eleazar and the family of seven brothers and their mother described in 2 Maccabees (Eleazar, 6:18–31; the brothers and their mother, 7:1–42)[30] form the raw material for a didactic text, in Greek, from the Roman period Diaspora. The Jewish author (or authors), possibly writing in Antioch-on-the-Orontes just prior to the destruction of Jerusalem by Titus, intended not only to inspire courage among Jews who were resisting foreign tyranny, but to prove—by means of an appeal to the methods of Greek philosophy—the superiority of the Torah. More specifically, this writer hoped to demonstrate that the teaching of the Platonic and Stoic philosophers was incorrect, namely, that reason based upon the powers of the human intellect allows the individual to master the emotions. Rather, so goes the argument of 4 Maccabees, only the wisdom derived from devotion to the Torah may do that. The author even goes so far as to insist that the four cardinal virtues embraced by Platonic and Stoic teachers—rational judgment, justice, courage, and self-control—may be attained only by knowledge of the Torah:

Our inquiry, accordingly, is whether reason is sovereign over the emotions . . . . Now reason is the mind that with sound logic prefers the life of wisdom. Wisdom, next, is the knowledge of divine and human matters and the causes of these. This, in turn, is education in the law, by which we learn divine matters reverently and human affairs to our advantage. Now the kinds of wisdom are rational judgment, justice, courage, and self-control.

(1:13–18)

Having stated this thesis, the author then proceeds to illustrate it in a variety of ways.

The Fourth Book Maccabees is distinctive in that it is the only surviving example of Jewish literature from the Greco-Roman world that, while exhibiting great interest in the traditions of Greek philosophy and Jewish history and theology, is cast in the form of a public oration. The rhetorical nature of the document has caused some scholars to conclude that it was an actual address delivered on an occasion intended to commemorate the sacrifices of Jewish martyrs, a view, however, that is far from certain. In addition to a setting in the period of the first Jewish War with Rome (66–74 AD), the period of tension associated with Caligula's plan for a statue of himself in the Jerusalem Temple (40 AD) has also been suggested.

Fourth Maccabees moves easily between the thought-world of the Greeks and Romans and that of the Jews. The author has read widely in the literature of philosophy, Plato's dialogue *Gorgias*—in which the art of rhetoric is praised and the philosophical virtues are held up as the models for one's manner of living and dying—has been suggested as one source of our author's inspiration.[31] In addition, the literature of Stoicism is another likely possibility, advocating, as it does, the duty of a person to live rationally and thus to be free of the power of the emotions.

But it is the centrality of the Torah that is the guiding principle of the thought of 4 Maccabees. Occasionally, the ability of a godly individual to control the emotions is linked directly to a Torah text, such as the quotation of Exodus 20:17 in connection with Joseph's mastery over his sexual desires (4 Macc. 2:1–6). On other occasions, however, Torah and reason are simply assumed to be the same, as in 6:31–35, cited below. In addition, the belief that God rewards the faithful and punishes the wicked in an eternal state of bliss or damnation is an important element in 4 Maccabees, as is the confidence that the death of devout Jewish martyrs has a redemptive power for the whole community of Israel. In this latter regard, 4 Maccabees expresses a view that, while not unique among Jewish writings of this period, was far from normative, and is one that finds a distant resonance in the New Testament understanding of the meaning of the death of Jesus (Rom. 4:25, and elsewhere).

the tyrant was punished, and the homeland purified—they [i.e., the martyrs] having become, as it were, a ransom for the sin of our nation. And through the blood of those devout ones and their death as an atoning sacrifice, divine Providence preserved Israel that previously had been mistreated.

(17:21–22)

Fourth Maccabees received its name from its close association, noted above, with 2 Maccabees, and it is included in some copies of the Septuagint

(Sinaiticus and Alexandrinus, but not Vaticanus). Jerome, however, omitted it from the Vulgate, and it has not achieved deuterocanonical status in the church.

After an introduction (chap. 1) in which the author addresses his subject—

The subject that I am about to discuss is most philosophical, that is, whether devout reason is sovereign over the emotions. . . .

(1:1)

he begins to provide examples from the traditions of Israel of persons who have demonstrated in their lives that reason is acquired by submission to the law, and that by means of that reason, the emotions may be controlled. Incidents from the lives of Joseph, Moses, Jacob, and David are cited (chaps. 2–3) as evidence that

the temperate mind can conquer the drives of the emotions and quench the flames of frenzied desires; it can overthrow bodily agonies even when they are extreme, and by nobility of reason spurn all domination by the emotions.

(3:17–18)

The most important evidences of these truths, however, are the martyrs of 2 Maccabees, and to an extended discussion of their sufferings and death 4 Maccabees now turns. First is the priest Eleazar. The background of events leading up to the persecutions of Antiochus Epiphanes, drawn largely from 2 Maccabees 3—6, is reviewed (3:19—5:38), then the tortures to which Eleazar was subjected are described in terrible detail that far exceeds the narrative in 2 Maccabees 6 (4 Macc. 6:1–30). Through it all, however, the aged priest is courageous and continues to witness to the values for which he is dying. As he nears death, Eleazar prays:

"You know, O God, that though I might have saved myself, I am dying in burning torments for the sake of the law. Be merciful to your people, and let our punishment suffice for them. Make my blood their purification, and take my life in exchange for theirs."

(6:27–29)

After noting the death of the brave man, the author draws the lesson.

Admittedly, then, devout reason is sovereign over the emotions. For if the emotions had prevailed over reason, we would have testified to their domination. But now that reason has conquered the emotions, we properly attribute to it the power to govern. It is right for us to acknowledge the dominance of reason when it masters even external agonies. It would be ridiculous to deny it. I have proved not only that reason has mastered agonies, but also that it masters pleasures and in no respect yields to them.

(6:31–35)

After a lengthy tribute to Eleazar (chap. 7), the text describes—again in excruciating detail—the tortures and deaths of the seven brothers and their mother (chaps. 8–17). The mother's death is the most inspiring of all and, as in the case of the death of Eleazar, elicits an instructive observation.

If, then, a woman, advanced in years and mother of seven sons, endured seeing her children tortured to death, it must be admitted that devout reason is sovereign over the emotions, . . . The lions surrounding Daniel were not so savage, nor was the raging fiery furnace of Mishael so intensely hot, as was her innate parental love, inflamed as she saw her seven sons tortured in such varied ways. But the mother quenched so many and such great emotions by devout reason.

(16:1–4)

A final statement in praise of the martyrs (chap. 17) includes an instruction addressed to the Jews that contains all of the major theological postulates that the author wished to declare.

O Israelite children, offspring of the seed of Abraham, obey this law and exercise piety in every way, knowing that devout reason is master of all emotions, not only of sufferings from within, but also of those from without.

Therefore those who gave over their bodies in suffering for the sake of religion were not only admired by mortals, but also were deemed worthy to share in a divine inheritance. Because of them the nation gained peace, and by reviving observance of the law in the homeland they ravaged the enemy.

(18:1–4)

F. Astrological Speculations:
The Treatise of Shem (first century ad)[32]

Astrology, with its claim that events in human life are controlled by celestial bodies, took firm root in the thought of many people in the ancient Near East, especially the Babylonians and other Mesopotamians. For their part, however, the Hebrews, at least during the Old Testament period, rejected such notions as being a violation of the conviction that only God was in control of human affairs. The Second Isaiah, for example, a devout Jew of Babylon who was an eyewitness to the work of the astrologers, mocked them and their pretended powers:

Stand fast [O Babylon] in your enchantments
  and your many sorceries,
  with which you have labored from your youth;
perhaps you may be able to succeed,
  perhaps you may inspire terror.
You are wearied with your many consultations
  let those who study the heavens
stand up and save you,
  those who gaze at the stars,
and at each new moon predict
  what shall befall you.
          (Isa. 47:12–13; cf. Jer. 10:2, Dan. 2:27–28)

But during the Hellenistic and Roman periods this Jewish resistance to those who affirmed the power of the stars was partly eroded, in some quarters at least, by the increasing Jewish contact with other cultures and systems of belief. Strong evidence for this Jewish, or perhaps Jewish-Christian, belief in astrological lore has come to light in the Treatise of Shem.

Although the oldest existing copy of this document is no earlier than the fifteenth century, internal evidence suggests that it was written during those turbulent times that surrounded the founding of the Roman Empire. Although some scholars have objected to this early dating, there are certain arguments that commend it, in that oblique references to Octavian (later Caesar Augustus) and his enemies Mark Antony and Cleopatra may be contained in the text of the document.[33] Almost surely it was written in either Hebrew or, more likely, Aramaic, and was composed in Egypt.

While it is assumed that the author of the Treatise of Shem was a Jew (or a Jewish-Christian, if the document is from later than about 70 AD) Jewish elements are scarce, being almost limited to the full title of the work: "The Treatise Composed by Shem, the Son of Noah, Concerning the Beginning of the Year and Whatever Occurs in It." Reference to God is made three times (8:3, 11:17, 12:9), the phrase "living God" being used twice.

If the treatise is the work of a Jew or a Jewish-Christian, the author reveals a set of theological values that are at odds with both Judaism and Christianity. Most obvious among these is the assumption that the events in the life of an individual or a nation will be determined by the position of the son in the heavens (i.e., in which zodiacal "house" it resides) at the beginning of the year. Added to this are hints of magic, such as the warning that persons whose names contain given letters of the alphabet will experience certain disasters during the year.

The document is composed of twelve parts, each of which predicts the events of a given year, depending upon which "house" the sun is in at the beginning of the year. Typical is the following section on Pisces:

> And if the year begins in Pisces: Everyone whose name contains [the letters] Kaph or Mim [will] become sick and [eventually] slain. The year will be good. And the grain will be good and healthy. And there will be spring rains . . . There will be wars and much desolation in cities; and villages will be transfered and displaced from one place to another. And robbers will come from Palestine and [many will wa]ge a great war against three cities. And the Romans (sometimes will be) victorious and (sometimes) easily overcome. And there will be great disease among men . . .
>
> (11:1–13)

One possible connection between the views expressed in the Treatise of Shem and the New Testament may be found in the story of the magi, Matthew 2:1–12. Here, as nowhere else in the New Testament, there is a description of a series of events set in motion by the activity of a celestial body. The likelihood is thus raised that among both Jews and Christians were those who gave credence to astrological lore and who believed in the power of the stars and planets to influence human life.[34]

ABBREVIATIONS

AB	*The Anchor Bible.* Garden City, N.Y.: Doubleday, various dates.
ANET	James B. Pritchard, ed. *Ancient Near Eastern Texts Relating to the Old Testament.* 3d ed. Princeton, N.J.: Princeton University Press, 1969.
AOT	H. F. D. Sparks, ed. *The Apocryphal Old Testament.* Oxford: The Clarendon Press, 1984.
APOT	R. H. Charles, ed. *The Apocrypha and Pseudepigrapha of the Old Testament.* 2 vols. Oxford: The Clarendon Press, 1913.
DSSE	G. Vermes, tr. *The Dead Sea Scrolls in English.* Harmondsworth: Penguin Books, 1962; rev. ed. 1987.
EJ	*Encyclopedia Judaica.* 16 vols. Ed. in chief Cecil Roth. Jerusalem: Keter Publishing Co.; New York: Macmillan, 1971.
HJP	Emil Schürer. *The History of the Jewish People in the Age of Jesus Christ (175 BC–AD 135).* Rev. and ed. Geza Vermes, et al., 3 vols. in 4 parts. Edinburgh: Clark, 1973–1987.
IDB	*The Interpreter's Dictionary of the Bible.* 4 vols., Gen. ed. G. A. Buttrick. Nashville: Abingdon, 1962.
IDBSup	*The Interpreter's Dictionary of the Bible.* Supplementary vol. Gen. ed. Keith Crim. Nashville: Abingdon, 1976.
JL	Geroge W. E. Nickelsburg. *Jewish Literature Between the Bible and the Mishnah.* Philadelphia: Fortress Press, 1981.
JW	Michael E. Stone, ed. *Jewish Writings of the Second Temple Period.* Sec. 2, vol. 2 in Compendia Rerum Iudaicarum ad Novum Testamentum. Philadelphia: Fortress Press, 1984.
NRSV	New Revised Standard Version of the Holy Bible. New York: National Council of the Churches of Christ in the United States of America, 1989.
OTP	James H. Charlesworth, ed. *The Old Testament Pseudepigrapha.* 2 vols. Garden City, N.Y.: Doubleday, 1983, 1985.
RSV	Revised Standard Version of the Holy Bible. New York: Division of Christian Education of the National Council of the Churches of Christ in the United States of America, 1946, 1952.
WHJP	Abraham Schalit, ed. *The World History of the Jewish People.* New Brunswick, N.J.: Rutgers University Press, 1972.

NOTES

PART ONE

CHAPTER 1. THE SPREAD OF HELLENISM

1. Because the exploits of Alexander have kindled the imagination of many people over the years, there are numerous accounts of his life and times. Yet in many ways he remains an elusive figure. No complete record has survived from a writer who knew Alexander personally, only fragments of once larger accounts. Five ancient writers, all of whom lived several centuries after Alexander, have left extended accounts: Arrian, Diodorus, Justin, Curtius, and Plutarch. Arrian, who frequently quotes Alexander's contemporaries Aristobulus and Ptolemy, is considered by many to be the most dependable of these writers, but none may be relied upon completely.

For the student who may be interested in pursuing the "real" Alexander, the following should prove helpful. W. W. Tarn, *Alexander the Great*. 2 vols. (1948; reprint. Cambridge: Cambridge Univ. Press, 1979). Vol. 1 is a narrative account of Alexander's life; Vol. 2 is an extended study of the historical sources and of particular problems encountered in reconstructing a life of Alexander. Charles A. Robinson Jr., *The History of Alexander the Great* (Providence, R.I.: Brown Univ. Press, 1953) provides a systematic overview of the ancient sources concerning Alexander. Robin L. Fox, *The Search for Alexander* (Boston: Little, Brown & Co., 1980) is a fine retelling of Alexander's story, lavishly illustrated with color photographs of artifacts and geographical sites connected with Alexander.

See also Peter Green, *Alexander the Great* (New York: Praeger, 1970); J. R. Hamilton, *Alexander the Great* (London: Hutchinson Univ. Press, 1973); Frank Lipsius, *Alexander the Great* (New York: Saturday Review Press, 1974); Lionel Pearson, *The Lost Histories of Alexander the Great* (Chico, Calif.: Scholars Press, 1983).

2. The question of the historical accuracy of Homer's tales about Troy, indeed the question of whether Homer himself was an real individual (as opposed to, say, a group of anonymous writers), is a matter of vigorous academic debate.

3. Josephus, *Antiquities*, IX, viii, 4–5. [hereafter cited as *Antiquities*]

4. It is widely held that, unlike Zech. 1—8 which dates from 520–518 BC, Zech. 9—14 is a product of the Hellenistic period. 9:9 is quoted in Matt. 21:5 in reference to Jesus' entry into Jerusalem on Palm Sunday.

5. It is reported that Darius was murdered by one of his generals.

6. The frequently repeated tale that Alexander wept because he had "no more worlds to conquer" appears in none of the most ancient sources.

7. Historians must contend with the fact that very little remains by way of a documentary record of the Ptolemaic Kingdom. What few papyri (the primary medium for the written word in Ptolemaic Egypt) have survived have come from the Nile valley, which is much drier than the Delta in which Alexandria is located. This means, however, that the provenance of many of the Ptolemaic documents are the political and cultural "backwaters," and not the administrative heart of the kingdom. Alexandria has yeilded very little archaeological evidence of any kind, due to a change in the level of the water table and to the fact that the modern city sits atop the ancient one. Even so, the documentary record of Ptolemaic Egypt is much better than that of the Seleucid Kingdom, from which even fewer written records exist.

8. One such group of successful rebels were the Parthians, who lived in a region that today is in northeast Iran. Parthia had been a satrapy within the Persian Empire, and had subsequently been ruled, in turn, by Alexander and the Seleucids. But in the middle of the third century BC the Parthians revolted against the Seleucids and established an independent kingdom that was successful in maintaining itelf even against the later incursions of the Romans, a feat of which few peoples could boast. Parthians (doubtless Jews of Parthia) are among those peoples mentioned as present for the Pentecost festival described in Acts 2 (v. 9).

9. Antioch-on-the-Orontes and Antioch-in-Pisidia figure prominently, of course, in the journeys of Paul, as described in the Book of Acts.

10. Polybius, *General History*, 29, 27, 1–8.

11. For further information on the history of the Greek language and the particular place of Koine Greek, the following should prove useful: B. C. F. Atkinson, *The Greek Language* (London: Faber & Faber, 1931); Procope S. Costas, *An Outline of the History of the Greek Language* (Chicago: Ares, 1979); Leonard R. Palmer, *The Greek Language* (Atlantic Highlands, N.J.: Humanities Press, 1980).

12. The discussion of the Septuagint is on 171–75.

13. Good discussions of Hellenistic literature may be found in the following: Charles Rowan Beye, *Ancient Greek Literature and Society*, rev. 2d ed. (Ithaca and London: Cornell Univ. Press, 1975, 1987); P. E. Easterling and B. M. W. Knox, *The Cambridge History of Classical Literature*, vol. 1: *Greek Literature* (Cambridge: Cambridge Univ. Press, 1985); Moses Hadas, *A History of Greek Literature* (New York: Columbia Univ. Press, 1950); Albin Lesky, *A History of Greek Literature*, tr. James Willis and Cornelis de Heer (New York: T. Y. Crowell, 1963); Peter Levi, *A History of Greek Literature* (New York: Viking, 1985).

14. The Museum in Alexandria was not the first such institution of its kind, since it was modeled on similar centers for scholarship and the worship of the Muses in classical Greece. (The Muses were nine daughters of Zeus who were considered to be the inspirers of artists and thinkers.) But the Alexandria Museum clearly overshadowed its prototypes in importance. The museum in

the modern sense of the word, i.e., as a repository of objects of art, is a creation of the European Renaissance, when many wealthy individuals built up extensive private collections. In some instances these became the nuclei of public museums, the first of which was probably the Ashmolean Museum of Oxford University, established in 1683 around the collection of a benefactor, Elias Ashmole. More recently, of course, the word *museum* has been applied not only to collections of art, but to a wide range of objects, so that there is now a Museum of Natural History, a Museum of Atomic Energy, and the like.

15. Beye, *Ancient Greek*, p. 262.

16. Like the Museum, the Library in Alexandria was based upon an idea that had a long history before the Hellenistic period. The first libraries were probably the royal archives established by many ancient monarchs for purposes of public record keeping, examples of which may be found as early as the third millennium BC. (In this connection, note the references to royal archives in ancient Israel and Judah in 1 Kings 14:29, 15:31, and the like). The Assyrian king Ashurbanipal (c. 668–629 BC) established an extensive collection of literary documents (poems, mythological texts, and the like) in connection with the royal archives at Nineveh, and ancient Egyptian pharaohs are known to have done the same. To the writer of the OT Book of Ecclesiastes, the world seemed to be awash in literary material (11:12). After the destruction of the Alexandria Library in 47 BC, there seems to have been an attempt to revive it. Plutarch reports that Mark Antony had the library of the city of Pergamum brought to Alexandria. But the institution never regained its prominence and it was reportedly destroyed forever by the caliph Omar in 642 AD, who declared that the writings of infidels did not deserve to be preserved.

17. For a discussion of Demeter, see 28–29.

18. In the *Hymn to Artemis*, for example, Artemis refers to Zeus as "Daddy" or "Pappa" and insistently but playfully asks the chief god for special favors that he repeatedly promises to grant.

19. See the excursus at the end of this chapter.

20. This is not to suggest that this account should be dismissed as a fictitious "romance." The story may have been included in the Acts narrative and may have been given in the shape that it has because its author intended it for a popular readership who knew and were fascinated by similar tales of maritime adventure.

21. For an annotated catalog of Hellenistic historians, see Lesky, *History of Greek Literature*, pp. 764ff.

22. Polybius' *General History*, 6.56.9, tr. W. R. Paton, as quoted in Hadas, *History of Greek Literature*, 230.

23. Diodorus, like Polybius, straddles both the Greek and Roman worlds. In spite of the fact that he lived within the Roman political system and made Rome the subject of much of his attention, he can be called a Hellenistic historian not only because he wrote in the Greek language but because the bulk of his historical material deals with the Greek past.

24. Quoted in Menahem Stern, ed., *Greek and Latin Authors on Jews and Judaism*, vol. 1: *From Herodotus to Plutarch* (Jerusalem: Israel Academy of Sciences and Humanities, 1976), 183.

25. Alexander Polyhistor is discussed on 176.

26. Quoted in Stern, *Greek and Latin Authors*, 59.

27. Other Hellenistic biographers whose work has survived in very fragmentary form include Satyrus (*Lives of the Dramatists*) and Antigonus of Carystus (*Lives of the Philosophers*), both of whom lived in the third century BC. The work of Antigonus, such as we have, is interesting because he draws upon his personal knowledge of his subjects.

28. For a discussion of the importance of the aretalogy and its possible influence on the writing of the Gospels, see Moses Hadas and Morton Smith, *Heros and Gods: Spiritual Biographies in Antiquity* (New York: Harper & Row, 1965); Carl R. Holladay, *Theios Aner in Ancient Judaism* (Missoula, Mont.: Scholars Press, 1977); David L. Tiede, *The Charismatic Figure as Miracle Worker*, SBL Dissertation Series 1 (Missoula, Mont.: Society of Biblical Literature, 1972).

29. Hans Windisch, *Paulus und Christus*, quoted in Tiede, *Charismatic Figure*, 15. Tiede quotes Windisch's original German; the English translation is the present author's. In evaluating Windisch's statement, one should remember that it was made in a cultural and political context where, out of anti-Semitic motives, serious efforts were underway to detach Christianity from its Jewish origins. For a discussion of Bar Kokhba, see chap. 9.

30. F. W. Walbank, *The Hellenistic World* (Cambridge: Harvard Univ. Press, 1982), 72.

31. *Ibid.*, 183f.

32. There are a number of excellent discussions of the philosophy of the Hellenistic period. Among them are: A. H. Armstrong, *An Introduction to Ancient Philosophy (London: Methuen, 1957)*; A. H. Armstrong, ed., *The Cambridge History of Later Greek and Early Medieval Philosophy* (Cambridge: Cambridge Univ. Press, 1967); Edwyn Bevan, *Stoics and Skeptics* (Cambridge: Heffer & Sons, 1913, 1959); Donald R. Dudley, *A History of Cynicism* (London: Methuen, 1937); Benjamin Farrington, *The Faith of Epicurus* (London: Weidenfeld & Nicolson, 1967); Andre-Jean Festugiere, *Epicurus and His Gods*, tr. C. W. Chilton (Oxford: Blackwell, 1955); W. K. C. Guthrie, *A History of Greek Philosophy*, 3 or 5 vols. (Cambridge: Cambridge Univ. Press, 1962–1975); R. D. Hicks, *Stoic and Epicurean* (New York: Scribner, 1910, 1962); A. A. Long and D. N. Sedley, eds., *The Hellenistic Philosophers* vol. 1, *Translations of Principal Sources with Philosophical Commentary,* (Cambridge: Cambridge Univ. Press, 1987); A. A. Long, *Hellenistic Philosophy: Stoics, Epicureans, Skeptics* (London: Duckworth, 1974, 1986); C. J. Rowe, *Plato* (Brighton, Sussex, Eng.: Harvester Press, 1984); F. H. Sandbach, *The Stoics* (London: Chatto & Windus, 1975).

33. This was also true in Israel, where close ties were maintained between the Davidic kings and the activities of the Jersualem Temple. The schismatic leader Jeroboam created new sanctuaries in the kingdom of Samaria, at Bethel

and Dan, in an effort further to sever the ties with Davidic Jerusalem (1 Kings 12:25–33). Apparently these shrines enjoyed the favor of the royal house of Samaria in the same manner that the Jerusalem Temple enjoyed Davidic patronage, for the priest Amaziah refers to Bethel as the "king's sanctuary" and "a temple of the kingdom" (Amos 7:13). Alexander's conquest of the East, however, introduced a new way of understanding the relation between religion and the state.

34. *Phaedo* 77, tr. Benjamin Jowett, *The Dialogues of Plato,* vol. 1 (New York: Random, 1937), 462.

35. Lucretius, *The Nature of the Universe,* tr. R. E. Latham (New York: Penguin Books, 1951, 1955), 60.

36. For a discussion of the wide range of meanings of the term *logos,* see H. Kleinknecht, "The Logos in the Greek and Hellenistic World," in Gerhard Kittel, ed., *Theological Dictionary of the New Testament,* tr. Geoffrey W. Bromiley, vol. 4 (Grand Rapids: Eerdmans, 1967), 77–91.

37. Quoted in Frederick C. Grant, ed., *Hellenistic Religions: The Age of Syncretism* (New York: Lib. Arts Press, 1953), 153.

38. Further discussions of the religions of the Hellenistic world may be found in Thomas Allen Brady, *Serapis and Isis: Collected Essays* (Chicago: Ares, 1978); Walter Burkert, *Greek Religion,* tr. John Raffan (Cambridge: Harvard Univ. Press, 1985); Franz Cumont, *The Oriental Religions in Roman Paganism* (New York: Dover, 1911, 1956); Lewis Richard Farnell, *The Cults of the Greek States,* 5 vols. (Oxford: Clarendon Press, 1896–1907); Andre-Jean Festugiere, *Personal Religion Among the Greeks* (Berkley: Univ. of California Press, 1954); J. Gwyn Griffiths, *The Origins of Osiris and His Cult* (Leiden: Brill, 1980); W. K. C. Guthrie, *The Greeks and their Gods* (London: Methuen; Boston: Beacon, 1951); Helmut Koester, *Introduction to the New Testament,* vol. 1: *History, Culture and Religion of the Hellenistic Age* (Philadelphia: Fortress Press, 1982.); Martin P. Nilsson, *The Dionysiac Mysteries of the Hellenistic and Roman Age* (New York: Arno, 1975); Walter R. Otto, *Dionysus: Myth and Cult,* tr. Robert Palmer (Bloomington and London: Univ. of Indiana Press, 1965).

39. From a Homeric Hymn *To Ceres,* found in Jane Harrison, *Prolegomena to the Study of Greek Religion* (London: Merlin, 1961), 274. A different translation of the same lines is found in John Ferguson, *Greek and Roman Religion: A Source Book* (Park Ridge, N.J.: Noyes Press, 1980), 157.

40. Ferguson, *Greek and Roman Religion,* 159.

41. *Ibid.,* 161.

42. Euripides, "The Bacchae," line 1 (see following note).

43. "The Bacchae," tr. Glibert Murray in *The Complete Greek Drama,* vol. 2, Whitney J. Oates and Eugene O'Neill Jr., eds. (New York: Random, 1938), 274–278.

44. Quoted in Felix Guirand, ed., *New Larousse Encyclopdia of Mythology,* tr. Richard Aldington and Delano Ames. (London: Hamlyn Publishing Group, 1968, 1976), 160.

45. The word *tragodia* (tragedy) is considered by some to be derived from *tragos*, (goat) an animal that was sometimes the sacrificial victim of Dionysian worship.

46. See Eric M. Meyers, Ehud Netzer, and Carol L. Meyers, "Artistry in Stone: The Mosaics of Ancient Sepphoris," *Biblical Archaeologist* 50 (December 1987):223–31.

EXCURSUS: NON-JEWISH HELLENISTIC WRITERS QUOTED IN THE
NEW TESTAMENT

1. Quoted from A. W. Bulloch, "Hellenistic Poetry," in P. E. Easterling and B. M. W. Knox, eds. *The Cambridge History of Classical Literature*, vol. 1: *Greek Literature* (Cambridge: Cambridge Univ. Press, 1985), 551.

2. For additional examples of the popularity of this line in the ancient world, see Martin Dibelius and Hans Conzelmann, *The Pastoral Epistles*, tr. by P. Buttolph and A. Yarbro, Hermeneia (Philadelphia: Fortress Press, 1972), 136–137.

3. All the known lines from *Thais*, including those quoted here, may be found in Francis G. Allison, *Menander: the Principal Fragments* (London: Heinemann; New York: Putnam, 1921), 357.

4. What is known of the plot of *Thais* is reconstructed in T. B. L. Webster, *Studies in Menander*, 2d ed. (Manchester: Manchester Univ. Press, 1960), 148.

5. Quoted from Bulloch, "Hellenistic Poetry," 600.

6. The quotations in Acts 17:28 are discussed in C. S. C. Williams, *A Commentary on the Acts of the Apostles* (New York: Harpers & Bros., 1957), 204–205.

CHAPTER 2.   JEWISH REACTIONS TO HELLENISM

1. There are a number of good discussions of political and military events in Palestine during the third and second centuries. Among the better are: Bezalel Bar-Kochva, *Judas Maccabaeus: The Jewish Struggle Against the Seleucids* (Cambridge: Cambridge Univ. Press, 1989); F. E. Adcock and M. P. Charlesworth, eds., *The Cambridge Ancient History*, 1928, vol. 7, pt. 1, *The Hellenistic Monarchies*, 1984; vol. 7, pts. 2, *The Rise of Rome to 220 B.C.*, 1990 (Cambridge: Cambridge Univ. Press); Abraham Schalit, ed., *The World History of the Jewish People. First Series: Ancient Times*. vol. 6, *The Hellenistic Age: Political History of Jewish Palestine From 332 B.C.E. to 67 B.C.E.* New Brunswick, N.J.: Rutgers Univ. Press, 1972, hereafter cited as *WHJP*; Emil Schürer, *The History of the Jewish People in the Age of Jesus Christ: 175 BC–AD 135*. 3 vols. New English Version revised and edited by Geza Vermes, et al. Edinburgh: Clark, 1983–87, hereafter cited as *HJP*.

2. For a discussion of the Zenon papyri, plus bibliography, see V. Tcherikover, "Social Conditions," in Schalit, 87–95.

3. Josephus (*Antiquities*, XII, 160ff.) deals at length with the career of Joseph the son of Tobias and of Joseph's son Hyrcanus, although the accuracy of Josephus' account has been called into question. See Tcherikover, *WHJP*, 98–101 and n. 25, 316f.

4. The terms "Maccabean" and "Hasmonean" are both used to refer to the family of Mattathias and to refer, as well, to the events surrounding their lives (as in "Maccabean" or "Hasmonean Period") and to the state over which some of the family members ruled. The term Maccabeus (perhaps "Hammer") seems to have been applied first to Judas (1 Macc. 2:4, 3:1; 2 Macc. 8:1), and in its original useage may have been meant only for him. Josephus provides the information (not given in 1 or 2 Maccabees) that Mattathias' great-grandfather was named Hasamonaios (*Antiquities*, XII, 265), thus Hasmonean is perhaps a preferable term when referring to the family or to the period which it dominated.

5. The primary sources are three in number: 1 Maccabees, 2 Maccabees and Josephus, each of which exhibits varying degrees of reliability. To these must be added the Book of Daniel which, although it is nearer in time to the actual events than any other ancient source, is written in such a style as to provide little concrete information. On Daniel see 76–81.

6. 2 Maccabees 3:22–40 describes how the Seleucid agent, Heliodorus, and his bodyguard were miraculously chased from the Temple when they attempted to loot the treasury:

> There appeared to them a magnificantly caparisoned horse, with a rider of freightening mein, and it rushed furiously at Heliodorus and struck him with its front hoofs . . . Two young men also appeared to him, remarkably strong, gloriously beautiful and splendidly dressed, who stood on each side of him and scourged him continuously.

Onias the high priest interceeds with God on Heliodorus' behalf, and the Seleucid envoy returns home to describe his adventures to the king. His speech concludes with a judgment in which one detects the hand of a pious Jewish writer:

> He who has his dwelling in heaven watches over that place [Jerusalem] himself and brings it aid, and he strikes and destroys those who do it injury.

7. Josephus (*Jewish War*, I, 33) reports that Onias fled to Egypt, where he constructed a Jewish temple at Heliopolis. 2 Macc. 4:33–34, however, describes how Onias was murdered in Antioch as a result of the treachery of Menelaus.

8. The Roman rebuff of Anitochus is discussed, 40.

9. The term "Hasidim" comes from *hesed*, a word often found in the Old Testament, where it usually means the constant, covenant love of God. The word may also mean the loyalty and commitment that God requires of people (e.g., Micah 6:8, where *hesed* is translated "kindness" in NRSV). Thus the Hasidim were not only the "pious ones" (the usual explanation of the term), but also the "committed ones," committed, that is, to God and to Torah. Their initial refusal to fight on the Sabbath had disastrous results (1 Macc. 2:29–38).

10. Questions have often been raised about Antiochus' motivation in imposing upon the Jews such terrible persecution. Answers have included the following:

Antiochus was angry over his rebuff by the Romans and ventilated his feelings upon the Jews; he was badly in need of money after his expensive military campaigns (this might explain his looting of the Temple treasures, but not his carnage and murder); he felt that he was suppressing a revolt against his authority; he believed that only the harshest measures would stamp out the traditions of the Jews and lead to their acceptance of Hellenism.

11. Cf. Josephus, *Antiquities*, XII, 246–256. The chronology of these events is very hard to establish. 1 and 2 Macc. speak of only one visit by Antiochus Epiphanes to Jerusalem, but Josephus describes two. 2 Macc. states (5:1) that the devastation of Jerusalem took place after Antiochus' second invasion of Egypt, the occasion of his rebuff by the Roman Popillius (Cf. Dan. 11:30). But Josephus' view is that Antiochus' initial visit to Jerusalem took place at that time, followed by a second, and much more destructive visit two years later (XII, 248). For its part, 1 Macc. (1:29–34) describes a second persecution after that imposed by Antiochus Epiphanes, this one conducted not by Antiochus himself, but by a "chief collector of tribute." This individual may be the same as the Apollonius described in 2 Macc. 5:24–26. For a discussion of the problems, see Goldstein, *II Maccabees*, AB, 41A, 89–96; HJP, 1:152, n. 37; V. Tcherikover, *Hellenistic Culture and the Jews*, tr. S. Applebaum (Philadelphia: Jewish Publication Society, 1959), 186–203.

12. See V. Tcherikover, *WHJP*, 131–144.

13. As for the primary sources, accounts of the exploits of Mattathias and Judas may be read in 1 Macc. 2:1—9:22, 2 Macc. 5:27, 8:1—15:39, Josephus, *Antiquities*, XXII, 265-434 and *Jewish War*, I, 34–47. An especially lucid treatment of the campaigns of Judas may be read in M. Avi-Yonah, *WHJP*, 150–178.

14. None of our primary sources describes exactly what the inhabitants of Modein were commanded to do, except that the sacrilege involved some kind of sacrifice (1 Macc. 2:15–23, Josephus, *Antiquities*, XII, 268). This may have simply been an effort at humiliation involving the sacrifice of pork (cf. 2 Macc. 6:18) or it may have been an attempt to force worship after the Greek manner (cf. 2 Macc. 6:7).

15. All of these are areas just north and west of Jerusalem. See an excellent map of Judas' early campaigns in Avi-Yonah, *WHJP*, 155. For maps relating to other campaigns of Judas, see *WHJP*, 166, 173.

16. Indian elephants had been used by Persian king Darius III at the Battle of Gaugamela against Alexander the Great in 331 BC, and these beasts were periodically employed by various armies during the Hellenistic period, their chief value lying in their ability to overwhelm lines of enemy infantry and cavalry. Probably the most celebrated use of elephants in ancient warfare is the invasion of Italy by the Carthagenian general Hannibal in 218 BC, who led his army, including the elephants, through both the Pyrenees and the Alps. The description in 1 Macc. 6:34–39 of the Seleucid elephants at Beth-Zechariah is quite interesting:

> They offered the elephants the juice of grapes and mulberries, to arouse them for battle. They distributed the animals among the phalanxes;

with each elephant they stationed a thousand men armed with coats of mail, and with brass helmets on their heads; and five hundred picked horsemen were assigned to each beast. These took their position beforehand wherever the animal was; wherever it went, they went with it, and they never left it. On the elephants were wooden towers, strong and covered; they were fastened on each animal by special harness, and on each were four armed men who fought from there, and also its Indian driver.

Cf. 1 Macc. 1:17.

17. Demetrius I Soter (162–151 BC) was the son of Antiochus III the Great (223–187 BC). But Antiochus' brother succeeded him upon his death as Seleucus IV Philopator (187–175 BC). Demetrius, who stood next in line, was subsequently sent to Rome as a hostage in exchange for Seleucus' brother Antiochus (later Antiochus IV Epiphanes), who had been in Roman hands since the battle of Magnesia in 188. Seleucus was assassinated in 175 and was succeeded by Antiochus IV Epiphanes, Demetrius remaining in Roman hands. After Antiochus Epiphanes' death, Demetrius escaped from the Romans (with the help of the historian Polybius), made his way home, assassinated young Antiochus V, and proclaimed himself king.

18. 2 Macc. 15:35 states that Nicanor's head was displayed from the Akra, but this would be highly unlikely in light of the fact that the Hasmoneans did not control this area. The following verse (15:36) calls attention to the fact that the date for the celebration of Judas' victory over Nicanor was thirteen Adar, one day before the celebration of Purim, or "Mordecai's day" (cf. 1 Macc. 7:49). Judas' victory over Nicanor is thus compared to that of the Jews in the time of Esther. With the account of Nicanor's defeat and death 2 Macc. comes to an end.

19. This is probably the same as the modern Khirbet Beit Bassa, just east of Tekoa in the wilderness of Judaea. Josephus, however, calls the place Bethalaga (*Antiquities*, XIII, 27).

20. The name Cleopatra was a favorite among the Ptolemaic family and Alexander Balas' wife is not, of course, the same Cleopatra who was the mistress of Julius Caesar and the wife of Mark Antony. This was Cleopatra VII, who ruled Egypt from 51 to 30 BC.

21. Coele-Syria (Greek for *hollow Syria*) was a name applied to the present Bekaa valley in Lebanon, but one that was ultimately (during the Hellenistic and Roman periods) extended to include all of Phoenicia and Palestine.

22. Josephus (*Antiquities*, XIII, 117) gives the Arab's name as Zabeilus, whereas the historian Diodorus (XXXII, 9) reports that Alexander was murdered by two of his own men, Heliades and Casius.

23. *Antiquities*, XIII, 135–141.

24. Demetrius II was subsequently captured by the Parthians while fighting in the East. Later, during the time of the Hasmonean leader John Hyrcanus I, Demetrius was released to attempt a return to his throne. See 51.

25. 1 Macc. 12:47 (followed by Josephus, *Antiquities*, XIII, 191) reports that a thousand of Jonathan's men went with him into Ptolemais, but that number

may be too large, in light of the apparent ease with which they were overcome there.

26. Interestingly, Josephus (*Antiquities*, XIII, 208) embellishes the simple statement in 1 Macc. 13:22 by saying: "A heavy snow, however, fell during the night, which covered the roads and lay so deep that it made the way impassable, especially for the feet of horses, and so prevented his [Trypho's] coming to Jerusalem."

27. Judas, Jonathan and John had been killed by their enemies. A fourth brother, Eleazar, had been killed in the Battle of Beth-Zechariah, where he acquitted himself with great courage (1 Macc. 6:40–47).

28. 1 Macc. 13:43 reports Simon's conquest of Gazara (biblical Gezer), while to that city Josephus (*Antiquities*, XIII, 215) adds Jaffa (or Joppa, cf. 1 Macc. 14:5) and Jamnia.

29. For a discussion of Jewish political councils, see below, 131–33.

30. Simon's other titles include Ethnarch (1 Macc. 15:1) and perhaps a designation of unknown meaning, "Asaramel" (1 Macc. 14:28); for possible explanations of this term, see J. Klausner, *WHJP*, 203, and Goldstein, *I Macc. AB* 41. Never is Simon referred to as king.

31. See the discussion on messianism, 240–48.

32. This Ptolemy is no known kin to the rulers of Egypt who bore the same name.

33. At this point the narrative in 1 Macc. comes to an end.

34. The only record of the Hasmonean state after the time of Simon that approaches completeness is that of Josephus (*Antiquities*, XIII and XIV; *Jewish War*, II–VII). Although he is sometimes unreliable in his details, there is no reason to doubt the basic integrity of Josephus' account.

35. This third son of Simon is referred to only as John in 1 Macc., but Josephus prefers the name Hyrcanus (see *Antiquities*, XIII, 228). This name was current in Jewish circles before the time of John Hyrcanus, and is perhaps to be traced to the fact that some Jews were resettled in the region of Hyrcania, on the southern shore of the Caspian Sea, during the Persian period. See *HJP* 1:201, n. 2.

36. See J. Klausner, *WHJP*, 211–221, especially the tributes to Hyrcanus in the Mishnah, 221.

37. *Antiquities*, XIII, 249 (cf. *Jewish War*, I, 61). Josephus also seems unsympathetic to the fact that Hyrcanus had hired non-Jewish mercenaries to fight for the Hasmonean state. In spite of Josephus' statement that Hyrcanus "became the first Judaean to support foreign troops," this was by no means a precedent, as mercenaries had fought in the armies of Israel as early as the time of David (cf. 2 Sam. 8:18). But it was a new departure for the Hasmoneans, and it may have seemed to Hyrcanus' more pious contemporaries, as it later seemed to Josephus, as a symbol of Hasmonean secularization under Hyrcanus.

38. Ptolemy's candidate for the Seleucid throne, Alexander Zebinas, pretended to be either an adopted son of Antiochus VII Sidetes (according to

some sources) or a natural son of Alexander Balas (according to others). He defeated Demetrius II in battle near Damascus, and not long after this Demetrius was murdered (125 BC). Demetrius' son, Antiochus VIII Grypus (126–96), however, continued the fight against Alexander Zebinas and in 123 defeated and killed the Ptolemaic-sponsored pretender. A period of relative quiet followed until 113 when Grypus' authority was challanged by his cousin and stepbrother who styled himself Antiochus IX Cyzicenus. Cyzicenus was unable to topple Grypus, but he did succeed in detaching Coele-Syria from Grypus' authority, and over this fragment of the Seleucid kingdom Cyzicenus ruled (113–95).

39. For a discussion of the Samaritans, see 122–27.

40. The most famous Idumaean is Herod the Great. In spite of the Idumaeans' conversion, most Jews continued to look with contempt upon them, calling them "semi-Jews" (*Antiquities*, XIV, 403). If the subtleties in Josephus' account may be relied upon (*Antiquities*, XIII, 257–258), Hyrcanus at least gave the Idumaeans the option of converting or going into exile. Yet it apparently does not occur to Josephus that the Jewish treatment of the Samaritans, the Idumaeans, and others was little different from the Seleucid treatment of the Jews.

41. Hyrcanus' three sons were originally named Judas, Mattathias, and Jonathan, after their Hasmonean ancestors. But they came to be known, in the Greek fashion, as Aristobolus, Antigonus, and Alexander Jannaeus.

42. Josephus (*Antiquities*, XIII, 282) says that a miraculous voice spoke to Hyrcanus, who was alone in the Jerusalem Temple at the time, at the very moment Samaria fell to Jewish arms.

43. For a discussion of Pharisees and Sadducees, see 113–19.

44. The origin of the name Pharisee is obscure, but it may be related to a Hebrew or Aramaic term that means *separate*. If this is so, while it is not clear what the Pharisees were originally thought to be separate from, some form of spiritual or theological purity is probably implied.

45. The term Sadducee is probably a corruption of the term *Zadok* and thus may emphasize the priestly role of this group (cf. 1 Kings 4:4). Another, less likely, possibility is that its root is the Hebrew word *zadik*, meaning *righteous*.

46. Reference to the Oniad and Tobiad families is on 37.

47. Wealth is a relative matter, of course, and one would imagine that the "wealth" of the Jewish aristocrats in the early days of the Hasmonean state was not very great, in light of the years of warfare that preceeded independence.

48. *Antiquities*, XII, 138. The word that Josephus uses here is *gerousia*, (senate). The term *sunedrion*, (Sanhedrin) is first used by him as a reference to the supreme Jewish council in his record of Herod the Great *Antiquities*, XIV, 167.

49. *Antiquities*, XIII, 288–298. Essentially the same story is told in the Babylonian Talmud. See A. Schalit, *WHJP*, 269–277.

50. The specific charge, according to Josephus, was as follows: "We have heard from our elders that your mother was a captive in the reign of Antiochus

Epiphanes." (It is essentially the same in the Babylonian Talmud. Both Josephus and the Babylonian Talmud inform the reader that the charge is false.) On the surface, the indictment points to Lev. 21:14, that says "a woman who has been defiled [female captives were routinely defiled] . . . he [a priest] shall not marry; but he shall take to wife a virgin of his own people." Thus below the surface the indictment implies that Hyrcanus may be a bastard, that is, that he may be the son not of Simon the Hasmonean, but of his mother's Seleucid captor. Small wonder that Hyrcanus was furious! But, as we suggest in the main body of the text, the real reason for Hyrcanus' break with the Pharisees may have had more to do with differences in political and cultural ideology, than with personal animosity.

51. This is the report of Josephus (*Antiquities*, XIII, 301; *Jewish War*, I, 70). On the other hand, the historian Strabo writes that Alexander Jannaeus was the first Hasmonean to style himself "king" (see *HJP*, 1:217, n. 5).

52. Fortress Antonia, or the Tower of Antonia, was possibly the location of Jesus' trial before Pilate and of his scouraging prior to his crucifixion (Mark 15:1–20 and parallels). It was also the site where Paul addressed his enemies, following his arrest in Jerusalem, and where he escaped flogging by appealing to his Roman citizenship (Acts 21:37—22:29). The Tower of Antonia of the Roman period was the result of one of Herod the Great's many rebuilding projects, and was called Antonia as a tribute to Mark Antony.

53. Josephus, as he sometimes does, uses the occasion to moralize: "Now his [Antigonus'] death clearly proves that there is nothing more powerful than envy and calumny, nor anything that more easily disrupts friendship and the ties of nature than these influences" (*Antiquities*, XIII, 310).

54. Josephus (*Antiquities*, XIII, 318) refers to the victims of Aristobulus' military campaigns as the Ituraeans, a people who lived in southern Lebanon, but who, during this time, also occupied parts of northern Galilee. By this conquest, all of Galilee was now in Hasmonean hands. It is interesting that, whereas the Idumaeans were looked upon scornfully by Jews into the first century AD, (see above, n. 8), this was apparently not the case with the Galileans who had been forcibly circumcised. The NT is careful to point out Jesus' genuine Jewish descent (Matt. 1:1–17; Luke 3:23–38), but this was apparently not true of all of his neighbors in Nazareth, and perhaps not true of all his Galilean disciples.

55. The split between Ptolemy VIII Lathyrus and his mother was apparently, among other things, a result of their taking sides in the struggle between Antiochus VIII Grypus (whom Cleopatra supported) and Antiochus IX Cyzicenus (supported by Lathyrus). See n. 6 above. Josephus reports (*Antiquities*, XIII, 349) that the leaders of Cleopatra's army were two Jews, Chelkias (Hellenized form of Hilkiah) and Ananias (Hananiah). Chelkias died during the campaign, but Ananias was instrumental in convincing Cleopatra that she should accept tribute from Alexander instead of occupying his land (XIII, 354–355).

56. *Antiquities*, XIII, 356.

57. See Klausner, *WHJP*, 226.

58. The Hebrew inscription on Alexander's coins, "King Jonathan" or "Jonathan is the King" (*yehonathan hamelek*) must have seemed to many pious Jews as a blasphemous echo of the phrase "The Lord is King" or "The Lord Reigns" (*yahweh malak*) in the Psalms (93:1, and elsewhere).

59. *Antiquities*, XIII, 373. Many scholars have questioned the large numbers employed by Josephus here and elsewhere in his account of the reign of Alexander Jannaeus. There may, indeed, be some exaggeration, but there is no reason for doubting the basic elements in his story.

60. There is a story in the Talmud that tells how an unnamed Sadduceean priest committed a sacrilegious act on the Feast of Tabernacles by pouring the water of libation not on the altar, as he was supposed to do, but upon his feet, whereupon he was showered with lemons by the people. Some scholars feel that this is a reflection of the incident involving Alexander. See Klausner, *WHJP*, 230; *HJP* 1:223, n. 16.

61. *Antiquities*, XIII, 376.

62. Demetrius was being challenged for his throne by a brother, Philip. (*Antiquities*, XIII, 384.)

63. Qumran is discussed on 134–69.

64. *Antiquities*, XIII, 398.

65. Alexandra was, of course, the queen's Greek name, Salome her Hebrew. Her Hebrew name actually occurs in several forms in the ancient sources, but most seem to be shortened forms of the phrase *sh^elom-ziyon*, meaning *Peace of Zion*. See Klausner, *WHJP* 6:242.

66. *Antiquities*, XIII, 401–404.

67. Klausner, IN *WHJP* 6:248.

68. *Antiquities*, XIII, 409.

69. Klausner, *WHJP* 6:247; also see *HJP*, 1:231–232.

70. Josephus says that the only fortresses that the queen excluded from Sadducean control were Hyrcania (east of Bethlehem), Alexandrium (in the Jordan valley north of the Dead Sea) and Machaerus (ease of the Dead Sea, in Moab), "where her most valuable possessions were" (*Antiquities*, XIII, 418). Machaerus was later (according to tradition) to be the site of the imprisonment of John the Baptizer.

71. Josephus states: "in barely fifteen days he [Aristobulus] had occupied twenty-two fortresses, and obtaining resources from these, he gathered an army from Lebanon, Trachonitis and the local princes." *Antiquities*, XIII, 427.

72. *Antiquities*, XIII, 419–421.

73. A helpful discussion of Rome's conquest of the eastern Mediterranean may be found in Walbank, *Hellenistic World*, 227–251.

74. The origins of the family of Antipater and Herod the Great are uncertain. Josephus struggles briefly with the problem, without solving it (*Antiquities*, XIV, 9). See *HJP*, 1:234, n. 3.

75. Gnaeus Pompeius Magnus, or Pompey the Great (106–48 BC) was an important Roman general and politican. After his conquests in the East, he organized, with Julius Caesar and Crassus, the First Triumvirate in 60. But he subsequently quarreled with Caesar and fled from Rome, to be defeated by his former ally at the Battle of Pharsalus (in Greece) in 48. He then attempted to find sanctuary in Egypt, but was murdered there.

76. Josephus gives two reasons for Scaurus' choice of Aristobulus. (1) He judged the more wealthy Aristobulus to be in a better position to pay the promised 400 talents, and (2) the entrenched forces of Aristobulus would have been harder to defeat than those of Hyrcanus and Aretas, which were encamped around Jerusalem. (*Antiquities*, XIV, 30–31.)

77. *Antiquitites*, XIV, 33, gives this brother's name as Phallion. Cf. *Jewish War*, VI, 130.

78. Under the Romans, Antioch-on-the-Orontes was an important administrative and commercial center. The city was beautified and expanded, and it became home to an important Jewish community and a center of early Christian activity (Acts 11:19, and elsewhere).

79. Josephus says that the Romans took advantage of the Jewish sabbath to raise their earthworks.

> But if it were not our national custom to rest on the Sabbath day, the earthworks would not have been finished, because the Jews would have prevented this; for the Law permits us to defend ourselves against those who begin a battle and strike us, but it does not allow us to fight against an enemy that does anything else. Of this fact the Romans were well aware, and on those days which we call the Sabbath, they did not shoot at the Jews or meet them in hand to hand combat, but instead they raised earthworks and towers, and brought up their siege-engines in order that these might be put to work the following day (*Antiquities*, XIV, 63–64. cf. 1 Macc. 2:41).

80. Lucius Cornelius Sulla (138–78 BC) was a Roman political and military leader. He was an ally of Pompey in the civil war against Marius (88 BC) and in the campaign against Mithradates of Pontus (87–82). From 82 to 79 he was dictator of Rome.

81. *Antiquities*, XIV, 71.

82. In the translation of R. B. Wright, *OTP*, 2:659.

83. Helpful discussions of Diaspora Judaism during the Hellenistic and Roman Periods may be found in S. Applebaum, "The Social and Economic Status of the Jews of the Diaspora," in S. Safrai and M. Stern, eds., *The Jewish People in the First Century* (Philadelphia: Fortress Press, 1976), 701–727; John J. Collins, *Between Athens and Jerusalem: Jewish Identity in the Hellenistic Diaspora* (New York: Crossroad, 1983); W. D. Davies and Louis Finkelstein, eds., *The Cambridge History of Judaism*, vol. 2: *The Hellenistic Age* (Cambridge: Cambridge Univ. Press, 1989); Michael Grant, *The Jews in the Roman World* (New York: Scribners, 1973); Helmut Koester, *Introduction to the New Testament*, vol. 1:

History, Culture and Religion of the Hellenistic Age (Philadelphia: Fortress Press; Berlin: Walter de Gruyter, 1982), 218–228; Jacob Neusner, *A History of the Jews in Babylonia*, vol. 1: *The Parthian Period* (Leiden: Brill, 1965); *HJB* 3:1:1–777; Tcherikover, *Hellenistic Culture and the Jews*, tr. S. Applebaum (Philadelphia: Jewish Publication Society, 1959), 186–203.

84. The work of the rabbis of Jamnia (Yavneh) is discussed, 311–12.

85. Hillel is discussed, 317–20.

86. The Babylonian Talmud is discussed, 64.

87. *Antiquities*, XII, 387–388. The Onias in question is apparently Onias III, although there is some uncertainty over the matter. See S. B. Hoenig, "Onias," *IDB* 3:603–604.

88. *Antiquities*, XIII, 284–287, 348–351.

89. Relevant passages from Manetho are to be found in Menaham Stern, ed. *Greek and Latin Authors on Jews and Judaism*, vol. 1: *From Herodotus to Plutarch* (Jerusalem: Israel Academy of Sciences and Humanities, 1976), 62–86.

CHAPTER 3. APOCALYPTIC

1. A large body of scholarly literature has been written on the subject of apocalyptic. The interested student may consult the following volumes, which should prove particularly helpful: S. B. Frost, *Old Testament Apocalyptic: Its Origin and Growth* (London: Epworth, 1952); Paul Hanson, *The Dawn of Apocalyptic* (Philadelphia: Fortress Press, 1975); Paul Hanson, *Old Testament Apocalyptic* (Nashville: Abingdon, 1988); Klaus Koch, *The Rediscovery of Apocalyptic*, tr. M. Kohl (London: SCM Press, 1972); George W. E. Nickelsburg, *Jewish Literature Between the Bible and the Mishnah* (Philadelphia: Fortress Press, 1981) hereafter cited as *JL*; Christopher Rowland, *The Open Heaven: A Study of Apocalyptic in Judaism and Early Christian History*, (London: SPCK, 1982); H. H. Rowley, *The Relevance of Apocalyptic* (New York: Association Press, 1944, 1964); D. S. Russell, *The Method and Message of Jewish Apocalyptic* (Philadelphia: Westminster Press, 1964).

2. The German scholar Gerhard von Rad, for example, argued that important roots of apocalyptic thought are to be found in Israel's Wisdom tradition, especially in connection with the concept of the "divine determination of times." See his *Wisdom in Israel* (Nashville: Abingdon, 1972), 263–283.

3. See discussion of messiah, 240–48.

4. This tendency to make God so majestic as to be unapproachable may be seen at Qumran where, as among other communities of Jews, it was forbidden even to speak the divine name Yahweh:

> If any man has uttered the [Most] Venerable Name, even though frivolously, or as a result of shock, or for any other reason whatever, while reading the Book of praying, he shall be dismissed and shall return to the Council of the Community no more. (The Community Rule, VI [also called the Manual of Discipline] *DSSE*, 83.)

5. For a full discussion of apocalyptic angelology and demonology, see D. S. Russell, *The Method and Message of Jewish Apocalyptic* (Philadelphia: Westminster Press, 1964), 235–262.

6. Satan is referred to in three OT passages: Job 1—2, Zech. 3:1–5, and 1 Chron. 21:1.

7. Some scholars have argued that the Similitudes of Enoch are a Christian-era interpolation into an otherwise pre-Christian work. This view has gained some support by the fact that, whereas fragments of 1 Enoch were found at Qumran, none of the fragments represent the Similitudes. If this should be so, it would, of course, rule out any influence of 1 Enoch on the writers of the NT. Most scholars, however, continue to argue for the unity of 1 Enoch, including the Similitudes. See *OTP,* 1:6f.

8. The references to an "anointed one" in Dan. 9:25, 26 appear to have nothing to do with a transcendent divine being, but are directed at, respectively, Zerubbabel (or Joshua, see Ezra 3:8, Zech. 6:9–14) and the high priest Onias III. The "son of man" (NRSV: "human being") of Dan. 7:13 seems to refer to the entire faithful community of Jews.

9. 1 Macc. 14:9–15 is quoted, 48.

10. Some texts in the Testaments of the Twelve Patriarchs seem to speak of two messiahs, a Davidic as well as a Levitical. But it has been objected that these texts may be later, Christian-era interpolations. See Russell, *Method and Message,* 310–316 and *OTP* 1:775–780. Some Qumran texts refer to two (or more) messiahs. See 242–43.

11. One interesting exception to apocalyptic's emphasis upon the resurrection of the dead is the Book of Jubilees that, instead, sometimes appears to teach a belief in the immortality of the soul (Jub. 23:31).

12. The members of the Qumran community may have held to a resurrection hope. See Russell, *Method and Message,* 373f.

13. ANET, 67.

14. See also especially Isa. 27:1. Job 26:12–13 and Ps. 89:10 (where there is also conflict between God and the monster), 40:15—41:11 (where Behemoth appears to be a hippopotamus, Leviathan a crocodile), Ps. 74:13–14 (where the carcass of the dragon also becomes food, here for wild beasts) are also interesting OT texts in which the dragon motif appears.

15. An intresting treatment of the dragon motif in creation and re-creation may be found in Bernhard Anderson, *Creation Versus Chaos* (New York: Association Press, 1957).

16. Cf. Amos 7:1, Jer. 1:11, Ezek. 1:1, Zech. 1:8, and elsewhere.

17. In Dan. 2:36–45, interestingly enough, it is Nebuchadnezzar who dreams, but Daniel who interprets. Cf. the story of Pharaoh's dream in Gen. 41.

18. There are a number of fine commentaries on the Book of Daniel that will add details to the discussion in this volume. They include: John J. Collins, *Daniel, First Maccabees, Second Maccabees* (Wilmington, Del.: M. Glazier, 1981);

John J. Collins, *The Forms of Old Testament Literature,* vol. 20: *Daniel: With an Introduction to Apocalypitc Literature* (Grand Rapids: Eerdmans, 1984); Louis F. Hartman and Alexander A. Di Lella, *The Book of Daniel, AB* 23; Andre Lacocque, *The Book of Daniel,* tr. David Pellance (Atlanta: John Knox Press, 1979); Norman W. Porteous, *Daniel: A Commentary,* Old Testament Library (Philadelphia: Westminster Press, 1965); W. Sibley Towner, *Daniel* (Atlanta: John Knox Press, 1984).

19. Other examples of OT literature which contain important apocalyptic elements include Isa. 24—27, Ezekiel, Joel, and Zechariah 1—8.

20. The Hebrew sections of Daniel are 1:1—2:4 and 8:1—12:13, with the Aramaic section sandwiched between them.

21. On the encounter in Egypt between Antiochus and the Romans, see 40.

22. ANET, 149–155.

23. It is interesting that the reference to Daniel is dropped in the Lucan parallel, Luke 21:20, although the sense is retained.

24. Helpful discussions of the contents and signficance of 1 Enoch may be found in the following: Matthew Black, *The Book of Enoch or I Enoch* (Leiden: Brill, 1985); R. H. Charles, APOT 2:163–281; R. H. Charles, *The Book of Enoch* (Oxford: Oxford Univ. Press, 1983); E. Isaac, *OTP* 1:5–89 (where there is also the most recent critical translation into English of the Ethiopic text); M. A. Knibb, *AOT,* 169–319; *JL,* 46–55, 90–94, 145–151, 214–223; H. H. Rowley, *The Relevance of Apocalyptic,* (New York: Association Press, 1964), 57–64. Quotations in this volume from 1 Enoch are from the translation of Isaac.

25. In addition to 1 Enoch, two other important apocalyptic writings are credited to this patriarch. 2 Enoch, also known as the Slavonic Apocalypse of Enoch, is a fanciful elaboration of the brief biblical account of the lives of Enoch and Methuselah in Gen. 5:21–32. The date and place of its composition have been subjects of wide disagreement (see F. I. Anderson, *OTP* 1:94–97). 3 Enoch, or the Hebrew Apocalypse of Enoch, is a piece of rabbinic speculative lore whose complex history of composition was completed about the fifth or sixth century AD. See P. Alexander, *OTP* 1:225–229.

26. Fragments of all five parts of 1 Enoch were discovered at Qumran, with the exception of the Similitudes.

27. Although the writers of the NT were familiar with a number of Jewish pseudepigraphal writings, only Enoch is cited by name in the NT. For a discussion of some of the issues raised by the special relationship between Jude and 1 Enoch, see *OTP* 2:25, 72–74, 137–141.

28. These examples are extracted from the much longer list of R. H. Charles, *APOT* 2:180–181, and the same author's *The Book of Enoch or 1 Enoch* (Oxford: Clarendon, 1912), xcv–ciii.

29. For a brief discussion of the role in 1 Enoch 37—71 in the development of messianism, see 243.

30. For further reading concerning the Testaments of the Twelve Patriarchs one should consult APOT 2:282–367; J. J. Collins, *Between Athens and Jerusalem* (New York: Crossroad, 1983), 154–162; H. W. Hollander and M. de Jonge, *The Testaments of the Twelve Patriarchs* (Leiden: Brill, 1985); M. de Jonge, *AOT*, 505–600; H. C. Kee, *OTP* 1:775–828 (where there is a recent translation of the text); *JL*, 231–241. Quotations from the Testaments in this volume are from the translation of Kee.

31. Cf. also Jub. 20–22.

32. See H. C. Kee, *OTP* 1:779.

33. For a fuller listing of NT texts influences by the Testaments of the Twelve Patriarchs, see R. H. Charles, *APOT* 2:291–292, and the same author's *The Testaments of the Twelve Patriarchs* (London: Black, 1908), lxxviii–xcii.

34. See, for example, 2 Enoch 3—22.

35. R. H. Charles, *APOT*, 2:293.

36. For further exploration of Jubilees see R. H. Charles, *APOT* 2:1–82; R. H. Charles and C. Rabin, *AOT*, 1–139; O. S. Wintermute, *OTP* 2:35–142 (where there is a recent translation); *JL*, 73–80. The quotations from Jubilees in this volume are from the translation of Wintermute.

37. As will be discussed, 310, Masada was the last Zealot stronghold to fall to the Romans (in 74 AD) after the insurrection of 66–70.

38. This is one of several places where Jubilees seems dependent upon 1 Enoch (or perhaps, vice versa).

39. For the text of the Jewish and Christian Sibylline Oracles see the recent translation (and accompanying critical commentary) by J. J. Collins, *OTP* 1:317–472. Helpful discussions also include: Collins, *Between Athens and Jerusalem*, 148–153; Collins, *JW*, 357–381; *JL*, 162–165, *HLP* 3:618–654. The quotations from the Sibylline Oracles in this volume are from the translation of Collins.

40. Because of discrepancies between the two collections, the books are numbered 1–8, 11–14.

41. This English translation of the *Dies Irae* is from Joseph Connelly, *Hymns of the Roman Liturgy* (Westminster, Md.: Newman Press, 1957), 252.

42. See the discussion, 245–47. It is uncertain whether 3:652–656 constitutes the end of an oracle or is part of the following passage, 3:657–808. Collins believes that 1.656 is the end of the fourth oracle of the main corpus (*OTP* 2:376), whereas *HJB* 2:501–502 understands there to be no seam between 11.656 and 657.

43. Additional information concerning the Psalms of Solomon may be found in S. P. Brock, *AOT*, 649–682; G. Buchanan Gray, *APOT* 2:625–652; R. B. Wright, *OTP* 2:639–670 (including a new translation); D. Flusser *JW*, 573–574; *JL*, 203–212. The quotations of Psalms of Solomon in this volume are from the translation of Wright.

44. The translation of this phrase as "Lord Messiah" is not completely certain. See *OTP* 2:667–668, n. z.

45. Discussions (including texts) of these examples of early apocalyptic may be found in *OTP* 1.

46. Qumran is discussed, 134–69.

47. For a discussion of midrash, see 106–10.

CHAPTER 4. THE THEOLOGY OF PALESTINIAN JUDAISM

1. The Hebrew word *torah* is traditionally translated "law," but its larger meaning is something like *teaching, instruction,* or even *revelation.* (See James Sanders, *Torah and Canon,* [Philadelphia: Fortress Press, 1972], 1–3). It is in this latter sense that the word, capitalized as Torah, is applied to the first five books of the OT or to significant parts of those books, for example, the Ten Commandments (Exod. 20:1–17, Deut. 5:6–21). Because there is no precise equivalent in English to this important term, the Hebrew form of the word is used in this volume.

2. The choice of the year 400 BC as the time by which the Pentateuch had received canonical status rests on the fact that this is the approximate time of the final schism between the Jews and the Samaritans, who also hold the Pentateuch to be sacred scripture.

3. The rabbi Gamaliel I was, according to one rabbinic tradition, the grandson of the venerated Hillel and, according to the NT, the teacher of the apostle Paul (Acts 22:3). See 317–20.

4. Quoted in *HJP* 2:333.

5. The bibliography relating to midrashim is extensive. For a basic bibliography and, in addition, a systematic description of major midrashim, see *HJP* 1:90–99.

6. H. D. Mantel in *WHJP* 8:41.

7. Jacob Z. Lauterbach, ed., *Mekilta de-Rabbi Ishmael,* vol. 2 (Philadelphia: Jewish Publication Society, 1933), 25. Palm branches and tents were associated with the autumn festivals of the Day of Atonement and Sukkoth (meaning "tents").

8. Quoted from *DSSE,* 218–219.

9. H. Freedman and Maurice Simon, eds., *Misrash Rabbah,* vol. 1 (London: Soncino, 1939), 80–86. The translation in this present volume has been slightly altered for purposes of clarity. A more recent translation of the same text may be found in Jacob Neusner, *Genesis Rabbah: The Judaic Comentary to the Book of Genesis,* Brown Judaic Studies 104 (Atlanta: Scholars Press, 1985), 109–118.

10. The canon of the Alexandrian Jews, as found in the Septuagint, was another matter, as we shall discuss, 171–75.

11. *Against Apion,* 1:8 (38–41). In arriving at the number 22, Josephus apparently considered each of the following to be one book: 1 & 2 Samuel; 1 & 2 Kings; Jeremiah + Lamentations; 1 & 2 Chronicles + Ezra-Nehemiah. The usual rabbinic enumeration was 24 (cf. 4 Ezra 14:44–46), a figure achieved by counting Chronicles and Ezra-Nehemiah as two books, and by regarding Jeremiah and Lamentations separately.

12. The rabbinic phrase that in the Mishnah and elsewhere is used to designate a canonical writing is "that which renders the hands unclean." This seems to imply that contact with a copy of the scriptures conveys an aspect of their holiness to the person's hands, so that the hands are no longer suitable for common use unless and until they are ritually purified.

13. *HJP* 2:319–320.

14. For references to Masada, see 304, 310.

15. Origen and Jerome, among other early Christian writers, stated that the Sadducees accepted only the Pentateuch as scripture, but that view is rejected by some modern scholars on the grounds that Josephus makes no mention of it. See *HJP* 2:408.

16. *Life*, 2. Josephus' claim concerning the popularity of the Pharisees has been called into question by some scholars. See especially E. P. Sanders, *Jesus and Judaism* (Philadelphia: Fortress Press, 1985), 188, 194–198.

17. See the following fine studies of the relationship between Jesus and early Judaism: Sanders, *Jesus and Judaism*, Geza Vermes, *Jesus the Jew* (New York: Macmillan, 1973); Geza Vermes, *Jesus and the World of Judaism* (Philadelphia: Fortress Press, 1983).

18. *Antiquities*, XVII, 42.

19. *Antiquities*, XIII, 288. But see n. 16, above.

20. Quoted in *HJP* 2:400.

21. For a discussion of the nature of "separateness" in Pharisaic life, see Sanders, *Jesus and Judaism*, 49.

22. E. P. Sanders argues against the identification of the *Haverim* with the Pharisees, *Jesus and Judaism*, 187–188.

23. *Jewish War*, II, 166.

24. *Antiquities*, XIII, 173.

25. *Jewish War*, II, 163.

26. *Jewish War*, II, 162.

27. Because of the negative portrait of the Pharisees in the NT, Christians have often entertained an incomplete understanding of the nature of Pharisaism. The literature of the church has frequently portrayed these sectarians as excessively legalistic, as being "narrow, censorious, self-righteous and conceited," in the words of one writer (Elmer W. K. Mould, *Essentials of Bible History* [New York: Ronald Press, 1951], 475, quoted with approval by Raymond F. Surburg, *Introduction to the Intertestamental Period* [St. Louis: Concordia, 1975], 56.) Indeed, the adjective "pharisaic" has long been used as a synonym for "hypocritical," while the Pharisee has become the whipping boy of much Christian exegesis. In this connection, two observations are in order. The first is that it should be remembered that those passages in the NT that describe the hypocrisy or excessive legalism of the Pharisees are part of a larger polemic directed by the early church toward the synogogue. Assuming that the anti-Pharisaic statements in the Gospels represent the actual words

of Jesus, the fact that they are recorded so often and so emphatically by the Evangelists indicates that they form part of an ongoing debate between early Christians and Jews.

A second thing to be remembered is that, like most polemic, this one is partial and distorted. Many Pharisees certainly must have represented a theological outlook that was wooden and sterile, especially when compared with the radical freedom preached by Jesus. But the case may be made, as it has been made by many scholars, that, when compared with other views of Torah, that of the Pharisees was progressive and open in the sense that it urged men and women to move beyond the letter of the Torah itself and to apply the meaning of God's instruction to every area of human life. During much of the history of the Pharisees the issue was not so much bondage to or freedom from the Law in the sense in which Paul posed the question, but whether the Torah had any claim upon human life at all. The Pharisees staked their lives upon their belief that it did.

28. *Antiquities*, XIII, 293.

29. This and previous excerpt quoted in *HJP* 2:384, 386.

30. *HJP* 2:409.

31. For other explanations of the possible derivation of the word *Sadducee*, see *HJP* 2:404–407.

32. An extensive survey of the scholarly literature on the Essenes may be found in *HJP* 2:555–558. See also G. Vermes, *The Dead Sea Scrolls: Qumran in Perspective* (Philadelphia: Fortress Press, 1977, 1985), 157–162.

33. For a description of the contributions of the various ancient sources, including that of the third century AD Christian writer, Hippolytus, see W. R. Farmer, "Essenes," *IDB* 2:143–145. See also *HJP* 2:562–574.

34. See the discussion of Essene origins in *HJP* 2:559.

35. From *DSSE*, 240.

36. The resettlement of the Qumran site (after its initial settlement in the eighth or seventh century BC) has been dated to a time not long before 135 BC. See Roland de Vaux, *Archaeology and the Dead Sea Scrolls* (London: Oxford Univ. Press, 1973), 5.

37. *Jewish War*, V, 145.

38. *Antiquities*, XV, 373–379.

39. *Jewish War*, II, 567; III, 11, 19.

40. *Jewish War*, II, 152–153.

41. *HJP* 2:572.

42. *Jewish War*, II, 145.

43. Philo, *Every Good Man is Free*, 81–82. The translation of this difficult passage is that of F. H. Colson, *Philo*, Loeb Classical Library, 9:59.

44. Josephus' precise words about the Essene belief concerning life after death portray a hope in the immortality of the soul rather than a belief in the

resurrection of the body. If Josephus is accurate, the possibility is thus raised of nonJewish influences upon the sects. On the other hand, Josephus, as he does elsewhere, may simply be using the language of Greek philosophy to convey a Jewish theological tenet. Josephus writes:

> It is their unmistakable conviction that bodies are corruptible and the material composing them impermanent, whereas the soul is immortal forever. Emanating from the most rarified ether they are trapped, as it were, in the prison house of the body, as if drawn down by one of nature's spells. But when they are released from the bonds of the flesh, then, as though liberated from a long servitude, they rejoice and soar aloft. Holding, I believe, to the same conception as the Greeks, they declare that for the good souls there waits a home beyond the ocean, a place not troubled by rain or snow or heat, but refreshed by a gentle west wind blowing gently from the ocean, while they consign bad souls to a murky, stormy abyss, full of punishments that know no end (*Jewish War*, II, 154–155).

45. See the discussion, 242–43.

46. Pliny the Elder, *Naturalis Historia*, 5:73. Quoted from Menahem Stern, ed., *Greek and Latin Authors on Jews and Judaism* (Jerusalem: Israel Academy of Sciences and Humanities, 1976), 472.

47. A helpful bibliography of books and articles that deal with various aspects of Samaritan studies may be found in Reinhard Pummer, *The Samaritans* (Leiden: Brill, 1987), xi–xiv. See also John Macdonald, *The Theology of the Samaritans* (London: SCM, 1964), 457–463.

48. In this regard it is perhaps instructive to note that the modern State of Israel has declared Samaritans to be Jews and has extended to them the privileges of the law of return.

48. The Samaritan Pentateuch also reads "Mount Gerizim" in Deut. 27:4 where the (Jewish) Masoretic text has "Mount Ebal." Gerizim and Ebal, which rise in the central hill country near the site of ancient Samaria, form between them a valley in which the ancient village of Shechem and the modern town of Nablus lie. The importance of the area as a cultic center is reflected in the accounts of Joshua's Shechem assembly in Josh. 24 and of the confrontation at Shechem between the leaders of the Northern tribes and King Rehoboam in 1 Kings 12:1–19.

50. The Chronicle Adler, in the form in which it is now known, dates from the nineteenth century AD, but there is every reason to believe that it contains some very old material. This account of the apostasy of the priest Eli, which is also contained in the older Samaritan Book of Joshua, would seem to be one of those ancient traditions. Since only the Torah is considered canonical by the Samaritans, none of the Samaritan accounts of their origins can claim scriptural authority, but that by no means diminishes their importance to the Samaritan community. This quotation is found in John Bowman, ed and tr.,

Samaritan Documents Relating to their History, Religion and Life (Pittsburg: Pick-wick, 1977), 89–90. This book is helpful not only for its fresh translations of selected Samaritan texts, but also for its critical discussions of Samaritan literature.

51. Ithamar is known from the OT as one of the four sons of Aaron (Exod. 6:23, and elsewhere).

52. ANET, 284–285.

53. One example of Chronicles' tolerant attitude toward the Samaritans is the story of the Samaritan prophet Oded in 2 Chron. 28:8–15, a beautiful narrative of compassion that is almost surely the literary inspiration for Jesus' parable of the good Samaritan in Luke 10:29–37. The relation between these two passages has often been overlooked by NT scholars, but is emphasized by the following comparison of a portion of the two texts:

Then those who were mentioned by name got up and took the captives, and with the booty they clothed all that were naked among them; they clothed them, gave them sandals, provided them with food and drink, and *anointed them;* and *carrying all the feeble among them on donkeys,* they brought them to their kindred

But a Samaritan while traveling came near him; and when he saw him, he was moved with pity. He went to him and bandaged his wounds, having

poured oil and wine on them. Then he put him on his own animal, brought him to an inn, and took care of him. The next day he took out two denarii and gave them to the innkeeper, and said, "Take care of him; and when I come back, I will repay you whatever more you spend."   (Luke 10:33f.)

*   *   *   *

at *Jericho,* the city of palms. Then they returned to Samaria.
(2 Chron. 28:15)

A man was going down from Jerusalem to *Jericho* . . .
(Luke 10:30)

For further discussion, see J. D. Crossan, *In Parables* (New York: Harper & Row, 1973), 65.

54. There is good reason to believe that this passage from the Book of Ezra has confused Zerubbabel with the earlier leader Sheshbazzar (cf. Ezra 1:8, and elsewhere), and that this Samaritan interference brought to a halt the first effort to rebuild the Temple, begun shortly after Sheshbazzar and his group arrived in Jerusalem in 538 BC. Zerubbabel, on the other hand, seems to have come to Jerusalem about 520 (Cf. Ezra 5:1–2, Hag. 1:1).

55. *Antiquities*, XI, 321–328. Despite the antiquity of the OT traditions concerning the importance of the Schechem-Mt. Gerizim area, evidence that the Samaritans looked to this spot as the center of their cult from the days of Joshua seems contradicted by the supremacy of Bethel, Dan, and Gilgal as the location of shrines in the North (cf. 1 Kings 12:29, Amos 4:4).

56. *Jewish War*, III, 307–315. Josephus makes no effort to suppress his disdain of the Samaritans, thus the authenticity of his account of their suffering in the time of Vespasian (which was also Josephus' own time) has much to commend it. Josephus places the figure of Samaritan deaths on Mt. Gerizim at 11,600.

57. Modern Samaritan theology is characterized by five principals: 1. Belief in one God. 2. Belief in Moses as God's supreme prophet. 3. Belief in the Holy Torah. 4. Belief in Mt. Gerizim as the most sacred place of worship. 5. Belief in the Day of Vengeance and Recompense. See John Bowman, ed., *The Samaritan Problem*, tr. Alfred M. Johnson, Jr., (Pittsburg: Pickwick, 1975), 29–56; T. H. Gaster, "Samaritans," IDB 4:190–197; John Macdonald, *The Theology of the Samaritans* (London: SCM, 1964).

58. For photographs of Samaritan synagogues in Holon and Nablus and on Mt. Gerizim, see Pummer, *The Samaritans*, Plates XVIII and XIX.

59. For the full text see Bowman, ed. and tr., *Samaritan Documents*, 23–24.

60. See Bowman, ed., *Samaritan Problem*, 91–118.

61. That the Samaritan custom of a sacrificial Passover has been continued since antiquity cannot be conclusively proved. It is interesting, however, that the Samaritans distinguish between Passover proper and the Festival of Unleavened Bread. These are spoken of as being identical in some OT texts (Deut. 16:1–8, 16), but, in fact, may originally have been independent festivals. See Pummer, 21–22.

62. For a discussion of Samaritan eschatology, see Macdonald, *Theology of the Samaritans*, 357–415.

63. Helpful literature on the synagogue includes, *HJP*, 2:423–463; I. Sonne, "Synagogue," IDB 4:476–491.

64. The importance of the synagogue among Greek-speaking Jews is evidenced by the fact that the name by which this particularly Jewish institution is widely known is its Greek designation, *synagoge*, not its Hebrew, *keneset*. Both words mean *a gathering together [of people]*, thus, a congregation. The Hebrew term, of course, has been preserved as the name of the parliamentary body in the modern State of Israel.

65. On synagogue worship, see Jacob J. Petuchowski, "The Liturgy of the Synagogue: History, Structure, and Contents," in William Scott Green, ed., *Approaches to Ancient Judaism*, Brown Judaic Studies 27, Vol. 4 (Chico, Calif.: Scholars Press, 1983), 1–64. The discussion in this volume is particularly dependent upon *HJP* 2:447–454.

66. For the text of the *Shemoneh 'Esreh* in both its Palestinian and Babylonian versions, see *HJP* 2:454–463.

67. Cf. Acts. 13:15, where Paul uncharacteristically stands to interpret the text.

68. The Targumim have come down to us in several traditions, the most important being the Targum Onkelos on the Pentateuch, the Targum Jonathan on the Prophets (both of which may have originated in Jewish circles in Babylonia) and the Palestinian Targumim. For a helpful discussion, see *HJP* 1:99–105.

69. Both Targum texts here are quoted from Bruce D. Chilton, *The Isaiah Targum*, The Aramaic Bible, Vol. 11 (Wilmington, Del.: M. Glazier, 1987), 15, 28. N. B. Chilton's note at the bottom of 15.

70. Quoted from Petuchowski, "The Liturgy," 33.

71. For a helpful discussion of the Sanhedrin, plus an extensive bibliography, see *HJP* 2:199–226.

72. *Antiquities*, XII, 138. The authenticity of this letter of Antiochus has been disputed.

73. In this connection a statement by the Hellenistic historian Hecataeus of Abdera is interesting. Hecataeus, who was a contemporary of Alexander the Great and Ptolemy I, transmits some interesting bits of misinformation about the Jews, namely, that Moses founded the city of Jerusalem and built its Temple. But in matters that have to do with his own time, he is perhaps more accurate, at least in his brief portrait of the power of the Jewish high priest. His work is now lost, and the following is from a fragment preserved by the first century BC writer Diodorus Siculus (i.e., the Sicilian):

> . . . authority over the people is regularly vested in whichever priest is regarded as superior to his colleagues in wisdom and virtue. This man they call the High Priest, and believe that he acts as a messenger to them of God's commandments. It is he, we are told, who in their assemblies and other gatherings announces what is ordained, and the Jews are so docile in such matters that straightway they fall to the ground and do reverence to the High Priest when he expounds the commandments to them. Quoted from Menahem Stern, ed., *Greek and Latin Authors on Jews and Judaism*, vol. 1:From Herodotus to Plutarch. (Jerusalem: Israel Academy of Sciences and Humanities), 1987), 28.

74. *Antiquities*, XIV, 175.

CHAPTER 5. QUMRAN

1. For further reading on the Qumran community and its literature, consult W. H. Brownlee, *The Meaning of the Qumran Scrolls for the Bible* (Oxford: Oxford Univ. Press, 1964); G. R. Driver, *The Judaean Scrolls: The Problem and A Solution* (Oxford: Blackwell, 1965); Menahem Mansoor, *The Dead Sea Scrolls*, 2d ed. (Grand Rapids: Baker, 1983); H. Ringgren, *The Faith of Qumran: Theology of the Dead Sea Scrolls* (Philadelphia: Fortress Press, 1963); Roland de Vaux, *Archaeology and the Dead Sea Scrolls* (Oxford: Oxford Univ. Press, 1973); Geza Vermes,

The Dead Sea Scrolls: Qumran in Perspective (Philadelphia: Fortress Press, 1977); Geza Vermes, *Discovery in the Judaean Desert* (New York: Desclee, 1956).

2. The name Qumran, taken from the nearby Wadi Qumran, was bestowed upon the ruined settlement by its first scholarly investigators, in the absence of any information concerning the name of the settlement in antiquity. The scrolls refer to the site and its inhabitants by various descriptive designations, such as "place of exile," "house of holiness," and the like.

3. See 122.

4. See 119.

5. As this volume was being prepared for publication the Henry E. Huntington Library of San Marino, CA, announced the release of photographs of hundreds of unpublished manuscripts from Qumran. The extent to which these documents, when carefully studied, will alter the scholarly consensus concerning Qumran is yet to be made clear. However, the discussion which this material will generate will be closely followed by all interested persons. See *Biblical Archaeology Review* 17:6 (Nov./Dec. 1991), 62–72, and articles in subsequent issues.

6. For this particular version of the history of the Qumran sect, I am indebted to Vermes, *Dead Sea Scrolls*. A helpful critique of the "Maccabean thesis" may be found in Philip R. Callaway, *The History of the Qumran Community* (Sheffield: J.S.O.T. Press, 1988). For a summary of different views concerning the identity of the Wicked Priest and the Teacher of Righteousness, see E. Jacob, "Dead Sea Scrolls," *IDB* 1:797.

7. The Habakkuk Commentary VIII, G. Vermes, *DSSE*, 240.

8. The Damascus Document I, *DSSE*, 97.

9. The Habakkuk Commentary XI, *DSSE*, 241–242.

10. Commentary on Psalm 37, *DSSE*, 245.

11. The Nahum Commentary I, *DSSE*, 232.

12. The Habakkuk Commentary II, *DSSE*, 236

13. The Habakkuk Commentary VII, *DSSE*, 239. Compare the manner in which some NT writers urge patience on the part of their readers in light of the delay of the *parousia*, as in 2 Pet. 3:3–9.

14. The discovery in the Zealot stronghold of Masada, which fell to the Romans in 74 AD, of a fragment of the Angelic Liturgy from Qumran has raised the possibility that Qumran was abandoned by the sectarians before the Roman destruction. It was then briefly occupied, so the theory goes, by a group of Zealots who later carried the Angelic Liturgy with them to Masada. However, this is but one of several theories to account for the presence of a Qumran document at Masada.

15. Vermes, *Dead Sea Scrolls*, 201.

16. The Damascus Rule XVI (*DSSE*, 109) and V (*DSSE*, 101).

17. The Community Rule V, *DSSE*, 78.

18. The Community Rule XIV, *DSSE*, 72.

19. The Community Rule III, *DSSE*, 75.

20. The War Scroll XV, *DSSE*, 144.

21. The Damascus Rule, B II, *DSSE*, 107.

22. Vermes, *Dead Sea Scrolls*, 183, sketches the following schematic for the final battle:

1. The Community fights against the "army of Satan"
   and wicked gentiles and moves to Jerusalem . . . .   6 years
2. A sabbatic year in which Temple worship is restored . . . . . .   1 year
3. War against the "Sons of Shem." . . . .   9 years
4. War against the "Sons of Ham.". . . . .   10 years
5. War against the "Sons of Japheth." . . . .   10 years
6. Four sabbatic years (during the 39 years of #3–5 above) . . . .   4 years

   Total: 40 years

23. The Messianic Rule II, *DSSE*, 121.

24. The Commentary on Isaiah (ii), *DSSE*, 227.

25. From the Blessing of the Prince of the Congregation, *DSSE*, 208–209.

26. The Community Rule IX, *DSSE*, 87.

27. The Heavenly Prince Melchizedek, *DSSE*, 267.

28. The Community Rule XI, *DSSE*, 94.

29. For a full discussion of the life of the sect see Vermes, *Dead Sea Scrolls*, 87–109.

30. The Community Rule V, *DSSE*, 79.

31. The Community Rule VI, *DSSE*, 81.

32. The War Rule II, *DSSE*, 125.

33. It is interesting that the Book of Jubilees describes essentially the same calendar as that followed at Qumran. Vermes (*Dead Sea Scrolls*, 177) has suggested that it was this calendrical difference that allowed the high priest Jonathan to go to Qumran on the Day of Atonement in order to torment the Teacher of Righteousness. It was the Day of Atonement at Qumran only, for if it had been the Day of Atonement in Jerusalem, the high priest could not have left the city.

34. This summary of arguments for and against identifying the Qumran community with the Essenes is based upon that in *HJP* 2:583–585, where further references may be found.

35. For this discussion and that on Qumran and the Early Christian Movement, I am indebted to Vermes, *Dead Sea Scrolls*, 198–209, 211–221.

36. The Habakkuk Commentary XI, *DSSE*, 242.

37. A fine discussion of individual documents from the Qumran library may be found in Vermes, *Dead Sea Scrolls*, 45–86. The quotations from the Qumran scrolls found here (with the exception of those from the Temple Scroll) are from *DSSE*.

38. The Community Rule, I, II, III, *DSSE*, 72, 75, 77.

39. The Comunity Rule, V, *DSSE*, 78–79.

40. The Community Rule, IX, *DSSE*, 87–88.

41. The Community Rule, X, *DSSE*, 89–90.

42. The definitive work on the Temple Scroll is that of Yigael Yadin, *The Temple Scroll*. 3 vols. Jerusalem: Israel Exploration Society, 1983). See also *HJP* 3:406–420.

43. In this connection, scholars have noticed similarities between the description of the Temple in the Scroll and that of Solomon's Temple in Josephus (*Antiquities*, VIII, 61–98).

44. Quotations here are in the translation of Yadin. See *Temple Scroll* 2:128–129.

45. *Ibid.*, 254.

46. S. Schechter, *Documents of Jewish Sectaries: Fragments of a Zadokite Work*. 1910. Reprint. (New York: Ktav, 1970).

47. The Damascus Rule, VII, *DSSE*, 104.

48. The Damascus Rule, X, XI, *DSSE*, 112–113.

49. The War Rule, I, *DSSE*, 124–125.

50. The War Rule, V, *DSSE*, 130.

51. The War Rule, VII, *DSSE*, 132.

52. The War Rule, XVII, *DSSE*, 145.

53. The War Rule, XVII, *DSSE*, 146.

54. The War Rule, XIV, *DSSE*, 141–142.

55. The Messianic Rule, II, *DSSE*, 121.

56. The Hymns, II, *DSSE*, 156.

57. The Hymns, III, *DSSE*, 160.

58. The Hymns, VIII, *DSSE*, 176–177.

59. The Hymns, X, *DSSE*, 182.

60. The Hymns, V, *DSSE*, 167.

61. The Genesis Apocryphon, II, *DSSE*, 216.

62. The Genesis Apocryphon, XX, *DSSE*, 218.

63. See the discussion of the Genesis Apocryphon above, 000–000.

64. The Genesis Apocryphon, XX, *DSSE*, 220.

65. The Genesis Apocryphon, XXII, *DSSE*, 222–223.

66. The Habakkuk Commentary, II, III, *DSSE*, 237.

CHAPTER 6. ADDITIONAL JEWISH LITERATURE OF THE HELLENISTIC PERIOD (1)

1. For further reading on the Septuagint, see Roger Beckwith, *The Old Testament Canon of the New Testament Church* (Grand Rapids: Eerdmans, 1985); Sidney Jellicoe, *The Septuagint and Modern Study* (Oxford: Oxford Univ. Press, 1968); Sidney Jellicoe, ed., *Studies in the Septuagint: Origins, Recensions, and Interpretations* (New York: Ktav, 1974); Bleddyn J. Roberts, *The Old Testament Text and Versions* (Cardiff: University of Wales Press, 1951); Albert C. Sundberg, *The Old Testament of the Early Church* (Cambridge, Mass.: Harvard Univ. Press,

1964); Henry B. Swete, *An Introduction to the Old Testament in Greek* (Cambridge: Cambridge Univ. Press, 1902).

2. The Letter of Aristeas is discussed, 208–11.

3. For information on Demetrius of Phalerum, see 14.

4. Philo is discussed, 368–72.

5. So reckon Oesterley and Robinson, quoted in B. J. Roberts, *The Old Testament Text and Versions* (Cardiff: Univ. of Wales Press, 1951), 186.

6. See Frank M. Cross, Jr., "The Oldest Manuscript from Qumran," *JBL* 74 (1955), 147–172. Reprinted in F. M. Cross and S. Talmon, *Qumran and the History of the Biblical Text* (Cambridge: Harvard Univ. Press, 1975), 147–176.

7. See James H. Charlesworth, ed., *The OT Pseudepigrapha and the New Testament* (Cambridge: Cambridge Univ. Press, 1985), 25–26, and Geza Vermes, *The Dead Sea Scrolls: Qumran in Perspective*, (Philadelphia: Fortress Press, 1977), 198–209.

8. For the discussion of the Targumim, see 129–31.

9. These statistics are cited in H. B. Swete, *An Introduction to the Old Testament in Greek* (Cambridge: Cambridge Univ. Press, 1902), 392. Swete's entire chapter, 381–405, on the subject of the Septuagint influence upon the NT writers, provides valuable information.

10. The text of the Letter of Jeremiah may be found in any standard translation of the Apocrypha. Quotations of the Letter of Jeremiah in this volume are from the NRSV. For helpful critical discussions, see Carey Moore, *Daniel, Esther and Jeremiah: The Additions, AB* 44, 315–358; George W. E. Nickelsburg, *JL*, 35–38; C. J. Ball, *APOT* 1:596–611 (where the document is referred to as the Epistle of Jeremy).

11. For the text of Artapanus and critical commentary (plus additional bibliography), see J. J. Collins in *OTP* 2:889–903. Quotations from Artapanus in this discussion are excerpted from the translation of Collins.

12. Polyhistor's real name was Cornelius Alexander and he was apparently a native of Miletus in Asia Minor. See the brief introduction by J. Strugnell in *OTP* 2:777–779.

13. For a brief discussion of Manetho, see 20.

14. *Against Apion*, 1, 75–105, 227–250.

15. Philo is discussed on 368–72.

16. *Stromata* I, XXIII, 154, 2–3.

17. For the text of the Ascension of Isaiah (including the Martyrdom), see M. A. Knibb, *OTP* 2:143–176 (where there is also a helpful critical introduction and bibliography). Quotations of the Ascension of Isaiah in this volume are from the translation of Knibb. See also R. H. Charles, *APOT* 2:155–162.

18. For the text of the Prayer of Manasseh see James H. Charlesworth, *OTP* 2:625–637 (where there is also a helpful critical introduction and bibliography). Quotations of the Prayer of Manasseh in this volume are from Charlesworth's translation. See also Herbert E. Ryle, *APOT* 1:612–624.

19. The text of the Additions to Esther may be found in the Apocrypha. Quotations in this volume are from the NRSV. Helpful critical discussions include the following: John J. Collins, *Between Athens and Jerusalem: Jewish Identity in the Hellenistic Diaspora* (New York: Crossroad, 1983), 87–89; D. Flusser *JW*, 552–554; J. A. F. Gregg *APOT*, 1:665–684; Carey A. Moore, *Daniel, Esther and Jeremiah: The Additions, AB* 44; *JL*, 172–175; E. W. Saunders, "Esther (Apocryphal)," *IDB*, 2:151–152.

20. There is evidence that some rabbis objected to the canonization of Esther. See Moore, *Daniel, Esther and Jeremiah*, xxiv–xxv.

21. The text of the Prayer of Azariah and the Song of the Three Young Men is in the Apocrypha. Quotations of the Additions to Daniel in this volume are from the NRSV. Helpful analyses are W. H. Bennett, *APOT* 1:625–637; Moore, *Daniel, Esther and Jeremiah, AB* 44; *JL*, 28–30.

22. For a discussion of the Greek OT attributed to Theodotion, see 174–75.

23. The text of the Testament of Moses in a critically annotated translation may be found (along with a helpful introduction and bibliography) in J. Priest, *OTP* 1:919–934. Quotations of the Testament of Moses in this volume are from Priest's translation. Priest argues that the document dates from the first century AD. The view that the Testament was written in the second century BC and expanded in the first century AD is presented in *JL*, 80–83, 212–214. See also R. H. Charles, *APOT* 2:407–424; R. H. Charles and J. P. M. Sweet, *AOT*, 601–616.

24. The text of the Wisdom of Ben Sirach may be found in any standard translation of the Apocrypha. Quotations of Sirach in this volume are from the NRSV. Helpful discussions are: G. H. Box and W. O. E. Oesterley, *APOT*, 268–517; T. A. Burkill, "Eclesiasticus," *IDB* 13–21; M. Gilbert in *JW*, 290–301; *JL*, 55–65; Patrick W. Skehan, *The Wisdom of Ben Sira, AB* 39; John G. Snaith, *Ecclesiasticus, or the Wisdom of Jesus Son of Sirach* (Cambridge Bible Commentaries, 1974).

25. The Wisdom of Ben Sirach is the only book of the Apocrypha "signed" by its author.

26. In this connection, the words of the nineteenth-century scholar Alfred Edersheim are interesting. "The Book of Ben-Sira represents an orthodox, but moderate and cold Judaism—before there were either Pharisees or Sadducees; before these two directions assumed separate form under the combined influence of political circumstances and theological controversies. In short, it contains, as yet undistinguishable and mostly in germ, all the elements developed in the later history of Jewish religious thinking. But beyond all this the book throws welcome light on the period in which it was written. If we would know what a cultured, liberal, and yet genuine Jew had thought and felt in view of the great questions of the day; if we would gain insight into the state of public opinion, morals, society, and even of manners at that period— we find the materials for it in the book Ecclesiasticus." Quoted by Box and Oesterley, *APOT* 2:292–293.

27. For a more detailed discussion of the influence of Ben Sirach upon the NT, see Box and Oesterley, *APOT* 2:294–196.

28. The text of Eupolemus, with a critical introduction, may be found in a new translation by F. Fallon in *OTP* 2:861–872. Quotations of Eupolemus in this volume are from the translation of Fallon. See also H. W. Attridge in *JW*, 162–165.

29. The text of 1 Macc. is in the Apocrypha. Quotations in this volume are from the NRSV. Critical discussions include H. W. Attridge, *JW*, 171–176; Joseph A. Goldstein, *I Maccabees AB* 41, 1976; *JL*, 145–117; Oesterley *APOT* 1:59–124.

30. The text of 2 Macc. may be read in the Apocrypha. Quotations in this volume are from the NRSV. Helpful critical discussions include: H. W. Attridge in *JW*, 176–183; Collins, *Between Athens and Jerusalem*, 72–81; James Moffatt, *APOT* 1:125–154; Jonathan A. Goldstein, *II Maccabees, AB* 41A; *JL*, 118–121; Solomon Zeitlin and Sidney Tedesche, *The Second Book of Maccabees* (New York: Harper, 1954).

31. See *JW*, 178ff., and *JL*, 118.

32. On the theory that Jonathan is the "Wicked Priest" in the literature of Qumran, see 135–36.

33. Other quotations from 2 Macc. appear on 39 and 42.

34. For the text of Philo the Epic Poet and critical commentary (plus additional bibliography), see Attridge, *OTP* 2:781–784. Quotations from Philo the Epic Poet in this discussion are excerpted from the translation of Attridge.

35. The surviving text of Theodotus' *On the Jews* may be read in the translation of F. Fallon in *OTP* 2:785–793. The text is accompanied by a critical introduction and bibliography. Quotations of Theodotus in this volume are from Fallon's translation. See also Nickelsburg, *JW*, 121–125.

CHAPTER 7. ADDITIONAL JEWISH LITERATURE OF THE HELLENISTIC PERIOD (2)

1. For the text of the Letter of Aristeas and critical commentary (plus additional bibliography), see Herbert T. Adams *APOT* 2:83–112; R. J. H. Shutt, *OTP* 2:7–34. Quotations in this volume are from the translation of Shutt. For helpful discussions of both the Letter and later expansions of the legends it contains, see Sidney Jelicoe, *The Septuagint and Modern Study* (Oxford: Oxford Univ. Press, 1968), 29–58. Additional helpful discussions are J. J. Collins, *Between Athens and Jerusalem* (New York: Crossroad, 1983), 81–86; George W. E. Nickelsburg, *JL*, 165–169.

2. The text of Tobit may be read in the Apocrypha. Among helpful critical discussions are the following: D. C. Simpson, *APOT* 1:174–241 and *JL*, 30–36; A. Wikgren, "Tobit, Book of," *IDB* 4:658–662; Frank Zimmerman, *The Book of Tobit* (New York: Harper & Bros., 1958).

3. For a discussion of foreign influences on Tobit, see Simpson, *APOT* 1:187–194. See also J. M. Lindenberger, *OTP* 2:488–490.

4. See *JL*, 30.

5. For possible influences of Tobit upon other literature, including the NT, see Simpson, *APOT* 1:198–199.

6. 1 Esdras may be found in standard editions of the Apocrypha. Quotations in this volume are from the NRSV. Critical discussions include S. A. Cook, *APOT* 1:1–58; Jacob A. Myers, *I and II Esdras, AB* 42.

7. There is considerable confusion over the manner in which the various versions of the Bible designate OT Ezra, OT Nehemiah, Septuagint Esdras A, and the Latin pseudepigraph usually called either 2 or 4 Esdras. For a very helpful chart that clarifies the matter, see N. Turner, "Esdras, Books of, *IDB* 2:141.

8. The text of Judith is in the Apocrypha. Quotations of Judith in this volume are from the NRSV. Critical discussions include A. E. Cowley, *APOT* 242–267; Carey A. Moore, *Judith, AB* 40; *JL,* 105–109.

9. Cf. the speeches in Acts (e.g., Acts 1:11–22).

10. The text of Susannah is in the Apocrypha. Quotations of Susannah in this volume are from the NRSV. Critical discussions include: D. M. Kay, *APOT* 1:638–651; Carey A. Moore, *Daniel, Esther and Jeremiah: The Additions, AB* 44, 77–116; *JL,* 25–26.

11. See 118.

12. The text of Bel and the Dragon is in the Apocrypha. Quotations in this volume are from the NRSV. Critical discussions include: Moore, *Daniel, Esther and Jeremiah AB* 44, 117–149; *JL,* 26–28; T. W. Davies *APOT* 2:652–664.

13. ANET, 60–72.

14. 3 Macc. may be found in some English language editions of the Apocrypha. Quotations of 3 Macc. in this volume are from the NRSV. A recent translation of the text, together with a critical discussion, is that of H. Anderson, *OTP* 2:509–529. See also Collins, *Between Athens and Jerusalem,* 104–111; Cyril W. Emmet, *APOT* 1:155–173; Moses Hadas, *The Third and Fourth Books of Maccabees* (New York: Ktav, 1953, 1976); *JL,* 169–172.

15. For a brief description of the military campaign of Antiochus III (the Great) of which the Battle of Raphia was a part, see 9, 11.

16. *Against Apion,* II, 53–54.

17. A recent translation of Ezekiel's *Exagoge* (along with critical commentary and bibliography) is that of R. G. Robertson, *OTP* 2:803–819. Texts quoted here are from Robertson's translation. Other helpful critical discussions include Collins, *Between Athens and Jerusalem,* 207–211; Nickelsburg, *JW,* 125–130.

18. For a discussion of Hellenistic drama, see 16–18.

19. Paul's citation of *Thais* is discussed on 34.

20. The possibility that Ezekiel's *Exagoge* may have been staged at Passover would mean that this Jewish-Greek drama may have been the first in a long line of dramatic presentations of biblical themes on the occasion of important religious festivals, a line which runs through the medieval Miracle plays to the Christmas pageant in the local parish or congregation of today.

21. A recent translation of Aristobulus, along with critical commentary and bibliography, is that of A. Yarbro Collins, *OTP* 2:831–842. Citations of Aristobulus here are from Collins' translation. Also see the critical discussion by P. Borgen, *JW*, 274–279.

22. Pythagoras (c. 580-500 BC) was an important mathematician from the island of Samos in the Aegean. The Pythagorean school of philosophy, which lasted well into the Hellenistic period, saw in numbers the key to understanding all reality. For many Pythagoreans, numbers possessed a mystic quality, the study of which almost amounted to a religion. The members of this order imposed upon themselves certain disciplines, including celibacy and dietary laws. See discussion, 271–72.

23. The Stoics are discussed on 26.

24. See the note on *Logos*, 385, n. 36.

25. See the Apocrypha for the text of Baruch. Quotations in this volume are from the NRSV. Helpful discussions include: Moore, *Daniel, Esther and Jeremiah AB* 44, 255–316; *JL*, 109–114; S. Tedesche, "Baruch, Book of," *IDB* 1:362–363; O. C. Whitehouse, *APOT* 1:569–595.

Excursus: Messianism in Late Hellenistic Period Jewish Literature

1. For helpful discussions of Jewish messianism of the Second Temple period, see F. H. Borsch, *The Son of Man in Myth and History* (Philadelphia: Westminster Press, 1967); Joseph Klausner, *The Messianic Idea in Israel from Its Beginning to the Completion of the Mishnah*, tr. by W. F. Stinespring (New York: Macmillan, 1955); W. Kramer, *Christ, Lord, Son of God*, tr. by Brian Hardy (Naperville, Ill.: Allenson, 1966); Jacob Neusner, *Messiah in Context: Israel's History and Destiny in Formative Judaism* (Philadelphia: Fortress Press, 1984); E. P. Sanders, *Jesus and Judaism* (Philadelphia: Fortress Press, 1985), 294–318; *HJP* 2:488–554; Geza Vermes, *Jesus the Jew* (New York: Macmillan, 1973), 129–159.

2. *DSSE*, 246.

3. *DSSE*, 87.

4. *DSSE*, 265–268.

5. H. C. Kee, *OTP* 1:795.

6. Kee, 824.

7. Kee, 816.

8. Kee, 827.

9. O. S. Wintermute, *OTP* 2:102.

10. Kee, 115–116.

11. John J. Collins, *OTP* 1:376.

12. Collins, *OTP* 2:376.

13. Collins, 379–380.

14. R. B. Wright, *OTP* 2:665–666.

15. Wright, 668.

CHAPTER 8. ROMAN RULE COMES TO PALESTINE

1. Readable and informative discussions of the early history of imperial Rome may be read in Michael Grant, *The Twelve Caesars* (New York: Scribners, 1975); Edward T. Salmon, *A History of the Roman World From 30 BC to 138 AD* (London: Methuen, 1920, 1944); Robert K. Sherk, *The Roman Empire: Augustus to Hadrian* (Cambridge: Cambridge Univ. Press, 1988).

2. For a helpful discussion of Tiberius, see *HJP* 2:178–183.

3. See the discussion of Agrippa I and Agrippa II, 297–99.

4. The JewishWar with Rome is discussed, 304–310.

5. *Jewish War*, III, 401.

6. See *HJP* 1:528.

7. For a description of the revolts during the reign of Trajan, see *HJP* 1:529–534.

8. More detailed treatments of Roman literature may be found in Frank O. Copley, *Latin Literature from the Beginnings to the Close of the Second Century AD* (Ann Arbor: Univ. of Michigan Press, 1969); J. Wright Duff, *A Literary History of Rome From the Origins to the Close of the Golden Age* (New York: Barnes & Noble Books, 1909, 1953); Frank Tenney, *Life and Literature of the Roman Republic* (Berkeley: Univ. of California Press, 1930).

9. From Cicero's First Oration Against Catiline, tr. Louis E. Lord, Basil Davenport, ed., *The Portable Roman Reader* (New York: Viking, 1951, 1969), 231–232.

10. Tr. A. F. Murison in Casper J. Kraemer, ed., *The Complete Works of Horace* The Modern Library, (New York: Random, 1936), 367.

11. Tr. H. W. Weeks, in Kraemer, ed., *Complete Works*, 15.

12. *Ibid.*, 39.

13. The original Latin of this quotation, *Dulce et decorum est pro patria mori,* is to be found, among other places, over the main entrance to Arlington National Cemetery.

14. For a discussion of the Sibylline Oracles, see 93–97.

15. E. V. Rieu, ed. and tr., *Virgil: The Pastoral Poems (The Eclogues)* (New York: Penguin Classics, 1954), 53–57.

16. Various interpretations of the Fourth Eclogue are discussed in Rieu, ed., *Virgil*, 136–143.

17. Tr. T. C. Williams in Addison Hibbard, ed., *Writers of the Western World* (Boston: Houghton Mifflin, 1942), 222.

18. Tr. by H. T. Riley in Hibbard, *Writers*, 404.

19. Polybius is discussed, 18.

20. Tr. B. O. Foster, from Basil Davenport, ed., *The Portable Roman Reader* (New York: Viking), 430–432.

21. Tacitus' "Histories," 2 × xxviii, tr. Clifford H. Moore, *Tacitus: The Histories and the Annals*, Loeb Classical Library, 1:223.

22. Tacitus' *Annals,* XIII, 32.

23. Tacitus' *Annals,* XV, 44.

24. Josephus is discussed, 360–63.

25. Plato is discussed, 23–24.

26. Plutarch's "Concerning Talkativeness" 1, tr. W. C. Helmbold, *Plutarch's Moralia,* Loeb's Classical Library, 6:419.

27. Plutarch's "Life of Solon," 7:1, tr. Bernadotte Perrin, *Plutarch's Lives,* Loeb Classical Library, 1:419.

28. From Suetonius' Life of Claudius, XXV. This often quoted sentence is discussed at length (including extensive bibliography) in Menahem Stern, ed., *Greek and Latin Authors on Jews and Judaism,* vol. 2: *From Tacitus to Simplicius* (Jerusalem: Israel Academy of Sciences and Humanities, 1976), 113–117.

29. Suetonius' Life of Nero, XVI.

30. Pliny's "Letters," 6:16, tr. William Welmoth, *Pliny,* Loeb Classical Library, 1:479–481.

31. Pliny's "Letters," 10:96, tr. William Welmoth, *Pliny,* Loeb Classical Library, 2:401–405.

32. Lucretius is discussed, 25.

33. The stoics are discussed, 26.

34. From Secena's "Epistle VIII," tr. R. M. Gummere, in the Loeb Classical Library. Reprinted in George Howe and G. A. Harrer, *Roman Literature in Translation,* rev. by Albert Suskin (New York: Harper & Bros., 1924, 1959), 542.

35. Among helpful discussions of Roman religion are the following: John Ferguson, *The Religions of the Roman Empire* (London: Thames & Hudson; Ithaca: Cornell Univ. Press, 1970); Michael Grant, *Roman Myths* (New York: Scribners, 1971); R. M. Ogilvie, *The Romans and Their Gods in theAge of Augustus* (London: Chatto & Windus, 1969).

36. The Mystery religions are discussed, 27–31.

37. For helpful discussions of Gnosticism see especially Giovanni Filoramo, *A History of Gnosticism,* tr. Anthony Alcock (Oxford: Blackwell, 1990) and Henry A. Green, *The Economic and Social Origins of Gnosticism* (Atlanta: Scholars Press, 1985). There are extensive bibliographies in both these works.

38. The worship of the Hellenistic ruler is discussed, 31–32.

39. *Antiquities,* XIV, 124.

40. *Antiquities,* XIV, 158. In *Jewish War,* I, 203, Josephus says that Hyrcanus was "sluggish and without the energy necessary to a king."

41. Josephus (*Antiquities,* XIV, 121; *Jewish War,* I, 181) relates that Antipater's wife, whose name was Cypros, was a member of a distinguished Arab (perhaps meaning Nabataean) family, and that she bore him four sons, Phasael, Herod, Joseph, and Peroras, and a daughter, Salome.

42. *Antiquities,* XIV, 176.

43. *Antiquities,* XIV, 467; *Jewish War,* I, 344.

44. *Antiquities,* XIV, 300.

45. That Mariamme's grandfathers were brothers resulted from the fact that her father, Alexander, was a son of Aristobulus II, while her mother, Alexandra, was a daughter of Hyrcanus II. In other words, her parents were first cousins. (See the chart of the Hasmonean family on 455.) Such royal marriages were by no means uncommon in the ancient world.

CHAPTER 9.   FROM HEROD THE GREAT TO THE REVOLT OF BAR KOKHBA

1. *Antiquities,* XV, 29.

2. For reference to the effect of the earthquake of 31 BC upon Qumran, see 283.

3. Hyrcanus was born to Alexander Jannaeus and Salome Alexandra about the year 100 BC, and would therefore have been in his early seventies at the time of his execution.

4. *Antiquities,* XV, 182. Cf. *Jewish War,* I, 434.

5. Inconsistencies between *Antiquities* and the *Jewish War* in the matter of Mariamme's death have caused some scholars to wonder about the accuracy of Josephus' reports. Also, the details connected with Mariamme's death are so similar to those involved with the story of the death of Joseph, Herod's uncle, that suspicion has been raised that Josephus (or his sources) may have confused some aspects of the two incidents. See *HJP* 1:302–303, n. 49.

6. Josephus applies this title to Herod in *Antiquities,* XVII, 246. There has been some scholarly reservation about whether Herod ever actually received this title, but he certainly ruled in a manner consistent with it. See *HJP* 1:316, n. 104.

7. On Herod's murder of the members of the Sanhedrin, see *Antiquities* XIV, 175; XV, 5. The history of the Sanhedrin during Herod's reign is not entirely clear, but that it ceased to function for a time is by no means unlikely. See *HJP* 2:205–206.

8. The fortress Antonia was possibly the site of Jesus' trial before Pilate.

9. Machaerus is, by tradition, the site of the execution of John the Baptist.

10. Josephus uses the designation "Great" in reference to Herod only one time, *Antiquities,* XVIII, 130.

11. A small village named Strato's Tower was the site of Herod's new harbor.

12. *Jewish War,* I, 410; *Antiquities,* XV, 332.

13. Josephus' descriptions of Caesarea Maritima (found principally in *Antiquities,* XV, 331–341, XVI, 136–141 and *Jewish War* I, 408–416) have been basically confirmed by modern archaeology. See Robert J. Bull, "Caesarea Maritima—The Search for Herod's City," and Robert L. Hohlfelder, "Caesarea Beneath the Sea," both articles in *Biblical Archaeology Review,* 8:3 (May/June 1982), 24–40. Also of interest is Robert L. Hohlfelder, et al, "Sebastos, Herod's Harbor at Caesarea Maritima," *Biblical Archaeology,* 46:3 (Summer 1983), 113–143.

14. *Antiquities,* XV, 390.

15. *Antiquities,* XV, 395.

16. *Antiquities,* XV, 411–412.

17. *Antiquities,* XV, 413.

18. Certain references in the Gospels assume added significance when the details of Herod's construction are recalled. The height of the Royal Portico, the "pinnacle of the Temple," is doubtless reflected in Matt. 4:5 and Luke 4:9. And the promise (or threat) of Mark 13:2 recalls the massive stones used by Herod's engineers.

Remains of Herod's structure may be seen today in the so-called Wailing Wall, part of the western retaining wall for the Temple Mount, in nearby Robinson's Arch, as well as in the so-called Huldah Gates, the double and triple arched portals in the southern wall that, although now blocked up, served as principal entrances in Herod's day. It is assumed by many scholars that other parts of Herod's vast complex lie beneath the present Muslim holy site, the Haram esh-Sharif, which occupies the former Temple Mount.

The literature on Herod's Temple is extensive, but a fine summary of what is known on the subject may be read in W. F. Stinespring, "Temple, Jerusalem," IDB 4:550–559. This article contains a lengthy bibliography. See also Hershel Shanks, "Excavating in the Shadow of the Temple Mount," *Biblical Archaeology Review,* 12 (Nov./Dec. 1986), 20–38; Meir Ben-Dov, "Herod's Mighty Temple Mount," *Biblical Archaeology Review,* 12 (Nov./Dec. 1986), 40–49.

19. The intrigues involving the royal princes are described in *Antiquities,* XVI, 300–XVI, 145; *Jewish War,* I, 431–646.

20. This, the only reference to an eclipse by Josephus, is recorded in *Antiquities,* XVI, 167.

21. Josephus (*Antiquities* XVII, 188–189; XI, 319; *Jewish War* II, 95) and the Gospel of Luke (3:1) differ somewhat is describing the extent of Philip's territory.

22. *Antiquities,* XVIII, 106–107.

23. *Jewish War,* III, 509–513.

24. According to Mark 6:17 (and in some manuscripts, Matt. 14:3 and Luke 3:19), Herodias' first husband was the tetrarch Philip. However, Josephus' statement in *Antiquities* XVIII, 109, 148, that Herodias' first husband was Herod, son of Mariamme II, appears to be correct.

25. The daughter of Herodias is not named in the NT, but Josephus (*Antiquities,* XVIII, 136) gives her name as Salome. Neither Josephus nor the NT reports anything about the "seven veils" which later tradition adorned Salome's dance.

26. *Antiquities,* VIII, 116–119, tr. Louis H. Feldman in the Loeb Classical Library.

27. Sejanus is referred to, 254.

28. *Antiquities,* XVII, 342. Cf. *Jewish War,* II, 111.

29. The Roman governors of Judaea are variously referred to in the literature of the time as *procurator* and *prefect.* See *HJP* 1:358–361.

30. See F. D. Gealy, "Praetorium," *IDB* 3:856.

31. Josephus' date of Quirinius' census (6 or 7 AD) differs from that in Luke 2:2 (about 6 BC). For a brief discussion of the problem and of proposed solutions, see S. Sandmel, "Quirinius," IDB 3:975–976. A more extensive treatment (with bibliography) may be found in *HJP* 1:399–427.

32. *Antiquities*, XVIII, 9.

33. *Antiquities* XVIII, 23–24.

34. Agrippa's letter to Tiberius (or Gaius) is preserved in Philo, *The Embassy to Gaius (Latin title, De legatione ad Gaium)*, 299–305. According to Philo, Agrippa relates how Pilate set up golden shields (associated with emperor worship) in Herod's Jerusalem palace, "not so much to honor Tiberius as to annoy the multitude." When the Jews protested and threatened to send a delegation to Tiberius, Pilate "feared that if they actually sent to an embassy they would also expose the rest of his conduct as governor by stating in full the briberies, the insults, the robberies, the outrages and wanton injuries, the executions without trial constantly repeated, with ceaseless and supremely grievious cruelty." In the end, Tiberius ordered Pilate to remove the offensive shields. The translation of this passage cited here is that of F. H. Colson, *Philo,* in the Loeb Classical Library.

35. *Antiquities*, XVIII, 55–59; *Jewish War*, II, 169–174.

36. *Antiquities*, XVIII, 60–62; *Jewish War*, II, 175–177.

37. *Antiquities*, XVIII, 85–89.

38. *Antiquities*, XVIII, 63–64. For a brief summary of the debate concerning the genuineness of this passage, see Louis H. Feldman, *Josephus,* Loeb Classical Library, 9:49–50, n. b. A more complete discussion (with extensive bibliography) may be read in *HJP* 1:428–441. There is another, passing reference to Jesus in *Antiquities*, XX, 200.

39. The translation is that of Feldman, *Antiquities,* in the Loeb Classical Library.

40. *Antiquities*, XIX, 293.

41. *Antiquities*, XIX, 346.

42. *Jewish War*, II, 224. *Antiquities*, XX, 108, reports that "one of the soldiers uncovered his genitals and exhibited them to the multitude."

43. *Antiquities*, XX, 113–117; *Jewish War*, II 228–231.

44. *Antiquities*, XX, 118–136; *Jewish War*, II, 232–246.

45. *Antiquities*, XX, 124.

46. Tacitus' *Histories,* V, 9, quoted in *HJP* 1:461.

47. *Antiquities*, XX, 161.

48. *Antiquities*, XX, 165–166. The translation is that of Feldman in the Loeb Classical Library. Cf. *Jewish War*, II, 256–257.

49. *Antiquities*, XX, 167–172; *Jewish War*, II, 261–263.

50. *Jewish War*, II, 264–265, tr. Gaalya Cornfeld, gen. ed., *Josephus: The Jewish War* (Grand Rapids: Zondervan, 1982), 167.

51. *Antiquities*, XX, 173–178; *Jewish War*, II, 266–270.

52. *Antiquities*, XX, 179–181.

53. *Antiquities*, XX, 253, tr. Feldman in the Loeb Classical Library. *Jewish War*, II, 277, says "Such a man was Albinus, but by comparison his successor Gessius Florus made him appear an angel." Having introduced Florus to the readers of his *Antiquities*, Josephus discontinues that narrative and refers us to his previously written *Jewish War* (*Antiquities*, XX, 259).

54. *Jewish War*, II, 283, which reads: . . . if peace had lasted, he [Florus] foresaw that he would have the Jews accuse him before Caesar; but if he contrived to make them revolt, he hoped that this greater outrage would forestall any inquiry into less serious offenses. So, to insure a nationwide revolt, he added daily to their sufferings. (Tr. Cornfeld in the Loeb Classical Library).

55. Josephus states (*Jewish War*, II, 284–285) that the spark that kindled the revolt was a dispute between the members of a Jewish synagogue in Cesarea Maritima and their gentile neighbors, an outgrowth of the larger Jewish-gentile conflict in the provincial capital. But as the first wide-scale violence erupted only after Florus' confiscation of the seventeen talents from the Temple treasury, perhaps that incident is more deserving of the "honor." However one may wish to characterize the matter, the revolt was the culmination of a long and often violent series of disputes between the Jews and their Roman oppressors, with the gentile, largely Greek-speaking element in the population frequently adding to the Jews' distress.

56. More about Josephus below (see 360–63), but attention may be drawn here to the reserved, third-person style of Josephus' account of his own rise to leadership in the rebel army (Jewish War, II, 568ff.). Josephus is part of a company of distinguished classical historians, including Polybius, who wrote of events to which they were witnesses.

57. Josephus' description of this moment goes like this:

Each man in turn offered his throat for the next man to cut, in the belief that his general would immediately share his fate; they thought death together with Josephus sweeter than life. He, however—should we say by fortune or by divine providence—was left with one other man; and anxious neither to be condemned by the lot, nor, if he were left as the last, to stain his hand with the blood of a fellow countryman, he persuaded this man also, under a pact, to remain alive. (tr. Feldman)

58. *Jewish War*, V, 513–516. Tr. Cornfeld.

59. *Jewish War*, VI, 249–253. Josephus goes to great lengths to paint the Romans in as favorable a light as possible, especially Vespasian and Titus, who were his patrons at the time he wrote. We shall discuss Josephus' methods later (see 360–63), but it may be noted here that some readers of Josephus have suspected that Titus intended from the very beginning to burn the Temple in order to deny to the Jews a rallying place for any future insurrections. It would also have been more expensive in terms of Roman lives to expel Jewish rebels from the Temple

by hand-to-hand combat than by simply burning the edifice to the ground (cf. *Jewish War*, VI, 228.).

60. *Jewish War*, VI, 267–270.

61. The date of the fall of Masada has traditionally been understood to be 73 AD, but new evidence suggests that Flavius Silva did not become governor of Judaea until 73. Thus it is likely that the spring of the following year was actually the time of Masada's capture. See *HJP* 1:512, n. 139 and the literature cited there.

62. *Jewish War*, VII, 3.

63. Cassius Dio's *History*, 12:1, states that Hadrian actually built his new city before the revolt, but other ancient authorities suggest that it was not built until after the cessation of fighting. It is likely, then, that Hadrian's plans for the city incited the Jews to revolt, but that the plans were not executed until later. For a discussion of the revolt of Bar Kokhba, see *HJP* 1:534–557. An especially helpful account is Yigael Yadin, *Bar Kokhba: The Rediscovery of the Legendary Hero of the Last Jewish Revolt Against Imperial Rome* (London: Weidenfeld & Nicolson, 1971). Also there is much valuable information concerning sources of our knowledge of the war, including the relevant passages from Dio's *History*, in Menachem Stern, ed., *Greek and Latin Authors on Jews and Judaism*, vol. 2, *From Tacitus to Simplicimus* (Jerusalem: Israel Academy of Sciences and Humanities, 1980), 392–405.

64. Dio, *History*, 12:2

65. Dio, *History*, 13:1. Tr. E. Cary in the Loeb Classical Library and reproduced in M. Stern, *Greek and Latin Authors.*

66. Eusebius, *Ecclesiastical History*, IV, 6. All references to Eusebius in this discussion are to this passage. Tr. Kirsopp Lake, *Eusebius: The Ecclesiastical History*, Loeb Classical Library, 1926, 1:311–313.

67. This is the present author's translation, based on the French. See P. Benoit, J. T. Milik and R. de Vaux, *Discoveries in the Judaean Desert II: Les Grottes de Murabba'at* (Oxford: Clarendon Press, 1961), 124–128.

68. Dio *History*, 14:2

69. See *HJP* 1:551 for a brief discussion of the site of Bar Kosiba's last battle. Also Yadin, *Bar Kokhba*, 193.

70. Dio, *History*, 14:3

71. Photographs of the Jerusalem portion of the Madeba mosaic may be seen in a number of publications. One of the most detailed is in Colin Thubron, *Jerusalem* (London: Heinemann, 1969), frontpiece and endpiece.

CHAPTER 10. PALESTINIAN JEWISH THOUGHT AND LITERATURE TO THE REVOLT OF BAR KOKHBA

1. From Sifre Deuteronomy 357. Quoted by Jacob Neusner, *A Life of Rabban Yohannan Ben Zakkai: Ca. 1–80 C.E.* (Leiden: Brill, 1962), 24.

2. See "Hillel," *EJ* 8:482–485. Helpful treatments of Hillel and other sages may be found in Shaye J. D. Cohen, *From the Macc. to the Mishnah* (Philadelphia:

Westminster Press, 1987); George Foot Moore, *Judaism*, 3 vols. (Cambridge: Harvard Univ. Press, 1966); Jacob Neusner, *A Life of Rabban Yohanan Ben Zakkai (Ca. 1–80 C.E.)* (Leiden: Brill, 1962); Ephraim Urbach, *The Sages: Their Concepts and Beliefs*, 2 vols. (Jerusalem: Magnes, 1979). See also Jacob Neusner, *The Rabbinic Traditions about the Pharisees Before 70*, pt. 1 (Leiden: Brill, 1971) for a systematic presentation of sayings by and about the sages.

For an interesting discussion of parallels between the literary traditions concerning the rabbis and the New Testament Gospels, see Michael Hilton and Gordian Marshall, *The Gospels and Rabbinic Judaism: A Study Guide* (Hoboken, N.J.: Ktav, 1988).

3. Neusner, *Rabbinic Traditions*, 288.

4. *Ibid.*, 322–323.

5. *Ibid.*, 329.

6. *Ibid.*, 286–289.

7. The quotation is from J. Goldin, "Hillel the Elder," *Journal of Religion* 26:263f., and is cited in Neusner, *A Life*, 18–19. Neusner also lists here the seven principles of Hillel's method.

8. See "Shammai," *EJ* 14:1291–1292.

9. See "Gamaliel, Rabban," *EJ* 7:295–296; E. P. Blair, "Gamaliel," *IDB* 2:351.

10. See Neusner, *Rabbinic Traditions*, pt. 1, 348–350.

11. See "Johanan ben Zakkai," *EJ* 10:148–154, from which the quotations cited here have been taken, except as noted below. A fuller treatment is in Neusner, *A Life*.

12. Halakhah and haggadah are discussed, 106–110.

13. Quoted by Neusner, *A Life*, 48.

14. The various versions of the meeting between Johanan and Vespasian have been brought together by Neusner, *A Life*, 115–120.

15. See "Rabban Gamaliel II," *EJ* 7:296–298, from which the citations in the text are drawn.

16. The *Shemoneh 'Eshreh*, or Eighteen Benedictions, is discussed, 129.

17. See Cohen, *Maccabees*, 227–228.

18. The question of the various canons of scripture is discussed on 150–52.

19. See "Akiva," *EJ* 15:488–492, from which the citations in the text are drawn.

20. Aquila is discussed on 174.

21. On the application of Num. 24:17, see 313.

22. A recent translation of the Apocalypse of Abraham, together with critical notes and bibliography, is that of R. Rubinkiewicz (rev. and notes added by H. G. Lunt), *OTP* 1:681–705. The quotations cited here are from the Rubinkiewicz translation. For further discussion, see *JL*, 294–299.

23. Daniel is discussed on 76–81, the Additions on 186–89 and 225–27.

24. It is possible that the figure of the "chosen one" is a Christian interpolation. However, since this individual's work seems to be little more than the bringing together of the scattered of Israel, that seems unlikely.

25. The title 4 Esdras is found in the Vulgate, and stems from the following enumeration found there:

1 Esdras = OT Ezra
2 Esdras = OT Nehemiah
3 Esdras = Septuagint 1 Esdras (including the Tale of the Three Guardsmen)

However, in some English translations of the Bible, including the NRSV, 4 Esdras is designated 2 Esdras, as the OT Books of Ezra and Nehemiah are called by the names of their principal personalities, and the Vulgate's 3 Esdras becomes 1 Esdras (as in the Septuagint).

26. 2 or 4 Esdras may be found in standard translations of the Apocrypha. Passages quoted here are from the NRSV. A recent translation, with critical introduction and bibliography, is that of B. M. Metzger in *OTP* 1:514–559. See also J. M. Myers, *I and II Esdras*, AB 42; *JL*, 287–294; *HJP* 3:294–306; Michael E. Stone in *JW*, 412–414.

27. For a discussion of messianism in 2/4 Esdras, see Myers, *I and II Esdras*, 126–129.

28. The reference to "twenty-four books" is to the Hebrew canon (5 books of the Torah, 8 of the combined Former and Latter Prophets, and 11 of the Writings [Ezra-Nehemiah = 1 book; 1 and 2 Chronicles = 1 book]). The "seventy that were written last" is an indeterminate number (70 is a symbolic figure) of works of apocalyptic.

29. See Metzger, *OTP* 1:522, expecially n. 19 at the bottom of the page that calls attention to the work of G. H. Box.

30. A recent translation of 2 Baruch, with critical commentary and bibliography, is that of A. F. J. Kiljn, *OTP* 1:615–652. Texts cited here are from Kiljn's translation. See also *JL*, 281–287; *HJP* 3:750–756; Stone, *JW*, 408–410.

31. A recent translation of the Life of Adam and Eve, including a critical introduction and bibliography, is that of M. D. Johnson, *OTP* 2:249–295. Quotations in this discussion are from Johnson's translation. See also John J. Collins, *Between Athens and Jerusalem: Jewish Identity in the Hellenistic Diaspora* (New York: Crossroad, 1983), 224–225; *JL*, 256–257; Nickelsburg, *JW*, 110–118; *HJP* 3:757–760.

32. The name of the Latin recension apparently derives from its preface: "The narrative and life of Adam and Eve the first-made, revealed by God to Moses his servant when he received the tablets of the law of the covenant from the hand of the Lord, after he had been taught by the archangel Michael." Moses does not otherwise figure in the document.

33. See especially the two essays by Nickelsburg, n. 31 above.

34. The text has apparently been corrupted here, for the same sentence that declares that Abel was 122 at the time of his murder, also provides Adam's age as 130.

35. See especially Johnson, *OTP* 254–255.

CHAPTER 11. SOME JEWISH LITERATURE OF PRESUMED DIASPORA ORIGIN
WRITTEN BEFORE 135 AD

1. A recent translation of 2 Enoch, accompanied by critical commentary and bibliography, is that of F. I. Anderson, *OTP* 1:91–221. Citations from 2 Enoch that are quoted here are from Anderson's translation. See also J. J. Collins, *Between Athens and Jerusalem: Jewish Identity in the Hellenistic Diaspora* (New York: Crossroad, 1983), 229–232; George W. E. Nickelsburg, *JL*, 185–188; *HJP* 3:746–750; Michael E. Stone, *JW*, 406–408.

2. The discussion of 1 Enoch may be found on 81–86.

3. On the role of Melchizedek in the literature of Qumran, see 145, 242.

4. A recent translation of Joseph and Aseneth, accompanied by critical notes and bibliography, is that of C. Burchard, *OTP* 2:177–247. Citations in this discussion are from Burchard's translation. See also Collins, *Between Athens and Jerusalem*, 211–218; *JL*, 258–263; *HJP* 3.1:546–552.

5. The Hellenistic romance is discussed above, 16–18.

6. The popularity of Joseph and Aseneth in Christian circles is discussed by Burchard, 195–199.

7. A recent translation of the Testament of Job, accompanied by critical commentary and bibliography, is that of R. P. Spittler, *OTP* 1:829–868. Quotations cited in this discussion are from the Spittler translation. See also Collins, *Between Athens and Jerusalem*, 220–224, J. J. Collins, *JW*, 349–354; *JL*, 241–248; *HJP* 3:552–555.

8. The Testaments of the Twelve Patriarchs is discussed on 86–90, the Testament of Moses on 189–92.

9. A recent translation of the Testament of Abraham (in both recensions), including critical introduction and bibliography, is that of E. P. Sanders, *OTP* 1:871–902. Quotations in this discussion are from Sanders' translation. See also Collins, *Between Athens and Jerusalem*, 226–228; Collins, *JW*, 60–64; *JL*, 248–253; *HJP* 3:761–767.

10. See *JL*, 249–250.

11. A brief, but helpful article on Josephus is J. Goldin, "Josephus, Flavius," *IDB* 2:987–988. See also William R. Farmer, *Macc., Zealots and Josephus* (New York: Columbia Univ. Press, 1957); Tessa Rajak, *Josephus: The Historian and His Society* (Philadelphia: Fortress Press, 1984); H. St. John Thackeray, *Josephus: The Man and The Historian*, reprint. (New York: Ktav, 1967).

12. Eupolemus is discussed, 197–98.

13. Josephus' statements about his ancestry provide the kind of (apparent?) inconsistency so frustrating to his readers. In *Life* 2 he writes "by my mother I am of the royal blood," but then goes on to trace the Hasmonean line to himself through the wife of his great-great-grandfather. Scholars have sought to reconcile this seeming contradiction by stating that Josephus is using the word "mother" in its larger meaning of "female ancestor." See Rajak, 15.

14. *Life* 19. The translation is that of William Whiston as revised by D. S. Margoliouth, *Flavius Josephus: The Great Roman-Jewish War: AD 66–70* (New York: Harper & Bros., 1960).

15. For Josephus' role in the Jewish War of 66–74 AD, see, 305–308.

16. *Antiquities* XX, 268, tr. Louis H. Feldman in the Loeb Classical Library.

17. The Wisdom of Solomon is found in standard translations of the Apocrypha. The translation quoted here is that of the NRSV. See also Collins, *Between Athens and Jerusalem*, 182–186; M. Gilbert, *JW*, 301–313; Samuel Holmes, *APOT* 1:518–568; *JL*, 175–185; *HJP* 3:568–579; David Winston, *The Wisdom of Solomon, AB* 43.

18. For a helpful discussion of the theology and philosophy of the Wisdom of Solomon (including an examination of parallels between this document and the writings of Philo), see Winston, 25–63.

19. See especially Holmes, *APOT* 1:525–527 and *JL*, 184–185.

20. The literature on Philo is extensive. A brief, but valuable overview is that of E. R. Goodenough, "Philo Judeus," *IDB* 3:796–799. See also P. Borgen, *JW*, 233–282; Collins, *Between Athens and Jerusalem*, 195–203; David Winston, *Philo of Alexandria* (New York: Paulist Press, 1981); H. A. Wolfson, *Philo*, 2 vols. (Cambridge, Mass.: Harvard Univ. Press, 1947).

21. Aristobulus is discussed, 234–37.

22. Caligula is discussed, 255.

23. This is the view, for example, of David Winston, *Philo of Alexandria*, 2–6.

24. On the Creation of the World, 70–71. See Winston, *Philo of Alexandria*, 173.

25. Allegory of the Law, 1:105. Winston, *Philo of Alexandria* 121.

26. *Life of Moses*, 1:1–2, 2:14. Winston, *Philo of Alexandria.MD0/ 267, 270.*

27. *Allegory of the Law*, 1:63–64. Winston, *Philo of Alexandria*, 225–226.

28. *Who is the Heir of Divine Things?*, 205. Winston, *Philo of Alexandria*, 94.

29. A recent translation of 4 Macc., accompanied by critical commentary and bibliography, is that of H. Anderson, *OTP* 2:531–564. See also Collins, *Between Athens and Jerusalem*, 187–191; Gilbert, *JW*, 316–319; *JL*, 223–227; *HJP* 3:588–593. Quotations in our discussion are from the NRSV.

30. 2 Macc. is discussed, 201–204.

31. See especially the discussion of Anderson, *OTP* 2:537–539. Discussions of Platonism and Stoicism on 23–26

32. For the text of the Treatise of Shem, see the recent translation (and accompanying critical commentary) by J. H. Charlesworth, *OTP* 1:473–486. The quotation cited is from Charlesworth's translation. See also *HJP* 3:369–372.

33. Charlesworth argues for a date shortly after the Battle of Actium (31 BC), and marshals impressive evidence to support this claim. (See *OTP* 1:474–475.) But for a different view, see *HJP* 3:369–372.

34. See Charlesworth's discussion, *OTP* 1:478–480.

BIBLIOGRAPHY

ANTHOLOGIES OF PRIMARY SOURCES

Austin, M. M., ed. *The Hellenistic World from Alexander to the Roman Conquest: A Selection of Ancient Sources in Translation.* Cambridge: Cambridge University Press, 1981.

Beyerlin, W. *Near Eastern Texts Relating to the Old Testament.* Philadelphia: Westminster Press, 1978.

Bowman, John. *Samaritan Documents Relating to Their History, Religion and Life.* Pittsburgh: Pickwick, 1977.

Charles, R. H., ed. *Apocrypha and Pseudepigrapha of the Old Testament in English.* 2 vols. Oxford: Clarendon Press, 1912.

Charlesworth, James H., ed. *The Old Testament Pseudepigrapha.* 2 vols. Garden City, N.Y.: Doubleday, 1983, 1985.

Ferguson, John. *Greek and Roman Religion: A Source Book.* Park Ridge, N.J.: Noyes Press, 1980.

The *Loeb Classical Library* contains texts (with notes) of important Greek and Latin writers of antiquity. A catalog has been published by the Harvard University Press, 1902.

Long, A. A., and D. N. Sedley, eds. The Hellenistic Philosophers. Vol. 1, *Translations of the Principal Sources with Philosophical Commentary.* Cambridge: Cambridge University Press, 1987.

Nickelsburg, George W. E., and Michael E. Stone, eds. *Faith and Piety in Early Judaism: Texts and Documents.* Philadelphia: Fortress Press, 1983.

Pritchard, James B., ed. *Ancient Near Eastern Texts Relating to the Old Testament.* Princeton, N.J.: Princeton University Press, 1969.

Sparks, H. F. D., ed. *TheApocryphal Old Testament.* Oxford: Clarendon Press, 1985.

Stern, Menahem, ed. *Greek and Latin Authors on Jews and Judaism.* Vol. 1, *From Herodotus to Plutarch.* Jerusalem: Israel Academy of Sciences and Humanities, 1976.

_____. *Greek and Latin Authors on Jews and Judaism.* Vol. 2, *From Tacitus to Simplicimus.* Jerusalem: Israel Academy of Sciences and Humanities, 1980.

Thomas, D. Winton, ed. *Documents from Old Testament Times.* New York: Nelson, 1958.

Vermes, Geza. *The Dead Sea Scrolls in English.* rev. ed. Harmondsworth: Penguin, 1987.

CHAPTER 1. THE SPREAD OF HELLENISM

GENERAL STUDIES OF THE HELLENISTIC WORLD

Austin, M. M., ed. *The Hellenistic World from Alexander to the Roman Conquest: A Selection of Ancient Sources in Translation.* Cambridge: Cambridge University Press, 1981.

Boardman, John, Jasper Griffin, and Oswyn Murray, eds. *The Oxford History of the Classical World.* Oxford: Oxford University Press, 1986.

Bury, J. B., S. A. Cook, and F. E. Adcock, eds. *The Cambridge Ancient History.* Vol. 6, *Macedon: 401–301 BC.* New York: Macmillan; Cambridge: Cambridge University Press, 1933.

Cook, S. A., F. E. Adcock, and M. P. Charlesworth, gen. eds. *The Cambridge Ancient History.* Vol. 7, *The Hellenistic Monarchies and the Rise of Rome.* Cambridge: Cambridge University Press, 1928.

Daiches, David, and Anthony Thorlby, eds. *The Classical World.* London: Aldus, 1972.

Davies, W. D., and Louis Finkelstein, eds. *The Cambridge History of Judaism,* vol. 2, *The Hellenistic Age.* Cambridge: Cambridge University Press, 1990.

Finley, Moses I., ed. *The Legacy of Greece: A New Appraisal.* Oxford: Clarendon Press, 1981.

Fraser, P. M. *Ptolemaic Alexandria.* 3 vols. Oxford: Oxford University Press, 1972.

Hadas, Moses. *Hellenistic Culture: Fusion and Diffusion.* New York: Columbia University Press, 1959.

Koester, Helmut. *History, Culture and Religion of the Hellenistic Age,* Vol. 1 of *Introduction to the New Testament.* Philadelphia: Fortress Press; Berlin: Walter de Gruyter, 1982.

Momigliano, Arnaldo. *Alien Wisdom: The Limits of Hellenization.* Cambridge: Cambridge University Press, 1975.

Roetzel, Calvin J. *The World That Shaped the New Testament.* Atlanta: John Knox Press, 1985.

Rostovtzeff, M. I. *Social and Ecomonic History of the Hellenistic World.* 3 vols. Oxford: Oxford University Press, 1941.

Schalit, Abraham, ed. *The World History of the Jewish People. First Series: Ancient Times.* vol. 6: *The Hellenistic Age: Political History of Jewish Palestine From 332 B.C.E. to 67 B.C.E.* New Brunswick, N.J.: Rutgers University Press, 1972. [abbreviated citation WHJP]

Schalit, Abraham, and G. T. Griffith. *Hellenistic Civilization.* New York: Barnes & Noble Books; Cambridge: Heffer, 1966.

Walbank, F. W. *The Hellenistic World.* Cambridge, Mass.: Harvard University Press, 1982.

Walbank, F. W., et al., eds. The Cambridge Ancient History. Vol. 8, Pt. 1: *The Hellenistic World,* 2d ed. Cambridge: Cambridge University Press, 1984.

Alexander the Great

Fox, Robin Lane. *The Search for Alexander.* Boston: Little, Brown & Co., 1980.

Green, Peter. *Alexander the Great.* New York: Praeger, 1970.

Hamilton, J. R. *Alexander the Great.* London: Hutchinson University Press, 1973.

Lipsius, Frank. *Alexander the Great.* New York: Saturday Review Press, 1974.

Pearson, Lionel. *The Lost Histories of Alexander the Great.* Chico, Calif.: Scholars Press, 1983.

Tarn, W. W. *Alexander the Great.* 2 vols. Cambridge: Cambridge University Press, 1948, 1979.

Welles, C. Bradford. *Alexander and the Hellenistic World.* Toronto: A. M. Hakkert, 1970.

Hellenistic Language and Literature

Atkinson, B. F. C. *The Greek Language.* London: Faber & Faber, 1931.

Aune, David E. *The New Testament in Its Literary Environment.* Philadelphia: Westminster Press, 1987.

Bengtson, Hermann. *Introduction to Ancient History.* Translated by R. I. Frank and F. D. Gilliard. Berkeley, Calif.: University of California Press, 1970.

Beye, Charles Rowan. *Ancient Greek Literature and Society.* Ithaca: Cornell University Press, 1975, 1987.

Costas, Procope S. *An Outline of the History of the Greek Language.* Chicago: Ares, 1979.

Cox, Patricia L. *Biography in Late Antiquity: A Quest for the Holy Man.* Berkeley, Calif.: University of California Press, 1983.

Easterling, P. E., and B. M. W. Knox, eds. *The Cambridge History of Classical Literature.* Vol. 1, *Greek Literature.* Cambridge: Cambridge University Press, 1985.

Fornara, Charles W. *The Nature of History in Ancient Greece and Rome.* Berkeley, Calif.: University of California Press, 1983.

Grant, Michael. *The Ancient Historians.* New York: Scribners, 1970.

Hadas, Moses. *Hellenistic Culture: Fusion and Diffusion.* New York: Columbia University Press, 1959.

_____. *A History of Greek Literature.* New York: Columbia University Press, 1950.

Hagg, Tomas. *The Novel in Antiquity.* Berkeley, Calif.: University of California Press, 1983.

Koester, Helmut. Introduction to the New Testament. Vol. 1, *History, Culture and Religion of the Hellenistic Age.* Philadelphia: Fortress Press, 1982.

Lesky, Albin. *A History of Greek Literature.* Translated by James Willis and Cornelis de Heer. New York: T. Y. Crowell, 1963.

Levi, Peter. *A History of Greek Literature.* New York: Viking, 1985.

Momigliano, Arnaldo. *Alien Wisdom: The Limits of Hellenization.* Cambridge: Cambridge University Press, 1975.

————. *The Development of Greek Biography.* Cambridge, Mass.: Harvard University Press, 1971.

Palmer, Leonard R. *The Greek Language.* Atlantic Highlands, N.J.: Humanities Press, 1980.

Perry, Ben Edwin. *The Ancient Romances: A Literary-Historical Account of Their Origins.* Berkeley, Calif.: University of California Press, 1967.

Scobie, Alexander. *Aspects of the Ancient Romance and Its Heritage.* Meisenheim am Glan: Hain, 1969.

Tarn, W. W., and G. T. Griffith. *Hellenistic Civilization.* New York: Barnes & Noble Books; Cambridge: Heffer, 1966.

Tiede, David L. *The Charismatic Figure as Miracle Worker.* SBL Dissertation Series 1. Missoula, Mont.: Society of Biblical Literature, 1972.

Hellenistic Education

Clark, M. L. *Higher Education in the Ancient World.* London: Routledge, Kegan & Paul, 1971.

Marrou, Henri I. *A History of Education in Antiquity.* Translated by George Lamb. London, New York: Sheed & Ward, 1956.

Smith, William A. *Ancient Education.* New York: Greenwood, 1955.

Walbank, F. W. *The Hellenistic World.* Cambridge, Mass.: Harvard University Press, 1982.

Hellenistic Philosophy

Armstrong, A. H., ed. *The Cambridge History of Later Greek and Early Medieval Philosophy.* Cambridge: Cambridge University Press, 1967.

————. *An Introduction to Ancient Philosophy.* London: Methuen, 1957.

Bevan, Edwyn. *Stoics and Sceptics.* Cambridge: Heffer, 1913, 1959.

Boardman, John, Jasper Griffin, and Oswyn Murray, eds. *The Oxford History of the Classical World.* New York: Oxford University Press, 1986.

Dudley, Donald R. *A History of Cynicism.* London: Methuen, 1937.

Farrington, Benjamin. *The Faith of Epicurus.* London: Weidenfeld & Nicolson, 1967.

Festugiere, Andre-Jean. *Epicurus and His Gods.* Translated by C. W. Chilton. Oxford: Blackwell, 1955.

Guthrie, W. K. C. *A History of Greek Philosophy.* 6 vols. Cambridge: Cambridge University Press, 1962–1975.

Hicks, R. D. *Stoic and Epicurean.* New York: Scribners, 1910, 1962.

Koester, Helmut. Introduction to the New Testament. Vol. 1, *History, Culture and Religion of the Hellenistic Age.* Philadelphia: Fortress Press, 1982.

Long, A. A., and D. N. Sedley, eds. The Hellenistic Philosophers. Vol. 1, *Translations of the Principal Sources with Philosophical Commentary*. Cambridge: Cambridge University Press, 1987.

Long, A. A. *Hellenistic Philosophy: Stoics, Epicureans, Sceptics*. London: Duckworth, 1974, 1986.

Rowe, C. J. *Plato*. Brighton, Sussex, Eng.: Harvester Press, 1984.

Sandbach, F. H. *The Stoics*. London: Chatto & Windus, 1975.

Tarn, W. W., and G. T. Griffith. *Hellenistic Civilization*. New York: Barnes & Noble Books; Cambridge: Heffer, 1966.

Walbank, F. W. *The Hellenistic World*. Cambridge, Mass.: Harvard University Press, 1982.

Hellenistic Religion

Brady, Thomas Allen. *Serapis and Osiris: Collected Essays*. Chicago: Ares, 1978.

Burkert, Walter. *Greek Religion* Translated by John Raffan. Cambridge, Mass.: Harvard University Press, 1985.

Cumont, Franz. *The Oriental Religions in the Roman Empire*. New York: Dover, 1911, 1956.

Farrell, Lewis Richard. *The Cults of the Greek States*. 5 vols. Oxford: Clarendon Press, 1896–1907.

———. *Greek Hero Cults and Ideas of Immortality*. Oxford: Clarendon Press, 1921.

Ferguson, John. *Greek and Roman Religion: A Source Book*. Park Ridge, N.J.: Noyes Press, 1980.

Festugiere, Andre-Jean. *Personal Religion Among the Greeks*. Berkeley, Calif.: University of California Press, 1954.

Grant, Frederick. *Hellenistic Religions: The Age of Syncretism*. New York: Lib. Arts Press, 1953.

Griffiths, J. Gwyn. *The Origins of Osiris and His Cult*. Leiden: Brill, 1980.

Guthrie, W. K. C. *The Greeks and Their Gods*. London: Methuen; Boston: Beacon, 1950.

Hadas, Moses, and Morton Smith. *Heros and Gods: Spiritual Biographies in Antiquity*. New York: Harper & Row, 1965.

Harrison, Jane E. *Prolegomena to the Study of Greek Religion*. 3d ed. 1921. Reprint. London: Merlin Press, 1961.

Hengel, Martin. *Jews, Greeks and Barbarians: Aspects of the Hellenization of Judaism in the Pre-Christian Period*. Philadelphia: Fortress Press, 1980.

Koester, Helmut. Introduction to the New Testament. Vol. 1, *History, Culture and Religion of the Hellenistic Age*. Philadelphia: Fortress Press, 1982.

Macchioro, Vittorio D. *From Orpheus to Paul*. New York: Holt, 1930.

Murray, Gilbert. *Five Stages of Greek Religion*. 3d ed. 1951. Reprint. Garden City, N.Y.: Doubleday, n.d.

Nilsson, Martin P. *The Dionysiac Mysteries of the Hellenistic and Roman Age*. New York: Arno, 1975.

Otto, Walter F. *Dionysus: Myth and Cult.* Translated by Robert B. Palmer. Bloomington: University of Indiana Press, 1965.

Scullard, H. H., gen. ed. Aspects of Greek and Roman Life Series. *The Religions of the Roman Empire,* ed. John Ferguson. Ithaca, N.Y.: Cornell University Press, 1970

Tarn, W. W., and G. T. Griffith. *Hellenistic Civilization.* New York: Barnes & Noble Books; Cambridge: Heffer, 1966.

Tiede, David L. *The Charismatic Figure as Miracle Worker.* SBL Dissertation Series 1. Missoula, Mont.: Society of Biblical Literature, 1972.

Walbank, F. W. *The Hellenistic World.* Cambridge, Mass.: Harvard University Press, 1982.

CHAPTER 2. JEWISH REACTIONS TO HELLENISM

GENERAL STUDIES

Bickerman, Elias. *The Jews in the Greek Age.* Cambridge, Mass.: Harvard University Press, 1988.

Boardman, John, Jasper Griffin, and Oswyn Murray, eds. *The Oxford History of the Classical World.* New York: Oxford University Press, 1986.

Cohen, Shaye J. D. *From the Maccabees to the Mishnah.* Philadelphia: Westminster Press, 1987.

Cook, S. A., F. E. Adcock, and M. P. Charlesworth, eds. The Cambridge Ancient History. 1928. Vol. 7, pt. 1, *The Hellenistic Monarchies,* 1984; *The Rise of Rome to 220 BC,* 1990. Cambridge: Cambridge University Press.

Davies, W. D., and Louis Finkelstein, eds. *The Cambridge History of Judaism.* Vol. 2, *The Hellenistic Age.* Cambridge: Cambridge University Press, 1989.

Gowan, Donald. *Bridge Between the Testaments: A Reappraisal of Judaism from the Exile to the Birth of Christianity.* 3d ed., rev. Philadelphia: Pickwick, 1986.

Hadas, Moses. *Hellenistic Culture: Fusion and Diffusion.* New York: Columbia University Press, 1959.

Hengel, Martin. *Jews, Greeks and Barbarians: Aspects of the Hellenization of Judaism in the Pre-Christian Period.* Philadelphia: Fortress Press, 1980.

————. *Judaism and Hellenism: Studies in Their Encounter in Palestine During the Early Hellenistic Period.* 2 vols. Philadelphia: Fortress Press, 1974.

Jagersma, Henk. *A History of Israel from Alexander the Great to Bar Kochba.* Translated by John Bowden. Philadelphia: Fortress Press, 1986.

Koester, Helmut. Introduction to the New Testament. Vol. 1, *History, Culture and Religion of the Hellenistic Age.* Philadelphia: Fortress Press, 1982.

Lieberman, Saul. *Hellenism in Jewish Palestine.* New York: Jewish Theological Seminary of America, 1962.

McCullough, W. Stewart. *The History and Literature of the Palestinian Jews from Cyrus To Herod: 550 BC to 4 BC.* Toronto: University of Toronto Press, 1975.

Oesterley, W. O. E. *The Jews and Judaism During the Greek Period: The Background of Christianity.* London: SPCK, 1941.

Roetzel, Calvin J. *The World That Shaped the New Testament.* Atlanta: John Knox Press, 1985.

Rostovtzeff, M. I. *Social and Ecomonic History of the Hellenistic World.* 3 vols. Oxford: Oxford University Press, 1941.

Russell, D. S. *From Early Judaism to Early Church.* Philadelphia: Fortress Press, 1986.

————. *The Jews from Alexander to Herod.* Oxford: Oxford University Press, 1967.

Schalit, Abraham, ed. *The World History of the Jewish People. First Series: Ancient Times.* Vol. 6, *The Hellenistic Age: Political History of Jewish Palestine From 332 B.C.E. to 67 B.C.E.* New Brunswick, N.J.: Rutgers University Press, 1972.

Schürer, Emil. *The History of the Jewish People in the Age of Jesus Christ.* 3 vols. New English Version revised and edited by Geza Vermes, et al. Edinburgh: Clark, 1973–87.

Smith, Morton. *Palestinian Parties and Politics that Shaped the Old Testament.* New York: Columbia University Press, 1971.

Tarn, W. W., and G. T. Griffith. *Hellenistic Civilization.* New York: Barnes & Noble Books; Cambridge: Heffer, 1966.

Walbank, F. W. *The Hellenistic World.* Cambridge, Mass.: Harvard University Press, 1982.

————, A. E. Austin, M. W. Frederiksen, and R. M. Ogilvie, eds. *The Cambridge Ancient History,* vol. 7, Pt. 1: *The Hellenistic World.* 2d ed. Cambridge: Cambridge University Press, 1984.

The Hasmonean Revolt and the Hasmonean State

Bar-Kochva, Bezalel. *Judas Maccabaeus: The Jewish Struggle Against the Seleucids.* Cambridge: Cambridge University Press, 1989.

Bickerman, Elias J. *The God of the Maccabees: Studies in the Meaning and Origin of the Maccabean Revolt.* Leiden: Brill, 1979.

————. *The Maccabees.* New York: Schocken Books, 1947.

Farmer, William R. *Maccabees, Zealots and Josephus.* New York: Columbia University Press, 1956.

Goldstein, Jonathan A. *I Maccabees.* AB 41, 1976.

————. *II Maccabees.* AB 41A, 1983.

Harrington, Daniel J. *The Maccabean Revolt: Anatomy of a Biblical Revolution.* Wilmington, Del.: Glazier, 1988.

Mendels, Doron. *The Land of Israel as a Political Concept in Hasmonean Literature: Recourse to History in Second Century BC Claims to the Holy Land.* Tübingen: Mohr-Siebeck, 1987.

Perlman, Moshe. *The Maccabees*. New York: Macmillan, 1973.

Zeitlin, S. *The Rise and Fall of the Judean State*. Vol. 1, Philadelphia: Jewish Pubns., 1962.

Jews of the Hellenistic Diaspora

Collins, John J. *Between Athens and Jerusalem: Jewish Identity in the Hellenistic Diaspora*. New York: Crossroad, 1983.

Fraser, P. M. *Ptolemaic Alexandria*. 3 vols. Oxford: Clarendon Press, 1972.

Grant, Michael. *The Jews in the Roman World*. New York: Scribners, 1973.

Neusner, Jacob. *A History of the Jews in Babylonia*. Vol. 1: *The Parthian Period*. Leiden: Brill, 1965.

Tcherikover, Victor. *Hellenistic Culture and the Jews*. Translated by S. Applebaum. Philadelphia: Jewish Publication Society, 1959.

CHAPTER 3. APOCALYPTIC

GENERAL STUDIES

Anderson, Bernard. *Creation Versus Chaos*. New York: Association Press, 1967.

Charles, R. H., ed. *The Apocrypha and Pseudepigrapha of the Old Testament*. 2 vols. 1913. Oxford: Oxford University Press, 1963.

⸺. *Religious Development Between the Old and New Testaments*. London: Williams & Norgate, 1914.

Charlesworth, James H. *The Old Testament Pseudepigrapha*. 2 vols. Garden City, N.Y.: Doubleday, 1983.

Charlesworth, James H., ed. *The Old Testament Pseudepigrapha and the New Testament*. Cambridge: Cambridge University Press, 1985.

Collins, John J. *The Apocalyptic Imagination: An Introduction to the Jewish Matrix of Christianity*. New York: Crossroad, 1984.

⸺. *Between Athens and Jerusalem: Jewish Identity in the Hellenistic Diaspora*. New York: Crossroad, 1983.

Dean-Otting, Mary. *Heavenly Journies. A Study of the Motif in Hellenistic Jewish Literature*. New York: Peter Lang, 1984.

Frost, S. B. *Old Testament Apocalyptic: Its Origin and Growth*. London: Epworth, 1952.

Hanson, Paul. *The Dawn of Apocalyptic*. Philadelphia: Fortress Press, 1975.

⸺. *Old Testament Apocalyptic*. Nashville: Abingdon, 1988.

⸺, ed. *Visionaries and Their Apocalypses*. Philadelphia: Fortress Press, 1983.

Hellholm, David, ed. *Apocalypticism in the Mediterranean World and the Near East*. Tübingen: J. C. B. Mohr (Paul Siebeck), 1983.

De Jonge, M. *Outside the Old Testament*. Cambridge: Cambridge University Press, 1985.

Koch, Klaus. *The Rediscovery of Apocalyptic*. Translated by M. Kohl. London: SCM Press, 1972.

Minear, Paul. *New Testament Apocalyptic*. Nashville: Abingdon, 1981.

Nickelsburg, George W. E. *Jewish Literature Between the Bible and the Mishnah*. Philadelphia: Fortress Press, 1981.

Ploger, Otto. *Theocracy and Eschatology*. Translated by S. Rodman. Richmond, Va.: John Knox Press, 1968.

Rost, Leonhard. *Judaism Outside the Hebrew Canon*. Translated by David E. Green. Nashville: Abingdon, 1974.

Rowland, Christopher. *The Open Heaven: A Study of Apocalyptic in Judaism and Early Christian History*. London: SPCK, 1982.

Rowley, H. H. *The Relevance of Apocalyptic*. New York: Association Press, 1944, 1964.

Russell, D. S. *Apocalyptic Ancient and Modern*. Philadelphia: Fortress Press, 1968.

_____. *The Method and Message of Jewish Apocalyptic*. Old Testament Library. Philadelphia: Westminster Press, 1964.

Schmithals, Walter. *The Apocalyptic Movement: Introduction and Interpretation*. Nashville: Abingdon, 1975.

Sneen, Donald. *Visions of Hope*. Minneapolis: Augsburg Press, 1978.

Stone, Michael E., ed. *Jewish Writings of the Second Temple Period*. Sec. 2, Vol. 2. Compendia Rerum Iudaicarum ad Novum Testamentum. Philadelphia: Fortress Press, 1984.

_____. *Scripture, Sects and Visions: A Profile of Judaism from Ezra to the Jewish Revolts*. Philadelphia: Fortress Press, 1980.

Individual Works

Black, Matthew. *The Book of Enoch or 1 Enoch: A New English Edition With Commentary and Textual Notes*. Leiden: Brill, 1985.

Charles, R. H. *The Book of Enoch, or I Enoch*. Oxford: Clarendon Press, 1925.

Collins, John J. *Daniel, First Maccabees, Second Maccabees*. Wilmington, Del.: M. Glazier, 1981.

Collins, John J., ed. Forms of the Old Testament Literature. Vol. 20, *Daniel with an Introduction to Apocalyptic Literature*. Grand Rapids: Eerdmans, 1984.

_____. *The Sibylline Oracles of Egyptian Judaism*. SBL Dissertation Series 13. Missoula, Mont.: Scholars Press, 1974.

Davenport, Gene L. *The Eschatology of the Book of Jubilees*. Leiden: Brill, 1971.

Hartman, Louis F., and Alexander A. Di Lella. *The Book of Daniel*, AB 23, 1978.

Hollander, H. W., H. J. de Jonge, and Th. Korteweg. *The Testaments of the Twelve Patriarchs*. Leiden: Brill, 1978.

Lacocque, Andre. *The Book of Daniel*. Translated by David Pellance. Atlanta: John Knox Press, 1979.

Porteous, Norman W. *Daniel: A Commentary.* Philadelphia: Westminster Press, 1965.

Slingerland, H. Dixon. *The Testaments of the Twelve Patriarchs.* Missoula, Mont.: Scholars Press, 1977.

Suter, David W. *Tradition and Composition in the Parables of Enoch.* SBL Dissertation Series 47. Missoula, Mont.: Scholars Press, 1979.

Towner, W. Sibley. *Daniel.* Atlanta: John Knox Press, 1984.

CHAPTER 4. THE THEOLOGY OF PALESTINIAN JUDAISM

General Studies

Avi-Yonah, Michael, and Zvi Baras, eds. *The World History of the Jewish People,* vol. 7: *The Herodian Period.* Jerusalem: Massada Publishing Ltd., 1977.

Cohen, Shaye J. D. *From the Maccabees to the Mishnah.* Philadelphia: Westminster Press, 1987.

Davies, W. D. *Christian Origins and Judaism.* Philadelphia: Westminster Press, 1962.

_____. *Torah in the Messianic Age and/or Age to Come.* Journal of Biblical Literature Monograph Series, Vol. 7. Missoula, Mont.: Scholars Press, 1952.

Falk, Zéev W. *Introduction to the Jewish Law of the Second Commonwealth.* Leiden: Brill, 1972.

Fohrer, G. *History of Israelite Religion.* Translated by David E. Green. Nashville: Abingdon, 1972.

Freedman, H., and Maurice Simon, eds. *Midrash Rabbah.* 10 vols. London: Soncino, 1939.

Gowan, Donald. *Bridge Between the Testaments: A Reappraisal of Judaism from the Exile to the Birth of Christianity.* 3d ed., rev. Philadelphia: Pickwick, 1986.

Guttmann, Alexander. *Rabbinic Judaism in the Making.* Detroit: Wayne State University Press, 1970.

Hengel, Martin. *Jews, Greeks and Barbarians: Aspects of the Hellenization of Judaism in the Pre-Christian Period.* Philadelphia: Fortress Press, 1980.

_____. *Judaism and Hellenism: Studies in Their Encounter in Palestine During the Early Hellenistic Period.* Translated by John Bowden. 2 vols. Philadelphia: Fortress Press, 1974.

Jeremias, Joachim. *Jerusalem in the Time of Jesus.* Translated by F. H. and C. H. Cave. London: SCM, 1969.

Koester, Helmut. Introduction to the New Testament. Vol. 1, *History, Culture and Religion of the Hellenistic Age.* Philadelphia: Fortress Press, 1982.

Levine, Etan. *The Aramaic Version of the Bible: Contents and Context.* Berlin: Walter de Gruyter, 1988.

McCullough, W. Stewart. *The History and Literature of the Palestinian Jews from Cyrus To Herod: 550 BC to 4 BC.* Toronto: University of Toronto Press, 1975.

Mulder, Martin J. *Mikra: Text, Translation, Reading and Interpretation of the Hebrew Bible in Ancient Judaism and Early Christianity.* Philadelphia: Fortress Press, 1988.

Murphy, Frederick J. *The Religious World of Jesus.* New York: Abingdon, 1991.

Neusner, Jacob. *Torah: From Scroll to Symbol in Formative Judaism.* Foundations of Judaism, Part 3. Philadelphia: Fortress Press, 1983.

———. *The Way of Torah: An Introduction to Judaism.* 3d ed. North Scituate, Mass.: Duxbury, 1979.

———. *What Is Midrash?* Philadelphia: Fortress Press, 1987.

Nickelsburg, George W. E. *Jewish Literature Between the Bible and the Mishna.* Philadelphia: Fortress Press, 1981.

Oesterley, W. O. E. *The Jews and Judaism During the Greek Period: The Background of Christianity.* London: SPCK, 1941.

Roetzel, Calvin J. *The World That Shaped the New Testament.* Atlanta: John Knox Press, 1985.

Roth, Cecil. *The Haggadah: A New Edition.* London: Soncino, 1934.

Rowley, H. H. *Worship in Ancient Israel: Its Forms and Meaning.* Philadelphia: Fortress Press, 1967.

Russell, D. S. *From Early Judaism to Early Church.* Philadelphia: Fortress Press, 1986.

Safrai, S., and M. Stern, eds. *The Jewish People in the First Century: Historical Geography, Political History, Social, Cultural and Religious Life and Institutions.* 2 vols. Compendia Rerum Judaicarum ad Novum Testamentum. Philadelphia: Fortress Press, 1974.

Sanders, James. *Torah and Canon.* Philadelphia: Fortress Press, 1972.

Sandmel, Samuel. *Judaism and Christian Beginnings.* New York: Oxford University Press, 1978.

Schalit, Abraham, ed. *The World History of the Jewish People. First Series: Ancient Times.* Vol. 6, *The Hellenistic Age: Political History of Jewish Palestine From 332 B.C.E. to 67 B.C.E.* New Brunswick, N.J.: Rutgers University Press, 1972.

Schürer, Emil. *The History of the Jewish People in the Age of Jesus Christ.* 3 vols. New English Version revised and edited by Geza Vermes, et al. Edinburgh: Clark, 1973–87.

Stone, Michael E., ed. *Jewish Writings of the Second Temple Period.* Sec. 2, Vol. 2. Compendia Rerum Iudaicarum ad Novum Testamentum. Philadelphia: Fortress Press, 1984.

Urbach, E. E. *The Sages, Their Concepts and Beliefs.* Translated by Israel Abrahams. Jerusalem: Magnes, 1975.

Vermes, Geza. *Post-Biblical Jewish Studies.* Leiden: Brill, 1975.

———. *Scripture and Tradition in Judaism. Haggadic Studies.* Leiden: Brill, 1961, 1973.

Sectarian Judaism

Beall, Todd S. *Josephus' Description of the Essenes Illustrated by the Dead Sea Scrolls.* Cambridge: Cambridge University Press, 1988.

Black, Matthew. *The Essene Problem.* London: Dr. William's Trust, 1961.

Bowker, John W. *Jesus and the Pharisees.* Cambridge: Cambridge University Press, 1973.

Bowman, John, ed. and trans. *Samaritan Documents Relating to Their History, Religion and Life.* Pittsburg: Pickwick, 1975.

_____, ed. *Samaritans and Jews.* Translated by Alfred M. Johnson Jr. Pittsburg: Pickwick, 1975.

Coggins, R. J. *Samaritans and Jews.* Atlanta: John Knox Press, 1975.

Finkelstein, L. *The Pharisees, the Sociological Background of Their Faith.* Philadelphia: Jewish Publication Society, 1938, 1962.

Howlett, Duncan. *The Essenes and Christianity: An Interpretation of the Dead Sea Scrolls.* New York: Harper & Bros., 1957.

Jospe, Raphael, and Stanley M. Wagner, eds. *Great Schisms in Jewish History.* Denver: Center for Judaic Studies; New York: Ktav, 1981.

Kampen, John. *The Hasideans and the Origins of Pharisaism: A Study in 1 and 2 Maccabees.* Atlanta: Scholars Press, 1988.

Macdonald, John. *The Theology of the Samaritans.* London: SCM, 1964.

Neusner, Jacob. *From Politics to Piety: The Emergence of Pharisaic Judaism.* Englewood Cliffs, N.J.: Prentice-Hall, 1973.

_____. *The Pharisees: Rabbinic Perspectives.* Hoboken, N.J.: Ktav, 1985.

_____. *Rabbinic Traditions About the Pharisees Before 70.* 3 vols. Leiden: Brill, 1971.

Pummer, Reinhard. *The Samaritans.* Leiden: Brill, 1987.

Rivkin, Ellis. *A Hidden Generation.* Nashville: Abingdon, 1978.

Saldarini, Anthony J. *Pharisees, Scribes and Sadducees in Palestinian Society.* Wilmington, Del.: M. Glazier, 1988.

Institutions of Judaism

de Vaux, Roland. *Ancient Israel: Its Life and Institutions.* Translated by John McHugh. London: Barton, Longman & Todd, 1961.

Gutmann, Joseph, ed. *The Synagogue: Studies in Origins, Archaeology and Architecture.* New York: Ktav, 1975.

Levine, Lee I., ed. *The Synagogue in Late Antiquity.* A Centennial Publication of the Jewish Theological Seminary in America. Philadelphia: Am. Sch. of Orient. Res., 1987.

Levy, I. *The Synagogue: Its History and Function.* London: Valentine, Mitchell, 1963.

Chapter 5. Qumran

General Studies Related to Qumran and the Times in Which the Community Flourished

Avi-Yonah, Michael, and Zvi Baras, eds. *The World History of the Jewish People.* Vol. 7: *The Herodian Period.* Jerusalem: Massada Publishing, 1975.

Beall, Todd S. *Josephus' Description of the Essenes Illustrated by the Dead Sea Scrolls.* Cambridge: Cambridge University Press, 1988.

Black, Matthew. *The Scrolls and Christian Origins.* Chico, Calif.: Scholars Press, 1961.

Brownlee, W. H. *The Meaning of the Qumran Scrolls for the Bible.* Oxford: Oxford University Press, 1964.

Bruce, F. F. *New Testament History.* London: Nelson, 1969.

Callaway, Phillip R. *The History of the Qumran Community: An Investigation.* Sheffield: J.S.O.T. Press, 1988.

Cross, Frank M. *The Ancient Library of Qumran and Modern Biblical Studies.* Garden City, N.Y.: Doubleday, 1958, 1961.

Cross, Frank M., and S. Talmon, eds. *Qumran and the History of the Biblical Text.* Cambridge, Mass.: Harvard University Press, 1975.

de Vaux, Roland. *Archaeology and the Dead Sea Scrolls.* Oxford: Oxford University Press, 1973.

Driver, G. R. *The Judean Scrolls: The Problem and A Solution.* Oxford: Blackwell, 1965.

Dupont-Sommer, A. *The Essene Writings from Qumran.* Translated by G. Vermes. Oxford: Blackwell, 1961.

Filson, Floyd. *A New Testament History.* London: SCM, 1975.

Gaster, Theodor H., trans. *The Dead Sea Scriptures.* Garden City, N.Y.: Doubleday, 1956.

Gowan, Donald. *Bridge Between the Testaments: A Reappraisal of Judaism from the Exile to the Birth of Christianity.* 3d ed., rev. Philadelphia: Pickwick, 1986.

Hengel, Martin. *Judaism and Hellenism: Studies in Their Encounter in Palestine During the Early Hellenistic Period.* Translated by John Bowden. 2 vols. Philadelphia: Fortress Press, 1974.

Knibb, Michael A. *The Qumran Community.* Cambridge Commentaries on Writings of the Jewish and Christian World 200 BC to AD 200 Series. Cambridge: Cambridge University Press, 1987.

Koester, Helmut. Introduction to the New Testament. Vol. 1, *History, Culture and Religion of the Hellenistic Age.* Philadelphia: Fortress Press, 1982.

Leaney, A. R. C. *A Guide to the Scrolls.* Naperville, Ill.: SCM Book Club, 1958.

Mansoor, Menahem. *The Dead Sea Scrolls.* 2d ed. Grand Rapids: Baker Bk., 1983.

McCullough, W. Stewart. *The History and Literature of the Palestinian Jews from Cyrus To Herod: 550 BC to 4 BC*. Toronto: University of Toronto Press, 1975.

Milik, J. T. *Ten Years of Discovery in the Wilderness of Judea*. Translated by John Strugnell. Naperville, Ill.: Allenson, 1959.

Nickelsburg, George W. E. *Jewish Literature Between the Bible and the Mishnah*. Philadelphia: Fortress Press, 1981.

Rabin, Chaim. *Qumran Studies*. London: Oxford University Press, 1957.

Reicke, Bo. *The New Testament Era*. Philadelphia: Fortress Press, 1968.

Ringren, H. *The Faith of Qumran: Theology of the Dead Sea Scrolls*. Philadelphia: Fortress Press, 1963.

Roetzel, Calvin J. *The World That Shaped the New Testament*. Atlanta: John Knox Press, 1985.

Roth, Cecil. *The Historical Background of the Dead Sea Scrolls*. Oxford: Blackwell, 1958.

Russell, D. S. *From Early Judaism to Early Church*. Philadelphia: Fortress Press, 1986.

Sandmel, Samuel. *Judaism and Christian Beginnings*. New York: Oxford University Press, 1978.

Sanders, E. P. *Paul and Palestinian Judaism*. Philadlephia: Fortress Press, 1977.

Schalit, Abraham, ed. *The World History of the Jewish People. First Series: Ancient Times. Volume 6: The Hellenistic Age: Political History of Jewish Palestine From 332 B.C.E. to 67 B.C.E.* New Brunswick, N.J.: Rutgers University Press, 1972.

Schiffmann, Lawrence H. *The Eschatological Community of the Dead Sea Scrolls: A Study of the Rule of the Congregation*. Atlanta: Scholars Press, 1989.

_____. *Sectarian Law in the Dead Sea Scrolls: Courts, Testimony and the Penal Code*. Atlanta: Scholars Press, 1983.

Schürer, Emil. *The History of the Jewish People in the Age of Jesus Christ*. 3 vols. New English Version revised and edited by Geza Vermes, et al. Edinburgh: Clark, 1973–87.

Stone, Michael E. *Jewish Writings of the Second Temple Period*. Sec. 2, Vol. 2. Compendia Rerum Iudaicarum ad Novum Testamentum. Philadelphia: Fortress Press, 1984.

Vermes, Geza. *The Dead Sea Scrolls: Qumran in Perspective*. Philadelphia: Fortress Press, 1977.

_____. *Discovery in the Judean Desert*. New York: Desclee, 1956.

_____. *Jesus the Jew*. New York: Macmillan, 1974.

Studies Related to Specific Qumran Texts

Allegro, J. M., and A. A. Anderson. *Discoveries in the Judean Desert of Jordan V: I*. Oxford: Clarendon Press, 1968.

Avigad, N., and Y. Yadin. *A Genesis Apocryphon*. Jerusalem: Bialik, 1956.

Barthélemy, D., and J. T. Milik. *Discoveries in the Judean Desert*, I: *Qumran Cave I*. Oxford: Clarendon Press, 1955.

Brownlee, W. H. "The Dead Sea Manual of Discipline." BASOR Supp. Studies 10–12 (1951).

———. *The Midrash Pesher of Habakkuk*. Missoula, Mont.: Scholars Press, 1979.

Burrows, Millar, J. C. Trevor, and W. H. Brownlee. *The Dead Sea Scrolls of St. Marks Monastery* 2 vols. New Haven: Am. Sch. of Orient. Res., 1950, 1951.

Davies, Philip R. *The Damascus Covenant: An Interpretation of the "Damascus Document."* Sheffield: J.S.O.T. Press, 1983.

de Vaux, Roland, and J. T. Milik. *Discoveries in the Judean Desert 6; Qumran Grotte 4 II*. Oxford: Clarendon Press, 1965.

Fitzmyer, J. A. *The Genesis Apocryphon of Qumran Cave I: A Commentary*. Rome: Biblica et Orientalia 18, 1966.

Holm-Neilsen, Svend. *Hodayot: Psalms from Qumran*. Universitetsforlaget I Aarhus, 1960.

Kittel, Bonnie P. *The Hymns of Qumran: Translation and Commentary*. Chico, Calif.: Scholars Press, 1981.

Knibb, Michael A. *The Qumran Community*. Cambridge Commentaries on Writings of the Jewish and Christian World 200 BC to AD 200. Cambridge: Cambridge University Press, 1987.

Leaney, A. R. C. *The Rule of Qumran and Its Meaning*. London: SCM, 1966.

Maier, Johann, ed. *The Temple Scroll: An Introduction, Translation and Commentary*. Translated by R. B. White. Sheffield: J.S.O.T. Press, 1985.

Mansoor, M. *The Thanksgiving Hymns*. Leiden: Brill, 1961.

Rabin, Chaim. *The Zadokite Documents*. Oxford: Clarendon Press, 1954.

Sanders, J. A. *Discoveries in the Judean Desert [of Jordan] Vol. 4. The Psalms Scroll of Qumran Cave 11 (11QPs^a)*. Oxford: Clarendon Press, 1965.

Sukenik, E. L. *The Dead Sea Scrolls of the Hebrew University*. Jerusalem: Bialik, 1955.

Weinfeld, Moshe. *The Organizational Pattern and the Penal Code of the Qumran Sect: A Comparison with Guilds and Religious Associations of the Hellenistic-Roman Period*. Göttingen: Vandenhoeck & Ruprecht, 1986.

Vermes. Geza. *The Dead Sea Scrolls in English*. rev. ed. Harmondsworth: Penguin, 1987.

———. *The Dead Sea Scrolls: Qumran in Perspective*. Philadelphia: Fortress Press, 1977, 1985.

Wernberg-Moller, P. *The Manual of Discipline: Translated and Annotated With An Introduction*. Leiden: Brill; Grand Rapids: Eerdmans, 1957.

Yadin, Yigael. *The Temple Scroll*. 3 vols. Jerusalem: Israel Exploration Society, 1983.

CHAPTERS 6 AND 7.   ADDITIONAL JEWISH LITERATURE OF THE
HELLENISTIC PERIOD

GENERAL OR INCLUSIVE STUDIES

Aune, David. E. *Greco-Roman Literature and the New Testament: Selected Forms and Genres.* Atlanta: Scholars Press, 1988

_____. *The New Testament in Its Literary Environment.* Philadelphia: Westminster Press, 1987.

Avi-Yonah, Michael, and Zvi Baras. *The World History of the Jewish People.* Jerusalem: Massada Publishing, 1977.

Beckwith, Roger. *The Old Testament Canon of the New Testament Church.* Grand Rapids: Eerdmans, 1985.

Charles, R. H. *The Apocrypha and Pseudepigrapha of the Old Testament in English.* Oxford: Oxford University Press, 1912.

Charlesworth, James H., ed. *The Old Testament Pseudepigrapha.* Prolegomena for the Study of Christian Origins. 2 vols. Garden City, N.Y.: Doubleday, 1983.

_____. *The Old Testament Pseudepigrapha and the New Testament.* Cambridge: Cambridge University Press, 1985.

Collins, John J. *Between Athens and Jerusalem: Jewish Identity in the Hellenistic Diaspora.* New York: Crossroad, 1983.

Cook, S. A., F. E. Adcock, and M. P. Charlesworth, eds. The Cambridge Ancient History. Vol. 7, pt. 1, *The Hellenistic Monarchies,* 1984; *The Rise of Rome to 220 BC,* 1990. Cambridge: Cambridge University Press, 1928.

Fraser, P. M. *Ptolemaic Alexandria.* 3 vols. Oxford: Clarendon Press, 1972.

Gowan, Donald. *Bridge Between the Testaments: A Reappraisal of Judaism from the Exile to the Birth of Christianity.* 3d ed., rev. Philadelphia: Pickwick, 1986.

Hadas, Moses. *Hellenistic Culture: Fusion and Diffusion.* New York: Columbia University Press, 1959.

Hengel, Martin. *Jews, Greeks and Barbarians: Aspects of the Hellenization of Judaism in the Pre-Christian Period.* Philadelphia: Fortress Press, 1980.

_____. *Judaism and Hellenism: Studies in Their Encounter in Palestine During the Early Hellenistic Period.* Translated by John Bowden. 2 vols. Philadelphia: Fortress Press, 1974.

Koester, Helmut. Introduction to the New Testament. Vol. 1, *History, Culture and Religion of the Hellenistic Age.* Philadelphia: Fortress Press, 1982.

McCullough, W. Stewart. *The History and Literature of the Palestinian Jews from Cyrus To Herod: 550 BC to 4 BC.* Toronto: University of Toronto Press, 1975.

Mendels, Doron. *The Land of Israel as a Political Concept in Hasmonean Literature: Recourse to History in Second Century BC Claims to the Holy Land.* Tübingen: Mohr-Siebeck, 1987.

Metzger, Bruce M. *An Introduction to the Apocrypha.* Oxford: Oxford University Press, 1957.

Momigliano, Arnaldo. *Alien Wisdom: The Limits of Hellenization.* Cambridge: Cambridge University Press, 1975.

Nickelsburg, George W. E. *Jewish Literature Between the Bible and the Mishnah.* Philadelphia: Fortress Press, 1981.

Oesterley, W. O. E. *An Introduction to the Books of the Apocrypha.* New York: Macmillan, 1935.

––––––. *The Jews and Judaism During the Greek Period: The Background of Christianity.* London: SPCK, 1941.

Roberts, Bleddyn J. *The Old Testament Text and Versions.* Cardiff, Wales: University of Wales Press, 1951.

Roetzel, Calvin J. *The World That Shaped the New Testament.* Atlanta: John Knox Press, 1985.

Russell, D. S. *From Early Judaism to Early Church.* Philadelphia: Fortress Press, 1986.

Sandmel, Samuel. *Judaism and Christian Beginnings.* New York: Oxford University Press, 1978.

Schürer, Emil. *The History of the Jewish People in the Age of Jesus Christ.* 3 vols. New English Version revised and edited by Geza Vermes, et al. Edinburgh: Clark, 1973–87.

Stone, Michael E., ed. *Jewish Writings of the Second Temple Period.* Sec. 2, Vol. 2. Compendia Rerum Judaicarum ad Novum Testamentum. Philadelphia: Fortress Press, 1984.

Tcherikover, Victor. *Hellenistic Culture and the Jews.* Translated by S. Applebaum. Philadelphia: Jewish Pubns., 1959.

Walbank, F. W. *The Hellenistic World.* Cambridge, Mass.: Harvard University Press, 1982.

Walbank, F. W., et al., eds. The Cambridge Ancient History. Vol. 8, Pt. 1, *The Hellenistic World,* 2d ed. Cambridge: Cambridge University Press, 1984.

Studies of Individual Writings

Bartlett, John R. *The First and Second Books of the Maccabees.* CBC, 1973.

––––––. *Jews in the Hellenistic World: Josephus, Aristeas, The Sibylline Oracles, Eupolemus.* Cambridge: Cambridge University Press, 1985.

Charles, R. H. *The Ascension of Isaiah.* London: SPCK, 1919.

Collins, John J. *Daniel, First Maccabees, Second Maccabees.* Wilmington, Del.: M. Glazier, 1981.

––––––. *The Sibylline Oracles of Egyptian Judaism.* SBL Dissertation Series 13. Missoula, Mont.: Scholars Press, 1974.

Dancy, J. C. *The Shorter Books of the Apocrypha.* CBC, 1972.

––––––. *A Commentary on I Maccabees.* Oxford: Blackwell, 1954.

Goldstein, Jonathan A. *I Maccabees. AB* 41, 1976.

———. *II Maccabees*. AB 41A, 1983.

Holladay, Carl R. *Theios Aner in Ancient Judaism*. Missoula, Mont.: Scholars Press, 1977.

Hadas, Moses. *The Third and Fourth Books of Maccabees*. New York: Ktav, 1953, 1976.

Jacobson, Howard. *The* Exagoge *of Ezekiel*. Cambridge: Cambridge University Press, 1983.

Jellico, Sidney. *The Septuagint and Modern Study*. Oxford: Clarendon Press, 1968.

———, ed. *Studies in the Septuagint: Origins, Recensions, and Interpretations*. New York: Ktav, 1974.

Martola, Nils. *Capture and Liberation: A Study in the Composition of the First Book of Maccabees*. Abo: Abo Akademi, 1984.

Moore, Carey A. *Daniel, Esther and Jeremiah: The Additions* AB 44, 1977.

Goldstein, Jonathan A. *I Maccabees*. AB 41, 1976.

Moore, Carey A. *Daniel, Esther and Jeremiah: The Additions*. AB 44, 1977.

———. *Judith: A New Translation with Introduction and Commentary*. AB 40. 1985.

Myers, Jacob M. *I and II Esdras*. AB 42, 1974.

Nickelsburg, George, W. E., ed. *Studies on the Testament of Moses*. Cambridge, Mass.: Society of Biblical Literature, 1973.

Skehan, W. Patrick. *The Wisdom of Ben Sira*. AB 39, 1987.

Snaith, John G. *Ecclesiasticus: Or, the Wisdom of Jesus Son of Sirach*. Cambridge Bible Commentary on the New English Bible, Old Testament Series. Cambridge: Cambridge University Press, 1974.

Sundberg, Albert C. *The Old Testament of the Early Church*. Cambridge, Mass.: Harvard University Press, 1964.

Swete, Henry B. *An Introduction to the Old Testament in Greek*. Cambridge: Cambridge University Press, 1902.

Wacholder, Ben Z. *Eupolemus: A Study of Judaeo-Greek Literature*. Cincinnati, New York: Hebrew Union College—Jewish Institute of Religion, 1974.

Zeltlin, Solomon, and Sidney Tedesche. *The Second Book of Maccabees*. New York: Harper & Bros., 1954.

Zimmerman, Frank. *The Book of Tobit*. New York: Harper & Bros., 1958.

EXCURSUS: Messianism in Late Hellenistic Jewish Literature

Borsch, F. H. *The Son of Man in Myth and History*. Philadelphia: Westminster Press, 1967.

Klausner, Joseph. *The Messianic Idea in Israel From Its Beginning to the Completion of the Mishnah*. Translated by W. F. Stinespring. New York: Macmillan, 1955.

Kramer, W. *Christ, Lord, Son of God*. Translated by Brian Hardy. Naperville, Ill.: Allenson, 1966.

Neusner, Jacob. *Messiah in Context: Israel's History and Destiny in Formative Judaism.* Philadelphia: Fortress Press, 1984.

Sanders, E. P. *Jesus and Judaism.* Philadelphia: Fortress Press, 1985.

Schürer, Emil. *The History of the Jewish People in the Age of Jesus Christ.* 3 vols. New English Version revised and edited by Geza Vermes, et al. Edinburgh: Clark, 1973–87.

Vermes, Geza. *Jesus the Jew.* New York: Macmillan, 1973.

CHAPTERS 8 AND 9.   ROMAN RULE COMES TO PALESTINE AND FROM HEROD THE GREAT TO THE REVOLT OF BAR KOKHBA

The History of Rome during the Late Republic and Early Empire

Barrow, R. H. *The Romans.* Baltimore: Penguin, 1953.

Ferguson, John. *Rome, The Augustan Age: A Source Book.* Oxford: Oxford University Press, 1981.

Grant, Michael. *The Twelve Caesars.* New York: Scribners, 1975.

Massie, Allan. *The Caesars.* London: Secher & Warburg, 1983.

Perowne, Stewart. *Hadrian.* London: Hoddon & Stoughton, 1960.

Salmon, Edward T. *A History of the Roman World From 30 BC to 138 AD* London: Methuen, 1920, 1944.

Sherk, Robert K., ed. *The Roman Empire: Augustus to Hadrian.* Cambridge: Cambridge University Press, 1988.

Roman Literature of the Late Republic and Early Empire

Barrow, R. H. *Plutarch and His Times.* Bloomington, Ind.: Indiana University Press, 1967.

Copley, Frank O. *Latin Literature From the Beginnings to the Close of the Second Century AD* Ann Arbor: University of Michigan Press, 1969.

Dorey, Thomas Alan, ed. *Latin Historians.* London: Routledge, Kegan & Paul, 1966.

Duff, J. Wight. *A Literary History of Rome From the Origins to the Close of the Golden Age.* New York: Barnes & Noble Books, 1909, 1953.

Fraekel, Eduard. *Horace.* Oxford: Clarendon Press, 1957.

Knight, W. F. Jackson. *Roman Virgil.* London: Faber & Faber, 1944, 1953.

Laistner, M. L. W. *The Greater Roman Historians.* Berkeley, Calif.: University of California Press, 1947.

Rawson, Elizabeth. *Cicero.* London: Allen Lane, 1975.

Syme, Ronald. *Tacitus.* 2 vols. Oxford: Clarendon Press, 1958.

Tenney, Frank. *Life and Literature in the Roman Republic.* Berkeley, Calif.: University of California Press, 1930.

Walsh, P. G. *Livy.* Oxford: Clarendon Press, 1974.

Religion in the Late Roman Republic and Early Roman Empire

Altheim, Franz. *A History of Roman Religion*. New York: Dutton, 1937.

Cumont, Franz. *The Mysteries of Mithra*. 1903. Reprint. New York: Dover, 1956.

_____. *The Oriental Religions in Roman Paganism*. 1911. Reprint. New York: Dover, 1956.

Ferguson, John. *Moral Values in the Ancient World*. New York: Arno, 1958, 1979.

_____. *The Religions of the Roman Empire*. Ithaca, N.Y.: Cornell University Press, 1970.

Filoramo, Giovanni. *A History of Gnosticism*. Translated by Anthony Alcock. Oxford: Blackwell, 1990.

Grant, Frederick, ed. *Ancient Roman Religion*. New York: Lib. Arts Press, 1957.

Grant, Michael. *Roman Myths*. New York: Scribners, 1971.

Grant, Robert, ed. *Gnosticism: A Source Book of Heretical Writings from the Early Christian Period*. New York: Harper & Bros., 1961.

Green, Henry A. *The Economic and Social Origins of Gnosticism*. Atlanta: Scholars Press, 1985.

Jonas, Hans. *The Gnostic Religion: The Message of the Alien God and the Beginnings of Christianity*. 2d rev. ed. Boston: Beacon Press, 1963.

Lacarriere, Jacques. *The Gnostics*. Translated by Nina Rootes. San Francisco: City Lights, 1989.

Ogilvie, R. M. *The Romans and Their Gods in the Age of Augustus*. London: Chatto & Windus, 1969.

Pearson, Birger A. *Gnosticism, Judaism, and Egyptian Christianity*. Minneapolis: Fortress Press, 1990.

Rose, Herbert Jennings. *Ancient Roman Religion*. London: Hutchinson University Library, 1948.

Rudolph, Kurt. *Gnosis: The Nature and History of Gnosticism*. Translated by R. M. Wilson. San Francisco: Harper & Row, 1983.

Taylor, L. Ross. *The Divinity of the Roman Emperor*. 1931. Reprint. Philadelphia: Porcupine, 1975.

Wynne-Tyson, Esme. *Mithras: The Fellow in the Cap*. 2d ed. New York: Barnes & Noble Books, 1972.

Roman Rule in Palestine

Avi-Yonah, Michael, and Z. Baras, eds. *The World History of the Jewish People*. Vol. 7, *The Herodian Period*. Jerusalem: Massada Publishing, 1977.

Ben-Gurion, David. *The Jews in Their Land*. Garden City, N.Y.: Doubleday, 1966, 1974.

Ben-Sasson, H. H., ed. *A History of the Jewish People*. Cambridge, Mass: Harvard University Press, 1976.

Dimont, Max I. *Jews, God and History.* New York: Simon & Schuster, 1962.

Farmer, William R. *Maccabees, Zealots and Josephus.* New York: Columbia University Press, 1957.

Goodman, Martin. *The Ruling Class of Judaea: The Origins of the Jewish Revolt Against Rome AD 66–70.* Cambridge: Cambridge University Press, 1987.

Grant, Michael. *Herod the Great.* New York: American Heritage Press, 1971.

_____. *The Jews in the Roman World.* New York: Scribners, 1973.

Hoehner, Harold. *Herod Antipas.* Cambridge: Cambridge University Press, 1972.

Horsley, Richard A., and John S. Hanson. *Bandits, Prophets and Messiahs: Popular Movements in the Time of Jesus.* Minneapolis: Winston Press, Seabury Books, 1985.

Jagersma, Henk. *A History of Israel from Alexander the Great to Bar Kokhba.* Translated by John Bowden. Philadelphia: Fortress Press, 1986.

Jeremias, Joachim. *Jerusalem in the Time of Jesus.* London: SCM; Philadelphia: Fortress Press, 1969.

Jones, A. H. M. *The Herods of Judaea.* 2d ed. Oxford: Clarendon Press, 1967.

Neusner, Jacob, ed. *Judaisms and Their Messiahs at the Turn of the Christian Era.* Cambridge: Cambridge University Press, 1987.

Noth, Martin. *The History of Israel.* New York: Harper & Bros., 1958.

Oesterley, W. O. E. *A History of Israel.* vol. 2: *From the Fall of Jerusalem, 586 BC, to the Bar Kokhba Revolt, AD 135.* Oxford: Clarendon Press, 1932.

Perowne, Stewart. *The Later Herods: The Political Background of the New Testament.* London: Hodder & Stoughton, 1958; New York: Abingdon, 1959.

_____. *The Life and Times of Herod the Great.* London: Hodder & Stoughton, 1956.

Rhoads, David M. *Israel in Revolution: 6–74 CE: A Political History Based on the Writings of Josephus.* Philadelphia: Fortress Press, 1976.

Robinson, Theodore H., J. W. Hunkin, and F. C. Burkitt. *Palestine in General History.* London: British Academy, 1929.

Safrai, Schmuel, and Michael E. Stern, eds. *The Jewish People in the First Century: Historical Geography, Political History, Social, Cultural and Religious Life and Institutions.* 2 vols. Compendia Rerum Judaicarum ad Novum Testamentum. Philadelphia: Fortress Press, 1974, 1976.

Sandmel, Samuel. *The First Christian Century in Judaism and Christianity.* Oxford: Oxford University Press, 1969.

Schürer, Emil. *The History of the Jewish People in the Age of Jesus Christ.* 3 vols. New English Version revised and edited by Geza Vermes, et al. Edinburgh: Clark, 1973–87.

Smallwood, E. Mary. *The Jews Under Roman Rule.* Leiden: Brill, 1976.

Soggin, J. Alberto. *A History of Ancient Israel.* Translated by John Bowden. Philadelphia: Westminster Press, 1984.

Yadin, Yigael. *Bar Kokhba: The Rediscovery of the Legendary Hero of the Last Jewish Revolt Against Imperial Rome.* New York: Random, 1971.

_____. *Masada: Herod's Fortress and the Zealot's Last Stand.* New York: Random, 1966.

CHAPTERS 10 AND 11. PALESTINIAN JEWISH THEOLOGY AND LITERATURE TO THE REVOLT OF BAR KOKHBA AND SOME JEWISH LITERATURE OF PRESUMED DIASPORA ORIGIN WRITTEN BEFORE 135 AD

Rabbinic Theology

Ben-Sasson, H. H., ed. *A History of the Jewish People.* Cambridge, Mass.: Harvard University Press, 1976.

Cohen, Shaye J. D. *From the Maccabees to the Mishnah.* Philadelphia: Westminster Press, 1987.

Grant, Michael. *Jews in the Roman World.* New York: Scribner's, 1973.

Green, William Scott, ed. *Approaches to Ancient Judaism.* 5 vols. Chico, Calif.: Scholars Press, 1980.

Hilton, Michael, and Gordian Marshall. *The Gospels and Rabbinic Judaism: A Study Guide.* Hoboken, N.J.: Ktav; New York: B'nai B'rith, 1988.

Moore, George Foote. *Judaism in the First Centuries of the Christian Era.* 3 vols. Cambridge, Mass.: Harvard University Press, 1927–1930.

Neusner, Jacob. *Judaism: The Evidence of the Mishnah.* Chicago: University of Chicago, 1981.

_____. *The Life of Johanan Ben Zakkai, c. 1–80 C.E.* Leiden: Brill, 1962.

_____. *The Mishnah Before 70.* Atlanta: Scholars Press, 1987.

_____. *Rabbinic Traditions About the Pharisees Before 70.* Leiden: Brill, 1971.

_____. *The Way of the Torah.* North Scituate, Mass.: Duxbury, 1979.

Sanders, E. P. *Paul and Palestinian Judaism.* Philadelphia: Fortress Press, 1977.

Simon, Marcel. *Jewish Sects at the Time of Jesus.* Translated by James Farley. Philadelphia: Fortress Press, 1967.

Stembaugh, John G., and David L. Balch. *The New Testament in Its Social Environment.* Philadelphia: Westminster Press, 1986.

Urbach, Ephraim. *The Sages: Their Concepts and Beliefs.* 2 vols. 2d ed. Jerusalem: Magnes, 1979.

GENERAL OR INCLUSIVE STUDIES ON JEWISH LITERATURE

See bibliography to chapters 6 and 7.

Individual Writings

Attridge, Harold W. *The Interpretation of Biblical History in the Antiquitates Judaicae of Flavius Josephus.* Missoula, Mont.: Scholars Press, 1976.

Bilde, Per. *Flavius Josephus Between Jerusalem and Rome: His Life, His Works and Their Importance.* Sheffield: Sheffield Academic Press, 1988.

Charles, R. H. *The Apocalypse of Baruch.* London: Black, 1896.

Cohen, Shaye J. D. *Josephus in Galilee and Rome.* Leiden: Brill, 1979.

Farmer, William R. *Maccabees, Zealots and Josephus.* New York: Columbia University Press, 1957.

Goodenough, E. R. *Introduction to Philo Judaeus.* New Haven: Yale University Press, 1940.

Hadas, Moses. *The Third and Fourth Books of Maccabees.* New York: Ktav, 1953, 1976.

Montefiore, Hugh. *Josephus and the New Testament.* London: Mowbray, 1962.

Murphy, Frederick J. *The Structure and Meaning of Second Baruch.* Atlanta: Scholars Press, 1985.

Myers, Jacob. *I and II Esdras.* AB 42. 1974.

Nickelsburg, George W. E., ed. *Studies on the Testament of Abraham.* Missoula, Mont.: Scholars Press, 1976.

Rajak, Tessa. *Josephus: The Historian and His Society.* Philadelphia: Fortress Press, 1984.

Thackery, Henry St. John. *Josephus: The Man and the Historian.* Reprint. New York: Ktav, 1967.

Williamson, Geoffrey A. *The World of Josephus.* Boston: Little, Brown, & Co., 1964.

Winston, David. *Philo of Alexandria.* New York: Paulist Press, 1981.

———. *The Wisdom of Solomon.* AB 43. 1979.

Wolfson, H. A. *Philo.* 2 vols. Cambridge, Mass.: Harvard University Press, 1947.

ANCIENT RULERS

PRINCIPAL RULERS OF PTOLEMAIC EGYPT (All dates are BC)

Ptolemy I Soter ("Savior")   323–285
  One of Alexander the Great's generals, founder of Ptolemaic dynasty.
  Founded the Library and Museum at Alexandria, which his successor
    made into the cultural center of the Hellenistic world.
  Wrote a biography of Alexander the Great, now lost.

Ptolemy II Philadelphus ("Brother-loving")   285–246
  Son of Ptolemy I Soter.
  Patron of literature and the arts.
  Letter of Aristeas (fictitiously) credits Ptolemy I with commissioning the
    translation into Greek of the Hebrew Bible known as the Septuagint.
  His relatively peaceful reign was a time of great political strength in the
    life of the kingdom.

Ptolemy III Euergetes ("Benefactor")   246–221
  Son of Ptolemy II Philadelphus.
  Invaded Seleucid kingdom to avenge death of his sister Bernice, wife of
    Seleucus II Callinicus.
  Continued predecessors' interest in artistic and literary matters.

Ptolemy IV Philopator ("Father-loving")   221–205
  Son of Ptolemy III Euergetes.
  Waged battles against Antiochus III the Great that demonstrated growing
    military weakness of Ptolemaic Egypt.

Ptolemy V Epiphanes ("Manifest God")   205–180
  Son of Ptolemy IV Philopator.
  Lost Palestine to Antiochus III the Great, 198.

Ptolemy VI Philometor ("Mother-loving")   180–145
  Son of Ptolemy V Epiphanes.
  Married his sister, Cleopatra II.
  Captured by Antiochus IV Epiphanes, but restored by the Romans.
  Supported Demetrius II of the Seleucid kingdom against Alexander Balas.
  Killed in battle with Balas.

Ptolemy VII Neos Philopator ("New Philopator")   145–116
    Also referred to as Physcon ("Fat Paunch").
    Son of Ptolemy V Epiphanes.
    Gained a reputation for cruelty and debauchery, temporarily expelled from
        Egypt, 131–129.

Ptolemy VIII Lathros ("Chickpea")   116–107, 88–80
    Son of Ptolemy VII.
    Ruled jointly with his mother, Cleopatra III, who expelled him to Cyprus.
    He returned to preside over a period of civil unrest, 88–80.

Ptolemy IX Alexander I   107–88
    Brother of Ptolemy VIII.
    Co-ruler with his mother, Cleopatra III.

Ptolemy X Alexander II   80
    Son of Ptolemy IX.
    Married his stepmother, but murdered her after reign of twenty days.
    Killed by a mob.

Ptolemy XI Auletes ("Flute-player")   80–51
    Son of Ptolemy VIII.
    Driven into exile, but restored by the Romans, with whom he was on
        friendly terms.

Ptolemy XII Theos Philopator I ("God loving the father")   51–47
    Son of Ptolemy VIII.
    Married his sister, Cleopatra, with whom he shared rule.
    Defeated by Julius Caesar and subsequently drowned.

Ptolemy XIV Theos Philopator II   47–44
    Son of Ptolemy VIII.
    Shared rule with sister, Cleopatra VII, who murdered him in order to ar-
        range for the succession of her son Caesarion.

Ptolemy XV Caesar, or Caesarion   44–30
    Son of Julius Caesar.
    Co-regent with his mother, Cleopatra VII.

Cleopatra VII Thea Philopator ("Goddess loving the father")   51–30
    Co-regent with her brothers: Ptolemy XIII 51–47; Ptolemy XIV 47–44.
    Co-regent with her son Ptolemy XV 44–30.
    Best remembered today for her affairs with Julius Caesar and Mark Antony,
        whom she married.

PRINCIPAL RULERS OF THE SELEUCID KINGDOM

Seleucus I Nicator ("Victor")   312–281
    One of the generals of Alexander the Great.
    Founder of the Seleucid kingdom.

Antiochus I Soter ("Savior")   281–261
Son of Seleucus I Nicator.
Campaigned against Ptolemy II Philadelphus.
Killed in battle.

Antiochus II Theos ("Divine")   261–246
Son of Antiochus I Soter.
Made peace with Ptolemy II Philadelphus, marrying his daughter Bernice,
whom he later abandoned.
Reportedly poisoned by his first wife, Laodice.

Seleucus II Callinicus ("Triumphant")   246–225
Son of Antiochus II.
Battled Ptolemy III Euergetes.

Seleucus III Soter Ceraunos   225–223
Son of Seleucus II.
Suffered defeat in attempt to conquer Asia Minor.

Antiochus III the Great   223–187
Son of Seleucus II.
Added large territories to the Seleucid domains, including southern Palestine
(Battle of Paneas, 200).
Defeated by Romans (188) and driven out of Asia Minor.

Seleucus IV Philopator ("Father-loving")   187–175
Son of Antiochus III.
Following his assassination, his throne seized by his brother, Antiochus IV.

Antiochus IV Epiphanes ("Manifest God")   175–164
Son of Antiochus III.
Educated in Rome where he had been taken as a hostage after father's de-
feat in 188.
Seized throne after murder of his brother, Seleucus IV.
His atrocities against Jews incited the Hasmonean revolt.

Antiochus V Eupator ("Of a good father")   164–162
Son of Antiochus IV.

Demetrius I Soter   162–150
Son of Seleucus IV Philopator.
Hostage in Rome with uncle, Antiochus IV Epiphanes.
Overthrew Antiochus V Eupator.
Intensive conflict with the Hasmoneans.
Killed in battle against Alexander Balas.

Alexander Epiphanes Balas   150–146
Pretender to throne who claimed to be son of Antiochus IV Epiphanes.
Son-in-law of Ptolemy VI Philometor.
Appointed Jonathan to the Jewish high priesthood, thus cementing an alliance with the Hasmoneans.
Murdered by obscure Arab in 146.

Demetrius II Nicator   145–139, 129–125
Son of Demetrius I
Overthrew Alexander Balas with the help of the Hasmonean Jonathan, who subsequently turned against him.
Taken prisoner in Parthian campaign, 139, but regained power in 129.

Antiochus VI Theos ("Divine") and Epiphanes Dionysus ("Dionysus Manifest")   143–142
Son of Alexander Balas, whose pretension he continued.
Ruled in opposition to Demetrius II Nicator.
Murdered by his general Trypho.

Antiochus VII Sidetes (Born in Side, Asia Minor)   139–129
Son of Demetrius I.
Campaigned against the Hasmoneans, led by Simon and, subsequently, John Hyrcanus.
Killed in campaign against the Parthians.

The final decades of the Seleucid kingdom were characterized by serious internal struggles for political power.

ROMAN EMPERORS 27 BC–138 AD

Augustus   27 BC–14 AD
Gaius Octavian, adopted son of Julius Caesar.
Undisputed ruler of the Empire, whose reign was marked by unparalled peace (the *Pax Romana*), commercial activity, and a flowering of the arts.

Tiberius   14–37
Stepson and adopted heir of Augustus.
Patron of Herod Antipas.
Reign characterized by cruelty and despotism.

Caligula   37–41
Nephew and adopted heir of Tiberius.
Insanity led to irrational and brutal policies.
Assassinated by members of the Praetorian Guard.

Claudius   41–54
Stepgrandson of Augustus, regarded as weak during his youth.
Proclaimed emperor by the military upon the death of Caligula.
Poisoned by his fourth wife, his niece Agrippina.

Nero   54–68
>   Son, by a previous marriage, of Claudius' fourth wife Agrippina.
>   Adopted as heir by Claudius over his own son Britannicus.
>   Ruled wisely at first, but fell into cruel and ruinous policies.
>   Instigated persecutions of Christians during which it is presumed that
>   Peter and Paul were martyred.
>   During his reign the Jews of Palestine revolted.
>   Declared public enemy by the Senate; committed suicide.

Galba   68–69
>   Noted Roman statesman who joined the conspiracy against Nero.
>   Made emperor by the Praetorian Guard, but soon alienated the powerful
>   Otho.
>   Assassinated after a reign of some six months.

Otho   69
>   Statesman who had served under Nero.
>   Conspired against Galba, after initially offering support.
>   Proclaimed emperor by the military, but committed suicide after his defeat
>   by the forces of Vitellius, having ruled three months.

Vitellius   69
>   Military leader and politician.
>   Ruled for less than a year before being overthrown by forces friendly to
>   Vespasian.

Vespasian   69–79
>   First of the three Falvian emperors.
>   Sent by Nero in 66 to quell the Jewish uprising in Palestine.
>   Acclaimed emperor by army in the East in an effort to end the political
>   instability in Rome.
>   Began several building projects, including the Colosseum.

Titus   79–81
>   Eldest son of Vespasian.
>   Commanded Roman legions which destroyed Jerusalem (70)
>   Brief reign marked by concern for public welfare.

Domitian   81–96
>   Second son of Vespasian.
>   Cruel and despotic as a ruler, he presided over persecutions of both Jews
>   and Christians.
>   Murdered as a result of a conspiracy involving his wife.

Nerva   96–98
>   Statesman who had served under the Flavian emperors.
>   Attempted, unsuccessfully, to curb the power of the military.

Trajan   98–117
  Soldier and statesman, adopted as heir by Nerva.
  Expanded the borders of the Empire in the East and elsewhere.
  Improved the Empire's system of roads and transportation.

Hadrian   117–138
  Nephew and comrade-in-arms of Trajan.
  Traveled widely through the Empire, establishing a Roman presence in the
    north of England (Hadrian's Wall) and fixing the Euphrates River as
    the limit of the Empire in the East.
  Oversaw and perhaps participated in the suppression of the revolt of Bar
    Kokhba.

Important Members of the Hasmonean family.

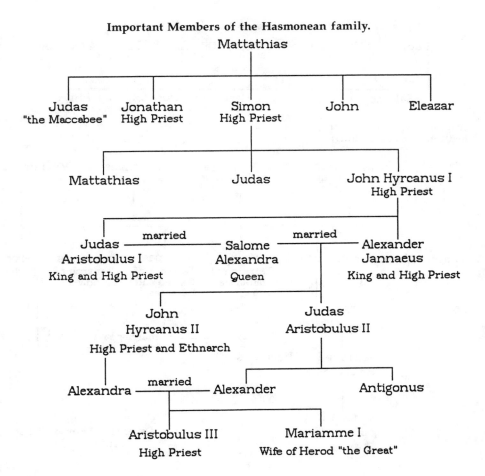

Important Members of the Herodian family.

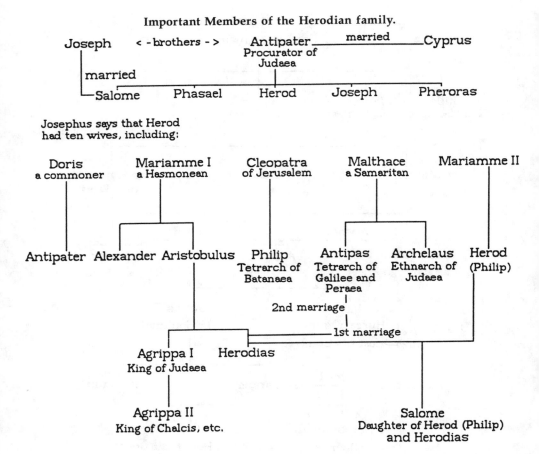

Joseph   < -brothers - >   Antipater ——————— married ——————— Cyprus
                         Procurator of
                           Judaea

married

Salome   Phasael   Herod   Joseph   Pheroras

Josephus says that Herod
had ten wives, including:

Doris	Mariamme I	Cleopatra	Malthace	Mariamme II
a commoner	a Hasmonean	of Jerusalem	a Samaritan	

Antipater   Alexander   Aristobulus   Philip   Antipas   Archelaus   Herod
                                    Tetrarch of   Tetrarch of   Ethnarch of   (Philip)
                                    Batanaea   Galilee and   Judaea
                                              Peraea

2nd marriage

——————————————— 1st marriage

Agrippa I   Herodias
King of Judaea

Agrippa II   Salome
King of Chalcis, etc.   Daughter of Herod (Philip)
                                    and Herodias

The Campaigns of Alexander 334–323 BC

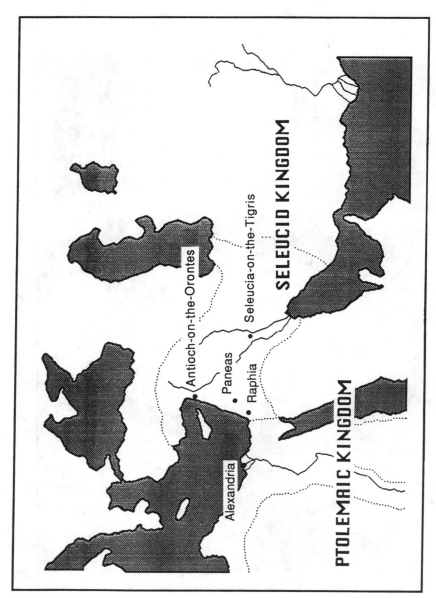

The Seleucid and Ptolemaic Kingdoms   About 200 BC

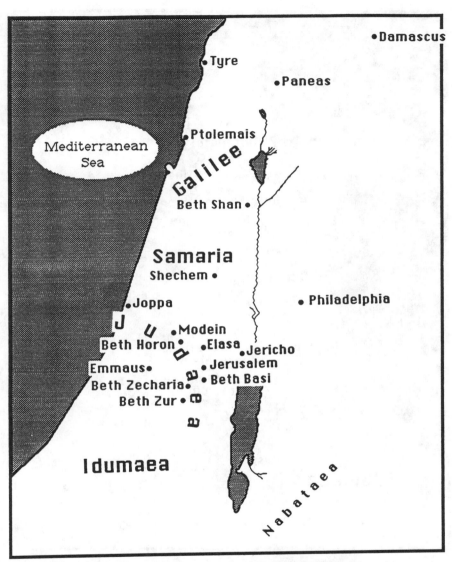

Important Sites in Palestine During the Hasmonean Period.

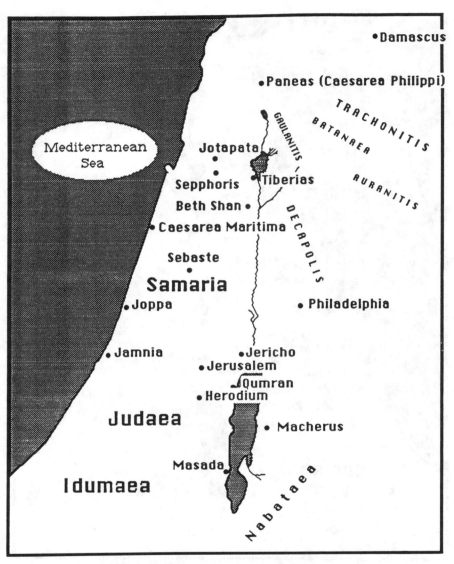

Important Sites in Palestine During the Herodian Period.

INDEX

461

Titus (Titus Flavius Sabinus Vespasianus): reign as emperor, 258; capture of Jerusalem, 258, 308–10; affair with Bernice, wife of Agrippa II, 299

Tobiad family: active in 2d century BC Palestine, 37; friction with Oniads, 38

Tobit, Book of: character of work, 211–16; influence upon Daniel and New Testament, 215–16

Torah: shapes life in future golden age, 69; central element in Jewish theology, 102–06; read in synagogue worship, 129–31; importance at Qumran, 140–41; definition of, 399 n. 1

Trachonitis, limits of rule of Alexander Jannaeus, 58

Trajan (Marcus Ulpius Trajanus): reign as emperor, 259; Jewish uprisings during his reign, 259

Treatise of Shem, character of work, 375–77

Trypho (Seleucid military leader): supports claims of Antiochus VI, 46; captures and murders Jonathan, 47; proclaims himself king, 47; defeated, 49

Tyre, conquered by Alexander, 5

Valentinus of Rome, Gnostic teacher, 273

Varus, Publius Quintilius, Roman governor of Syria, 290

Vespasian (Titus Flavius Sabinus Vespasianus): reign as emperor, 257–58; sent to quell Jewish revolt, 257; attitude toward his divinity, 258; friendship with Pliny the Elder, 267; not divinized, 275; assumes control of army in Palestine, 306; meeting with Josephus, 307; meeting with Johanan ben Zakkai, 322–23

Vesuvius, Mt.: eruption during the reign of Titus, 258; eruption described by Pliny the Younger, 267–68

Virgil (Publius Virgilius Naso): active during Augustan Age, 254; character of his poetry, 262–63

Visions: See Dreams and Visions

War Rule, The, character of work, 160–63

Watchers, as supernatural beings, 70, 92

Wine, use in Dionysian Mystery, 29

Wisdom of Jesus the Son of Sirach, The: character of work, 192–96; possible influence upon New Testament, 195–96

Wisdom of Solomon, The: character of work, 363–68; possible influence upon New Testament, 367

Worship, in Hellenistic synagogue, 128–31

Worship of the Ruler: in Hellenistic period, 31–32; in early Roman period, 274–76

"Writings" (as a part of the Hebrew canon), acceptance as scripture, 110–12

Xenophon, biographical writings, 20

Yavneh. See Jamnia

Zabdiel, the Arab, assassin of Alexander Balas, 46

Zaddok, a Pharisee, Zealot founder, 295

Zealots: origins, 295–96; during administration of Cumanus, 300; during administration of Felix, 301–02; during war with Rome, 305, 308–10; survival beyond 70 AD, 311

Zebinas, Alexander. See Alexander Zebinas

Zeno of Citium, founder of Stoicism, views, 26

Zenon Papyri, information concerning Ptolemaic Palestine, 36

Zerubbabel, leader of returning exiles, 64; portrayed in 1 Esdras, 216–19

Zeus. See also Ammon: father of Dionysus, 29; chief deity of Seleucid kingdom, 32